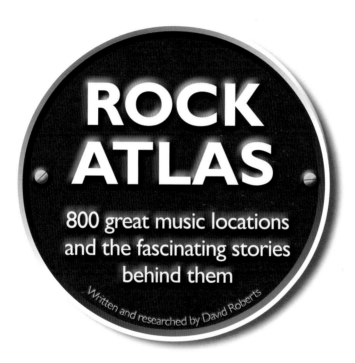

ROCK ATLAS

800 great music locations
and the fascinating stories
behind them

Written and researched by David Roberts

red
planet

Rock Atlas is a trade mark of Red Planet Publishing Ltd

Rock Atlas UK & Ireland

Second revised and expanded edition published March 2015
First edition published October 2011
Text © David Roberts 2011-2015
This work © Red Planet Publishing Ltd 2015
Paperback ISBN: 978 1 9059 5957 0
Hardback ISBN: 978 1 9059 5958 7

Where locations are private residences, we particularly ask all readers to respect absolutely the privacy of those who live there.

This book is dedicated to the late Peter Tarleton

Design: Mark Young
Proofreader: Matthew White
Publisher: Mark Neeter
Bowie cover image colouring: Terry Pastor (www.terrypastor.co.uk)

Printed in the Czech Republic by Finidr

For more information visit: www.redplanetzone.com

UNITED KINGDOM & IRELAND
SECOND EDITION

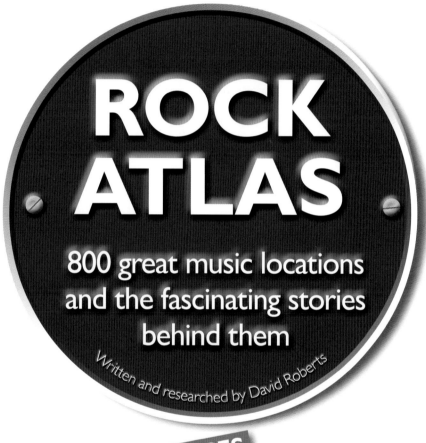

ROCK ATLAS

800 great music locations
and the fascinating stories
behind them

Written and researched by David Roberts

PLACES
TO VISIT

Album cover & music video locations
Statues, graves, memorials & plaques
Venues, festivals & places that influenced songs

Rock Atlas

"Particularly satisfying was my trip to Savoy Steps in London's West End to **FIND THE SPOT** where Dylan tossed his hand-written cue cards to the ground during the film accompanying 'Subterranean Homesick Blues'..."

Introduction
Welcome to Rock Atlas UK & Ireland

What's marvellous about a second edition of Rock Atlas UK & Ireland – apart from the obvious conclusion that enough people purchased the first edition to make it possible at all – is that the first book generated feedback that certainly makes the book you are now reading appreciably better.

Rock Atlas has now developed its own community of fans who have written to me with new information, new pictures and some helpful suggestions. It was nice to find that I wasn't the only music fan with an obsession for the important places in rock history. What hasn't changed at all from edition one is my continued fascination for the venues, statues, album cover photo shoot locations and recording studios that have created so much pleasure. Since Rock Atlas first published I've added many new entries to the book, some after recent trips to locations such as The Kinks' 'Dead End Street', The

Small Faces' 'Lazy Sunday' garden and new rock memorials like the unusual representation of The Jam in Woking. There's also been time to catch up with visits on my long list of iconic locations left over from book one. Particularly satisfying was my trip to Savoy Steps in London's West End to find the spot where Bob Dylan tossed his hand-written cue cards to the ground during the film accompanying 'Subterranean Homesick Blues'. With the help of old friend and big Rock Atlas supporter Martin Downham, I was able to reproduce the moment Dylan stood on the same spot more than four decades earlier and get a goosebumps moment, an experience repeated on many of these excursions Martin and I like to call our Rock Atlas safaris.

A final note about another way in which things have improved since the first Rock Atlas in 2011: the book is now better illustrated. This is

thanks specifically to the excellent work and enthusiasm of Chesterfield photographer Peter Tarleton, who scoured the UK for new opportunities to capture his astonishing images of sometimes rather ordinary Rock Atlas subjects. Peter's pictures of everything from the bridge over troubled water in Devon to Rock City in Nottingham have helped make Rock Atlas beautiful.

So, thanks to all who submitted feedback – and for those that suggested it, you'll be pleased to see this book now has an index – so please do keep in touch.

David Roberts, Wivenhoe, UK

Contact David regarding Rock Atlas content at: poppublishing@gmail.com or the publisher Red Planet Publishing at: info@redplanetzone.com

Keep up to date via our Facebook page at www.facebook.com/rockatlas and our website at www.redplanetzone.com

Acknowledgements

Thanks to Jeff Adams, Lynne Ball, Nigel Bones, John Breeze, Sue and Ian Bruce, Mick Bute, Jonathan Byrne, Ian Cater, Mike Charity, Pete Clemons, Barry Cleveland, Jules and Emma Cole, Pete Compton, Mike Crawley, Ian Dalgliesh, John Daniel, Stephen Davies, Tony Dawson-Hill, Geoff Docherty, Phil Elcome, Jim Farrell, Dr Dick Farrow, Pete Fielding, Linda Fisher, Craig Fleming, Patrick Graham, Dick Greener, Claire Hamill, Laura Jade Heseltine, Chris Hillman, Steve Johnson, Sheena Lemon, Graham Lowe, Manchester District Music Archive, Peter O'Donnell, Dave Okomah, Alison Parsons, Phil Pegler, Al Read, Roy Richardson, David Rush, Trevor Simpson, Brian Smith, Mark Steer, Janice Storey, Alex Surtees, David Tangye, Abigail Ward, Neil Watson, Paul Webster, Rupert White, Joyce Williamson, and finally, special big thanks to my wife Janet Roberts.

Bibliography and other sources used to create Rock Atlas:
A Promoter's Tale – Rock at the Sharp End by Geoff Docherty
Banned on the Run by Brian Southall
Comfortably Numb – The Inside Story of Pink Floyd by Mark Blake
FAB – An Intimate Life of Paul McCartney by Howard Sounes
Exorcising Ghosts – The Autobiography of Dave Mason Exploring The Networked David Mason
Worlds Of Popular Music: Milieu Cultures by Peter Webb
Life by Keith Richards
Guinness Book of British Hit Singles & Albums Editor David Roberts
How Black Was Our Sabbath by David Tangye and Graham Wright
Love Will Tear Us Apart blog
http://ljlovewilltearusapart-spacegirlcurtis.blogspot.co.uk/
Neil Young – Zero to Sixty by Johnny Rogan
Pompey Pop Pix byDave Allen and Mick Cooper
Queen in Cornwall by Rupert White
Rock Chronicles Editor David Roberts
Thirty Years of the Cambridge Folk Festival by Dave Laing and Richard Newman
Small Town Saturday Night by Trevor Simpson
Wild Tales by Graham Nash
Yeah Yeah Yeah – The Beatles & Bournemouth by Nick Churchill

Rock Atlas

650
GREAT MUSIC LOCATIONS

ROCK ATLAS USA

David Roberts

The musical landscape of America

Album cover & music video locations

Venues, festivals & places that influenced songs

Statues, graves museums, memorials & plaques

Exclusive interviews and more than 500 fascinating photographs

Crosby, Stills & Nash Cover shoot by Henry Diltz, West Hollywood 1969

"Here's a guidebook with a side order of stories about America's great music locations"
DAVID ROBERTS
on the sister book to Rock Atlas UK & Ireland

PLUS! THE BRILL BUILDING • DEAD MAN'S CURVE • THE JOSHUA TREE • PAISLEY PARK AND MORE

Contents

Rock Atlas

Contents

Rock Atlas

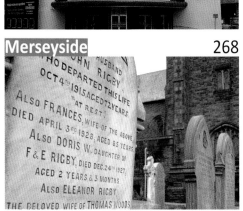

Contents

Rock Atlas

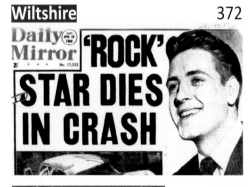

Contents

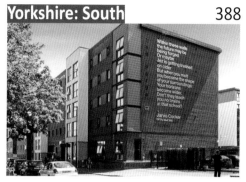

Key to English regional and UK and Ireland country colour-coding

East
Greater London
Midlands
North East
North West
South East

South West
Yorkshire and Humber
Wales
Scotland
Northern Ireland
Republic of Ireland

Bedfordshire

*T*here's an air of transience about Bedfordshire's rock claims to fame, which may have something to do with the two main roads (the A1M and the M1) that link north and south through the county. It was late one night after Christmas 1978 that Joy Division's Ian Curtis was rushed to Luton & Dunstable Hospital when travelling home north from a gig, suffering from what was later diagnosed as the singer's first epileptic seizure. On a brighter note, the Duke and Duchess of Bedford were among the first landowners to welcome hippies and rock music into their home at Woburn Abbey and Dunstable punches above its weight with two of British music's historically important venues.

Dunstable
Soul central at the California Ballroom

Gone but not forgotten by thousands of soul fans, the building that was the California Ballroom was demolished to make way for a Dunstable housing estate. A familiar gig for beat groups in the early Sixties, the second half of the decade saw a succession of soul greats from Ike and Tina Turner to James Brown double ticket prices and crank up the excitement. Running from 1960 to 1979, this extraordinary venue became the southern epicentre of Britain's obsession with soul and Motown music, although the likes of Cream, The Who, Traffic and Jimi Hendrix kept up a fine tradition of outstanding rock performances, with a healthy number of glam rock acts booked as the Seventies wore on. But if you grooved to the records of Percy Sledge, Jimmy James & The Vagabonds, Johnny Johnson & The Bandwagon, Arthur Conley and Edwin Starr, the 'Cali' was the first place to check out your favourites live. All that remains today to mark the location is a reference on a standard street sign for Royce Close, which reads 'Site of the California Ballroom 1960-1979 & pool 1935-1970'.

LOCATION 001: Royce Close, postcode LU 2NT. For the extended history of the 'Cali', visit: www.california-ballroom.info

Serial Sixties hit-makers The Searchers pack out the California Ballroom, the band's favouirite gig outside of London according to Mike Pender (second from right). Below: Royce Close marks the spot

Cardington
The giant hangars of rock

The giant airship hangars at RAF Cardington form the dramatic backdrop to the cover of the Propellerheads' 1998 hit album Decksandrumsandrockandroll. Since the demise of airship travel, the sheds have been used for movie-making and rock rehearsals. Easily big enough to house two Wembley Stadiums inside, one shed has been booked for tour practice by The Rolling Stones, Paul McCartney, AC/DC, Rod Stewart and U2. In 2011, the Take That production team built the group's entire outdoor show stage for secret rehearsals for their Progress Live tour inside one of the giant Cardington hangars.

LOCATION 002: three miles south-east of Bedford at Shortstown, near Cardington, postcode MK42 0TF

Bedfordshire

Photo by Oz Hardwick

Dunstable
The space-age Queensway Hall

With its flying saucer-like 100-foot-long dome, Queensway Hall/Civic Hall was the California Ballroom's equal in terms of Dunstable's place in British music history and an architectural treasure in its own right. Opened in April 1964, it promoted a broad spectrum of music genres and kicked off with a rather innocuous 'Top Twenty Disc Nite' attended by 1,300 teenagers who reportedly voted the new structure "Fab!" By the Seventies and Eighties, the more challenging sounds of Pink Floyd, Sex Pistols, Iron Maiden and R.E.M. were experienced by Dunstable and Luton music fans. One noteworthy event, under the Friars concert promotion banner on Midsummer Night 1972, coincided with the advent of David Bowie mania.

Riding a wave of music press excitement created by the recent release of the Ziggy Stardust album, the newly crowned golden boy of rock played Dunstable accompanied by his Spiders from Mars and supported on the bill by San Francisco's Flamin' Groovies. Perhaps Hawkwind fans remember the place with most affection. The band made a total of 15 appearances at The Queensway Hall, which served as the location for the making of a BBC film to accompany their signature hit 'Silver Machine', seen by millions on Top of the Pops during the summer of 1972. Some rock legends didn't share Hawkwind's obvious love of the place. An exuberant but threatening atmosphere at a 1978 Blondie gig caused Debbie Harry to flatly refuse to remain on stage and an appearance by The Clash caused more long-lasting

aggravation. When their 'London's Burning' was performed as 'Dunstable is Burning' a headline-grabbing mini riot is said to have broken out. The local authority, who ran the Queensway, acted forcefully to avoid any further damage to the venue's reputation and the fixtures and fittings and promptly cancelled the next scheduled concert, for which The Boomtown Rats received a compensation payment. Just as well the Hawkwind and Bowie videos are still around to give some indication of the great atmosphere Queensway Hall generated – It's now an Asda superstore.

LOCATION 003: Before the site became a superstore in 2000, Queensway Hall's futuristic structure stood on Queensway, Dunstable town centre, postcode LU5 4JD

Hawkwind play the saucer-like Queensway Hall, the venue where their Top of the Pops performance of 1972 hit 'Silver Machine' was filmed

Woburn
The Festival of the Flower Children

One of Britain's earliest pop festivals, a three-day "happening" at Woburn Abbey in 1967's Summer of Love, saw a bill topped by The Small Faces, The Move, Eric Burdon and Jeff Beck. Taking place "by kind permission of his Grace the Duke of Bedford", an advertisement at the time went on to describe the August Bank Holiday event as a "Festival of the Flower Children". This new initiative by the Duke provided some spectacular moments for the national press to report. During the proceedings a hot-air balloon floated over, dropping flowers on the 12,000-strong crowd below, and disaster was averted when a stage awning caught light, which was quickly dealt with before anyone was hurt. Although not exactly rife, capitalism did rear its ugly head according to reports in one Sunday newspaper. An interview revealed that a disgruntled hippie had paid 30 shillings (£1.50) for a three-day ticket and then been disgusted to discover that a hot dog would set him back a further one shilling and nine pence (8p). The following summer saw a second event promoted as the Woburn Music Festival at which Jimi Hendrix, Pentangle, Geno Washington, Family, Roy Harper and Donovan all featured.

LOCATION 004: Woburn Abbey (postcode MK17 9WA) is close by junction 12 or 13 of the M1

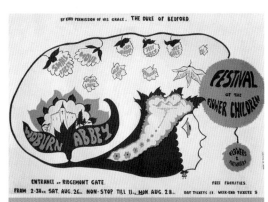

BY KIND PERMISSION OF HIS GRACE, THE DUKE OF BEDFORD. FESTIVAL OF THE FLOWER CHILDREN. WOBURN ABBEY. ENTRANCE AT RIDGEMONT GATE. FROM 2·30 SAT. AUG. 26. NON-STOP TILL 11. MON. AUG. 28. DAY TICKETS £1. WEEK-END TICKETS S FREE FACILITIES. FLOWERS & FIREWORKS

Note the tiny statement (bottom right) for "Flowers & Fireworks". During Marmalade's set, excited fans started tossing lighted sparklers, some of which landed on the stage canopy, resulting in DJ turned fire officer John Peel requesting that the crowd move back from the stage

> **"** I saw people starting to tear trees down to make fires because they were camping out for the night and the Duke of Bedford and his wife came along. I said **'I'M VERY SORRY SIR ABOUT THE TREES, IT'S REALLY DISGUSTING.'** He says, 'Oh never mind – we can always grow some more.'
>
> **WOW MAN, HOW LOOSE CAN YOU GET? "**
> **ERIC BURDON**

Born in
BEDFORDSHIRE

Mick Abrahams (below), guitar, (b. 7 Apr 1943, Luton)
David Arnold, composer, (b. 23 Jan 1962, Luton)
Badly Drawn Boy, singer-songwriter, (b. Damon Gough, 2 Oct 1969, Dunstable)
Clive Bunker, drums, Jethro Tull (b. 30 Dec 1946, Luton)
Neil Conti, drums, Prefab Sprout (b. 12 Feb 1959, Luton)
Duke D'Mond, vocals, The Barron Knights (b. 25 Feb 1943, Dunstable, d. 9 Apr 2009)
Gilson Lavis, drums, Squeeze (b. 27 Jun 1951, Bedford)
Martin McCarrick, guitar/cello, Therapy? (b. 29 Jul 1962, Luton)
Paul Young (b. 17 Jan 1956, Luton)

Big hair in Bedfordshire: captured in an early 1970s Chrysalis Records press picture, Luton-born blues guitarist Mick Abrahams was a founder member of Jethro Tull before forming his own band, Blodwyn Pig

Poster Courtesy Oscar Wilson

Berkshire

Less rock evocative perhaps than the Mississippi, but the River Thames running through this royal county has drawn a host of well-heeled and indeed high-heeled rock glitterati to its towns and villages. Aside from gathering together the individuals who would be Led Zeppelin and the Spice Girls, Berkshire played a huge part in the mod movement's enjoyment of some terrific live music at the various Ricky-Tick clubs around the county. Berkshire can also proudly claim to have Elton John as a resident, one of the world's best established annual festivals at Reading, the grandeur of John Lennon's Tittenhurst home and the less grand but charming Reading pub where he and Paul McCartney played a gig as holidaying teenagers in 1960.

Eton
The Jam's posh school protest

"Sup up your beer and collect your fags, there's a row going on down near Slough" wrote The Jam's Paul Weller. Eton public school is the destination in the class war song by Britain's angry young mod trio. Paul Weller wrote and recorded 'The Eton Rifles' in 1979, prompted by reports a year earlier of a march by Right to Work and Rock Against Racism protestors who congregated outside the school, a symbol of posh privilege and wealth to the burgeoning socialist movement during the years of Margaret Thatcher's Conservative government.

LOCATION 005: there is no direct access for vehicles over the Thames from Windsor to Eton. Pedestrians can walk across Windsor Bridge and up Eton High Street to Eton College, a distance of about half a mile. Postcode: SL4 6DW

Hook End
The studios where pigs might fly

Until recently a superbly appointed residential studio complex, Hook End Manor has variously been owned by Ten Years After's Alvin Lee, Pink Floyd's Dave Gilmour and producer and all-round pop person Trevor Horn. However well-appointed the recording facilities might be, it is the 16th-century former monastery and surrounding countryside that has drawn the likes of Radiohead, Morrissey, Iron Maiden, Kaiser Chiefs, Robbie Williams and Megadeth to book in and work. In addition to Dave Gilmour's floating recording studio aboard the

Astoria houseboat, nearby on the Thames, Hook End Manor was used to record parts of Pink Floyd's 1987 album A Momentary Lapse of Reason. During Gilmour's ownership of Hook End, one of the group's famous giant inflatable pig stage props was stored in an outbuilding of the property. At least one report suggests that it was the presence of the well-documented Hook End ghosts that was a factor in Gilmour's wife Ginger wanting the couple to move out.

LOCATION 006: the village of Hook End is slightly north-east of the A4074 that joins Reading and Wallingford, postcode RG8 0UE. The house and studio are a private residence

Archer and dirt biker Alvin Lee purchased Hook End in 1972, set about constructing a recording studio soon after with the help of his father Sam, before selling the high maintenance estate to Dave Gilmour in 1980

"It happened for each person at **TEN PAST FOUR** in the morning. It felt **LIKE A HAND** on your **CHEST**"

MORRISSEY
explaining how he experienced the Hook End ghost, like many a visitor before him

Berkshire

Pangbourne
Boathouse birthplace for Led Zeppelin

Jimmy Page's beautiful riverside home at Pangbourne was the location where the component parts of Led Zeppelin were assembled. In 1968, Yardbirds guitarist Page decided to start a new group and enlisted the services of organist and bass player John Paul Jones, vocalist Robert Plant and drummer John Bonham. Page owned the Boathouse between 1967 and 1975 and the property was the band's early HQ, where they first met and later rehearsed by climbing a ladder to the first floor. The property, the hub of what Page jokingly referred to as "the New Renaissance of Berkshire", has attracted many visiting Led Zeppelin pilgrims down the

years. According to a report in the Sunday Times, one inquisitive visitor in 2003, apologising for any intrusion, asked the then owner Graham Gore, "Did you know that a group used to be here?" Gore broke off from mending his son's car in the Boathouse garage to reply, "You mean Led Zeppelin?

"Once the sun comes out, we all go on the river and EVERY DAY IS A HOLIDAY"

JIMMY PAGE

Jimmy Page at home on the river

The former Boathouse, Pangbourne, home of Jimmy Page

Why, are you a fan?" "No," replied a no doubt amused Robert Plant, "I was the singer."

LOCATION 007: the Boathouse, 4 Shooters Hill, Pangbourne, postcode RG8 7DU. Best viewed from the opposite bank of the River Thames, this private residence is a short walk from the centre of the village of Pangbourne

Old Windsor
White Tie and Tiara Balls at Elton's Woodside mansion

Two miles south of the royal residence of Windsor Castle lies the only slightly more modest home of Elton John. World statesmen and women, footballers and fellow musicians and entertainers are all regular visitors to either establishment, particularly since Elton began hosting his annual White Tie & Tiara Summer Ball to benefit the Elton John AIDS Foundation at his Woodside home. Sir Elton's eight-bedroom, Queen Anne-style property is accessed through electric gates and a gravelled drive flanked by immaculately tended white rose bushes. Inside, floral opulence is everywhere in a house full of vases of flowers. Outside, the obsessive nature of the owner is reflected in the formerly laid-out gardens on the 37-acre property which feature a lake, orangery, the White Scented Gardens, an Italian garden, a Roman terrace, a secret garden and enough garaging for a fleet of cars that once made most motor museums green with envy but now houses his burgeoning collection of modern art.

LOCATION 008: on the road going south out of Old Windsor, turn right on to Crimp Hill, where the private residence of Woodside is approximately one mile on your left. Postcode: SL4 2HL

Reading
The Thames-side festival that saw Nirvana's last stand

It's testament to the success of this annual festival by the River Thames that so many legendary performances have ended up on CD and DVD. Nirvana, Hawkwind, Level 42, Samson, Ten Years After and Marillion have all been captured and given the 'Live at Reading' treatment. But it was Nirvana's greatest (and final) UK performance at the 1992 Reading Festival that fans remember with most enthusiasm. This festival hasn't always been located in its current Richfield Avenue site. Perpetually close to the River Thames, the festival began in 1961 as a jazz and blues-based event at Richmond Athletic Ground before settling at Reading.

LOCATION 009: Richfield Avenue, postcode RG1 8EQ

Reading
The Nerk Twins pay (and play) their dues at The Fox and Hounds

During the 1960 Easter weekend, John Lennon and Paul McCartney played a couple of acoustic sessions to drinkers at The Fox and Hounds in Reading. The two friends had hitch-hiked down to stay at Paul's cousin Betty's pub in the Reading suburb of Caversham. Both lads served behind the bar and absorbed some good show-business advice from Betty's husband, a former Butlins entertainments manager. He advised them on what to play to his Saturday night punters and suggested the duo kick off with a lively instrumental number instead of launching straight into Paul's favoured 'Be-Bop-a-Lula'. So, this unique rock 'n' roll meets country and western gig saw Lennon and McCartney perched on stools with their guitars beginning with their version of Les Paul and Mary Ford's 'The World is Waiting for the Sunrise'. When new landlords Kevin Durkan and wife Kerri took over The Fox and Hounds in 2011

The Fox and Hounds: now a Beatles shrine

they set about turning the pub poolroom into a Beatles shrine.

LOCATION 010: north of the centre of Reading over the River Thames at 51 Gosbrook Road, Caversham, postcode RG4 8BS

> "At the end of the week **WE PLAYED IN THE PUB AS THE NERK TWINS.** We even made our own **POSTERS** "
> **PAUL McCARTNEY**

Berkshire

Sunningdale
Ringo, John and Yoko at Tittenhurst Park

This Georgian house was home to John Lennon and Yoko Ono from 1969 too 1971 before the house, estate and recording studio were purchased by Ringo Starr, who owned it between 1973 and 1988. The place is familiar to so many music fans due to its frequent appearance in Beatles film footage and photos. Two days after The Beatles' final recording session, John, Paul, George and Ringo wandered the 72-acre estate for the group's last photocall on August 22nd 1969. The Daily Mail's Monte Fresco, the group's assistant Mal Evans and American Ethan Russell all snapped away and Russell's Tittenhurst pictures were included on the front and back of The Beatles' US album release Hey Jude. Most memorable of all are the images from the 'Imagine' video (taken from the album/movie Imagine) of John and Yoko outside and inside Tittenhurst's white walls. At the beginning of the 'Imagine' video, as John and Yoko entered the house, the couple's equivalent of a welcome mat was weirdly and typically a simple message etched into the glass above Tittenhurst's front door: 'THIS IS NOT HERE'.

Pete Nash www.britishbeatlesfanclub.co.uk

Revered singer-songwriter Nick Drake was an excited house guest at Tittenhurst in 1971. John and Yoko had relocated to New York, leaving domestic staff in charge of the upkeep of the house in readiness for their return. Caretaker Paul Wheeler had been a friend of Drake at Cambridge University, and following the completion of his Pink Moon album Drake spent at least one visit soaking up the atmosphere of the rock star lifestyle at the house that had been home and creative hub for Lennon's Imagine recordings earlier that year.

LOCATION 011: north of the village of Sunningdale on the A329, postcode SL5 0PN. Status: private

The Tittenhurst Park house and grounds

The cover for US album Hey Jude photographed at Tittenhurst

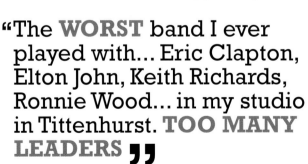

> "The **WORST** band I ever played with... Eric Clapton, Elton John, Keith Richards, Ronnie Wood... in my studio in Tittenhurst. **TOO MANY LEADERS** "
>
> **RINGO STARR**

Windsor & Newbury
The Ricky-Tick clubs

Perhaps Berkshire's biggest contribution to rock history came with the establishing of the wonderfully titled Ricky-Tick club. The name was coined in the 1920s and 30s as a description for syncopated music, but it was the organ-based, jazz-influenced rhythm and blues sounds that encouraged fans to flock to the Ricky-Tick's various locations across Berkshire. Promoter John Mansfield tapped into the rapidly growing enthusiasm for new bands like The Rolling Stones, who broke big at the first Ricky-Tick location at the Star & Garter hotel in Windsor back in January 1963. They literally brought the house down, with walls and ceilings shedding crumbling masonry, forcing a move down to the riverside Thames Hotel. By May 1964, the Ricky-Tick had a very different home at Clewer Mead. This derelict mansion was a mecca to mods, who travelled from as far as north London to groove to the music provided by the likes of Zoot Money, Graham Bond and Georgie Fame. Like most music clubs at the time there was no alcohol to be had, but the old house had a room converted into a coffee bar, a games room and a room set aside for the new early-60s recreation of TV watching. You can see a perfect reconstruction of the club in the 1966 movie Blow-Up. The director, Michelangelo Antonioni, was keen to use the real Windsor venue but the local council was in the process of trying to oust the Ricky-Tick from Clewer Mead. At great expense and effort, the club's fixtures and fittings were transported to the film's studio in Borehamwood, Hertfordshire,

> " It ended up as an almighty punch-up on stage as punches are thrown on stage and cymbals are being thrown around and guitars smashed on heads and **ROGER DALTREY WAS GOING WILD SHOUTING FOR THE CROWD TO RIOT** "
>
> **JOHN MANSFIELD**

where the Ricky-Tick was recreated for a sequence in the movie where The Yardbirds (featuring both Jeff Beck and Jimmy Page) performed in front of a bussed-in crowd of the club's mods. On May 20th 1966, the Ricky-Tick in Newbury was the setting for a massive falling-out by members of The Who. Famously fiesty on stage, this particular gig took their trademark aggression a stage further when John Entwistle and Keith Moon arrived late and Pete Townshend and Roger Daltrey took to the stage backed by support band The Jimmy Brown Sound. Entwistle and Moon finally arrived midway through the performance of 'My Generation', prompting Townshend to strike Moon over the head with his guitar in front of 800 Ricky-Tick club witnesses. Worse was to come. When refused payment for the gig, The Who's van ran out of petrol a short distance down the A4 on the journey back to London. With his injuries from the gig requiring stitches, Moon recuperated in a nursing home before going on to announce that he and Entwistle would be leaving The Who. Both rejoined within a week.

LOCATIONS 012, 013, 014, 015 and 016: at Windsor (all gone), Newbury (Corn Exchange), Maidenhead, Hounslow, and at The Stoke hotel Guildford, and Hounslow

Berkshire

Sunningdale
Big bands at The Old Trout

Local music fans didn't have to travel far to see some of rock's finest bands perform in the 1990s. A trip to The Old Trout Inn, on the Thames promenade, was as far as they needed to go to see Reading Festival warm-up gigs there by the Pixies, The Stranglers, House of Love, Suede, The Verve, Carter the Unstoppable Sex Machine and Blur. London promoter Jim Robertson was the man with all the right contacts to enable a steady stream of superstars to play the venue between 1989 and 1995. Robertson also drew plenty of record company scouts to this riverside location to check out the young up-and-coming talent performing when superstars weren't hogging the stage.

LOCATION 017: The Old Trout Inn is now Browns restaurant, Barry Avenue Windsor, SL4 1QX

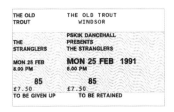

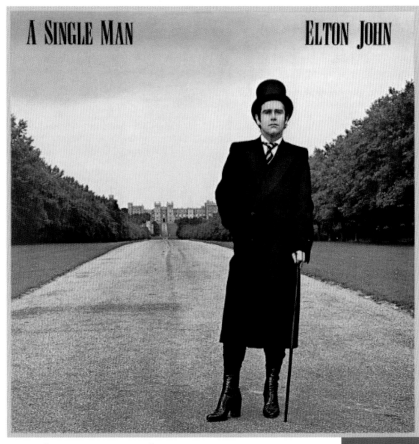

A SINGLE MAN   ELTON JOHN

Windsor Great Park
Elton John on The Long Walk

Windsor Castle and Windsor Great Park are where the front cover for his 1978 album A Single Man was shot. The photo features an uncharacteristically soberly dressed Elton in undertaker black. Some tracks on the LP were recorded nearby at The Mill, Cookham.

LOCATION 018: south of the castle (postcode SL4 1NJ) on The Long Walk, which is a public right of way

Elton John's 15th hit album featured this portrait in Windsor Great Park, snapped by photographer Terry O'Neill

Born in BERKSHIRE

Cliff Bennett (b. 4 Jun 1940, Slough)
Mark Brzezicki, drums, Big Country (b. 21 Jun 1957, Slough)
Tim Dorney, keyboards, Republica (b. 30 Mar 1965, Ascot)
Danny Goffey, drums, Supergrass (b. 7 Feb 1974, Slough)
Sarah Harding, Girls Aloud (b. 17 Nov 1981, Ascot)

Chesney Hawkes (b. 22 Sep 1971, Windsor)
Jonny Male, guitar, Republica (b. 10 Oct 1963, Windsor)
Mike Oldfield (b. 15 May 1953, Reading)
Irwin Sparkes, vocals/guitar, The Hoosiers (b. 5 Mar 1981, Reading)
Will Young (b. 20 Jan 1979, Wokingham)

Bristol

U K hip-hop, and more specifically trip-hop, was responsible for a 'Bristol sound' in the city famous for its historical tobacco and slave trade links. Massive Attack, Tricky and Portishead all evolved from late 80s collective The Wild Bunch to do their bit in putting Bristol on rock's atlas in the 90s and Tricky even named an album after his birthplace, 2008's Knowle West Boy. At the beginning of the decade, music papers eager for the next new sound descended on Bristol. The Face even likened Bristol's

Massive Attack to "Pink Floyd with bigger bass sounds and better drum patterns" to underline the new order of things. Towards the end of the Nineties, fellow Bristolian Roni Size brought yet more critical acclaim to the city when pioneering drum 'n' bass and bagging the 1997 Mercury Prize for debut album New Forms. As you'd expect for a city with its own music scene Bristol has some legendary clubs and venues, which sadly number among them the place where American Eddie Cochran played his last gig before ascending his own stairway to heaven.

Bristol
Eleanor Rigby's Bristol connection

While acknowledging that a real-life Eleanor Rigby lived, was buried and has a gravestone etched with her name in Liverpool, the origins of the Beatles song partly come from Bristol. In January 1966, when the song's creator Paul McCartney was visiting the Theatre Royal, where his actress girlfriend Jane Asher was performing in St Trinian's-style comedy The Happiest Days of Your Life, he observed a sign for Bristol wine merchants Rigby & Evens. Linked to this are reports indicating that at the time, Beatles Help! movie star Eleanor Bron was the Eleanor he had on his mind when 'Eleanor Rigby' was being written. This author would like to think that all three – Miss Bron, Rigby & Evens and the Liverpool gravestone must have been equally responsible for the completion of one of The Beatles' finest and saddest songs. And it does seem likely that a Bristol-based wine merchant's name plate was the final crucial piece in Paul McCartney's lyrical jigsaw.

Bonhams

LOCATION 019: Rigby & Evens once traded from No. 22 King Street, a short stroll from the Old Vic's home at the Theatre Royal (No.35). Postcode BS1 4ED

Bristol

Bristol
The Granary: Bristol's Byzantine home of rock

If a venue that closed in 1988 is still remembered by reunion events, a website and a book, it has to have done something right in its glory years. The Granary really began to make a name for itself during the prog rock boom of the early 1970s when bands of the order of Yes, King Crimson and Supertramp played the place, establishing it as a fantastically popular rock venue for over two decades. Originally a magnificently appointed 10-storey grain store, built in 1869, the windows were non-glazed to allow air to circulate the grain. Prior to its use as a rock venue The Granary had been a jazz club hosting performances by the likes of the ever-popular Somerset local Acker Bilk. When opened as a rock club in 1968 the organisers used the first three floors of the listed building with the entrance and offices on the ground floor and a first-floor dance area, stage and main bar. The centre of the second floor was removed to create a balcony for projecting light shows, incorporating a DJ booth, small bar and viewing areas. The new venture used its 500-capacity area to host up-and-coming acts as live rock blossomed in the late 60s and early 70s. Emulating the success of early underground counter-culture newspapers OZ and Rolling Stone, The Granary even had its own magazine, Dogpress, complete with some highly original graphics. By the late Seventies The Granary was a Bristol rock institution attracting bigger bands on the

upward arc of their careers. On one occasion Dire Straits had the temerity to question a £200 or so performance fee contract that included a case of beer. The reported haggling by the band wasn't over the size of the fee but over the fact that they demanded a second case of beer, which the management politely refused. The advent of punk and new wave meant the arrival of performers such as Generation X, Bauhaus and The Stranglers which kept the fans coming, but in the mid-Eighties the overheads involved in running such a big place meant that The Granary's most popular

The igloo-like windows and the DJ box above the Granary stage are clearly visible as Robert Plant struts his stuff at an early post-Led Zeppelin gig with The Honeydrippers at The Granary on May 19th 1981

draw was the regular rock DJ nights hosted by Adrian Coleman. By 1988 it was no longer a going concern and closed, but the important part it played in so many

"I suppose the biggest gig was Robert Plant's first solo appearance after leaving Led Zep. Picking a favourite? Dire Straits were unforgettable but they were so new we lost money. Booking **SUPERTRAMP AND JUDAS PRIEST** on the same night **FOR £95**"

AL READ
Former entertainments organiser, DJ and licensee of the club for the first 14 years of its existence

young lives is happily celebrated by the organisers' regular reunion events. Added unconnected interesting fact: According to a website dedicated to the hugely popular BBC TV sitcom Only Fools and Horses, The Granary was the exterior location for the famous episode when David Jason, as Del Boy, hilariously fell through a bar hatch.

LOCATION 020: These days the magnificent Granary is a very well appointed block of apartments, a short walk south-east of the city centre at Welsh Back, Bristol. Postcode BS1 4HQ

Above: The Bristol Byzantine gem that was the Granary, now converted into a block of apartments. Right: Stargazer face a late-70s Granary crowd of flares

Bristol

Bristol
The Dug Out Club

The foundations for a new music genre, which Mixmag magazine are said to have dubbed trip-hop, were conceived in the small clubs, bedrooms and front rooms in and around the St Pauls area of 1980s Bristol. A wide cultural mix of the city's young population made it the place to be to hear long-established soul, punk and reggae music, but what made Bristol extra interesting was its platform as an experimental sounding board for mixing and mashing up all kinds of music, and eventually hitting upon the lo-fi, bass-heavy vibe of trip-hop. Here on the edge of one of the most deprived areas of Bristol were definite similarities to Harlem and South Bronx's New York City 1970 invention, Hip-Hop. Like any happening scene, for a short while at least, it had its focal point. The right people found the right place at the right time and that place was The Dug Out Club. If a German research group are to be

believed, it was here in the club's cramped basement that the Jamaican DJs of Bristol first created rap/toasting. The Dug Out even had a psychedelic rock night in the 60s before the tiny capacity encouraged organisers to move that increasingly popular brand of music to bigger premises at Bristol's Granary. Later, during the Eighties, when the innovative Afro-Caribbean music-makers mingled with the university students from the bohemian bedsits of Clifton, an altogether different music genre took route at The Dug Out. The Bristol sound, some dubbed trip hop, was the result of a melting pot of music emanating from the basement, while upstairs a video lounge screened all the best must-see cult movies. Eighties turntable residents at The Dug Out were The Wild Bunch, who eventually morphed into the world-famous Massive Attack. But long before

the 1990s heyday of drum 'n' bass and trip hop, The Dug Out was no more. This legendary piece of Bristol's cultural history closed its doors for the last time in 1986.

LOCATION 021: The Dug Out Club is now Surakhan, a Korean restaurant, at 52 Park Row, Bristol. Postcode BS1 5LH

"The Dug Out was a meeting spot for the ghetto and poshville. **IT WAS OUR STUDIO 54,** and it put Bristol on the map"

PETER WEBB
Author of Exploring the Networked Worlds of Popular Music: Milieu Cultures

Bristol
Rock 'n' Roll's
Colston Hall of Fame

A glittering list of rock's finest have played Bristol's premier rock venue down the decades. Jimi Hendrix, The Stones, Bowie, Roxy Music, Elton, Thin Lizzy, Lou Reed and Bob Marley all played the hall in their heyday. At the end of their 1964 UK tour, The Beatles sportingly played, despite being the victims of a stunt that saw them showered in flour from the lighting gantry by four students. Two decades later Bob Dylan, with supporting roles for Ronnie Wood, Ian Dury and Richie

Havens, played in front of 1,000 extras hired for the filming of scenes for his Hearts of Fire movie.

LOCATION 022: the city centre at 13 Colston Street, postcode BS1 5AR

Colston Hall has staged 140 years of music concerts. Left: Bob Dylan and Fiona Flanagan filming a scene from Hearts of Fire on the Colston Hall stage

Eddie Cochran's last stand: Bristol saw his final performance on 16th April 1960, aged just 21

The framed tribute presented to the Hippodrome by Cochran fan Gwen Hale, who attended Eddie's final show

Bristol
Eddie Cochran's final show

The Bristol Hippodrome was Eddie Cochran's final stop on his UK tour before returning to America in 1960. Cochran never made the plane home, dying as a result of a car crash on the A40 heading east for Heathrow Airport. Aside from a plaque in Cirencester and a memorial in Bath, Cochran is also remembered here by a small framed presentation plaque located in the Hippodrome Cast Bar. These days the Hippodrome majors in musicals.

LOCATION 023: 10 St Augustine's Parade in the city centre, postcode BS1 4UZ

Born in
BRISTOL

Mercury Prize-winning Bristolian Roni Size

Julie Burchill, writer/columnist (b. 3 Jul 1959)
Russ Conway (b. 2 Sep 1925, d. 16 Nov 2000)
Roger Cook, songwriter (b. 19 Aug 1940)
Sara Dallin, vocals, Bananarama (b. 17 Dec 1961)
Rob Ellis, drums, PJ Harvey (b. 13 Feb 1962)
Roger Greenaway, songwriter (b. 23 Aug 1938)
Abi Harding, saxophone, The Zutons (b. 1982)
Nellee Hooper, producer (b. 7 Jan 1963)
Wayne Hussey, vocals, The Mission (b. 26 May 1958)
Nik Kershaw (b. 1 Mar 1958)
Grantley Marshall (Daddy G), vocals, Massive Attack (b. 18 Dec 1959)
Roni Size (above), DJ/producer (b. 29 Oct 1969)
Tricky (b. 27 Jan 1968)
Andrew Vowles (Mushroom), keyboards, Massive Attack (b. 10 Nov 1967)
Keren Woodward, vocals, Bananarama (b. 2 Apr 1961)
Robert Wyatt (b. 28 Jan 1945)

ROCK ATLAS UK & IRELAND EDITION **29**

Buckinghamshire

The former home of Three Men in a Boat author Jerome K Jerome invaded by the Small Faces, a Denham pub's three-pint songwriting method enjoyed by Mike Oldfield, an unscheduled Sex Pistols gig at Wycombe College, an eye-popping High Wycombe hostelry enjoyed by the Kings of Leon and a Victorian railway station timewarp for Welsh band Man are some of the key stories in the annals of Buckinghamshire rock. Noel Gallagher is a Little Chalfont resident and Paul Weller writes a less than loving lyric about Milton Keynes, but it's the cast of characters passing through the county town of Aylesbury (on a par with San Francisco according to Ian Hunter) with its significant court, club and market square that perhaps gives the county its greatest rock 'n' roll claim to fame.

Aylesbury
'Market Square Heroes' and the British San Francisco

Aylesbury was the spiritual setting for 'Market Square Heroes', the song that gave the Buckinghamshire-formed band Marillion their first hit in 1982. Inspired by the inner-city riots across England the previous year, Marillion's vocalist Fish remembers writing the song's lyrics in nearby St Mary's churchyard. Mott the Hoople's Ian Hunter is another to have gained inspiration from the town. Talking to Mojo in 2009, he said: "Aylesbury is like a little San Francisco. It's one of those places where everything seems to start... The people there seem to sense what's going to happen. In fact, the atmosphere of Aylesbury got to me to such an extent that I was seriously considering moving there... but I moved to America instead."

LOCATION 024: the town centre, postcode HP20 1UF

Aylesbury
'Keef' in court

In January, at the start of what would become a particularly difficult 1977 for Keith Richards, Aylesbury Crown Court was the setting for a high-profile court case for The Rolling Stones' guitarist. Found guilty on some but not all of a catalogue of drug possession charges, he was also fined £25 for failing to produce a current MOT certificate or tax disc while driving. When Tony Parsons reported for NME he described the trial thus:"The next day, The Final Day, can only be likened to Cup Final Fever. Oop fer der bust, and so on. By this time the big, forbidding-looking front gates of Aylesbury Crown Court were locked up to keep the maddening crowd at bay." Keith's misdemeanours escalated to an altogether more international level in February when he was infamously arrested by the Canadian Mounties in Toronto.

LOCATION 025: Market Square, postcode HP20 1XD

Born in BUCKINGHAMSHIRE

Nicholas Bracegirdle, aka Chicane (b. 28 Feb 1971, Chalfont St Giles)
Terry Cox, drums, Pentangle (b. 13 Mar 1937, High Wycombe)
Paul Ferguson, drums, Killing Joke (b. 31 Mar 1958, High Wycombe)
Adam Ficek, drums, Babyshambles (b. 1974, Bletchley, Milton Keynes)
Kris Ife, singer-songwriter (b. 16 Jun 1946, Aylesbury)
John Otway (b. 2 Oct 1952, Aylesbury)
Tim Rice, lyricist (b. 10 Nov 1944, Amersham)
Justin Sullivan, vocals, New Model Army (b. 8 Apr 1956, Jordans)

Denham and Chalfont St Giles
Songwriting inspiration for Mike Oldfield down the pub

A lapsed songwriter from his time as a performer around the folk clubs in and around Reading, Mike Oldfield had another stab at lyric writing after the success of his instrumental albums. A concerted effort saw him create some memorable songs such as 'Moonlight Shadow', which became a huge hit in 1983 for him and Maggie Reilly who sang vocals. The lyric writing seemed to flow best when he decamped from his home in Tilehouse Lane, Denham (where he had a recording studio built on to his 100-year-old property in 1981), to his local pub, The Crown in Chalfont St Giles. However,

according to Mike Oldfield's son Luke, the pub where his dad rediscovered his songwriting skills was more likely to be The Swan in Denham. In 1987 Mike Oldfield moved a short distance away to Roughwood Croft, in Chalfont St Giles.

LOCATIONS 026 and 027:
Tilehouse Studios, currently run by Mike's son Luke Oldfield, is at Little Halings, Tilehouse Lane, Denham: Postcode UB9 5DG. The property at Roughwood Croft is nearby in Nightingales Lane, Chalfont St Giles. Postcode HP8 4SJ

"I lived in Denham and I'd go down the pub, The Crown, with my rhyming dictionary, my thesaurus and my writing pad, and line up my pints of Guinness. By the time I'd got through **THREE PINTS I'D COME UP WITH A SONG**"

MIKE OLDFIELD

Buckinghamshire

Aylesbury
From Mandrake Paddle Steamer to Ziggy at Friars

Even if you never attended a gig there - the club had 87,000 members by the time it closed in 1984, so many did - no-one who bought a music paper in the Seventies could have failed to notice the weekly gig ads topped by the distinctive gothic Friars logo. Opening with Mike Cooper and Mandrake Paddle Steamer on June 2nd 1969 at New Friarage Hall, Friars relocated to the Borough Assembly Hall from 1971 until 1975, when it moved to its current Civic Centre home. Promoter David Stopps oversaw the conveyor belt of prog rock's finest that put Aylesbury on the music map and managed the 2009 40th anniversary gig that saw Friars return to the town once more. No band has been as crucial to the ongoing success story as The Groundhogs, who returned to play the anniversary gig along with early Friars favourites Edgar Broughton and The Pretty Things. Back in the day, Captain Beefheart, Genesis, Mott the Hoople and Fleetwood Mac all appeared before new-wavers, and punks became the Friars' new customers when The Flamin' Groovies and The Vibrators took the place by storm in 1976. That same year saw American hopefuls Blondie play a career-changing gig at Friars that kick-started their love affair with British audiences and record-buyers – the polar opposite to their luke warm reception back home. Before the end came, The Clash, U2, The Jam, The Ramones and The Police all put in memorable appearances. Friars played an important part in David Bowie's development from thoughtful singer-songwriter to full-blown rock 'n' roll superstar. September 25th 1971 was the date of his memorable first performance at the club in front of the Friars' faithful, who each paid ten shillings to watch a captivating performance that left him promising, "When I come back I'm going to be completely different." How focused, driven and true to his word was he? January 29th, 1972 saw his return in the guise of Ziggy Stardust. It was a life-changing introduction to a whole new direction in music for him. It was equally life-changing for many in the audience that night who witnessed a set list including the new Ziggy album plus revved-up classics 'I Feel Free' by Cream and 'Around and Around' by Chuck Berry.

LOCATION 028: Civic Centre, Market Square, postcode HP20 1UF. For the continuing Friars drama and more information about the various Friars locations visit the website: www.aylesburyfriars.co.uk

"Up until then we had only been playing in New York, where everyone was a cool beatnik and nobody showed any enthusiasm whatsoever. But from the moment we went on stage at Friars the audience went crazy. That was **THE BEGINNING OF BLONDIE AS A BIG BAND"**

CHRIS STEIN
Blondie's guitarist, talking to Mojo in 2013

Photo Geoffrey Tyrell

Buckinghamshire

High Wycombe
Strip pub debut for Kings of Leon

Oklahoma's biggest rock export, the Kings of Leon, made their UK debut at High Wycombe's extraordinary White Horse pub in February 2003. The young band's first impression of the British live circuit was not what they were expecting but not altogether unfavourable. In addition to beer and big-screen football, The White Horse offered entertainment of a more exotic nature. This warm-up gig and an encounter with the pub's naked dancers was followed the next day by a rather more traditional introduction to Britain's music venues up the A40 at The Zodiac in Oxford.

LOCATION 029: The White Horse, 95 West Wycombe Road, postcode HP11 2LR

"It was a strip joint by day then at night they'd have bands playing, so when we got there, there was a bunch of **NAKED WOMEN IN OUR DRESSING ROOM**, changing clothes. We thought this is definitely the life!

MATTHEW FOLLOWILL
Kings of Leon, talking to Mojo magazine

Kings of Leon's UK debut found them sharing a dressing room at The White Horse, High Wycombe

High Wycombe
Blondie and Lightnin' Hopkins at The Nag's Head

The rather ordinary-looking Nag's Head pub had a rather extra ordinary life as a music venue. Blues fan and promoter Ron Watts was the driving force behind the pub's Blues Loft in the 1960s, which played host to an unbelievable list of soon-to-be massive bands including blues and rock outfits Lightnin' Hopkins, Fleetwood Mac, Thin Lizzy and Status Quo. The Nag's Head continued its successful run through to the punk and new wave era when Siouxsie and The Banshees, The Damned, Sex Pistols and even The Jam and Blondie came to play. Its popularity has ebbed and flowed but its continued use as a live music venue appeared to have ended in 2013.

LOCATION 030: still standing, the Nag's Head was the subject of a save our venue petition by music fans who weren't chuffed about the idea of their iconic pub being converted to an 11-bedroom hotel. The pub (or maybe hotel by the time you read this) is at 63 London Road, High Wycombe. Postcode HP11 1BN

Geoffrey Tyrell

Buckinghamshire

Marlowe
Small Faces at Monks Corner

The former home of writer Jerome K Jerome was the spot for a final burst of creativity for the Small Faces in the period around their No.1 album Ogdens' Nut Gone Flake. According to keyboards man Ian McLagan, Monks Corner was where 1968 hit single 'The Universal' was written and partly recorded. The birdsong, barking dog and Steve Marriott's acoustic guitar were all taped in the garden on their old mono cassette machine. Sharing the house with Steve and wife Jenny were Ian and Ronnie Lane and their other halves. Marlow was also the starting point for Lane's new venture in 1974, The Passing Show, a rock and folk tour travelling the country in a circus-style big top.

LOCATION 031: west of Marlow, Monks Corner, Marlow Common, postcode SL7 2QR Status: private residence

SMALL FACES

IMMEDIATE

THE UNIVERSAL
Donkey rides, a penny a glass

Birdsong and barking dogs at Monks Corner for the Small Faces' 11th hit single

"It was a very beautiful house... and it was in that garden that Steve wrote 'The Universal' **WITH THE DOGS BARKING** in the background"

JENNY MARRIOTT

High Wycombe
Sex Pistols chaos and a Buzzcocks pilgrimage

When future Buzzcocks Pete Shelley and Howard Devoto read a review describing a "musical experience" featuring new band the Sex Pistols in NME in February 1976 they were excited enough to drive down from their native Manchester to catch the "chaos", as the band described what they stood for, at High Wycombe College. It turned out to be an experience that changed their lives, as Devoto later admitted, prompting them to form the Buzzcocks. The Sex Pistols were booked to support Screaming Lord Sutch for High Wycombe College's Rag Week Ball on February 20th and they were at their attention-seeking best. The college social secretary had secured the band by offering half a case of Carlsberg lager and acceding to Johnny Rotten's request that the DJ should play some "loud, out of tune guitar music", which he duly did by selecting New York Dolls' 'White Punks on Dope'. But when the Pistols took to the stage to perform what eyewitnesses described in equal measure as either "mesmerising" or "unintelligible noise" they over-ran into the time allotted for headliner Lord Sutch's set. Although the crowd that night was boosted by a dozen or so Pistols fans up from London sporting safety pins and dressed in bin liners the vast majority were disco fans who began booing when the Pistols made it clear they weren't going to stop playing anytime soon. Scuffles broke out and efforts by the DJ to drown the Pistols out by playing disco on the PA system only stiffened the band's resolve until brute force was employed. Order was only restored when, after Johnny Rotten had been forcibly lifted off the stage, the plugs were pulled on them and the shambles of a climax to their set had ended. The chaos didn't deter Pete Shelley and Howard Devoto. The two promptly booked the Pistols for what would prove to be a seminal gig in British pop music history when they played Manchester's Lesser Free Trade Hall on June 4th 1976 for slightly more than half a case of lager – but still only £32. According to the then assistant Wycombe College social secretary, Patrick Graham, "The college venue was a cavernous 60s-built theatrical hall with

Taplow
Station cover for Man's first chart album

The fine Victorian architecture of Taplow station is pictured on Man's 1973 album cover Back into the Future, photographed by Ruan O'Laughran. The Victorian characters pictured on the platform (from left to right on the gatefold sleeve) were Man people Angie Davies, Will Youatt, Plug's daughter, Howard 'Plug' Davies (tour manager/roadie), Ella Ryan, Phil Ryan, Linda Williams, Micky Jones, Terry Williams, Jenny Jones, Noel Ryan and Jeff Hooper (sound engineer). Micky Jones came up with the idea for the title of the album and Youatt the concept for the sleeve design. The double LP was the Welsh band's first to chart and it gave them a No.23 hit, which remains their highest-placed entry. "The photo session was a good laugh." said Jones. "We turned up at Taplow station, which was derelict.

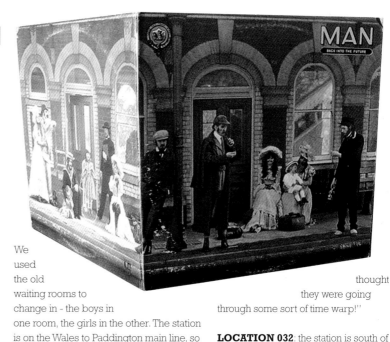

We used the old waiting rooms to change in - the boys in one room, the girls in the other. The station is on the Wales to Paddington main line, so every 15 minutes an express would come thundering through. I think passengers thought they were going through some sort of time warp!"

LOCATION 032: the station is south of Taplow, east of Maidenhead, postcode SL6 0NU

polished parquet floor. It was integral to the rest of the college buildings - big drape curtains, and on one side a little side stage (where I did the disco with the social secretary, Tony Wilkins, who was the one who booked the Pistols for half a crate of Carlsberg). At the west end of the building was the high, main theatre-style stage where a kick from a performer would naturally hit a front row mosher in the neck." What a pity that nobody had the presence of mind to snap any photos on the night!

LOCATION 033: The College of Further Education is now Bucks New University, Queen Alexandra Road, High Wycombe, Bucks. Postcode HP11 2JZ

" I was a local reporter and interviewed John Lydon afterwards. He was lovely and fascinating, but staggering around behind him was a drugged up Sid Vicious (not yet in the band, but a mate). Vicious was bleeding from an arm and Lydon told me he had done it SMASHING A WINDOW OF THEIR VAN TO GET IN FOR A KIP "
JANICE RAYCROFT

Cambridgeshire

Cambridge
The Cambridge Folk Festival

Popular Alabama folk import Emmylou Harris completes her headlining set at the 2006 Cambridge Folk Festival

Attracting artists from all over the world, this annual long weekend is Britain's most famous folk festival. Celebrating its 50th anniversary in July 2014 with headline appearances from Van Morrison and Sinéad O'Connor, the Cambridge Folk Festival has become a hot ticket, selling out quickly each year. Everyone you would expect to see at such a popular event has appeared, beginning with young British folk pilgrim Paul Simon. He played a week after a TV appearance on Ready, Steady, Go! where he'd sung his new composition 'I Am a Rock'. The New Jersey-born musician performed a half-hour set on the main stage at Cherry Hinton Hall, the new venue for the festival in its second year, 1965. Other international acts to grace the stage at Cherry Hinton Hall down the years have included Emmylou Harris, Joan Baez, Steve Earle, Jackson Browne, Jimmy Cliff and James Taylor. UK stalwarts of the folk scene Fairport Convention, Pentangle, Kate Rusby, Bellowhead and Mumford & Sons have all played to enthusiastic Cambridge Folk Festival attendees, who are treated to some of the festival circuit's best-appointed facilities. What began as an attempt to combine the excitement witnessed at the

Photo: CamPlus

Spiritual home to Pink Floyd, Cambridge oozes rock sophistication and can also claim to be Britain's annual central pilgrimage point for folk fans with the famous festival, located at Cherry Hinton Hall. The Beatles, The Rolling Stones and Jimi Hendrix have all played the wider county, although few of the original venues they played (none in the case of Peterborough) are still intact. Wisbech is a town that saw more than its fair share of Sixties beat groups leave an impression at the town's opulent Corn Exchange, which turned out to be a particularly significant destination on The Rolling Stones' 1963 schedule of appearances. But back to sophisticated Cambridge for a moment: a riot at a Drifters concert? Surely not...

A proliferation of panama hats, rugs and garden chairs at the 2012 Cambridge Folk Festival

US 1958 Newport Jazz Festival with the socialist ideals linked to the British folk movement is now a world-famous event broadcast nationally by the BBC. The man charged with organizing the first festivals was local fireman Ken Woollard and his legacy continues as his former assistant Eddie Barcan still programmes the festival to this day.

LOCATION 034: four miles south-east of the city centre at Cherry Hinton Hall, Cherry Hinton Road. Postcode CB1 8DW

" **CBS desperately wanted Paul Simon to play the festival. But we were full up, totally full up, and WE COULDN'T PAY HIM, even though they only wanted minimal money. So they paid for a page of advertising in the programme... and he appeared as a guest artist** "

KEN WOOLLARD
Cambridge Folk Festival's former Director, recalls Paul Simon's July 31 1965 appearance, when he was incorrectly billed as 'Paul Simons'

Cambridgeshire

Cambridge
Rioting Drifters fans and Syd's last stand at the Corn Exchange

It wasn't until 1965 that the good folk of Cambridge ceased exchanging corn and hired out this magnificent asset as a place of entertainment. The best of British has performed here including The Beatles, Iron Maiden and Dizzee Rascal. In 1972, in the same year it was converted into a properly designated concert venue, the place witnessed the final public appearance of local legend Syd Barrett when his band Stars supported The MC5. Two years later and the management were faced with a near riot when 1,000 Drifters fans showed their displeasure when informed that the band would not be appearing.

LOCATION 035: Wheeler Street in Cambridge city centre, postcode CB2 3QB

Cambridge Corn Exchange

The former St Margaret's Square home of Syd Barrett

Cambridge
Syd Barrett's semi-detached

The madcap genius Syd Barrett retreated from the fame and success he once enjoyed in Pink Floyd, penning classic hits 'Arnold Layne' and 'See Emily Play', by living as something of a recluse until his death aged just 60. In a semi-detached house in the cul-de-sac at 6 St Margaret's Square, he spent his days painting pictures and making his own furniture but leaving the 1930s three-bedroom house largely lacking any modernisation from the time his mother owned the property in the 1950s. A shrine to a hugely creative but ultimately troubled soul who settled for the simple life, the house has attracted much interest from Syd's fans: one or two were even reported to have camped in the long, narrow garden during his tenancy. Like most of his followers, they were no doubt feeling the need to in some way protect the fragile but precious character that helped spark the British psychedelic music movement.

LOCATION 036: private residence to the south-east of the city centre, postcode CB1 8AQ

Chatteris
Half Man Half Biscuit's 'envy of the Fens'

The track 'For What Is Chatteris...' appears on Half Man Half Biscuit's 2005 album Achtung Bono. The song appears to sound like a tourist information leaflet, promoting an apparently perfect Fenland town with three good butchers, two fine chandlers and a first-class cake shop, not to mention its famed brass band. But as the Half Man Half Biscuit song goes, "...if you're not there, I may as well be in Ely or St Ives".

LOCATION 037: 20 miles north of Cambridge where the A141 meets the A142, postcode PE16

Gog Magog Hills
Where Syd saw Emily play

A range of low chalk hills, south-east of Cambridge, is where Syd Barrett would play as a child when heading out of the family home in Cherry Hinton. The trees en route to the Gog Magog Hills was where he is thought to have set his Pink Floyd psychedelic pop masterpiece, 'See Emily Play'. Roger Waters revealed the spot that helped inspire the images conjured up in Pink Floyd's second hit single: "I know which woods Syd's talking about in 'See Emily Play'. We all used to go to these woods as kids. It's a very specific area – one specific wood on the road to the Gog Magog Hills."

LOCATION 038: a few miles south-east of Cambridge. Postcode CB22 3AD

David Roberts x 2

Grantchester
Pink Floyd's Grantchester Meadows

Pink Floyd's Dave Gilmour actually lived at 109 Grantchester Meadows, Cambridge, from the age of ten but it was Roger Waters who penned the band's 'Grantchester Meadows' album track. Pick the right day in early summer and you can see and feel why Grantchester Meadows was such an inspirational location for his song of the same name. The pastoral track, all birdsong and acoustic guitar strumming with Waters' lyrics and vocals, appeared on the band's 1969 album Ummagumma. The recommended method of discovering this idyllic spot is to wander lazily out of Cambridge on the River Cam's footpath to Grantchester with the seven-minute-plus track on repeat on your mp3 player.

LOCATIONS 039 and 040: from the M11 at junction 12, head towards Grantchester village High Street. Turn left at the green and enter the meadows at the end of the road, past the Red Lion pub, postcode CB3 9NF. Dave Gilmour's boyhood home was at 109 Grantchester Meadows, Cambridge, CB3 9JN

David Roberts

Right: the post-Barrett Pink Floyd line-up with Roger Waters (front), who penned the song 'Grantchester Meadows', and Dave Gilmour (far right), who lived there. 'Grantchester Meadows' appears on Ummagumma, whose front cover artwork by Hipgnosis was created at Storm Thorgerson's girlfriend's home in Long Shelford, a village two miles south of Grantchester

Cambridgeshire

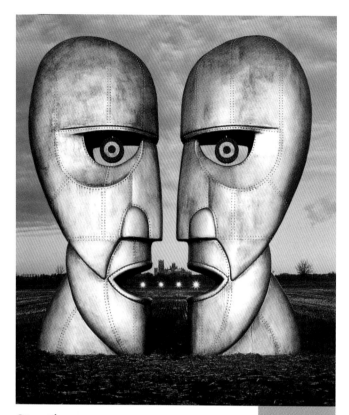

Stretham
The Division Bell album cover

A field near Stretham was the temporary site for the three-metre-high sculptures photographed for the cover of Pink Floyd's album The Division Bell. Created by Storm Thorgerson, these vast metallic busts were sculpted by Aden Hynes and John Robertson from artist Keith Breeden's illustrations and photographed with Ely Cathedral clearly visible in the background. The two sculptures are currently on display as museum exhibits in the US at Cleveland, Ohio's, Rock and Roll Hall of Fame.

Ely Cathedral and the flat fields outside Stretham form the setting for Pink Floyd's The Division Bell album cover

LOCATION 041: east out of Stretham on the A1123, the Division Bell field is on your left just before the bridge over the River Cam, with views of Ely Cathedral in the distance. Postcode: CB6 3LJ

Wisbech
The emerging Rolling Stones upsize at the Wisbech Corn Exchange

Wisbech was no music outpost, hosting a growing number of rock and pop shows in the Sixties. It played a significant part in the development of the increasing popularity of The Rolling Stones in the summer of 1963. That July proved to be a career-defining milestone. A week or two before their first hit 'Come On' entered the chart, the band made their TV debut on Thank Your Lucky Stars and made the jump from the club circuit to ballrooms around the country. Wisbech was the place where the band made their debut in this larger type of venue, when they appeared at the Corn Exchange on July 20. Despite the significance of the gig, there seems little empathy between the Corn Exchange crowd and Keith Richards in particular, who referred to the male Wisbech fans as hostile 'yokels' in his autobiography Life.

LOCATION 042: still standing near the town centre at 1 North Brink, postcode PE13 1JR

Born in CAMBRIDGESHIRE

Syd Barrett, vocals/guitar, Pink Floyd (b. 6 Jan 1946, d. 7 Jul 2006, Cambridge)
Andy Bell, vocals, Erasure (b. 25 Apr 1964, Peterborough)
Matthew Bellamy, vocals/guitar, Muse (b. 9 Jun 1978, Cambridge)
Andrew Eldritch, vocals, The Sisters of Mercy (b. 15 May 1959, Ely)
David Gilmour, vocals/guitar, Pink Floyd (b. 6 Mar 1946, Cambridge)
Maxim, (aka Keith Palmer) vocals, The Prodigy (b. 21 Mar 1967, Peterborough)
Aston Merrygold, JLS (b. 13 Feb 1988, Peterborough)
Olivia Newton-John (b. 26 Sep 1948, Cambridge)
Owen Powell, guitar, Catatonia (b. 9 Jul 1967, Cambridge)
Tom Robinson (b. 1 Jun 1950, Cambridge)
Phil Selway, drums, Radiohead (b. 23 May 1967, Hemingford Grey)

Cheshire

*T*he county, famed for its Premier League footballers' palatial piles, gave birth to Gary Barlow and Ian Brown, has absorbed huge musical influences from nearby metropolis' Manchester and Liverpool, and come up with its own brooding bunch of rock locations. Cheshire is where Doves and The Charlatans developed and prospered, Paul Simon and Elvis Costello were inspired to write some fine railway-inspired lyrics, Spike Island became the live event of the Nineties, and Ian Curtis lived and died.

Macclesfield
The beginning and end of Joy Division

Fifteen miles south of Manchester lies the silk town of Macclesfield, where Joy Division singer Ian Curtis grew up and died. Born in Old Trafford, Manchester, Curtis' early childhood was spent in the family home at Balmoral Crescent, Hurdsfield, a short walk north-west of the centre of Macclesfield, before moving to a flat nearer the centre of town. A schoolboy at the town's King's School in Cumberland Street, along with future Joy Division drummer Stephen Morris, Curtis later married Deborah Woodruff at St. Thomas' Church, Henbury, west of Macclesfield. After two years living on the Manchester outskirts, the couple moved back to Macclesfield in 1977. Much of the Joy Division catalogue of songs was written at this time in the terraced house at No.77 Barton Street, Macclesfield. It was also the setting for Curtis' tragic suicide. In the early hours of Sunday May 18 1980, the day before the band were due to fly out of the UK bound for their first US tour, the 23-year-old singer hung himself in the kitchen. A memorial stone inscribed with the title of Joy Division's best-known song,

Ian Curtis fan Laura Jade Heseltine from London visits the singer's memorial stone in his hometown of Macclesfield

Photo: Laura Jade Heseltine

'Love Will Tear Us Apart', can be found at Macclesfield Crematorium. Pretty much a kerbstone, the small memorial to Curtis is usually decorated with fans' gifts and is therefore relatively easy to find.

LOCATIONS 043, 044, 045, 046 and 047: Macclesfield is 15 miles south of Manchester: Balmoral Crescent (postcode SK10 2NP); The King's School is in Cumberland Street (SK10 1DA); St.

Thomas', Henbury, is three miles west of Macclesfield on the A537 (SK11 9NN); 77 Barton Street (SK11 6); the memorial stone is at 87 Prestbury Road (SK10 3BU). A walking tour including some of these locations, plus Armitt Street Labour Exchange, where Curtis worked, and his favourite haunts, the Travellers Rest and Krumbles, have been included on a Joy Division tour, available by contacting the Macclesfield Visitor Information Centre

Cheshire

Lower Withington
Science meets music at Jodrell Bank

Here's another contender for the UK and Ireland's most spectacular gig venue. 'Live from Jodrell Bank' is the catch-all title for the series of music events first launched at the site of the world-famous observatory in Cheshire. With its big name acts (Elbow, The Flaming Lips, New Order, Sigur Rós) and additional science activities and workshops, organizers claim that all this has made for a new chapter in live music experiences.

LOCATION 048: Jodrell Bank Observatory and Discovery Centre, near Lower Withington is 10 miles west of Macclesfield and 20 miles south of Manchester on the A535 between junctions 17 and 18 of the M6 motorway. Postcode SK11 9DL

Left: Astronomically good: Bernard Sumner concentrates as New Order take Jodrell Bank by storm. Main picture: Jodrell Bank Live, "making for a new chapter in live music experiences", as they say

Photo: Keith Ainsworth

" Jodrell was a dream come true. All the thrills of space exploration for **A BAND OF THE STAR WARS GENERATION**, plus some pretty amazing **COLD WAR ERA HARDWARE**. Thanks to everyone who stood in the rain right through to the end, you made it the best gig ever!… Ooooooh Jodrellites "

GUY GARVEY
Elbow

Cheshire

Northwich
The Charlatans' Melting Pot Café

Fondly remembered by The Charlatans as the place
they first met after signing a recording deal with the
Beggars Banquet label, Weaverdale Café appears on
the cover of the band's 1998 greatest hits album Melting
Pot. Less than five miles north-east of Northwich,
where The Charlatans were formed, lies Pickmere
Lake, pictured on the band's 2004 album cover for Up
at the Lake. Tim Burgess said: "It's 18 miles south of
Manchester, and 20 miles away from Liverpool. So I've
had the most brilliant musical upbringing."

LOCATION 049: Weaverdale Café is now the
Melting Pot Cafe at 96 Witton Street, near the centre of
Northwich. Postcode: CW9 5AB

Runcorn
Elvis Costello's inter-city song

From Elvis Costello's 1977 debut album My Aim Is True, '(The
Angels Wanna Wear My) Red Shoes' was a song written and
stored in the Elvis memory banks during a train journey from
Runcorn to Liverpool. A 20-minute section of the rail trip took
the then 22-year-old songwriter north over the River Mersey and
west to Lime Street station, Liverpool, before hastily returning
home to safely capture the words and music. Describing the
experience, Costello said: "I had to keep the song in my head
until I got to my mother's house, where I kept an old Spanish
guitar that I had had since I was a kid."

LOCATION 050: to duplicate Elvis Costello's inspirational
songwriting rail journey, board a Liverpool-bound train at
Runcorn station, Shaw Street, Runcorn, postcode WA7 5UB

Wilmslow
Doves kick against their roots

Doves' 2005 atmospheric single 'Black and White Town' was written
about this satellite town outside Manchester. The band's formation began
when brothers Jez and Andy Williams met Jimi Goodwin at Wilmslow
High School back in the mid-80s. Early gigging at the local leisure
centre followed and eventually led to the formation of Sub Sub. A fire that
destroyed the band's studio at nearby Ancoats forced a fresh start, but by
1998 Doves were born. Wilmslow High School is getting a reputation for
turning out rock bands. Members of 2013 album chart-toppers The 1975
(Matthew Healy, Ross MacDonald, Adam Hann and George Daniel) also
met there. In 2005, Jimi Goodwin told the the Wilmslow Express: "I think
it's normal to be frustrated and resent where you're from. That's what the
song 'Black And White Town' is about. It's something to kick against."

LOCATION 051: Wilmslow High School, Holly Road, postcode SK9 1LZ

Born in CHESHIRE

Gary Barlow (b. 20 Jan 1971, Frodsham)
Ian Brown, vocals, The Stone Roses/solo (b. 20 Feb 1963,
Warrington)
Ben Byrne, drums, Starsailor (b. 8 Mar 1977, Warrington)
Chris Evans, presenter (b. 1 Apr 1966, Warrington)
Nigel Harrison, bass, Blondie (b. 24 Apr 1951, Stockport)
Robert Heaton, drums, New Model Army (b. 6 Jul 1961,
Knutsford, d. 4 Nov 2004)
Steven Hewitt, drums, Placebo (b. 22 Mar 1971, Northwich)
Rupert Holmes, singer-songwriter (b. 24 Feb 1947, Northwich)

Stove King, bass, Mansun (b. 8 Jan 1975, Ellesmere Port)
John Mayall, guitar, The Bluesbreakers (b. 29 Nov 1933,
Macclesfield)
Jim Moray, folk singer-songwriter (b. 20 Aug 1981, Macclesfield)
Paul Morley, writer (b. 26 Mar 1957, Stockport)
Stephen Morris, drums, New Order/Joy Division/The Other
Two/Bad Lieutenant (b. 28 Oct 1957, Macclesfield)
Nemone (Nemone Metaxas), DJ (b. 3 Nov 1973, Chester)
Andie Rathbone, drums, Mansun (b. 8 Sep 1969, Blacon)
James Stelfox, bass, Starsailor (b. 23 Mar 1976, Warrington)

Spike Island
The Stone Roses' finest hour

A former toxic waste site in Widnes was the location for one of the most memorable events in British rock. It was here on May 27, 1990 that the whole baggy, "Madchester" movement had its day in the sun when 28,000 mostly stoned Roses fans gathered for the biggest northern cool party of their lives. Due to the watery surroundings there were supposedly frogmen employed to rescue any fans who either accidentally or intentionally went for a swim. Despite the ramshackle nature of the organisation and the incredibly high consumption of fast food, lager, ecstasy and dope, this giant rave recorded just four arrests for unruly behaviour. No doubt its legendary status as a key event in Britain's cultural history has grown out of all proportion due to the lack of filmed evidence of what was The Stone Roses' finest hour. Despite this, the "Baggy Woodstock", as it became known, did, like its 1969 hippie festival predecessor, inspire its own movie. In 2013, director Mat Whitecross's drama about a group of Stone Roses fans and their pilgrimage to attend the gig of their lives faithfully captured the euphoria of a golden summer when British music and the 1990 football World Cup created a cultural high.

LOCATION 052: east off the A533 on the north side of the River Mersey, postcode WA8 0DG

Spike Island – the movie. A bold attempt, more than two decades after the event, to capture a special moment

A band's-eye view of the Spike Island masses and belching chimneys

" I know some people have said there was a problem with **CHEMICALS IN THE AIR**... but I only know of a couple of people who now have six fingers "

STEVE ADGE
Stone Roses tour manager interviewed by the Observer

Cheshire

Widnes
Paul Simon writes 'Homeward Bound': But where?

A thoroughly confusing story surrounds one of Britain's best-known music locations. While touring England's folk clubs in 1965, the American singer-songwriter apparently wrote 'Homeward Bound' on a Widnes railway station platform, but which one? Uncertainty comes from the man himself as to which railway station he was actually "sitting in", as the lyrics to the song says. Closed in 1994, Ditton railway station to the west of Widnes is the most likely location, although Simon may well have penned Simon and Garfunkel's first UK hit single as far away as Warrington Bank Quay station, seven miles east of Widnes. What is certain is that there is a plaque commemorating the Paul Simon connection situated in the ticket office on the Liverpool-bound platform of the main Widnes railway station and that Simon was 'Homeward Bound' by train to girlfriend Kathy Chitty in London. So, the Widnes/Paul Simon association is certainly no rock myth. The station song-writing legend aside, he performed at Howff Folk Club, Geoff Speed's local club, in September 1965 and stayed several nights at Speed's parents' home in the town's Coroner's Lane.

LOCATION 053: Widnes station (and plaque) can be found north of the town centre at Victoria Avenue, postcode WA8 7TJ

Welcome to Widnes

Widnes

Left: Paul Simon and Kathy Chitty on a London street, pictured on Simon's solo debut album. Main picture: "Arriving at Widnes station I initially thought the 'Homeward Bound' plaque had been stolen again, but the ticket office guy told me it wasn't on the platform but on the wall adjacent to his ticket office. When I told him I wanted to photograph it he played a clip of 'Homeward Bound' by Simon and Garfunkel on the station PA system!" Photographer Peter Tarleton

At Widnes Station in 1965 Paul Simon wrote the song Homeward Bound

Photos: Peter Tarleton

Cornwall

*T*he county of ship wrecks, tin mines, pasties and a staunchly independent people also boasts some of Britain's finest surfing beaches. At least one Beach Boy puts Cornwall on a par with the Big Sur when it comes to inspirational locations. Speaking from his Santa Barbara home to rock paper *Melody Maker* back in 1974, Mike Love waxed lyrical on the subject. "I'm very fond of England and have always thought of leasing an estate in Cornwall, just to be able to write. The whole atmosphere and mood of the countryside as well as the tradition there would lend itself to some serious writing." Fellow Americans Gram Parsons and Blondie also gained tcreative inspiration here, but it was British folkies Ralph McTell and Donovan that are best associated with the laidback Cornish vibe, honing their skills as 1960s beachniks. Thanks to 21st century musicians like Seth Lakeman, that vibe is still alive and well today.

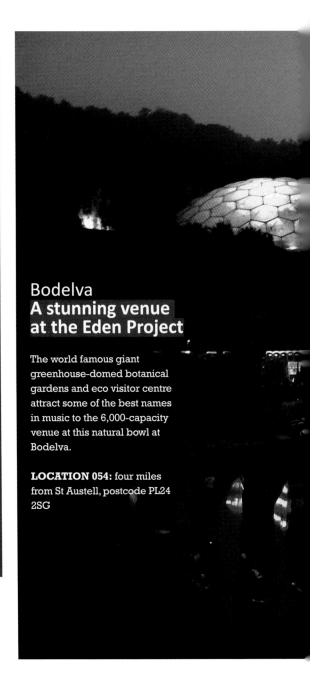

Bodelva
A stunning venue at the Eden Project

The world famous giant greenhouse-domed botanical gardens and eco visitor centre attract some of the best names in music to the 6,000-capacity venue at this natural bowl at Bodelva.

LOCATION 054: four miles from St Austell, postcode PL24 2SG

Born in CORNWALL

Mick Fleetwood, drums, Fleetwood Mac (b. 24 Jun 1947, **Redruth**)
Andy Mackay, saxophone, Roxy Music (b. 23 Jul 1946, **Lostwithiel**)

" No mud, **NO PUSHY SPONSORS**, no dodgy burgers, just lots of greenery "

JARVIS COCKER

Eden Sessions at the Eden Project: Biomes form a back drop to the acoustically outstanding natural amphitheatre Above: Chic, featuring Nile Rodgers, celebrate good times and get everybody dancing at the 2013 Eden Sessions

Photo: Ben Foster

Photo: Apex

Cornwall

Golant
Up the creek at the Sawmills studio

Oasis in a rowing boat? This could have been a regular sight on the River Fowey near Golant, location of the extraordinary Sawmills studio. Tucked away in its own private tidal creek, the only way to access the secluded recording complex is by dinghy or canoe. "No neighbours make it a great place to make noise and plenty of bands have recorded outside on the lawn by the water," states studio manager Ruth Taylor. Oasis, Muse, Terrorvision, Supergrass and The Verve are just some of the visitors that have recorded albums in this beautiful hideaway. The Stone Roses, Robert Plant and The Kooks have also experienced Sawmills' welcoming directions to the 17th-century water mill. "Down into the village and past the Fisherman's Arms until you reach a car park and level crossing. This is where we'll meet you with the boat," as the Sawmills website so invitingly

Photo: Neil Walsh - 2010 session: Smoke Fairies - Through Low Light and Trees

puts it. Ruth Taylor also reveals: "We've had lots of boat-related shenanigans."

LOCATION 055: Arrive by boat! Four miles east of the A390 and four miles north of Fowey, postcode PL23 1LW. Status: private property www. sawmills.co.uk

> Oasis worked on Definitely Maybe here in February 1994

Indian Queens
Nick Lowe's driving song

It was the "pretty name" rather than the place itself that inspired Nick Lowe to write 'Indian Queens', a track on his 2001 album The Convincer. Lowe owned a little retreat down in Cornwall for writing and merry-making with his mates. In order to get there he had to drive past the village on the main A30 route down through the county. Lowe recalled: "I was driving back up to London after one of these bacchanals and I was a bit hung over and I get kind of soulful and the next thing I know I'm pulling up outside my house in West London where I live and I found I'd written this little song."

LOCATION 056: on the main A30 in the centre of Cornwall, postcode TR9 6TF

NICK LOWE
The Convincer

Mitchell
The Folk Cottage Club

The Folk Cottage Club was variously located in the old church hall at Rose, near Perranporth, and later in a backroom at The Swan Inn, Truro, but its heyday was when based in an old ramshackle former farmworkers building outside the village of Mitchell. Resident musician, Monday to Friday, in the summer of 1967 was 22-year-old Ralph McTell, who played the 100-capacity club on the first floor above a downstairs coffee and snack bar. Years later McTell, who lived that summer in a rented caravan north of Mitchell, remembered his Cornish folk apprenticeship fondly: "Its unique spirit got to me, a mix of swashbuckling seafarer bravado and Methodist rectitude." Kent born McTell's first paid gigs when he arrived from London were at The Mermaid Inn, Porth, Newquay. This is where he was talent-scouted for the nearby Folk Cottage residency by local musician John Hayday.

LOCATION 057: at Lower Landrine Farm, near Mitchell. Postcode TR8 5BB. Now a private residence

Newquay
The Magical Mystery Tour hits town

A rectangular plaque on the grassy park by the sea at the Killacourt, Newquay, marks the most westerly point of The Beatles' Magical Mystery Tour. The Fab Four and a coach load of passengers arrived in Newquay in September 1967, shooting scenes for the movie that made its debut on BBC TV on Boxing Day that year. Based at the Atlantic Hotel, the group, crew and entourage also filmed a number of other Cornish scenes at Porth, Watergate Bay, Holywell Bay and Tregurrian.

LOCATIONS 058 and 059: The Atlantic Hotel is still standing and flourishing at Dane Road, Newquay. Postcode TR7 1EN. The Magical Mystery Tour commemorative plaque can be found at the top of the Killacourt, above Towan beach, Newquay. Postcode TR7 1UJ

The Beatles' Magical Mystery Tours, aboard this reproduction of the original coach, can be made daily during the holiday peak season from Newquay bus station

Cornwall

Seth Lakeman tests out the acoustics in North Tamerton church

North Tamerton
Word of Mouth: Seth Lakeman's stories of everyday folk

When Seth Lakeman gathered together a bunch of songs and recorded interviews based on people's stories and the local history of his native Devon and Cornwall, he found the perfect location to record them. In June 2013 he set up a temporary studio in North Tamerton church and the result was his 2014 album Word of Mouth. Folk pin-up boy Lakeman was certainly in tune with his environment. Having previously recorded in a copper mine and a cooperage he made North Tamerton's tiny church his creative hub for Word of Mouth, clearly intent on "capturing the sound of the room", as he put it. Church warden Ernie Hicks, who supplied the band with daily lunchtime pasties, helped rig up the many microphones and enabled Lakeman to use the church organ and, in particular, the bells, which had a starring role on the album.

LOCATION 060: North Tamerton church is 10 miles south-east of Bude. Postcode EX22 6RY

" It was quite funny actually, because **THE BELL RINGERS WOULD COME ALONG** and we would have to stop for them quite a few times. It was a bit like the Vicar of Dibley! **"**

SETH LAKEMAN

St Ives
Donovan's Bohemian beach party

St Ives was a sanctuary for free-spirited young poets, artists and musicians in the early Sixties. A teenage Donovan hitch-hiked there in 1962 from his Hatfield, Hertfordshire, home to busk his guitar-accompanied poetry for cash to feed himself and his companion Gypsy Dave. Describing himself as a "beachnik", Donovan supplemented his earnings by waiting tables. "I earned my bread by waiting in coffee bars and they fired me because my hair was too long." Resisting the Bohemian invasion, some St Ives locals would display signs demanding 'No Undesirables', articulating their distaste for male visitors sporting hair curling over their collar. Good days saw Donovan bed down in an art studio, but when money was scarce he frequently slept the night on the beach. By 1966, a then internationally famous Donovan returned to St Ives with an ITV film crew to make a documentary about his early days as a musician in the town. Keen to recreate his earlier lifestyle living on Porthminster beach, the crew gathered together his old friends from the town, paying them an extravagant £3 per day as beatnik extras.

LOCATION 061: near the tip of Cornwall, three miles north of the A30, postcode TR26 2

St Martin
Gram's Cornish holiday

Country-rock pioneer Gram Parsons' visits to England, hanging out with The Rolling Stones, are well documented elsewhere, but in 1971 he also spent extended periods holidaying in Cornwall. The location was the Tregidden Mill home of fellow Flying Burrito Brothers and International Submarine Band member Ian Dunlop, near the village of St Martin. Dunlop, still a touring musician to this day, had moved from the American West Coast to England's West Country, where he now works as an artist from his Cornish studio – the same place where Gram Parsons visited his friend decades ago. Parsons was so taken with the Lizard peninsula that he proposed to girlfriend

Echo chamber: Ocean Rain in Carnglaze Caverns

St Neot
Echo & The Bunnymen's finest hour

The cover for what many consider to be Echo & The Bunnymen's finest album was shot here in the cathedral-like Carnglaze Caverns near Liskeard. A public tourist attraction that also doubles as a music venue, the caverns were the location for photographer Brian Griffin's picture of the band that accompanies the Ocean Rain album.

LOCATION 062: one mile north of the village of St Neot, postcode PL14 6HQ. www.carnglaze.com

Gretchen Burrell here before marrying back in the USA. Remembering that summer well, Dunlop recalls how he and Parsons walked the Kennack, Cadgwith, Lizard and Mullion stretches of the South West Coast Path and visited the local pubs. Two years on from his Cornish vacation, Parsons was dead, amid sensational reports surrounding his infamous botched cremation in California's Joshua Tree National Park. "We used to go up for a pint to the Prince of Wales, a mile up the lane in Newtown, or, three miles away on the coast, to the Five Pilchards at the [then] fishing cove of Porthallow, near St Keverne" says Dunlop.

LOCATION 063: the Lizard peninsula, south Cornwall, postcode TR12 6DS. Status: private

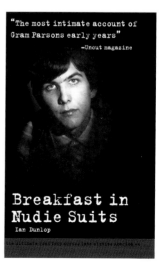

"The most intimate account of Gram Parsons early years"
—Uncut magazine

Breakfast in Nudie Suits
Ian Dunlop

Cornwall

Tintagel
Seth Lakeman's Camelot cover shoot

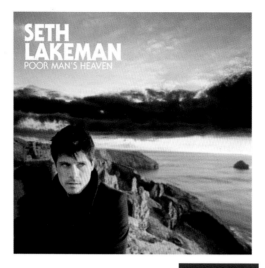

The mid-noughties saw West Country musician Seth Lakeman grab a Mercury Prize nomination and Best Album and Singer trophy at the BBC Radio 2 Folk Awards, swiftly followed by Top 10 album status with the release of Poor Man's Heaven. This 2008 rhythm-driven offering was made in Cornwall with the addition of a rugged album cover shot of the wreckers' coast at Tintagel. The cover shot by photographer Andrew Whitton was accomplished near Tregatta, with views facing south-west. Whitton explains: "The shoot was conceived to reflect the coastal, maritime influence of the music.

Seth has strong, definite themes to his albums. He's inspired by his surroundings and the stories he heard as a child, which make this part of Cornwall perfect. It was our intention to shoot the artwork on a

Andrew Whitton's stunning view of the Cornish coastline

stormy day, with rough seas and hellish-looking skies. But shoot day came and the skies cleared, leaving us with the beautiful scenery you see in the artwork. Tintagel offered us many options, fishing villages, a seafaring cemetery, a stunning coastline and the site of what is thought to be the location of Camelot, home of King Arthur. One thing that strikes you as you wander around is how life for villages like that are built up on folklore. Once you experience this you can really delve into and appreciate the songs of an artist like Seth. For me, it just gave me an exquisite location of meaning and relevance to Seth as an artist and his work."

LOCATION 064: near the village of Tintagel, about six miles west of the A39 in north Cornwall, postcode PL34 0AH

Truro
A beginning for Queen

On June 27, June 1970, singer Freddie Mercury, guitarist Brian May and drummer (and local boy) Roger Taylor made their debut as Smile. The venue for their gig was Truro City Hall (later renamed The Hall for Cornwall), hired as a fundraiser for the Red Cross by Taylor's mother. On bass guitar that night was Mike Grose. It would be a further 12 months before John Deacon would fill that role on stage and complete the classic Queen line-up.

LOCATION 065: postcode TR1 2LL, accessed via Boscawen Street or Back Quay

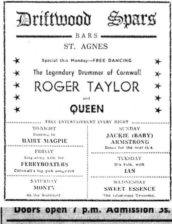

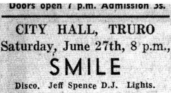

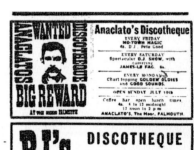

Three early Queen gigs in Cornwall, including the Freddie Mercury, Brian May, Roger Taylor and Mike Grose debut as Smile. Roger's mother placed the ad around April 1970 when vocalist Tim Staffell was still in the band. The remaining two ads actually billing "Queen" are from 1971.

Images from Rupert White's book Queen in Cornwall

Tresco
Blondie's 'Island of Lost Souls'

Blondie found the perfect location to promote their 1982 single 'Island of Lost Souls' when the second largest of the Scilly Isles was chosen. The video for what turned out to be Blondie's last Top 20 chart hit for almost 17 years was shot amid the tropical plants and statues at the Abbey Garden on the island of Tresco. The band made the crossing for the photo shoot by small boat, with Debbie Harry clutching her cellophane-protected collection of outfits and blonde wig to disguise her dark hair.

LOCATION 066: Tresco is 30 miles from the Cornish coast, postcode TR24 0QQ

Photo: Brian Aris

County Durham

*R*oger Whittaker's 1969 debut hit 'Durham Town (The Leavin')' maybe the most obvious county connection, but dig deeper and there's a varied bunch of locations awaiting rock pilgrimage. Worthy sons and daughters of County Durham include singer-songwriters Claire Hamill and Lesley Duncan, Prefab Sprout's McAloon brothers and Sixties singing starlet Susan Maughan. There's a Peterlee pub that booked Led Zeppelin, the aforementioned Sprouts' Langley Park, a visit by The Beatles to Stockton touched by tragedy, 'Summer Holiday' penned at the town's Globe Theatre and a visually memorable album cover photo shoot for The Who at Easington.

Langley Park
Prefab Sprout's search for excitement

Prefab Sprout actually hailed from the neighbouring village of Witton Gilbert, but maybe Witton Gilbert to Memphis lacked the more obvious geographical connection of From Langley Park to Memphis, the group's third and highest charting studio album release. The final track, 'The Venus of the Soup Kitchen', also namechecks the 1988 album's title. Speaking at the time, Prefab Sprout's Paddy McAloon said: "Langley Park is a small village in County Durham where I come from in the north of England. Nowhere seemed more exotic to someone from there than a place like Memphis where Presley came from, so really it's

Prefab Sprout's highest-charting studio album had a title that revealed both their childhood base and the imagined, more exotic, Elvis equivalent

about looking across the sea from where you live and thinking the rest of the world is much more exciting."

LOCATION 067: south of the A691, about five miles east of Durham. Postcode: DH7

Born in COUNTY DURHAM

Gem Archer, guitar, Oasis (b. 7 Dec 1966, Durham)
Eds Chesters, drums, The Bluetones (b. 24 Oct 1970, Bishop Auckland, Darlington)
Lesley Duncan, singer-songwriter (b. 12 Aug 1943, Stockton-on-Tees, d. 12 Mar 2010)
Keith Gregory, bass, The Wedding Present (b. 2 Jan 1963, Darlington)
Claire Hamill, singer-songwriter (b. 4 Aug 1954, PortClarence, Stockton-on-Tees)
Liam Howe, Sneaker Pimps (b. 1974, Elwick, Hartlepool)
Susan Maughan, (b. 1 Jul 1938, Consett)
Martin McAloon, bass, Prefab Sprout (b. 4 Jan 1962, Durham)
Paddy McAloon, vocals, Prefab Sprout (b. 7 Jun 1957, Consett)
Wendy Smith, vocals, Prefab Sprout (b. 31 May 1963, Durham)
Alan White, drums, Yes (b. 14 Jun 1949, Pelton, Chester-le-Street)

Who's next

Peterlee
Led Zeppelin at The Argus Butterfly

This pub, named after an endangered local butterfly, once played host to a few of rock's biggest attractions. March 23, 1969 saw Led Zeppelin perform for a £100 fee a fortnight before their debut album scorched into the chart. Deep Purple, Family, Jethro Tull, Taste and Ten Years After also appeared at the tiny venue, billed as Peterlee Jazz Club. Joint promoters Brian Stoker and David Richards had the knack of booking big names on the verge of superstardom. Typically, Free appeared at the pub just a week before 'All Right Now' rocketed to No.2 in the singles chart.

> **"I said 'What are you doing next month?', AND PAGE SAID they were playing the Hollywood Bowl, so that was the last we saw of [Zep]"**

BRIAN STOKER
Promoter interviewed by the
Hartlepool Mail in 2008

LOCATION 069: Peterlee is between the A19 and the coast. The Argus Butterfly is on York Road, postcode SR8 2DP

Easington Colliery
The Who's Next album cover

Easington is the colliery that made headlines in 1951 when 83 men lost their lives in a tragic mining disaster. It was here that The Who assembled in 1971 for photographer Ethan A Russell to snap them for the sleeve of Who's Next. The album that would become the band's first chart-topper featured the front cover image of a huge man-made monolith rising from the barren slag heap landscape. They say the camera never lies but the photo shoot concept that Pete Townshend, Roger Daltrey, John Entwistle and Keith Moon had evidently just relieved themselves on the concrete structure was not completely authentic. At least a couple of the band members couldn't 'go', so rain water from an empty film canister was splashed against the concrete to get the desired effect.

The end result of Ethan A Russell's Easington Colliery photo shoot

LOCATION 068: the colliery, which ceased mining in 1994, is between Easington village and the sea on Seaside Lane, postcode SR8 3

> " The north-east runs **THROUGH MY VEINS** like the river Tees runs through the valley... I feel privileged to call it 'home' "
>
> **CLAIRE HAMILL**

PortClarence
Claire Hamill: at home on both banks of the River Tees

When new Island Records label singer-songwriter Claire Hamill needed a location for her debut album cover shoot in 1972 she looked no further than the place of her birth. Port Clarence lies on the northern side of the River Tees and is connected to the south side by the iconic Middlesbrough Transporter Bridge. Hamill, who chose a 1920s black panne velvet dress she found in a Darlington Oxfam shop for the shoot, was born about 200 yards from the base of the famous bridge, which appears behind her in the photograph selected for the sleeve of One House Left Standing.

LOCATION 070: an abandoned goods yard which later became the site of the company that built the Thames Barrier and the Dartford Crossing bridge. Port Clarence Road. Postcode TS2 1TW

Port Clarence-born Claire Hamill, pictured on the cover of her debut album One House Left Standing, released in 1972, and in 2013 on the southern side of the Tees estuary at South Gare, near Redcar

grahamlowephotography.com

Stockton-on-Tees
Tragic news as The Beatles play The Globe

Although the Fab Four played Stockton's Globe Theatre on October 15, 1964 at the height of
Beatlemania, it was their earlier visit on November 22, 1963 that would be most powerfully etched in
the minds of the young fans that day. As those present at the first of two shows that evening left and
fans for the second show filed into The Globe, news began filtering through that President John F
Kennedy had been assassinated in Dallas, Texas. Other superstar visits to the Globe included Buddy
Holly, Chuck Berry, The Everly Brothers, The Rolling Stones, The Supremes and Cliff Richard and The
Shadows. One number sure to have been played live at The Globe when The Shadows (featuring
local boys Hank Marvin and Bruce Welch) appeared was their 'Wonderful Land' B-side 'Stars Fell on
Stockton'. Shadows group members and songwriters Welch and Brian Bennett are reported to have
penned chart-topper 'Summer Holiday' in The Globe's orchestra pit while passing the time during a
break one January afternoon in 1962 when Cliff and co were starring in their 1962 pantomime, Dick
Whittington. Status Quo were the last rock band to play The Globe in 1974 before the place closed in
1996. Moves are afoot to restore it to its former art deco magnificence and host more live music and
entertainment in the not too distant future. On some future date, perhaps Cliff and the Shads or Quo
should reopen the place.

LOCATION 071: at 101 High Street, postcode TS18 1BD

A stunning
printed mural
protects The
Globe during
its renovation.
Begun in 2013,
the lengthy
project provided
an opportunity
to remind
Stockton's
music fans just
which legendary
performers had
appeared at this
historic building
down the years

Cumbria

*E*ngland's third largest county was where Spooky Tooth and British Sea Power were rooted, but not since The Beatles played Carlisle has there been as rocktastic an event as that which saw Lady Gaga arrive on stage in a coffin at BBC's travelling circus, Radio 1's Big Weekend, in front of 20,000 damp fans in a field in Cumbria in May 2011. "Just put your paws up, 'coz you were born this way Carlisle!" was how she acknowledged her Cumbrian 'Little Monsters', as the New York City-born entertainer likes to dub her fans. Those aforementioned Beatles made two newsworthy appearances in Carlisle that saw them ejected then fêted in the Sixties, and Black Sabbath paid their dues at Carlisle's Cosmo. Then there's Maryport's beat boom mecca and, more recently, the seriously funny Half Man Half Biscuit, honouring Ambleside by selecting the Lake District town to appear on an album cover.

Ambleside
The Half Man Half Biscuit CSI franchise

The Half Man Half Biscuit album cover for the band's 2008 release CSI: Ambleside pictures the Lake District town's Church Street and the Priest Hole restaurant.

LOCATION 072: Church Street, Ambleside, postcode LA22 0BU

Maryport
Beat boom stars at the Palace

Built on the site of an old brewery and opened in 1934, the Palace Ballroom was one of British music's significant outposts on the beat boom tour circuit. The Hollies, Manfred Mann, The Animals and The Small Faces were among the hugely popular chart stars that headed to Cumbria's east coast.

LOCATION 073: off the A596 north-west of the Lake District, on the coast at Lower Church Street, Maryport. More recently known as the Civic Hall, the building was demolished to make way for housing in 2009. Postcode: CA15 6LE

Carlisle
Beatles ejected then fêted

The Beatles made two memorable visits to Carlisle. The first came just a few days before their first recording sessions for debut album Please Please Me when they managed to get themselves ejected from the Crown & Mitre Hotel ballroom on February 8, 1963. On tour supporting Helen Shapiro, both the band and the 16-year-old chart starlet were in the hotel bar next to where Carlisle Golf Club's annual dinner dance was in full swing in the ballroom. They were invited to join in by one local lad, but when the club chairman spotted the four leather-clad Beatles sampling the buffet and twisting on the dance floor with Shapiro he asked them all to leave. The Beatles were clearly not too upset by their treatment, although Shapiro was "mortified" by a Daily Express story about the incident. They returned later that year on November 21 as chart-toppers to an ecstatic reception from fans, who in some cases had queued for 36 hours for a chance to get a ticket. The ABC cinema where The Beatles performed on both occasions became Lonsdale City, and despite the art deco building's inactivity as a music venue, or indeed a cinema, it still stands today in Warwick Road. The Beatles never played in Cumbria again. However, Paul McCartney certainly must have recalled the county favourably. In 2001 he proposed to Heather Mills at the Sharrow Bay hotel on Lake Ullswater. A year later he revealed how he liked to shop in Carlisle as he was rarely recognised in the city.

LOCATIONS 074 and 075: the Crown & Mitre Hotel still stands in the centre of Carlisle at 4 English Street, postcode CA3 8HZ. The old ABC cinema is a few minutes walk away on Warwick Road, postcode CA1 1DN

Carlisle
Sabbath's return to the Cosmo

When local band Earth played an end-of-school year dance for £40 in Carlisle and promised to return for a second booking a year later, the student organisers reasoned that with the December 15, 1970 date approaching they might have a no-show on their hands. In the period between the two bookings, Earth had gone through a line-up change down in Birmingham and turned into album chart-toppers Black Sabbath. But the 1970 school dance wasn't disappointed when the band and truck duly rolled into the Cosmopolitan venue car park and performed to the hall's capacity crowd for the agreed £70 fee. The Who, Pink Floyd and The Moody Blues also played more conventional gigs at the Cosmo and, no doubt, for certainly more money than the honourable Sabbath. The Yardbirds, The Pretty Things and The Groundhogs also played the place, and in the 1970s this partly rural outpost was said to host some sensational Young Farmers dances and a star-studded conveyor belt of chart acts such as Mud, Bay City Rollers and Johnny Nash.

LOCATION 076: the Cosmo opened in 1962. The building formerly used at various times as a cinema, bingo hall and even a roller-skating rink was situated just south of Eastern Way in Harraby, south-east of the centre of Carlisle. Demolished in 2004, the only connection to the Cosmo's illustrious past is the recently constructed Argyll Drive, named after the building that was once the Argyll Cinema. Postcode: CA1 3PB

Born in CUMBRIA

Glenn Cornick, bass, Jethro Tull (b. 23 Apr 1947, Barrow)
Mike Harrison, vocals, Spooky Tooth (b. 30 Sep 1942, Carlisle)
Steve Hogarth, vocals, Marillion (b. 14 May 1959, Kendal)
Greg Ridley, bass, Humble Pie (b. 23 Oct 1942, Aspatria)
Neil Hamilton Wilkinson, vocals/bass, British Sea Power (b. Kendal)
Yan Scott Wilkinson, vocals, British Sea Power (b. Kendal)
Matthew Wood, drums, British Sea Power (b. Kendal)

It's hard to imagine a band more geographically conscious of their surroundings than British Sea Power. The band, featuring three Cumbrians (Wood, Wilkinson and Wilkinson), have numbered Westminster library, an Arctic church, a Thames cruiser, Jersey Opera House, the Natural History Museum and Jodrell Bank among their venues

Derbyshire

A surreal Oasis photo shoot, The Rolling Stones at Swarkestone Pavilion and Harry Webb's unveiling as Cliff Richard are four of the best Derbyshire rock spots. Years after the Buxton Festivals of 1973 and '74, Donington Park has hosted Monsters of Rock then Download in the county. Derby music fans are well catered for at the Flower Pot pub, but it's hard to envisage a more atmospheric venue for live music than Derbyshire's Peak Cavern. Sadly, Nick Cave and The Bad Seeds are yet to make an appearance.

Castleton
Rock formations inside the Devil's Arse

Richard Hawley is no stranger to playing the odd unusual venue. But when he performed inside a Peak District cavern, even for him it must have topped his other unconventional gig venues, which have included a Sheffield tyre and exhaust centre. The occasion was a pre-Christmas gig in 2008 at a cave called the Devil's Arse (or the Peak Cavern in polite company). The acoustics couldn't have been better, especially when Hawley delivered his beautifully atmospheric version of 'Silent Night'. The Devil's Arse might not be open for gigs all that often, but judging by the reactions of music fans who've witnessed this special setting it's definitely worth heading for next time a concert is scheduled. Where else can several hundred fans sit in the mouth of a cave and listen to good live music?

LOCATION 077: aside from its attributes as a music venue, the Devil's Arse (or Peak Cavern) is open for business as a tourist attraction daily (April to October) and at weekends (November to March). Head for Castleton, Hope Valley, postcode S33 8WS

"The Devil's Arse is an **AWE-INSPIRING** venue. Getting a great sound for a rock band in a cave takes a lot of skill. The logistics of getting a PA and lights there is a **SERIOUS CHALLENGE** too but if you get both right then you simply cannot beat it for a memorable venue "
JOHN REILLY

Photo: Peter Tarleton

Rocking the Devil's Arse: Locally popular Boy on a Dolphin lead singer, John Reilly, plays a gig inside Britain's largest natural cave entrance in the summer of 2012

Now: the beautifully refurbished Cromford station as it is today... and then: the Gallagher brothers, Carla the barmaid, various members of art director Brian Cannon's family and his assistant pose for photographer Michael Spencer Jones' surreal shoot

Photo: Peter Tarleton

Cromford
A surreal Oasis photo shoot

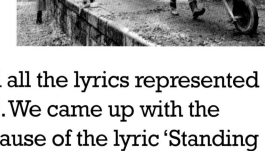

The quaint little grade II-listed railway station buildings at Cromford was the location selected when Microdot art director Brian Cannon created the cover for what turned out to be the first No.1 single for Oasis in 1995. The surreal photographic sleeve for 'Some Might Say' featured Liam Gallagher waving from the railway bridge and Noel Gallagher dousing raincoat-wearing barmaid Carla Knox with water from a watering can on the platform. Others enlisted for the shoot included Cannon family members Brian Cannon Sr (with wheelbarrow), Helen Cannon (with mop) and assistant Matthew

Sankey (begging for "education please").

LOCATION 078: just outside the village of Cromford, two miles south of Matlock. Cromford railway station, Lea Road, postcode DE4 5JJ. Status: currently advertised as The Waiting Room Holiday Cottage, available to rent as a holiday home

> "Noel... wanted all the lyrics represented in the IMAGE. We came up with the concept... because of the lyric 'Standing at the station/In need of education'"
>
> **BRIAN CANNON**

Photo: Peter Tarleton

The Flower Pot's unassuming exterior hides a 250-capacity rock and blues venue

Derby
Real ale and real music at The Flower Pot

In the Cathedral Quarter of Derby you'll find a pub with a winning combination. Famous for both real ale (it is home to the Black Iris Brewery) and live music, this rather ordinary-looking pub has managed to attract a rather extraordinary list of performers down the years. Included in their list of notables is Nils Lofgren, Midge Ure, Squeeze, Joe Bonamassa, John Martyn, Wilko Johnson and, at the time of writing this, Focus were up on the Flower Pot's tiny stage

next. Like most small venues with an exceptional pedigree for live music it's the pub's promoters who have turned The Flower Pot into the Derby blues and rock mecca it is today. Alan and Lisa Woolley are the dynamic duo responsible for attracting crowds of up to 250 to The Flower Pot for special nights.

LOCATION 079: The Flower Pot is at 19-25 King Street, Derby. Postcode DE1 3DZ

Born in DERBYSHIRE

Long John Baldry (right) (b. 12 Jan 1941, Haddon, d. 21 Jul 2005)
Martyn P Casey, keyboards, Nick Cave and The Bad Seeds (b. 10 Jul 1960, Chesterfield)
Lloyd Cole, vocals/guitar, Lloyd Cole and The Commotions (b. 31 Jan 1961, Buxton)
Kevin Coyne, vocals/guitar (b. 27 Jan 1944, Derby)

Mark Shaw, vocals, Then Jerico (b. 10 Jun 1961, Chesterfield)
Dave Lee Travis, radio DJ (b. 25 May 1945, Buxton)
Mark Webber, guitar, Pulp (b. 14 Sep 1970, Chesterfield)
John Wetton, vocals/bass, Asia/King Crimson (b. 12 Jun 1949, Willington)

Long John Baldry was a British blues legend and mentor to Rod Stewart

Derbyshire

Swarkestone
Beggar's Banquet revisited

A crumbling Jacobean grandstand
was the chosen location for a classic
Rolling Stones photo shoot on June 8,
1968. The event caused quite a stir in
the tiny village of Swarkestone as the
black limos rolled up transporting the
Stones and their props, prompting
local teenagers to head to the centre
of the excitement, clutching their
autograph books. The band, along
with photographer Michael Joseph,
assembled at Swarkestone Pavilion
to shoot a sequence of pictures to
promote The Rolling Stones' new
album release, Beggar's Banquet.
Chosen for its grand dereliction by
Joseph and Mick Jagger, the photo
shoot had the Stones, in medieval
garb, playing cricket in the long
grass outside, lounging around
among the local herd of Friesian
cows and clambering up the ruined
front face of the pavilion building.
The Swarkestone photos taken of the
Stones never featured on the cover of
Beggar's Banquet and there was no
little acrimony between the band and
their record company Decca over what
should be used, delaying the album's
release until late 1968. However, the
pictures were too good, and ultimately
too memorable, to be wasted and got
used extensively to promote the album.
One picture did eventually surface
prominently as the back cover to the
band's 1990 compilation album, Hot
Rocks 1964-1971.

LOCATION 080: owned by The
Landmark Trust and now beautifully
renovated and available for hire as a
holiday home, Swarkestone Pavilion is
less than 10 miles south of the centre
of Derby and about four miles north of
Ticknall. Postcode DE73 7JB

BEGGAR'S BANQUET
THE ROLLING STONES
* SKL 4955 * LK 4955

DECCA

Photo: Peter Tarleton

The beautifully restored Swarkestone
Pavilion as it is now (above), and in 1968
(top and main picture) when the Stones
descended on Derbyshire

Derbyshire

Ripley
Harry Webb makes his debut as Cliff Richard

The Regal ballroom in Ripley played a huge part in Cliff Richard's personal musical history. On May 3, 1958, having ditched real name Harry Webb, he performed for the first time under new name Cliff Richard. Billed as Cliff Richard and The Drifters' first appearance outside London and the group's home county of Hertfordshire, it was dance hall manager Harry Greatorex who was the catalyst in the name change. Greatorex demanded an Elvis or Jerry Lee Lewis-like name for his posters, which resulted in a frantic discussion back in London to arrive at something that would excite Ripley's teenagers. A plaque marking the 50th anniversary of this historic gig was unveiled at the venue in 2008. The gig finished too late for the group to get a southbound train back to London, forcing Cliff and the boys to sleep on the ballroom's benches. However, band member Ian Samwell recalled the ballroom's proper stage, with curtains unlike the cramped conditions they were familiar with back at Soho's 2i's club. "The curtains parted, we were standing there and really rocked. The place was absolutely jam-packed and the response was fantastic."

LOCATION 081: Ripley is midway between Derby and Mansfield and the ballroom is at 34 Nottingham Road, postcode DE5 3DJ. Current status: still advertising as an entertainment venue

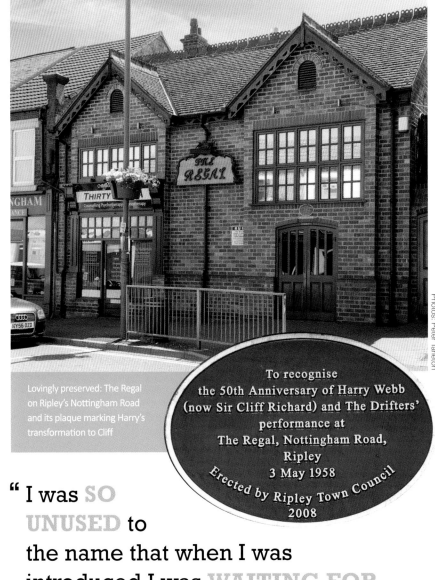

Lovingly preserved: The Regal on Ripley's Nottingham Road and its plaque marking Harry's transformation to Cliff

To recognise the 50th Anniversary of Harry Webb (now Sir Cliff Richard) and The Drifters' performance at The Regal, Nottingham Road, Ripley 3 May 1958 Erected by Ripley Town Council 2008

Photos: Peter Tarleton

" I was SO UNUSED to the name that when I was introduced I was WAITING FOR SOMEONE ELSE to walk out on to the stage "

CLIFF RICHARD
admits he wasn't ready for the switch from Harry to Cliff at Ripley

Devon

*C*overing a large chunk of the county, even the wild and untamed Dartmoor National Park is not immune from rock music associations. The rocky granite landscape prompted an artistic strop by Rick Wakeman, provided folk legends for Seth Lakeman's gritty ballads and, in its gentler, nearby rolling South Hams, bolt-hole seclusion for rock's glitterati. The small seaside town of Teignmouth gets a hat-trick of Rock Atlas mentions if you include Patrick Wolf's homage 'Teignmouth', from his 2005 album Wind in the Wires, and the fact that The Beatles broke their Magical Mystery journey to Cornwall there. But it's the north coast you need to head for to discover Britain's most expansive and romantic rock location at Saunton Sands. Here, a windswept Robbie Williams filmed his 1997 'Angels' video and Pink Floyd, less romantically, turned the beach into a giant hospital and battleground.

Peter Tarleton

East Prawle
The rocking Pigs Nose

The Pigs Nose Inn is situated in the village of East Prawle, and for its eccentricity alone deserves a place in any guide book, let alone one specifically related to rock locations. Chris Farlowe, Terry Reid, former- Monkee Peter Tork and His Shoe Suede Blues, Wishbone Ash, The Animals, The Yardbirds, It's a Beautiful Day, The Boomtown Rats and Curiosity Killed the Cat have all played Pigs Nose gigs at the hall next door. Damon Albarn, who owns a house a few miles north at Beesands, chose the Pigs Nose to launch his new project, The Good, The Bad & The Queen. Band members Albarn, Paul Simonon, Simon Tong and Tony Allen made their live debut in front of 150 people there in 2006.

LOCATION 082: opposite the village green at East Prawle, near the southernmost tip of Devon. Postcode TQ7 2BY

Dittisham
Old Rectory rehearsals for Led Zeppelin

In the early Eighties, Led Zeppelin band member John Paul Jones owned the Old Rectory, a perfect Devonshire retreat for the band to rehearse with its recording studio, swimming pool and nine bedrooms. Rebuilt after a fire in the Seventies almost destroyed it, the house was, until recently, the property of Duran Duran manager Michael Berrow.

LOCATION 083: at the end of Rectory Lane, Dittisham. Postcode TQ6 0HD. Status: private house

Devon

The facts add up. Only Paul Simon, who stayed right here in the Sixties, can quash rumours that this is THE 'Bridge Over Troubled Water'

Peter Tarleton

Bickleigh
The 'Bridge Over Troubled Water'

Staying at The Fisherman's Cot on the banks of the River Exe, Paul Simon was reported to have drawn inspiration to later write the Simon and Garfunkel classic 'Bridge Over Troubled Water'. Stopping at the Devon hostelry while touring Britain's folk haunts as a performer and observer back in the Sixties, the New Jersey-born singer-songwriter was able to gaze out over the bridge at Bickleigh from in front of his room (No.6). Though the facts are sketchy, the river is susceptible to flooding at this point on the Exe and Simon was, according to locals, apparently aware of a reported drowning at nearby Thorverton during his stay, which may have contributed to the maudlin nature of arguably his most famous recording.

LOCATION 084: on the A396 Exeter Road as it crosses the River Exe at Bickleigh. Postcode EX16 8RW

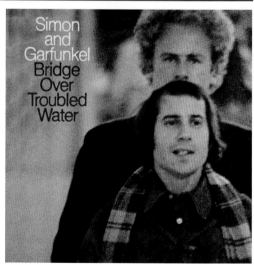

Saunton Sands
Robbie Williams shoots 'Angels'

The miles of flat sands and dunes on Devon's north coast were the location for shooting the video that accompanied Robbie's 1997 single 'Angels'. A life time's worth of brownie points would surely be secured by any guy selecting this spot to propose to his very own 'angel'.

LOCATION 085: nine miles from Barnstaple on Devon's north coast, postcode EX33 1LQ

Wistman's Wood
Lakeman country

Seth Lakeman's 2005 album Kitty Jay features a cover with the Devon-born folk singer crouching pensively at Wistman's Wood near his Dartmoor home. The title track relates to the legend of an 18th-century pregnant servant girl who committed suicide and was buried on the moor. Mysteriously, her grave near Hound Tor is still decorated with flowers by unseen visitors to this day.

LOCATION 086: north of Two Bridges and the B3212. Two Bridges postcode: PL20 6SW

Seth Lakeman on the cover of his Kitty Jay album

Teignbridge District Council

Teignmouth
Muse come home

"We used to spend all our time hanging out there," revealed Matt Bellamy to the hordes of Muse fans. Bellamy was pointing at the old Teignmouth pier at a huge outdoor homecoming gig, staged for the band who hailed from this genteel seaside town on Devon's south coast. Bellamy and drummer Dominic Howard met for the very first time at The Den, the large grassy area on the seafront that hosted 10,000 fans on two nights in September 2009 for their "Seaside Rendezvous". The trio's bass guitarist, Chris Wolstenholme, still a Teignmouth resident, was even involved in the council meeting that gave the go-ahead to road closures in the town and approval for the band's giant Punch and Judy-styled stage. Muse have frequently returned to their hometown, rehearsing for their 2003 world tour in the local college and opening a £3-million arts centre a year later. In 2012, the trio returned to yet another big Teignmouth crowd when they were chosen to carry the Olympic torch from the nearby bridge connecting Shaldon and Teignmouth.

LOCATION 087: at The Den, a grassy expanse on the Teignmouth seafront, postcode TQ14 8BD

Muse bring the Olympic torch into Teignmouth. All three members of the band grew up in the town, having met as pupils at Teignmouth Community College

Devon

Saunton Sands
Pink Floyd's beds and bombers on the beach

More than 700 hospital beds stretch along Saunton Sands on the cover of Pink Floyd's 1987 album A Momentary Lapse of Reason. The concept was dreamt up by artist Storm Thorgerson, who zeroed in on a lyric, "a vision of an empty bed", from the album's track six, 'Yet Another Movie', and multiplied that thought. Inevitably interrupted by rain, the shoot took two weeks to complete. Five years earlier the vast expanse of Saunton Sands and sea also provided the perfect spot for filming World War II troop-landing scenes in Pink Floyd's movie The Wall.

For authenticity, six wartime vehicles were loaned from the Cobbaton Combat Collection military museum and tourist attraction in nearby Chittlehampton. Sadly, one of the two half-sized German enemy Stuka bombers used for filming crash-landed in the sea. Saunton Sands is literally a hot spot for movie and photo shoots. In 1990, the South West's hottest temperature was recorded here (35.4C).

LOCATION 088: nine miles from Barnstaple on Devon's north coast, postcode EX33 1LQ

In the days before computerised imagery, these beds were manhandled into place to create this memorable cover shot by Robert Dowling, who bagged a gold award at the Association of Photographers Awards for the image

Yes Tor
Rick Wakeman says "No" to Yes cover

The second highest point on Dartmoor, Yes Tor, appears on 1978 Yes album cover Tormato. Designs for the cover did not go down well with the band's keyboard wizard Rick Wakeman. He threw a tomato at the originally titled Yestor album sleeve artwork in disgust, prompting a change of name to Tormato. Wakeman's contribution to the design process was adopted on the finished cover. The tenth Yes hit album, Tormato heralded the departure of both Wakeman (for the second time) and vocalist Jon Anderson.

LOCATION 089: grid reference SX580901: about five miles south of the A30 at Okehampton

The Tormato cover, complete with Rick Wakeman's artistic contribution

Born in DEVON

David Cross, violin/keyboards, King Crimson (b. 23 Apr 1949, Plymouth)
Beth Gibbons, vocals, Portishead (b. 4 Jan 1965, Exeter)
Dave Hill, guitar, Slade (b. 4 Apr 1946, Holbeton)
Seth Lakeman (b. 26 Mar 1977, Buckland Monachorum)
Chris Martin, vocals, Coldplay (b. 2 Mar 1977, Exeter)
Serge Pizzorno, vocals/guitar, Kasabian (b. 15 Dec 1980, Newton Abbot)

Pete Quaife (above), bass, The Kinks (b. 31 Dec 1943, Tavistock, d. 23 Jun 2010)
Danny Thompson, double bass, (b. 4 Apr 1939, Teignmouth)

Woodcombe
Kate Bush's Aerial inspiration

Kate Bush bought her South Hams hideaway in 2004. The 1920s house appealed to the UK's first woman to record a No.1 album due to its remote, beautiful and private position. The 17 acres incorporate a pebble beach, boathouse and two small offshore islands, the perfect inspiration for the maritime themes explored on her 2005 album Aerial.

LOCATION 090: seven miles south-west of Kingsbridge, postcode TQ7 2NJ. Status: private property

Dorset

*D*orset's Jurassic Coast is a visual delight not lost on album and single sleeve creators. Artwork adorning releases by Phish, Ocean Colour Scene and Martha and The Muffins all feature. Other visual treats include the video adventures of Big Country on the beautiful Isle of Purbeck, Coldplay's 'Yellow' at Studland Bay and a classic Beatles album cover shoot in Bournemouth. And the draw of her home county brought PJ Harvey back to the Dorset clifftops when she needed a new recording base.

Bournemouth
Robert Freeman's With the Beatles photo shoot

Just how significant a place Bournemouth was in the history of The Beatles is evident when you realise that the Fab Four played more shows at the Gaumont in the town than any other British theatre outside of London, managing 16 shows in 14 months from August 1963. In addition, Bournemouth was the location for Robert Freeman's photo shoot for the iconic With the Beatles album cover. Their shadowy black and white portraits, created in just one hour on August 22, 1963 - the day before single 'She Loves You' was released - was hurriedly completed in an area of the dining room at Bournemouth's Palace Court Hotel. With no make-up and the use of the available midday light from a window, it was no meticulously organized fashion shoot. However, The Beatles did dress for the camera, wearing their specially acquired black roll-neck sweaters, and just two rolls of film later Freeman had captured what became one of the classiest album covers of the period. "There was no make-up, hairdresser or stylist – just myself, The Beatles and a camera – a Pentax SLR, with an 18mm

telephoto lens. The aperture was set at F22 to ensure depth of focus and the effect of the telephoto was to compress them into a tight group shot", according to Freeman. Further proof that Bournemouth was almost like Liverpool-on-Sea to the Fab Four comes via one significant show they performed at the old Bournemouth Winter Gardens. Here they were filmed by a US TV crew, enabling the American public to get their first glimpse of the group two months before their famous Ed Sullivan Show appearances.

LOCATION 091: the Gaumont cinema building and the Palace Court Hotel are next door to each other on Westover Road, Bournemouth. The hotel is now a Premier Inn. Postcode BH1 2BZ

Robert Freeman was paid £75 for the impromptu With the Beatles cover shoot at the Palace Court Hotel. Amazingly the group picture was one shot, with Ringo having to duck down below Paul to accommodate the square format required

Chesil Beach
Echoes of a beach in Canada

Martha and The Muffins' 1980 Top 10 hit 'Echo Beach' was a fictitious location dreamed up by the band's Mark Gane. Though inspired by his local Sunnyside Beach on Lake Ontario, Canada, Gane's song was released as a single in a picture sleeve showing a map of the extraordinary 18-mile-long Chesil Beach.

LOCATION 092: eastern end of the beach. Take the B3157 south to the Abbotsbury Swannery. Postcode DT3 4JG

Hengistbury Head
Great balls of Phish wool!

The Slip Stitch and Pass album cover from US rock band Phish features a giant ball of wool pursuing a running figure on the shoreline at Hengistbury Head. A 1997 live offering, the cover was yet another classic image created by Storm Thorgerson.

LOCATION 093: turn left on to The Broadway from the B3059 in Southbourne, postcode BH6 4NA

Durdle Door
An Ocean album cover scene

Completing a trio of Dorset coastal record covers is Ocean Colour Scene's album North Atlantic Drift, which carries images of the natural coastal archway Durdle Door on its cover. The band's May 2003 photo shoot was the work of renowned snapper Lawrence Watson.

LOCATION 094: approximately five miles south of the A352 at West Lulworth, postcode BH20 5RS

Puddletown
Arthur Brown and 'A Horse with No Name' down on the farm

When Arthur Brown – he of the flaming head and Crazy World – made a small fortune from his 1968 hit 'Fire' he decamped near to the quaintly named village of Puddletown in Dorset. He made a home base at nearby Ilsington Farm, reportedly making regular trips to the local, The Kings Arms, in the band's Rolls Royce. When not down the pub he would enjoy the bucolic life style the surrounding countryside offered and hunker down in the farm's Jabberwocky recording studio, where his album Strangelands was created, (ominously it was not released until 1988). Rumours of his agricultural eccentricity at the time include one report of him fitting lights to the local cows. Ilsington Farm has a couple of other minor claims to fame. While inhabited by Brown and his commune, the BBC used the place for filming a documentary about Tess of the D'Urbervilles and the book's author, Thomas Hardy. There has been much additional music activity here. Among the various musicians availing themselves of the farm's recording facilities were the band America, who are said to have completed the writing and demoing of their most famous song, 'A Horse with No Name', there in the summer of 1971.

LOCATIONS 095 and 096: the manor at Ilsington lies a couple of miles south of Puddletown, which is on the main A35. Postcode DT2 8QW. Just like Arthur did you can still have a drink in the Kings Arms Hotel at 30 High East Street, Dorchester, postcode DT1 1HF

Dorset

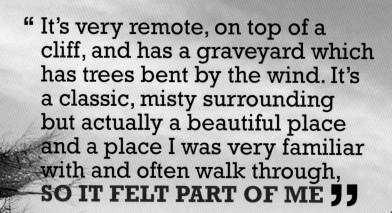

" It's very remote, on top of a cliff, and has a graveyard which has trees bent by the wind. It's a classic, misty surrounding but actually a beautiful place and a place I was very familiar with and often walk through, **SO IT FELT PART OF ME** "

PJ HARVEY
describes the church where she
recorded Let England Shake

Photo: Cat Stevens

Eype
PJ Harvey's clifftop recording base

Having first contemplated London or Berlin as a recording base for her eighth album, PJ Harvey eventually settled on a magical place closer to home. The clifftop church of St Peter's, a few miles from where she grew up in the Dorset village of Corscombe, was rehearsal space and studio for her second Top 10 album Let England Shake. For a five-week period in 2010, the remote 19th-century church,

now the coastal village of Eype's Centre for the Arts, became the project's creative hub. On a snowy night in December that year, St Peter's was fittingly also the album's launch venue when PJ Harvey previewed Let England Shake ahead of its critically acclaimed release and Mercury Prize in 2011.

LOCATION 097: St Peter's Church and Eype Centre for the Arts can be accessed at Mounts Lane in the village of Eype, a mile west of Bridport, just south of the A35, postcode DT6 6AL

Left: Photographer Cat Stevens captures the Let England Shake sessions. "I was struck by what a lovely atmosphere had been created in St Peter's. A group of old friends recording the songs live, in one take. I had a wonderful time documenting it."

Main pic:ture: PJ Harvey's album launch was held on a snowy December night in 2011

Photo: Mike Jack

Dorset

Poole
Tour of Life tragedy for Kate Bush

When Kate Bush decided to tour an ambitious live show following early single and album success in her chart debut year of 1978, she sensibly began with a trial performance in Dorset. Poole Arts Centre was the venue for the warm-up show on April 1, 1979, where Kate could road-test all aspects of a complex and innovative stage show. As Kate would be singing and dancing, she pioneered the use of a head mic to replace a conventional microphone to give herself that extra degree of freedom on stage. The first date at Poole would have been a resounding success had tragedy not struck at the end of the night when lighting director Bill Duffield, completing a final check of the stage, fell 20 feet through a cavity, suffering injuries that would eventually lead to his death. As a result, the tour very nearly got cancelled before it had started with Kate and the crew left devastated. But, when the tour reached London's Hammersmith Odeon, Kate, with support from Peter Gabriel and Steve Harley, turned a special performance of her Tour of

Life into a memorial concert to Duffield to benefit his family. Gabriel and Harley had both worked with Duffield on their own stage shows previously. Poole Arts Centre has many other claims to fame, having hosted gigs by U2, Michael Jackson, KISS and The Smiths, but it is Kate Bush's warm-up gig for her only tour until 2014 that it is most associated with.

LOCATION 098: in the centre of Poole, the building (expensively refurbished in 2002), is now called The Lighthouse (Poole's Centre for the Arts) at 21 Kingland Road, postcode BH15 1UG

Kate Bush 'captured' in one of her earliest EMI press shoots by photographer Gered Mankowitz

Isle of Purbeck
In a Big Country

The Big Country video for the band's 1983 hit 'In a Big Country' was shot at various locations on the Isle of Purbeck. Not a real island, the Dorset peninsula's tourist hotspots, Corfe Castle, the seaside resort of Swanage and the white cliffs of Old Harry Rocks, are all locations for what proves to be an almost Enid Blyton-esque, Famous Five-like storyline

involving the band members and a mysterious dark-haired girl. All that's missing are the lashings of ginger beer.

LOCATIONS 099 and 100: the A351 to the coast at Swanage (postcode BH19 1) takes in Corfe Castle (postcode BH20 5ED) on route

Studland Bay
Chris Martin gets drenched for 'Yellow'

Sand and sun was what was required, but the weather wasn't exactly what Coldplay had envisaged when the day came to shoot the music video for their breakthrough hit single in 2000. Chris Martin got a drenching on Studland Bay beach during the filming of the video for 'Yellow'. The gloomy rain and seaspray-lashed location was in keeping with the mood of the band that day. Apparently drummer Will Champion's mother's funeral was on the same day as the video shoot and it was decided by the band members that only frontman Chris would appear in front of the camera. The depressing background and simple, continuous take didn't harm prospects of 'Yellow' becoming a hit. It remained on the singles chart for 11 weeks and helped boost the album from which it came, Parachutes, to No.1 and a limpet-like grip on that chart for more than two years.

LOCATION 101: Studland is two miles north of Swanage. Postcode BH19 3AP

According to Chris Martin, "'Yellow' refers to the mood of the band. Brightness and hope and devotion." The conditions on the day of the video shoot were anything but

Born in DORSET

Robert Fripp (b. 16 May 1946, Wimborne)
Alex James, bass, Blur (b. 21 Nov 1968, Boscombe)
Rick Kemp, bass, Steeleye Span (b. 15 Nov 1941, Little Hanford)
Lee Kerslake, drums, Uriah Heep (b. 16 Apr 1947, Bournemouth)
Greg Lake (b. 10 Nov 1948, Bournemouth)
Darrell Sweet, drums, Nazareth (b. 16 May 1947, Bournemouth)

Dorset rock stars Greg Lake (left) and Robert Fripp

Photo: Barry Garvey

Rock Atlas

Essex

Did Essex once stage the UK's equivalent of Woodstock? Well, according to the locals, if the effect on the tiny village of Weeley is anything to go by – yes they did! These days there's the mega V Festival with its swanky, all mod cons approach to satisfy live music watchers but there's also a gritty determination about Essex's musical activity dating back over more than half a century. After all, this is the coastline that was washed away in the tragic floods of 1953 and witnessed the brave resistance movement that was pirate radio off the port of Harwich (Radio Caroline South). It has its fair share of posh rock star homes and gardens: Rod Stewart's is particularly magnificent and there's the "all too beautiful" cottage homes of Steve Marriott. But it's the glorious seaside locations of Southend and Canvey Island that helped create a small but significant music revolution. This was a raw, no frills, but appealingly flash sound that pushed the likes of pub rock innovators Dr Feelgood into the national limelight.

Arkesden
Steve Marriott's cottage fire and tragic death

This is the village where mod icon Steve Marriott lived and tragically died in 1991. The former Small Faces and Humble Pie band member was found dead at the scene of a fire at the 16th-century cottage he rented in the village High Street. At 6.30 on the morning of April 20, a passing motorist saw the property ablaze and called the fire brigade. One officer attending the emergency call-out was Keith Dunatis, a fan of Marriott's, who identified the rock star's body immediately and successfully rescued his collection of guitars and recording equipment. Compounding the tragedy was the fact that Marriott, after a period of relative inactivity, had returned the day before from a productive trip to the US, where he'd been working once more on an album with former Humble Pie bandmate Peter Frampton.

LOCATION 102: approximately eight miles north of Bishop's Stortford, just west of the M11. The cottage is opposite the Axe & Compasses pub (Marriott's local) in Arkesden village High Street, postcode CB11 4EX. Status: private residence

Billericay
Ian Dury's 'Billericay Dickie'

When Ian Dury incorporated a British music hall sensibility into his songs, 'Billericay Dickie', from his most popular album New Boots and Panties!!, created his sauciest seaside postcard character yet. The 40,000 townspeople of Billericay have been trying to live it down ever since. Essex girls from Shoeburyness and Burnham-on-Crouch also get a namecheck, but it's the randy bricklayer that constantly brings a smirk whenever the name of the town gets an airing.

LOCATION 103: Billericay is east of the A12 between the M25 and Chelmsford, postcode CM12

Canvey Island
A warning from British Sea Power

'Canvey Island', a track on British Sea Power's 2008 Top 10 album Do You Like Rock Music?, is a song written by the band's Yan (Peter Wilkinson) as an obvious warning of the problems of climate change, remembered through the dreadful floods in 1953 that so devastated Canvey, claiming the lives of 58 of the island's inhabitants. The band was memorably filmed for the BBC's Culture Show, playing the track at waterfront pub The Monico.

LOCATION 104: The Monico is at 1-3 Eastern Esplanade, postcode SS8 7DN

Born in ESSEX

Najma Akhtar, singer (b. 1964, Chelmsford)
Victoria Beckham, Spice Girls (b. 17 Apr 1974, Harlow)
Jet Black, drums, The Stranglers (b. 26 Aug 1938, Ilford)
Pauline Black, vocals, The Selecter (b. 23 Oct 1953, Coggeshall)
Graham Bond, British R&B musician (b. 28 Oct 1937, Romford, d. 8 May 1974)
David Byron, vocals, Uriah Heep (b. 29 Jan 1947, Epping, d. 28 Feb 1985)
Keith Christmas, singer-songwriter (b. 13 Oct 1946, Wivenhoe)
Vic Collins, guitar, Kursaal Flyers (b. 10 Sep 1950, Rochford)
Tony Connor, drums, Hot Chocolate (b. 6 Apr 1947, Romford)
Tina Cousins, singer (b. 20 Apr 1974, Leigh-on-Sea)
Sarah Cracknell, vocals, Saint Etienne (b. 12 Apr 1967, Chelmsford)
Jamie Cullum, jazz musician/presenter (b. 20 Aug 1979, Rochford)
Graeme Douglas, guitar, Kursaal Flyers (b. 22 Jan 1950, Rochford)
Dave Gahan, vocals, Depeche Mode (b. 9 May 1962, North Weald)
Paul Gray, bass, Eddie & The Hot Rods (b. 1 Aug 1958, Rochford)
Roy Hay, guitar/keyboards, Culture Club (b. 12 Aug 1961, Southend-on-Sea)
John Hendy, East 17 (b. 26 Mar 1971, Barking)
Steve Hillage (b. 2 Aug 1951, Chingford)
Liam Howlett, keyboards, The Prodigy (b. 21 Aug 1971, Braintree)
Neil Innes, Bonzo Dog Doo-Dah Band/The Rutles (b. 9 Dec 1944, Danbury)
Wilko Johnson, guitar, Dr Feelgood (b. 12 Jul 1947, Canvey Island)
Nick Kamen (b. 15 Apr 1962, Harlow)

Sonja Kristina, vocals, violin/Curved Air (b. 14 Apr 1949, Brentwood)
John Leyton (b. 17 Feb 1939, Frinton-on-Sea)
Alison Moyet (b. 18 Jun 1961, Billericay)
Peter Nelson, bass, New Model Army (b. 22 Sep 1958, Colchester)
Scott Robinson, Five (b. 22 Nov 1979, Basildon)
Dave Rowntree, drums, Blur (b. 8 May 1964, Colchester)
Jon Sevink, violin, Levellers (b. 15 May 1965, Harlow)
Twink (John Alder), drums/vocals, The Pink Fairies/The Pretty Things (b. 29 Nov 1944, Colchester)
Cliff Williams, bass, AC/DC (b. 14 Dec 1949, Romford)

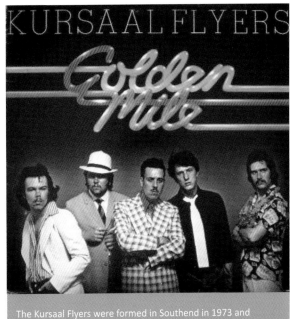

The Kursaal Flyers were formed in Southend in 1973 and featured Essex-born guitarists Graeme Douglas and Vic Collins

Essex

Canvey Island
'Down by the Jetty' with Dr Feelgood

" The **MURKY WATER.** The flaming towers on the horizon at the oil refineries. I think it's **BEAUTIFUL.**

In the evening the mists surge around, like dry ice at a concert **"**

Wilko Johnson
In an interview with Mojo

Spiritual home to Dr Feelgood, Canvey Island has a salty character and special atmosphere preserved in something of a decades-old timewarp. The band probably rejected any thoughts that the landscape was anything other than a petrochemical wasteland when their brand of pub rock helped spearhead the new genre that turned them from local heroes into R&B media favourites. Mid-Seventies albums Down by the Jetty and Malpractice sounded as belligerent and gloriously seedy as their surroundings, but a certain affection for the place was obvious on album covers picturing the band at home in Canvey Island locations. The jetty in question can be found a stone's throw from the waterfront Lobster Smack pub. The band's last single featuring frontman Lee Brilleaux was titled 'Down at the Doctors' simply because it was recorded down at Canvey's Dr Feelgood Music Bar in January 1994, 10 weeks before the singer's death. The venue is, like Lee, no longer standing and sadly missed, but the cover of this live album

The Wilko-less Dr Feelgood line-up spell out their background on the beach in front of the Labworth restaurant on Canvey Island

carries an image of the band in front of the place at 21 Knightswick Road where now stands the Oysterfleet Hotel and a plaque honouring Brilleaux. The 2009 Julien Temple-directed movie Oil City Confidential provides the perfect introduction to the band and this oddly romantic Essex outpost.

LOCATIONS 105, 106, 107 and 108: there's only one way into Canvey Island. The favoured spot for more than one photoshoot was the art deco building currently called The Labworth, a restaurant situated on the beach front, postcode SS8 7DW. The Oysterfleet Hotel is at 21 Knightswick Road, postcode SS8 9PA, and the Lobster Smack pub, down by the jetty, is on Haven Road, postcode SS8 0NR. The Admiral Jellicoe pub, pictured on the cover of the band's fifth album, Be Seeing You, is at 283 High Street, postcode SS8 7RS

SITE OF DR FEELGOOD MUSIC BAR

The singer LEE BRILLEAUX 1952 – 1994 performed here 25th January 1994

Look for this commemorative plaque on the wall outside the Oysterfleet Hotel

Left: Wilko Johnson and co-author Zoë Howe give a lively Essex Book Festival talk about Wilko's autobiography, Looking Back at Me at the Lobster Smack pub on Canvey Island in 2012

Above: a Feelgood pub 'Down by the Jetty' – The Lobster Smack

Photos: David Roberts

Photo: Johnny Williams

PRS
for MUSIC

Blur
first gigged here
1989
Presented to
East Anglian Railway Museum

PRS for Music Heritage Award

Chappel and Wakes Colne
Blur's railway shed reunion

Honoured by a PRS for Music plaque, the
East Anglian Railway Museum was the
unusual location for Blur's first gig. Damon
Albarn, Graham Coxon, Alex James and
Dave Rowntree returned to the Colchester
museum's Goods Shed 20 years on from their
first public performance in 1989 as a starter to
kick off their much-publicised 2009
reunion tour.

LOCATION 109: north of the A1124, eight
miles west of Colchester at Station Road,
postcode CO6 2DS. Website: www.earm.co.uk

Above: Fittingly Blur
song 'Essex Dogs'
gets an airing at the
June 13, 2009 gig
where it all started

Right: The first PRS
for Music plaque, awarded
to commemorate Blur's first gig

Colchester
Beer House shoot for Marillion's best

The bar-room setting for the cover shoot for Marillion's 1987 No.2 album Clutching at Straws was photographed at Colchester's Beer House pub. In the cut-and-paste days before computer graphics, images of Robert Burns, Dylan Thomas, Truman Capote and Lenny Bruce were added to the front cover bar scene at what was then called The Baker's Arms. Hurriedly put together by a designer working against an impossible deadline, the sleeve unsurprisingly didn't meet with lead singer Fish's approval. "The worst Marillion sleeve, which also housed our best album to date," he later reflected.

LOCATION 111: a short walk south-east of the centre of Colchester at 126 Magdalen Street, postcode CO1 2LF

Famous faces prop up the bar at the Beer House pub

Harlow
Free rock for all at Harlow Town Park

Harlow Town Council upset some residents but hugely impressed others with their free rock concerts staged at Harlow Town Park during the Seventies. A broad selection of rock, pop and folk acts helped make Harlow hip, attracting decent crowds – 20,000 in the case of a riotous visit by the Bay City Rollers in 1974 – to the new town's futuristic park bandstand. Five dates were set during the spring and summer of 1973 with Atomic Rooster, Chicken Shack, Arthur Brown, Mungo Jerry and Hawkwind all headlining. Space- rockers Hawkwind made a memorable return in 1974, supported by Magic Michael and Michael Moorcock, the year in which Fairport Convention, Clancy and Sassafras also made appearances. Thin Lizzy and Man topped the bill in 1975. Others putting in an appearance, before the council's initiative was scaled down, included Judas Priest and 10cc. Perhaps more councils should follow Harlow's lead and put rock on their list of public services...

LOCATION 110: the showground bandstand still hosts concerts (although not currently of the scale of the Seventies events) in the town park, framed by Edinburgh Way to the north and Mandela Avenue to the south. Postcode: CM20

Harlow
Catholic church album cover for The Chemical Brothers

The Chemical Brothers' album cover image for Brothers Gonna Work It Out is an extraordinary architectural gem that would not look out of keeping in the US Mid-West. But it's the Our Lady of Fatima Catholic Church in Harlow new town that adorns the DJ duo's DJ 1998 compilation album.

LOCATION 112: a short distance east of the town centre at Howard Way, postcode CM20 2NS

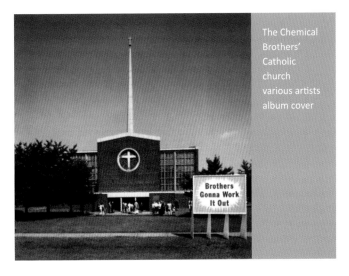

The Chemical Brothers' Catholic church various artists album cover

Essex

Photo: David Roberts

Epping
Rod Stewart's country life

Rod Stewart's country home near Epping famously boasts a full-sized football pitch, complete with dug-outs, where Rod the former mod's Vagabonds FC have staged many a match down the years. When his beloved Celtic needed a pre-season training pitch in 2005 Rod (and his amazing facilities) eagerly obliged. The estate only became Rod's place when he successfully outbid King Constantine of Greece for the property in 1986. Completing the archetypal British setting for the man who no doubt yearns for California when in Essex and

Main picture: Rod first spotted Wood House in the pages of Country Life magazine in 1986

Inset: not bad for a boy from the Archway Road: Celtic fan Rod on a day off at his Epping home. Now which Ferrari shall I take out today?

Essex when on the West Coast is Rod's good old English local, the Theydon Oak, where he has been frequently spotted downing the odd red wine or two. Putting a whole new meaning on the description "free house", so good for trade and so pally with the landlord and landlady is Rod that apparently he hasn't bought a drink there in more than 20 years. Sadly, one unfulfilled footnote to this location's entry remains just that: shortly before his death, Michael Jackson was reported to have plumped for Wood House as his base for the relatively easy trip down the nearby M11 into London for his projected marathon of O2 gigs in 2009 and 2010. Rod Stewart revealed an interesting wartime

fact about Wood House in Rod – The Autobiography (2012). Apparently this part of Essex had once been the constituency of MP Winston Churchill, who stayed at Wood House and would watch the World War II German bombing raids on nearby London from an upstairs window.

LOCATIONS 113 and 114: originally part of the vast estate belonging to Copped Hall, Wood House is south of Epping High Street and almost within earshot of the M25. Postcode: CM16 5HT. Status: private residence. The Theydon Oak pub can be found at 9 Coopersale Street, Epping, postcode CM16 7QJ

Moreton
Humble Pie's hideaway at Beehive Cottage

Spotted driving around the winding lanes of this part of Essex in a white Aston Martin fitted with a record player, Steve Marriott lived the rock 'n' roll lifestyle in this remote setting just west of the small village of Moreton. Here the guitarist and singer-songwriter resided along with wife Jenny, dogs, cats, geese and a horse that he would famously ride to the local pub. Purchased in 1968 shortly before his career took an international upturn with the formation of Humble Pie, the property boasted a detached building for guests and recording studio, which became Clearsound Studio, a place where Peter Frampton was a frequent visitor during the secret formation and rehearsing of the supergroup's new material. Larger scale band rehearsals would take place at nearby Magdalen Laver Village Hall. Watch out for the High Laver Bridge if you are driving around these parts. Rock legend has it Marriott once bounced over it a

Photo: Micky Walker

little too quickly in the Aston Martin and landed in the river below.

LOCATION 115: three miles north of the A414 Harlow Road, at Moreton. Postcode: CM5 0DR. Status: private residence

"In order to buy the house we had to get an ADVANCE FROM IMMEDIATE RECORDS and I remember borrowing a further £500 from Arthur Howes, the promoter "

JENNY MARRIOTT

Photo: David Roberts

Top: Steve Marriott and his dogs outside the cottage he shared with wife Jenny and Ronnie Lane and his wife Sue

Above: Steve Marriott's Beehive Cottage studio

Essex

Westcliff-on-Sea
Nash and Young at the Essex seaside

When Crosby, Stills, Nash & Young completed their mammoth US coast-to-coast stadium tour in 1974 and wound-up proceedings in front of 72,000 fans at Wembley, they quite reasonably needed a break. But the first destination Neil Young and Graham Nash headed for on their vacation may surprise a few people. When Young's newly acquired 1934 Rolls-Royce Shooting Brake - purchased at Antiques World in Fulham and nicknamed "Wembley" - headed out of London the duo and a bunch of friends ended up in the seaside town of Westcliff-on-Sea. Here, in the Boston Hall Hotel, Young began writing a series of songs which continued when the party headed for the next leg of their vacation, across the North Sea to Amsterdam. Photos from the few days on the Essex coast pop up in Graham Nash's 2004 photographic book Eye to Eye, including the cover self-portrait, shot in a seafront arcade photo booth.

LOCATION 116: the Boston Hall Hotel was knocked down a while back to make way for Admirals Place, The Leas, postcode SS0 7BF

Photo: Matthew Lloyd. http://www.arthurlloyd.co.uk

Southend-on-Sea
The Kursaal's Flyers and Feelgoods

Although the last live music gig was as far back as 1977, the Kursaal Ballroom's opulent foyer, exterior walls and famous dome still stand today as a reminder of some memorable occasions since its opening in 1901 at the heart of what was claimed to be the world's first theme park. Now converted as a venue for ten-pin bowling, this remarkable structure saw Thin Lizzy turn out for the dubious honour of performing at the place for the final time. Among the many acts gracing this fine venue during its pre-punk heyday were the Kursaal Flyers, who took their name from a mocked-up wild-west train that featured in the annual Southend Carnival. Around half the tracks on Dr Feelgood's 1976 chart-topping live album Stupidity were recorded here.

LOCATION 117: Eastern Esplanade, Southend-on-Sea. Postcode SS1 27G

Feelgood factor: live at Southend's Kursaal

Weeley

'The People's Festival': Weeley becomes Woodstock

August Bank Holiday weekend 1971 saw over 130,000 rock fans descend on this 200-acre site five miles from the coast at Clacton-on-Sea for an event headlined by The Faces and T.Rex that bore all the hallmarks of a UK version of Woodstock. Like the legendary 1969 festival in New York state, Weeley was located in a farming community and grew from modest beginnings to something quite out of control. In Weeley's case, it developed from such tiny aspirations that the final end to the story is all the more mind-boggling. No doubt intrigued by the money-making potential of a small music festival, the local Round Table ditched their time-honoured annual fete and donkey derby fundraisers in favour of a music festival in the summer of 1971. Very definitely "not a bread trip", as the committee put it, every penny raised would go to aid Bangladesh, Shelter and other important community charities. But just how did one set about organising a pop festival? With little or no knowledge of a type of event new to Britain at the time, the committee were innocently undaunted. The local plumbers and electricians were soon on board and galvanised into action, with the three solicitors in the Clacton Round Table put in charge of the car parks. Medical affairs were the responsibility of Clacton GP Dr Dick Farrow, who was informed by his Round

Pictured with the bus that transported the performers to the festival from London, Marc Bolan arrives at Weeley

Table chairman Vic Speck that "I might need a bit of first aid." As the weekend of the festival arrived, this off-the-cuff request turned out to be something of an understatement when it transpired that Farrow would be forced to hastily enlist the help of 75 nurses to cope with the growing number of fans tripping on LSD or overdosing on heroin. But the person mostly responsible for turning an ambitious fundraising event into a gigantic news story, making the front pages of the national Sunday papers, was promoter Colin King. Hired by the Round Table to book a few ▶

Essex

"Rod Stewart went up to the mic on stage and said 'We'll have a quick tune up and we'll be right wiv ya.' And they were brilliant. Later he announced one song: 'This is about a school boy who falls in love with a dirty old prostitute!"
Young fan Keith Page describes the first live performance of 'Maggie May'

"Rod had two bottles of Liebfraumilch on stage – I was filming Rod in his pink satin suit from the side of the stage"
Dr Dick Farrow, who supervised the festival's first-aid tents and administered some sound advice to fans over the festival PA system

"Thump, thump, thump: I could hear the music as far away as Clacton-on-Sea pier, where I was fishing for bass, skate and eels. My father Bill was a 19-stone master builder but worked on the gate at the festival and was intimidated enough by some of the Hells Angels to warn me not to attend saying, 'I'm not going back'"
16-year-old school leaver Ian Bruce

"The biggest draw for me was The Faces, but it was an immense bill. Some of the acts I had seen previously, including Hackensack, who I think opened. The memories that stick with me are the splendour of Barclay James Harvest performing with orchestra, and waking up to Status Quo, who had morphed from pop band to outrageous, hairy blues sluggers. Not all the performers impressed, obviously – I was nonplussed by Julie Felix and Richie Havens but I'm not sure if that was Weeley!"
16-year-old Braintree schoolboy Nigel Bones

"THE POP PUNCH-UP: A savage running battle broke out at a pop festival yesterday when leather-jacketed Hells Angels clashed with security guards and catering staff"
How the Sunday Mirror reported the festival

▶ "names", King bagged a huge line-up. "I approached Rod Stewart and Marc Bolan. I wanted Pink Floyd but they weren't in the country. That was the only band I couldn't get hold of. I didn't want Led Zeppelin because they were too expensive." An outside appointment, King turned an interesting new venture for Clacton Round Table with an expected 10,000 ticket-holder limit into an east Essex pop fan invasion of biblical proportions. Promoted as "The People's Festival", tickets were £1.50 for the entire weekend, for an event that had everything - a great British bill including Barclay James Harvest complete with 45-piece orchestra, fires, gang fights, Hells Angels, confiscated shotguns, knives and metal pipes… and some decent weather. The on-site sanitation might not have been up to the standard of the music, though. Marc

Bolan was rumoured to have ventured into the village and blagged a hot bath from a local resident, who accepted £1 for the privilege of inviting the T.Rex star into her cottage. The festival finally came to a protracted end with Stray (accompanied by a firework display) playing until dawn on the Tuesday, long after the expected Bank Holiday Monday shut-down. Post Weeley, lessons were learned - not least by the government of the day, which was prompted to publish a guidebook (Pop Festivals: Report and Code of Practice) for future events, with contributions from Weeley's overworked 'first aid' hero Dick Farrow. The good doctor also had a paper published in The Practitioner in 1972 which became the template for dealing with the many festivals of Weeley's magnitude that would follow.

LOCATIONS 118 and 119: the festival site is bordered by a railway line to the north, the B1441 to the west and bisected by public footpaths close to Hall Farm and St Andrews Church. Postcode CO16 9JW. Festival Close, named to commemorate Weeley's great event, is bizarrely north of the village, as far away from the old festival site as it can be. Postcode CO16 9AT

It wasn't all bonfires, Hells Angels and mayhem: the sunny weather and great music made Weeley a fantastic, memorable experience for most of the fans

Police reports suggested that the Weeley crowd could have been as much as 150,000 strong, which put a strain on the carefully prepared but ultimately overwhelmed toilet facilities

Event photos: Jules and Emma Cole

Rock Atlas

Gloucestershire

While not quite conjuring up images of a Severn delta steeped in roots music, the county dominated by the wide and often muddy river throws up its own rock ghosts. Pictured famously in the estuary's open landscape are Bob Dylan and Echo & The Bunnymen, while the unsolved mystery of Manic Street Preacher Richey Edwards and the early death of blues-rock pioneer Brian Jones are reminders of how heavy a price was paid for rock immortality by the county's two most influential young musicians. The Gloucestershire gloom is lifted by the enthusiastic folk of Stroud, who welcomed The Beatles to their town for the Fab Four's first proper UK gig outside their native north-west, and Cheltenham can claim to have witnessed the birth of that phrase "Beatlemania". Slade performing in a nuclear power station? Heavy rock recordings at Clearwell Castle? Gloucestershire has the lot…

Aust
Dylan crosses the River Severn

One of the most iconic photographs taken of Bob Dylan was snapped here on the south bank of the River Severn by Barry Feinstein. The picture appears on DVD and CD covers for the Martin Scorsese movie No Direction Home and portrays an inscrutable Dylan waiting for the next Aust Ferry en route to a concert in Cardiff. His mode of transport, an Austin Princess loaned by The Rolling Stones, waits patiently at the end of a slipway terminal closed for business shortly after the picture was taken on May 11,

Photo: David Roberts

Photo: David Roberts

Opposite page: Barry Feinstein's No Direction Home cover shot shows Dylan about to cross the Severn in 1966. Above: the same view today

Left: A fan left this delicately created graffiti on what remains of the Aust Ferry terminal site

Cheltenham
The Blue Moon and The Night Owl

Currently known as The Night Owl, this high street venue began its pop life as a milk bar called Egg & Bacon in the 60s. By the end of the decade as the Blue Moon Club, it attracted The Rolling Stones, Mott the Hoople, Cream and Jimi Hendrix. At this time the club was expertly run by two partners, Bill Reid and Eddie Norman, who had a knack for booking the next big thing in pop. A reputation built on a mod audience saw Rod Stewart's early incarnation with Steampacket. Happily, the venue has survived down the decades and into the 21st century, attracting the likes of Stereophonics and Feeder despite changing names from The Night Owl, Misty's, The Attic and back to The Night Owl again. Perhaps the club's biggest claim to fame came in the Sixties when The Four Tops made their UK debut there.

LOCATION 121: 170 High Street, postcode GL50 1EP

"There was no sign of drink or drugs, no… ego, just a gentle… **ACCEPTANCE** of a guy wanting to take a few snaps"
MIKE CHARITY
photographer, meets Hendrix backstage at The Blue Moon

1966. The times were certainly a-changing, as can be seen by the new Severn Bridge nearing completion in the photograph's background, which rendered the quaint old Aust Ferry redundant. All that remains today are the overgrown, weed-infested platform and ruins of the terminal building, turnstile and slipway stretching out into the muddy banks of the Severn.

LOCATION 120: leave the A403, join Passage Road and head for the banks of the River Severn

Gloucestershire

The Beatles play
Cheltenham
facing a barrage
of screams and
a shower of Jelly
Babies

Cheltenham
'Beatlemania invented' in Cheltenham

The phrase "Beatlemania" was coined when The Beatles played Cheltenham's Odeon cinema on November 1st 1963 and the Daily Mirror invented the word to describe the scenes of hysteria the band created. This just emphasises the degree to which the band were stirring up the emotions of teenage pop fans up and down the country at the time. Words like "excitement" just wouldn't do. A measure of their success in the week of the Odeon shows was the fact that although their latest hit 'She Loves You' had just been toppled from the top of the singles chart it was soon to return to No. 1 and then be overtaken by their own 'I Want to Hold Your Hand' at the top in the run up to Christmas.

With the Beatles: Freelance photo-journalist Mike Charity was present at the birth of Beatlemania ▶

A Cheltenham fan adopts a Beatles-worshipping position

Photos: Mike Charity

Gloucestershire

but admits he was still rather 'green' when it came to asking questions at the press call that day.

"Eventually they arrived backstage and for some reason I was sure there were five Beatles, so in all innocence I asked the group member nearest to me, "Where's the other one?"

Of course it would be John Lennon who answered the question. 'What do you mean the other one - there's only bloody four of us.'

After this slight upset, things returned to normal, the scribes got their notes and we took our photographs. Within 15 minutes the 'presser' was over, the four cheerfully waved their goodbyes and we wished them good luck.

After the John Lennon retort, I vowed to myself that in future I would be sure to check my facts before meeting other subjects to be photographed. In later years I learned there had in fact been a fifth Beatle - or possibly two, and I wondered if at the time [John] thought I was trying to being clever or sarcastic with my question! Myself and two other local paper

snappers arranged with the cinema manager to let us in during the evening's final support act's stage entrance and we were guided down to the front-of-house orchestra pits, which was to be our base for The Beatles' half -hour performance. I was totally unprepared as the curtain rose for the giant front wave of sound that accompanied their entrance and the wall of female screams attacking from the rear. The auditorium decibels increased with each number The Beatles played, deafening both melody and lyrics - even The Beatles' amplified speakers could not match the volume of noise produced by the frenetic fans, causing John Lennon at one point during their performance to yell out, 'Shut Up!'

The non-stop noise was very unpleasant - but oh, the atmosphere! Teenage girls were kneeling, hands raised, as if in prayer to their onstage gods. Some just sat and cried. Others threw 'Jelly Babies' on to the stage, often showering us with a bad-aimed lob.

At the end, after no more than a couple of encores, the group left

the stage with what appeared a slightly hurried exit. Unseen by us in the orchestra pits, they had spotted a horde of whirling dervish devotees flowing down the aisles in a determined race for the stage. Slinging our cameras over the footlights, we also leapt up on to the boards and ran for the wings. Backstage all was darkness as strong hands grabbed hold and firmly guided us out to the stage door into some sort of truck. The vehicle, with no interior lighting, sped off, leaving us literally in the dark regarding our destination. Some eight minutes later it came to a sudden halt, the doors were yanked open, and as we alighted from the vehicle we were amazed to find John, Paul, Ringo and George had been our travelling companions. The venue was Cheltenham's Savoy hotel, where the group were staying for the night before their next day's concert."

The setting for this first sighting and sounding of Beatlemania was the large art deco cinema, whose redeeming decorative feature was the two naked silver ladies tangled in celluloid on the building's façade.

LOCATION 122: the place where Beatlemania began may be rubble or a new apartment block by the time you read this. Like most of these old art deco cinemas, it was replaced by a multiplex elsewhere in Cheltenham. The crumbling building is at the crossroads of Winchcombe Street and Albion Street. Postcode GL52 2LZ

Beatlemania began at the Odeon Cinema, Cheltenham

Left: 'What do you mean, the other one?' Mike Charity gets a ticking off from John Lennon

Photo: Jeff Adams

Gloucestershire

Cheltenham
Brian Jones' home city

In the unlikely setting of a sunken tropical garden in the Beechwood Shopping Centre you can find the bust of Brian Jones. The founder member of The Rolling Stones was a key figure in the development of the British blues and R&B movements. His childhood home near the centre of Cheltenham still stands largely unchanged since the 1950s at the quaintly named 17 Eldorado Road. The guitarist's gravestone can be located in Prestbury cemetery, a short distance to the north of the city.

LOCATIONS 123, 124 and 125: Beechwood Shopping Centre is at 123 High Street, postcode GL50 1DQ. Brian Jones' childhood home is located at 17 Eldorado Road, postcode GL50 2PU. Prestbury cemetery can be found by taking the B4632 north-east out of Cheltenham city centre

Right: Fans still make the pilgrimage to the grave of Brian Jones on the anniversary of his birth and death

Bottom right: Charlie Watts and Bill Wyman in the middle of the huge numbers of fans, family and friends at Brian Jones' funeral in Cheltenham. Filming Ned Kelly down under in Australia, Mick Jagger was unable to attend the 1969 ceremony, which saw Jones' remains borne in a silver and bronze coffin rumoured to have been sent by Bob Dylan (Photo: Mike Charity)

In Affectionate Remembrance of BRIAN JONES born 28th february 1942 died 3rd July 1969 at Hartfield, Sussex

Right: The city centre bust of the original Rolling Stone Brian Jones

Photo: Peter Tarleton   Photo: David Roberts

Clearwell Castle
A heavy rock haven

The dungeons at Clearwell Castle proved an inspirational rehearsal and recording location for the cream of British heavy rock in the 1970s. Black Sabbath's Sabbath Bloody Sabbath and Deep Purple's Burn albums were written there. Work by Led Zeppelin on In Through the Out Door also owed much to the atmosphere at the mock Gothic mansion, where the band composed and rehearsed new material for the album in 1978. Looked after royally with breakfasts at 5pm by Clearwell's owner's son Bernie Yeates and using Ronnie Lane's mobile recording unit, Bad Company were typical of groups eschewing the London studios at the time in favour of a live

Lords of the manor: Deep Purple pose in the grounds of Clearwell Castle

recording vibe. Hawkwind and The Sweet were also visitors to this heavy haven, now a popular venue for weddings.

LOCATION 126: a mile west of the B4228 south of Coleford, postcode GL16 8LG

"OZZY TOOK US TO THE WYNDHAM ARMS where we got well and truly oiled. We managed to give the local darts team a good thrashing 🗩

DAVID TANGYE
Sabbath roadie who spent an eventful time during rehearsals for Sabbath Bloody Sabbath

Oldbury Naite
Nuclear power performance by Slade

A nuclear power station must surely be a contender for the craziest venue Slade has ever played. When the BBC wanted to crank up the excitement for a performance by Noddy Holder and co for a 1972 edition of Top of the Pops, they used film of the band delivering smash hit 'Gudbuy T'Jane' from Oldbury, on the banks of the Severn Estuary. Their dramatic appearance wasn't just *at* the place, it was very much *in* it. Sadly, no footage remains of the band in white coats acting out some pop science inside the

reactor on one of the fuelling machines atop the pilecap! "We were making a special film for Top of the Pops at a power station. I was wearing a silver suit so they decided to film me walking along an overhead ledge as though I was a spaceman who'd just landed. It was very high up and I suddenly looked down at the ground. That was a mistake because I just froze. I had this terror of falling and I just froze completely, like a cat does when it gets stuck up a tree," Slade's guitarist Dave Hill recalled.

LOCATION 127: Four miles north-east of Thornbury, the power station was decommissioned in 2012. Postcode BS35 1RQ

Photo: Polydor

The comparatively soberly dressed Slade, who donned white coats and stomped around Oldbury Nuclear Power Station in 1972

Gloucestershire

Newent
Joe Meek's childhood home

Joe Meek, the pioneer of home-produced smash hits such as 'Telstar' by the Tornados, was raised in Newent. As a child Joe would spend hours in the Meek family's garden shed building all sorts of electronic equipment, including what some reports suggest might have been this part of Gloucestershire's first television set. His short but eventful life producing pop records from his flat in London's Holloway Road ended on February 3, 1967 when he shot himself aged just 37. Newent remembers the man often dubbed a pop genius with a plaque at his birthplace and the recent naming of Meek Road elsewhere in the town. There's a large marble headstone marking Joe Meek's grave in the Newent cemetery.

LOCATIONS 128, 129 and 130: the plaque outside Joe Meek's birthplace is in the centre of Newent at 1 Market Square, postcode GL18 1PS. Meek Road is a short walk away on the south-eastern outskirts of town, postcode GL18 1UB. The gravesite is at plot 99, Newent cemetery, Watery Lane, postcode GL18 1QG

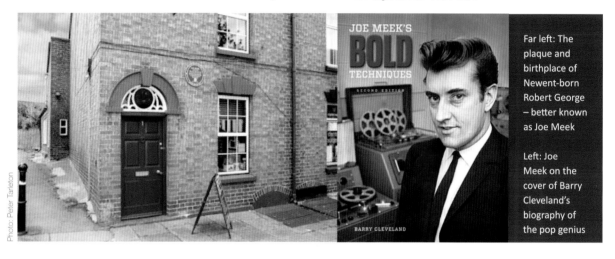

Photo: Peter Tarleton

Far left: The plaque and birthplace of Newent-born Robert George – better known as Joe Meek

Left: Joe Meek on the cover of Barry Cleveland's biography of the pop genius

Severn View services
The Richey Edwards mystery

Richey Edwards disappeared on the day he and Manic Street Preachers lead vocalist James Dean Bradfield were due to fly to the States on a promotional tour. This Gloucestershire spot marks the location where the guitarist effectively vanished, in what has become British rock's most famous tragic mystery. Here at Severn View services on February 15, 1995 his silver Vauxhall Cavalier was found abandoned just a short distance from the Severn Bridge. With no further sign of him, Edwards was officially declared missing and "presumed dead" in 2008.

LOCATION 131: at the Moto service station on the M48, which replaced the original Aust services – in existence when Richey Edwards vanished. Postcode: BS35 4BH

Born in GLOUCESTERSHIRE

James Atkin, vocals, EMF (b. 28 Mar 1969, **Cinderford**)
Derry Brownson, keyboards, EMF (b. 10 Nov 1970, **Gloucester**)
Dominic Chad, guitar, Mansun (b. 5 Jun 1972, **Cheltenham**)
Jaz Coleman, vocals, Killing Joke (b. 26 Feb 1960, **Cheltenham**)
Mark Decloedt, drums, EMF (b. 26 Jun 1969, **Gloucester**)
Ian Dench, guitar, EMF (b. 7 Aug 1964, **Cheltenham**)
Zachary Foley, bass, EMF (b. 9 Dec 1970, **Gloucester**, d. 3 Jan 2002)
Brian Jones, The Rolling Stones (b. 28 Feb 1942, **Cheltenham**, d. 3 Jul 1969)
Alex Kapranos, vocals/guitar, Franz Ferdinand (b. 20 Mar 1972, **Almondsbury**)
Joe Meek, producer (b. 5 Apr 1929, **Newent**, d. 3 Feb 1967)
Tom Smith, vocals, Editors (b. 29 Apr 1981, **Stroud**)

Stroud
A Beatles first at The Subscription Rooms

Stroud, March 31, 1962: an important place and time in Beatles history as The Subscription Rooms saw the first UK performance of the group outside their native north-west in front of a paying audience. John, Paul, George and Pete Best (Ringo was yet to join) were still seven months shy of their UK chart debut, but significantly were just three months into new manager Brian Epstein's tenure. The Shadows, Helen Shapiro and Roy Orbison were the top three chart acts that week, but the beat group era was about to begin.

Phil Pegler, a young mod from Whiteshill at the time, remembers a close encounter with The Beatles in Stroud:
"In 1962 I was probably one of the first mods in Stroud and had just bought my dream scooter, a Lambretta Li 175 Rallymaster, fully dressed with spot and fog lamps, side crash bars and a load of other accessories. On the Saturday evening in question my pal, Bow, another mod, and I parked our scooters at the rear of The Sub Rooms, alongside an old black van. From the back of the van two lads were unloading their gear, drums, guitars, etc. On seeing our scooters they came over for a closer look. Candy, my scooter, was a striking, good-looking machine. George and Pete introduced themselves but it meant nothing to us at that time. The guy called George was really taken with my scooter and spent some time trying the lights, sitting on and starting her up, and seemed quite amused that I called her Candy. Later of course we realized that it was George Harrison and Pete Best, the drummer before Ringo. We helped carry some of their gear into The Subs, where we met John and Paul. When they had set up they met up with Bow and myself in the Railway, a public house opposite the Sub Rooms, and we gave them a game of darts. So my claim to fame is that George Harrison sat on my scooter, although he did decline coming for a spin with me!"

The Beatles returned for a second concert on September 1 later that year. This time they were just two short months from experiencing their first UK chart entry when 'Love Me Do' crept into the Top 40 at No.32 in the first week of November.

LOCATION 132: The Subscription Rooms, George Street, postcode GL5 1AE

Severn Estuary
Severn heaven for Echo & The Bunnymen

The south bank of the River Severn was the setting for the cover shoot for Echo & The Bunnymen's first Top 10 album, Heaven Up Here.

LOCATION 133: postcode BS35 1RQ

Heaven Up Here
Echo And The Bunnymen

The cover image was shot on a day off from recording across the River Severn in Wales at Rockfield Studios

Tockington
Mike Oldfield's home on 'the edge of England'

When rock stars move house, or upsize, it usually isn't for an extra bedroom or a bigger garden. When Mike Oldfield was looking for a new property in 2004 his motivation was somewhere drier for the horses. 'Roughwood' in Buckinghamshire had suffered a prolonged wet spell that meant that his fields and paddocks had turned to mud and in Oldfield's words, "It was time to move on." His first thought was a move to the New Forest, but a random internet search brought up Old Down House, a 54-acre former country park and zoo built in Cotswold stone overlooking the Severn Estuary. "I stuck the cursor north of Bristol – 'What about there?' – and up this house popped, Old Down House, a big house with lots of land. So that day we got in the car and drove up there. It feels to me as if the place is right on the edge of England, because England stops at the Severn, and then you're in Wales. And being on the edge of something is rather nice, I think." By 2007 Oldfield was off again, this time to move out of the UK entirely amid tabloid news reports that he was quitting the country due to draconian anti-smoking laws, too many CCTV cameras and, inevitably, the British weather.

LOCATION 134: Old Down is now a country house visitor attraction with added wedding and business conference accommodation. Old Down Manor, Foxholes Lane, Tockington. Postcode: BS32 4PG. Public access

Rock Atlas

Greater London

With the exception of Liverpool and Manchester for short spells, London has been the undisputed heartbeat of the British music scene and the nation's capital of rock. London's domination is split up into a number of geographical centres of excellence with very distinctive contributions to British popular music. In the middle of it all, Soho gave us the clubs and coffee bars that propagated pop and rock from jazz, blues, skiffle and R&B roots. North London had its The Kinks and The Dave Clark Five, from the East came geezers The Small Faces, Ian Dury, Dizzee Rascal and Billy Bragg, south of the river gave us the kitchen-sink drama of homebodies Squeeze and a black, urban, DIY and pirate radio scene, and out West was where those well-heeled enclaves of Richmond, Twickenham and Harrow had the venues that propelled The Stones, The Who and Cream to worldwide fame from exotic but ramshackle places like Crawdaddy, Eel Pie and Klooks Kleek.

Never the easiest of places to organise for listings books like this one, the London entries in Rock Atlas have been arranged by postcode, beginning with North London (N) and moving clockwise through the East (E), South-East (SE), South-West (SW), West (W) and finally the North-West (NW).

N1
Richard Ashcroft and Fat Les: doing the Hoxton walk

Fans of mega hit single 'Bitter Sweet Symphony' by The Verve can, if they care to, walk in Richard Ashcroft's footsteps to recreate the video filmed in Hoxton. The famous video walk begins where Falkirk Street joins Hoxton Street then heads north on the eastern side of the street. This short journey promoting The Verve's 1997 No.2 hit was reproduced to promote World Cup record 'Vindaloo' a year later, when Fat Les (Keith Allen and a growing gang of walkers including young daughter Lily Allen) parodied Ashcroft's deadpan walk to camera.

LOCATION 135: Hoxton Street, postcode N1 6SH

Richard Ashcroft doing the Hoxton walk in the award-winning video for 'Bitter Sweet Symphony'

Academy Pictures

N1
Pub rock, pints and punk at the Hope & Anchor

The early to mid-Seventies revival of basic, no frills country, rock and blues, dubbed pub rock, was chiefly associated with this Islington boozer. Hardly a genre, it was rock and it was played in pubs during an economically depressed decade. Pub landlords began to realise that to chase the younger punters' pound they needed the added attraction of live music, something that pre-Seventies would have been a deterrent to increased takings. Nowhere epitomised the new London-based scene better than the Hope & Anchor, where Ducks Deluxe, Brinsley Schwarz, Chilli Willi and The Red Hot Peppers, Bees Make Honey, Kilburn and The High Roads and Dr Feelgood strutted their stuff on the small stage and at a growing number of pubs - the Tally Ho (where it all began), The Greyhound and The Bull and Gate - in pub rock's London heartland. When pub rock morphed into punk, the Hope & Anchor took this proper new genre in its stride, which is more than can be said for TV star Jonathan Ross. Attending his first ever gig at the Hope & Anchor in 1977, he cracked his head on the low ceiling pogo-ing along to X-Ray Spex. Despite the allure of punk, that same year saw the pub struggling for survival. Promoter Ian Grant hit on the idea of a live album to raise awareness and cash. The pub's three-week- long Front Row Festival provided bands ranging from XTC to The Stranglers, who recorded enough material to keep engineer John Leckie busy in the RAK mobile recording truck outside. The album resurrected enough interest to reach No.28 on the albums chart and the Hope & Anchor became the place to go once again, boosted by a photo of all the performers pictured outside the pub on the front cover of Melody Maker. Wilko Johnson remembers the lack of space at the Hope & Anchor: "It was quite an art playing there. I was constantly clonking people with my guitar."

LOCATION 136: 207 Upper Street, Islington, postcode N1 1RL

Above: Cover of the Live album that helped make the Hope & Anchor more widely known outside of London

Left: The Front Row Festival performers pose outside the Hope & Anchor for a photo that made the cover of Melody Maker

Greater London

Photo: David Roberts

N2
The Fortis Green Kinks konnections

Linking Muswell Hill to East Finchley is the area and road called Fortis Green, the place where Kinks Ray and Dave Davies spent their childhood growing up in Denmark Terrace. Across the road from the Davies household is local pub The Clissold Arms, which once remembered the brothers with pictures and memorabilia including a plaque marking this spot as the site in 1960 of Ray and Dave's Kinks debut. The Clissold Arms even got a namecheck in Dave's 2002 Bug album track 'Fortis Green', but currently The Kinks association only stretches to a few framed photos.

LOCATIONS 137 and 138: the Davies' childhood home is at 6 Denmark Terrace and The Clissold Arms is opposite at 115 Fortis Green, postcode N2 9HR

The front room (with bay window) in Denmark Terrace where Ray (right) and Dave Davies (left) constructed the 'You Really Got Me' riff on the family piano

N4
The Finsbury Park Madness earthquake

August 1992 saw all seven original members of Madness reunite for their Madstock! concerts at Finsbury Park. The eight years apart had done little to dampen down enthusiasm from their fans. But even the most avid among them could hardly have anticipated the effect the band's absence would have on the immediate and surrounding areas of Finsbury Park. The cumulative effect of tens of thousands of fans po-going up and down during ska classic 'One Step Beyond' actually caused earth tremors significant enough for police to evacuate three local eight-storey tower blocks. Seismologists confirmed it was indeed the synchronized jumping of so many fans that had caused the noise and ground movement, a phenomenon repeated on Madstock!'s second day at exactly the same time.

"The anticipation building up to them appearing on stage was beyond compare! 30,000 fans danced for over two hours to an endless set of classic ska anthems which resulted in 4.5 on the Richter scale being registered... and I was one of them!" Recalled Rotherham's Music Factory Group Product Development Manager Richard Lee

LOCATION 139: the park has hosted many other notable outdoor music events down the years, including performances by Bob Dylan (on more than one occasion), Neil Young, KISS, a 1996 Sex Pistols reunion gig, a free concert by Limp Bizkit in 2003 and a Stone Roses comeback show in 2013. Postcode N4 2AP

N6
The Highgate home to Pink Floyd

In a quiet residential road sandwiched between Archway Road and Crouch End lies the semi-detached house Pink Floyd called home during their earliest musical activity. The property was owned by Mike Leonard, their friend, Regent Street Polytechnic tutor and landlord. All four original members of Pink Floyd lodged here as students from 1963. Leonard was a lighting technician and experimented at home with enthusiastic musical backing from his lodgers. In 1968, the BBC filmed an edition of the popular science programme Tomorrow's World at Stanhope Gardens with Leonard tinkering with his lighting effects while Pink Floyd played an instrumental number seated in the same room. Leonard was also briefly a member of the band, playing keyboards, but his other activities and his older age were obstacles to him becoming a permanent addition. Despite his short musical involvement, Leonard did at one time feature in one of the various names Syd Barrett, Roger Waters, Rick Wright and Nick Mason gave their band before settling on Pink Floyd. For a short period they appropriately called themselves Leonard's Lodgers. When Leonard died in 2012 the semi-detached house was still pretty much as it would have been in the Sixties. The loft was full of dust-covered musical instruments that the band would have used. The house sold at auction for a reported £1.2 million later that same year.

LOCATION 140: 39 Stanhope Gardens. Highgate. Postcode N6 5TT

N3
A Northern Line love song at 'Finchley Central'

The subject of The New Vaudeville Band's third hit single was a jaunty story of love lost on London Underground's Northern Line. 'Finchley Central' was a 1967 No.11 hit for the septet, led by 1920s dance band fan Geoff Stephens, born in nearby New Southgate. Mega hits about British locations don't end there. See their million-selling 'Winchester Cathedral' entry in Rock Atlas Hampshire.

LOCATION 141: Station Road, Finchley, postcode N3 2RY

N4
Slade on Rock Street

Never a hit album, Whatever Happened to Slade (1977) nevertheless makes a thoroughly essential entry in Rock Atlas. The band were photographed up against the wall for the album cover in the appropriately named Rock Street. Standing next to billboard images of their earlier skinhead selves, the band were also photographed farther down Rock Street outside house numbers 6 and 8.

LOCATION 142: Rock Street, Finsbury Park, postcode N4 2DN

With glam rock's glitter fading, Slade recorded this out-and-out rock offering in 1977

Greater London

N4
Finsbury Park's rocking Rainbow

Originally a cinema, this prominently situated Finsbury Park structure was well known to rock fans in the Seventies as the Rainbow Theatre. The Moorish-styled interior had been lavishly designed to reproduce the look of a Spanish village. Formerly the Astoria, the 3,000-seat venue played host to Cliff Richard, The Beatles and The Beach Boys in the Sixties before its transformation as north London's stylish home of rock music on November 4, 1971, when The Who performed the Rainbow's opening gig. In its heyday, the Rainbow saw memorable performances by David Bowie (1972), Stephen Stills' Manassas (1972), Van Morrison (1973), Stevie Wonder (1974) and Little Feat (1975) before finally closing its doors to rock music in January 1982. The venue's last post, so to speak, was sounded by the heavy metal band UFO, who were reported to have been using the venue as a rehearsal space the week the building's lease was offered for sale. The building is once again in constant public use as the UK HQ for the Universal Church of the Kingdom of God, whose owners have beautifully maintained the grade II-listed interior. Rock fans who remember cramming into the grand foyer, pint in hand, will be pleased to know that the famous star-shaped fish pond they avoided falling into remains in all its glory.

LOCATION 143: in the fork between Isledon Road and Seven Sisters Road, 232-238 Seven Sisters Road, postcode N4 3NX

David Roberts

Beautifully restored and maintained by the present owners: the Rainbow's grand entrance hall and fish pond

N7
Music and mayhem at Joe Meek's home on Holloway Road

High up on a wall on Holloway Road is a small plaque dedicated to one of British pop's larger-than-life characters. The plaque tells anyone who chances to glance up above a grocery store that it marks the spot where record producer Joe Meek lived and worked. Carrying an image of the Telstar satellite and dubbing him "The Telstar Man", the small black disc can only hint at the innovation and mayhem that went on in the three-storey flat where the Gloucestershire-born Meek created his unearthly recordings. Europe's first independent producer led a volatile existence, which ended when he shot dead his landlady Violet Shenton (who owned the ground-floor leather handbag and suitcase

shop). He then turned the gun, owned by his protégé and lover Heinz, on himself that fateful day back in February 1967. The chaotic surroundings inside 304 Holloway Road were brilliantly reconstructed for the Joe Meek biopic Telstar in 2008.

LOCATION 144: the plaque and Meek's former flat and recording studio are at 304 Holloway Road. Postcode N7 6NJ

Joe Meek's Holloway Road plaque, complete with the image reminding everyone of his involvement in producing a 1962 trans-atlantic chart-topper

David Roberts

N8
Konk Studios and Ray's café

When the brothers Ray and Dave Davies decided to invest some of the proceeds from new songs like 'Lola' and 'Apeman' in a recording studio, they settled on a base close to home for their new venture. Created by The Kinks for their own recordings in the early Seventies, Konk would come to play host to Blur, Depeche Mode, The Stone Roses, Massive Attack and the Arctic Monkeys. A short walk turning right out of Konk to the parade

Ray Davies pictured in the doorway on Tottenham Lane, for the cover of his Working Man's Café album

of shops curving round into Church Lane sees you arrive at the doorway where the photo shoot for the 2007 Ray Davies solo album Working Man's Café took place. The café pictured on the remainder of the CD packaging (The Lane Cafe) is a further minute's walk away, heading south on Tottenham Lane.

LOCATIONS 145 and 146:
Konk is at 84-86 Tottenham Lane, near the corner with Church Lane, Crouch End, postcode N8 7EE. The Lane Cafe is at 55 Tottenham Lane, postcode N8 9BD

Greater London

N8
'Sweet Dreams' at the Church Studios

Once an Agapemone church, then utilised by animators Bob Bura and John Hardwick for the creation of their Trumpton, Camberwick Green and Captain Pugwash children's TV shows, this beautiful church (and the house next door) was eventually bought as a recording studio by musician Dave Stewart in the Seventies. A five-minute walk north from Church Studios, The Broadway is where Dave and Annie Lennox formed The Tourists when living above the Spanish Moon record shop. Back at The Church, they later went on to complete work on their Sweet Dreams (Are Made of This) album as the Eurythmics. With Dave Stewart's many connections in the music business, not surprisingly, this beautiful church has seen many legendary visitors. In the Nineties, Bob Dylan came calling on his friend at The Church. Unaware that he'd arrived at the wrong address on nearby Crouch End Hill, he asked the woman who answered the door if Dave was at home. As she happened to be the

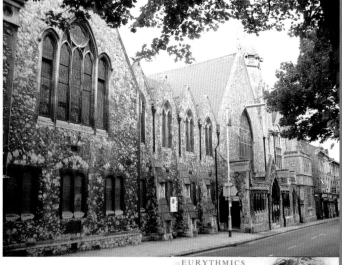

Dave Stewart and Annie Lennox would work at the Crouch Hill Church Studios while living in a flat on The Broadway

wife of a plumber called Dave, she invited her visitor in to wait for his return. Minutes later the plumber returned home to find Dylan waiting for him in the living room drinking a cup of tea. Fortunately, when this amazing place was sold it thankfully remained as a recording studio. In 2004, singer-songwriter David Gray bought it and subsequently recorded his next four studio albums here before passing the baton on to producer and songwriter Paul Epworth, who purchased the property in 2013 and set about improving the facilities still further.

LOCATIONS 147 and 148: just south of the centre of Hornsey on the A1201 at 145H Crouch Hill, postcode N8 9QH. Dave and Annie's flat was at 28 The Broadway, a five-minute walk away, postcode N8 9SU

N10
Viv Stanshall's neighbourly plaque

Viv Stanshall, who was born in Oxford, died in a fire at his London flat in Muswell Hill in the early hours of March 6, 1995. This eccentric presence, best known as the leading loony in the magnificent Bonzo Dog Doo-Dah Band, is remembered by his many friends and neighbours with a plaque they

organized and erected outside his former residence.

LOCATION 149: the Viv Stanshall plaque is to the right of the gates to his former Muswell Hill flat on the corner of Hill Park and Hill Park Mews. Postcode N10 3QT

N10
A Fairport Convention

Can there have been a more naturally chosen band name than Fairport Convention? The group that has sported a myriad of line-up changes began life in the childhood home of guitarist Simon Nicol. The name of his family's house was the large north London property called 'Fairport', and as Nicol's friends, first Ashley Hutchings then Richard Thompson, 'convened' there to rehearse, Fairport Convention presented itself as their perfectly logical new group name.

LOCATION 150: 'Fairport' stands at the corner of Fortismere Avenue and Fortis Green Road, postcode N10 3BQ. Status: private residence

The Muswell Hill house where Fairport Convention began in 1967

Photo: David Roberts

N16
Amy Winehouse 'Back to Black' at Abney Park

The sombre video to singer-songwriter Amy Winehouse's signature hit song 'Back to Black' was filmed in the grounds of Abney Park Cemetery. The magnificently gothic Abney Park Chapel is the backdrop to the end of the funeral procession as Amy symbolically buries her broken heart. Abney Park additionally gave its name to the American band of that name, who also titled their first album after the cemetery. The band's Washington-born frontman Robert Brown once lived close to the cemetery when studying in London.

LOCATION 151: entrance to the cemetery is from Stoke Newington High Street, postcode N16 0LH. Nearby Gibson Gardens (opposite the cemetery entrance a fork

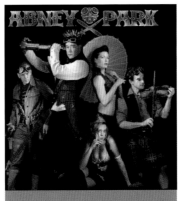

Abney Park named themselves after the north London cemetery, which was a stone's throw from where the band's Robert Brown once lived

left) and Chesholm Road (a little way south) feature during earlier scenes in the video

N15
Dave Clark's boyhood home

Dave Clark, drummer and leader of the stomping Dave Clark Five, who patented the "Tottenham Sound", grew up at 208 Philip Lane, Tottenham. Situated above the Williams Brothers grocery store and opposite what was the Greyhound (now the Botany Bay) pub, this was the rented family home of a teenager whose group briefly gave The Beatles a run for their money in the transatlantic superstar stakes in the mid-Sixties. It was here that The Dave Clark Five rehearsed for what would be a stratospheric rise from the band's home base at the Tottenham Royal to the top of the American singles chart and 18 appearances on The Ed Sullivan Show.

LOCATION 152: on the corner with Kitchener Road at 208 Philip Lane, Tottenham, postcode N15 4HH. Status: private residence

Greater London

N19 & N6
The Muswell Hillbillies

The pub scene depicted on the front cover of The Kinks' 1971 album Muswell Hillbillies was, confusingly, photographed two miles from the band's spiritual home in Muswell Hill. To find the right kind of pub and stage a back cover picture of the band posing under a sign to Muswell Hill, they decamped to the Archway Tavern and, for the signpost, to a small traffic island where Castle Yard meets Southwood Lane.

LOCATIONS 153 and 154: the Archway Tavern, Archway Close, postcode N19 3TD and the Castle Yard/ Southwood Lane junction, postcode N6, are a mile apart

Above: Not exactly Muswell Hill at all: The Kinks prop up the bar at the nearby Archway Tavern

Left: The Kinks look reluctant to pose for the Southwood Lane, Highgate photograph which appeared on the back cover of their Muswell Hillbillies album

N22
Wood Green photo call for 10cc album cover

The picture of 10cc on the cover of their 1974 album Sheet Music was shot inside what was formerly the Odeon cinema/ Gaumont Palace in Wood Green. Those wishing to experience the crazy lighting and thick carpets of the cinema interior borrowed for the band's photo call will be disappointed. However, the grand old cinema exterior is still very much intact and displays its old Gaumont Palace sign.

LOCATION 155: the building in the centre of Wood Green's busy shopping area is now the Dominion centre community church, 9 The Broadway High Road, Wood Green, postcode N22 6DS

N22
Technicolor Dreams, MTV and the Dead at 'Ally Pally'

Always a music venue able to offer that little bit more, Alexandra Palace has staged the annual BRIT Awards, with its attendant indoor funfair, and many a large scale rock event, beginning with the epic 14-Hour Technicolor Dream, staged to benefit underground newspaper The International Times in 1967. On the bill that April night, and the next morning until sunrise when Pink Floyd brought proceedings to a dramatic end, were a succession of the counter-culture's most far-out acts including Yoko Ono, Soft Machine and The Crazy World of Arthur Brown. Most of the 6,000 present inside were 'stoned', some taking advantage of the banana skin joints freely available while watching more than 30 musicians and poets, some playing simultaneously on two stages. The Sunday Mirror's 1967 review of the 14-Hour Technicolor Dream described it as: "The whole thing was rather like the last struggle of a doomed tribe to save itself from extinction." In between 1967 and recent enormous events such as the MTV Europe Music Awards, The Grateful Dead, The Stone Roses, Blur, Travis and The Strokes have all played noteworthy gigs here.

LOCATION 156: Alexandra Palace Way, Wood Green, postcode N22 7AY

Then: John "Hoppy" Hopkins, one of the organisers of the 14-Hour Technicolor Dream, snapped this shot of Brian Jones at an Ally Pally Stones concert in 1967. Now(ish): 'Ally Pally' is treated to Wayne Coyne's crowd-surfing act during a Flaming Lips gig

Greater London

Born in NORTH LONDON

Adele (b. 5 May 1988, Tottenham)
Jazzie B (Trevor Beresford Romeo), DJ/producer, Soul II Soul (b. 26 Jan 1963, Hornsey)
Mark Bedford, bass, Madness (b. 24 Aug 1961, Islington)
Brian Bennett, drums, The Shadows (b. 9 Feb 1940, Palmers Green)
Melanie Blatt, All Saints (b. 25 Mar 1975, Camden)
Johnny Borrell, vocals/guitar, Razorlight (b. 4 Apr 1980, Muswell Hill)
Wallis Buchanan, didgeridoo, Jamiroquai (b. 29 Nov 1965, Crouch End)
Jonny Buckland, guitar, Coldplay (b. 11 Sep 1977, Islington)
Emma Bunton, Spice Girls (b. 21 Jan 1976, Finchley)
Clem Cattini, drums, The Tornados/ Johnny Kidd & The Pirates (b. 28 Aug 1937, Stoke Newington)
Dave Clark, drums, The Dave Clark Five (b. 15 Dec 1942, Tottenham)
Terry Coldwell, East 17 (b. 21 Jul 1974, Islington)
B.J. Cole, pedal steel guitar (b. 17 Jun 1946, Enfield)
Chris Cross, bass, Ultravox (b. 14 Jul 1952, Tottenham)
Dana (b. 30 Aug 1951, Islington)
Lenny Davidson, guitar, The Dave Clark Five (b. 30 May 1944, Enfield)
Dave Davies, guitar/vocals, The Kinks (b. 3 Feb 1947, Fortis Green)
Ray Davies, vocals, The Kinks (b. 21 Jun 1944, Fortis Green)
Alison Goldfrapp, vocals, Goldfrapp, (b. 13 May 1966, Enfield)
Tony Hadley, vocals, Spandau Ballet (b. 2 Jun 1960, Islington)
Brian Harvey, East 17 (b. 8 Aug 1974, Walthamstow)
Chas Hodges, Chas & Dave (b. 28 Dec 1943, Edmonton)

Mark Hollis, vocals/guitar, Talk Talk (b. 4 Jan 1955, Tottenham)
Steve Howe, guitar, Asia/Yes (b. 8 Apr 1947, Holloway)
Ashley Hutchings, guitar, Fairport Convention (b. 26 Jan 1945, Southgate)
Bob Johnson, guitar/vocals, Steeleye Span (b. 18 Mar 1944, Enfield)
John Keeble, drums, Spandau Ballet (b. 6 Jul 1959, Islington)
Martin Kemp, bass, Spandau Ballet (b. 10 Oct 1961, Islington)
Dave Knights, bass, Procol Harum (b. 28 Jun 1945, Islington)
Joe Leeway, vocals/percussion, Thompson Twins (b. 15 Nov 1955, Islington)
Leona Lewis (b. 3 Apr 1985, Islington)

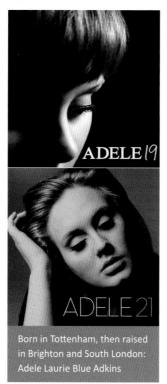

Born in Tottenham, then raised in Brighton and South London: Adele Laurie Blue Adkins

Shaznay Lewis, All Saints (b. 14 Oct 1975, Islington)
John Lydon (aka Johnny Rotten) (b. 31 Jan 1956, Finsbury Park)
Derrick McKenzie, drums, Jamiroquai (b. 27 Mar 1962, Islington)
Malcolm McLaren (b. 22 Jan 1946, Stoke Newington, d. 8 Apr 2010)
Sir George Martin, producer (b. 3 Jan 1926, Highbury)
George Michael (b. 25 Jun 1963, East Finchley)
Alan Murphy, guitar, Level 42 (b. 28 Nov 1953, Islington, d. 19 Oct 1989)
Dave Murray, guitar, Iron Maiden (b. 23 Dec 1956, Edmonton)
Simon Nicol, guitar, Fairport Convention (b. 13 Oct 1950, Muswell Hill)
Dave Peacock, Chas & Dave (b. 24 May 1945, Enfield)
Marco Pirroni, guitar/vocals, Adam & The Ants (b. 27 Apr 1959, Camden)
Simon Raymonde, Cocteau Twins (b. 3 Apr 1962, Tottenham)
Martin Rushent, producer (b. 11 Jul 1948, Enfield, d. 4 Jun 2011)
Mike Smith, vocals/keyboards, The Dave Clark Five (b. 6 Dec 1943, Edmonton, d. 28 Feb 2008)
Alvin Stardust (Bernard Jewry) (b. 27 Sep 1942, Muswell Hill)
Geoff Stephens, The New Vaudeville Band/songwriter (b. 1 Oct 1934, New Southgate)
Rod Stewart (b. 10 Jan 1945, Highgate)
Charlie Watts, drums, The Rolling Stones (b. 2 Jun 1941, Islington)
Sean Welch, bass, The Beautiful South (b. 12 Apr 1965, Enfield)
Chris White, bass, The Zombies (b. 7 Mar 1943, Barnet)
Amy Winehouse (b. 14 Sep 1983, Southgate, d. 23 Jul 2011)

EC1
Folk promoted and world music 'invented' at the Empress of Russia

The Empress of Russia pub was a key venue in the promoting of two music genres. It was home to one of London's leading folk establishments, Islington Folk Club, from 1978 during three spells, and it's said that it was here that Bob Dylan paid his last known visit to a London folk club in 1987. Although invited to perform, he declined, explaining, "I've come to listen and enjoy myself, not to work." Islington Folk Club is now based at the Horseshoe pub at Clerkenwell Close, where it has carried on the tradition, every Thursday, since 1999. The Empress of Russia played an important part in the development of another music genre when a series of meetings took place there to establish the term and the marketability of what we now know and buy as 'world music'.

> " It was the most **COST-EFFECTIVE** thing you could imagine. You know, £3,500 and you get a **WHOLE GENRE** – and a whole section in record stores today "
>
> **JOE BOYD**

A short walk from Liverpool Street station takes you to the strange world of Norton Folgate

World music as a marketing genre took off after a series of meetings that began on June 29, 1987. They were attended by like-minded enthusiasts and indie record label champions including broadcaster Charlie Gillett, writer Ian Anderson, producer Joe Boyd and record label owner Iain Scott. Their aim was to focus attention on properly categorising what, thanks to them, became world music by establishing a block of the genre's records in stores. This they achieved, bankrolled by 11 independent record labels investing £3,500 in the initiative.

LOCATION 157: the Empress of Russia is now The Brasserie at 362 St John Street, Islington, postcode EC1V4NR

EC1
The history of Norton Folgate by Madness

The Liberty of Norton Folgate, the ninth studio album from Madness, helped draw attention to one of the oddest districts of London. The lengthy title track tells the story of an area of east London that was, until 1900, a real independent state in the manner of the 1949 fictitious subject of the Ealing comedy film Passport to Pimlico.

LOCATION 158: follow the cobbled Folgate Street, east of the A10 and Broadgate Tower, postcode EC1 6DB

Greater London

German photographer Rut Blees Luxemburg's photo for the 2002 album

The Jam photographed at St Katharine Docks by the River Thames

Four lads down from Liverpool make a stand in the City of London

EC1
Tower block cover for The Streets' debut

A beautifully photographed Islington tower block appears on the cover of the debut album by Mike Skinner (aka The Streets). Birmingham-born Skinner admitted loving London (Hampstead Heath in particular), without ever living in a tower block, when quizzed by Time Out.

LOCATION 159: Kestrel House, City Road, Islington, postcode EC1

E1W
The Jam snapped at St Katharine Docks

The Jam's compilation album of all their hits, Snap!, carries a cover snap of the three band members out for a stroll at St Katharine Docks. The trio were photographed well before the break-up of the band and release of this 1983 album.

LOCATION 160: St Katharine Docks, off the River Thames, postcode E1W 1LA

EC3
Cast in the city for All Change cover

Surprisingly, Liverpool band Cast chose a spot outside The Royal Exchange, between Cornhill and Threadneedle Street in the City of London, to pose in typical four-lads-down-from-Liverpool style for the cover of their 1995 album All Change.

LOCATION 161: The Royal Exchange, postcode EC3V 3LL

E2
The 'Up the Bracket Alley'

The video for the title song from The Libertines' 2002 album Up the Bracket was filmed in an alley in Bethnal Green and namechecks nearby Vallance Road (once home to the Kray twins at No.178) in the opening line. Fans have turned 'Up the Bracket Alley' into a Libertines-based message wall. This spot, just south of Regent's Canal (seen briefly in the video), is a short walk from the flat in Teesdale Street once shared by the band's Carl Barât and Pete Doherty. Most of the debut album's tracks were written and conceived here. Adding further interest to these locations was the 2011 movie There Are No Innocent Bystanders, in which Barât revisits the area for a spot of nostalgia.

LOCATIONS 162 and 163: 'Up the Bracket Alley' (real name Hare Row) is off Cambridge Heath Road, postcode E2 9BT. Barât and Doherty's former flat, nicknamed the Albion Rooms, is at 112a Teesdale Street, postcode E2 6PU

E12
Little Ilford's 'Itchycoo Park'

Close to Steve Marriott's childhood home in East Ham and bordered by the North Circular Road is this small park immortalised in the Small Faces song. Twice a Top 10 hit, in 1967 and 1975, Itchycoo Park was a favourite haunt well known to the band members from their childhood. It was full of stinging nettles that, according to Ronnie Lane, caused the itching and scratching that led to the song's title.

LOCATION 164: Little Ilford Park is bordered on the eastern side by the A406 North Circular Road. Accessed by Church Road and Dore Avenue, postcode E12 6JT

E17
East 17 and Parklife

East 17 (also named E-17 and East Seventeen) named themselves after the postcode of the area they came from and titled their 1993 chart-topping debut album Walthamstow. The North-East London district, famous for its greyhound stadium, was also the location for photo shoots for the cover of a second Walthamstow-based No.1 album when Blur's Parklife pictures were shot there in 1994.

LOCATION 165: the greyhound stadium, still standing but closed for racing, is off the A112 in Walthamstow, postcode E4 8SJ

Dagenham
Village Blues at the Roundhouse

Still a music venue to this day, the Roundhouse pub has been described as East London's premier location for rock during the period between 1969 and 1975, when promoting bands as the Village Blues Club. Everyone from Led Zeppelin in the early days to Dr Feelgood during the height of pub rock have played the distinctive white building. And how about this for an east end honour? In 1999, Barking-born Billy Bragg, said to be lined up to narrate a locally made documentary movie about the place, had a road named after him on the site of the old Roundhouse car park. Before leaving Dagenham, ponder this. Is Terry Venables 'Dagenham Dave'? The 1995 Morrissey single of that name carried a photo of the Dagenham-born footballer on the cover.

LOCATION 166: Lodge Avenue and Bragg Close, Dagenham, postcode RM8 2HY

Born in EAST LONDON

Damon Albarn (b. 23 Mar 1968, Whitechapel)

John Ashton, guitar, The Psychedelic Furs (b. 30 Nov 1957, Forest Gate)

Kenny Ball, trumpeter (b. 22 May 1930, Ilford)

Jet Black, drums, The Stranglers (b. 26 Aug 1938, Ilford)

Marc Bolan (b. 30 Sep 1947, Hackney, (d. 16 Sep 1977)

Graham Bond, British R&B musician (b. 28 Oct 1937, Romford, d. 8 May 1974)

Andy Bown, keyboards, Status Quo (b. 27 Mar 1946, City of London)

Mick Box, guitar, Uriah Heep (b. 8 Jun 1947, Walthamstow)

Billy Bragg (b. 20 Dec 1957, Barking)

Vince Clarke, keyboards/guitar, Erasure (b. 3 Jul 1960, South Woodford)

Phil Collen, guitar, Def Leppard (b. 8 Dec 1957, Hackney)

Jamie Cullum (b. 20 Aug 1979, Rochford)

Jules De Martino, multi-instrumentalist, The Ting Tings (b. 16 Jul 1969, East London)

Rob Dean, guitar, Japan (b. 23 Apr 1953, Clapton)

Dizzee Rascal (b. 1 Oct 1985, Bow)

Darren Emerson, DJ, Underworld (b. 30 Apr 1971, Hornchurch)

Dave Evans (The Edge), guitar, U2 (b. 8 Aug 1961, Barking)

Paloma Faith (b. 21 Jul 1985, Hackney) Gabrielle (b. 16 April 1970, Hackney)

Tim Gane, guitar/keyboards, Stereolab (b. 12 Jul 1964, Barking)

Martin Gore, keyboards/guitar, Depeche Mode (b. 23 Jul 1961, Dagenham)

Steve Harris, bass, Iron Maiden (b. 12 Mar 1956, Leytonstone)

Brian Harvey, East 17 (b. 8 Aug 1974, Walthamstow)

Imogen Heap, singer/songwriter (b. 9 Dec 1977, Havering)

John Hendy, East 17 (b. 26 Mar 1971, Barking)

Steve Hillage (b. 2 Aug 1951, Chingford)

Alan Howard, bass, Brian Poole & The Tremeloes (b. 17 Oct 1941, Dagenham)

Kenney Jones, drums, The Small Faces/Faces/The Who (b. 16 Sep 1948, Stepney)

Kano, rapper (b. 21 May 1985, East Ham)

Gary Kemp, guitar, Spandau Ballet (b. 16 Oct 1959, Smithfield)

Ronnie Lane (b. 1 Apr 1946, Plaistow, (d. 4 Jun 1997)

Nicko McBrain, drums, Iron Maiden (b. 5 Jun 1952, Hackney)

Steve Marriott, vocals/guitar, (b. 30 Jan 1947, East Ham, d. 20 Apr 1991)

Tony Mortimer, East 17 (b. 21 Oct 1970, Stepney)

Dave Munden, drums, Brian Poole & The Tremeloes (b. 2 Dec 1943, Dagenham)

Plan B (Ben Drew), rapper (b. 22 Oct 1983, Forest Gate)

Brian Poole, vocals, Brian Poole & The Tremeloes (b. 2 Nov 1941, Barking)

Andy Powell, guitar, Wishbone Ash (b. 19 Feb 1950, Stepney)

Jeff Rich, drums, Status Quo (b. 8 Jun 1953, Hackney)

Helen Shapiro (b. 28 Sep 1946, Bethnal Green)

Sandie Shaw (b. 26 Feb 1947, Dagenham)

Leeroy Thornhill, The Prodigy (b. 8 Oct 1968, Barking)

Louise Wener, vocals, Sleeper (b. 30 Jul 1966, Gants Hill)

Keith West (b. 6 Dec 1943, Dagenham)

Ricky West, guitar, Brian Poole & The Tremeloes (b. 7 May 1943, Dagenham)

Wiley, rapper (b. 19 Jan 1979, Bow)

Cliff Williams, bass, AC/DC (b. 14 Dec 1949, Romford)

Jah Wobble (b. 11 Aug 1958, Stepney)

East end girls Paloma Faith and Sandie Shaw

The plaque and first appearance of Dire Straits at Farrer House

Photo: Glenda Bogdanovs

SE8
Dire Straits' Deptford debut marked by a plaque

In 2009, the Deptford birthplace of Dire Straits was marked by a plaque. Original members of the band, Mark and David Knopfler, John Illsley and Pick Withers, made their debut at a punk festival performed on waste ground behind

Farrer House on Church Street in June 1977, and 32 years later Mark Knopfler and Illsley returned to the council estate where they lived to unveil the PRS for Music heritage plaque. Speaking at the unveiling, Mark Knopfler remembered Dire Straits' debut outside his council flat in 1977: "This was my bedroom and we ran the power out of the back window over the balcony to the set next to the road and waited for a crowd to gather." The spontaneous punk festival saw Dire

Straits perform a very un-punk-like set. Keen guitarist Illsley remembered trying to help the punk bands that turned up by tuning their guitars for them – a gesture not appreciated by the musicians, who, he recalled, promptly un-tuned them again before performing to no doubt capture the true spirit of the genre.

LOCATION 167: the plaque is outside on the wall of Farrer House, Church Street, Deptford, postcode SE8 3DY

SE1
Wapping Wings over London Town

Wings' 1978 album London Town has a picture of band members Paul McCartney, Linda McCartney and Denny Laine standing on the bank of the River Thames in Wapping, with Tower Bridge

in the background. The title track, featuring 'barkers' and 'rozzers', was a Paul and Denny co-written song created just about as far away from London as you can get. The duo penned

it a couple of years earlier while on tour in Perth, Western Australia.

LOCATION 168: Tower Bridge, River Thames, postcode SE1 2UP

LONDON TOWN

SE7
The Who put the boot in at Charlton

Charlton Athletic football ground has changed much since the damp day in 1976 when The Who made a record-breaking appearance there on a bill titled Who Put the Boot In. The Harvey Goldsmith-promoted concert was one of three visits to English (Charlton), Welsh (Swansea City) and Scottish (Celtic) football stadia. At Charlton's Valley ground on May 31, The Who set the unenviable record as the world's loudest group when their 120-decibel output bagged them a place in The Guinness Book of Records. Responsibly, Pete Townshend would later write to the book's editor, Norris McWhirter, to politely make a case for the removal of the record-breaking category that had begun to seriously affect his hearing. Other acts playing on a day when 76,000 official ticket-holders were joined by many with forgeries

included Little Feat and The Sensational Alex Harvey Band. The Who had played the football ground two years earlier in the summer of 1974 when Lou Reed, Humble Pie and Bad Company also rocked the Valley on a sunny day marred by outbreaks of crowd violence.

LOCATION 169: the much-changed football ground is at Floyd Road, Charlton, postcode SE7 8BL

The drenched crowd packed into Charlton Athletic football ground in 1976

SE9
When Quo came together at The Welcome Inn

Before you can begin rockin' all over the world, you have to pay your dues. Eltham turned out to be a good place to start when Status Quo members Francis Rossi and Rick Parfitt hitched up for the first time. The Welcome Inn (now the Edens residential development) where Status Quo first performed in 1967 may have burned down in 2006 but that fact didn't stop PRS for Music marking the event with a plaque on the site in 2010. That very first gig saw support from Episode Six an outfit that later evolved into Deep Purple. "I remember the gig very well. It was the first we played after Rick [Parfitt] joined us. He wore the green and yellow striped blazer I got married in," recalled Francis Rossi at the unveiling.

LOCATION 170: in Well Hall Road, Eltham, postcode SE9 6UB

Quo get back to where it all started, at Well Hall Road

Greater London

Welling
Kate Bush's family farmhouse

East Wickham Farm was the family home where Kate Bush lived with her doctor father, mother and two older brothers, John and Paddy. Her inbuilt wonder and love of music and outpouring of songs, written when a schoolgirl, all began here, surrounded by her musical family. Famously 'discovered' and encouraged by David Gilmour and signed to EMI as a songwriting prodigy, the teenage Kate Bush also formed the KT Bush Band with brother Paddy and three friends, playing south London pubs. The secluded 350-year-old farmhouse offered a base for an idyllic childhood and subsequently a secure and private environment for her work. The conversion of one of the farm's barns into a 24-track studio in 1983 was significant. It gave Kate, who now had four Top 10 albums to her credit, a financial and creative independence to take as long as she wanted over future projects.

LOCATION 171: the former Bush family farmhouse property is almost impossible to see through impenetrable undergrowth and is situated in a surprisingly built-up area on Wickham Street, Welling, postcode DA16 3DA. Status: private residence

Kate Bush, who shares a birthday with Wuthering Heights author Emily Brontë, wrote her 'version' at East Wickham Farm

Photo: Warren King

Squeezed together under the plaque on Royal Hill

SE10
Early Greenwich gigging for Squeeze

Some of pop's most thoughtful songwriting came out of south London in the 1970s courtesy of Greenwich-based band Squeeze. Their lyrical kitchen-sink dramas incorporated a number of key local locations. One of the best examples was 'King George Street', a single from the 1985 album Cosi Fan Tutti Frutti. The band were propelled to fame on the back of gigs in the Greenwich area at The Bricklayer's Arms, the now demolished Northover (Catford), Hardy's Free House, the Deptford Arms and The Bell. A plaque to commemorate one of their earliest gigs was unveiled at the Greenwich Dance Agency, Borough Hall, Greenwich, in 2010.

"I've always stayed in this area and I love this area – I don't think I'll ever leave," said Glenn Tilbrook at the time, "But I've seen it change, and it's now harder for bands to get started."

LOCATIONS 172 and 173: King George Street, postcode SE10 8QB. The Borough Hall plaque is on Royal Hill, postcode SE10 8RE

SE14
Goldsmiths college of rock

Specialising in the arts and culture, this magnate for creative types was where students Damon Albarn, Graham Coxon and Alex James formed the nucleus of Blur. Others benefiting from what this constituent college of the University of London had to offer were John Cale, Bonzo's Neil Innes, Malcolm McLaren, Placebo frontman Brian Molko and DJ Rob da Bank.

LOCATION 174: 8 Lewisham Way, postcode SE14 6YZ

SE15
Jarvis Cocker's Camberwell concern

A B-side to the single 'Razzmatazz', and the final track on Pulp's 1993 Intro album that recalled an utterly awful party that Jarvis Cocker attended, '59 Lyndhurst Grove' was written as a well-intentioned warning to the wife of an architect he met there. His concern that she was headed for a life of misery "married to this prick", as he put it, led him to write to her enclosing a copy of the CD. No reply was forthcoming.

LOCATION 175: 59 Lyndhurst Grove, Camberwell, SE15 5AW. Status: private residence

Greater London

SE10
The record-breaking O2

Once famously dubbed a hugely expensive white elephant, London's Millennium Dome was regenerated by AEG Europe as the world's most popular music arena, overtaking New York's Madison Square Garden's record for most tickets sold in a year. Imagine turning the O2 structure upside-down as a giant dish: O2 boffins have calculated that it would take Niagara Falls 15 minutes to fill it with water or, if you prefer, 3.8 billion pints of beer. In addition to the 20,000-capacity arena, the O2 boasts nightclubs, cinema screens and a curving mall of eateries. Sadly, the once excellent interactive museum of popular music called the British Music Experience, which opened in 2009 closed in 2014. The whereabouts of the collection of handwritten lyrics, memorabilia and famous outfits from 60 years of British music history may pop up elsewhere, but at the time of writing plans were sketchy.

LOCATION 176: with access by tube, road and river, the O2 lies in a bend in the Thames at Peninsula Square, Greenwich, postcode SE10 0DX

The magnificent O2 attracts all the biggest international touring performers. Nine Inch Nails, the Eagles and Lady Gaga were just three of the acts which played the arena in 2014

Greater London

SE18
The house that made Boy George

In 1974, the 14-year-old George O'Dowd moved house to 171 Shooter's Hill, where his metamorphosis into chart-topping Culture Club singer and DJ Boy George began. George, together with mum, dad, his sister and four brothers, moved to this Edwardian semi from their cramped 1930s council house at 29 Joan Crescent, two miles away on Eltham's Middle Park estate. Both homes were featured in the 2010 Channel 4 TV documentary The House that Made Me, enabling George, somewhat reluctantly at first, to return to his childhood surroundings, where the programme makers had reproduced the 70s interiors in both houses.

LOCATIONS 177 and 178: both private residences, at 29 Joan Crescent, Eltham, postcode SE9 5KR, and 171 Shooter's Hill, postcode SE18 3HP

> " I would never **DARE** go knock on the door and say 'I used to live here, can I come in?' **"**
>
> **BOY GEORGE**
> when filming the Channel 4 documentary about his childhood homes

Born in SOUTH-EAST LONDON

Ginger Baker, drums, Cream (b. 19 Aug 1939, Lewisham)

Easther Bennett, Eternal (b. 11 Dec 1972, Croydon)

Vernie Bennett, Eternal (b. 17 May 1971, Croydon)

John Bentley, bass, Squeeze (b. 16 Apr 1951, Deptford)

Alan Blakley, Brian Poole & The Tremeloes (b. 1 Apr 1942, Bromley, d. 1 Jun 1996)

Boy George, vocals, Culture Club (b. George O'Dowd, 14 Jun 1961, Bexley)

Kéllé Bryan, Eternal (b. 12 Mar 1975, Lewisham)

Kate Bush (b. 30 Jul 1958, Bexleyheath)

Captain Sensible (Ray Burns), bass, The Damned/solo (b. 23 Apr 1955, Balham)

Norman Cook (Fatboy Slim), DJ/producer/keyboards (b. 31 Jul 1963, Bromley)

Jay Darlington, keyboards, Kula Shaker (b. 3 May 1968, Sidcup)

Chris Difford, guitar, Squeeze (b. 4 Nov 1954, Greenwich)

Mickey Finn, drums, T. Rex (b. 3 Jun 1947, Thornton Heath, d. 11 Jan 2003)

Matthew Fisher, guitar, Procol Harum (b. 7 Mar 1946, Croydon)

Jerome Flynn, Robson & Jerome (b. 16 Mar 1963, Bromley)

Simon Friend, guitar, Levellers (b. 17 May 1967, Upper Norwood)

Peter Grant, music manager (b. 5 Apr 1935, South Norwood, d. 21 Nov 1995)

Steve Harley (b. 27 Feb 1951, Deptford)

Charlie Heather, drums, Levellers (b. 2 Feb 1964, Bromley)

Ken Hensley, keyboards, Uriah Heep (b. 24 Aug 1945, Plumstead)

Nick Heyward (b. 20 May 1961, Beckenham)

Jools Holland (b. 24 Jan 1958, Blackheath)

Steve Jansen, drums, Japan (b. 1 Dec 1959, Beckenham)

John Paul Jones, bass, Led Zeppelin (b. 3 Jan 1946, Sidcup)

Louise (Redknapp, née Nurding) (b. 4 Nov 1974, Lewisham)

Jacqui McShee, vocals, Pentangle (b. 25 Dec 1943, Catford)

Les Nemes, bass, Haircut 100 (b. 5 Dec 1960, Croydon)

Horace Panter (Sir Horace Gentleman), bass, The Specials (b. 30 Aug 1953, Croydon)

Mica Paris (b. 27 Apr 1969, Lewisham)

Maxi Priest (b. 10 Jun 1961, Lewisham)

Danny Rampling, DJ (b. 15 Jul 1961, Streatham)

Francis Rossi, vocals/guitar, Status Quo (b. 29 May 1949, Forest Hill)

Siouxsie Sioux (b. 27 May 1957, Southwark)

Tommy Steele (b. 17 Dec 1936, Bermondsey)

Poly Styrene, vocals, X-Ray Spex (b. 3 Jul 1957, Bromley d. 25 Apr 2011)

David Sylvian, vocals, Japan (b. 23 Feb 1958, Beckenham)

Glenn Tilbrook, vocals/guitar, Squeeze (b. 31 Aug 1957, Woolwich)

Tinie Tempah, rapper (b. 7 Nov 1988, Plumstead)

Steve Peregrin Took, drums, T. Rex (b. 28 Jul 1949, Eltham, d. 27 Oct 1980)

Paul Tucker, keyboards, Lighthouse Family (b. 12 Aug 1968, Crystal Palace)

Florence Welch, vocals, Florence + The Machine (b. 28 Aug 1986, Camberwell)

Alan White, drums, Oasis (b. 26 May 1972, Eltham)

Steve White, drums, The Style Council (b. 31 May 1965, Bermondsey)

Marty Wilde (b. 15 Apr 1939, Blackheath)

Bill Wyman (b. 24 Oct 1936, Lewisham)

Bexley-born Boy George

SW1
Big Ben photo ops for The Who and The Jam

One of the best spots to have your picture taken anywhere in the world is under London's Big Ben, a fact not lost on The Who in 1965 and The Jam who emulated them in 1979.

LOCATION 179: Victoria Embankment underneath Big Ben, Westminster, postcode SW1A 2JH

SW1
The New Boots and Panties!! shop

Axford's was the clothing shop on Vauxhall Bridge Road where Ian Dury posed with his six-year-old son Baxter for the image that adorns the cover of the singer-songwriter's 1977 album New Boots and Panties!! Suggested by Dury to photographer Chris Gabrin, the location was chosen after an abortive attempt to get a cover picture outside Dury's flat at The Oval. The three then made the short journey to Vauxhall Bridge Road. Gabrin's hastily parked Mini van can be seen across the road outside Woolworths in the window reflection. Axford's had originally been pointed out to Drury by his friend, the artist Peter Blake. Hardly worth recommending for a pilgrimage, just about all that's left of this location is the pavement. But, here is one visual stop on pop's timeline that should be marked with a plaque. The photo shoot was lovingly recreated in the 2010 Ian Dury biopic Sex & Drugs & Rock & Roll.

LOCATION 180: 306 Vauxhall Bridge Road, postcode SW1V 1

SW1
'Boris the Spider' at The Scotch of St James

A favourite haunt for musicians in London's swinging Sixties, The Beatles (and in particular Paul McCartney) found The Scotch of St James a haven of relative privacy and a conveniently short distance from their Savile Row daytime base. It was at this late-night bolthole that the Fab Four could escape from public pressure and keep up-to-date with the fast-changing music scene. The tartan-decorated club was where Jimi Hendrix first caused a stir on his arrival in the UK. An impromptu performance on September 24, 1966 accompanied by the club's house band was his first astonishing appearance, followed quickly by a Jimi Hendrix Experience private showcase on October 19. Although the media would ramp up the competitiveness between the Sixties acts, it was at The Scotch of St James where The Who, The Rolling Stones and The Beatles could relax together with a drink and a smoke and compare notes. One typical night out enjoyed by The Who's John Entwistle and Rolling Stone Bill Wyman saw the two bass guitarists playing a naming game listing imaginary pet animals. This particular creative conversation led to Entwistle recording Who track 'Boris the Spider', a creature born at The Scotch of St James.

LOCATION 181: The Scotch of St James is now the Directors Lodge Club, 13 Mason's Yard, Duke Street, postcode SW1Y 6BU

Greater London

SW1
'Party Central' for The Small Faces

Described as 'Party Central' by keyboards man Ian McLagan, 22 Westmoreland Terrace was The Small Faces' home for 12 glorious months, during which time the band racked up four Top 10 singles. Under the watchful eye of an Austrian housekeeper, McLagan, Steve Marriott and Ronnie Lane arrived in the Pimlico property rented for them by manager Don Arden at the tail end of 1965. Drummer Kenney Jones stayed with his mum and dad in Stepney, and as a result probably missed much of the mayhem that took place at Westmoreland Terrace. One memorable visit by Brian Epstein to No.22 saw The Beatles manager experience his first LSD trip. The house was sparsely furnished with, apart from their beds, just the odd wooden chair, an old sofa and Ronnie Lane's precious Dansette record player. Following the most creative and productive period in their career, they left

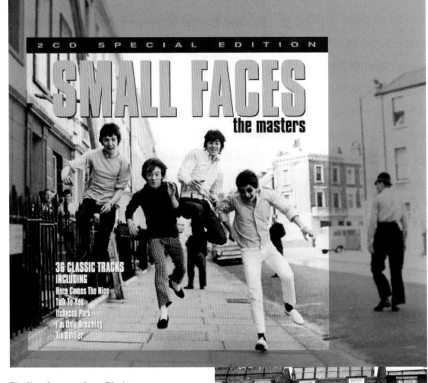

Photo: Pictorial Press

Pimlico for good on Christmas Eve 1966.

LOCATION 182:
22 Westmoreland Terrace, Pimlico, postcode SW1V 4.
Status: private residence

Photo: David Roberts

Top: the full picture shows a 'Bobby' apparently taking no notice of the leaping Small Faces. Above: No.22 today is still recognisable

" Steve, typically, had chosen the biggest bedroom at the top of the house... and as I was the new boy in town who hoped for some **PEACE AND QUIET**, I took the small room next to Steve's on the top floor 🗩

IAN MCLAGAN

SW1
Brian Epstein's Chapel Street home

This is the exclusive Belgravia property where Brian Epstein lived and then tragically died in 1967. His home, from December 1964 (and from 1966 his work base), was like the man himself, fashionably smart and immaculately turned out. Often parked outside would be his choice of transport for the day - the red Rolls-Royce or the silver Bentley. A launch party for the press for the Sgt Pepper's Lonely Hearts Club Band album was held here on May 19, 1967, when Paul McCartney met photographer Linda Eastman for only the second time.

LOCATION 183: 24 Chapel Street, postcode SW1X 7. Status: private residence

Photo: David Roberts

The Soul II Soul plaque unveiling was followed by an exclusive live set inside the Electric

Photo: Warren King

SW2
Soul II Soul honoured in Brixton

The Fridge was the venue where Soul II Soul played their debut gig back in 1991. On June 21, 2012, the group returned for the unveiling of a plaque to mark their first full live performance at the same venue, now called Electric Brixton. The PRS Heritage Award was made in the presence of Soul II Soul's members, including Jazzie B, vocalist Caron Wheeler, Aitch and Q. ''It is ironic that it's the Jubilee year and that's when Soul II Soul started and flourished - during a time of recession. That's what the kids need to do today.'' Said Jazzie B, speaking at the Electric in 2012.

''We went from Hackney to New York and around the world, [but] Brixton has such a special place in our story and this venue is where things really took off.''

LOCATION 184: Electric Brixton, Town Hall Parade, postcode SW2 1RJ

Greater London

SW3
Chelsea songs, King's Road hippies and punks at the World's End

Immediately north of the River Thames, hip, trendy and wealthy Chelsea has been regularly referenced in pop and rock, but not always positively. Elvis Costello's critical hit '(I Don't Want to Go to) Chelsea' in 1978 was an attempt to articulate what he thought the place stood for. Less critical was Jon Bon Jovi's biggest UK solo hit 'Midnight in Chelsea', written with the assistance of Dave Stewart and Bruce Willis. Chief inspiration for the 1997 No.4 hit was the New Jersey frontman's stay in a Chelsea basement observing and writing about London's red buses, homeless drunks, goths and "Sloane Rangers". Disappointingly, the single's video was shot in Manhattan. The open-all-hours three-storey Chelsea Drugstore where Mick Jagger sang about standing in line "with Mr Jimmy" from the Stones' 'You Can't Always Get What You Want' has long since ceased trading. This architectural icon of the Sixties was an early attempt to introduce a US-style drug store to London. Drugs, records, coffee and alcohol bars and magazines are no longer on offer as the building has adopted a more recent US import. The junction of Royal Avenue and No.49 King's Road is currently a McDonald's restaurant. Around the same time in the late Sixties, the western, World's End district of King's Road began to attract a steady stream of rock stars raiding a new wave of clothes emporiums. The uniquely styled shop Granny Takes a Trip led the

Photo: David Roberts

way and fed a craving for more exotic stage gear, championed by regular customers Marc Bolan and Rod Stewart. In 1971, Malcolm McLaren and Vivienne Westwood began a cultural revolution at the then shabby end of King's Road. They kick-started the Fifties rock 'n' roll revival look that so dominated early to mid-Seventies pop with their Let It Rock shop. With the best jukebox for miles and shelves stocked with brothel creepers,

luminous ties and socks, the shop at No.430 evolved into SEX, the famous punk boutique, a magnet for the fast-developing punk movement, which sported that new fashion by using The King's Road as a vast al fresco catwalk. Tom Petty gives a more up-to-date guided tour of this rag bag of clothing stores on 'Kings Road', from his 1981 hit album Hard Promises.

LOCATION 185: The King's Road, postcode SW3

It was here in 1975 at the boutique called SEX, now Vivienne Westwood's World's End, that a green-haired John Lydon auditioned for the Sex Pistols

SW5
Dylan heads for the Troubadour in 1962

A Bohemian-style coffee house since 1954, the Troubadour has played host to a wide variety of performers including Sammy Davis Jr, Jimi Hendrix, Paul Simon, Joni Mitchell and Adele. Said to be London's oldest folk club and still a wonderfully atmospheric place to eat, drink and take in live music, the Troubadour's best claim to fame came from Bob Dylan's first UK gig on a cold November night in 1962. The emerging folk singer was in Britain to record a part acting in the BBC TV play Madhouse on Castle Street. Before heading for London, established US folk singer Pete Seeger had singled out the Troubadour as a place the 21-year-old Dylan must visit. The coffee bar's Tuesday night folk organiser, Anthea Joseph, only recognised him on his arrival from the front cover of US folk magazine Sing Out!, which fans could buy from Collets record shop in Tottenham Court Road. During this same winter, Dylan also made impromptu appearances at other key folk spots, the King & Queen in Foley Street and the Pindar of Wakefield in Gray's Inn Road.

LOCATION 186: Old Brompton Road, Earls Court, postcode SWA 9JA

> "Dylan didn't seem as interested in **PERFORMING** as he was in listening. I felt quite like a native in the presence of an anthropologist"
>
> **ANTHEA JOSEPH**
> Troubadour folk night organiser

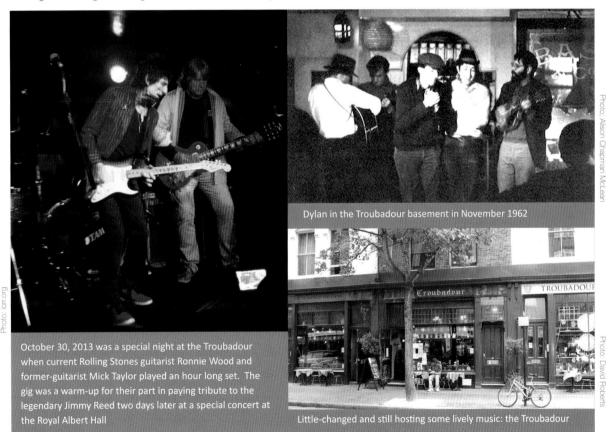

Photo: ior.org

Photo: Alison Chapman McLean

Photo: David Roberts

Dylan in the Troubadour basement in November 1962

October 30, 2013 was a special night at the Troubadour when current Rolling Stones guitarist Ronnie Wood and former-guitarist Mick Taylor played an hour long set. The gig was a warm-up for their part in paying tribute to the legendary Jimmy Reed two days later at a special concert at the Royal Albert Hall

Little-changed and still hosting some lively music: the Troubadour

Greater London

SW6
Mumford & Sons at Pimpernel & Partners

UK folk-rock outfit Mumford & Sons were pictured in the window of an address on south-west London's grooviest thoroughfare when snapped for their Sigh No More album cover in 2009. Photographer Max Knight spent nine hours getting the finished result at the location on The King's Road. The cover shows all four band members plus their friend (and Laura Marling's multi-instrumentalist) Pete Roe looking out of a floor window in the building next door. Max Knight rates the shoot as one

Mumford & Sons at No.596 King's Road

of his toughest assignments. "We had to battle the heat, the traffic (shooting across the main road) and the reflection off the glass window. The shoot also took place on Wimbledon finals day... It was super distracting as it was a boiling hot day and the pub across the road was full of people with ice-cold beers, cheering on the tennis."

LOCATION 187: at the vintage and replica French furniture shop called Pimpernel & Partners, 596 King's Road, postcode SW6 2DX

SW8
Pink Floyd's pig

The inclusion of a pig on the sleeve of Pink Floyd's Animals album cover in 1977 began a close association with the animal throughout the band's stop-start career. The LP cover's inflatable pig, conceived by the band's Roger Waters, was launched and tethered floating above the defunct Battersea Power Station for the photo shoot. After three days of airborne activity, the 40-foot-long helium-filled balloon broke free and famously caused mayhem with flights at nearby Heathrow Airport. The pig eventually crash-landed in a Kent farm but was hastily puncture-repaired and returned for one last attempt at a perfect photo - which failed. The final cover was a composite of at least two different photographs to get the desired effect.

LOCATION 188: 188 Kirtling Street, Nine Elms, postcode SW8 5BP

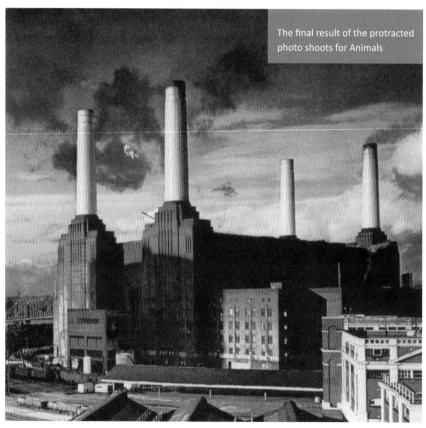

The final result of the protracted photo shoots for Animals

Photo: Evening Standard/Stringer

SW7
'A Host of Stars' at The Royal Albert Hall

Opened in 1871 and one of very few music venues to offer a performer the experience of being virtually surrounded by their audience, the grand Royal Albert Hall continues to operate as a special venue for rock-watching. Said to be Paul Weller's favourite place to play, the building was almost 100 years old before pop and rock made their debuts in the mid-Sixties. Billed back then as 'A Host of Stars', the old place echoed to the music of The Spencer Davis Group, The Yardbirds, The Small Faces, The Mindbenders, Them, The Moody Blues, Unit 4 Plus 2, The Nashville Teens and The Zombies in 1966 for a Dick Clark US TV show. Both Cream and Led Zeppelin have particularly memorable associations with the venue that also hosted late-Eighties BRIT Awards shows. And, when Eric Clapton (probably the Royal Albert Hall's most

regular performer) and friends wanted the perfect venue for an opportunity to say a musical goodbye to George Harrison, here is where the great and good paid tribute to the former Beatle a year after his death, at the Concert for George in 2002. Sixteen-year-old East Molesey schoolboy David Rush vividly recalls the 1970 Led Zeppelin gig at the Royal Albert Hall. "Tickets were completely sold out but a friend managed to secure the top tickets from an agency for about £1.20, which at the time was the highest price I'd paid to see a band. Oddly, we were directed to the main floor to sit in large swivel armchairs! We didn't stay in those for very long. After the gig we decided to climb on stage as they were packing away and have a look around. My friend saw Page's black Les Paul (the one that subsequently got nicked) on top of an

Zapped! The Royal Albert Hall cancelled a performance of Frank Zappa's film score 200 Motels in 1971. "Filth for filth's sake" was how the hall's general manager described the work. Below: When Led Zeppelin played the venue in January 1970 Led Zeppelin II was about to knock Abbey Road by The Beatles off No. 1 in the UK

amp and held the guitar for a few minutes. One of the roadies politely asked him if he could put it down as they had to pack away. Imagine doing that now at the O2!"

LOCATION 189: Kensington Gore, postcode SW7 2AP

Roger Taylor, PRS Chairman Guy Fletcher and Brian May at the unveiling of the PRS for Music heritage plaque in 2013

SW7
Imperial College: spiritual base for Queen

What Brian May referred to as Queen's "first proper gig" took place in the Union Hall at Imperial College on July 18, 1970. This was the year Mike Grose joined them as bass player and Imperial College was where his replacement, John Deacon, was auditioned in 1971. Brian May's personal associations with the place have lasted for four decades. After completing a degree in physics, he went on to study a PhD. The launch of the Queen II album in 1974 led to the realisation that his music career was assured. As a result, May left college to devote more time to the band before returning in 2007 when gaining his doctorate in astronomy. His early memories of Imperial College are exciting enough even without his participation in the development of Queen. His involvement as a music fan and member of the College Entertainment Committee enabled him to attend and book a regular rock concert every Saturday, which saw early Seventies bands like Spooky Tooth, Mott

the Hoople and Procol Harum play the Union Hall. A special highlight was the committee's successful attempt to book Jimi Hendrix in 1967, a particular hero of May's. In 2013, May and Queen drummer Roger Taylor attended the unveiling of an Imperial College plaque to commemorate the building's special place as a major stepping stone in the band's road to rock stardom. More specifically, it was their first London concert – a gig that would kick-start a belief that rock music, and not physics or astronomy, would become the dominant career for guitarist May. A final thought from Roger Taylor: "Imperial College was effectively our positional and spiritual base and so means a lot to Queen. Many good memories. Without it… who knows?"

LOCATION 190: the plaque is situated by the entrance to Beit Quadrangle, Imperial College, Prince Consort Road, Kensington, SW7 2BB

SW9
'Electric Avenue', 'The Guns of Brixton' and Bob Marley Way

Built in the 19th century, Brixton's Electric Avenue was named to mark one of the earliest shopping streets to enjoy electric lighting. This lively thoroughfare was the title of Eddy Grant's biggest hit, which made No.2 on both sides of the Atlantic. A frequent topic for songwriters, Brixton and its recent volatile history has featured in graphic tracks by The Clash ('The Guns of Brixton') and Carter - The Unstoppable Sex Machine ('And God Created Brixton'). Recent local exports Alabama 3 were formed in Brixton in the Nineties, becoming world famous for 'Woke Up this Morning', the theme to US TV's The Sopranos. This track features on the band's 1997 album Exile on Coldharbour Lane, which is a mile-long stretch of road from Brixton to Camberwell.

LOCATIONS 191 and 192: Electric Avenue and Brixton market are bordered by the A23, the B223 and the A2217 (Coldharbour Lane), postcode SW9 8JX. A short walk south from the market on the B223 Railton Road brings you to Bob Marley Way, postcode SE24 0LP

SW10
Home to the embryonic Stones

"Truly disgusting" was how Keith Richards described the living conditions at the address where The Rolling Stones spent the cold winter of 1962-63. Most importantly it was a base for obsessionally honing the skills to enable them to emulate Mick Jagger, Keith Richards and Brian Jones' American blues heroes. Here they studied and copied the Muddy Waters and Bo Diddley records they would listen to on the flat's one luxury item, Brian Jones' huge radiogram. When the cold and squalor got too much they would cash-in empty bottles and head for the nearby Wetherby Arms pub at 500 King's Road, for a drink and a warm, to ponder their future.

LOCATION 193: 102 Edith Grove, Chelsea, sandwiched between the River Thames and The King's Road, postcode SW10 0NH

Main photo: Philip Townsend. Inset: David Roberts

Greater London

SW13
Recording heaven at Olympic Studios

This former theatre, then film studio, in Barnes began its new life as a recording studio in the mid-Sixties. For any young rock fan hell-bent on filling their autograph book, the doorway of Olympic Studios must have made for the most profitable hovering point. Attracted by the smart Barnes location and superior acoustics, the likes of Led Zeppelin, The Rolling Stones, The Who and Dusty Springfield were all regular visitors. Even The Beatles strayed from Abbey Road to commence recordings for 'All You Need Is Love'. Olympic was where supergroup Blind Faith assembled to record their transatlantic chart topping debut album, Procol Harum delivered 'A Whiter Shade of Pale', The Small Faces created 'Lazy Sunday' and the Eagles began their recording career with 'Take It Easy' and the remaining bunch of songs on their first two albums. According to Ian McLagan's biography All the Rage, 'Lazy Sunday' was recorded at Olympic while The Small Faces were living in Marlow. Apparently, the song started life as a rather slow, uninspiring number when Steve Marriott first introduced it to the rest of the band during a session at Olympic. They goofed around with it and added the 'Roo de doo de doo, roo de doo de di do'' (courtesy of a little ditty Who roadie Bob Pridden contributed) and a short burst of the Stones' hit 'Satisfaction', with comb and paper accompaniment. Later beneficiaries of the Olympic acoustics were Queen, who selected the place for A Night at the Opera, and The Verve, who recorded the classic Urban Hymns here. Despite recent album recordings by Babyshambles (Shotter's Nation in 2007) and U2 completing work on No Line on the Horizon in 2008, the famous old studio is now closed, with the building's future as a recording facility uncertain after EMI sold it in 2009.

LOCATION 194: now a cinema with cafe and dining room, 117 Church Road, Barnes, postcode SW13 9HL

Photo: Martin Downham

The entrance to Olympic Studios where classic single 'Itchycoo Park' by The Small Faces and tracks for Traffic's Mr Fantasy album were recorded on the same day in 1967

SW17
A Tooting turning point for Status Quo

Around the time Status Quo were enjoying the success of their fourth hit single 'Down the Dustpipe', they played a significant gig in Tooting. The year was 1970 and, booked to play the Castle pub, they realised their audience was evolving. That night Status Quo evolved too. For the first time the band played to a crowd sitting cross-legged in their trench coats on the floor. Clutching their pints and nodding their heads, Quo adapted their performance accordingly. As the Castle stage was no more than a few inches high, Quo guitarists Rick Parfitt and Francis Rossi ''had to get down to the audience'', as Parfitt put it. So, heads bowed and legs apart, the famous Quo stance came into being. Musically, this also marked their development into mega-selling album rock property. Currently live music takes a back seat at The Castle, which these days advertises quiz nights and salsa classes.

LOCATION 195: 38 Tooting High Street, postcode SW17 0RG

SW15
Marc Bolan's roadside shrine

When Marc Bolan died in a car crash on September 16, 1977, his devoted fans decided to mark the location of the tragedy with a shrine to the T.Rex glam-rock icon. This is the spot in Barnes where the purple Mini he and girlfriend Gloria were travelling in struck a tree at speed near the railway bridge on Queens Ride. It is the focal point for fans to pay their respects and leave a memento, message or flowers. The message board, sculptured bust and memorial stone of Bolan are all situated on the steep, heavily wooded embankment that drops away from the stretch of road where Bolan met his death.

LOCATION 196: at the junction of Queens Ride and Gipsy Lane, Barnes, postcode SW15

The Bolan shrine is hidden away on a shady embankment surrounded by trees at the spot where the rock star was killed in a car crash in 1977

Photos: David Roberts and Martin Downham

SW15
Sandy Denny's Putney Vale gravestone

Sandy Denny, the honey-voiced folk singer who suffered a brain haemorrhage in 1978 and died in a Wimbledon hospital, is buried at Putney Vale Cemetery. At her burial, a lone piper played 'Flowers of the Forest' as her coffin was lowered into the ground.

LOCATION 197: Putney Vale Cemetery, Stag Lane, postcode SW15 3DZ

Sandy Denny was just 31 when she died

SW11
'The girl from Clapham' and the 'windy common'

Clapham Common and railway station junction is the setting and euphemism for one of Britain's greatest song stories. Referencing 'the girl from Clapham' and 'the windy common', 'Up the Junction' by Squeeze was a No.2 hit in 1979 for the south London band, who nabbed the title from the 1963 novel, TV drama and subsequent movie of the same name. Manfred Mann failed to chart with their 'Up the Junction' theme song to the 1968 movie but the track and the storyline of teenage abortion and social depravation was picked up and turned into a late-Seventies pop classic by Squeeze songwriters Chris Difford and Glenn Tilbrook.

LOCATIONS 198 and 199: Clapham Junction, postcode SW11 2QP, and Clapham Common, postcode SW4 7

Photo: Martin Downham

Greater London

SW15
The Half Moon pub rolls with the times

This Putney pub's first regularly organised music nights began under the Folksville banner in 1963. American folk and blues legends Sonny Terry and Brownie McGhee, Champion Jack Dupree and Arthur Crudup all played The Half Moon, augmented by the best of new British folk, Roy Harper, Ralph McTell, Bert Jansch and John Martyn. The venue has rolled with the times, and British R&B and pub rock movements saw top exponents John Mayall's Bluesbreakers and Dr Feelgood also play The Half Moon. U2 and Kate Bush have a particular soft spot for the place: U2 played their first sold-out gig on their debut UK tour here and Kate made her public performance debut billed as the KT Bush Band. In May 2000, The Half Moon played host to a private Rolling Stones get-together

Photo: David Roberts

The Half Moon has reverberated to the sounds of every milestone music genre since 1963

in memory of Keith Richards' personal assistant Joe Seabrook, who had died just a month or so earlier. The band, who had played the venue four decades previously, all assembled to party, with Ronnie Wood and Richards jamming with the night's hired band. Pictures of the acts that have played the place

decorate the walls of this traditional pub, which was thankfully saved from gastro-pub anonymity in 2009 to continue a menu of wall-to-wall live music.

LOCATION 200: 93 Lower Richmond Road, Putney, postcode SW15 1EU

Born in SOUTH-WEST LONDON

Emma Anderson, vocals, Lush (b. 10 Jun 1967, Wimbledon)
Iain Baker, keyboards, Jesus Jones (b. 29 Sep 1965, Carshalton)
Jeff Beck (b. 24 Jun 1944, Wallington)
David Bowie (b. 8 Jan 1947, Brixton)
Dave Brock, vocals/guitar, Hawkwind (b. 20 Aug 1941, Isleworth)
Richard Butler, vocals, The Psychedelic Furs (b. 5 Jun 1956, Kingston upon Thames)
Tim Butler, bass, The Psychedelic Furs (b. 7 Dec 1958, Teddington)
Sandy Denny, vocals, Fairport Convention (b. 6 Jan 1947, Merton Park, d. 21 Apr 1978)
Chris Dreja, guitar, The Yardbirds (b. 11 Nov 1945, Surbiton)
Mel Gaynor, drums, Simple Minds (b. 29 May 1960, Balham)
Ed Harcourt, singer-songwriter (b. 14 Aug 1977, Wimbledon)
Mick Jones, guitar, The Clash (b. 26 Jun 1955, Brixton)
Simon Kirke, drums, Bad Company/Free (b. 28 Jul 1949, Lambeth)
Dee C. Lee, vocals, The Style Council/solo (b. 6 Jun 1961, Balham)

Benjamin Lovett, Mumford & Sons (b. 30 Sep 1986, Wimbledon)
Tom McGuinness, bass, Manfred Mann (b. 2 Dec 1941, Wimbledon)
John Martyn (b. 11 Sep 1948, New Malden, d. 29 Jan 2009)
Alex Paterson, The Orb (b. 15 Oct 1959, Battersea)
Rat Scabies (Christopher Millar), drums, The Damned (b. 30 Jul 1957, Kingston upon Thames)
Tom Rowlands, keyboards, The Chemical Brothers (b. 11 Jan 1971, Kingston upon Thames)
Paul Simonon, bass, The Clash (b. 15 Dec 1955, Brixton)
Skin (Deborah Dyer), vocals, Skunk Anansie (b. 3 Aug 1967, Brixton)
Dave Swarbrick, violin, Fairport Convention (b. 5 Apr 1941, New Malden)
Mick Talbot, keyboards, The Style Council (b. 11 Sep 1958, Wimbledon)
Porl Thompson, guitar, The Cure (b. 8 Nov 1957, Wimbledon)
Ben Watt, guitar/keyboards, Everything but the Girl (b. 6 Dec 1962, Barnes)

KT3
A Fairport Convention cover shoot in Wimbledon

The cover photograph for Fairport Convention's first hit album Unhalfbricking was shot at Arthur Road in Wimbledon. The composition of this 1969 cover, sans band name or album title, depicts Fairport Convention singer Sandy Denny's parents Edna and Neil outside their home. Sandy and the rest of the band are assembled in the background on the lawn, and the precise location is pinpointed by the appearance of St Mary's Church (Broadway Court) in the photo's misty background.

LOCATION 201: Arthur Road, Wimbledon, postcode KT3 6LX

Eric Hayes' photo of Edna and Neil (and Fairport Convention) at Arthur Road, Wimbledon, was shot in the early spring of 1969

Surbiton
Toby Jug debut for Ziggy Stardust

Strange fact alert: John Lennon's dad, Freddie, once worked behind the bar at the now demolished Toby Jug, and a bunch of blues-rock outfits played the solid but less than beautiful old pub. But good as the likes of Ten Years After, Jethro Tull, Fleetwood Mac and King Crimson must have been, it was the beginning of a particular tour on February 10th 1972 that really put this Tolworth hostelry on the music map. That was the day David Bowie performed the first date of his Ziggy Stardust tour backed by his Spiders from Mars. The function-room crowd numbered some 60 inquisitive rock fans who had seen Bowie adorn the cover of Melody Maker just a couple of weeks previously and appear on BBC TV's The Old Grey Whistle Test just two nights earlier. It might have been just a pub gig but Bowie had his 'main man'

persona lit by a dramatic theatrical spotlight. The lucky few who paid on the night, without so much as a queue, probably witnessed the best pub gig of this or any century. Stephen King, who later made a career as a sound engineer working for The Who, The Kinks and XTC, remembers the event well: "I couldn't blink for fear of missing something. The sound was fantastic - so loud my ears were ringing for days afterwards. I can still remember feeling the sheer power of the opening chords of 'Ziggy Stardust'."

LOCATION 202: now a building site on the roundabout where the A3 meets Kingston Road, Tolworth, Surbiton. Not forgotten, even by the local powers that be, the loop of road behind where the pub once stood is called Toby Way. Postcode KT5 9PA

Proof that the Toby Jug attracted some great bands, even if their spelling wasn't up to much, and Bowie on the cover of Melody Maker less than three weeks before his Ziggy debut at the Toby Jug

Greater London

WC2
Dylan's 'Subterranean Homesick Blues'

Immortalised in D. A. Pennebaker's movie Dont Look Back, a sequence filmed in an alley close to the Savoy hotel has become one of the all-time great music videos. When Bob Dylan visited London in the spring of 1965 he stayed at the Savoy. On May 8 he left his hotel suite with Pennebaker and friends, American singer-songwriter Bob Neuwirth and US beat poet Allen Ginsberg, and headed for the back streets behind the Savoy, taking a set of handwritten cue cards to accompany the lyrics to 'Subterranean Homesick Blues'. At the entrance to Savoy Steps, instead of miming to the song he captioned key words and phrases from the lyrics as the camera rolled with the cue cards earlier painted by Dylan, girlfriend Joan Baez and his new British friends Alan Price and Donovan. At his Savoy suite, a day after the 'Subterranean Homesick Blues' shoot, Dylan met Donovan again and all four Beatles (in London filming Help!), who brought along Alma Cogan.

LOCATION 203: little has changed since the shooting of the memorable promotional film in 1965. The exact spot where Dylan performed his much-copied, inventive cue-card routine is at the entrance to Savoy Steps (position yourself with your back to Savoy Hill). Next to The Queen's Chapel of the Savoy, postcode WC2R 0DA

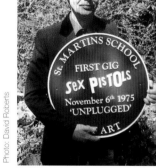

WC1
St Martins debut for the Sex Pistols

St Martins School of Art was the place where the Sex Pistols launched their bid to get noticed. Here, after lugging their equipment on foot from their nearby base in Denmark Street, they played their first gig, which lasted no longer than 20 minutes. The raucous debut on November 6, 1975 ended in chaos

Glen Matlock with his copy of the St Martins plaque

when, legend has it, they had the plug pulled on them by St Martins student Stuart Goddard, who, years later, would transform himself into Adam Ant. Other former St Martins students who made a name for themselves in music include Jarvis Cocker, Polly Jean Harvey, Sade, Shane MacGowan, Clash members Joe Strummer, Paul Simonon and Mick Jones, and Bonzo Dog Doo-Dah men Vivian Stanshall and Neil Innes. Student and Sex Pistol Glen Matlock states, "I would like to say that punk started when we did our first show at St Martins School of Art. I don't know if that's quite true or not, but we certainly put the cat among the pigeons. Remember, this was a good year before any other bands were really playing around."

LOCATION 204: the 7th floor of the Central Saint Martins College of Art & Design, 107 Charing Cross Road, postcode WC1B 4AP

WC2
The Beatles fan club on Monmouth Street

When Beatles manager Brian Epstein moved his business HQ down from Liverpool, he relocated the centre of his NEMS organisation to this trendy street near Seven Dials, Covent Garden. His arrival here in 1963 created a massive increase in work for the local postal service, as this became the address of the group's fan club at the start of Beatlemania. In 2010, a plaque marking this spot was unveiled by Cilla Black, another of Epstein's management stable of stars.

LOCATION 205: at 13 Monmouth Street, postcode WC2H 9DD

WC2
Tin Pan Alley on Denmark Street

London's equivalent of the original New York City-based Tin Pan Alley is stuffed with music history. Musicians and fans still get a buzz and a tingle of nostalgia wandering down the street where instrument shops and offices look much as they did back in the post-war period when songwriters and publishers set up shop. At various times, Denmark Street has seen the recording of the first Rolling Stones album at No.4 (Regent Sounds Studio), the launch of the New Musical Express at No.5, the address where both the Sex Pistols and The Clash made their base at No.6, the launch of Melody Maker at No.19, Mills Music,

Photo: David Roberts

The studio where the Stones recorded their debut album

where Elton John once worked as a £5-a-week office boy, at No.20, and the street's only remaining recording facility, Tin Pan Alley Studios, at No.22.

LOCATION 206: Denmark Street, postcode WC2H 8LU

WC1
Bob Marley remembered at Ridgmount Gardens

When Bob Marley first came to the UK in 1972, he lived at this quiet, rather stately mansion block at Ridgmount Gardens, a short stroll from the busy Tottenham Court Road. In 2006, Mayor of London Ken Livingstone, who organised a commemorative plaque in partnership with the Nubian Jak Community Trust, described the internationally famous reggae artist as "quite simply a musical genius." The plaque unveiling was attended by children from Paddington Green Primary School, who read aloud a potted history of Marley's life's work, and students from St Martin-in-the-Fields High School for Girls, who sang 'Redemption Song' from the 1980 Bob Marley and The Wailers album Uprising.

LOCATION 207: 34 Ridgmount Gardens, postcode WC1E 7

Photo: David Roberts

MAYOR OF LONDON

ROBERT NESTA MARLEY
1945-1981

SINGER, LYRICIST AND RASTAFARIAN ICON

LIVED HERE
1972

NUBIAN JAK COMMUNITY TRUST

WC2
The Blitz Club

Originally centred around a few dozen extraordinarily flamboyant art students, mostly from St Martins, a new movement developed its identity at The Blitz Club near Holborn tube station. Three key characters were the pioneers-in-chief of the New Romantic fashion and music explosion based at this former World War II wine bar. Taking care of the Blitz cloakroom was a young Boy George, DJ duties were handled by Rusty Egan, and Steve Strange played the host with, at his discretion, only those weird or wonderful enough permitted entry.

LOCATION 208: 4 Great Queen Street, Holborn, postcode WC2B 5DG

Greater London

W1
The Stones, Blind Faith, Blur, Live 8 and James Taylor at Hyde Park

At 2.30 pm precisely on Friday June 13, 1969 the bandstand at the south-east corner of Hyde Park was the venue for an unconventional photo call. "Mick, Keith, Bill and Charlie invite you to meet their new guitarist" read the invitation to the press. Joining The Rolling Stones that day was Welwyn Garden City-born Mick Taylor. The former John Mayall's Bluesbreakers guitarist's arrival in the Stones was a PR masterstroke, on a par with the signing of a star footballer. The event preceded the famous Stones in the Park free concert, when the band remembered the recently deceased founding member Brian Jones, found dead in his Cotchford Farm swimming pool 2 days earlier. However, it was The Pink Floyd, Jethro Tull, Roy Harper and Tyrannosaurus Rex who first started the tradition of playing free in Hyde Park when their June 29, 1968 event kicked off proceedings. A year later supergroup Blind Faith (Eric Clapton, Steve Winwood and Ric Grech) made their debut in front of another free audience. Major concert events, sadly no longer 'free', have been frequent down the decades. Recent highlights include Live 8 (2006) and the reformation of Blur (2009).

In this eyewitness account, photographer Mike Charity remembers the Stones at Hyde Park vividly...

"We were led into the cordoned-off area behind the stage. An hour or so later a sand-coloured WW2 armoured truck - no windows, just slits in the steel walls - rolled up and there alighted the Stones and, to my surprise, a lady very much in the news at the time - Christine Keeler. Eventually the photographic press were gathered together and ushered out front for the start of the show, where we were sandwiched between the stage frontage and a line of formidable Hells Angels acting as minders, keeping fans

Photographer Mike Charity was in front of the stage for the Stones' legendary Hyde Park gig

away. It seemed the whole world had descended on the park. There was a wall of people as far as the eye could see. In the far distance fans had climbed up lamp posts, poles and trees, anywhere they could plonk or park themselves to be sure of being there and partaking of the rock 'n' roll atmosphere. Whatever position us snappers found ourselves in at the start of the concert, that was where we stayed, pinned to the spot. Not happy with fluttering creatures at the best of times, I found I was in direct line of flight for hundreds of white butterflies, released from the stage as a tribute to Brian Jones, who was found dead in his swimming pool just two days before the concert."

On a somewhat smaller scale, Hyde Park has always had its fair share of

buskers, none more celebrated than the newly signed Apple label artist James Taylor back in 1968. In between Beatles recording breaks on the White Album, the young American singer-songwriter used the downtime to record his debut album. And, with no time for gigging and rent to pay, Taylor would make the journey from his temporary home in Earls Court to busk in the Hyde Park subway to raise some cash. He remembers, "There was this underground passage by Hyde Park where people liked to play, because the echo was good. You couldn't walk across the street there, so people had no choice but to come past you."

LOCATION 209: west of Park Lane, postcode W1

W1
Hendrix audience blown away at the Bag O' Nails

The dramatic rise in popularity of Jimi Hendrix can be traced back to a significant performance in Kingly Street. Having made his UK public debut in October at the nearby Scotch of St James, Hendrix (now billed as The Jimi Hendrix Experience) literally blew some of his audience away on November 25, 1966 at a special reception for inquisitive musicians and journalists. At the showcase gig for the new group, some of the audience fled the tiny Bag O' Nails club battered by the trio's high-volume performance. Among those present who stayed to witness a hugely significant gig were The Beatles, The Who and Donovan. That night, The Jimi Hendrix Experience enjoyed a promotion push generated by thrilled musicians' word-of-mouth recommendations and an interview with Record Mirror. By the end of the following month, The Jimi Hendrix Experience were a national TV curiosity, as seen on Ready Steady Go! and Top of the Pops, interviewed by Radio Caroline and courting contract offers from the likes of Who management duo Chris Stamp and Kit Lambert. The Bag O' Nails was also a favourite after-hours Beatles haunt and the place where Paul McCartney met his future wife Linda at a Georgie Fame gig in May 1967. The young photographer Linda Eastman was in the UK from the US checking out the London rock scene. Elsewhere in Kingly Street, look out for the former studio and darkroom at Picture Story Publications Ltd at No.21, where The Beatles posed for a photo session with Fiona Adams behind the camera. No.62 was once La Valbonne, another nightclub frequented by the Fab Four.

LOCATION 210: 9 Kingly Street, Soho, postcode W1B 5PH

The HMV plaque unveiled by Beatles producer George Martin in 2000

Photo: Martin Downham

W1
HMV plaque marks a key Beatles event

Between the Boots and Foot Locker stores on Oxford Street is the location of the original HMV store. Here, Beatles manager Brian Epstein was directed to get The Beatles' demo tapes transferred to disc for convenience when touting them round the record labels. The engineer, liking what he heard during the transfer, suggested Epstein approach EMI Publishing on the top floor, which eventually resulted in their first hit 'Love Me Do' being released in 1962. Look out for the large wall plaque, which reminds passers-by that this was once a prestigious record store with an important connection to The Beatles' eventual success story.

LOCATION 211: 363-367 Oxford Street, postcode W1C 2LA

W1
Kirsty MacColl's Soho Square bench

Soho Square is the fitting location of a memorial to singer-songwriter Kirsty MacColl, who died tragically in Mexico in 2000. A ceremony when a bench was unveiled in her memory was witnessed by 150 family, friends and fans, accompanied by a broadcast of her song 'Soho Square', from the 1993 album Titanic Days, in which MacColl sang about shivering pigeons, naked trees and 'an empty bench in Soho Square'.

LOCATION 212: the bench and plaque can be found at the southern end of Soho Square, postcode W1D 3QE

Greater London

On a snowy lunchtime in December 2010 Paul McCartney performed an intimate two-hour gig at the 100 Club to aid its battle against closure

W1
Seven decades of new music at the 100 Club

The 100 Club has promoted live music in the same premises since 1942, when jazz was the draw. The subterranean venue at No.100 on London's busy Oxford Street has witnessed a number of significant music events, not least Britain's first punk festival over two chaotic nights in September 1976. Newly assembled acts sporting provocative names such as The Damned, The Clash, Siouxsie and The Banshees, Buzzcocks and a headlining Sex Pistols took to the stage in an atmosphere of mutual aggression between the audience and the performers. This was a catch-all opportunity for the British music press to witness several bands desperate to prove themselves at the vanguard of the new punk movement. The 100 Club event provided the many assembled journalists with all the copy they needed to spread the news about this new, largely London-based phenomenon nationwide. An equally important introduction to a new era occurred in 1992 when the 100 Club hosted new outfit Suede, a gig that revitalised interest in the club and led to the venue enjoying jam-packed houses for visits by a conveyor belt of indie-rock bands such as Oasis, Travis, Catatonia and Kula Shaker. Recently threatened with closure due to the spiralling cost of rent on Oxford Street, the place has gained much superstar support in its battle to survive, and thankfully the 2014 gig schedule seems to suggest that it won't be dying anytime soon if events like July's 50th anniversary concert by The Pretty Things was anything to go by.

LOCATION 213: 100 Oxford Street, postcode W1D 1LL

100 CLUB

NO SMOKING.
It is against the law to smoke in these premises

Greater London

W1

Skiffle is born and Cliff finds Shadows at the 2i's

The 2i's Coffee Bar in Old Compton Street billed itself as the 'home of the stars'. Musicians Hank Marvin, Joe Brown, Tommy Steele, Bruce Welch, Cliff Richard and Adam Faith were all fans and performers at the centre of a new youth movement. Professional wrestler Paul Lincoln ran the 2i's, which encouraged the new breed of Fifties teenagers to enjoy whooshing, frothy coffee at Formica tables and skiffle music in the cramped basement. Skiffle found a home at the 2i's thanks to Wally Whyton's request to the owners for a place to 'busk' for his group The Vipers. Business at the coffee bar had been poor but The Vipers' regular performances began to create the packed atmosphere where regular fans, musicians and agents made it the place to be seen, perform and do business. Long before either did the big business they became famous for in the Sixties and Seventies, producer and label boss Mickie Most and Led Zeppelin manager Peter Grant worked at the 2i's – Most was a waiter and Grant was doorman. About the same time, back in early 1958, Harry Webb, Norman Mitcham and Terry Smart were three school friends looking for bookings. Billed as The Drifters, acting manager John Foster sensed the potential evident in singer Webb (Cliff Richard) and managed a booking for the Hertfordshire trio at the 2i's. Mitcham and Smart were enthusiastic amateurs but lacked the charisma of singer Webb, who was soon grabbing rave reviews on Jack Good's Oh Boy! TV show. By 1959,

and with a national tour looming, the search for more accomplished musicians by Foster bore fruit on another visit to the 2i's. Cliff recalled, "He came back from the 2i's club and said, 'I've found a guitarist. He plays like James Burton, who played for Ricky Nelson and ultimately ended up playing for Elvis, and he looks like Buddy Holly. And, he's got a friend.' So, Bruce Welch and Hank Marvin came home and we sang and played together. It was obvious we were going to click so I asked them to join me." Welch and Marvin, who in addition to performing at the club also worked behind the bar

serving the customers orange juice, were soon joined by Jet Harris and Tony Meehan and the newly named Shadows line-up was complete.

LOCATION 214: the 2i's is currently the Boulevard Bar & Dining Room, 59 Old Compton Street, Soho, postcode W1D 6HR

The downstairs performance area is now storage for the bar and restaurant that occupies No.59 on this still vibrant Soho street

CITY OF WESTMINSTER

SITE OF THE 2i's COFFEE BAR (1956-1970)

BIRTHPLACE OF BRITISH ROCK 'N ROLL AND THE POPULAR MUSIC INDUSTRY

ROBERT MANDRY

" In 1958 the 2i's... was just a little cafe with an old battered piano in the basement in Old Compton Street. But **IT HAD A SOUL** and a buzz "

JOE MORETTI
Guitarist

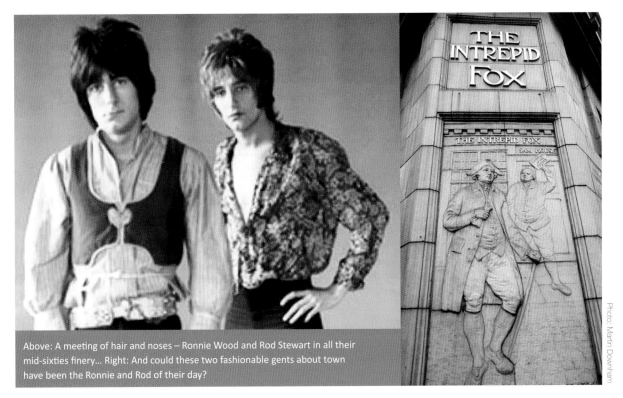

Above: A meeting of hair and noses – Ronnie Wood and Rod Stewart in all their mid-sixties finery... Right: And could these two fashionable gents about town have been the Ronnie and Rod of their day?

W1
Ronnie meets Rod at The Intrepid Fox

Before The Jeff Beck Group and The Faces found an outlet for their combined talents, Rod Stewart and Ronnie Wood met for the first time and forged a lifelong friendship when they crossed paths at The Intrepid Fox in Soho. This historic pub, where it's rumoured that Mick Jagger talked Ronnie into joining The Rolling Stones, and favoured by other music types including Motörhead's Lemmy, Malcolm McLaren and the Sex Pistols, was closed down in 2006. Happily, the building (now a classy burger restaurant) still stands and the ornate stone pub sign still remains as a memorial to one of rock's great watering holes.

LOCATION 215: 97-99 Wardour Street, W1F 0UD

" It was The Intrepid Fox in Wardour Street. We bumped into each other... He was with The Birds and we recognised a nice big nose and a fairly **SIMILAR HAIRCUT** "

ROD STEWART

" He came up to me - we had similar hair – and he said "**HELLO FACE!**", and I'll never forget it. And years later we were in The Faces! "

RONNIE WOOD

Greater London

W1
Keith Moon remembered at the Marquee

Owned by Harold Pendleton and based at 165 Oxford Street, the Marquee Club was said to have been the first venue where a London audience saw an electric guitar. This seminal moment occurred in 1958 when Pendleton and Chris Barber tracked down US bluesman Muddy Waters and brought him to the former Marquee ballroom, in a cinema basement. In the Sixties it was Pendleton who introduced the predominantly jazz-based audiences to the music of the new British R&B movement, featuring the genre's innovators Alexis Korner and Cyril Davies (Blues Incorporated). Young R&B band The Rolling Stones made their Marquee debut supporting Davies, and by 1964 the venue had moved to Wardour Street where the likes of The Who and The Yardbirds became fixtures. Progressive and punk sounds found a home at the club before yet another move to 105-107 Charing Cross Road until 1995, when the name vanished. Years later the Marquee reappeared, launched at the Islington Academy (16 Parkfield Street) in 2002, and between 2004 and 2005 Leicester Square was its home. What appears to be the absolute end came following a short period at 14 Upper St Martin's Lane on February 12, 2008. A plaque remembering Keith Moon at the best-known

> "I used to **SWEEP THE FLOOR** and put the chairs out"
>
> **PHIL COLLINS**

CITY OF WESTMINSTER

KEITH MOON
1946–1978

LEGENDARY ROCK DRUMMER
WITH 'THE WHO'

PERFORMED HERE AT
THE SITE OF THE
MARQUEE CLUB
IN THE 1960s

THE HERITAGE FOUNDATION

Photo: David Roberts

Marquee location in Wardour Street is all that remains of one of Britain's best-loved music brands. The Who drummer, who died in 1978, was honoured at the plaque's unveiling in 2009, an event attended by his 88-year-old mother and Roger Daltrey. Teenager and future rock star Phil Collins has some very early memories of the place. "I used to go to the Marquee three or four times a week. I was always at the front of the queue because I went straight from school. I went so often that the management got to know me. They invited me in and I used to sweep the floor and put the chairs out before the audience arrived."

LOCATION 216: the Marquee commemorative plaque is at 90 Wardour Street, Soho, postcode W1F 0TH

Keith Moon's plaque marks the position of the world-famous Marquee and the familiar arched front entrance on Wardour Street

W1
The tragic deaths of two rock legends at Harry Nilsson's Mayfair flat

A top-floor flat in Mayfair is perhaps one of the unhappiest locations in Rock Atlas as it was here, just off Curzon Street, that not one but two rock legends coincidentally met their early deaths. Cass Elliot (Mama Cass) had completed two weeks of successful solo shows at the London Palladium when she returned to this Mayfair flat and died from a heart attack aged just 32 on July 28, 1974. Tragedy struck again when Keith Moon, who occupied the very same flat No.12, died there on September 7, 1978, also aged 32. Moon, who had been a guest of Paul McCartney at the Buddy Holly movie preview the night before, returned to the Curzon Square (then Curzon Place) flat and died from heart failure after spending his last hours alive watching Vincent Price movie The Abominable Dr Phibes on TV. This unlucky flat was not owned or rented by Keith Moon. It was his benevolent fellow Who band member Pete Townshend who rented the place to encourage Moon to get his life back on track after years of drugs and alcohol dependency. And the owner of this unfortunate property from whom Townshend rented? American singer-songwriter Harry Nilsson bought the place and let it out at the time of both deaths. And the rock connections don't end there. Apparently Nilsson hired good friend Ringo Starr and Robin Cruikshank,

Above: Rock Atlas researcher Martin Downham trains his camera on the top-floor flat once owned by Harry Nilsson

The 1971 album Nilsson (inset) was recorded a short distance from his Mayfair flat at Trident Studios

who had set up a 1970s furniture design partnership, to help redecorate the place. These days the entire block of apartments has been given a complete makeover with a rather sombre black paint job outside - perhaps an appropriate colour under the circumstances surrounding this striking but tragic property.

LOCATION 217: Curzon Square, near the western end of Curzon Street, postcode W1J 7SX

"From one balcony you could read the time from **BIG BEN**, and from the other balcony you could watch the **BUNNIES** go up and down"

HARRY NILSSON
describes the position of his Curzon Square flat, close to the Playboy Club

Greater London

Photo: Martin Downham

W1
(What's the Story) Berwick Street?

The Oasis best-selling album (What's the Story) Morning Glory? features a cover shot of radio DJ Sean Rowley and the album's producer Owen Morris passing each other in an otherwise deserted Berwick Street. So, the cover doesn't picture either of the Gallagher brothers, as some people originally thought. However, the Soho street, which was once a mecca for fans of independent record shop browsing, coincidentally joins the conveniently named Noel Street. This second Oasis album went on to become the UK's third best-selling studio album.

LOCATION 218: Berwick Street, Soho, postcode W1F 8TD

No Gallaghers: Berwick Street, as pictured on the UK's third best-selling studio album, and the little-changed street today

W1
When Harry became Cliff at the Swiss Tavern

A short walk from the site of the 2i's Coffee Bar was the Swiss Tavern (now Comptons), the pub where in 1958 a young singer entered as Harry Webb and left as Cliff Richard. Harry Greatorex, who ran a ballroom in Ripley, Derbyshire, was on a scouting mission in London at the 2i's Coffee Bar and wanted to book Harry Webb and The Drifters, but the young Harry was adamant that the posters must advertise just "The Drifters". Greatorex insisted that he had to have an Elvis or Jerry Lee Lewis type of name up front to promote the act, so the band set about thinking one up. Cliff takes up the story: "We went to a little pub round the corner, ordered a shandy, sat down and thought of names. The last combination of names was Russ Clifford [then] Cliff Russard. I thought, wait a minute, forget Russard – Cliff, (rock face!), then we got to Cliff Richards with an 's' on the end and then Ian Samwell, who wrote 'Move It!' for me said, 'Take the 's' off. That means you've got two Christian names - Cliff Richard – and it could be a tribute to Little Richard.' And that's how it came about. I thought, that sounds good - Cliff Richard and The Drifters. Then of course we changed Drifters to Shadows. The 'd' I think was important. The 'd' of Richard, the 'D' of Drifters and the 'd' of Shadows. There was a link and it was rhythmical." For the full story of Cliff's life-changing Ripley concert, check out the Derbyshire section of Rock Atlas

LOCATION 219: "the world-famous Old Dame of Compton Street", Comptons, is at 51-53 Old Compton Street, Soho, postcode W1D 6HN

Photo: David Roberts

IMPRESARIO
DON ARDEN
AND MOD BAND
"SMALL FACES"
(STEVE MARRIOTT, RONNIE
LANE, KENNEY JONES,
IAN MCLAGAN AND
JIMMY WINSTON)
WORKED HERE
1965-1967

W1
Carnaby Street: Small Faces "worked here"

The epicentre of the swinging Sixties, Carnaby Street was more specifically the hub of the mod movement's universe, a fact still evident today judging by the target iconography, scooters and parkers on display. The street became a new base for London's rag trade out of necessity when World War II bombs destroyed much of the east end's tailoring businesses. Those most fashionable of Mods, The Small Faces, were managed from an office in Carnaby Street by the highly efficient and some would say downright frightening, larger-than-life character Don Arden. From this base, Arden would pay the band in clothes tokens for the local boutiques and shops rather than actual cash. The office was also the home of The Small Faces'

fan club, where sacks of mail would arrive containing requests for signed photos, offers of marriage, a variety of gifts and, on one occasion, a dog. In 2007, the band's drummer, Kenney Jones, unveiled a plaque at the building

where Don Arden and The Small Faces worked.

LOCATION 220: the former Small Faces HQ and plaque are at the south end of Carnaby Street (Nos.52-54), postcode W1F 9QD

Carnaby Street: still a hub of chic mod fashion in the 21st century

"We had accounts in the shops down there and so we spent a lot of money on shirts. In other words, that's how we got our money, because we couldn't get it any other way, so we became **FASHION GURUS** walking about in the latest togs"

KENNEY JONES

Greater London

W1
Beatles at The Palladium and Brian Epstein's office

Argyll Street's Palladium theatre hosted three concerts by The Beatles between 1963 and 1964. Most memorable was their appearance on the hugely popular weekly TV show Val Parnell's Sunday Night at the London Palladium. Broadcast nationwide on October 13, 1963 at a time when, in the UK, there were only two television channels, this performance was a pivotal point in their career. It enabled their by now well-honed act to be broadcast into millions of homes for maximum impact. Reporting on the Palladium performance the following day, newspapers printed "Beatlemania!" headlines and pictured the crowds of screaming girls who caused chaos on the pavements outside. Across Argyll Street from the Palladium at Nos. 5-6 is the office block where Beatles manager Brian Epstein held court. His North End Music Stores (NEMS) HQ office was set up here in 1964 after a brief spell in Covent Garden. Argyll Street provided a more convenient central venue for The Beatles and other artists belonging to the Epstein management stable. Once the business base had shifted from Liverpool to London, press interviews and management of The Beatles, Cilla Black, Gerry and The Pacemakers and Billy J Kramer and The Dakotas was taken care of here in Argyll Street.

LOCATIONS 221 and 222: Argyll Street, Oxford Circus, postcode W1F 7TF

W1
McCartney's 'Yesterday' written at the Asher family home

Doctor and Mrs Asher lived in Wimpole Street along with their talented actress daughter Jane and fledgling pop singer son Peter. They obligingly provided a London base for Jane's boyfriend Paul McCartney, who was their attic-room lodger for three years until 1966. To avoid the press and fans, Paul would often gain access to and from the property via back doors, side doors and adjacent rooftops. Paul thrived at No.57 in this naturally artistic and creative environment, rattling off a few tunes along the way, including 'Yesterday', pop's most-covered song, begun here and finished on holiday at Shadows guitarist Bruce Welch's villa in Portugal.

LOCATION 223: 57 Wimpole Street, postcode W1G 8YW. This private residence is close to the intersection with New Cavendish Street

Left: Paul McCartney lodged here in the attic at the top of No.57 Wimpole Street
Above: Jane Asher and the Asher family lodger, Paul McCartney

W1
The Beatles' last stand on the Savile Row rooftop

The Beatles, as a public unified band, ended on January 30, 1969 with an extraordinary lunchtime concert on the rooftop of their Apple HQ at Savile Row. Paul McCartney had worked at trying to reinvigorate the band by getting them to play to a live audience. The filmed rehearsals in the cold, cavernous Twickenham Film Studios had stretched them to bad-tempered breaking point. Lennon remained exasperatingly uncommunicative, Harrison was frustrated at the lack of attention given to his songs and the usually affable Starr was impatient to get the project out of the way so that he could start on his movie, The Magic Christian. Decamping to the new Apple Studios in the basement of their Savile Row HQ, they had at least managed some semblance of rehearsing, but a location for the live show could not be agreed.

The Roundhouse, the Royal Albert Hall, the Cavern and even makeshift stages in India or Africa were all discussed and dismissed until, with overall interest in the project waning, they all agreed to play up on the roof of the central London building. On that bitterly cold winter's lunchtime, The Beatles, plus Billy Preston, assembled on the roof and ran through their repertoire of new songs, including 'Don't Let Me Down' and 'I've Got a Feeling', plus an oldie from 1962, 'One After 909'. A local bank manager objected to the noise and disruption and called in the police to stop the gig.

Fears that they might be dragged from the stage and arrested came to nothing. The police merely asked them to turn their amps down. It was left to Lennon, at the end of their last run-through of 'Get Back', at the end of their last ever public live performance, to turn to the onlookers, assembled on adjacent rooftops and swarming below in Savile Row, and announce, "I'd like to say thank you on behalf of the group and ourselves and I hope we passed the audition."

LOCATION 224: 3 Savile Row, postcode W1S 3

W1
The Apple Boutique

The Beatles' well-intended but ultimately unsuccessful adventure into retail marketing opened in December 1967. The exterior of their clothes and fashion shop on Baker Street represented the optimism of the time, with a building-wide psychedelic landscape painted by Dutch artists The Fool. Months later, at the bureaucratic insistence of local councillors, the building was whitewashed over, heralding the end of this altruistic folly. Having lost money virtually since it opened, The Beatles decided to close the store in July 1968 and give away the remaining stock, although they craftily

spent a night or two beforehand helping themselves to some of the finer items. Once the shop had finally closed, Paul McCartney, ever the opportunist, wrote the title of their forthcoming single 'Hey Jude' in the whitewashed shop windows. Look out for the building's blue plaque, which namechecks only John Lennon and George Harrison and not the other two living Beatles.

LOCATION 225: 94 Baker Street, at the junction with Paddington Street, postcode W1U 6FZ. The building is currently occupied by an employment agency

> " I got into the Apple building [and the owners] told me... when they took it over it was in **A TERRIBLE STATE** and they had to paint over a lot of scribblings on walls from Lennon "
> **WILL CAMPBELL**
> Former journalist

The Manchester Square staircase

"Loads of fans used to come by to try and **RE-CREATE THE PHOTO** but were usually chased off by security because... EMI weren't having any of that! "

BRIAN SOUTHALL
former EMI PR director

Photo: David Roberts

W1
EMI Manchester Square and the iconic Beatles balcony

The original location of this iconic stairway was on a first-floor landing at EMI's London HQ in Manchester Square, where if you leant over the balcony you looked down into the EMI reception area. This is the spot where photographer Angus McBean looked up to snap The Beatles for their Please Please Me debut album cover. The balcony featured again on covers for the band's Red (62-66) and Blue (67-70) greatest hits albums. The Blue album's updated shot of the Fab Four was a picture originally shot by McBean for the cover of the shelved Get Back album. Neither EMI nor the balcony remain at Manchester Square. Moving offices to Hammersmith in 1995, EMI also moved the increasingly iconic staircase, which they described as "a very important part of Beatles history and EMI history". Re-erected in the Hammersmith office's staff café, together with a commemorative plaque, there it stayed until the structure moved once more to EMI Group HQ in Wrights Lane, Kensington. Describing the EMI fixtures and fittings as "like fragments of the true cross" in his biography McCartney, author Christopher Sandford revealed that the current owner of the banisters and staircase is none other than Paul McCartney himself.

LOCATION 226: No.20 Manchester Square, postcode W1U 3PZ. Status: private offices

Circus

...Howlin' Wolf visited London to record a super... ...hose fans included Eric Clapton, Steve Winwood,... ...the resulting album of recordings at Olympic... ...rk depicting the all-star band on the steps of the...

...ircus, postcode W1J 9EY

vv⊥
Gerry Rafferty's 'Baker Street'

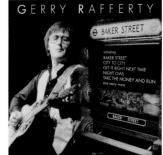

Sherlock Holmes and Gerry Rafferty – they both made this London thoroughfare world famous. Rafferty's biggest hit was a biographical song recalling his days spent busking in the capital. He would stay in a friend's flat off Baker Street when visiting London from his home in Scotland, and this homesick song was written as a joyous end to a period of isolation from releasing music following legal problems when he was a member of Stealers Wheel.

LOCATION 228: Baker Street tube station, postcode W1U 6SF

W1
Rock stars wind down at The Speakeasy

Four consecutive nights at The Speakeasy Club by Bob Marley and The Wailers helped the band create a name for themselves during their first British tour as a newly signed act with the Island label. That short, sold-out residency in May 1973 was witnessed by audience members including Eric Clapton, Jeff Beck and members of Deep Purple and The Who. Other Speakeasy acts you didn't get to see every night of the week in Britain included the extraordinary Mothers of Invention featuring Frank Zappa in 1967 and King Crimson's debut there in May 1969. Back in the day when the nearby Marquee club didn't have a bar, and the local pub The Ship chucked out after last orders, The Speakeasy would come into its own as an after-midnight wind-down place where musicians, journalists and photographers would mingle the night away. One night, on the eve of the

release of Sgt Pepper's Lonely Hearts Club Band, American group The Turtles arrived in London and headed straight for The Speakeasy to find The Beatles in a booth enjoying a quiet night out. Additionally, as The Turtles' Howard Kaylan later boasted, in one night he met Graham Nash, Donovan, Brian Jones and Jimi Hendrix, who, in turn, legend has it, once jammed with Paul McCartney's girlfriend Jane Asher's mum and failed in an attempt to lure Marianne Faithfull away from boyfriend Mick Jagger. The Speakeasy ceased being London's great rock 'n' roll hangout in the late 70s, but not before The Who's Pete Townshend had met up with the Sex Pistols' Steve Jones and Paul Cook to famously tell them they were 'the future of rock'.

LOCATION 229: north of the junction of Oxford Street and Regent Street, 48 Margaret Street, postcode W1W 8SE

> "The Speakeasy [was] where bands could **GO AFTER GIGS** - it was a late club and I often used to see John Lennon or Keith Moon...**"**
>
> **JIM MCCARTY**
> Yardbirds drummer

Greater London

W1
Ziggy Stardust materialises on Heddon Street

The subject of a recent renovation as an area of pavement eateries, Heddon Street is famously the spot where David Bowie was photographed for his Ziggy Stardust and the Spiders from Mars album cover. Although the prominent, illuminated 'K. West' sign (auctioned off a while back) and the back cover original red telephone box are long gone, the street has changed little and a replacement phone box has been installed for those Bowie pilgrims wishing to emulate his back cover pose. Bowie's 'motivation' for photographer Brian Ward's cover shoot that wet night in January 1971 was to carry off a look inspired by characters from A Clockwork Orange and William S. Burroughs' novel The Wild Boys. The photo shoot was booked for the studio in Heddon Street but Ward persuaded Bowie to step outside for a few shots on the street, although rumour has it he couldn't persuade the Spiders from Mars band members to join them due to the cold and damp weather that night. The result of the photo session produced a truly iconic rock 'n' roll moment. The colour-tinted front cover picture was nearer to an alien landing in London and remains one of the most powerful pop images, selected for the series of British album cover designs reproduced on Royal Mail postage stamps in 2010. The Heddon Street location was honoured again in 2012 when a Ziggy Stardust plaque was positioned to mark the spot where the iconic cover was created. Bowie fan Gary Kemp unveiled the plaque in a ceremony also attended by Spiders from Mars band members Trevor Bolder and Mick Woodmansey.

LOCATION 230: Ziggy Stardust front cover: 23 Heddon Street; back cover: the Heddon Street alleyway, postcode W1B 4BQ

The black Heddon Street Ziggy Stardust plaque is one of only two in London created to honour fictional characters – the second was for Sherlock Holmes. Above right: Terry Pastor, who designed, retouched and coloured the original black and white shots for the album cover, has worked on new digital versions like this one, available to buy from his website

"It was cold and it rained and **I FELT LIKE AN ACTOR**"

DAVID BOWIE
recalls the cover shoot

Photo © The David Bowie Archive®

An outtake from photographer
Brian Ward's Ziggy session with the
famous telephone box featured on
the album's back cover

Greater London

W1
John, Paul, Jimi and Ringo at Montagu Square

The English Heritage blue plaque on the wall of 34 Montagu Square indicates only a small proportion of the rock history associated with this ground-floor and basement flat. The plaque unveiled by Yoko Ono in 2010 informs that John Lennon lived there in 1968, but understates this regency

house's important role in the lives of three other rock legends. The first home that John and Yoko shared together, it was here that the two were photographed naked for the couple's Two Virgins album cover and Lennon worked on material for The

Beatles' White Album. The capital's most celebrated rock and pop residence began its colourful history in 1965 when flat No.1 at No.34 was purchased and lived in by Ringo Starr and wife Maureen. Needing more space with the arrival of son Zak, the Starrs soon vacated Montagu Square and Paul McCartney moved in during 1966, utilising the basement as a recording studio and working on, among other things, 'Eleanor Rigby'. The next tenant, later that same year, was Jimi Hendrix, who set up home in the basement with girlfriend Kathy Etchingham and his manager Chas Chandler, who, along with his girlfriend Lotta, took the first floor. Here Hendrix formed the Experience and wrote at least one classic hit, 'The Wind Cries Mary', and in a less productive mood reportedly threw paint at the walls during an acid trip. This led owner/landlord Ringo to re-decorate the place with white interiors throughout, a look that prevails to this day. After Hendrix moved to nearby Brook Street, in came John and Yoko before Ringo eventually sold up in 1969. The most desirable rock 'n' roll pad in London has attracted many tourist visitors down the years and at least one would-be rock star purchaser in Noel Gallagher, who was thwarted in his plans to buy in 2001. "People from all corners of the world will come to London and see this plaque with love for John and the memory of what he was," said Yoko Ono at the unveiling in 2010

LOCATION 231: 34 Montagu Square is a private residence, postcode W1H 2LJ

Picture lower left: London's most celebrated rock 'n' roll residence and the plaque at No.34. Main picture: Montagu Square was Montagu Place back in the days when Jimi Hendrix lived there

Greater London

W1
Pill-popping to the latest R&B sounds at the Flamingo

Early-Sixties London clubs, previously set up for jazz fans, grudgingly allowed the new R&B acts a session or two. The Flamingo Club in Wardour Street was a good example, with its famous all-nighters. Georgie Fame and The Blue Flames were at the forefront of acts who were now incorporating soul, bluebeat and pop-style sounds into the jazz they had been playing since the mid-Fifties. Fame's own British take on R&B had been accelerated by his switch from piano to Hammond organ, backed up by The Blue Flames' powerful rhythm base of saxophone, guitar and congas. Dancing to this music through to dawn, Flamingo Club-goers kept their energy levels up by amphetamine pill-popping and the relatively new British crazes for drinking Coca-Cola and scoffing American-style hotdogs.

LOCATION 232: 33-37 Wardour Street, Soho, postcode W1F 6PU

Georgie Fame outside the club on Wardour Street where he recorded his 1964 debut album Rhythm and Blues at the Flamingo

" I would come out of the Flamingo at 4 O'CLOCK IN THE MORNING after a night of watching bands when I couldn't take the heat anymore and I had to get some air. As I was leaving, John Mayall WOULD BE COMING IN carrying his keyboard on his shoulders down into the depths to set up "

ERIC BURDON

Photo: David Roberts

The first- floor flat where Jimi Hendrix lived with girlfriend Kathy Etchingham. The blue plaque was the first in London to be dedicated to a rock musician

W1
Hendrix and Handel in Brook Street

A blue plaque on the wall at 23 Brook Street marks the former home of Jimi Hendrix, where the guitarist lived on and off between 1968 and 1969. Unveiled by Pete Townshend in 1997, the plaque sits next door to another at No.25, where, 200 years earlier, the composer Handel once lived. Handily placed, it was little more than a 10-minute walk across Regent Street and into Soho for Hendrix to relax or jam at the Bag O' Nails or head north of Oxford Street to The Speakeasy.

LOCATION 233: 23 Brook Street, postcode W1K 4HA

W1
Tommy rocking at Ronnie Scott's

East London-born Ronald Schatt later changed his name to Ronnie Scott, and with the help of fellow sax-playing friend Pete King opened his first jazz club at 39 Gerrard Street in 1959. The former tea bar was the perfect refuge for like-minded fans of American jazz. The club moved to larger premises at 47 Frith Street in the '60s, when rock acts appeared in addition to the jazz legends who had helped make it the coolest place to play in London. Special Ronnie Scott's nights included the premiere of rock opera Tommy by The Who, an appearance by Jimi Hendrix days before his death and a debut showcase by the much-vaunted Humble Pie. The smaller venue within a venue, Upstairs at Ronnie's, also played host to a stream of hopefuls including Soft Machine, The Jam and XTC.

LOCATION 234: in 1965, Ronnie Scott's moved to 47 Frith Street, Soho, postcode W1D 4HT

W1
The Bee Gees' London base

Bee Gees manager and producer Robert Stigwood's Brook Street home was the base for all the band's significant activities from 1968 to 1980. During this 12-year period at Brook Street the trio composed songs, took care of Bee Gees business and first met John Travolta, the star of Saturday Night Fever, the movie that re-ignited the Gibb brothers' astonishing career as disco superstars. The house carries a green plaque, which was unveiled by Robin Gibb in 2008.

LOCATION 235: 67 Brook Street, postcode W1K 4NJ

W1
Les Cousins in Greek Street

The oddly named Les Cousins Club was formerly a skiffle hang-out before opening as a folk and blues venue in 1965. Les Cousins wasn't a person at all, the club being appropriately named after the boy in the 1959 French movie of the same name who moved to the city under the influence of his decadent cousin. The club was briefly re-opened in 2004 for a special tribute concert to Nick Drake.

LOCATION 236: 49 Greek Street, postcode W1D 4EG

Greater London

W1
World's first Hard Rock Café

This Hard Rock Café was the original and first of 163 (and counting) Hard Rock's to open, back in 1971. Famous for food and rock memorabilia, the original restaurant has created its own niche in music history and still houses Eric Clapton's Lead II Fender guitar, the first ever item of memorabilia donated to the chain. Also on display: Pete Townshend's Gibson Les Paul guitar, Mitch Mitchell's Jimi Hendrix Experience black Gretsch drum kit and Adam Clayton's Fender Telecaster bass. This first Hard Rock Café houses a special collection of its most prized memorabilia in what it calls the Vault Museum, located in the old Coutts bank, now the Hard Rock Café, London Rock Shop, for which there's no extra admission charge. The vault's London rock treasures include the first guitar owned by the Sex Pistols' Glen Matlock, the harpsichord used by The Beatles to record 'All You Need Is Love' and 'Lucy in the Sky with Diamonds' and the silver suit Eric Clapton wore on the cover of Cream's Goodbye Cream LP.

LOCATION 237: 150 Old Park Lane, postcode W1K 1QZ

Right: the unique Gibson Flying V guitar Jimi Hendrix played at the Isle of Wight Festival is just one of many treasures in the Hard Rock Café Vault Museum

W2
Crosby, Stills & Nash on Moscow Road

In November 1968, Californian David Crosby and Texan Stephen Stills departed the US West Coast vibe of Laurel Canyon for the cold winter of London's Bayswater to meet up with Lancastrian Graham Nash. Mixing Everly Brothers-style harmonies with lyrics as insightful as anything Dylan was producing at the time, the three decamped to a flat on Moscow Road to rehearse material for what would turn out to be their debut album. Amid the joint-smoking fog of creativity – Crosby famously borrowed a local Bayswater butcher's shop sign, "All Joints Must Be Re-Weighed at Time of Purchase", and displayed it in the flat window - the place soon became open house for journalists and inquisitive record company types. Visitors who heard CSN play live, acoustic and as yet unrecorded versions of 'Marrakesh Express' and 'Suite: Judy Blue Eyes' included George Harrison, who surprisingly declined to sign them for Apple. Ironically, once signed to Atlantic and back in the US, some in the music press began describing CSN as "America's answer to The Beatles". "They had guitars and enough money to rent a flat on Moscow Road with a little upstairs studio in it," said Graham Nash on his move to Moscow Road, as remembered in his autobiography Wild Tales. "I moved right in with them for three weeks. We went to local stores and stocked our refrigerator; we had ladies come by, plenty of dope. And we sang our asses off."

LOCATION 238: 16 Moscow Road is the unconfirmed address, near the junction with Salem Road, postcode W2 4BT

The top-floor Bayswater flat where Crosby, Stills & Nash perfected songs on their 1969 debut album

Photo: Archant

W2 and W11
West London Clash sites

There are two West London locations worth a visit if you have a particular passion for The Clash. A busy thoroughfare under, Edgware Road named Joe Strummer Subway leads you down steps to Mick Jones' Rock & Roll Public Library, housed in what was once the subway's large confectionery kiosk. The subway was named to commemorate the place where

Joe Strummer frequently busked for loose change before taking to the world's stages as a member of The 101ers, The Clash, and in his own band, Joe Strummer and The Mescaleros. Clash guitarist Mick Jones' extraordinary collection of memorabilia has its home in the kiosk, which has been attractively transformed into the Subway Gallery below the Edgware Road and Harrow Road crossing. The second Clash location is a couple of miles west, just off Portobello Road, where an enterprising fan of the band, Gary Loveridge,

conceived and organised the creation of a larger than life-size mural of Joe Strummer. Painted on a vacant shop front by artist Emma Harrison, the mural was inspired by Loveridge's visit to the equally striking Strummer mural in New York City's East Village.

LOCATIONS 239 and 240: Joe Strummer Subway is under the junction of Edgware Road and Harrow Road, postcode W2 1DX. The mural is on Blenheim Crescent ,near the junction with Portobello Road, postcode W11 2EE

Gary Loveridge and Emma Harrison join Mick Jones at the 2013 unveiling of the Joe Strummer mural. Inset: Subway Gallery founder Robert McHarg III and Mick Jones at the Joe Strummer Subway

Greater London

W2
Stiff and Blackwell at Alexander Street

This Bayswater address was the HQ for Stiff Records, where the business side of things was overseen by Jake Riviera and Dave Robinson. Through this door passed Elvis Costello, Nick Lowe, Ian Dury, Madness and The Pogues en route to their meteoric rise to critical acclaim in the late-Seventies' new wave era. With the punk and new wave scenes unsettling the old order of progressive rock, it was perhaps symbolic that the Stiff premises had once been the home of Pink Floyd's Roger Waters. Blackhill Enterprises, who looked after Floyd's interests, had also been based at No.32, which makes this tiny portal with managed artists Marc Bolan, Kevin Ayers, The Clash and Roy Harper a veritable music business hotbed. It was from these offices that Blackhill Enterprises organised the early free Hyde Park music festivals starring the likes of Blind Faith.

The Damned behaving badly outside the Alexander Street Stiff address, from which the UK's first punk single, 'New Rose', was released in 1976

LOCATION 241: Stiff Records was at 32 Alexander Street, which is now Gallery 32, postcode W2 5NU

Kula Shaker's fourth album release, covered by Peter Pan

W2
Kula Shaker's Peter Pan pilgrimage

Kula Shaker's 2010 album Pilgrims Progress features Kensington Gardens' famous Peter Pan statue on the cover. The band's video for the album's first single, 'Peter Pan R.I.P', was also shot in the royal park.

LOCATION 242: enter Kensington Gardens from the north side Bayswater Road entrance, near Lancaster Gate tube station. Postcode: W2 2UE

Photo: David Roberts

Above: the 'Lazy Sunday' house and garden at Eyot Green as it is today
Right: 'Wouldn't it be nice, to get on with me neighbours': Steve Marriott in a still from the 'Lazy Sunday' promotional film set at his Eyot Green home

W4
The Small Faces' 'Lazy Sunday' at Eyot Green

A modern terraced town house built in 1962, a stone's throw from a beautiful stretch of the River Thames, was where Steve Marriott set up home a few years later. Here on Netheravon Road South, The Small Faces frontman gained his inspiration, wrote and even recorded the promotional film for 1968 hit single 'Lazy Sunday'. His neighbours in this quiet spot of Chiswick named Eyot Green "made it very clear they've got no room for ravers", as the song's lyrics go. The rather unsophisticated video to accompany the release of the band's 10th hit shows Marriott alone in the communal gardens attached to the house, surrounded by first one then four huge Wharfedale speakers borrowed from Olympic Studios,

where The Small Faces recorded the track. Later in the video all four band members run and dance around the garden, presumably much to the bemusement of the neighbours, who, as the song goes, banged on the windows and doors in disapproval when Marriott had previously pumped up the volume. The fact that the elderly neighbours really did feel that the pop stars next door were rather "dreadful" (in the words of the owners of the house who later bought the place) must have been compounded by the steady stream of rock 'n' roll visitors, including Rod Stewart and various local music types from this Bohemian corner of London, who would party long and loud. Jenny Marriott, who lived with Steve at Eyot

Green in 1968, had some sympathy with the neighbours. She says:"He [Steve] was having a lot of hassle with his neighbours, the Hasselewaithes, and ended up writing 'Lazy Sunday' about his time there. Mind you I didn't blame the neighbours. It must have been hard living next door to him. They complained continuously about the noise and rightly so. Steve had installed Wharfedale speakers from Olympic Studios in the living room, which measured approximately 14 feet by 12 feet!"

LOCATION 243: one road back from the river behind Chiswick Mall, Netheravon Road South, Eyot Green, Chiswick, postcode W4 2PZ

Greater London

W4
A Beatles film set at Strand-on-the-Green

A running theme of The Beatles' second movie Help! was the pursuit of Ringo Starr, who at one point is chased down Post Office Alley and into the City Barge pub on one of the most picturesque stretches of the Thames' Embankment. The scene, involving all four Beatles in and around this location at Strand-on-the-Green, climaxes with Ringo's encounter with a fully-grown tiger in the pub's basement. Scenes inside the pub were shot in the studio.

LOCATIONS 244 and 245: The City Barge, 27 Strand-on-the-Green, and Post Office Alley, postcode W4 3PH

Strand-on-the-Green: a Beatles Help! location

Photo: Martin Downham

W6
Wild matinees at The Greyhound

Nazareth, Blackfoot Sue and Free were just three of the hard-working outfits that played The Greyhound during its wild existence. The pub's music venue had a stage in one corner with little balconies before being knocked into one large room as the 1970s progressed and the bands and crowds became livelier. In 1974, The Jam got their chance to shine here as support to Thin Lizzy, and before long The Greyhound was becoming a favourite on the punk circuit. Local music fan John Daniel recalls some of the mayhem: "They held Saturday afternoon matinee shows, such as the UK Subs. At the time they were a band playing major venues. Hundreds of punks were outside, all pushing at the doors, until eventually the doors broke off. A police coach travelling to the Fulham FC match drove past and a punk threw a brick at the coach window, so we then had 50 annoyed police chasing us away".

LOCATION 246: the building still stands but The Greyhound disappeared long ago at 175 Fulham Palace Road, postcode W6 8QT

W9
BBC Maida Vale Studios

When the BBC broadcast live sessions by guest musicians, here is where they have frequently taken place down the years. Most famous of these were the Peel Sessions recorded for John Peel's radio shows from 1967 to 2004. Many broadcasts ended up as record releases, a trend kick-started by the Fab Four, whose 1994 release Live at the BBC gathered together 69 songs recorded for shows such as Top Gear and Saturday Club from 1963 to 1965. There's a small plaque on the wall in Studio 3 which marks Bing Crosby's last recording here on October 11, 1977, and electronic music buffs will know that it was at Maida Vale where the BBC Radiophonic Workshop conjured up the theme tune to Doctor Who.

LOCATION 247: Delaware Road, postcode W9 2LG

W5
British blues made in Ealing

When Keith Richards says that without The Ealing Club there "might have been nothing", you know its contribution to the development of British rhythm and blues and ultimately rock music must have been huge. Strictly speaking, The Rolling Stones guitarist was referring to two significant characters behind the club – Alexis Korner and Cyril Davies – but Richards' own contribution shouldn't be underestimated in the development of a new sound propagated in west London back in the early Sixties. With the encouragement and mentoring of Korner and Davies, the Stones were regular performers at The Ealing Club where they cut their teeth along with a tidal wave of other bands, led by the highly influential Blues Incorporated, then The Yardbirds, Manfred Mann, John Mayall, The Pretty Things, Rod Stewart and Long John Baldry. All that remains today is a plaque funded by Ealing music fans on the building where it all began on 17, March 1962 and a lively website that keeps 21st-century British blues fans informed and entertained. With the spirit of the club very much in mind, enthusiasts have staged an Ealing Blues Festival every year since 1987, which attracts up to 10,000 fans to Walpole Park.

LOCATIONS 248 and 249: The Ealing Club is now the Red Room nightclub, opposite Ealing Broadway station at 42a The Broadway, postcode W5 2NP. The annual summer Ealing Blues Festival is held at Walpole Park, Mattock Lane, postcode W5 5EQ

The very private entrance to a very private world: Freddie Mercury's Kensington home

Photo: David Roberts

W7
Freddie Mercury's final home

Garden Lodge, Kensington, is where Freddie Mercury lived, and then died, on Sunday November 24, 1991, leaving behind the woman who he referred to as "the love of my life", Mary Austin. The house and garden, still occupied by Austin, who was left the bulk of Freddie's vast fortune, has been little changed since the Queen frontman died tragically from AIDS aged just 45. When Mary made a promise to Freddie to keep secret the location of where his ashes were scattered or buried, rumours suggested that she may have chosen to bury them under a cherry tree in the Japanese garden of their mansion home. Without revealing the location, Mary revealed in an interview with The Daily Mail that she had secretly left Garden Lodge one day to accede to Freddie's final request that his remains be scattered or buried in the agreed place, where they would not be disturbed or defiled. She said: "One morning, I just sneaked out of the house with the urn. It had to be like a normal day so the staff wouldn't suspect anything – because staff gossip. They just cannot resist it. But nobody will ever know where he is buried because that was his wish."

LOCATION 250: a high wall surrounds Freddie and Mary's home at Garden Lodge, 1 Logan Place. Fortunately, respectful fans now visiting the place no longer spread graffiti on the walls, in accordance with the wishes of the local residents. Postcode W7 6QN

Greater London

W8
Dusty Springfield's Kensington home

The house in Aubrey Walk was where Dusty Springfield lived from 1968 until she relocated to the USA in 1972. Two years after the singer's death in 1999, a plaque was unveiled on the front wall in memory of what many music fans would regard as Britain's most talented and charismatic female singer. Following rebuilding work, a second plaque was unveiled in 2011 at a ceremony attended by Dusty's close friends Simon Bell, Robin Gibb, Madeline Bell and Dusty's secretary Pat Rhodes.

LOCATION 251: 38 Aubrey Walk, postcode W8 7JG. Status: private residence

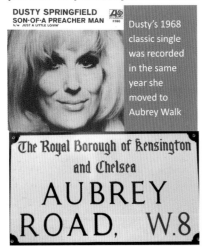

Dusty's 1968 classic single was recorded in the same year she moved to Aubrey Walk

W9
Duffy's 'Warwick Avenue'

When Duffy met up with co-writers Eg White and Jimmy Hogarth to finish work on 'Warwick Avenue', she had already completed most of the lyrics. At the time, the subject of the Rockferry album track was a place she had never visited, a name she plucked with no specific reason from a London Underground tube map. The resulting saturation radio play of the spring 2008 smash hit single means few can journey in or out of this station on the Bakerloo Line without recalling the waves of defiant emotion from Duffy's tearful back-of-a-taxi-cab video performance, now forever linked to this posh pop location.

Never having visited Warwick Avenue before writing the song, Duffy was quickly snapped there for this press shot

LOCATION 253: near Little Venice, Paddington, postcode W9 2PT

W8
Bill Wyman's Sticky Fingers

The American-style restaurant opened by owner Bill Wyman in 1989 was named after the Rolling Stones album released 18 years earlier. The walls of Sticky Fingers are crammed full of rock memorabilia from the bass guitarist's collection.

LOCATION 252: 1A Phillimore Gardens, Kensington, postcode W8 7QG

W12
Kinks collapse and Pete Townshend's White City

In 1985, The Who's Pete Townshend released White City: A Novel, which was actually an album about this area in west London where the White City Stadium (venue for London's 1908 Olympic Games) once stood. The demolition of the stadium was the subject of a song ('White City') written by Shane MacGowan for The Pogues' 1989 album Peace and Love. White City Stadium was also the venue for a less-than-together Ray Davies famously quitting The Kinks on stage back in 1973, shortly before collapsing and being rushed to hospital.

LOCATION 254: White City, postcode W12 7TS

W10
Westway Flyover: a kiss, Clash, Jam and a Blur...

The Westway flyover is hardly as evocative an inspiration to songwriters as Route 66 or the New Jersey Turnpike, but this stark, functional, elevated carriageway has not been lost on Britain's grittier bands. The Clash were, it would seem, most lyrically and photographically attached to it. The Westway gets a starring role in 'London's Burning', features in the title of the band's documentary movie Westway to the World, and is pictured on the cover of their 1999 live album From Here to Eternity. Others to share their fascination for the massive escape route out of the capital include The Jam, whose 1977 album cover This Is the Modern World pictures the trio looking all smart casual in the structure's shadows, Bloc Party, who use an aerial view on their 2007 album A Weekend in the

City, and Blur, The Pretty Things and Pete Doherty, who each weave the Westway into their song lyrics. A photograph shot here by Jimmy Page's daughter Scarlet was dominated by the apparently 'wasted' model Lucy Joplin, on the receiving end of a full-on kiss by a male model at a football pitch under the Westway, which provided the cover image for the Stereophonics' No.1 album Performance and Cocktails. More recently, in 2012, the aforementioned Blur released their evocative reunion single 'Under the Westway' – perhaps the most descriptive song so far written about this large expanse of concrete.

LOCATION 255: Westway flyover, postcode W10

TW1
The Beatles' Help! houses in Twickenham

Although indoor shots of the linked Beatles homes in Help! the movie were filmed at nearby Twickenham Film Studios, the external scenes showing the Fab Four entering each of their individual terraced houses were shot in Ailsa Avenue. For the record, Ringo Starr lived at No.5, John Lennon next door at No.7, Paul McCartney at No.9 and George Harrison at No.11.

LOCATION 256: 5, 7, 9 and 11 Ailsa Avenue, Twickenham, postcode TW1 1NF. Status: private residences

John Lennon outside his Help! home No.7 Ailsa Avenue, greets movie co-stars Leo McKern and Eleanor Bron

TW1
Strawbs launched from Twickenham

In 1963, a banjo, guitar and mandolin trio, Dave Cousins, Tony Hooper and Arthur Phillips, made their debut in a back-room folk club in Clapham. Without a name to call themselves, Cousins quickly rectified the problem by deciding on The Strawberry Hill Boys as band rehearsals were frequently based at Strawberry Hill in Twickenham. A couple of years passed before the band's name morphed with familiarity into The Strawbs, whose line-up and genre changes would deliver the massive hits 'Lay Down' and 'Part of the Union'.

LOCATION 257: Waldegrave Road, Twickenham, postcode TW1 4SX

Greater London

W14
Queen's Kensington mile

There are several key Kensington locations in the personal band history of Queen, all within a mile of each other. First, there's a crucially important pub. The Kensington was the Queen local where Freddie Mercury met Brian May and Roger Taylor and would often hold meetings to talk Queen business over a drink or two. It's also the place where Freddie met the woman he called "the love of my life", Mary Austin, with whom he shared the final years of his life across Kensington at Garden Lodge. Nearby is the first-floor building where Freddie and Roger both sold the latest fashions in the early Seventies at Kensington Market. The market building has been demolished but the flat once shared by all the group at times in Sinclair Road, Kensington, still stands. The Garden Lodge home of Freddie Mercury is close by but covered elsewhere in W7.

LOCATIONS 258, 259 and 260: the Kensington pub is at 54 Russell Gardens, postcode W14 8EZ. The Queen flat is at 36 Sinclair Road, postcode W14 0NH

Top: where Queen met and drank. The Kensington was also where Dr Feelgood enjoyed a lengthy residency at the height of pub-rock mania

Above: made in Kensington. The band's first single and track one from their debut album was not a hit, but success came quickly

Above: various members of Queen shared a first-floor flat here at No.37 Sinclair Road

TW1
Ringo stars at The Turk's Head

Twickenham pub The Turk's Head was the location used during a scene involving Ringo Starr in The Beatles' first movie, A Hard Day's Night, in 1964. A popular local with staff at nearby Twickenham Film Studios, the pub was also the venue for the traditional wrap party for A Hard Day's Night with cast and crew attending.

LOCATION 261: 28 Winchester Road, Twickenham, postcode TW1 1LF

TW9
Strawbs photocall at Osterley Park

According to the band's Dave Cousins, The Strawbs' first photo call was for a picture that eventually got used on the cover of their 2012 album Of a Time. The image is one of the band shot in front of Osterley House. The album was based on the original 1960s LP of songs that was presented to A&M but rejected.

LOCATION 262: Osterley House, in Osterley Park, is a National Trust property, less than two miles from Isleworth on Jersey Road, postcode TW7 4RB

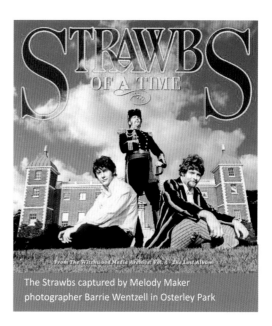

The Strawbs captured by Melody Maker photographer Barrie Wentzell in Osterley Park

TW9
Richmond's Crawdaddy clubs

In 1963, The Crawdaddy Club was made famous due to its increasingly popular resident band, The Rolling Stones. This crucial venue in the development of the Stones was perfectly situated for drawing large groups of R&B fans from all over London due to its location opposite Richmond station. This was where The Beatles ventured out to west London for their first opportunity to see the Stones play. The club was named after the Bo Diddley song 'Hey Crawdaddy' or 'Craw Dad', with which the Stones would close their performances. Once they had charted with 'Come On', their fan base began spilling out on to the streets of Richmond and they moved to larger venues, to be replaced at the Crawdaddy by The Yardbirds. The importance of this key club is underlined by the first major rock magazine in America naming itself Crawdaddy! in 1966. The popularity of the brand name saw a larger live venue take off at Richmond Athletic Ground, where the Richmond Athletic Association's clubhouse and grandstand area presented

Crawdaddy performances as R&B groups made way for future rock gods Led Zeppelin and Pink Floyd.

LOCATION 263: formerly the Station Hotel, now a bar and dining establishment called One Kew Road, 1 Kew Road, Richmond, postcode TW9 2NQ

"My **FAVOURITE PLACE**, looking back, was the Station Hotel, Richmond, just because everything really **KICKED OFF** from there **"**

KEITH RICHARDS reflects in his autobiography, Life

Greater London

TW1
A mecca for music fans at Eel Pie Island

Connected to the real world by a slender footbridge, Eel Pie Island is a fantasy island in the River Thames which drew musicians and fans in the Fifties and Sixties to the hotel, which sadly burned to the ground in 1971 and was demolished. The hotel, once described by Eric Clapton as a "creaky wooden gin palace", began promoting jazz in the Fifties at a time when the island was bridgeless and gig-goers would ferry across or even swim in some cases. Never the easiest of places to play, even in the Sixties, groups would have to manhandle their amps and instruments over the new, tiny pedestrian bridge. Acker Bilk, The Who, The Rolling Stones, The Yardbirds and Rod Stewart all played this unique location during their early careers. The isolated community still has a wind-chime resonance that, on a sunny summer's day, gives off a Laurel Canyon, hippie-style vibe. Although the island is liberally sprinkled with arts and crafts studios, the Eel Pie Recording Studios isn't one of them. The currently redundant Pete Townshend-owned recording facility is situated on the mainland on the Thames' south-west bank, downriver of Richmond Lock at The Boathouse, Ranelagh Drive.

LOCATION 264: cross the bridge to Eel Pie Island in the River Thames, at Twickenham, postcode TW1 3DY

Top: the Eel Pie Island Hotel. Middle: the dance hall in 1964. Bottom: a view of the fire-ravaged dance hall looking towards the stage

The Rolling Stones on Eel Pie Island: Brian Jones, Bill Wyman and Mick Jagger performing one of their sets during a weekly residency that began in April 1963

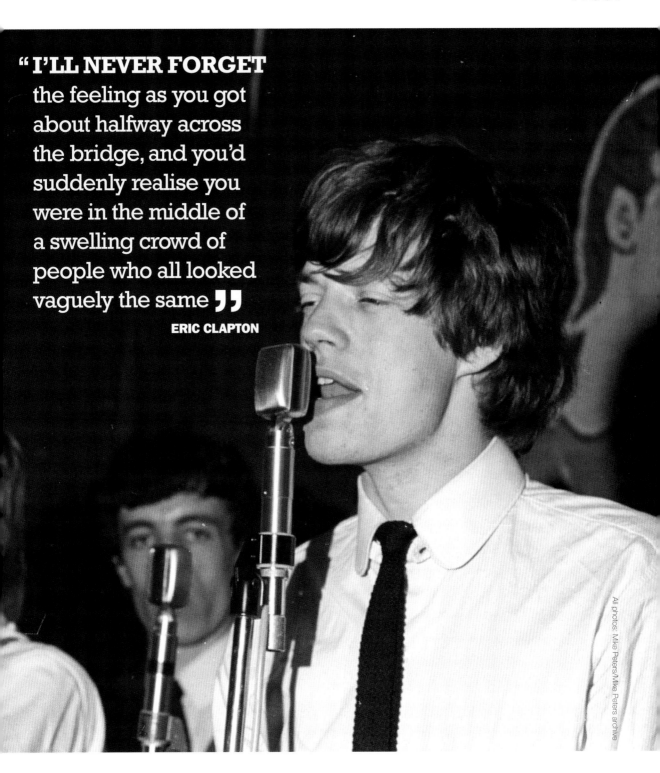

"**I'LL NEVER FORGET** the feeling as you got about halfway across the bridge, and you'd suddenly realise you were in the middle of a swelling crowd of people who all looked vaguely the same **"**

ERIC CLAPTON

David Gilmour's private floating studio is an Edwardian houseboat built in 1911 for theatre impresario Fred Karno. The recording facilities are used mostly for the exclusive use of Pink Floyd and Gilmour's solo albums

Photo: Peter Tarleton

TW12
David Gilmour's Astoria houseboat

Moored on the River Thames at Hampton, the Astoria is a palatial houseboat owned by Pink Floyd's David Gilmour since 1986 and converted for use as a recording studio. Ninety-foot long in total, the studio control room is surprisingly large at 30 ft x 20 ft considering the restrictions of the water-based craft, which once also accommodated a 90-piece concert orchestra on deck. The Pink Floyd guitarist thought no more about the craft until a while later. "I was in the dentist waiting room and I picked up a Country Life [magazine] and there it was for sale in this Country Life by pure coincidence," recalled Gilmour. "So I rang them up and came down and had a look and bought it. I didn't even think about putting a studio in it at first. It was just very, very beautiful, a magical place."

LOCATION 265: moored on the River Thames at Hampton Court Road, postcode TW12 2EN

TW10
Ian Dury's solar-powered musical bench

Donated by his family, Ian Dury's extraordinary memorial is tucked away in a quiet garden in Richmond Park. On the face of it, an inscribed park bench in peaceful Poet's Corner would seem an inappropriate way to remember one of pop music's larger-than-life characters. Closer inspection reveals a large 'Reasons to be Cheerful' carved inscription, but it's the solar-powered armrests that make the bench special. By plugging in any standard set of headphones, visitors can enjoy a number of Dury's tracks and hear the great man's Desert Island Discs BBC radio interview, broadcast four years before his death in

Photo: David Roberts

2000. The bench's location in Richmond Park marks a favourite place that Dury often visited during his life.

"My luxury would be a working item... an 8-track home recording studio with a solar panel... that would keep me happy forever." Ian Dury, who would have approved of his solar-powered memorial, chooses his luxury item on Desert Island Discs.

LOCATION 266: Poet's Corner, near Pembroke Lodge, Richmond Park, postcode TW10

TW10
Two Ronnies at The Wick

When advertised for sale in 1971, The Wick came complete with its own separate cottage, gypsy caravan and gardens sloping down to the River Thames. Currently owned by Pete Townshend, The Wick has 'previous' in rock star home ownership terms. Originally the property of Ronnie Wood, the guitarist shared the bank-busting purchase, persuading fellow Faces mate Ronnie Lane to buy the cottage at the bottom of the garden. The Wick is where Wood lived and rehearsed his 1974 solo album I've Got My Own Album to Do in the house's purpose-built basement studio. Mick Jagger, Keith Richards, Mick Taylor, George Harrison, Ian McLagan and Rod Stewart all made musical contributions at the Wick studio and no doubt enjoyed a frame or two on Ronnie's snooker table, once owned by the sport's legendary champion Joe Davis.

LOCATION 267: Richmond Hill, Richmond, postcode TW10 6RN. Status: private residence

"It's COMMANDING ASPECT could equal any in Europe, and has been the subject of many an artist's painting 🙙

RONNIE WOOD
guitarist and artist waxes lyrical about the Wick in his autobiography, Ronnie

Built in 1775, The Wick has stunning views of the River Thames and was purchased for £140,000 in 1971 by Ronnie Wood from the actor Sir John Mills

Greater London

TW13
Freddie Mercury's Feltham star

Born in Zanzibar, the less exotic Feltham was where the boy who became Freddie Mercury first made his home in the UK, a fact honoured by the unveiling of a large decorative plaque in November 2009. Freddie's fellow Queen band member Brian May, who also grew up in Feltham, joined Freddie's mother Jer Bulsara to pay tribute to the rock legend, who died in 1991, at the unveiling of the Hollywood-style star imbedded in the pavement of

the Centre shopping piazza. More than 2,000 of the singer's fans, together with the local Mayor and Queen tribute band Mercury attended the ceremony. The four years at his family home in Feltham from 1964 to 1968 coincided with his discovery and passion for music, shared with local boy Brian May, who recalled often visiting Freddie at his Gladstone Avenue home."I grew up in Walsham Avenue about 200 yards from where [Freddie] lived but we never met until later", May said of his teenage friend." Freddie invited me around to his house and we sat listening to Jimi Hendrix."

LOCATION 268: The Centre, Feltham, postcode TW13 4GU

Photo: David Roberts

Freddie Mercury's huge pavement star in Feltham

Born in WEST LONDON

Lily Allen (b. 2 May 1985, Hammersmith)
Adam Ant (b. 3 Nov 1954, Marylebone)
Simon Bartholomew, guitar, The Brand New Heavies (b. 16 Oct 1965, Ealing)
Betty Boo (b. 6 Mar 1970, Kensington)
Keisha Buchanan, Sugababes (b. 30 Sep 1984, Westminster)
Jean-Jacques Burnel, bass, The Stranglers (b. 21 Feb 1952, Notting Hill)
Tony Butler, bass, Big Country (b. 13 Feb 1957, Shepherd's Bush)
Phil Collins (b. 30 Jan 1951, Chiswick)
Paul Cook, drums, Sex Pistols (b. 20 Jul 1956, Hammersmith)
Elvis Costello (b. 25 Aug 1954, Paddington)
Mikey Craig, bass, Culture Club (b. 15 Feb 1960, Hammersmith)
Roger Daltrey (b. 1 Mar 1944, Hammersmith)
Adam Devlin, guitar, The Bluetones (b. 17 Sep 1969, Hounslow)
Eliza Doolittle (b. Aliza Caird, 15 Apr 1988, Westminster)
John 'Rhino' Edwards, bass, Status Quo (b. 9 May 1953, Chiswick)
John Entwistle, bass/vocals, The Who (b. 9 Oct 1944, Chiswick, d. 27 Jun 2000)
Adam Faith (b. 23 Jun 1940, Acton, d. 8 Mar 2003)
Andy Fraser, bass, Free (b. 3 Jul 1952, Paddington)
Justine Frischmann, vocals/guitar, Elastica (b. 16 Sep 1969, Twickenham)
Ian Gillan, vocals, Deep Purple (b. 19 Aug 1945, Hounslow)
Charlotte Hatherley, guitar, Ash/solo (b. 20 Jun 1979, Chiswick)
Steve Jones, guitar, Sex Pistols (b. 3 Sep 1955, Shepherd's Bush)
John "Speedy" Keen, Thunderclap Newman (b. 29 Mar 1945, Ealing, d. 12 Mar 2002)
Bob Kerr, Bonzo Dog Doo-Dah Band (b. 14 Feb 1940, Kensington)
Jan Kincaid, drums/keyboards, The Brand New Heavies (b. 17 May 1966, Ealing)

Andrew Levy, bass, The Brand New Heavies (b. 20 Jul 1966, Ealing)
Ian McLagan, keyboards, The Small Faces/The Faces (b. 12 May 1945, Hounslow)
John McVie, bass, Fleetwood Mac (b. 26 Nov 1945, Ealing)
Glen Matlock, bass, Sex Pistols (b. 27 Aug 1956, Paddington)
Brian May (b. 19 Jul 1947, Hampton)
Crispian Mills, vocals, Kula Shaker (b. 18 Jan 1973, Hammersmith)
Mark Morriss, vocals, The Bluetones (b. 18 Oct 1971, Hounslow)
Scott Morriss, bass, The Bluetones (b. 10 Oct 1973, Hounslow)
Ian Mosley, drums, Marillion (b. 16 Jun 1953, Paddington)
Annie Nightingale, broadcaster (b. 1 Apr 1942, Osterley)
Gary Numan (b. 8 Mar 1958, Hammersmith)
Andrew Loog Oldham, manager (b. 29 Jan 1944, Paddington)
David O'List, guitar, The Attack/The Nice (b. 13 Dec 1948, Chiswick)
Jimmy Page (b. 9 Jan 1944, Heston)
Andrew Ranken, drums, The Pogues (b. 13 Nov 1953, Ladbroke Grove)
Keith Relf, vocals/harmonica, The Yardbirds (b. 22 Mar 1943, Richmond, d. 14 May 1976)
John Renbourn, guitar, Pentangle (b. 8 Aug 1944, Marylebone)
Paul Samwell-Smith, bass, The Yardbirds (b. 8 May 1943, Richmond)
Seal (Seal Henry Samuel) (b. 19 Feb 1963, Paddington)
Labi Siffre (b. 25 Jun 1945, Hammersmith)
Heather Small, vocals, M People (b. 20 Jan 1965, Ladbroke Grove)
Roger Ruskin Spear, multi-instrumentalist, Bonzo Dog Doo-Dah Band (b. 29 Jun 1943, Hammersmith)
Richard Thompson, vocals, Fairport Convention (b. 3 Apr 1949, Notting Hill)
Daniel Woodgate, drums, Madness (b. 19 Oct 1960, Maida Vale)

NW1
The London Beatles Store

An ideal place to stock up on Beatles memorabilia, the London Beatles Store has a superb selection of Fab Four merchandise, ranging from badges and posters for a few pounds to collectable figurines and limited editions for several hundred pounds.

LOCATION 269: a short walk north up Baker Street from Baker Street tube station at 231/233 Baker Street, London, NW1 6XE

NW1
The Beatles are waxed, wedded and sentenced

The imposing Marylebone Register Office is where Paul McCartney married Linda Eastman in March 1969, breaking the hearts of numerous Beatlemaniacs who still thought, after nearly 10 years, they might just be 'in with a chance' with the last remaining Beatle bachelor. Ringo Starr married Bond girl Barbara Bach at the same venue in 1981, with his two surviving bandmates as guests of honour. Meanwhile, a short distance away at Marylebone Magistrates Court in November 1968, John Lennon pleaded guilty to unauthorised drugs possession. A short walk east along Marylebone Road will take you to Madame Tussauds, where the four wax figures of The Beatles are displayed, depicting them in happier days.

LOCATION 270: Marylebone Road, postcode NW1 5PT

Photo: David Roberts

NW1
Dublin Castle break for the 'Nutty Boys'

Claims to fame for this busy pub include the setting for Coldplay's first gig, the location for Madness video 'My Girl', and career kick-starts for Travis and a number of others who made their first tentative steps here courtesy of the much-missed, landlord Alo Conlon, who turned the pub into a music venue in 1979. The spiritual home of local 'Nutty Boys' Madness in their early days, the hundreds of acts who have graced the 150-capacity Dublin Castle include The Specials, Arctic Monkeys and Babyshambles.

LOCATION 271: 94 Parkway, Camden, postcode NW1 7AN

A proper pub on the outside, The Dublin Castle wears its music history well inside, with posters and pictures reminding every punter of its colourful past

"He asked us what we **PLAYED** and we said country and western, and jazz – we thought that would be the thing to say when going... for a gig at an **IRISH PUB** "

SUGGS
reveals how he blagged a crucial early break for Madness with Alo Conlon

Greater London

Inside and outside the magnificent Roundhouse which, these days, is open for music, theatre, cinema, conferences and creative mentoring for 11-25 year-olds, as part of the Roundhouse Trust scheme

"I think that was one of the BEST CONCERTS I've ever done"

JIM MORRISON rates a Roundhouse performance fronting The Doors in 1968

NW1
Rock history made at the Roundhouse

Once a gin-barrel storehouse and 19th-century railway engine shed and turntable, this circular structure first became a music venue when hosting an all-night rave featuring Pink Floyd and Soft Machine to celebrate the launch of underground newspaper The International Times on October 14, 1966. When, in the following spring, the UFO club moved out of its Tottenham Court Road basement, the Roundhouse seemed like a sensible new venue, until a few months there saw the club continually make a loss and fold. But by this point the Roundhouse had built a name as a music venue and in the autumn of 1968 The Doors and Jefferson Airplane played

a double-billed gig under the Middle Earth club banner. Making an even bigger mark on British music history was the July 4, 1976 performances by American prototype punks the Ramones and The Flamin' Groovies. The insolent stage presence, a high-speed 30-minute set and Dee Dee Ramone spurting blood from a cut finger all over his white Fender Precision bass left an instant impression that something shocking was happening. The Ramones' appearance accidentally prompted the beginning of a rethink in rock values that would trigger a backlash against established rock superstars and lay the foundations of the UK punk movement. Although closed as a music

venue in 1983, the Roundhouse returned to the live music scene again in 2006. Revamped but still retaining the best of what Sixties UFO club organiser Joe Boyd described as a "magnificently decaying brick hulk", the Roundhouse has recently rocked its 3,000-capacity foundations to memorable gigs by Paul McCartney, Morrissey and Robbie Williams. Talking Heads founder David Byrne literally played the building when his innovative 2009 project invited fans to make music from a pump organ wired up to the Roundhouse's pillars, pipes and beams.

LOCATION 272: Chalk Farm Road, postcode NW1 8EH

Greater London

NW1
Faithless honoured at the Jazz Café

Originally called Camden's Jazz Café this was exclusively a jazz venue until MAMA & Company took over the former bank building, and now jazz, soul, funk, dance, hip hop and pretty much anything else goes these days. The Jazz Café was where London dance music hit-makers Faithless gained their big break in 1996, which led in 2012 to a special ceremony at the place to honour that fact. In recognition of the group's first full live gig at the Jazz Café, a PRS for Music heritage plaque was unveiled in front of Faithless, media, local government and key music industry figures, followed by a DJ set from Maxi Jazz inside the venue.

LOCATION 273: 5 Parkway, Camden, London NW1 7PG

Photos: Warren King and David Roberts

Sister Bliss and Maxi Jazz representing Faithless at the unveiling of the Jazz Café plaque, and Maxi Jazz's DJ set closes the proceedings

NW1
'Rhythm 'n' booze' at Dingwalls

Situated in the heart of the vibrant atmosphere at Camden Lock Market, Dingwalls has been a music venue since 1973. Named after the Victorian building's original owner, you can still see timber-yard owner T.E. Dingwall's name painted on the outside wall. The large shed-like building began its new life as a live music venue during the advent of glam-rock and flourished as a punk hotspot when The Ramones played there in 1976, watched,

significantly, by impressionable members of the recently formed but still little-known bands The Clash, Sex Pistols and The Damned. Advertised as purveyors of 'Rhythm 'n' Booze' in the Eighties, various artists including Blondie, The Doors, Dr Feelgood and the Foo Fighters have performed at this canal-side music mecca.

LOCATION 274: Middle Yard, Camden Lock, postcode NW1 8AB

NW1
The Electric Ballroom

The former Carousel Ballroom got a new name and a new purpose in 1978 when live music took centre stage at the Electric Ballroom on Camden High Street. Dizzee Rascal, Stereophonics, Paolo Nutini and Public Image Ltd have been recent additions to a gig list that has included U2, Wings, Oasis and Red Hot Chili Peppers down the years. The Electric Ballroom was also once a convenient rehearsal space for new punk bands connected to neighbouring Chiswick Records. Others using the facility in this way were The Clash and Frank Zappa.

As popular as ever, the venue has added themed club nights to the 1,100-capacity venue on two levels. However, the Ballroom's close proximity to Camden Town tube station is a blessing and a curse. Redevelopment plans around the station and the threat of a compulsory purchase order were an issue in 2003, but fortunately the Ballroom soldiers on as that rare thing these days, a great historic music venue which still has a future.

LOCATION 275: 184 Camden High Street, postcode NW1 8QP

STRAIGHT MUSIC PRESENTS

THE SPECIALS
MADNESS
DEXY'S MIDNIGHT RUNNERS
THE SELECTOR

ELECTRIC BALLROOM
184 CAMDEN HIGH ST. NW1 (NEAREST TUBE CAMDEN TOWN)
SATURDAY 21st JULY at 7·30
TICKETS £2·00 (INC.VAT) ADVANCE ELECTRIC BALLROOM BOX OFFICE. TEL: 485 9006
LONDON THEATRE BOOKINGS, SHAFTESBURY AVE., TEL: 439 3371; PREMIER BOX OFFICE, TEL: 240 2245,
OR ROCK ON RECORDS, 3 KENTISH TOWN RD., NW1, TEL: 485 5088

A stage-eye view of the Electric Ballroom and a poster for what looks like one hell of a night's entertainment at No.184 Camden High Street

Greater London

NW1
Bob Dylan's Camden

Reportedly tempted to buy a house in north London to be near his friend, musician and producer Dave Stewart, Bob Dylan has a soft spot for the environs of Camden, a fact underlined by Stewart's video to accompany Dylan's World Gone Wrong album. The 1993 film for the album's stand-out track, 'Blood in My Eyes', followed the top-hatted Dylan as he mingled with the locals on the streets and sat at a table in, what was at the time, the Fluke's Cradle café. The cover of the album pictures Dylan at Fluke's Cradle, sitting below a painting by Irish artist Peter Gallagher, which received an enormous boost in value as a result of its inclusion.

LOCATION 276: the Fluke's Cradle café is now the Max Orient restaurant at 275 Camden High Street, postcode NW1 8QS

Dylan sits below Peter Gallagher's L'Etranger, the subject of a legal wrangle when the painting was featured in this album cover shot at Fluke's Cradle

NW1
Rock celebrity sanctuary at The Hawley Arms

Famous as the pub that Razorlight and Pete Doherty frequent, and a favourite location of the late Amy Winehouse, the Hawley Arms was very nearly demolished as a result of the 2008 Camden Market fire. An eclectic schedule of music takes place in the first-floor bar, but it's the music-themed wall decorations, jukebox and positive feel of a place that has survived some tough times that make this pub so special.

LOCATION 277: near Camden Market at 2 Castlehaven Road, postcode NW1 8QU

NW3
Supernova Heights

When your second album threatens to become the biggest-selling UK release since The Beatles' Sgt Pepper's Lonely Hearts Club Band, you are entitled to name your new gaff to reflect your elevation to rock superstardom. The track 'Champagne Supernova' from (What's the Story) Morning Glory? was Noel Gallagher's inspiration for decoratively naming his home Supernova Heights. The Oasis guitarist and songwriter left Primrose Hill and moved to the country in 1999.

LOCATION 278: 9 Steele's Road, Belsize Park, postcode NW3 4SE. Status: private residence

NW3
Chalk Farm Madness

The attractive Edwardian frontage of Chalk Farm tube station was actually a late replacement location for the cover shoot of the Madness album Absolutely in 1980. The band were to have assembled outside Camden station, but with too many pedestrians and cars about Madness and their photographer headed half-a-mile north-west to the quieter Chalk Farm station.

LOCATION 279: Adelaide Road, postcode NW3 2BP

NW5
Bull and Gate break for Coldplay

The future of the Bull and Gate pub may be uncertain, but you can't erase its important history in hosting some of rock's biggest names' early steps to stardom. Blur, Coldplay, Keane and Manic Street Preachers all have a lot to thank this sometimes unkindly labelled top "toilet circuit" venue. Coldplay were Bull and Gate regulars in 1999, and it was here where one particular gig prompted a rave review in NME that the band all agree changed their lives forever.

LOCATION 280: no longer the music venue of old but still a pub, at 389 Kentish Town Road, NW5 2TJ

NW3
Madness on Primrose Hill

Madness LP The Rise & Fall (1982) features an almost Penny Lane-like tour on the track 'Primrose Hill'. The cover photograph for this, their fifth hit album, is a panoramic view of London from Primrose Hill, with the band typically engaged in a variety of whacky activities.

LOCATION 282: postcode NW3

NW5
Tally Ho! It's pub-rock

The precise point at which a new music genre takes off is naturally impossible to pin down. But in the case of pub rock it was very much a location-associated accidental birth. On May 3, 1971, the Tally Ho pub's Sunday lunchtime jazz combo were about to disappoint the regulars with a no-show when the landlord enlisted the help of local band Eggs Over Easy to fill the slot. Formed by New Yorkers Austin de Lone and Jack O'Hara, the band were conveniently billeted a short stroll way at 10 Alma Street. A pub residency flourished, and once they eschewed the jazz covers and began trotting out their own three- or four-hour sets of country-rock, pub-rock was up and running, with the Tally Ho geographically at the centre of the movement.

LOCATION 281: the Tally Ho at 9 Fortess Road was reduced to a pile of rubble for redevelopment in 2006. No.10 Alma Street, postcode NW5 3DJ

NW5
Jefferson Airplane at Parliament Hill Fields

Vaguely advertised, heavily rained upon, and with an anti-hippie, hostile element amongst the crowd, a nevertheless "happy to be here" Jefferson Airplane played the first of a series of free festivals at Parliament Hill Fields. This Camden Council initiative on September 4, 1968 saw Fairport Convention also perform on the tiny bandstand in front of a crowd estimated in the low hundreds. The following May brought three more Camden Fringe free festivals at the bandstand, headlined by Pink Floyd, Procol Harum and Fleetwood Mac.

LOCATION 283: Highgate Road, Hampstead, postcode NW5 1QR

Jefferson Airplane at Parliament Hill Fields

Photo: Brian Richards

Greater London

NW5
Kinks on 'Dead End Street'

In days of old when the word 'video' hadn't entered common vocabulary, beat groups (as they were called in the mid-Sixties) only had one way to visually promote each new single. Miming to the records on TV pop shows was all well and good, but The Kinks wanted more. Their ground-breaking mini movie to promote 1966 release 'Dead End Street' saw the band dressed as undertakers manhandling a coffin (carrying their roadie) up, down and inside No.4 Little Green Street. Reminiscent of an old silent black and white movie, the band were also filmed down the adjacent pedestrian railway tunnel. Chosen for its Dickensian feel back then, Little Green Street thankfully retains all its olde worlde cobbled charm to this day, although residents are up in arms about rumoured redevelopment plans. Although not filmed on Little Green Street, the Oasis video accompanying the band's 2005 chart-topping single 'The Importance of Being Idle' tips an undertaker's hat in the direction of The Kinks' early attempt at a mini kitchen-sink drama. "I was so pleased to see, a few months ago, that none of it had changed, including the little tunnel and one of the actual houses where we made the music video" said Dave Davies of The Kinks, on a visit to Little Green Street in 2007.

LOCATION 284: a 10-minute walk from Tufnell Park tube station, Little Green Street, postcode NW5 1BL

Little Green Street was the location for the 'Dead End Street' Kinks promo film, of which the BBC allegedly disapproved, suggesting the undertaker theme was in bad taste

Photos: David Roberts

NW8
Scouse rock legends at home in St John's Wood

No.7 Cavendish Avenue has been owned by Paul McCartney since 1966. A conveniently short stroll from Abbey Road, this provided relatively easy access for fans to get close to the only London-based Beatle during the mid-Sixties, whereas John, George and Ringo had retreated to secluded private outer-London estates in Esher and Weybridge. Patient fans were treated to regular glimpses of their idol, with some exceptionally lucky ones witnessing Paul perched on a windowsill late one evening premiering his new song, 'Blackbird'. The garden featured a unique domed sun house where The Beatles, as part of a day-long photo session that took them from London's Docklands to St John's Wood, assembled for a few final shots, along with Paul's sheepdog, Martha. Across the road, marked by a blue plaque, is the former home of Paul's neighbour and fellow Scouser Billy Fury.

LOCATIONS 285 and 286: 7 Cavendish Avenue (McCartney) and 1 Cavendish Avenue (Billy Fury), St John's Wood, postcode NW8 9JE. Status: private residences

NW6
'Rock Island Line' at Broadhurst Gardens

The Decca recording studios in West Hampstead created some of Britain's most historically vital music moments. Not so vital for The Beatles, but nevertheless worthy of note, is the fact that these studios were the first port of call in London on the Fab Four's rise to becoming the greatest band in popular music history, a rise that would cause Decca no little embarrassment after they decided to pass on the opportunity to sign them following the band's demo-session audition at Broadhurst Gardens on New Year's Day 1962. Acts who did end up passing the audition for Decca in the early Sixties included The Rolling Stones, Fleetwood Mac and John Mayall's Bluesbreakers, but the studios' seminal moment came with a recording by Lonnie Donegan several years earlier on July 13, 1954. Recorded in the still standing Studio 2, his revved-up version of an old American country-blues song by Lead Belly would prove to be a skiffle classic and just what the new breed of British teenagers had been waiting for. Evidence suggests that Decca's release of 'Rock Island Line' was a major jolt forward in British popular music's development into a new, independent youth movement.

LOCATION 287: the building is currently the rehearsal space for the English National Opera at 165 Broadhurst Gardens, West Hampstead, postcode NW6 3AX

The Broadhurst Gardens building still contains the walls, if not the fixtures and fittings, to Studio 2. Inset: the Decca release recorded at Broadhurst Gardens that helped kick-start British rock

Photo: David Roberts

NW6
Klooks Kleek and Moonlight at The Railway Hotel

Aside from being around the corner from the Decca recording studios and a handy place to relax after a hard day's recording, The Railway Hotel was the home of R&B club Klooks Kleek. The club catered for an R&B audience entertained by John Mayall, Graham Bond, Georgie Fame and their various combos. Encouraged by a growing demand for British blues, the club's upstairs room (with no stage) helped develop lengthy careers for Eric Clapton, The Rolling Stones, Peter Green, Jethro Tull, Ten Years After and Cream. The club closed in 1970, only to re-open again soon after to support a new wave of young live performers including The Jam, The Cure and Uriah Heep, at what was then called The Moonlight Club.

LOCATION 288: The Railway Hotel or, more recently, Railway Tavern, 100 West End Lane, postcode NW6 2LU

Photo: David Roberts

The West End Lane location at The Railway Hotel for what was once the Klooks Kleek club

Greater London

The plaque honouring Mickie Most and the extensive RAK Studios building (a former Victorian school house) on Charlbert Street, where everyone from Adele to Radiohead have recorded

NW8
RAK Studios and Mickie Most's plaque

In 1969, after a highly successful career as a pop star in South Africa, Hampshire-born producer and music entrepreneur Mickie Most created his own RAK record label, and from 1976 recorded a conveyor belt of hit records from the RAK recording studios in St John's Wood. Things got off to a shaky start. The studios' opening coincided with electricity power cuts – a common occurrence in 1970s Britain. An incredulous American producer overseeing the first ever recordings at RAK with clients Gallagher & Lyle eventually got through the interruptions before a steady stream of rock legends – Pink Floyd, The Who, The Moody Blues – worked and played here. Never one to be hindered by schedules, The Who's Keith Moon insisted he didn't want to see any clocks inside RAK and quite literally didn't know what time of day it was when the band recorded their Who Are You album with Glyn Johns at the helm. Most, who died aged 64 in 2003, is remembered for RAK pop classics by Mud, Racey, Suzi Quatro, Kim Wilde, Hot Chocolate, Steve Harley and CCS and, pre-RAK, the production credit on the astonishing recording of 'The House of the Rising Sun' by The Animals. The studio carries a blue plaque to remember the man next to the front entrance.

LOCATION 289: private studios, 42-48 Charlbert Street, St John's Wood, postcode NW8 7BU

NW10
Cream jam in Ginger's front room

In 1966, bass player Jack Bruce and guitarist Eric Clapton arrived at Ginger Baker's north London house to rehearse together for the first time. The blues jam that day in Baker's small front room was so successful that the trio decided they were on to something and Cream was born. The Braemar Avenue property became a hive of band activity and a silk-screen press set-up in Ginger's garden shed was used to run off the band's first posters.

LOCATION 290: 154 Braemar Avenue, off the A4088, south-west of Brent Reservoir, postcode NW10 0DS

> "It was very obvious we had **SOMETHING UNIQUE**"
>
> **JACK BRUCE** on that first rehearsal at Ginger Baker's house

Main picture: Steve Levine at the Red Bus Studios' console in Studio One. Inset: the Red Bus tour, featuring an assortment of new talent including Geordie, gets ready to depart from the company's previous base in Soho

NW8
On the road and in the studio with Red Bus

A friendly vibe and a sound quality considered to be up there with the world's best is what has attracted top recording artists to Red Bus Studios since it began business in 1978. Culture Club were so impressed they made the place their recording base for three years in the early Eighties. The studio flourished at a time when synths and drum machines were the must-have addition to new recordings, even for established legends like The Beach Boys, who dropped by to record material for their 1985 eponymous album at Red Bus, with Steve Levine at the production helm. The business had originally been built on the success of Red Bus founders Eliot Cohen, Ellis Elias and Leslie Grade's management and promotion of 70s artists including Mungo Jerry. One of Cohen's ground-breaking ideas saw bands promoted around the country as part of an innovative tour in a double-decker red bus, affording great exposure to Red Bus acts, while college and university students paid the affordable entry price of 1 pence for each gig. The trio's recording business proved to be equally successful and reached a peak with the production of Spandau Ballet tracks such as 'Gold' and 'Lifeline' for the band's huge No.1 album True in 1982. "When Culture Club recorded their first major No.1 multi-million-seller 'Do You Really Want to Hurt Me,' Red Bus Studios had 500 kids waiting outside the studio on a permanent basis to see Boy George", recalled Eliot Cohen.

LOCATION 291: a short walk north-west of Marylebone Station, 34 Salisbury Street, postcode NW8 8QE

Greater London

NW8
The Abbey Road Studios and world-famous zebra crossing

The most famous zebra crossing in the world is featured on The Beatles' Abbey Road album cover and the image is one of only six photographs taken on August 8, 1969 by photographer Iain Macmillan. It's almost impossible to replicate the photograph yourself without teetering atop a stepladder placed in the middle of the road. Given the sheer volume of traffic in the area, this is not recommended. A few metres from the zebra crossing is the recording home of The Beatles, where most – but not all – of their 200-plus songs were recorded under the guidance of producer and so-called fifth Beatle George Martin. Favouring Studio 2, The Beatles went from straight rock 'n' rollers, recording their first album in a day, through to the epic Sgt Pepper's Lonely Hearts Club Band album. During the final splintered days, The Beatles could be found solo in other studios, or even corridors, within Abbey Road, recording their separate parts for later releases such as the White Album. But The Beatles' reliance on the studios is just one chapter of the Abbey Road story's impact on British popular music. Glenn Miller made his final recording here in 1944 and Cliff Richard and The Drifters' sensational 'Move It!' (1958), Pink Floyd's psychedelic masterpiece The Piper at the Gates of Dawn (1967), Kate Bush's first No.1 album Never for Ever (1980) and Radiohead's transatlantic chart-topper Kid A (2000) were all created in this white, rather plain Georgian townhouse.

LOCATIONS 292 and 293: 3 Abbey Road, St John's Wood, postcode NW8 9AY. Status: private studios. The zebra crossing is outside the studios

Above: The studio entrance, complete with the ever present messages from the hordes of tourists who visit every day

Right: One of the UK's biggest tourist attractions as a result of one hastily concocted Beatles album cover shoot. The most photographed zebra crossing in the world was given Grade II-listed status in 2010

Greater London

★ "SENSATIONAL - WEIRD!" *Daily Sketch.*

" *Must be one of the trendsetting groups of 1965".* Melody Maker.
" *The Who deserve a big success!"* Record Mirror.

★ *Latest Disc " I Can't Explain" Fast entering the charts in the States*
In the top 10 in Watford & Harrow area!

BACK BY POPULAR DEMAND !

THE WHO !

THIS SUNDAY, FEB 14th
Railway Hotel Harrow & Wealdstone

HA3
A Who legacy in Harrow and Wealdstone

The Who's 1971 album Meaty Beaty Big and Bouncy nicely rounded up their hits to that point, with the cover artwork reflecting a pictorial history from the band's beginnings. Photos appearing on the inside of the gatefold package depict a key venue in their rise to fame, The Railway Hotel. Destroyed in a fire in 2002 and sadly no longer standing, this is where The Who became a regular draw for their loyal mod fan base from 1964 and where Pete Townshend began his famously destructive on-stage guitar-smashing activities. The relatively new development of flats on the old Railway Hotel site have been fittingly named after the band's drummer and vocalist. Keith Moon House and Roger Daltrey House serve as a constant reminder of the incredibly exciting music and mayhem created in this otherwise quiet suburban corner of north-west London.

LOCATION 294: a plaque marking the spot "where The Who made rock history" at the site of the old Railway Hotel appears to have been removed, but Keith Moon House and Roger Daltrey House are at least some kind of memorial next to the station, High Street, postcode HA3 5BP

HA8
The Edgware Amy Winehouse memorial

Amy Winehouse, who died in 2011 aged just 27, was cremated at Golders Green Crematorium before her ashes were buried at the Edgwarebury Cemetery, in a plot next to her grandmother Cynthia Levy. Here she shares a black headstone with a pink inscription of a songbird with her grandmother, at a spot much visited by her fans judging by the floral tributes.

LOCATION 295: between the A41 and M1 north of Edgware, Edgwarebury Lane, postcode HA8 8QP

HA5 / HA6
Elton's childhood homes

Reginald Dwight's early years, right up until his initial success as singer-songwriter Elton John, were spent here in this corner of north-west London. His first childhood home was at 55 Pinner Hill Road, where he lived with his grandparents Fred and Ivy Harris, before moving a short distance to 111 Potter Street and then to Flat 3A at Frome Court, on Pinner Road, where he spent his teenage years (1962-1971) with his mother and stepfather, Fred Fairbrother. The Northwood Hills hotel was the place where he made his performance debut as a 15-year-old in 1962. Paid £25 a week, his repertoire back then extended little further than Jim Reeves and Ray Charles covers. Still hosting live music but now operating as modern Indian sports club Namaste Lounge, the building proudly displays a PRS for music plaque to mark Reggie's Thursday-through-to-Sunday evening performances that began a career spanning six decades (and counting) as Elton John.

LOCATIONS 296, 297, 298 and 299: 55 Pinner Hill Road, Pinner, postcode HA5 1LD; 111 Potter Street, Northwood, postcode HA6 1QH; Frome Court, Pinner Road, postcode HA6 1QP; and former Northwood Hills hotel is at 66 Joel Street, Northwood Hills, postcode HA6 1LL. There's a handy 'Pinner Walks' website if you want more details on how to walk 'in the footsteps of Sir Elton'

Reg Dwight at 111 Potter Street, Pinner in a family snap included on the inside cover of Elton John's 1973 album, Don't Shoot Me, I'm Only the Piano Player

Photo: DJM Records

HA9
Wembley hosts Live Aid

A common location for the world's largest bands to strut their stuff these days, but it wasn't always so. Stadium rock at the home of English football kicked off in the early Seventies when a half-filled stadium hosted a rock 'n' roll revival concert. By 1974, the old ground was packed to capacity when 72,000 attended the final date for Crosby, Stills, Nash & Young, after what had been a gruelling stadium tour of the USA. This one-off British appearance saw the supergroup top a bill also featuring The Band and Joni Mitchell. So successful was the day that summer concerts became something of a fixture with Elton John, the Eagles and The Beach Boys entertaining fans on the hallowed turf next. By 1985, there was no other

British venue capable of hosting the most publicised outdoor music event since Woodstock and the combination of Wembley and a perfect sun-drenched summer's day did Live Aid proud. The newly built stadium, complete with spectacular arch, replaced the old Wembley with its twin towers in 2007 and continues to host some of the world's biggest music events. For indoor concerts requiring a more modest capacity there's Wembley Arena. Built in just six months as a swimming pool for the 1934 Empire Games, hence the original name Empire Pool, this building in the shadow of Wembley Stadium became London's 12,000-capacity indoor concert venue in 1978. The renamed Wembley Arena attracted mega draws the Eagles, Madonna and Bruce Springsteen and was the subject of a major 2006 revamp by LiveNation.

LOCATIONS 300 and 301: Wembley Stadium is Empire Way, postcode HA9 0WS, and Wembley Arena is next door at Arena Square, Engineers Way, postcode HA9 0AA

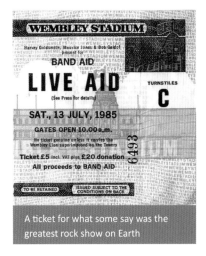

A ticket for what some say was the greatest rock show on Earth

Born in NORTH-WEST LONDON

Hugh Cornwell, vocals, The Stranglers (b. 28 Aug 1949, Tufnell Park)
Fearne Cotton, presenter (b. 3 Sep 1981, Northwood)
Jerry De Borg, Jesus Jones (b. 30 Oct 1960, Kentish Town)
Ian Dury (b. 12 May 1942, Harrow, d. 27 Mar 2000)
Steve Ellis, vocals, Love Affair (b. 7 Apr 1950, Edgware)
Marianne Faithfull (b. 29 Dec 1946, Hampstead)
Harvey Goldsmith, promoter (b. 4 May 1946, Edgware)
Jack Good, producer (b. 7 Aug 1931, Greenford)
Jet Harris, bass, The Searchers (b. 6 Jul 1939, Kingsbury, d. 18 Mar 2011)
Billy Idol (b. 30 Nov 1955, Stanmore)
Elton John (b. 25 Mar 1947, Pinner)
Tony Kanal, bass, No Doubt (b. 27 Aug 1970, Kingsbury)
Johnny Kidd, vocals, Johnny Kidd & The Pirates (b. 23 Dec 1935, Willesden, d. 7 Oct 1966)
Paul Kossoff, guitar, Free (b. 14 Sep 1950, Hampstead, d. 19 Mar 1976)
Hugh McDowell, cello, Electric Light Orchestra (b. 31 Jul 1953, Hampstead)
Dave Mattacks, drums, Fairport Convention (b. 13 Mar 1948, Edgware)
Tony Meehan, drums, The Shadows (b. 2 Mar 1943, Hampstead, d. 28 Nov 2005)

Keith Moon, drums, The Who (b. 23 Aug 1946, Wembley, d. 7 Sep 1978)
Richard Oakes, guitar, Suede (b. 1 Oct 1976, Perivale)
Larry Parnes, manager (b. 3 Sep 1929, Willesden, d. 4 Aug 1989)
Dave Parsons, bass, Bush (b. 2 Jul 1965, Hillingdon)
Steve Priest, bass, The Sweet (b. 23 Feb 1948, Hayes)
Gavin Rossdale, vocals, Bush (b. 30 Oct 1965, Kilburn)
Slash (Saul Hudson), guitar, Guns N' Roses (b. 23 Jul 1965, Hampstead)
Dusty Springfield (b. 16 Apr 1939, West Hampstead, d. 2 Mar 1999)
Chris Squire, bass, Yes (b. 4 Mar 1948, Kingsbury)
Screaming Lord Sutch (David Sutch) (b. 10 Nov 1940, Hampstead, d. 16 Jun 1999)
Chris Thomas, producer (b. 13 Jan 1947, Perivale)
Mick Tucker, drums, The Sweet (b. 17 Jul 1947, Harlesden, d. 14 Feb 2002)
Rick Wakeman, keyboards, Strawbs, Yes (b. 18 May 1949, Perivale)
Ronnie Wood, guitar, The Birds, The Faces, The Rolling Stones (b. 1 Jun 1947, Hillingdon)
Richard Wright, keyboards, Pink Floyd (b. 28 Jul 1943, Hatch End, d. 15 Sep 2008)

Greater Manchester

*R*ock pilgrimages to Greater Manchester should be enjoyed while listening to The Beautiful South's 'Manchester'. The track from their 2006 album Superbi pulls no punches when describing it in all its rainy glory, but it's done optimistically in a 'never mind' sort of way while name-checking just about everywhere from Altrincham to Wythenshawe. Elbow, Doves, The Smiths and even Take That also bring Manchester locations into songs with the delightful Bury, the M62, Whalley Range, Rusholme and the Mancunian Way as a backdrop, and who can blame them for their emotional attachment to the city and its surrounding area that gave birth to Manc exports ranging from Herman's Hermits to Oasis. Few places have as rich a small community feel in such a vast area, throwing up classic soap-opera song stories like The Freshies' 'I'm in Love with the Girl on a Certain Manchester Megastore Check-Out Desk' and some of the best comic rock from that band's Chris Sievey, creator of the Timperley papier-mache-headed troubadour Frank Sidebottom. Greater Manchester boasted some world famous clubs until one by one they disappeared. Wigan Casino? Gone. Haçienda? Gone. And more recently, the building that once saw Rod Stewart and Cream make significant live debuts has now joined the ranks of these legendary places spoken of in the past tense. But the Twisted Wheel lives on in the memory, at least, thanks to some excellent work in this edition of Rock Atlas courtesy of photographers Brian Smith and Bill Armstrong...

Bickershaw
The festival that inspired Joe and Elvis

Photo: Chris Hewitt, www.tractor-ozft.com

The promoter and driving force behind the epic Bickershaw Festival in 1972 was Jeremy Beadle. The professional practical joker and broadcaster persuaded 40,000 rock fans to attend what many present agree was one of the best and also one of the wettest outdoor music gatherings of the Seventies. The tiny village of Bickershaw was host to the Grateful Dead, who played for five hours, and the extraordinary Captain Beefheart. Among the soggy gathering excited and inspired by what they saw over the three days from May 5 to 7 were two young fans who would later make their own revered music, Joe Strummer and Elvis Costello.

LOCATION 302: the fields used for the festival still remain pretty much as they did in the Seventies, just off the B5237 where it joins Bolton House Road, approximately five miles south-east of Wigan. Postcode: WN2 4XU

Right: the Grateful Dead's Jerry Garcia braves the elements at Jeremy Beadle's Bickershaw Festival in 1972

Bury
Guy Garvey's wedding bus ride

'Great Expectations', from the 2005 Elbow album Leaders of the Free World, is vocalist Guy Garvey's charming imagined wedding story set on a bus ride between Manchester and Bury.

LOCATION 304: the 135 bus route to Bury, north of Manchester. Postcode: BL9

> "I got married... on the 135 bus to Bury. It was such a LOW-KEY affair... even the bride didn't know"
>
> **GUY GARVEY**
> explains 'Great Expectations'

Elbow were honoured with the freedom of Bury in 2009. Pictured in their natural habitat, they created their own beer 'Charge' in 2014, named after the track on their The Take Off and Landing of Everything album

Bolton
Dancing all night at Va-Va

Spanish for "Go-Go", Va-Va was perhaps the best-appointed and most modern of all the Northern Soul clubs. Promoting "All-Nighters Every Friday of the Year", the club was regularly packed to its 400 capacity with fans journeying from all over the north. By 1973 it was a nationally popular venue. Lavishly designed with Perspex and tiles, Va-Va tended to overshadow three equally worthy Bolton locations for rare soul aficionados: the Cromwellian, the Bolton Palais, and Troggs in Farnworth.

LOCATION 303: the original site is close to the job centre, Elizabeth House, just off Great Moor Street, in the centre of Bolton. Postcode: BL1 1TP

Greater Manchester

Manchester 1
The end of the Twisted Wheel

The city's Twisted Wheel Club claimed to be the only surviving soul club still spinning Sixties R'n'B classic vinyl in the original club building the last time out in the first edition of Rock Atlas. Sadly, there's nothing to see now as the building it inhabited was razed to the ground in 2013. Whatever happened to the old wheel that hung on the wall that gave the place its name? Prior to its location in Whitworth Street as a pivotal purveyor of Northern Soul, The Twisted Wheel began life as a rhythm and blues venue in 1963 at Brazennose Street. This funky little coffee-bar club was founded by Ivor Abadi and soon provided The Small Faces with their first public appearance and local band The Hollies with a residency. In 1965, the club relocated to nearby Whitworth Street, where a second notable debut took place when rock supergroup Cream played their first gig. The trio were indebted to Eric Clapton's keyboards player Ben Palmer, who drove them up north in a black Austin Westminster to make the

Main picture: A rare photograph taken by Bill Armstrong of the now famous Cream debut at Manchester's Twisted Wheel on July 29 1966. Far left: A very nervous Rod Stewart performed for the first time with Long John Baldry (left) at The Twisted Wheel in January 1964 – an all-nighter they performed under the billing of The Cyril Davies All-Stars, Cyril having died earlier that month. Long John Baldry (with Rod as his new vocalist) would rename the band The Hoochie Coochie Men. Both men are pictured outside the club as photographer Brian Smith remembers inside was "so hot, packed and sweaty, the camera fogged up!"

Photos: Brian Smith and Bill Armstrong

appearance as late replacement for US soul singer Joe Tex. So Cream played The Twisted Wheel on July 29 1966 as a warm-up gig for their formally advertised debut down south in Windsor two days later. Cream's Jack Bruce confirms: "The first concert we did was at The Twisted Wheel in Manchester. It was just called Cream. It wasn't advertised. Somebody had pulled out of the gig and we just took the gig up as a practice the day before doing the Windsor Jazz Festival. That was our first official concert."

LOCATION 305: sadly, this is currently a building site for a new hotel. The Twisted Wheel last stood at the London Road end of Whitworth Street at No.6. Postcode: M1 3QW

Greater Manchester

Manchester 1
Elbow work, rest and play at the Roadhouse

In the late Nighties, this basement club was where local band Elbow literally worked, rested and played. All the band members with the exception of Mark Potter served behind the bar or helped out at some point before the boys from Bury made their debut on the tiny Roadhouse stage as Elbow. Guy Garvey spent so much time there that he would give record company types the club number as his contact point. Further proof that this place must be Elbow's spiritual home comes from the fact that Roadhouse co-owner Steve Lloyd was a big early supporter of the band and produced their first release, 1998's limited edition, The Noisebox EP. Typical of the band, they continue to return to their roots, even performing at recent Roadhouse birthday and Christmas parties to 200-capacity crowds. Roadhouse manager and co-owner Kate Mountain recalls the early days: "...it was a logistical nightmare when [Elbow] actually performed because I lost all my staff!" The club continues to thrive today on the strength of its rich history of stand-out appearances from acts as diverse as Aphex Twin, Death in Vegas, The Verve, Super Furry Animals and The White Stripes.

LOCATION 306: at 8 Newton Street, Piccadilly, postcode M1 2AN

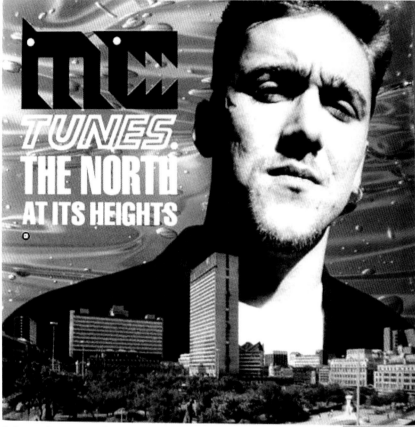

Manchester 1
Elbow, Gomez and MC Tunes

The station, or area of the city centre called Piccadilly, gets name-checked in the Elbow track 'Station Approach' and 'Whippin' Piccadilly' by Gomez, with Piccadilly Gardens pictured on the cover of MC Tunes' The North at its Heights album. The rear of Piccadilly station in Fairfield Street was where Manchester's first warehouse rave 'happened', starring The Stone Roses.

LOCATION 307: Piccadilly station at Station Approach, postcode M1 2PA

Moss-side rapper Nicky Lockett (aka MC Tunes) looms above the Manchester skyline

Heywood
The John Peel-funded Tractor Sound Studios

A plaque marks the place where John Peel financed a Heywood recording studio after the DJ had struck up a friendship with local band Tractor, who sent him a demo tape in 1973. Nearby Townhead cotton mill had been his place of work during a happy six months prior to his life-changing trip to the US and debut as a radio DJ in the Sixties.

LOCATION 308: 58 Market Street, Rochdale, postcode OL10 1UK

Manchester 1
The world-famous Haçienda

Now rebuilt as a block of apartments still carrying the Haçienda name, the site of this former yacht showroom and Bollywood cinema on Whitworth Street became a focal point for Greater Manchester's rave and acid house fans during its heyday in the late 1980s. The facilities on offer included a dance floor, DJ balcony, downstairs cocktail bar, conventional bar and café, kitted out in the strikingly memorable yellow-and-black-striped hazard warning décor. Financed by Factory Records (allocated the Factory catalogue number 51) and therefore primarily by Factory's biggest earners and stakeholders New Order, it finally closed for business following a drugs raid in 1997. The building was demolished in 2002 and some fixtures and fittings, artefacts and posters, including items from Rob Gretton's Haçienda collection, are now at the Manchester Museum of

Manchester Evening News

Science & Industry. Despite the club's strong association with the Madchester music and fashion scene, its international fame was fanned by an appearance on the cover of influential American magazine Newsweek and an early appearance by the relatively unknown Madonna in 1983. There are two plaques on the new apartment block:

a subtle engraved 'FAC 51 Haçienda' greets visitors at the entrance and a wall plaque awarded by PRS for Music displays the fact that Manchester band James played their first gig at the Haçienda on November 17, 1982.

LOCATIONS 309 and 310: south-west of Manchester city centre, The Haçienda Apartments, on Whitworth Street West, on the south side of the canal. Postcode: M1 5DE. The Manchester Museum of Science & Industry is at Liverpool Road, Castlefield, postcode M3 4FP

Former New Order and Joy Division bass guitarist Peter Hook, who owns the Haçienda brand trademark, outside the new apartment block that stands on the site of the famous club

> " The most famous nightclub
> **EVER**, in my opinion "
> **CLINT BOON**
> Inspiral Carpets

Haigh
The Verve's Haigh Hall homecoming

Guaranteed to reach fever pitch, homecoming gigs by world-conquering heroes almost always hit the spot and few have been bigger and better than The Verve's at Haigh Hall in 1998. The Wigan band's May 24 appearance drew 33,000 fans to the country parkland six months after their third hit album Urban Hymns had topped the UK chart.

LOCATION 311: about three miles north of Wigan, accessed from the B5239 near the village of Haigh, Haigh Hall and Country Park is open to the public, postcode WN2 1PE

Manchester 2
Dylan and the Sex Pistols make history at the Free Trade Hall

One of British music history's most controversial concerts occurred on May 17, 1966 when Bob Dylan and The Hawks took to the Free Trade Hall stage and launched into 'Like a Rolling Stone'. It wasn't Dylan's first appearance at the grand old venue more familiar to fans of the Halle Orchestra. Just over a year earlier he had performed solo and acoustic to the delight of Manchester's folk fraternity. But in 1966 he ditched his acoustic guitar and plugged in a Stratocaster and introduced a whole new loud, electric take on his revered folk back catalogue. Not all the audience that night disapproved, but one among the dissenters did become audibly vocal among the jeers and slow handclaps. Recordings of the concert include Keith Butler yelling out rock music's most famous heckle. "Judas!" was the damning one-word criticism shouted out by the young Keele University student during Dylan's regeneration from folk minstrel to rock star. Less well reported but equally disgruntled was the demonstration by one female fan who had drawn lots with her friends to determine who would make the long walk down the aisle to the Free Trade Hall stage to deliver a scribbled note to Bob

LESSER FREE TRADE HALL
MANCHESTER

SLAUGHTER & THE DOGS
PRESENTED BY R. & B.

THE SEX PISTOLS
PRESENTED BY MALCOLM McLAREN

PLUS SUPPORT

TUES. 20th JULY 1976
from 7.30 p.m.

requesting he unplug and tell his band to go home. Also in the audience was 17-year-old Mark Makin, who captured the historic gig for posterity on his camera.

Dylan's much-documented 1966 appearance was matched 10 years later by another significant gig in British music history. This time, the Lesser Free Trade Hall was the venue for the now legendary Sex Pistols gig on June 4, 1976. When Bolton College students Pete McNeish (later Pete Shelley) and Howard Trafford (later Howard Devoto) failed to persuade the powers that be at Bolton Institute of Technology that they should play host to the Pistols, they audaciously booked one of Manchester's grandest cultural venues. Where Dylan had controversially played in the main hall a decade earlier, the Sex Pistols played in front of a crowd estimated at no more than 40 in the smaller, upstairs, Lesser Free Trade Hall. This gig, along with a much better attended second

appearance on July 20, saw the then little-known punk outfit from London create an indelibly strong impression on an impressionable Manchester audience of budding musicians. "Expecting a band in silver trousers, like Iggy Pop or the New York Dolls" was how Penetration fanzine editor Paul Welsh put it. What the crowd witnessed was "... ugly bastards in strategically ripped charity shop clothing". But, the Pistols' loud, stripped-down, aggressive bunch of Stooges and mod cover versions and a few of their own songs struck a chord with a group of local fans present at the birth of a new genre of music. Aside from Buzzcocks' Shelley, Devoto and Steve Diggle, the audiences for one or both Pistols appearances included Morrissey, Tony Wilson, Bernard Sumner, Peter Hook, Ian Curtis, Mark E. Smith and writer Paul Morley. Enthused by the experience, Hook headed for the city centre shop Mazel Radio Musicals the very next day to purchase a bass guitar. He paid £35 for the instrument from the second-hand electrical emporium at 124-136 London Road, which has long since disappeared.

LOCATION 312: now a Radisson hotel, the still imposing Manchester Free Trade Hall is situated in the city centre on Peter Street, postcode M2 5GP

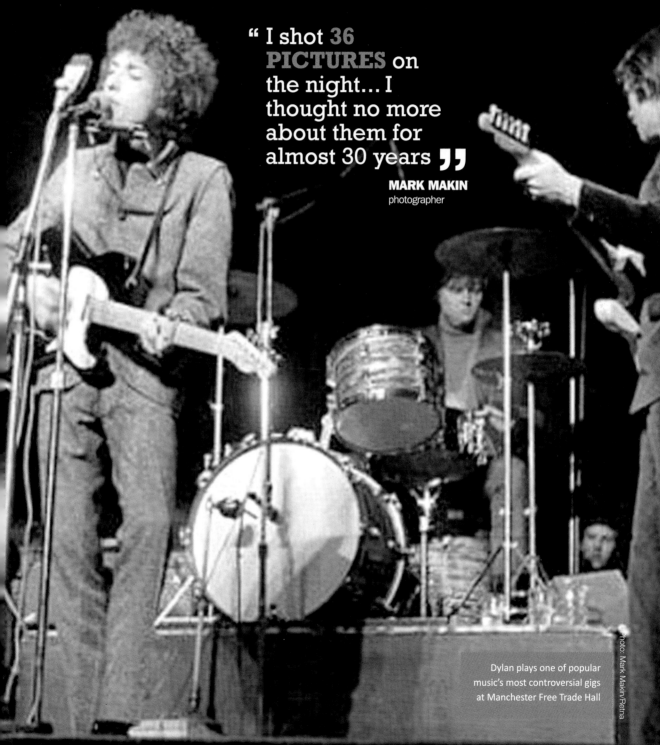

" I shot **36 PICTURES** on the night... I thought no more about them for almost 30 years "

MARK MAKIN
photographer

Dylan plays one of popular music's most controversial gigs at Manchester Free Trade Hall

Photo: Mark Makin/Retna

Photo: Peter Tarleton

Manchester 5
Smiths' photo shoot puts the Lads Club on the map

Opened in 1904 by Boy Scouts leader Robert Baden-Powell, Salford Lads Club became a location worthy of pilgrimage for thousands of Smiths fans when the red-brick building formed a backdrop for an iconic group photo in 1986. The famous inside cover picture for the band's fourth hit album The Queen Is Dead became the archetypal bedroom wall poster at the time. In 2005, photographer Stephen Wright's famous image was accepted into the National Portrait Gallery collection. There's a Smiths room at the club that acts as a focal point and shrine to visitors. A film featuring Smiths vocalist Morrissey cycling round Salford and revisiting the club's front

doorway a year later was shot for the intended video 'Stop Me If You Think You've Heard this One Before', but the release's airplay was banned by the BBC due to the song's "plan a mass murder" line in the wake of the infamous Hungerford massacre. Former members of Salford Lads Club include Joy Division

and New Order's Peter Hook. Graham Nash and Allan Clarke also used the club for early Hollies band rehearsals.

LOCATION 313: Salford Lads Club is roughly a mile west of Manchester city centre, on the corner of the 'real' Coronation Street, Salford, postcode M5 3RS

Above: the magnificent, world-famous Lads Club as it is today

Right: Salford Lads Club and The Smiths: in the National Portrait Gallery collection

"We started the session at the Salford Lads Club at **MORRISSEY'S REQUEST**. The rotten light and the casual pose help the photo have a relaxed nature " **STEPHEN WRIGHT** Photographer

Greater Manchester

Manchester 4
Michael Jackson transferred from Fulham to Manchester

When Michael Jackson died in 2009, Mohamed Al-Fayed commissioned an extraordinary statue in memory of his friend. Originally, the memorial to "The King of Pop" was to have been sited at the multi-millionaire's Harrods store in Knightsbridge, but when Al-Fayed sold the property he then had the statue erected at the home of Fulham Football Club, where he was Chairman. The 7-ft 6-in-tall plaster and resin Jacko sat on a 2.5-tonne granite base inscribed with the words and music from the singer's 1988 single 'Man in The Mirror'. When the statue was unveiled at a home game versus Blackpool in 2011, not all Fulham fans thought the location was appropriate, and even Jackson may have wondered how this memorial ended up inside a football ground overlooking the River Thames, where he did once attend a game at Craven Cottage and sat in the director's box with Al-Fayed. But in May 2014, Michael was on the move. With Al-Fayed no longer the club's owner, a new home for the statue was found when an approach to the National Football Museum resulted in the

donation of surely one of the most spectacular and bizarre additions to its collection of exhibits.

LOCATION 314: just north of Manchester Arndale shopping centre, the National Football Museum can be found at the Urbis Building, Cathedral Gardens, postcode M4 3BG

Michael Jackson's statue was unveiled before the Premier League game between Fulham and Blackpool on April 3, 2011

Manchester 2 & 5
The Hollies at the Oasis

Local Manchester band The Hollies made their debut at the Oasis Club in December 1962. The Oasis was a mecca for all the best groups in the north west and attracted all of the city's up-and-coming beat groups and many from Liverpool, including The Beatles. When Graham Nash and Allan Clarke met as Salford schoolboys, the pair formed first The Two 'Teens, then The Fourtones, The Deltas and, most famously, The Hollies. Blackpool-born Nash was raised in a two-bedroom terraced house at 1 Skinner Street – just a stone's throw away from the now legendary Salford Lads Club where he and Clarke were members and later rehearsed their groups.

LOCATIONS 316 and 317: the Oasis club (now the Manchester Registration Service at Heron House) was at 45/47 Lloyd Street, off Albert Square, postcode M2 5LE. Skinner Street is now renamed and rebuilt as James Henry Avenue, postcode M5 3HR

Manchester 8
Mark E. Smith's 'Cheetham Hill'

The Manchester area known as Cheetham Hill was the inspiration for the song of the same name that appeared on The Fall's 1996 album The Light User Syndrome. According to the band's Broughton-born frontman Mark E. Smith, Cheetham Hill, formerly a run-down and dangerous place, isn't what it once

was when he was a street gang lad. Ah, those were the days!

LOCATION 315: Cheetham Hill Road runs from south to north in north Manchester, a short distance from Prestwich, where The Fall's Mark E. Smith grew up. Postcode: M8 8

Manchester 7
Ewan MacColl's 'Dirty Old Town'

The city of Salford is the subject of Ewan MacColl's song 'Dirty Old Town'. Most familiar versions of the gritty description of the large chunk of urban Greater Manchester are by The Pogues, The Dubliners and The Clancy Brothers, which has led to a case of mistaken identity. The assumption that the song had been written about an Irish location is wide of the mark. Folk musician MacColl was born and grew up in the Broughton area of Salford, vividly bringing to life the canal, gas works, factory and docks in 'Dirty Old Town', which he wrote in his early thirties in 1949. Local band Doves followed in MacColl's footsteps, painting an equally moody industrial picture on 'Shadows of Salford', a track from their 2005 chart-topping album Some Cities.

LOCATION 318: Ewan MacColl was born in Heath Avenue, Lower Broughton, Salford, postcode M7 1

Manchester 13
'From Atlanta, Georgia to Longsight, Manchester'

The Stone Roses' spiritual heartland appears to be located in this edgy region of south-east Manchester. Famous for all the wrong reasons in the Nineties with its weekly news headlines of guns, gangs and drugs, the place gets a mention in Roses track 'Daybreak' ('from Atlanta, Georgia to Longsight, Manchester'), and 'Longsight M13' was the opener on Roses vocalist Ian Brown's Solarized solo album. The Madchester movement had its roots in places like Longsight and Moss Side, where, alongside gang graffiti for local footy giants United and City, baggy hieroglyphics for the Roses, Happy Mondays and Inspiral Carpets sat side-by-side.

LOCATION 319: Longsight is about three miles out of Manchester city centre on the A6, postcode M13

Brian Smith captures Johnny Cash's after midnight performance back in 1963 at the Astoria

Photo: Brian Smith Photography

Manchester 13
Johnny Cash makes his UK stage debut at the Astoria Irish Club

On October 10, 1963, three years before he undertook his first full UK tour, Johnny Cash played a one-night stand (his first live stage show in the UK) at Manchester's Astoria Irish Club. Popular with the packed audience, who had no doubt enjoyed Cash's 1961 recording of his Irish song 'Forty Shades of Green', he was supported on his live UK concert debut by his backing group The Tennessee Three. The venue, later named the Carousel, Sloskys and International 2, was where Noel and Liam Gallagher's mother and father first met, and it has hosted a variety of acts from The Pogues to Public Enemy.

LOCATION 320: 210 Plymouth Grove, Longsight, postcode M13 0AS

Greater Manchester

Manchester 14
'Rusholme Ruffians' and Top of the Pops

Home to Manchester's famously tasty Curry Mile restaurants, Rusholme has appeared in at least two hit songs and was home to BBC's Top of the Pops shows for over a decade. The Smiths' 'Rusholme Ruffians' appeared on their 1985 album Meat Is Murder, and the cleverly titled 'From Rusholme with Love' was included on Mint Royale's 1999 debut On the Ropes. The former church and then film studio on Dickenson Road was where the BBC first began broadcasting Top of the Pops from January 1964.

LOCATION 321: Rusholme is two miles south of the city centre. The Top of the Pops studio in the converted Wesleyan Church is on the western end of Dickenson Road and is remembered by a green plaque. Postcode M14 5AT

Manchester 15
T J Davidson

It's the long, shabby, bare-brick room in this converted warehouse that was the setting for Joy Division's performance in the 'Love Will Tear Us Apart' video. The recording and rehearsal business was run by Tony Davidson, son of the owner of well-known Manchester jeweller Davidson's on Oldham Street.

LOCATION 322: at 35 Little Peter Street, Knott Mill, until demolition in the 80s, postcode M15 4QJ

Manchester 15
The Joy Division bridge

One of a series of Joy Division photos shot one winter's day in 1979 appears on the cover of the band's Best Of album. Photographed by Kevin Cummins, Ian Curtis, Bernard Sumner, Peter Hook and Stephen Morris are pictured on the Epping Walk Bridge in Hulme, an area packed full of locations familiar to the band. On a route leading to the site of the Haçienda, the bridge is also close to the Russel Club in Royce Road, where Joy Division played some of their earliest gigs. Also nearby are T J Davidson's rehearsal rooms, the Boardwalk club and Tony Wilson's former flat, making the bridge in Hulme the perfect memorial to the late Ian Curtis. A petition to have the structure named after the singer was set up in 2010.

LOCATION 323: the footbridge is over the A5103 Princess Road, leading to Princess Parkway, south of Manchester city centre. The bridge is best accessed from Poynton Street on the eastern side. Postcode: M15 6PN

> **"It's the photograph that sums the band's sound up because of the sparseness, space and BLEAKNESS"**
>
> **KEVIN CUMMINS**
> talking to the Manchester Evening News

THE BEST OF
JOY DIVISION

Manchester 15
Yellow and smiley at The Boardwalk

A yellow smiley face beams out from the traditional blue plaque that marks the spot where famous Madchester venue and nightclub The Boardwalk operated between 1984 and 1999. The club's last seven years saw the popular Yellow night provide a unique atmosphere, offering the very best in house, soul, disco and funk. The building also provided Oasis with their first proper rehearsal space in the below-ground-level area behind the glass tiles, which are still evident today on the swanky, upmarket structure, now converted to offices. Yellow/Boardwalk DJ Dave Haslam sums the place up best when he describes The Boardwalk on his website www.davehaslam.com: "Very Manchester; a brilliant mix of black and white, students, single mothers from Sale and Droylsden, dental nurses from Chorlton, Cheshire girls, Moss Side boys. You get that kind of club once in a generation."

LOCATION 324: close to Deansgate train station, Manchester city centre, at 21 Little Peter Street, postcode M15 4PS

Photo: Brian Smith Photography

Muddy Waters performs for the TV cameras at the fictitious Chorltonville Station

Manchester 16
'Chorltonville': Home of the blues

On a typically damp south Manchester day in 1964, an ambitious Granada TV production was filmed and broadcast featuring American blues legends Muddy Waters, Sister Rosetta Tharpe and Sonny Terry and Brownie McGhee. An astonishing makeover of what was once Wilbraham Road station by Granada saw the platform and station buildings transform into a typical railroad scene from the southern states of America. Station platform signs were substituted to read 'Chorltonville', in keeping with the American theme, and it was also the name of the nearby 20th-century garden village.

LOCATION 325: the railway line still runs through what was Wilbraham Road station at the end of Athol Road, Chorlton-cum-Hardy, about 3 miles south of Manchester city centre. Postcode: M16 8QW

PLEASE BE AT CENTRAL STATION – 7.30 p.m. PROMPT

GRANADA TV MANCHESTER 3

invites you to the

BLUES AND GOSPEL TRAIN

with

MUDDY WATERS
SONNY TERRY · BROWNIE McGHEE
SISTER ROSETTA THARPE
REV. GARY DAVIS · OTIS SPANN
COUSIN JOE PLEASANTS

THURSDAY MAY 7th at 7-30 prompt

Casual gear essential: Denims, Sweaters.

The show will be recorded in the open at the old disused Wilbraham Road Railway Station, Chorlton-cum-Hardy. Entrance to Station is in Atholl Road, off Wilbraham Road, near the junction of Alexandra Road and Wilbraham Road. Come early !

Photo: Peter Goldsmith

A signed invitation to an extraordinary evening's entertainment in south Manchester

Greater Manchester

Manchester 19
The Gallagher family home

In 1972, the Gallagher family moved home from Longsight to a cul-de-sac in Burnage. This three-bedroomed house was home to Tommy and Peggy Gallagher and their three boys, Paul, Noel and Liam. Here Noel began to write a steady stream of songs, some that would appear on Oasis albums in the Nineties. The teenage Noel scrawled words and notes on what he called his 'Wonderwall', in the small bedroom he shared with younger brother Liam.

LOCATION 326: Ashburn Avenue, Burnage, postcode M19 IDQ

The Gallaghers, pictured when they were still in a band together, and their childhood home on Ashburn Avenue where Noel wrote 'Wonderwall'

Manchester 20
Sifters-Oasis' 'Shakermaker' record shop

A regular haunt of the Gallagher brothers in their teenage years, Sifters second-hand record shop also made an appearance in Oasis' 1994 hit single 'Shakermaker'. The reference to ''Mr Sifter'' in the song was a line apparently hurriedly created to complete the lyrics en route to the recording studio. The Gallaghers' taxi stopped at some traffic lights outside Sifters and Noel quickly added the lines to polish off another hit, with Mr Sifter, traffic lights and all.

LOCATION 327: south of the city centre, Sifters is still 'selling songs' at 177 Fog Lane, Burnage, postcode M20 6FJ

Manchester 21
The Bee Gees harmonize on Keppel Road

Born on the Isle of Man, Keppel Road, Chorlton-cum-Hardy became home to the brothers Gibb until the family left to build a new life in Australia in the late Fifties. During their eight years at Keppel Road, Barry, Robin and Maurice began singing three-part harmony before their teenage years, performing live as The Rattlesnakes. The location of their singing debut was at the Gaumont cinema on Manchester Road East, a few minutes walk from their home.

LOCATIONS 328 and 329: the Bee Gees' home still stands at 51 Keppel Road, postcode M21 0BP. You can trace the footsteps of the three brothers as they ran to their live singing debut at the Gaumont (now The Co-operative Funeral Care) on Manchester Road East (postcode M21 9PN) by turning out of Keppel Road into Selborne Road and then crossing Manchester Road East.

Spirits Having Flown: The Bee Gees return to their childhood Chorlton-cum-Hardy home on Keppel Road in 1981

Rochdale
Mike Harding's wild north-west

The wild north-west was the subject for comedian and folkie Mike Harding's 1975 hit single. Expressing how difficult it was to attach spurs to clogs, 'Rochdale Cowboy' put Rochdale on the map much as songstress Gracie Fields had done decades earlier.

LOCATION 330: to search for the song's local "pie and pea saloon", head for the town centre, postcode OL16 1LR

Greater Manchester

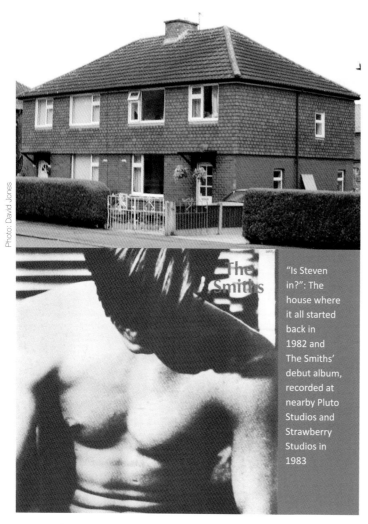

Photo: David Jones

"Is Steven in?": The house where it all started back in 1982 and The Smiths' debut album, recorded at nearby Pluto Studios and Strawberry Studios in 1983

Manchester 32
Marr calls on Morrissey

Sandwiched between the railway line and Longford Park in Stretford is the house where Smiths vocalist Morrissey lived as a teenager. The red-bricked semi-detached house on Kings Road is where The Smiths first came into being in 1982 when John Maher (later Johnny Marr) first arrived to discuss the forming of a band that May with Steven Patrick Morrissey. Almost two years after this meeting The Smiths released their eponymous debut album, featuring 'Still Ill', a song that refers to the iron bridge on Kings Road next to house number 502.

LOCATION 331: about three miles south-west of Manchester city centre at 384 Kings Road, postcode M32 8GW

Manchester 21
Chuck Berry at the Princess

Here's a music venue that provided the perfect ambience for the 1960s and 70s stag night. Chorlton-cum-Hardy's Princess Theatre Club attracted a working-men's club/pub type crowd inside a building which had formerly been the Princess Ballroom (aka Chorlton Palais). Its life as a thriving rock 'n' roll venue began when ex-wrestler Bill Kerfoot took on the place and another former cinema five miles northeast called the Domino. Kerfoot's idea was to book double headers on the same night at both the Princess and The Domino on Grey Mare Lane, Openshaw, a plan that somehow worked with big stars like Chuck Berry, first at the Domino and then racing across Manchester to perform his second show of the evening at the affectionately called "Prinny". The clientele were a hard crowd to please, and when a band weren't appreciated they were often fortunate to simply be booed off stage. Perhaps it was the time-honoured rivalry between Manchester and Liverpool that brought things to a head when The Merseybeats once played The Princess and were forced off in a shower of coins. Faring rather better were the star US imports that appeared – a list that included Little Richard, Duane Eddy, Gene Vincent and Del Shannon, whose album Del Shannon Live in England was recorded there. Maybe big American acts were attracted to this Chorlton-cum-Hardy palace of entertainment by the added delights of the Princess's Western ranch-style Ponderosa club (complete with strippers) which later transformed into the Princess casino.

LOCATION 332: The Princess is now a McDonald's restaurant on Barlow Moor Road, Chorlton-cum-Hardy, postcode M21 8AY

Right: Chuck Berry plays the Princess backed by pick-up band The Canadians, having already performed at the Domino earlier that same night

"The Princess
housed a small
Ponderosa club
with Western
ranch decor
and mainly
STRIPPERS"
BRIAN SMITH
Photographer

Photo: Brian Smith Photography

Greater Manchester

Rochdale
The Deeply Vale free festivals

Fondness for the Deeply Vale mid-to-late-Seventies series of free festivals set in an idyllic valley on the moors outside Rochdale has spawned a hugely informative website, its own T-shirts and a lovingly put-together DVD released in 2007. Drawing inspiration from the success of the neighbouring, earlier Bickershaw Festival, Deeply Vale began tentatively, drawing just a few hundred fans in 1976. Popularity accelerated sharply until, in 1978, 20,000 hippies and punk fans flooded into the site to camp and groove to the sounds of Steve Hillage, The Fall, The Durutti Column and a young, flame-haired Mick Hucknall fronting The Frantic Elevators. Deeply Vale provided the inspiration for a new generation of musicians in the north-west. Making up the audience were Tractor manager and Deeply Vale co-organiser Chris Hewitt, Ian Brown, future Wedding Present band member Dave Gedge, future Smiths bass guitarist Andy Rourke, assorted members of The Mock Turtles and an eight-year-old Jimi Goodwin, who would find success with Doves two decades later. One of the few events to combine the great outdoors with new-wave music, Deeply Vale still attracts a few rambling punk-era pilgrims in search of the site of this locally produced success story.

LOCATION 333: the festival site lies in a moorland valley and can be reached easily by heading west out of Rochdale on the A680 and turning left on to Ashworth Road just as the A680 reaches Ashworth Moor Reservoir. Postcode OL11 5UN

The crowd awaits the arrival on stage of Steve Hillage in 1978

"It was far more **ORGANISED** than early Glastonburys. My day job was running musical events... so we took some of the **CHAOS** out of the stage arrangements that happened at Stonehenge and early Glastos – things ran to a timetable and all types of bands were welcome "

CHRIS HEWITT
Deeply Vale stage manager and co-organiser

Photo: Chris Hewitt / www.tractor-oz1t.com

Greater Manchester

Rochdale
Party People at Cargo Studios

Home to Tractor Music, Cargo Studios and Suite 16 down the years, this location played a vital role in the development of some of the north-west's ground-breaking bands. Closely linked to the place, bass guitarist Peter Hook participated in Joy Division's first Factory Records recordings at Cargo Studios and later owned the building when named Suite 16. Architecturally rather nondescript, 16 Kenion Street nevertheless made an authentic appearance as itself in music movie 24 Hour Party People and was awarded a plaque in 2009.

LOCATION 334: 16 Kenion Street, postcode OL16 1SJ

> **"Watching The Stone Roses, Happy Mondays... The Charlatans... walk through those [Cargo Studios] doors had [an effect] on Rochdale... as IAN CURTIS had on Macclesfield "**
> **PETER HOOK**

Wigan
The 'world's best disco'

World-famous but hardly worthy of a visit today, the site where hoards of British Northern Soul fans trekked to in the Seventies has latterly become a shopping centre and car park. That said, Wigan's Casino was the nation's best-known and most popular venue for a music and fashion movement that escaped the mainstream in pop's nearest thing to a secret society. The Casino's all-nighters ran from 1973 to 1981, and if the present-day websites, books and internet forums are any indication, the teenagers that attended back then still continue to celebrate what American music magazine Billboard voted the 'world's best disco' in 1974.

LOCATION 335: the site of the former Casino club is at Station Road, Wigan, postcode WN1 1

Stockport
Keeping it local at Strawberry Studios

Strawberry Studios was opened in 1967 by former Sixties beat groups road manager Peter Tattersall and Mindbenders band member Eric Stewart, back in the days when recording studios outside London were uncommon. The duo named their new business venture after the then current Beatles track 'Strawberry Fields Forever', and support from another investor, Graham Gouldman, and session help from local musicians Kevin Godley and Lol Creme quickly established the studios as a thriving concern. Aside from recording artists including Neil Sedaka, the team behind Strawberry Studios recorded themselves as Hotlegs and eventually, in 1972, began a run of massively successful singles and albums as 10cc. By the late Seventies, an association with local producer Martin Hannett opened up a whole new raft of talent hungry to make a recording, and a second cut-price facility across the road was used by a wave of new, up-and-coming Manchester bands. Stockport's hive of activity welcomed The Durutti Column, Happy Mondays, The Stone Roses, Buzzcocks, Simply Red, James and New Order. But what makes misty-eyed fans of Manchester music most excited is the fact that Joy Division's debut album was made here during the first 17 days of April 1979. Unknown Pleasures was recorded on the now famous Strawberry Studios Helios desk, which has recently been renovated at great expense. There's no music-making inside the facility these days, but a plaque marks the spot of this legendary recording and mixing outpost.

LOCATION 336: Strawberry Studios ended its association with Stockport in 1993. The original site has private offices that still retain the name at 3 Waterloo Road, Stockport, postcode SK1 3BD

STOCKPORT HERITAGE TRUST

STRAWBERRY RECORDING STUDIOS
1968 to 1993
Association with the band 10cc resulted in some of the most memorable music being produced at these Studios. Paul McCartney, Neil Sedaka, Stone Roses, The Syd Lawrence Orchestra and many others also recorded here.

THE METROPOLITAN BOROUGH OF STOCKPORT

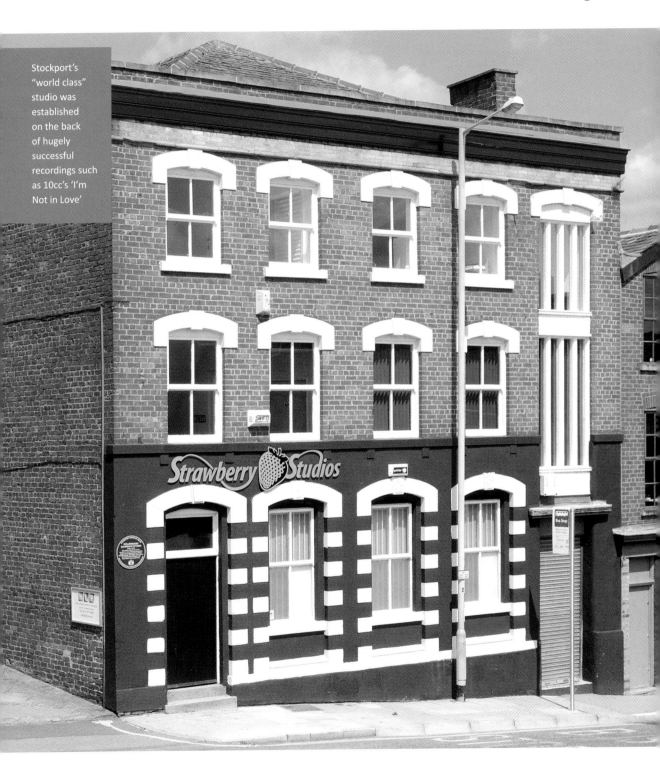

Stockport's "world class" studio was established on the back of hugely successful recordings such as 10cc's 'I'm Not in Love'

Manchester 60
Strangeways warning by The Smiths

A category A correctional facility familiar to all Mancunians, Strangeways prison was renamed HM Prison Manchester in the 1990s. But it is the former weirdly named institution that attracted songwriters and included singer Ian Brown as an inmate following his conviction on an 'air rage' charge in the late Nineties. Deep Purple's 1987 album The House of Blue Light carried a 'Strangeways' track, but it is The Smiths' final album, Strangeways, Here We Come, that gives the "Victorian monstrosity of a prison", as Smiths singer Morrissey put it, its biggest claim to fame.

LOCATION 337: north of Manchester city centre at 1 Southall Street, postcode M60 9AH

"I was always INTRIGUED by the word STRANGEWAYS. I remember as a kid, when I first heard that the prison was really called that, I WONDERED, had it not occurred to anybody to change the name? "

JOHNNY MARR
The Smiths

Born in GREATER MANCHESTER

Stuart Adamson, vocals, Big Country (b. 11 Apr 1958, Manchester, d. 16 Dec 2001)

Paul 'Bonehead' Arthurs, guitar, Oasis (b. 23 Jun 1965, Burnage, Manchester)

Richard Ashcroft, vocals, The Verve/solo (b. 11 Sep 1971, Wigan)

Bez (Mark Berry), percussion, Black Grape/Happy Mondays (b. 18 Apr 1964, Salford)

Clint Boon, vocals/keyboards, Inspiral Carpets (b. 28 Jun 1959, Oldham)

Elkie Brooks (b. 25 Feb 1945, Salford)

Tim Burgess, vocals, The Charlatans (b. 30 May 1967, Salford)

Dean Butterworth, drums, Good Charlotte (b. 26 Sep 1976, Rochdale)

Allan Clarke, vocals, The Hollies (b. 5 Apr 1942, Salford)

John Cooper Clarke (b. 25 Jan 1949, Salford)

Lol Creme, guitar/vocals, 10cc (b. 19 Sep 1947, Prestwich)

Chris Curtis, drums, The Searchers (b. 26 Aug 1941, Oldham, d. 28 Feb 2005)

Ian Curtis, vocals, Joy Division (b. 15 Jul 1956, Stretford, d. 18 May 1980)

Saul Davies, guitar/violin, James (b. 28 Jun 1965, Oldham)

Paul Davis, keyboards, Happy Mondays (b. 7 Mar 1966, Swinton)

Mark Day, guitar, Happy Mondays (b. 29 Dec 1961, Manchester)

Steve Diggle, guitar/vocals, Buzzcocks (b. 7 May 1955, Manchester)

Howard Donald, Take That (b. 28 Apr 1968, Droylsden)

Billy Duffy, guitar, The Cult (b. 12 May 1961, Hulme, Manchester)

Georgie Fame (b. 26 Jun 1943, Leigh)

James Fearnley, accordion, The Pogues (b. 9 Oct 1954, Worsley)

Martin Fry, vocals, ABC (b. 9 Mar 1958, Stockport)

Liam Gallagher, vocals, Oasis/Beady Eye (b. 21 Sep 1972, Burnage, Manchester)

Noel Gallagher, guitar/vocals, Oasis/Noel Gallagher's High Flying Birds (b. 29 May 1967, Longsight, Manchester)

Freddie Garrity, vocals, Freddie and The Dreamers (b. 14 Nov 1936, Manchester, d. 19 May 2006)

Guy Garvey, vocals/guitar, Elbow (b. 6 Mar 1974, Bury)

Andy Gibb (b. 5 Mar 1958, Manchester, d. 10 Mar 1988)

Gillian Gilbert, keyboards/vocals, New Order (b. 27 Jan 1961, Whalley Range, Manchester)

Craig Gill, drums, Inspiral Carpets (b. 5 Dec 1971, Salford)

Kevin Godley, drums/vocals, 10cc (b. 7 Oct 1945, Prestwich)

Jimi Goodwin, vocals/guitar, Doves (b. 28 May 1970, Manchester)

Larry Gott, guitar, James (b. 24 Jul 1957, Manchester)

Graham Gouldman, bass/vocals, 10cc (b. 10 May 1946, Salford)

Karl Green, bass, Herman's Hermits (b. 31 Jul 1947, Davyhulme)

Martin Hannett, record producer (b. 31 May 1948, Miles Platting, Manchester, d. 18 Apr 1991)

Mike Harding, folk singer-songwriter/broadcaster (b. 23 Oct 1944, Crumpsall, Manchester)

Roy Harper, singer-songwriter/guitarist (b. 12 Jun 1941, Rusholme, Manchester)

Les Holroyd, bass/vocals, Barclay James Harvest (b. 12 Mar 1948, Oldham)

Peter Hook, bass, Joy Division/New Order (b. 13 Feb 1956, Salford)

Dominic Howard, drums, Muse (b. 7 Dec 1977, Stockport)

Mick Hucknall, vocals, Simply Red (b. 8 Jun 1960, Denton)

Davy Jones, vocals, The Monkees (b. 30 Dec 1945, Manchester, d. 29 Feb 2012)

Mike Joyce, drums, The Smiths (b. 1 Jun 1963, Fallowfield, Manchester)

Richard Jupp, drums, Elbow (b. Bury)

Jay Kay (Jason Cheetham), vocals, Jamiroquai (b. 30 Dec 1969, Stretford)

Andy Kershaw, presenter (b. 9 Nov 1959, Rochdale)

Liz Kershaw, presenter (b. 30 Jul 1958, Rochdale)

Graham Lambert, guitar, Inspiral Carpets (b. 10 Jul 1964, Oldham)

John Lees, guitar/vocals, Barclay James Harvest (b. 13 Jan 1947, Oldham)

Paul 'Kermit' Leveridge, vocals, Black Grape (b. 10 Nov 1969, Manchester)

Ewan MacColl, singer-songwriter (b. 25 Jan 1915, Salford, d. 22 Oct 1989)

Paul 'Guigsy' McGuigan, bass, Oasis (b. 9 May 1971, Manchester)

Johnny Marr, guitar, The Smiths/Electronic/The The/Modest Mouse/The Cribs (b. 31 Oct 1963, Ardwick, Manchester)

Graham Massey, keyboards, 808 State (b. 4 Aug 1960, Manchester)

MC Tunes (b. Nicholas Hodgson, 28 Mar 1970, Moss Side, Manchester)

Morrissey (b. 22 May 1959, Davyhulme, Manchester)

Gary 'Mani' Mounfield, bass, Primal Scream/The Stone Roses (b. 16 Nov 1962, Crumpsall, Manchester)

Martin Noble, guitar, British Sea Power (b. 28 Jan 1986, Bury)

Peter Noone, vocals, Herman's Hermits (b. 5 Nov 1947, Davyhulme, Trafford, Manchester)

Jason Orange, Take That (b. 10 Jul 1970, Crumpsall, Manchester)

Mark Owen, Take That (b. 27 Jan 1972, Oldham)

Lyn Paul, The New Seekers (b. 16 Feb 1949, Wythenshawe, Manchester)

Craig Potter, guitar, Elbow (b. Bury)

Mark Potter, keyboards, Elbow (b. Bury)

Mel Pritchard, drums, Barclay James Harvest (b. 20 Jan 1948, Oldham, d. 28 Jan 2004)

Mark Radcliffe, broadcaster (b. 29 Jun 1958, Bolton)

Mike Read, broadcaster (b. 1 Mar 1947, Manchester)

Andy Rourke, bass, The Smiths (b. 17 Jan 1964, Manchester)

Paul Ryder, bass, Happy Mondays (b. 24 Apr 1964, Manchester)

Shaun Ryder, vocals, Black Grape/Happy Mondays (b. 23 Aug 1962, Salford)

Dave Sharp, guitar, The Alarm (b. 28 Jan 1959, Salford)

Pete Shelley, guitar/vocals, Buzzcocks (b. 17 Apr 1955, Leigh)

Mark E. Smith, vocals, The Fall (b. 5 Mar 1957, Salford)

John Squire, guitar, The Stone Roses/The Seahorses (b. 24 Nov 1962, Altrincham)

Lisa Stansfield (b. 11 Apr 1966, Rochdale)

Eric Stewart, guitar/vocals, 10cc (b. 20 Jan 1945, Droylsden)

Bernard Sumner, vocals/guitar, Joy Division/New Order/Electronic/Bad Lieutenant (b. 4 Jan 1956, Salford)

Simon Tong, guitar/keyboards, The Verve (b. 9 Jul 1972, Wigan)

Pete Turner, bass, Elbow (b. 28 Aug 1974, Bury)

Nigel Twist, drums, The Alarm (b. 18 Jul 1958, Manchester)

Paul 'Wags' Wagstaff, guitar, Black Grape (b. 28 Dec 1964, Stockport)

Martyn Walsh, bass, Inspiral Carpets (b. 3 Jul 1968, Rusholme, Manchester)

Barry Westhead, keyboards, Starsailor (b. 13 May 1977, Wigan)

Gary Whelan, drums, Happy Mondays (b. 12 Feb 1966, Manchester)

Katie White, vocals, The Ting Tings (b. 3 Mar 1983, Wigan)

Andy Williams, vocals/drums, Doves (b. 22 Feb 1970, Manchester)

Jez Williams, vocals/guitar, Doves (b. 22 Feb 1970, Manchester)

Tony Wilson, record label owner/presenter (b. 20 Feb 1950, Salford, d. 10 Aug 2007)

Stewart 'Woolly' Wolstenholme, vocals/keyboards, Barclay James Harvest (b. 15 Apr 1947, Chadderton, d. 13 Dec 2010)

Alan 'Reni' Wren, drums, The Stone Roses (b. 10 Apr 1964, Manchester)

Hampshire

*W*as Hampshire the birthplace of British rock 'n' roll? Devotees of Tony Crombie's Rockets put up a strong case centred round their ''feverish'' and ''riotous''1956 Theatre Royal show in Portsmouth. The affluent county has more than its fair share of inspirational homes and houses where popular music's classic chords were struck. Benifold, Farley House, Headley Grange and Stargroves played host to increasingly wealthy Seventies rock stars who hit upon a new way of recording their music away from the claustrophobia of London's studios. Hampshire also boasts one of England's finest cathedrals, Winchester, which inspired two very different stories - three if you count the fact that Led Zeppelin's John Paul Jones came within a whisker of leaving the band to become the cathedral's organist in 1971. Then there's what amounts to The Beatles' least successful gig (Aldershot), a rare 90s protest song ('Twyford Down') and the UK's only Top 10 hornpipe ('Portsmouth'). Quite why the county has given birth to a preponderance of drummers is anyone's guess but, at various times, Coldplay, King Crimson, Manfred Mann, Razorlight, The Troggs, Uriah Heep and The Zombies have all been driven on rhythmically by a Hampshire sticksman. And finally, if sea shanties float your boat, Mike Oldfield's update of a traditional folk melody from 1701 gave him his highest-placed single when 'Portsmouth' peaked at No.3 in the chart in 1976.

Aldershot
The Beatles play to 18 fans at the Palais

The good people of Hampshire's military town weren't to know, but they could have witnessed history in the making on December 9, 1961. Just 18 fans turned out to see what was supposed to be The Beatles' first gig outside Hamburg and their native north-west. The booking by northern promoter Sam Leach went horribly wrong. John, Paul, George and Pete Best were scheduled to do a show at Aldershot's Palais Ballroom, but a pre-arranged sizeable advertisement heralding the band's appearance in local newspaper The Aldershot News failed to appear and The Beatles were left to perform to a scattering of non-paying punters, some of whom had been persuaded to attend following a quick dash round the local pubs to press-gang a crowd of fans. Drummer Pete Best recalls what happened halfway through a song. ''George and Paul put on their overcoats and took to the floor to dance the foxtrot together, while the rest of us struggled along, making enough music for them and the handful of spectators.''

LOCATION 338: The Palais Ballroom, corner of Queens Road and Perowne Street, postcode GU11

Beaulieu
Rod finds his real life 'Maggie May' at the Beaulieu Jazz Festival

The innovative forerunner to many more great British music festivals was in its sixth year in 1961 when the 16-year-old Rod Stewart lost his virginity and gained the necessary experience to later write his trademark song 'Maggie May'. The "key personal milestone" with a woman Rod described in his autobiography as "older (and larger)" began in the Beaulieu Jazz Festival beer tent and reached its satisfactory conclusion on a secluded patch of grass. Rod and his group of friends had earlier made their entrance to the festival via an unusual route. The festival grounds lay on one side of a tidal river, and knowing the price of an entrance ticket was beyond their means, Rod and friends crossed the river, crawling through a four-foot-diameter overflow pipe, before making their entrance. They'd been tipped-off that the discomfort of a bit of wading and crawling would soon have them inside the festival for free. Even the wait to see the water level fall as the tide receded wasn't a hardship: Rod and co simply bided their time by drinking in the rather splendid Montagu Arms on the opposite bank of the river to the festival. Back in 1961, Rod was a self-confessed beatnik, whose anti-social behaviour was mostly confined to the new fad for growing your hair long and never washing or changing your clothes. Although the music may have drawn Rod and his pals to this corner of the New Forest, they may have also been influenced by the festival's unruly reputation. The previous summer saw outbreaks of violence make national headlines as jazz fans rioted, even cutting short live

ROD STEWART

A product of Phonogram, Inc.

Mercury Records

BBC TV transmissions of the festival. The great unwashed youth cult of Britain was revolting, but a year after his visit to Beaulieu Rod the beatnik had become the subject of a cult conversion. By 1962 he'd transformed into "Rod the Mod".

LOCATION 339: The Montagu Arms Hotel, Beaulieu, postcode SO42 7ZL

The 'Maggie May'-era Rod Stewart, a song inspired by his trip to Hampshire in 1961

East End
The Stones, The Who and Led Zeppelin at Stargroves

Stargroves ticks all the boxes in any competition for the most rock 'n' roll mansion in Britain. Oliver Cromwell famously stayed there, and more recent visitors have recorded some of rock's most popular albums. The Rolling Stones (Sticky Fingers and Exile on Main St) and Led Zeppelin (Physical Graffiti and Houses of the Holy) were among a number to be created inside the old walls. At various times owned by Mick Jagger and Rod Stewart, the estate also attracted The Who, utilising the grand surroundings and The Rolling Stones' mobile recording unit to good effect when recording their tour de force, 'Won't Get Fooled Again'.

LOCATION 340: three miles west of the A34 at the village of East End (part of the larger village of East Woodhay), postcode RG20 0AE. Stargroves is a private house, but there are public footpaths around the estate

Hampshire

Farley Chamberlayne
The birth of British folk-rock at Farley House

According to Q magazine, "folk-rock's defining moment" came with the release of Fairport Convention's album Liege & Lief. The beginning of something special in British folk can be traced back to the group's eight-week stay at Farley House in the remote village of Farley Chamberlayne during the summer of 1969. Fairport's bass guitarist Ashley Hutchings recalled what he remembered as "a sense of adventure" and the "uplifting" atmosphere of the large Queen Anne house where they wrote, rehearsed and lived

the Liege & Lief experience. In between the periods spent inventing British folk-rock, the group lived the rural lifestyle to the full with kite-flying, football on the lawn, trips to the local pub and even a spot of busking in nearby Winchester.

LOCATION 341: near the village of Braishfield, on the A3090, Farley House, Farley Lane, Farley Chamberlayne, postcode SO51 0QR. Status: private residence

"Being in that HOUSE certainly helped FORM the music 🙶
ASHLEY HUTCHINGS

Above: Fairport Convention, with new members Dave Mattacks and Dave Swarbrick, meet on the lawn at Farley House in 1969 during the creation of Liege & Lief

Headley
Radical recordings at Headley Grange

Some of Led Zeppelin's best work was created at Headley Grange. Built in 1795, the rambling retreat certainly had an atmosphere when the band moved in for the duration of their stay 176 years later. "It was very Charles Dickens", according to guitarist Jimmy Page, whose room was at the very top of the former poorhouse. "Dank and spooky" is how he remembered it. "It became lighter as a result of our stay there," he told Guitar magazine. Using The Rolling Stones' mobile recording unit, the band harnessed the house's acoustics to maximum effect with John Bonham's drumming captured in the hall on tracks such as 'When the Levee Breaks'. Although most famous as the place where Robert Plant was

216 UK & IRELAND EDITION **ROCK ATLAS**

Photo: David Roberts

reported to have completed the lyrics for 'Stairway to Heaven', the rural retreat was already a favourite of Fleetwood Mac, who recommended it to Led Zeppelin. Genesis created much of The Lamb Lies Down on Broadway here and Ian Dury and Elvis Costello also recorded or rehearsed there. A footnote about Headley Grange from a concerned Jimmy Page when speaking to Mojo magazine about his return to the place while filming the movie It Might Get Loud. "There's this kind of Zeppelin heritage and it's fine for us to be glib about that, but the family there had had their gates nicked in the run-up to the O2

> **" We did 'Going to California' with all of us sitting OUTSIDE ON THE GRASS playing mandolins and whatever else was around "**
>
> **JOHN PAUL JONES**
> recalls a winter recording

[gig in 2007] because they had Headley Grange written on them! I felt bad about that."

LOCATION 342: just south of the B3002, Liphook Road, Headley, postcode GU35 8N. Status: private house. Don't make Jimmy Page feel 'bad' - stay away from those gates!

Above: Headley Grange: once a poorhouse, now one of rock's stateliest of homes

Opposite page: Led Zeppelin IV and Peter Gabriel's final album as a member of Genesis, The Lamb Lies Down on Broadway, were both created at Headley Grange

Hampshire

Headley
Fleetwood Mac's Benifold home

With a population of under 6,000, Headley has certainly punched above its weight when counting rock star inhabitants. Even before Led Zeppelin commandeered Headley Grange on Liphook Road, Fleetwood Mac had made the small village their base. In 1970, the same year that Peter Green left and the band began their transformation from blues-rock band to multi-million-album-selling supergroup, Fleetwood Mac and manager Clifford Davis bought a three-storey, 20-room mansion called Benifold on Headley Hill Road. Purchased for a reported £23,000, the former religious retreat, with the addition of recording and rehearsal space, became the Fleetwood Mac commune during a period when they made four albums, Future Games, Bare Trees, Penguin and Mystery to Me, hitched up to The Rolling Stones' mobile recording studio parked outside. After four years of the usual rock star disagreements, departures and drinking sessions at local pubs (The Crown and The Wheatsheaf), the band upped and left for California in 1974.

LOCATION 343: Benifold, Headley Hill Road, Headley, postcode GU35 8DU

Fleetwood Mac's Bob Welch (far right) was inspired to write 'Hypnotized' (the single on the Mystery to Me album) following a dream he experienced when a UFO piloted by Navajo shaman landed on the tennis court at Benifold

Built in 1899, Benifold (originally called Pinehurst) was home to Fleetwood Mac for four years while they shuttled back and forth to the States during their rise to supergroup status

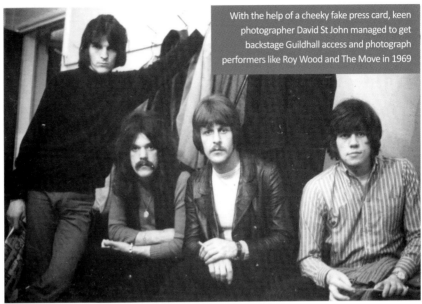

With the help of a cheeky fake press card, keen photographer David St John managed to get backstage Guildhall access and photograph performers like Roy Wood and The Move in 1969

Photo: David St John

Southampton
Access all areas for David St John at the Guildhall

Advertised as the south's largest multi-purpose entertainment venue, Southampton's opulent-looking Guildhall has hosted concerts from a who's who of music legends including The Rolling Stones, David Bowie, Pink Floyd, Biffy Clyro, Jake Bugg, Arctic Monkeys and Amy Winehouse. Promoting gigs under the Friars and Ricky-Tick banners in the sixties and Seventies, the Guildhall has catered for all music tastes from prog to mod balls. Local celebrity and rock and roller David St John was an enthusiastic, regular concert-goer and is well qualified to rate some of the Guildhall's classic gigs. St John managed to catch The Jimi Hendrix Experience twice, both as support to Cat Stevens and The Walker Brothers, then for the headlining Geno Washington and his Ram Jam Band. Of the progressive bands, he singles out the "amazing, weird showmanship" of Jethro Tull but rates an appearance by The Move as perhaps his most memorable night at the Guildhall, where he got to support them and photograph them. Now a comedy entertainer and frequent contestant on TV quiz shows who lives in the West Midlands, David remembers The Move's Guildhall gig vividly. "I turned up at the Guildhall early and found out that the support band had let [The Move] down. I made a couple of quick calls and managed to scrape up a band and we set up, then played a made-up 'busking' set which went well. Roy Wood was watching us from the wings and when we came off he complimented me on my blues harmonica playing. I asked if I could take a couple of quick backstage pics in their dressing room and they were all great. Woody asked if he could buy the photos! He gave me his address (Birmingham) and sent a cheque." Unlike a number of city centre venues, Southampton's Guildhall continues to promote sizeable concerts with big-name billing.

LOCATION 344: the O2 Guildhall, as it is called now, is in the heart of the city centre, West Marlands Road, postcode SO14 7LP

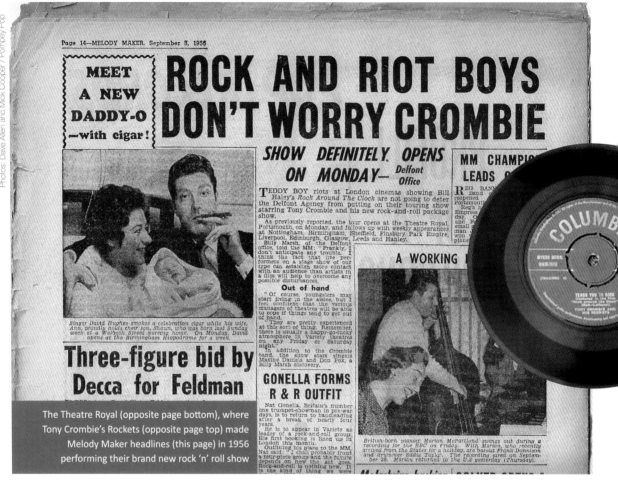

Photos: Dave Allen and Mick Cooper / Pompey Pop

Page 14—MELODY MAKER. September 8, 1956

MEET A NEW DADDY-O —with cigar!

ROCK AND RIOT BOYS DON'T WORRY CROMBIE

SHOW DEFINITELY OPENS ON MONDAY— *Delfont Office*

TEDDY BOY riots at London cinemas showing Bill Haley's *Rock Around The Clock* are not going to deter the Delfont Agency from putting on their touring show starring Tony Crombie and his new rock-and-roll package show.

As previously reported, the tour opens at the Theatre Royal, Portsmouth, on Monday, and follows up with weekly appearances at Nottingham, Birmingham, Sheffield, Finsbury Park Empire, Liverpool, Edinburgh, Glasgow, Leeds and Hanley.

Billy Marsh, of the Delfont office, told the MM: "Frankly, I don't anticipate any trouble. I think the fact that live performers on a stage show of our type can establish more contact with an audience than artists in a film will help to overcome any possible disturbances.

Out of hand

"Of course, youngsters may start jiving in the aisles, but I feel confident that the various managers of theatres will be able to cope if things tend to get out of hand.

"They are pretty experienced at this sort of thing. Remember, there is usually a happy-go-lucky atmosphere in Variety theatres on any Friday or Saturday night."

In addition to the Crombie band, the show stars singers Maxine Daniels and Don Fox, a Billy Marsh discovery.

GONELLA FORMS R & R OUTFIT

Nat Gonella, Britain's number one trumpet-showman in pre-war days, is to return to bandleading after a break of nearly four years.

He is to appear in Variety as leader of a rock-and-roll group. His first booking is lined up in London this month.

Outlining his plans to the MM, Nat said: "I shall probably front a four-piece group and the future depends on how the act goes. Rock-and-roll is nothing new. It is the kind of thing we were

MM CHAMPIO... LEADS ...

REG BAN... Band reopened Portsmouth Reg's h... Empress day. ... small man ... won ... pions...

A WORKING ...

Singer David Hughes smokes a celebration cigar while his wife, Ann, proudly holds their son, Shaun, who was born last Sunday week at a Welbeck Street nursing home. On Monday, David opens at the Birmingham Hippodrome for a week.

Three-figure bid by Decca for Feldman

British-born pianist Marian McPartland swings out during a recording for the BBC on Friday. With Marian, who recently arrived from the States for a holiday, are bassist Frank Donnison and drummer Eddie Taylor. The recording aired on September 28. Marian returned to the US yesterday (Thursday).

The Theatre Royal (opposite page bottom), where Tony Crombie's Rockets (opposite page top) made Melody Maker headlines (this page) in 1956 performing their brand new rock 'n' roll show

Portsmouth
A British rock 'n' roll first

Portsmouth's Evening News dubbed it "the most controversial music craze since the Charleston" when rock 'n' roll first got a live airing on the stage of the Theatre Royal. More significantly, it would appear that the good teenagers of Portsmouth witnessed what may have been the first British rock 'n' roll show when Tony Crombie and his Rockets performed that night on September 10, 1956.

This was more than four months before Bill Haley and his Comets set foot on British soil up the coast at Southampton. For his new rock 'n' roll tour, drummer Crombie had spent £400 assembling a group to emulate the sounds of the new genre coming out of the US and is thought to be the first British rocker to have won a recording contract, having penned a 1956 deal with EMI Columbia's Norrie Paramor.

LOCATION 345: the Theatre Royal, 20-24 Guildhall Walk, PO1 2DD

"Screams, **STAMPING** feet, and the... clap, clap, clap of a feverish, shirt-sleeved and sweatered teenage audience launched 'Rock 'n' Roll' on to the British variety stage 🗨

EVENING NEWS
report of the event in 1956

Winchester
Graham Nash's birthday 'trip' to the cathedral

"Standing on the grave of a soldier that died in 1799, and the day he died was a birthday and I noticed it was mine" was the poignant line written by Graham Nash in 'Cathedral', the epic five-minute track on Crosby, Stills & Nash's 1977 album CSN. Nash had visited the cathedral on his 32nd birthday while under the influence of LSD in 1974. The spontaneous trip to Winchester, along with his road manager Leo Makota in a chauffeur-driven 1928 Rolls-Royce, was made the morning after a gig at the Royal Albert Hall. Both wanted to touch the famous Stonehenge standing stones, which they did, but they also wound up in Winchester, where they visited the Great Hall (seeking out King Arthur's Round Table) and the cathedral. The subject of the song he wrote as a result of his visit to the cathedral was based around a grave inscription to British Army officer Hugh Foulkes, prominently marked on Winchester Cathedral's central aisle floor, whose birthday Nash saw was identical to his own. "There were graves on the floor and one of them attracted my attention and my legs started to waver, not shake, but just waver, you know, like a divining rod - it was real strange" was how Nash later described his moving experience while "flying in Winchester Cathedral", as the song says.

LOCATION 346: Winchester Cathedral, 9 The Close, postcode SO23 9LS

> **"...getting up in the morning at six, getting into this old Rolls-Royce that we'd hired for the day, going over to this dealer's in London and picking up some acid, dropping the ACID and then going through Richmond Park with the ultimate goal of ending up in STONEHENGE – and we went through Winchester on the way "**
>
> **GRAHAM NASH**

Hampshire

Twyford Down
Galliano's M3 madness protest

'Twyford Down' was a hit single for acid jazz exponents Galliano, taken from their 1994 Top 10 album The Plot Thickens. The track was created as their protest at the excavation of a large chunk of an 'Area of Outstanding Natural Beauty' near Winchester to lay a new two-mile stretch of the M3.

LOCATION 347: the distinctive M3 motorway cutting near Winchester

Drums over Twyford Down: a still from Galliano's video promoting the plight of this Hampshire beauty spot

Winchester
A Grammy-winning cathedral song

Foundations for Winchester's vast cathedral were laid in 1079. The best part of a thousand years later it became the inspiration for an astonishingly successful transatlantic hit single. The New Vaudeville Band's 'Winchester Cathedral' was a UK No.4 hit and topped the US Billboard Hot 100 for three weeks in 1966, selling more than a million copies in the process. The British sextet were the creation of Geoff Stephens, who, hired as a staff songwriter in London's Denmark Street, was gazing one day at a calendar on the office wall. Stephens was intrigued by the architecture on a picture of Winchester Cathedral below the dates and set about writing a song to capture his enthusiasm for the subject.

LOCATION 348: Winchester Cathedral, 9 The Close, postcode SO23 9LS

The small but perfectly formed "most relevant venue in the south" is still going strong in 2014.

Southampton
Seal of approval for The Joiners

The Joiners first promoted live music as far back as the late Sixties, when Jimi Hendrix is rumoured to have dropped in en route to or from the Isle of Wight Festival. By 1988, every other Tuesday was set aside for the legendary 'Next Big Thing' nights. The organiser's clever knack of booking bands already popular but about to hit huge saw 600 queue down the street for The Charlatans in 1990, and a similar level of excitement greeted the visit of the Manic Street Preachers in 1991. Brett Anderson of Suede and The Verve's Richard Ashcroft each rate their gigs at The Joiners in 1992 as among their best ever. The Joiners has a reputation for superb hospitality, which may have encouraged Oasis, Coldplay, The Libertines and Radiohead to also play what NME announced as "undoubtedly the most relevant venue in the south".

LOCATION 349: 141 St Mary's Street, postcode SO14 1NS

Born in HAMPSHIRE

Rob da Bank (Robert Gorham) DJ and festival promoter (b. 24 Jun 1974, Warsash)
Carl Barât, guitar/vocals, The Libertines (b. 6 Jun 1978, Basingstoke)
Amelle Berrabah, Sugababes (b. 22 Apr 1984, Aldershot)
Ronnie Bond, drums, The Troggs (b. 4 May 1940, Andover, d. 13 Nov 1992)
Andy Burrows, drums, Razorlight (b. 30 Jun 1979, Winchester)
Will Champion, drums, Coldplay (b. 31 Jul 1978, Southampton)
Craig David (b. 5 May 1981, Southampton)
Michael Giles, drums, King Crimson (b. 1 Mar 1942, Waterlooville)
Hugh Grundy, drums, The Zombies (b. 6 Mar 1945, Winchester)
Steve Hillier, keyboards, Dubstar (b. 14 May 1969, Southampton)
Roger Hodgson, vocals, Supertramp (b. 21 Mar 1950, Portsmouth)
Mike Hugg, drums, Manfred Mann (b. 11 Aug 1942, Gosport)
Howard Jones (b. 23 Feb 1955, Southampton)
Paul Jones, vocals/harmonica, Manfred Mann (b. 24 Feb 1942, Portsmouth)
Steve Lamacq, presenter (b. 16 Oct 1965, Basingstoke)
Laura Marling (b. 1 Feb 1990, Eversley)
Scott Mills, DJ and radio presenter (b. 28 Mar 1973, Eastleigh)
Mickie Most, producer/music mogul (b. 20 Jun 1938, Aldershot, d. 30 May 2003)
Paul Newton, bass, Uriah Heep (b. 21 Feb 1948, Andover)
Roland Orzabal, vocals/guitar, Tears for Fears (b. 22 Aug 1961, Portsmouth)
Reg Presley, vocals, The Troggs (b. 12 Jun 1941, Andover, d. 4 Feb 2013)
Peter Staples, bass, The Troggs (b. 3 May 1944, Andover)
Jef Streatfield, guitar, The Wildhearts (b. 8 Jun 1971, Southampton)
Mike Vickers, guitar/saxophone, Manfred Mann (b. 18 Apr 1940, Southampton)
Dave Wright, guitar, The Troggs (b. 21 Jan 1944, Winchester, d. 10 Oct 2008)

Herefordshire

J̃ust about every major act apart from The Beatles played Hereford's Hillside Ballroom back in the Sixties, but it's the less obvious venues at Grosmont Wood Farm and Hereford United football ground that are perhaps most noteworthy. Black Sabbath drummer Bill Ward's extraordinary and ingenious wrought-iron homage to the band's track 'Paranoid' just begs the question why no other rock star mansions have followed suit. The county can claim to have also given us the majority of the line-ups for The Pretenders and Mott the Hoople, but it's Mike Oldfield's retreat to escape the pressures of stardom at Hergest Ridge that has to be the jewel in Herefordshire's rock crown.

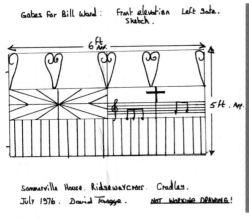

The rough sketch made by Black Sabbath blacksmith David Tangye for drummer Bill Ward's decorative gates to Somerville House

Cradley
The Black Sabbath blacksmith calls

It was near this upmarket Herefordshire village that Black Sabbath drummer Bill Ward commissioned the distinctive 'Paranoid'-themed entrance gates to his Somerville House home. Knowing that David Tangye was employed by Sabbath frontman Ozzy Osbourne but was also a blacksmith by profession, Ward called on his craftsmanship to fashion the gates displaying the opening musical notes to 'Paranoid', Black Sabbath's best known track. Tangye was a man of many talents: the Ozzy emissary and blacksmith also went on to co-author the Black Sabbath biography, How Black Was Our Sabbath.

LOCATION 350: Somerville House is on Bromyard Road, postcode WR13 5JL. Status: private residence

Grosmont
Floyd, Tull and Mac on the farm

With no neighbours and a decent traffic-free route in, this location could have claimed to be the perfect rave venue - with police approval! Grosmont Wood Farm barn was the remote rural venue for some extraordinary rock concerts. The Gwent Constabulary Spring Bank Holiday Barn Dance in 1967 saw recent chart debutants Pink Floyd performing, while Jethro Tull, Fleetwood Mac and Arthur Brown stormed the barn almost exactly two years later.

LOCATION 351: about two miles north-west off the B4521 at Cross Ash, postcode NP7 8LB. Status: private farm

Born in HEREFORDSHIRE

Martin Chambers, drums, The Pretenders (b. 4 Sep 1951, **Hereford**)
Pete Farndon, bass, The Pretenders (b. 12 Jun 1952, **Hereford**, d. 14 Apr 1983)
Ellie Goulding (b. 30 Dec 1986, **Lyonshall**)
Dale 'Buffin' Griffin, drums, Mott the Hoople (b. 24 Oct 1948, **Ross-on-Wye**)
James Honeyman-Scott, guitar, The Pretenders (b. 4 Nov 1956, **Hereford**, d. 16 Jun 1982)
Albert Lee, guitar (b. 21 Dec 1943, **Lingen**)
Mick Ralphs, guitar, Bad Company/Mott the Hoople (b. 31 Mar 1944, **Stoke Lacy**)

Hereford
United in rock at Edgar Street

Island Records recording artists Mott the Hoople, Heads, Hands & Feet, Amazing Blondel and Karakorum (whatever happened to them?) formed the line-up for one of the earliest ever football stadium concerts at Hereford United's Edgar Street ground. No Woodstock, the August Bank Holiday event in 1971 drew a crowd of more than 3,000 rock fans: still substantially more than non-league United's attendances for football matches at the time, at least until their epic FA Cup giant-killing of Newcastle United the following winter.

LOCATION 352: the Hereford United football ground is in the centre of Hereford, at Edgar Street, postcode HR4 9JU

Formed in Herefordshire, Mott the Hoople pictured on the cover of their Wildlife album, released just prior to their appearance at Hereford United football ground

Kington
High on Hergest Ridge

A distorted view of Hergest Ridge featuring Mike Oldfield's Irish wolfhound 'Bootleg' and his remote-controlled model glider decorated the cover of his follow-up album to the enormously successful Tubular Bells. The 1974 release was named after the 1,000-foot-high Herefordshire beauty spot which inspired the 20-year-old Oldfield to record it. The house where he lived and worked on Hergest Ridge was The Beacon on Bradnor Hill, just outside the market town of Kington, near the Welsh/English border. Before work could begin, with no road to the house to speak of back then, Oldfield was forced to drag a grand piano 200 yards up the hillside and then remove a window as the treasured instrument would not squeeze through the house door. Oldfield's third album, Ommadawn, was also conceived and written at this remote country retreat, where Oldfield experienced problems. "There were neighbours all around, and they turned up en masse one afternoon, complaining about the noise. It was a bit like the Frankenstein movie, when they all come to get the monster. I put [The Beacon] up for sale the next day. Ever since then, I've lived where there aren't any neighbours." Forgetting Oldfield's reservations, there is no better way to reacquaint yourself with the delights of both his classic albums than by plugging in your MP3 player, following the National Trail out of Kington and striding up the ridge.

LOCATION 353: The Beacon, which has now reverted to a private residence, is on Bradnor Hill near Kington. Hergest Ridge can be visited by following the National Trail out of Kington, which is situated on the A44, postcode HR5

Mike Oldfield indulging his passion for model glider-flying high on Hergest Ridge

Hertfordshire

*W*ithin the Hertfordshire county boundary you can explore Knebworth's 'stately home of rock', the spot where British rock 'n' roll ignited for Cliff Richard when he first heard a new song called 'Heartbreak Hotel', a Welwyn Garden City pub where Led Zeppelin played a seminal gig and the 350-year-old country house where Ritchie Blackmore named a new group Deep Purple. This is the county for Zombies, video shoots, location beginning and ending eras in the Queen timeline, the birthplace of jazz man and (crucially) skiffle enthusiast Chris Barber and a village pub with no beer where Fairport Convention made their home. There's Elton John's obsession with his local football club, the talented Tewin family Wilde, plus Little Richard's rock 'n' roll rescue act in Watford. And, if you travel a short distance up the A1, there remains a reminder, every time you head out of London, of the Canterbury prog rock outfit Hatfield and the North, who took their name from a road sign now irritatingly reworded to read "The North and Hatfield".

Aldbury
Oasis were there then

An Oasis folly? Not the complete disaster of a release many have panned, the band's Be Here Now set a record for the UK's fastest-selling album in 1997, shifting an incredible 663,389 copies in just three days. The setting for the cover shoot was certainly no architectural folly. Photographed at the suitably opulent former home of Playboy Club chief Victor Lownes, Stocks House was the perfect location for sinking a Rolls-Royce in the swimming pool and arranging a selection of thought-provoking items chosen by Noel Gallagher from the BBC props department. When a hotel, Stocks House was a favourite watering hole for Who drummer Keith Moon, and the house and grounds became a video director's dream when selected for filming Madness ('It Must Be Love'), Fun Boy Three ('Summertime') and Kajagoogoo ('Hang On Now'). The house is currently the private residence of former jockey and trainer Walter Swinburn.

LOCATION 354: north of the picturesque village of Aldbury, Stocks Road, Aldbury, postcode HP23 5RX

Stocks House provides the setting for the cover of Oasis' record-breaking follow-up to (What's the Story) Morning Glory?

Cheshunt
The Wolsey Hall Who gigs

A seemingly unremarkable venue, Cheshunt's Wolsey Hall was a regular stepping stone for The Who on their career curve upwards. The band made four appearances here, the first of which was as The High Numbers on October 11, 1964. The venue's "Sunday Scene" promised "raving R&B" at a ticket price of five shillings to see the band, who had recently changed their name from what had been The Who. They returned a month later to Cheshunt, this time billed as The Who. Their act at this time, which was peppered with Motown covers – Martha Reeves' 'Heatwave' was a particular favourite – was about to get a boost with a 23-date residency at London's Marquee Club. Back to Wolsey Hall they came "by popular request" on November 18, 1965 before their final Cheshunt appearance on December 1 of that year. Four weeks before this gig, the band's 'My Generation' had stormed the singles chart and by 1966 Wolsey Hall was just not big enough to accommodate the increasing number of fans who wanted to witness their popular brand of power pop.

LOCATION 355: close to the town centre in Windmill Lane, postcode EN8 9AA

Wolsey Hall attracted bands of the calibre of The Moody Blues and Them in its heyday, but The Who made the biggest impression when they performed there just as their 'My Generation' single was charting

Cheshunt
Noisy and uncooperative: Cliff upsets the neighbours!

Born in India and raised in Hertfordshire, Cliff Richard (Harry Webb as he was then) moved into a new family home on the Bury Green Estate in Cheshunt in 1951. The new, modern, three-bedroom council house at 12 Hargreaves Close was a massive improvement for a family forced to share temporary accommodation with relatives since moving to England two years previously. This is the house where Cliff practised with his mates Terry Smart and Norman Mitcham when forming the original Drifters. Steve Turner's biography shows just what a rebel the young Cliff could be. In it he researched the local council files and discovered a complaint about the noise emanating from No.12 by a neighbour at No.11, requesting that the late-night skiffle sessions cease. The resulting hand-written council record read "son not willing to cooperate". There's a plaque to mark Cliff's association with the house and a development of retirement flats nearby in Cheshunt has been named after the singer at Cliff Richard Court.

LOCATIONS 356 and 357: the house at Hargreaves Close (postcode EN7 5BB) is west of the A10 Great Cambridge Road. Cliff Richard Court is at High Street, Cheshunt, postcode EN8 0BE. Status: both are private residences

Hertfordshire

Knebworth
The 'stately home of rock'

The gothic mansion and grounds that doubled as Wayne Manor in the first Tim Burton-directed Batman movie, Knebworth House has the distinction of being the largest single-stage rock venue in the country, hosting some of Britain's largest outdoor music events. The estate began temporarily shipping out the herds of deer and opening its gates to live rock shows as early as 1974's Bucolic Frolic, which attracted 60,000 fans to watch The Allman Brothers headline a bill also boasting Van Morrison, The Doobie Brothers, The Sensational Alex Harvey Band, Mahavishnu Orchestra and Tim Buckley. In 1975, with the sound travelling as far as the county town of Hertford, 80,000 attended Knebworth Park, excited by the prospect of witnessing performances

from Pink Floyd, Steve Miller Band, Captain Beefheart, Roy Harper and Linda Lewis. Then 1976 saw Mick Jagger drop in for tea and leave his Y-fronts at the foot of his four-poster guest room bed when The Rolling Stones drew 100,000 to Knebworth Fair, joined by 10cc, Hot Tuna, Lynyrd Skynyrd, Todd Rundgren's Utopia and The Don Harrison Band. The Stones were massively late on stage due to someone pouring a bottle of beer into the mixing desk.

A Midsummer Night's Dream in 1978 saw a more modest 60,000 turn out for Genesis, Jefferson Starship, Tom Petty, Devo, Brand X and The Atlanta Rhythm Section and 45,000 attended the advertised Oh God, Not Another Boring Old Knebworth with Frank Zappa

headlining a cutting-edge bill featuring The Tubes, Peter Gabriel, The Boomtown Rats, Rockpile and Wilko Johnson's Solid Senders. The more stately titled 1979 Knebworth Festival saw Led Zeppelin play over two Saturdays to a crowd of 200,000, supported by The New Barbarians, Todd Rundgren, Southside Johnny and The Asbury Dukes, The New Commander Cody Band, Chas & Dave and Fairport Convention. Knebworth 80, with The Beach Boys, Mike Oldfield, Elkie Brooks, Santana, Lindisfarne and The Blues Band, attracted a crowd of 45,000 but signalled the end of rock at Knebworth for a time while jazz and Cliff Richard took over. However, The Return of the Knebworth Fayre in 1985 laid on a heavy-duty line-up featuring Deep Purple, Scorpions, Meat Loaf, UFO,

SJM CONCERTS & MCP PRESENT
By Arrangement With Primary Talent International

oasis
plus special guests
SATURDAY 10th AUGUST 1996
KNEBWORTH PARK
STEVENAGE, HERTFORDSHIRE
(SUBJECT TO LICENCE)

GATES 12 NOON SHOW STARTS 2.15PM PRICE £22.50 INC. VAT (Subject to Booking Fee)   123404

Above left: Beach Boy Al Jardine chats to Henry Lytton-Cobbold and friends on the roof of Knebworth House. The occasion coincided with Henry's brother's 12th birthday party, when the band's Dennis Wilson ate the entire birthday cake. Above: The UK's largest single-stage rock venue packed for the appearance of Robbie Williams in 2003. Left: a ticket to a record-breaking event

Mountain, Mama's Boys and Alaska, boosting the attendance to 80,000.

It's a Kind of Magic had Queen (their last gig with Freddie Mercury), Status Quo, Big Country and Belouis Some, drawing 120,000 punters in 1986 before a four-year gap, after which the same number attended Pink Floyd, Paul McCartney, Mark Knopfler, Eric Clapton, Elton John, Phil Collins, Genesis, Robert Plant and Jimmy Page, Cliff Richard and The Shadows, Status Quo and Tears for Fears. Genesis came back in 1992, supported this time by The Saw Doctors and Lisa Stansfield, watched by 90,000.

The Knebworth attendance record was smashed when Oasis drew 250,000 fans over two days in 1996. The Prodigy, Manic Street Preachers, Ocean Colour Scene, The Charlatans, Cast, The Chemical Brothers, Kula Shaker and The Bootleg Beatles were in support for the most oversubscribed tickets in British rock history. 2001 saw a return to live music with 35,000 grooving to a Ministry of Sound event in nine marquees, before the massive 2003 Robbie Williams concerts drew 375,000 over three nights, the Robster ably assisted by Moby, Ash, Kelly Osbourne and The Darkness. Hedgestock with The Who in 2006 preceded a lull in activity until the Sonisphere Festival arrived in 2009 and repeated its occupancy of Knebworth in 2010, 2011 and back again in 2014, featuring the heavy metal likes of Metallica, Iron Maiden, Alice Cooper, Limp Bizkit and all the usual suspects.

LOCATION 358: Knebworth House and park are a short distance off the A1(M) at Stevenage

Knebworth has become the destination for a summer pilgrimage by hard rock and heavy metal fans since Sonisphere set down roots in Hertfordshire

" I was 14 [when the Stones played] and we have LITTLE MEMENTOS of that. We have a pair of very SMART RED UNDERPANTS left at the bottom of Mick Jagger's bed which are now in the safe 🎵

HENRY LYTTON-COBBOLD
Current owner of Knebworth House

Hertfordshire

Little Hadham
Fairport Convention at The Angel

Following the band's living, working and sharing a house ethos that worked so successfully in Hampshire a year earlier, Fairport Convention moved to the Hertfordshire village of Little Hadham in 1969. They made their home for more than a year in what had been a village pub, The Angel. More than a dozen band members, wives, children and roadies shared one bathroom and one kettle in the basic accommodation. Despite the spartan conditions, the band enjoyed visits from many musicians keen to share their hippie-style hospitality. Drummers Cozy Powell and John Bonham and Nick Drake (rehearsing material for his Bryter Layter album) would all make the trek out to Hertfordshire. After a hard day's writing and rehearsing, local pub The Nags Head was the destination most nights for a spot of unwinding. The band were made welcome by the local community and even staged fundraising gigs for St Cecilia's church organ fund and the Hertfordshire Police benevolent fund, with a crowd of around 3,000 turning up in a meadow in nearby Much Hadham. Their stay at The Angel came to an enforced end shortly after the release of their

1971 Top 10 album Angel Delight, named after their stay in the former pub. Positioned precariously on a sharp corner of the main A120, the building was struck by a lorry, which careered into what was band member Dave Swarbrick's living quarters. The Dutch lorry driver died instantly but Fairport's fiddle player miraculously survived the accident. The band's Simon Nicol recalls, "Swarb's was the [room] with the chevrons on the wall, Richard's [Thompson] is the one above. The entire front wall and the chimney in the corner collapsed on the truck, leaving the floor of RT's room hanging loose in space. A bottle of poteen was rescued from the rubble and was shared with the fire service once the body of the driver and his rather bashed-up co-pilot were removed. As a palliative for extreme shock, it's right up there with hot, sweet tea!"

LOCATIONS 359 and 360: the former Angel inn is on the A120 at the crossroads in Little Hadham, postcode SG11 2DQ. Status: private residence. The Nags Head pub Fairport Convention visited as their local is in nearby Hadham Ford, postcode SG11 2AX

Photo: David Roberts

Left: Dave Swarbrick's room (above the chevrons) was the one hit by the truck

Right: Neighbourly Fairport Convention play a 1970 fete opposite Little Hadham's Nags Head

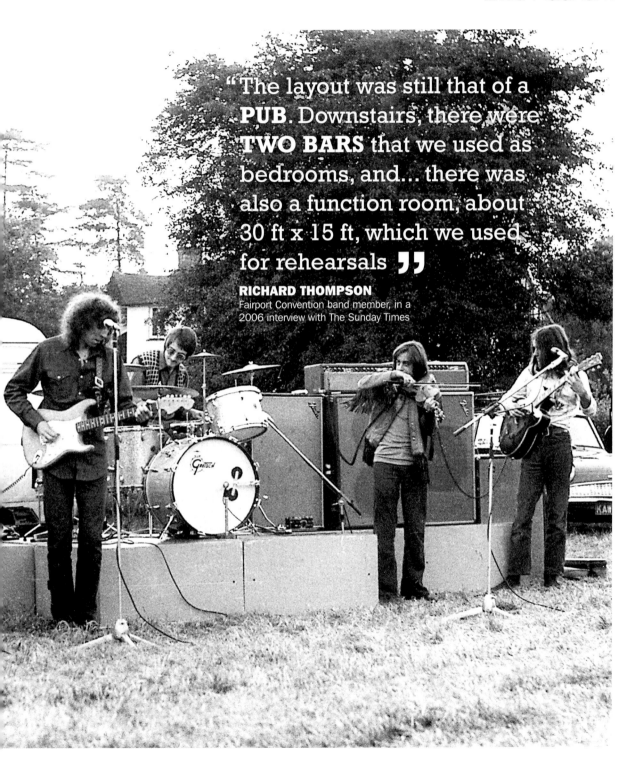

"The layout was still that of a **PUB**. Downstairs, there were **TWO BARS** that we used as bedrooms, and... there was also a function room, about 30 ft x 15 ft, which we used for rehearsals "

RICHARD THOMPSON
Fairport Convention band member, in a
2006 interview with The Sunday Times

Hertfordshire

Hoddesdon
Cliff Richard 'discovered' at the Five Horse Shoes

In March 1958, The Drifters featuring Harry Webb made their debut at Forty Hill Badminton Club, a short distance down the A10 from Webb's Cheshunt home. But their most significant gig came farther north up the A10 a little later, one mid-week evening, at the Five Horse Shoes pub in Burford Street, Hoddesdon. There they met 'Teddy Boy' John Foster, who would become their manager. Foster, crucially, had both a telephone (rare at the time) and enough experience of Soho's legendary 2i's Coffee Bar venue to blag them a booking there that would prove crucial.

LOCATION 361: the pub, now demolished, stood in Burford Street, postcode EN11 8JW

The future Cliff Richard was 'discovered' here: Demolished in 1967, the Five Horse Shoes pub where John Foster discovered what he saw as Britain's own Elvis

" I looked at the singer in his white shirt and black trousers and I saw ELVIS. Something told me, yes, he's going to be BIG "

JOHN FOSTER
Talent-scouting in Hoddesdon
(From Steve Turner's Cliff Richard: The Biography)

Markyate
The Zombies' 'Beechwood Park'

Once a nunnery, now a prep school, Beechwood Park gave its name to The Zombies song that appeared on their 1967 album Odessey and Oracle. The atmospheric track was written by the group's Barnet-born bass guitarist Chris White, whose father owned a local general store from where he and Chris would deliver goods to the girl's school.

LOCATION 362: Beechwood Park School (now co-ed) is south-west of the A5 at Markyate. Postcode: AL3 8AW

Hertford
Balls Park incident as Smile become Queen

November 14, 1970 was the day Queen first played a gig under that name. Balls Park College was the venue for the crowning of Queen, with local outfit Full Frontal Nudity filling the support slot. Booked originally for the college's winter ball as Smile, organisers thought they might be imposters when Roger Taylor's drum kit was set up bearing the bass drum logo "Queen". When quizzed about this, the band explained that they had recently decided on a name change after their previous gig at The Cavern Club, made famous by The Beatles on Liverpool's Mathew Street.

LOCATION 363: no longer a college, the buildings are in private ownership. Postcode: SG13 8AR

Ridge
Deep Purple at Deeves Hall

Deeves Hall in the village of Ridge was the setting for auditions that led to the formation of Deep Purple. An advertisement in the pages of Melody Maker in 1967 assembled the remaining musicians that would create the group Roundabout, who name-changed to Deep Purple in April 1968, but not before a wall of names was democratically drawn up here, which included Orpheus, Sugarlump and Concrete God! The barn at Deeves Hall was perfectly isolated from any neighbours who might have objected to the noise levels of the band as they rehearsed both new songs and the personnel that would see them perform their first gigs in Denmark and release debut album Shades of Deep Purple later that same year. When they weren't road-testing new songs, popping out for provisions at nearby Shenley Stores or dashing back and forth to favourite London

hang-out the Speakeasy, the band would hold séances, and yes - of course - Deeves Hall had its fair share of supernatural activity, either experienced by Ritchie Blackmore or created by one of his frequent, elaborate practical jokes. Was Deeves Hall actually haunted? The previous occupants were sure it was, but if the rocking chair which appeared to move back and forth of its own accord was anything to go by it certainly was not. That was just another of Blackmore's pranks using a tiny hole in the floorboards and a thin piece of string attached to the leg of the chair!

LOCATION 364: Deeves Hall, Deeves Hall Lane, Ridge, postcode EN6 3LS. Located close to South Mimms and junction 23 of the M25 at its intersection with the A1. Status: private

" We had a list [of band names] on the wall at Deeves Hall. One morning DEEP PURPLE was on it... it turned out Ritchie [Blackmore] had put it up... it was his grandmother's favourite song "

JON LORD

Photo: David Roberts

Left: Deeves Hall, where a succession of vocalists were auditioned (including, legend has it, Rod Stewart) for the group that was finally named Deep Purple. Above: The band spent a sleepness night at haunted Deeves Hall on the eve of the photo session for the picture on the cover of their debut album

Hertfordshire

St Albans
Where it all began for The Zombies

Arguably Hertfordshire's best-known international rock exports, The Zombies got together in the best tradition of all British bands - down the pub. All five original members met for the very first time outside the Blacksmiths Arms in St Albans back in 1961. It's a fact commemorated by a stylish, traditional wall plaque with an extraordinary story behind it. Husband and wife Zombies fans Tony and Gill Dawson-Hill were the driving force behind the plaque to mark the band's roots in St Albans – Tony having witnessed them live for the first time as a 13-year-old schoolboy at the city's Ballito stocking factory canteen around the time of their breakthrough hit, 'She's Not There', in 1964. Although they had no luck when approaching English Heritage about their idea for a commemorative plaque (recipients have to be dead, after all), local history, and civic societies and the local council were more enthusiastic but still had no spare cash to fund such a project. Undaunted by a lack of financial support and difficulties with permission from the freeholders to erect a plaque on the building, Tony and Gill finally found their benefactor when the Stonegate Pub Company responded favourably. As the pub's leaseholders they agreed to fund both the plaque and its installation. A year-long campaign by the Dawson-Hills culminated in their plaque being unveiled outside the Blacksmiths Arms on April 27, 2012, 51 years after five local schoolboys became The Zombies.

LOCATION 365: the Blacksmiths Arms, 56 St Peter's Street, in the centre of St Albans. Postcode: AL1 3HG

The plaque was unveiled by The Zombies in 2012 in the presence of Tony and Gill Dawson-Hill, who coordinated the whole project to honour the band's first meeting outside the Blacksmiths Arms. Hertfordshire's best-known international rock exports now draw overseas fans to St Albans, who head for the pub specifically to see the plaque

> "I remember standing outside the Blacksmiths Arms on that Saturday, waiting for the others to arrive. We were going to get a band together, and we had agreed to meet in front of the pub because it was just around the corner from where we used to see bands play in the BLACKSMITHS HALL next door. When we started out, we used to rehearse just behind the pub in a little place called the Pioneer Hall "

COLIN BLUNSTONE
Zombies vocalist, talking to Lemonrock

Tewin
The Wilde family home

The Thatched Rest is the aptly named home of one of British rock 'n' roll's earliest stars. Marty Wilde's family base is where high-profile music careers began for daughter Kim Wilde and son Ricky Wilde. Marty's wife and mother to Kim and Ricky had her own noteworthy pop moment as a member of The Vernons Girls. Joyce Baker, as she was back in the Fifties, married Marty in the first heavily publicised pop star wedding before the couple moved to Hertfordshire. In 1996, Kim Wilde managed a slightly quieter ceremony of her own in nearby Codicote, where she would live with her future husband, the actor Hal Fowler. The wedding did nevertheless have its rock 'n' roll photo opportunity when Kim arrived at Codicote's St Giles Church accompanied by father Marty.

LOCATION 366: The Thatched Rest is on Queen Hoo Lane, postcode AL6 0LT. Status: private residence

Top: Hertfordshire's rock 'n' roll wedding: Kim arrives at St Giles Church with father Marty

Above and left: The Wilde family's Hertfordshire home and Marty Wilde's music room

Hertfordshire

Waltham Cross
Cliff hears Elvis for the first time

A massively important few minutes in the future career of the teenage Cliff Richard took place on the streets of Waltham Cross one Saturday in May 1956, when he unknowingly discovered Elvis Presley on a car radio. Picture the scene and let Cliff describe what happened that spring day that changed his life:

''I can remember the moment I first heard Elvis because I was with some buddies of mine and we were walking round a town called Waltham Cross, which was a few miles away from where I lived. And I remember this car pulling up. It was a little tiny store, a hole-in-the-wall type place, a newsagents, Asplans it was called. Anyway, the car pulled up and he must have been in a rush. The engine was still running, the windows were down. He ran in to buy, perhaps, cigarettes and a newspaper. We're all going 'Ahhh, I'm going to have one of these when I grow up. You know – that sort of thing. And then we heard Elvis singing – well we didn't know who it was – we heard 'Heartbreak Hotel', didn't know what the title was. And before it had finished the car had gone. And we thought – we were – deflated thinking: 'We've got to find out who this person is.''

LOCATION 367: the shop formerly known as Asplan's was in the Four Swannes area of Waltham Cross, postcode EN8 7HH

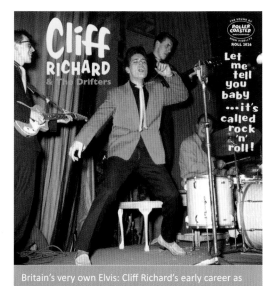

Britain's very own Elvis: Cliff Richard's early career as a rock 'n' roll star owed everything to Elvis' sound and stage moves

Watford
Elton supports his local football club

With his Seventies pop career skyrocketing and his local football team languishing in the old Third Division, Elton John put on what the Watford Observer claimed was the first outdoor rock concert to be staged at a British football stadium. The 1974 gig, which raised almost £30,000 for his beloved Watford FC, drew a crowd of 30,200 to the Vicarage Road football ground to see a bill that included Nazareth and Rod Stewart. According to the local paper, many fans deliberately fainted in order to be helped backstage by the St John Ambulance crew in a bid to get near the show's stars. Elton, who later became Watford Chairman during some of the club's most successful years, returned to play al fresco football fund raisers at the stadium in 2005 and 2010.

LOCATION 368: Vicarage Road is a short walk from the town centre. Postcode: WD18 0ER

The Watford FC nickname is The Hornets: Elton dresses as one for the ground-breaking gig at Vicarage Road in 1974. Left: How the Watford Observer reported "the first ever [concert] to be staged in a British football stadium"

Watford

Little Richard to the rescue at the Gaumont

Carrying on the British music hall tradition of great variety bills, promoter Don Arden was attempting the teenage equivalent for pop music in the early Sixties. By the time his 1963 package tour arrived at the Watford Gaumont, the advertised Everly Brothers, Bo Diddley, Rolling Stones and Mickie Most line-up was failing to attract sufficient interest at the box office. The Watford leg of the tour on October 5 hit a significant turning point when Little Richard was added to the mix. Arden took typically forceful action, and after reportedly phoning the American star 20 times, Richard relented and joined the tour in Hertfordshire. The excitable rock 'n' roller didn't disappoint his audience, pounding out his hits, at one point clambering on top of his piano, stripping off everything but his trousers and giving an incendiary performance that garnered four encores.

LOCATION 369: tragically, all that remains of the old cinema is the road name Gaumont Approach, a stone's throw from the building's original site at 65 High Street, Watford. Postcode: WD17 1LJ

Welwyn Garden City

Led Zeppelin take off at The Cherry Tree

A Waitrose supermarket now dominates the building where the Cherry Tree pub once entertained music fans. In the same week their debut album first stormed the chart, Led Zeppelin played here at the pub's Bluesville '69 Club in April 1969. The Cherry Tree also catered for Tamla and soul fans on various nights of the week, but it was the staggering performance by a group who were on the cusp of rock superstardom that most will recall best.

LOCATION 370: Welwyn Garden City town centre, Bridge Road, postcode AL8 6AB

> " I remember Page's strange antics with his weird box of sounds. An **INCREDIBLE**, powerful noise vibrating the wooden floorboards "

ANDY CLARE Baldock schoolboy, remembers Jimmy Page at The Cherry Tree

Born in HERTFORDSHIRE

Rod Argent, vocals/keyboards, The Zombies/Argent (b. 14 Jun 1945, St Albans)

Paul Atkinson, guitar, The Zombies (b. 19 Mar 1946, Cuffley, d. 1 Apr 2004)

Russ Ballard, guitar/vocals, Argent (b. 31 Oct 1945, Waltham Cross)

Chris Barber (b. 17 Apr 1930, Welwyn Garden City)

Colin Blunstone, vocals, The Zombies (b. 24 Jun 1945, Hatfield)

Chris Britton, guitar, The Troggs (b. 21 Jan 1944, Watford)

Martin Carthy (b. 21 May 1941, Hatfield)

Ray Cooper, percussionist (b. 19 Sep 1942, Watford)

Alesha Dixon (b. 7 Oct 1978, Welwyn Garden City)

Robert 'Lu' Edmonds, guitar, Public Image Ltd (b. 9 Sep 1957, Welwyn Garden City)

Bruce Gilbert, guitar, Wire (b. 18 May 1946, Watford)

Geri Halliwell, Spice Girls (b. 6 Aug 1972, Watford)

Bob Henrit, drums, Argent (b. 2 May 1944, Broxbourne)

Simon Le Bon, vocals, Duran Duran (b. 27 Oct 1958, Bushey)

David 'Buster' Meikle, vocals/guitar, Unit 4 + 2 (b. 1 Mar 1942, Goffs Oak)

Peter Moules, bass, Unit 4 + 2 (b. 14 Oct 1944, Barnet)

Mat Osman, bass, Suede (b. 9 Oct 1967, Welwyn Garden City)

Brian Parker, vocals/guitar, Unit 4 + 2 (b. 1940, Cheshunt, d. 17 Feb 2001)

Jim Rodford, bass, Argent (b. 7 Jul 1941, St Albans)

Jerry Shirley, drums, Humble Pie (b. 4 Feb 1952, Waltham Cross)

Mick Taylor, guitar, John Mayall's Bluesbreakers/The Rolling Stones (b. 17 Jan 1949, Welwyn Garden City)

Storm Thorgerson, album cover designer (b. 1944, Potters Bar, d. 18 Apr 2013)

Tracey Thorn, vocals, Everything but the Girl (b. 26 Sep 1962, Brookmans Park)

Dave Vanian (David Lett) vocals, The Damned (b. 12 Oct 1956, Hemel Hempstead)

Chris White, bass, The Zombies (b. 7 Mar 1943, Barnet)

Isle of Man

*T*he island's chief rockular claim to fame is as the birthplace of the Bee Gees. Justifiably proud of the Gibb brothers, the place has set about honouring the trio in a number of ways. They have even been the subject of a set of stamps. By happy coincidence, their mother once worked behind the counter at the local post office. The island's Palace ballroom was a favourite stopping-off point for chart acts in the Sixties. The Stones appeared twice, in August 1964 and September 1965, and The Who's Pete Townshend even wrote a song set on the Isle of Man following a gig in 1966. That August's visit inspired 'Happy Jack', their 1967 No.3 smash hit written about a man who "lived in the sand at the Isle of Man." By the time Mott the Hoople played their last British gig here, at the Palace in 1974, the island's booming tourist years were in decline and the rock and pop visits declined with them.

Born in ISLE OF MAN

Christine Collister, singer-songwriter (b. 28 Dec 1961, Douglas)

Barry Gibb (b. 1 Sep 1946, Douglas)

Maurice Gibb (b. 22 Dec 1949, Douglas, d. 12 Jan 2003)

Robin Gibb (b. 22 Dec 1949, Douglas, d. 20 May 2012)

Davy Knowles, Back Door Slam (b. 30 Apr 1987, Port St Mary)

Douglas
Birthplace of the Bee Gees

Bee Gees Barry, Robin and Maurice were all born in the island's capital Douglas. In 1999, on the 50th anniversary of Robin and Maurice's birthday, the brothers were honoured in a unique way. Six sets of postage stamps, each themed around a Bee Gees song, were issued by the Isle of Man Post Office in recognition of the world-famous trio's achievements, with a second philatelic tribute in 2009. In 2010, the two surviving brothers, Barry and Robin returned to Douglas where they were honoured as freemen of their home borough in a ceremony at the town hall:

Maurice was also honoured posthumously. Home to the brothers had been a spacious three-bedroomed semi-detached at 50 St Catherine's Drive. By 1952, the family had moved to 43 Snaefell Road on the Willaston estate and in 1955 they left the island for Manchester. In 2013, a blue plaque marking the brothers' St Catherine's Drive home was unveiled by Robin-John, son of Robin Gibb, who had died a year earlier. A second plaque

commemorates the Bee Gees outside the Union Mills Post Office, where the brothers' mother Barbara once worked.

LOCATION 371: St Catherine's Drive is a short walk east of the seafront at Douglas, postcode IM1 4BF. Snaefell Road is north of the town centre, postcode IM2 6. Union Mills Post Office is on Main Road, Union Mills, a mile north west of the centre of Douglas on the A1, postcode IM4 4AD

The Douglas-born Gibb brothers get the Isle of Man stamp of approval, and the Bee Gees plaques in Douglas and the village of Union Mills

Douglas
Unhappy Stones squeeze in a gig at the Lido

Sandwiched between a lengthy spell of recording in Hollywood, California, and a tour of Germany, The Rolling Stones tried unsuccessfully to get their gig in Douglas on September 8, 1965 cancelled. A telegram from Mick, Keith and Andy [manager Andrew Loog Oldham] failed to prevent their appearance at the Palace Lido, despite their "It is impossible" plea. The Stones' flying visit (a year after their only other performance on the island) did allow one night at the Castle Mona Hotel, next door to the venue. The obligatory band photo call was staged on the hotel balcony with screaming fans below. Amid all the hysteria, Mick, Keith, Brian, Bill and Charlie were forced to make their entrance to the venue via a toilet window. Despite their seeming reluctance to fulfil their contracted booking they put on a storming show.

LOCATION 372: the ornate Palace Ballroom, later called the Lido, was said to be the largest in Europe at one time. Demolished to extend the casino, this imposing structure stood next to the once magnificent and still standing, Castle Mona Hotel, Central Promenade, Douglas, postcode IM2 4LY

Keith Richards and Brian Jones get in some practice backstage at the Lido for the gig the Stones suggested was "impossible to do"

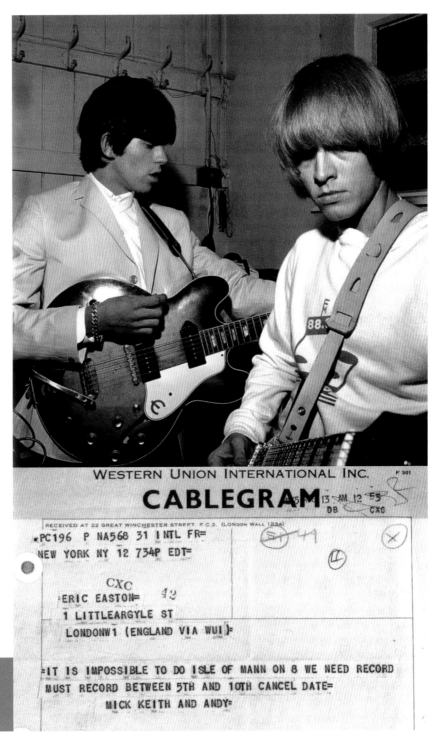

WESTERN UNION INTERNATIONAL INC.

CABLEGRAM

RECEIVED AT 22 GREAT WINCHESTER STREET. E.C.2. (LONDON WALL 1234)

PC196 P NA568 31 INTL FR=
NEW YORK NY 12 734P EDT=

CXC
ERIC EASTON= 42
1 LITTLEARGYLE ST
LONDONW1 (ENGLAND VIA WUI)=

=IT IS IMPOSSIBLE TO DO ISLE OF MANN ON 8 WE NEED RECORD
MUST RECORD BETWEEN 5TH AND 10TH CANCEL DATE=
MICK KEITH AND ANDY=

Isle of Wight

*H*ome to poet Alfred Lord Tennyson, the Isle of Wight attracted the new order of pop poetry when the likes of Bob Dylan, Leonard Cohen, Joni Mitchell and Joan Baez arrived to make the Isle of Wight Festivals some of the most significant events in British pop history. With a larger gathering than Woodstock, the island's 1970 festival was also Britain's biggest. It showcased Jimi Hendrix's final UK performance, a fact commemorated by a statue to the guitarist at Freshwater. Happily, the strong connection between the Isle of Wight and contemporary music continues to this day where the annual festival takes place in the heart of the island at Newport. Retro rock 'n' roll movie That'll Be The Day was filmed at Shanklin and Ryde, where actor pop stars David Essex, Ringo Starr, Billy Fury, Keith Moon and Viv Stanshall expressed their love for the place. In the spirit of Tennyson, who surrounded himself with island visitors Edward Lear, Gilbert and Sullivan and Jenny Lind, the singer-songwriter Robyn Hitchcock is perhaps the modern-day equivalent, finding the place an inspiration that draws him back regularly for performances to charm his loyal followers. The island features poetically in his song 'Airscape': "cliffs suspended in the heat" and "the sun reflected from the waves. Inshore it spangles."

Bembridge
Bob Dylan's B&B

When Bob Dylan was invited to appear at the second Isle of Wight Festival in 1969, the organisers sold him on the idea by sending both their own movie and booklet of the island's best features. Dylan and family were invited to spend a two-week, all expenses paid holiday on the island with a $50,000 festival appearance fee for dad. As it turned out, an accident on board the ocean liner Queen Elizabeth II prevented son Jesse, and as a consequence daughter Maria, joining Dylan and wife Sara when the couple agreed to come and settle into their holiday hideaway at Forelands Farm, Bembridge. Visited by George Harrison,

Ringo Starr and John Lennon while enjoying all the home comforts of the idyllic farm bed and breakfast, Dylan spent the fortnight consuming healthy quantities of pies, porridge, tea and honey, playing tennis (badly according to housekeeper Judy Gascoyne), sailing and making excursions to Queen Victoria's Osborne House and Quarr Abbey to experience the monks chanting. Meanwhile, Dylan's backing group, The Band, made good use of the farm's barn and set up their equipment for rehearsals for what would be Dylan's first major live performance since his serious motorcycle accident in 1966.

LOCATION 373: Forelands Farm Lane, postcode PO35 5TJ. Status: private residence

Freshwater
The Jimi Hendrix statue

As a lasting memorial to Jimi Hendrix and the historic 1970 music festival, Dimbola Lodge Museum is the location for a statue of the world's most famous guitarist, who died just three weeks after his performance at the third Isle of Wight Festival close by at East Afton Farm. Decisions regarding the placing of the statue, commissioned by music promoter John Giddings, have been controversial. The National Trust denied permission to site it at the original festival location and Dimbola Lodge curator Brian Hinton checked out the planning permission regulations before the life-size Hendrix bronze was positioned outside in the museum grounds. A local faction, vehemently opposed to the honouring of the American rock star, campaigned to stop what some considered an outrageous monument to a "junkie". Happily, the statue still survives in its spot at the former residence of Julia Margaret Cameron, the home of the celebrated Victorian photographer. The building is now a museum to her work and also provides visitors with an exhibition of the colourful history behind the Isle of Wight's music festivals. A final word from Brian Hinton: "Janie Hendrix wrote to me from Seattle thanking me for helping to save the statue and saying how Jimi would have been proud to be associated with the great Victorian poets and artists whose work he so loved."

LOCATION 374: the Jimi Hendrix statue is in the garden at Dimbola Lodge Museum, Terrace Lane, Freshwater Bay. Postcode: PO40 9QE

Photo: Alan Simpkins: Isle of Wight Images

The Jimi Hendrix statue was created by Putney-based sculptor John Swindells

Bob Dylan gets some exercise ahead of his appearance at the 1969 Isle of Wight Festival with some help from George Harrison, on court at Bob's Bembridge bed and breakfast accommodation

" After supper some evenings [Bob] would ask if I would like him to sing something. I would **DEMOTE** George Harrison to go fetch things from the kitchen and help me do the washing up so I would not **MISS** anything "
JUDY GASCOYNE

ISLE OF WIGHT FESTIVAL

FRIDAY 28th AUG
CHICAGO · FAMILY · TASTE
· JAMES TAYLOR · ARRIVAL ·
LIGHTHOUSE · PROCOL HARUM
MELANIE · VOICES OF EAST HARLEM

SATURDAY 29th
DOORS · JONI MITCHELL · WHO
FREE · SLY AND THE FAMILY STONE
CAT MOTHER · JOHN SEBASTIAN
· EMERSON, LAKE AND PALMER ·
MUNGO JERRY · SPIRIT

SUNDAY 30th AUG
JIMI HENDRIX EXPERIENCE
JOAN BAEZ · LEONARD COHEN
· DONOVAN · RICHIE HAVENS ·
MOODY BLUES · RALPH McTELL
· PENTANGLE · GOOD NEWS

Latest addition MILES DAVIS
JETHRO TULL · TEN YEARS AFTER

East Afton
Hendrix headlines UK's biggest festival

Originally scheduled for Churchills Farm, Calbourne, the county council found the site unsuitably "high, windy and damp" for the third Isle of Wight Festival and agreed that East Afton Farm near Freshwater should host a gathering later reported as being larger than that at Woodstock. A good case could be put forward for this event being better organised and boasting an even better line-up than the most famous festival in rock history a summer earlier. Jimi Hendrix, John Sebastian, Ten Years After, The Who, Sly & The Family Stone, Richie Havens and Joan Baez all reprised their Woodstock performances on a bill that also included Joni Mitchell (whose performance drew four encores), Leonard Cohen, Miles Davis, The Doors, Free, Jethro Tull, Taste, Emerson, Lake and Palmer, Chicago and Donovan. What Woodstock had that the East Afton festival did not was a blockbuster movie watched by millions. Had the 600,000 who made it to the Isle of Wight in 1970 been immortalised on the big screen in the same way, then Hendrix's version of 'God Save the Queen' might have lived in the memory just as long as his wonderfully distorted reworking of 'The Star Spangled Banner' did at Woodstock.

LOCATION 375: east out of Freshwater on the B3399 Newport Road. Postcode: PO40 9UF

A great festival for ticketless rock fans: the East Afton site boasted elevated hillside viewpoints of the whole event in 1970, although in the days before big screens Jimi Hendrix would have been virtually invisible to the naked eye

"No I'm not getting £30,000, or whatever, for this one... Leonard Cohen and I are living in a **NICE LITTLE HOTEL**... with breakfast at a quarter-to-nine"
JOAN BAEZ

Godshill
The 1968 'Isle of Wight Pop Festivity'

The story of pop festivals on the Isle of Wight began when used as a means to raise funds for the island's swimming pool association. The one-hundred-acre Hells Field at Ford Farm, in the south of the island near Godshill, was the setting for what was advertised as "The Great South Coast Bank Holiday Pop Festivity". The August 1968 one-nighter was compered by John Peel, and those present saw headliners Jefferson Airplane make their British debut. The 10,000 fans also enjoyed performances by the Crazy World of Arthur Brown, Tyrannosaurus Rex, The Move, The Pretty Things and Fairport Convention, whose vocalist Iain Matthews (who sang with his eyes tight shut) recalled: "I started Leonard Cohen's 'Suzanne' in darkness, when I opened my eyes at the end of the song it was dawn."

LOCATION 376: north of Niton on the A3055. Postcode PO38 2BP

Born on ISLE OF WIGHT

Boon Gould, guitar, Level 42 (b. 4 Mar 1955, **Shanklin**)
Phill Jupitus, presenter (b. 25 Jun 1962, **Newport**)
Mark King, vocals, Level 42 (b. 20 Oct 1958, **Cowes**)
Nathan King, vocals, Level 42 (b. 29 Aug 1970, **Cowes**)
David Steele, bass/keyboards, Fine Young Cannibals (b. 8 Sep 1960, **Cowes**)

Quarr Abbey
Scott Walker's walk on the quiet side

At the height of his fame, The Walker Brothers' Scott Walker discovered he hadn't the temperament to deal with being a swinging 60s pop star and spent some time at Quarr Abbey. This beautiful medieval monastery provided both peace and seclusion and the opportunity for the singer to study the Gregorian chanting of the Abbey's monks, something Bob Dylan witnessed on a day trip when staying locally while performing at the island's 1969 pop festival. Sadly for Walker, his adoring fans soon discovered his whereabouts and would hammer on the Abbey doors or enter the grounds to catch a glimpse of their idol.

LOCATION 377: north of the A3054 between Fishbourne and Binstead, postcode PO33 4ES. The Abbey invites organised group tours

After his stay at Quarr Abbey, in December 1966, Scott Walker wore the key to his monastery room around his neck for this LP cover shoot

Wootton
Dylan headlines the 1969 Isle of Wight Festival of Music

The second Isle of Wight Festival attracted 150,000 music fans from around the world - a greatly increased gathering compared to the first festival assembled in the fields a short distance from Woodside Bay, to the north of the island. Bob Dylan was the big draw for a crowd that included Beatles John Lennon, George Harrison and Ringo Starr and assorted celebrities including Jane Fonda, Roger Vadim, Keith Richards, Mick Jagger, Peter Wyngarde, Terence Stamp and Cilla Black. The Who (whose helicopter was involved in an accident on landing), Pentangle, Richie Havens, Tom Paxton, The Moody Blues, Joe Cocker, Family, The Nice and The Pretty Things provided the supporting bill. The most entertaining performance of the weekend came from the Bonzo Dog Doo-Dah Band's explosions, bubble-blowing machine and Viv Stanshall's public information announcements, which kept the crowd informed about the comings and goings at the festival site.

LOCATION 378: north of the A3054 at Wootton Bridge. Postcode: (approx.) PO33 4JP

Ryde
The Beatles' 'Ticket to Ride'

'Ticket to Ryde' anyone? The seaside town to the island's north is said to have been the inspiration for The Beatles' 1965 chart-topper 'Ticket to Ride'. In 1960, before they found worldwide fame, Paul McCartney and John Lennon hitch-hiked down to the Isle of Wight to visit Paul's cousin Elizabeth and her husband Mike Robbins, who ran the Bow Bars pub in Ryde. McCartney revealed that the line had come about as a memory of a British Railways ticket issued for a trip to the town of Ryde. The island also gets a mention in McCartney's Sgt Pepper's Lonely Hearts Club Band album track 'When I'm Sixty-Four': "Every summer we can rent a cottage in the Isle of Wight."

LOCATION 379: 74 Union Street, Ryde, postcode PO33 2LN

Kent

Bowie on the lawns of Haddon Hall: Ziggy Stardust and a surge of early Seventies classic songs were created in the room with the veranda to Bowie's right

*S*tations, caves, a castle and even a sea fort provide Kent's 'Garden of England' with a vigorous crop of music locations. Responsible for the birth of Mick Jagger and Keith Richards, Dartford was the starting point for the formation of Britain's most enduring rock 'n' roll band, The Rolling Stones. Their arch-but-friendly rivals The Beatles favoured the county, with significant visits in 1967. Though 250 miles from the real Strawberry Fields, Kent's Knole Park was the setting for rock's first music video by the Fab Four, who also finished off filming their Magical Mystery Tour 10 miles east at West Malling. The remarkable tunnelled music venue that was Chislehurst Caves, the inspirational big 'listening ears' at Dungeness and Chas Hodges' 'Margate' all fall within the county that also gave birth to Keane, Shane MacGowan, Kevin Ayers and Joss Stone.

Beckenham
Everything's Hunky Dory at Haddon Hall

Beckenham was the place where David Bowie's alter-ego Ziggy Stardust was born and where the ideas flowed on some of his most enduring songs such as 'Life on Mars', conceived and composed late one afternoon after "a beautiful day, sitting on the steps of the bandstand" at Beckenham Park. The park was just a short walk from home at Haddon Hall, a fake gothic mansion where young David's early Seventies transformation from misfit and misfiring songwriter to man on a mission to create an extraordinary career and persona took place. First in the basement, then elevated to a room overlooking the gardens, Bowie slaved away on an endless diet of cigarettes, coffee and tea supplied by doting wife Angie. This period of creative energy and determination paid off and songs written and composed at this time formed the classic albums Hunky Dory and Ziggy Stardust

and the Spiders from Mars, which would confirm his place in the rock star firmament. With nothing left of Haddon Hall these days, the only recognition of Bowie's presence in Beckenham is at the spot where, as plain David Jones, he played some of his earliest gigs at the Three Tuns pub in the High Street, now a restaurant, but a least a restaurant that acknowledges and embraces its Bowie connections. Folk recitals at The Three Tuns gradually evolved into more experimental performances, an initiative Bowie dubbed 'The Arts Lab'. A red plaque marks this key location in Bowie's development as an international superstar, a vital and solitary point of pilgrimage for those seeking out Bowie's Beckenham.

LOCATIONS 380 and 381: the wall plaque is at Zizzi, 157 High Street, Beckenham, postcode BR3 1AE. The demolished Haddon Hall was at 42 Southend Road, now Shannon Way, postcode BR3 1WG

Kent

Chislehurst
Siouxsie's 'Hong Kong Garden'

The inspiration behind Siouxsie and The Banshees' 1978 single 'Hong Kong Garden' was a small Chinese restaurant on the busy Chislehurst High Street. The local band's (Siouxsie grew up in the town) debut hit made No.7 and the lyrics were written as a result of Siouxsie's experiences of the racial abuse suffered by the staff at the hands of local thugs.

LOCATION 382:
Noble House, 101 High Street, Chislehurst, postcode BR7 5AG

" There was a Chinese restaurant in Chislehurst called 'The Hong Kong Garden'. Occasionally the **SKINHEADS** would turn up... en masse and just terrorise these Chinese people who were working there. It was a kind of tribute **"**
SIOUXSIE SIOUX

Photo: Polydor Records

Chislehurst Caves
Kent caves echo to the sound of rock's finest

These man-made subterranean tunnels echoed to the sounds of rock's finest when used as Britain's weirdest music venue in the Sixties and Seventies. Far out and deep down, Chislehurst Caves attracted The Rolling Stones, David Bowie and Jimi Hendrix. DJ Johnny Stewart wasn't impressed by the innovative sounds of The Pink Floyd in 1966. He responded to a radio commercial for a "Radio Caroline night out at Chislehurst Caves - this week Pink Floyd" by jumping on his Lambretta GT 200 and riding in a small mod convoy from Bromley to the caves. "What a load of rubbish, I thought at the time. Five tunes and five shillings to get in. What a waste of money! Status Quo were on the following week but I never returned." In 1974, the caves proved the perfect extravagant underground location for a media bash to celebrate the release of Silk Torpedo by The Pretty Things, the first record on Led Zeppelin's new Swan Song label. An NME report by Steve Turner listed scantily-clad nymphets, nuns in stockings and suspenders, escapologists and fire-eaters, all laid on courtesy of Swan Song's (then) generous £5,000 party budget.

LOCATION 383: between the B264 and the A222 at Caveside Close, postcode BR7 5NL. Status: now a visitor attraction

Denge
Rock art at the 'Listening Ears'

The Dungeness coastal landscape is shaped by the strange architectural splendour of the sound mirrors that are featured as cover artwork on Turin Brakes' Ether Song album and hit single 'Long Distance'. Constructed as a Royal Air Force early warning system for incoming aircraft, the Denge mirrors are often referred to as 'Listening Ears' and have also featured in The Prodigy's video for 'Invaders Must Die' and Blank & Jones' Monument album cover and video for 'A Forest'.

LOCATION 384:
between Lydd-on-Sea and Greatstone-on-Sea. Postcode: TN29 9NL. There's access with guided walks. Visit: www.andrewgrantham.co.uk/soundmirrors for more info

Dartford
A railway epiphany for Jagger and Richards

Although they had met years before when both attended Wentworth Primary School, the significant meeting place for two young students who would form the world's most enduring rock band happened in October 1961 at Dartford railway station. Rock legend has it that Mick Jagger and Keith Richards got into conversation when sharing a railway carriage on a Sidcup-bound train from Dartford station. Richards had noticed, with admiration, the records Jagger had with him that day, hard-to-buy releases that Jagger had purchased by mail order. Other reports suggest the two simply exchanged words on the platform, but what is certain is that they immediately bonded through their enthusiasm for American blues music. At the time of writing, a plaque and even a bronze statue to mark the meeting place is at the planning stage. In the meantime Stones fans can seek out a graphic steel sculpture of Mick Jagger in Dartford's Central Park, paired with a similarly designed representation of a Vox amplifier. The essential piece of rock 'n' roll kit was, according to the nearby plaque, first created by the town's Jennings Musical Industries. A 20-minute walk south-east brings you to local music and arts venue The Mick Jagger Centre, and the local council have honoured the two Stones by naming streets in a new estate near to Keith's Spielman Road boyhood home Stones Avenue, Babylon Close, Ruby Tuesday Drive, Dandelion Row, Little Red Walk, Lady Jane Walk, Angie Mews, Rainbow Close, Cloud Close, Satisfaction Street and Sympathy Street.

LOCATIONS 385, 386, 387 and 388: for Mick and Keith's meeting of minds, go to Station Approach, postcode DA1 1BP. Less than a mile west of the station is The Mick Jagger Centre, Shepherds Lane, postcode DA1 2JZ. The Stones streets are at new housing development The Bridge, less than two miles from the town centre just south of the Queen Elizabeth II Thames crossing, postcode DA1 5PA. The sculptures of Jagger and the Vox amplifier are located next to the Darent Valley Path, just beside the entrance to the Ecology of Colour project in Central Park, Dartford, postcode DA1 1EU

Central Park celebrates Dartford's rock heritage with a sculpture celebrating Mick Jagger and Vox amplifiers: both products of this Kent town

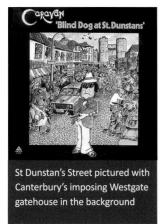

St Dunstan's Street pictured with Canterbury's imposing Westgate gatehouse in the background

Canterbury
Caravan's St Dunstans album cover

Local prog-rockers Caravan featured an illustration of a Canterbury street on the cover of their 1976 hit album Blind Dog at St Dunstans. The band members were frequent visitors to the pubs in the St Dunstans area of the city. The cover illustration depicts the busy St Dunstans Street with the medieval Westgate gatehouse in the background, said to be the oldest in England. Caravan were one of a number of groups in the Sixties that began what became known as the Canterbury scene. Emanating from the group The Wilde Flowers, those associated with the movement, Robert Wyatt, Hugh Hopper, Steve Hillage, Kevin Ayers and Daevid Allen, were not all locals but formed various bands when meeting in the city as students.

LOCATION 389: to find the spot where the blind dog stood, head for Westgate, located where the main A290 crosses the Great Stour river in Canterbury city centre. Postcode: CT1 2BQ

Kent

Photo: P.A. Woodhead www.flickr.com/photos/pawoodhead

Herne Bay
Pirate radio and Slade at Shivering Sands

Shivering Sands is the somewhat dispiriting-sounding location where Screaming Lord Sutch launched his Radio Sutch pirate radio station in the Thames Estuary in 1964. Situated on an abandoned World War II sea fort, the station then became Radio City and was dogged by controversy before its government shutdown in 1967. A year earlier, the station's boss, Reg Calvert, had been killed in an incident following a notorious invasion of the remote station by a business rival (Major Oliver Smedley) who employed strong-arm tactics to close down Radio City in revenge for money owed and unpaid. A resulting altercation at Smedley's Essex home ended with the Major shooting Calvert fatally with a 12-bore shotgun. The 1975 movie Slade in Flame used the rusting but spectacular fort as a location for some dramatic scenes of the fictitious band Flame (played by Slade) visiting Radio City.

LOCATION 390: off the coast from the town of Herne Bay, postcode CT6 5NE

Top: The sci-fi-like sea fort that harboured pirate DJs and Slade, where the band played out dramatic scenes from their 1975 movie. Above: The Slade in Flame poster, which featured an image of the sea fort

Margate
Chas & Dave's seaside hit

A big fan of the whole cockle, whelk, jellied eel eating, bucket-and-spade business of British seaside holidays, Chas Hodges chose Margate as a subject for song-writing for purely commercial reasons. "We were doing an advert for Courage Best Bitter about going down to Margate, so we used that to give it an extra plug on the telly." 'Margate' hit the chart in 1982 and was memorably included in The Jolly Boys, a feature-length episode of the BBC comedy show Only Fools and Horses. Here's an elocution lesson from Chas Hodges: "Margate is pronounced "Margit" where I'm from!"

LOCATION 391: at the end of the A28 on the north-eastern tip of the Kent coast. Postcode: CT9 1HG

Rochester
A Clannad castle cover

The group were Irish, the location ought to have been Nottingham, but Clannad's cover artwork for their 1984 Legend album, sound-tracking the TV series Robin of Sherwood, was photographed at Rochester Castle.

LOCATION 393: open to the public, the castle is in the centre of Rochester, close by the bridge over the River Medway. Postcode: ME1 1SW

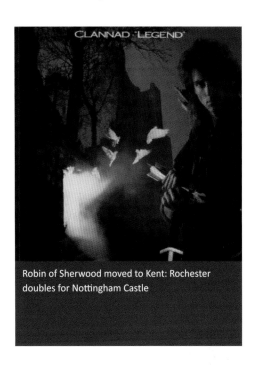

Robin of Sherwood moved to Kent: Rochester doubles for Nottingham Castle

Rolvenden
Ian Dury and Chaz Jankel at Toad Hall

When Ian Dury and The Blockheads' success began to realise a degree of financial security, Dury rented his very own rock star mansion. Toad Hall in the village of Rolvenden had a swimming pool and a spiral staircase leading to a tower with views over the Kent countryside which, despite his disability, Dury would ascend with the aid of his minder, Fred "Spider" Rowe. Author Will Birch's Ian Dury: The Definitive Biography points to Toad Hall as the place where both Dury and writing partner Chaz Jankel completed work on what would become the new wave No.1 single 'Hit Me with Your Rhythm Stick'. Jankel worked diligently in the garage to create the keyboard melody while Dury finalised the lyrics, which he'd kept on a scrap of paper since the song's conception three years earlier.

LOCATION 392: Toad Hall is west of Rolvenden, south of the B2086, in Sandhurst Lane, TN17 4QP. Status: private residence

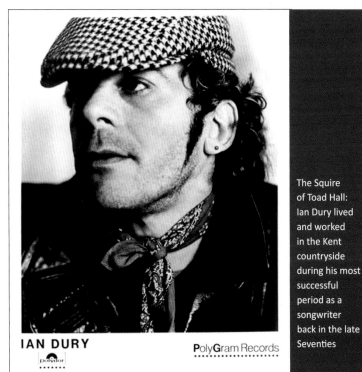

The Squire of Toad Hall: Ian Dury lived and worked in the Kent countryside during his most successful period as a songwriter back in the late Seventies

Photo: Polydor/PolyGram Records

IAN DURY

PolyGram Records

Kent

Sevenoaks
'Strawberry Fields Forever' at Knole Park

Knole Park, with its stately home surrounded by a deer park, provided the location for the mini-movie The Beatles made to accompany their psychedelic masterpiece 'Strawberry Fields Forever'. Over two cold, crisp winter days in early 1967, the four Beatles arrived on set driving their black Mini Coopers and rode around the park on large white horses. At one point an observer witnessed John Lennon larking about singing "Hey, Hey, We're The Monkees", the theme song from the brand new US TV show, as the group filmed a scene jumping from a tree. While staying in the town, Lennon also happened upon the subject matter for a new song that would end up on the group's next album, Sgt Pepper's Lonely Hearts Club Band. He wandered into a local antique shop and purchased an old Victorian circus poster. The names of the performers on the bill that so fascinated him would become the characters included in the lyrics of 'Being for the Benefit of Mr Kite'.

LOCATION 394: Knole Park is within a short walk east of Sevenoaks town centre. Postcode: TN15 0RP. Status: open to the public. The exact site of the antique shop is unknown

John Lennon's visit to a Sevenoaks antique shop saw him purchase this poster, which carried the inspirational line 'Being for the Benefit of Mr Kite'

West Malling
The Magical Mystery Tour finale

The Beatles' Magical Mystery Tour of the south-west of England in 1967 should have seen the band end their journey at Shepperton Film Studios for filming interior scenes for the movie. Instead, they were forced to switch location to West Malling when it transpired that nobody had booked Shepperton for shooting the outstanding scenes. The movie's ballroom sequence for 'Your Mother Should Know' was filmed in the disused aircraft hangar at RAF West Malling and 'I Am the Walrus' was shot on the airfield's tarmac. A ticket-selling scene was filmed in the town's High Street at local shopkeeper Sam

Brown's tobacconists.

LOCATION 395: only sections of the airfield remain at the former RAF West Malling, south of the town just off the A228. Postcode ME19

Tonbridge
Keane formed at Tonbridge School

All three members of Keane first met as primary school children in Battle, East Sussex, before forming their first band, The Lotus Eaters, while at public school in 1995. As boarding students at Tonbridge School, Tim Rice-Oxley, Tom Chaplin and Richard Hughes would mostly cover the latest Oasis or U2 material before a band name change to Keane became essential, when they discovered that a duo calling themselves The Lotus Eaters had already charted a decade earlier.

LOCATION 396: High Street, Tonbridge, postcode TN9 1JP

Rochester
Schoolboy Jagger inspired by Ramblin' Jack

When Ramblin' Jack Elliott travelled to Rochester Docks and then back to London in the Fifties, his impromptu performance for a bunch of schoolboys, which included Mick Jagger, inspired the Kent's future Rolling Stone to instantly buy a guitar

Bob Dylan famously counts Ramblin' Jack Elliott as a huge influence on his music, but the New York-born folk legend also had a very immediate effect on the young Mick Jagger. Ramblin' Jack found himself at Rochester railway station after a visit to a ship back in the Fifties and put on an impromptu performance for Jagger. "We were waiting for a train back to London and there was a group of schoolchildren on the other platform across the tracks from us and I thought, 'Well, look at those kids just standing around bored. I think I'll play them a little music. What the heck.' And I just got the guitar out of my case and started yodelling and playing cowboy songs to these kids across the way. They appreciated it and I think they even clapped. But I didn't know one of those kids was young Mick Jagger. He told me about it when I met him about 20 years later in a hotel in Canada. He said that was the first time he'd seen me and that he ran right out the next day and bought a guitar. He must have been about 12, 14 years old or something like that."

LOCATION 397: the station is off the High Street. Postcode: ME1 1HQ

Born in KENT

Kevin Ayers (b. 16 Aug 1944, Herne Bay, d.18 Feb 2013)

Gary Barden, vocals, Michael Schenker Group (b. 27 Aug 1955, Tunbridge Wells)

Peter Blake, pop artist (b. 25 Jun 1932, Dartford)

Bill Bruford, drums, King Crimson (b. 17 May 1949, Sevenoaks)

Billy Childish, vocals/guitar (b. 1 Dec 1959, Chatham)

Richard Coughlan, drums, Caravan (b. 2 Sep 1947, Herne Bay, d.1 Dec 2013)

Roger Dean, album cover artist (b. 31 Aug 1944, Ashford)

Anne Dudley, keyboards, Art of Noise (b. 7 May 1956, Chatham)

Guy Fletcher, keyboards/guitar, Dire Straits (b. 24 May 1960, Maidstone)

Gordon Giltrap, guitarist (b. 6 Apr 1948, Brenchley)

Paul Hartnoll, keyboards, Orbital (b. 19 May 1968, Dartford)

Phil Hartnoll, keyboards, Orbital (b. 9 Jan 1964, Dartford)

Richard Hughes, drums, Keane (b. 8 Sep 1975, Gravesend)

Rick Huxley, guitar, The Dave Clark Five (b. 5 Aug 1942, Dartford, d.11 Feb 2013)

Mick Jagger, vocals, The Rolling Stones (b. 26 Jul 1943, Dartford)

Matt Letley, drums, Status Quo (b. 29 Mar 1961, Dartford)

Shane MacGowan (b. 25 Dec 1957, Tunbridge Wells)

Phil May, vocals, The Pretty Things (b. 9 Nov 1944, Dartford)

Mike Ratledge, keyboards, Soft Machine (b. May 1943, Maidstone)

Noel Redding, bass, The Jimi Hendrix Experience (b. 25 Dec 1945, Folkestone, d. 11 May 2003)

Keith Richards, guitar, The Rolling Stones (b. 18 Dec 1943, Dartford)

Crispian St Peters, singer-songwriter (b. 5 Apr 1939, Swanley, d. 8 Jun 2010)

Dave Sinclair, keyboards, Caravan (b. 24 Nov 1947, Herne Bay)

Richard Sinclair, guitar, Caravan (b. 6 Jun 1948, Canterbury)

Joss Stone (b. 11 Apr 1987, Dover)

Dick Taylor, guitar, The Pretty Things (b. 28 Jan 1943, Dartford)

Pete Tong, DJ (b. 30 Jul 1960, Hartley)

Lancashire

*T*ragically, a good deal of Lancashire's great rock heritage has been demolished. Nelson's incredible Imperial Ballroom, which attracted just about every major Sixties act to the small mill town, has long since burned to the ground, Blackpool's Northern Soul mecca succumbed to the wrecking ball in 2009 and Ribchester's location for major punk bands, the Lodestar, has an uncertain future. Despite demolition and uncertainty, there are still stories to tell and plenty of Lancashire locations worthy of pilgrimage that have survived the years, and in one case the centuries. Black Sabbath's Heysham graves date back to the 11th century, the Blackpool church hall where Jethro Tull began life still stands, and the town's magnificent Empress Ballroom has experienced extraordinary scenes involving The Rolling Stones, The Stone Roses and The White Stripes, while Blackburn's Reidys music store is a magnet for musos, even if the town's 4,000 holes are best avoided. Ironically, the very area where rhythm and blues flourished in the Sixties venues now laid to waste hosts the thriving and award-winning Great British Rhythm & Blues Festival in Colne.

Born in LANCASHIRE

Chris Acland, drums, Lush (b. 7 Sep 1966, Lancaster, d. 17 Oct 1996)

Jon Anderson, vocals, Yes (b. 25 Oct 1944, Accrington)

Neil Arthur, vocals, Blancmange (b. 15 Jun 1958, Darwen)

Tony Ashton, keyboards, Ashton, Gardner & Dyke (b. 1 Mar 1946, Blackburn, d. 28 May 2001)

Dave Ball, Soft Cell (b. 3 May 1959, Blackpool)

Bobby Elliott, drums, The Hollies (b. 8 Dec 1941, Burnley)

John Foxx, vocals, Ultravox (b. 26 Sep 1947, Chorley)

Charlie Gillett, broadcaster (b. 20 Feb 1942, Morecambe, d. 17 Mar 2010)

Keef Hartley, drummer (b. 8 Apr 1944, Preston, d. 26 Nov 2011)

Eric Haydock, bass, The Hollies (b. 3 Feb 1942, Burnley)

Victoria Hesketh (aka Little Boots) (b. 4 May 1984, Blackpool)

Tony Hicks, guitar, The Hollies (b. 16 Dec 1945, Nelson)

Chris Lowe, keyboards, Pet Shop Boys (b. 4 Oct 1959, Blackpool)

Nicholas McCarthy, guitar, Franz Ferdinand (b. 13 Dec 1974, Blackpool)

Sarah Martin, violin, Belle & Sebastian (b. 12 Feb 1974, Blackburn)

Lionel Morton, guitar/vocals, The Four Pennies (b. 14 Aug 1941, Blackburn)

Graham Nash, The Hollies, Crosby, Stills & Nash (b. 2 Feb 1942, Blackpool)

Ken Nicol, guitar, Steeleye Span (b. 27 May 1951, Preston)

Danbert Nobacon, Chumbawamba (b. 16 Jan 1962, Burnley)

Les Pattinson, bass, Echo & The Bunnymen (b. 18 Apr 1958, Ormskirk)

Mike Pickering, musician/DJ (b. 24 Feb 1958, Accrington)

Maddy Prior, vocals, Steeleye Span (b. 14 Aug 1947, Blackpool)

Robert Smith, vocals, The Cure (b. 21 Apr 1959, Blackpool)

Andy Summers, guitar, The Police (b. 31 Dec 1942, Poulton-le-Fylde)

Diana Vickers (b. 30 Jul 1991, Blackburn)

John Waite, vocals, The Babys (b. 4 Jul 1952, Lancaster)

James Walsh, vocals/guitar, Starsailor (b. 9 Jun 1980, Chorley)

Blackburn
The "holes in our roads" story that inspired John Lennon

A national newspaper article that caught the eye of John Lennon was responsible for a memorable lyric line in The Beatles 'A Day in the Life', recorded in 1967. The story about 4,000 holes in Blackburn found its way into the Sgt Pepper's album track following a Daily Mail feature about the state of the potholed roads in the Lancashire town. The same edition of the paper also carried an account of the death in a car crash of Tara Browne, heir to the Guinness fortune. This prompted Lennon to include the line "he blew his mind out in a car" in one of the last true Lennon and McCartney compositions.

LOCATION 398: Blackburn lies 25 miles north of Manchester, just off the M65 motorway. Postcode: BB1 5AF. Don't feel obliged to visit every pothole!

FAR&NEAR
The holes in our roads

THERE are 4,000 holes in the road in Blackburn, Lancashire, or one twenty-sixth of a hole per person, according to a council survey.

If Blackburn is typical there are two million holes in Britain's roads and 300,000 in London.

£225,0000 sea defence scheme for Felixstowe is being urged on the Government by East Suffolk River Board.

1,000 ratepayers in Harrow, Middlesex, said the Exchequer

The 1967 story that Lennon included in 'A Day in the Life'

Blackpool
Church hall debut for embryonic Tull

A plaque at Blackpool's Holy Family R.C. Church hall has been erected in honour of Jethro Tull. In 1964, local teenagers Ian Anderson, Jeffrey Hammond and John Evan, then playing as The Blades, performed their first gig and one of Britain's most enduring rock bands was born. "I don't even think there was a stage here at the time and, in my memory, it was so much bigger," recalled Anderson at the plaque unveiling in 2010. "To us at the time it was like playing Madison Square Garden in New York."

LOCATION 399: Holy Family R.C. Church, Links Road, North Shore, Blackpool. Postcode FY1 2RU

Ian Anderson returns to his roots with flute

News & Pictures North

Blackpool
The seaside Mecca for sun and soul

Demolished in 2009, the Blackpool Mecca hosted Northern Soul nights from 1971 to 1979. Without an all-night licence to compete with Wigan's Casino, the Mecca still packed in soul enthusiasts at its Highland Room between 8pm and 2am thanks to dedicated expert DJs Ian Levine and Colin Curtis. Fans of the venue were given the opportunity to buy their own tiny piece of the much-loved venue when it was pulled down. Small sections of the wooden dance floor went on sale at £10.

LOCATION 400: was situated on Central Drive, postcode FY1 5

" The **RIVALRY** between Blackpool Mecca and Wigan Casino was tribal, like two football clubs who hate each other "

DJ COLIN CURTIS
Who kept the fans happy during the Mecca's heyday

Lancashire

Blackburn
The Four Pennies at Reidys

The town's chart-toppers, The Four Pennies, named themselves after Penny Street in Blackburn town centre. The street's music store, Reidys, was where the group bought all their gear and they were at the grand opening of a new store in 1964, the same year their biggest hit 'Juliet' made No.1. Quite the men about town, the band even played at Ewood Park in front of thousands of Blackburn Rovers football fans.

LOCATIONS 401 and 402: Reidys 'home of music' was at 9-13 Penny Street, Blackburn, postcode BB1 6HJ. In 2013, they moved again to bigger premises (including a performance stage) at 1 Nab Lane, off Feilden Street, Blackburn, postcode BB2 1LN

Above: Chart-topping Blackburn band The Four Pennies might have been the "Lionel Morton Four" but for a meeting above Reidys in Penny Street

Right: Guitar heaven at Reidys "The Musician's Superstore" in Blackburn

Lancashire

Blackpool
Stones, Roses and Stripes at the Empress Ballroom

Commonly hired as a genteel dancing venue, or for trade fairs and conferences, the Empress Ballroom was the setting for a Rolling Stones riot and the first really big gig The Stone Roses performed. The Rolling Stones' visit in 1964 saw the band forced to exit the stage when fans began throwing bottles, smashing the ballroom chandeliers and wrecking a Steinway piano. The aggressive behaviour of some of the 7,000 crowd squeezed into the ballroom on July 24, and the injuries to 50 teenage fans requiring hospital treatment, led to the band being barred from ever returning to Blackpool's grandest venue. But what part did the Stones actually play in creating what Blackpool Gazette headlines said was a "Ballroom Riot"? Many eye-witness accounts point to the violent scenes emanating from a large group from north of the border

chanting "Scotland, Scotland" in front of the stage - the concert coincided with the traditional Scottish invasion at the end of holiday week in the town. It wasn't just the Stones who suffered at the hands of the unruly element in the crowd. Earlier local support group The Executives had decided to wisely cut short their set following coin-throwing and threats which saw their brand new amp and speakers totally smashed, along with the Stones' gear, that was dragged from the stage and destroyed by the mob when the Stones were forced to escape the carnage. Twenty-five years later, The Stone Roses, by comparison, were greeted almost reverentially by at least 4,000 of their followers, who descended on the town one hot August day in 1989 and witnessed what many observers reckoned to be the band's finest moment. The Blackpool gig would prove to be a defining moment for the band who decided that they would have their first big performance away from London and give their growing fan base a day out at the seaside. Fortunately The Stone Roses filmed their Empress Ballroom

appearances. In 2004, The White Stripes chose this spectacular venue to create their first DVD, Under Blackpool Lights.

LOCATION 403: a short walk from the promenade seafront, the Empress Ballroom is inside the Winter Gardens, Church Street, postcode FY1 1HU

Opposite: The location for two of Britain's most talked-about concerts when The Rolling Stones and The Stone Roses came to Blackpool

Below: No doubt inspired by the Empress Ballroom's rock history, The White Stripes filmed their debut DVD there

Right: The calm before the storm: The Rolling Stones minutes into their 1964 Blackpool date that ended in a riot. Far right: All of The Stone Roses knew and loved Blackpool from their childhood trips to the seaside there, so the Winter Gardens' Empress Ballroom was a popular choice as venue for the band's special 1989 summer gig

WINTER GARDENS

LIVE SHOWS · CABARET · BARS

Lancashire

Colne
East Lancashire boasts Europe's best blues

Celebrating its 25th year in 2014, The Great British Rhythm & Blues Festival is an annual event in Colne every August Bank Holiday weekend. Rated Best Blues Festival by the European Blues Awards in 2013, the popularity of this festival has grown to the point where 600 artists perform over eight venues. In addition to the International Stage at the Colne Municipal Hall, local hostelries including The Crown Hotel, Colne Legion, The Admiral Lord Rodney, Colne and Nelson Rugby Union Football Club and the Green Chimney have all been added as venues at this Lancashire blues hotbed.

LOCATION 404: Colne is in east Lancashire. One of eight official festival venues, the International Stage is at Colne Municipal Hall (Muni Theatre), Albert Road, Colne. Postcode BB8 0AE

Blackpool
Birthplace of Graham Nash

The maternity ward where Graham Nash was born, famously "in an upstairs room in Blackpool by the side of a Northern Sea", is now part of the Kimberley hotel. His birthplace, which Nash included in the lyrics to 1971 song 'Military Madness' (on his solo debut album Songs for Beginners), was, according to Nash, "a windowless bunker" which he revisited in 1996 along with his two sons Jackson and Will for a family history lesson. Less dramatically, it turns out the maternity ward may have been sited where the ground-floor dining room of the hotel is now, which afforded sea views before the building descended into the decaying state it is in today.

LOCATION 405: the decaying Kimberley hotel is in need of a great deal of TLC. On the seafront, 585-589 New South Promenade. Postcode FY4 1NQ

Inside and out - old blues and new blues: Phil May (The Pretty Things), below, and Alan Nimmo (King King), left, on the International Stage at Colne's Great British Rhythm & Blues Festival

Photos x 3: Peter Tarleton

Heysham
Black Sabbath's rock graves

The ruins of St Patrick's Chapel, Lower Heysham, provided the atmospheric cover for Black Sabbath's Best Of album in 2000. The row of six stone graves, which are said to date from the 11th-century, are located in a timeless, windswept spot overlooking the coast at Morecambe Bay. The graves' original contents and stone covers disappeared centuries ago.

LOCATION 406: easily accessed in a beautiful location, the row of graves at St Patrick's Chapel are next to the small church of St Peter's, in the village of Heysham, postcode LA3 2RW

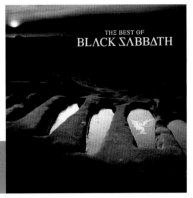

The 11th-century graves overlooking Morecambe Bay

Ribchester
Pistols and Rats at the Lodestar

With bookings impossible to get in and around London, Irish new-wavers The Boomtown Rats hit the provinces to make their mark. The Lodestar Hotel was the setting for the band's first UK gig on May 6, 1977. Bob Geldof recalled only 12 people being there that night, but 180 rammed into the place when they returned later that same year in August. While in the area, Geldof and co stayed overnight at the Victoria hotel in nearby Clitheroe. The Lodestar must have developed a reputation for harbouring punk and new wave waifs and strays as this remote venue had previously played host to the Sex Pistols on August 18, 1976. Remarkably, this Pistols gig came after their legendary June 4, and July 20, appearances at Manchester's Lesser Free Trade Hall in the same year.

LOCATIONS 407 and 408: just north of the Ribchester Bridge over the River Ribble lies the renamed Lodestar Hotel (formerly De Tabley Arms). Postcode: PR3 3ZQ. In 1977, the original Lodestar was further up the hill towards Blackburn (now a private house). Clitheroe's Victoria hotel is on the corner of King Street and York Street, postcode BB7 2BZ

Nelson
Small town, huge stars at 'The Imp'

This book doesn't generally resort to lists to emphasise a point, but in Nelson's case we will make an exception. The Imperial Ballroom, in a town with a population of less than 30,000, is a venue that has attracted The Beatles, The Rolling Stones, The Who, Jimi Hendrix, The Small Faces, The Kinks, Otis Redding, Smokey Robinson, The Animals, Pink Floyd, Ike and Tina Turner, Cream, Free, Stevie Wonder, Bo Diddley and Little Richard. The man responsible for booking so many household names was Bob Caine, the extraordinarily successful manager of the venue affectionately known as The Imp. Shortly after changing its name to The Column, this imposing building was destroyed by fire. The ballroom's legacy of hosting the cream of 60s and 70s pop acts lives on. Imperial Gardens – a sheltered housing development – occupies the spot where Lennon and Hendrix strutted their stuff.

LOCATION 409: 'The Imp' stood in Carr Road, where Imperial Gardens stands today. Postcode BB9 7TG

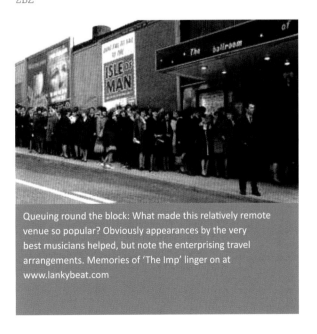

Queuing round the block: What made this relatively remote venue so popular? Obviously appearances by the very best musicians helped, but note the enterprising travel arrangements. Memories of 'The Imp' linger on at www.lankybeat.com

Leicestershire

*T*he city of Leicester can be proud that it gave the world Family, one of the most distinctive-sounding rock bands, featuring Roger Chapman's magnificent rasping vocals. More famously perhaps, the Human League's Phil Oakey was born here, while Engelbert Humperdinck and Mark Morrison grew up in Leicester, the city that also gave birth to Diesel Park West and Gaye Bykers on Acid. From the city's southern outskirts, Blaby and Countesthorpe gave Kasabian to the world and Ashby-de-la-Zouch delivered up that tweedy trio Young Knives. The claims to rock fame keep coming with Stevie Wonder performing on his first visit to the UK as a 14-year-old and the wonderfully idiosyncratic Leicestershire creations that were Showaddywaddy and Cornershop. But it's the variety of live venues, big (De Montfort Hall), small (the Musician pub) and gone forever (The Charlotte), that best boost Leicester's rock CV.

Leicester
The accidental birth of Showaddywaddy

Little changed since it was the Fosseway pub, the Indigo restaurant is the spot where Showaddywaddy were born. Ever wondered why there were so many band members? The eight glam-rock Teddy Boys came into being one night in 1973 when the panic-stricken Fosseway landlord realised he had accidentally double-booked two bands. Both Choise and Golden Hammers were persuaded to play together and enjoyed themselves so much that they decided to team-up. As Showaddywaddy, they quickly sky-rocketed to success via TV show New Faces and a string of 10 Top 10 hits, beginning in 1974.

LOCATION 410: the Indigo at the Fosseway is at 432 Melton Road, three miles north of the city centre, postcode LE4 7SN

Leicester
The Charlotte: gone but not forgotten

Noel Gallagher once lost a shoe escaping an over-enthusiastic crowd at The Princess Charlotte, Blur were filmed appearing here on their Starshaped DVD and Diesel Park West's John Butler referred to the place as "Leicester's version of [London's] Marquee Club". Gallagher nominated The Charlotte as the setting for his second favourite Oasis gig of all time. "It was that mental that I knew after the encore of 'I Am the Walrus' they were going to invade the stage," he said. "So, I put my guitar down and set the delay pedal going, then ran for my life. I ended up in the dressing room with one shoe." The much-loved pub on Oxford Street was successful partly due to its close proximity for students at the nearby De Montfort University. Many bands including Coldplay, Arctic Monkeys and local favourites Kasabian have good reason to thank The Charlotte for boosting their early careers, but future generations will only be able to read about the place as confirmation of its closure as a music venue came through in spring 2010.

LOCATION 411: no longer a music venue, The Charlotte re-opened as a pub in 2014. You'll find it in Leicester city centre, 8 Oxford Street, postcode LE1 5XZ

"The Charlotte is part of Leicester FOLKLORE 🙶
JOHN BUTLER

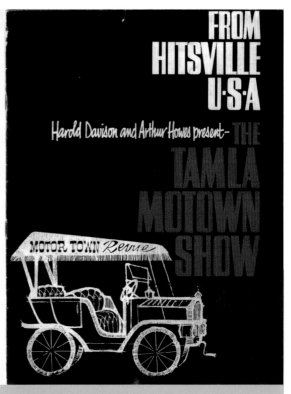

A Motown press picture of the young Stevie Wonder. The year he played Leicester he also had his first writing credit on a hit single when 'Uptight (Everything's Alright)' crashed the Billboard chart in America before making its chart debut in the UK in February 1966

Above: The Motown programme cover for the Leicester show in 1965. Below: The Tamla Motown tour of the UK played at the Odeon in 1965

Leicester
14-year-old Stevie Wonder at the Odeon

Fabulously restored to its original art deco glory as the Athena, the Odeon cinema once played host to the 1965 touring Tamla Motown Show. What struck 26-year-old local music fan Keith Dickens first was the excitement at seeing Martha and The Vandellas belting out their latest single 'Nowhere to Run', their debut on the UK Tamla Motown label. "But my most memorable recollection of the event was of seeing the 14-year-old, blind Stevie Wonder performing like an animated puppet." Surprisingly, the 21-date tour was considered a flop as attendances were low enough to necessitate Britain's own Georgie Fame being added to the show. But, as Dickens points out, "By the end of the 60s, any of the acts on that bill could have headlined their own show."

LOCATION 412: the city centre, at Queen Street, postcode LE1 1QD

Leicestershire

Leicester
The Ultima Thule 'weird rock' experience

Perhaps this is a rock pilgrimage best enjoyed in the mind. Despite the lack any longer of a physical presence in the city centre, this Leicester institution is still worth flagging up. "Purveyors of Progressive Music from Around the World", Conduit Street was once home to the imaginatively monikered Ultima Thule Record Shop. The owners of the shop were old-fashioned enough to encourage visitors to chat and first listen to the album they were about to consider purchasing. And where else could you possibly shop for progressive, psych, fusion, Krautrock, RIO, Zeuhl, Canterbury, Eurorock, weird, experimental and electronic rock? Now a mail-order operation only, manager Alan Freeman insists that the shop's name is a combination of several philosophical and mystical influences, but appropriately 'Ultima Thule' was also the title of an extremely rare Tangerine Dream single on Ohr Records from 1971.

LOCATION 413: once a retail shop, now a Tesco Express, the business relocated a mile or so south of the city centre at 21 Heather Road, postcode LE2 6DF. Now a mail-order operation with visitors by appointment. Website: www.ultimathulerecords.com

Deep in the heart of Leicester: the Musician pub rocks to the sound of Ian Hunter in 2010

Photo: Paul Needham / Mohawk Visuals

Leicester
Indoors and out at De Montfort Hall

Leicester's premier concert hall saw Frank Sinatra, The Beatles, the Stones, The Jam, The Clash and Louis Armstrong appear in their heyday, and a varied programme of visitors in 2014 included the likes of Counting Crows, Joan Armatrading, Imelda May, Paloma Faith and John Mayall. The growing British obsession with summer festivals has encouraged De Montfort Hall and Victoria Park to host June's folk-orientated Big Session Festival and the Summer Sundae Weekender outdoor events every year since 2001.

LOCATION 414: the century-old concert hall is in Leicester city centre, 7 Granville Road, postcode LE1 7RU

Born in LEICESTERSHIRE

Dave Bartram, vocals, Showaddywaddy (b. 23 Mar 1952, Leicester)

Roger Chapman, vocals, Family (b. 8 Apr 1942, Leicester)

Brian Davison, drums, The Nice (b. 25 May 1942, Leicester, d. 15 Apr 2008)

John Deacon, bass, Queen (b. 19 Aug 1951, Oadby)

Chris Edwards, bass, Kasabian (b. 20 Dec 1980, Leicester)

Robert Gotobed, drums, Wire (b. 21 Apr 1952, Leicester)

Davey (Davy) Graham, guitarist (b. 26 Nov 1940,

Leicester
Americana on Clyde Street

Abandoned and derelict at the end of the 20th century, but on the back of a growing interest in roots music the Bakers Arms near Leicester city centre gradually transformed into The Musician. Hosting live music every night, the beautifully refurbished "Borderline of the Midlands" became Leicester's good news story. With so many music venues closing, local record label boss and gig promoter Darren Nockles turned his attention to filling the 220-capacity Americana-themed venue and bar and even enticing the likes of Ryan Adams and Ian Hunter to play the former back-street boozer.

LOCATION 415: The Musician is close to the city centre in Clyde Street, postcode LE1 2DE

" **Ryan Adams had a classic rock and roll rider – a bottle of VODKA and 40 Marlboro Lights** "
DARREN NOCKLES
Musician pub gig promoter

The ingenious front doors to the Musician pub on Clyde Street

Leicester, d. 15 Dec 2008)
John Illsley, bass, Dire Straits (b. 24 Jun 1949, Leicester)
Jon Lord, keyboards, Deep Purple (b. 9 Jun 1941, Leicester d. 16 Jul 2012)
Tom Meighan, vocals, Kasabian (b. 11 Jan 1981, Leicester)
Philip Oakey, Human League (b. 2 Oct 1955, Leicester)
Viv Prince, drums, The Pretty Things (b. 9 Aug 1941, Loughborough)
Rob Townsend, drums, Family, Medicine Head, The Blues Band (b. 7 Jul 1947, Leicester)
Pick Withers, drums, Dire Straits (b. 4 Apr 1948, Leicester)

Kasabian were formed by three Leicestershire students: Chris Edwards (left) and Tom Meighan (third left) - both Leicester born - and Sergio Pizzorno (second left), born in Devon. Ian Matthews (right), born in Bristol, joined later in 2004

Lincolnshire

*T*his is a county boasting two exceptional wordsmiths. Lyricist Bernie Taupin loved Lincolnshire, living there and writing some of popular music's best-known lyrics from his times in Grimsby, Market Rasen, Owmby by Spital and, most importantly, Tealby, where Britain's best-selling song was conceived. Rod Temperton is another lyrical Lincolnshire lad with a worldwide reputation. He has Michael Jackson's 'Thriller' among many songwriting credits to his name. Worthy of mention in passing is the fact that 'The Devil Went Down to Scunthorpe' by The Toy Dolls was a 1997 reworking of the Charlie Daniels Band smash hit, which had the horn-ed one originally visiting Georgia. The none-more-Cockney British skiffle and rock 'n' roll pioneer Joe Brown was born in the county, in the village of Swarby, before moving south. Travelling in the other direction, Robert Wyatt has made the Lincolnshire town of Louth his home and recording base for more than two decades. And, best claim to fame of all: where would The Beatles have been without a significant Skegness incident?

Born in LINCOLNSHIRE

Joe Brown (b. 13 May 1941, Swarby)
Raymond 'Boz' Burrell, bass, Bad Company (b. 1 Aug 1946, Lincoln, d. 21 Sep 2006)
Steve Currie, bass, T. Rex (b. 19 May 1947, Grimsby, d. 28 Apr 1981)
Howard Devoto, vocals, Magazine (b. 15 Mar 1952, Scunthorpe)
Vince Eager, singer (b. 4 Jun 1940, Grantham)
Stephen Fretwell, singer-songwriter (b. 10 Nov 1981, Scunthorpe)
Tim Hart, guitar/vocals, Steeleye Span (b. 9 Jan 1948, Lincoln, d. 24 Dec 2009)
Graham Lewis, bass, Wire (b. 22 Feb 1953, Grantham)
Tony McPhee, guitar, The Groundhogs (b. 23 Mar 1944, Humberston)
Iain Matthews, vocals, Fairport Convention/Matthews' Southern Comfort (b. 16 Jun 1946, Scunthorpe)
Nicola Roberts, Girls Aloud (b. 5 Oct 1985, Stamford)
Martin Simpson, folk singer/guitarist (b. 5 May 1953, Scunthorpe)
Rodney Slater, multi-instrumentalist, Bonzo Dog Doo-Dah Band (b. 8 Nov 1941, Crowland)
Bernie Taupin, lyricist (b. 22 May 1950, Anwick)
Rod Temperton, songwriter/producer/musician (b. 15 Oct 1947, Cleethorpes)

The none-more-Cockney Joe Brown was actually born in the remote Lincolnshire village of Swarby

Market Rasen

Elton's 'Saturday Night' rocker at the Aston Arms

The Aston Arms is where lyricist Bernie Taupin absorbed all his reference material for Elton John's classic rocker 'Saturday Night's Alright for Fighting'. As a teenager he visited Market Rasen to "get a little action in", as the song says, playing snooker, downing pints and watching the "aggravation" develop on a Saturday night. The track was included on Elton's double album Goodbye Yellow Brick Road, but the Aston Arms was pictured on the sleeve notes for follow-up LP Captain Fantastic and the Brown Dirt Cowboy. Another Lincolnshire location immortalised by Taupin was 'Grimsby', a love song on Caribou dedicated to the North Sea fishing port where a pub called the Skinner's Arms gets a mention. Research reveals that there is not and never has been a pub of that name in Grimsby – apparently Elton and Bernie were big fans of the London-based BBC TV sitcom Steptoe & Son, whose Shepherd's Bush local bore that name.

LOCATION 416: the Aston Arms is located at the back of the market square, 18 Market Place, postcode LN8 3HL

Elton John's 1973 hit single (right) and the Lincolnshire pub (top) that inspired lyricist Bernie Taupin to write it

Photo: Peter Tarleton

Lincolnshire

Owmby by Spital
Bernie Taupin's home village

Born near the village of Anwick at Flatters, a farmhouse in the south Lincolnshire countryside, it was at the isolated village of Owmby by Spital where lyricist Bernie Taupin lived from the age of eight until his first marriage, to Maxine Feibelman, in 1971. Taupin's former bungalow home at Maltkiln Farm lies at the opposite end of Church Lane. He drew inspiration for his songwriting with Elton John through his affection for this remote area. Unconfirmed reports suggest he wrote 'Skyline Pigeon' for Elton's Empty Sky album from happy childhood memories of times spent exploring the village's Norman church of St Peter & St Paul. The young Taupin would clamber up to the roof and its bell tower, with three bells dating back to 1687.

LOCATION 417: Owmby by Spital lies eight miles south of Lincoln. Both the bungalow (a private residence) and the church are in Church Lane, postcode LN8 2HN

From Lincolnshire farm hand to lyricist: Bernie Taupin's debut solo album in 1971 was a spoken-word recording of his poetry

> " The area I was living in was sort of akin to living in Indiana or Nebraska where you have TWO OPPORTUNITIES after you leave school: you either work on the land and drive a tractor or you go and work in the... towns. Living in Lincolnshire, I did both **"**

BERNIE TAUPIN
Talking to Music
Connection in 1989

North Thoresby
Lincolnshire's rock 'n' roll wedding

When guitarist Gary Moore married Kerry Booth (the daughter of the then Grimsby Town football manager Dave Booth) in 1985 the wedding was bound to attract media interest. Former Thin Lizzy bandmate Phil Lynott was a guest at the ceremony at St Helen's Parish Church in the village of North Thoresby and is thought to have turned up late and in a state that would suggest he had already liberally toasted the happy couple long before they had been joined in holy matrimony. Realising they could get to see not one but two rock legends at the appointed time of the wedding, local rock fans turned out in large numbers outside the tiny village's church. In addition to his marriage, 1985 was a good year for Gary Moore and indeed Phil Lynott. As a duo they released 'Out in the Fields', which peaked at No.5 on the UK singles chart, a solo career high for both of them.

LOCATION 418: North Thoresby is about seven miles inland from Grimsby. St Helen's Parish Church, Church Lane, postcode DN36 5QG

Skegness
Triumph and tragedy: the Rory Storm story

An important incident in the development of The Beatles took place in the bracing Lincolnshire seaside resort of Skegness. Merseyside rock 'n' roll outfit Rory Storm and The Hurricanes (with Richard Starkey, aka Ringo Starr, on drums) had a season-long booking at the Butlins holiday camp back in 1962. During this summer residency, John Lennon and Paul McCartney drove from Liverpool to Skegness on August 15, to ask Starr to join The Beatles. Before their arrival, Starr had agreed to join Kingsize Taylor in Hamburg, as Taylor had suggested a £20 weekly pay packet. Lennon and McCartney offered £25 a week, which Starr accepted. Although revered in Liverpool and hugely popular at Butlins, the young Rory Storm was not bound for Ringo's glorious route to worldwide fame and died a tragic death aged just 33 in 1972. John Scoles, a Butlins employee back in the summer season of 1962, remembers Rory well: "Rory was very tall and slim, had bleached-blond hair – rare then – and used to run the mile race at the weekly [Butlins] sports day for a bit of fun. He made a pact with his mother saying that if he didn't emerge as the top Liverpool group he would take his own life. About 10 years later, sadly, both him and his mother did this together."

LOCATION 419: Skegness holiday resort, postcode PE25 1NU

Tealby
UK's best-selling single was written here

There is no plaque to mark the spot, but it was in this house, called affectionately "Piglet-in-the-Wild" by Bernie Taupin, that Elton John's songwriting partner penned the original lyrics for 'Candle in the Wind', the song that would become Britain's biggest-selling single. First released on the 1973 Elton album Goodbye Yellow Brick Road, the song was reworked as a tribute to Diana, Princess of Wales in 1997, eventually selling 4.65 million copies in the UK and 33 million worldwide. Many more of Elton's hits that dominated the airwaves and charts in the Seventies were created under the roof of this little-changed cottage Taupin once shared with first wife Maxine.

LOCATION 420: south of the B1203 at Beck Hill, Tealby, postcode LN8 3. Status: private residence

Made in Lincolnshire: Britain's all-time best-seller and Bernie Taupin's former cottage, Piglet-in-the-Wild in Tealby

Merseyside

*D*espite The Beatles' utter domination of this section of Rock Atlas, there are 21st-century bands that still epitomise what's so special about Merseyside. Take The Coral: absorbing all that's great from the history of the place and adding their own American West Coast take on things, they refuse to imagine a better base or recording location than their much-loved Wirral peninsula seaside town of Hoylake. Alongside The Farm, Cast, The La's and The Zutons, they add to the tradition of local bands naturally and defiantly singing with a Scouse accent. Across the world's most music-associated river this side of the Mississippi, American beat poet Allen Ginsberg pronounced Liverpool in 1965 "the centre of consciousness of the human universe", and music maverick Bill Drummond put forward the theory that a ley line of creative cosmic energy ran up the city's Mathew Street, linked to the thoroughfare's statue of psychologist Carl Jung. There is most definitely something in the Mersey water: Liverpool born and bred artists have conjured up more than 50 No.1 singles since the chart began in 1952 and the city has had its fair share of hits written about it. Little Jimmy Osmond's 'Long Haired Lover from Liverpool (No.1), Liverpool F.C.'s 'Anfield Rap' (No.3), The Scaffold's 'Liverpool Lou' (No.7) and Gerry and The Pacemakers' 'Ferry Cross the Mersey' (No.8) all fit the smash hit category, with less well remembered but really rather good releases 'In Liverpool' by Suzanne Vega and 'Going Down to Liverpool' by The Bangles propping up the nether regions of the chart. But, indisputedly top of the pops, it is The Beatles for which the area is so hugely famous. Thanks to John Lennon, Paul McCartney, George Harrison and Ringo Starr, nowhere else in Britain can boast such a tightly packed plethora of iconic locations worthy of rock pilgrimage.

Liverpool 1
The Eleanor Rigby statue

Set back from the road in Stanley Street sits a statue of the character from The Beatles' saddest song, 'Eleanor Rigby'. The figure of Eleanor Rigby was the subject of a project by actor, artist and rock 'n' roller Tommy Steele, who created the sculpture. It is dedicated to "all the lonely people", a line from the lyrics written by Paul McCartney, who was reportedly influenced in a variety of ways, explained elsewhere in the Liverpool and Bristol pages of Rock Atlas. Also close by were the music shops where The Beatles bought their early instruments. No.60 Stanley Street was the location where Hessy's Music Centre famously sold a 1958 Hofner Senator guitar to John Lennon's Aunt Mimi. On July 31, 1960, she paid a £17 deposit, followed by further instalments of £13 and nine shillings, to provide John with the guitar he would later take with him to Hamburg. The Beatles were also customers at Rushworths Music House, a short distance away in Whitechapel.

LOCATION 421: Stanley Street, postcode L1 6AL

Tommy Steele's Eleanor Rigby statue on Stanley Street

Photo: Peter Tarleton

Merseyside

Liverpool 1
Bill Harry's Mersey Beat HQ

An important aspect in the rapidly growing appeal of the Liverpool beat groups in the Sixties was the way in which the news of this great phenomenon spread. Created in 1961 to report on the extraordinary beat boom that occurred, the Mersey Beat music paper was devised and put together by Bill Harry and his girlfriend Virginia Sowry from premises in Renshaw Street.

LOCATION 422: 81a Renshaw Street, postcode L1 4EN. Website: www.merseybeat.com

" [Brian] Epstein **ORDERED 144 COPIES** of issue No.2, in which the entire front cover story was of The Beatles recording in Hamburg, which led him to ask me to arrange for him to visit The Cavern to see The Beatles 🙿
BILL HARRY

Right: Mersey Beat was created on Renshaw Street by Bill Harry and Virginia Sowry

Liverpool 2
The Hard Days Night Hotel

Claiming to be the world's only Beatles-inspired hotel, with Beatles-themed bars, a restaurant, lounge and bedrooms, the Hard Days Night Hotel provides luxurious 4-star accommodation in its grade II-listed city centre building. Open to 'day trippers' as well as residents, Blake's Bar - named after Sir Peter Blake, who designed the Sgt Pepper's Lonely Hearts Club Band album cover - and BarFour are suitably decorated to reflect the different eras of Beatles history. Visitors wishing to enjoy an 'Imagine'-themed night's sleep can book the Lennon Suite, which comes complete with white furnishings and white piano. The grand exterior of the hotel includes four individual statues by sculptor Dave Webster of each Beatle. The hotel is very well placed for Beatles tours, being situated at the end of Mathew Street.

LOCATION 423: North John Street, postcode L2 6RR

Photo: Peter Tarleton

This plaque marks the spot where Liverpool's second most popular venue once entertained beat music fans

Liverpool 2
The 'From Us to You' sculpture at The Beatles Shop

Above the entrance to a shop devoted to all things Beatles-related is a sculpture erected in 1984 of all four Beatles by David Hughes. The local sculptor's bronze carries the inscription "From Us to You" and was funded by fans from around the world through the initiative of the shop's owner, Ian Wallace.

LOCATION 424: the sculpture is above the entrance to The Beatles Shop, 31 Mathew Street, postcode L2 6RE

Liverpool 2
The 'cradle of Mersey Beat' at The Iron Door

A short walk north of The Cavern is the site where Liverpool's second most popular venue for beat music attracted crowds of more than 1,000. The Iron Door was a particular favourite of Cilla Black and The Searchers during its short four-year life.

LOCATION 425: the distinctive Iron Door plaque sits proudly among the swanky new office blocks at 13 Temple Street, postcode L2 5RH

"I'm only 15, maybe 16... We used to have **ALL-NIGHT SESSIONS** that started at eight o'clock and finished at eight the following morning "

CILLA BLACK
who worked hard at
The Iron Door

Merseyside

Liverpool 2
The Mathew Street Lennon statue

This statue is one of two solo figures commemorating John Lennon - the second is at John Lennon Airport. The Mathew Street fibreglass sculpture is the work of Dave Webster and captures the young Lennon perfectly, casually leaning against the wall gazing at the teenagers heading for The Cavern.

LOCATION 426: at the north end of Mathew Street, postcode L2 6RE

John Lennon watches the tourists in Mathew Street

Liverpool 2
Arthur Dooley's Beatle Street sculpture

Looking down from the wall of Mathew Street opposite Cavern Walks is the unconventional sculpture by Liverpool artist Arthur Dooley titled "Beatle Street", with the slogan "Four Lads that Shook the World". Constructed from wood, bronze and plastic dolls, it depicts Paul McCartney, George Harrison and Ringo Starr as three cherubs in the arms of the Madonna (or Mother Liverpool), with John Lennon represented as another small cherub to the right. At various points down the years, since it was first created in 1974, the original McCartney cherub has disappeared (a fact acknowledged by a plaque reading "Paul has taken wings and flown") and a new Lennon cherub was added following his death in 1980 with a plaque reading "Lennon Lives".

LOCATION 427: Mathew Street, postcode L2 6RE

Photo: Peter Tarleton

Photos: Cavernclub.org / Peter Tarleton

These days the world-famous Cavern is open from 10.30am until after midnight, seven days a week

Liverpool 2
The Cavern Club

Opened originally as a jazz club in 1957, The Beatles played their first of 292 bookings at The Cavern on February 9, 1961. The Beatles' association with the Mathew Street club goes back even earlier when proto-Beatles, The Quarry Men, played the famous basement as a skiffle group in 1957. When local bands in the early Sixties performed their rock 'n' roll (often at lunchtime), the venue attracted capacity crowds of almost 1,000 fans. If you climb down the 30 steps off Mathew Street it's hard to imagine how such a small, damp, warehouse cellar could accommodate so many people and generate so much excitement. With nowhere for the stench of sweat and cigarette smoke to escape, the walls dripped with perspiration and were frequently washed down with bleach, which gave The Cavern a unique aroma that fans who were present 50 years ago

remember to this day. Doorman Paddy Delaney, resident DJ Bob Wooler and owner Ray McFall were the men that ran the club in its heyday, witnessing the birth of the Mersey beat sound and the group that would go on to make Liverpool famous worldwide for its music. In many ways, The Cavern was just as significant a venue for The Hollies as it was for The Beatles. It was here in 1963 that the Manchester group were 'discovered' by EMI producer Ron Richards, which led to their Parlophone signing. Photographer Wyck Gerson Lohman remembers a unique day in the life of The Cavern from 1966:"Prime Minister Harold Wilson was to re-open The Cavern Club in Liverpool, in a slightly different location from the original one where The Beatles had played their first gigs. On that day my friend Rolf and I joined Ronan O'Rahilly, the head of Radio Caroline, when he boarded the train to Liverpool. None of us had the slightest idea where to go once we'd get to Liverpool, but this problem was soon

solved. As we were looking for a seat on the train we passed Harold Wilson, who was actually travelling second class – impossible to imagine nowadays – and was, for some reason, surrounded by a team of women. Ronan O'Rahilly, in fact, hated Harold Wilson since he had vowed to close down all Pirate Radio Stations, but when we got to Liverpool, all we had to do to get to the Cavern was to follow in his wake as they walked from the Railway Station to the Club."

The current Cavern Club is a faithfully reconstructed 1982 version of the the real thing using much of the same area and more than 15,000 of the original bricks. Situated 15 yards away from its old entrance near Cavern Walks, the present site is still a great place for a drink and venue for great music. Paul McCartney returned here in 1999 to perform a special ground-breaking internet broadcast gig.

LOCATION 428: 10 Mathew Street, postcode L2 6RE

Merseyside

Liverpool 2
The walls of fame

Two walls of fame are situated in the street opposite The Cavern Club, paying tribute to Liverpool's music heritage. Building bricks are engraved with the names of the many performers who have graced the stage of The Cavern. This commemorative display is joined by a second display of more than 50 discs, one for each act that has achieved a British No.1 hit single since the chart began in 1952.

LOCATION 429: opposite the Cavern Club entrance, Mathew Street, postcode L2 6RE

John Doubleday's bronze representation of The Beatles didn't gain too many complimentary remarks from Mike McGear

Photo: David Roberts

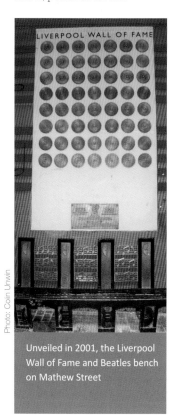

Photo: Colin Unwin

Unveiled in 2001, the Liverpool Wall of Fame and Beatles bench on Mathew Street

Liverpool 2
John Doubleday's bronze Beatles

A statue of all four Beatles playing guitars and drums greets visitors to the ground floor of the Cavern Walks shopping arcade. Created by Essex sculptor John Doubleday, this bronze representation was officially unveiled in 1984 by Paul McCartney's brother Mike. Apparently, he was none too impressed and reportedly had difficulty recognising which of the four figures was his brother. Other Beatles-related artwork includes terracotta relief dove and rose imagery on the walls of the centre, designed by Cynthia Lennon in memory of husband John.

LOCATION 431: in Cavern Walks shopping centre, Mathew Street, postcode L2 6RE

Liverpool 2
The Grapes: a Beatles bolt-hole

The famous Grapes pub is where Sixties Merseybeat groups escaped to in between performances at the nearby Cavern Club. The pub has been updated but still retains the backroom area where The Beatles sat to enjoy a beer and a smoke. In the early Sixties, The Cavern was unlicensed, so The Grapes was an attractive bolt-hole for performers wanting something stronger. On the wall of the snug, marking the location of The Beatles' favourite table, is a photograph of the four of them in the pub and a preserved piece of Sixties wallpaper that appears in the photo behind them. The Grapes was the first place Pete Best headed for, to drown his sorrows, when informed by manager Brian Epstein that he'd been replaced by Ringo Starr.

LOCATION 430: 25 Mathew Street, postcode L2 6RE

The Gerry Marsden-penned trans-atlantic Top 10 hit 'Ferry Cross the Mersey' finally made UK No.1 when re-recorded by Marsden and a bunch of other Liverpool musicians for charity single release in aid of the Hillsborough football disaster fund in 1989. The 1965 cinema release featuring many Liverpool stars of the day is a perfect Merseybeat snapshot of the times that has sadly never made it to DVD

Photo: Peter Tarleton

Liverpool 3
The 'Ferry Cross the Mersey'

There's the West Coast sound, Seattle Sound, music of the Delta, Motown and more but the UK's most successfully named musical export comes courtesy of the sludgy, brown and quite often oily stretch of water running by Liverpool. Perhaps local outfit Gerry and The Pacemakers best summed up the love for the river with their recording of 'Ferry Cross the Mersey' in 1964. A Brian Epstein-produced and presented movie of the same name and starring many Liverpool musicians and places was released a year later.

LOCATION 432: you can take your own ferry cross the Mersey by boarding at the Pier Head Ferry Terminal, Georges Parade, postcode L3 1DP

Liverpool 3
John and Cynthia's Mount Pleasant wedding

The Georgian building at No.64 Mount Pleasant was the registry office where John Lennon married Cynthia Powell on August 23, 1962. The small wedding party consisted of Cynthia's brother Tony, John's best man, Brian Epstein, Paul McCartney and George Harrison.

LOCATION 433: 64 Mount Pleasant is east of Liverpool city centre. The building is no longer a registry office. Postcode: L3 5SD

Liverpool 3
The European Peace Monument

ACC Liverpool has become the permanent home of a European Peace Monument dedicated to John Lennon. The 18-foot sculpture, created by American artist Lauren Voiers, forms part of the global peace initiative which aims to position one sculpture of peace on each of the continents of the world. The structure was unveiled by Julian Lennon and his mother Cynthia Lennon (John's first wife) on October 9, 2010, the day the former Beatle would have celebrated his 70th birthday.

LOCATION 434: the monument is outside the recently built ACC Liverpool, which combines the 11,000-capacity Echo Arena venue and the BT Convention Centre, Kings Dock, Liverpool Waterfront, Postcode: L3 4FP

Merseyside

"**CHARISMATIC** live performer, songwriter, animal lover and gentle man "

Some of the words on the plaque at the foot of Billy Fury's statue

Liverpool 3
The Billy Fury statue

A few steps from the River Mersey is a striking likeness of Billy Fury sculpted by Tom Murphy. It depicts a Liverpool rock 'n' roller who had already enjoyed 13 hit singles before The Beatles first charted in 1962. But as Jack Good, the man responsible for 50s pop TV shows Oh Boy! and Six-Five Special, said when unveiling the statue in 2003, there was another reason Billy was so special: "Billy was the first one of that stature to write his own songs. People say that it all started with The Beatles, but it was Billy Fury who did it first," said Good, as quoted in Spencer Leigh's book Wondrous Face.

LOCATION 435: situated on a patch of grass next to the Piermaster's House, on the banks of the River Mersey at Albert Dock, postcode L3 4AN

If there was a Rock Atlas award for the best rock 'n' roll statue in the book, Billy Fury's would surely win it

Liverpool 2
Eric's: a members-only punk paradise

With an entrance opposite Merseyside music mecca The Cavern, Eric's became a new venue for a new wave of music when it opened for the first time on October 1st 1976. Like its famous neighbour, Eric's was a basement club with jazz connections and co-owner Roger Eagle named the new venture he started with Ken Testi and Pete Fulwell after L.A.-born jazz musician Eric Dolphy. A membership-only club, Eric's benefited from a wider fanbase than the Merseybeat-based Cavern had done, attracting bands and members from way beyond the Liverpool city limits. Punk and new wave acts The Teardrop Explodes, OMD, Elvis Costello, Dead or Alive and Echo & The Bunnymen were local regulars, with visits from nationally hot bands The Clash, Buzzcocks, Joy Division and Simple Minds. Visual memories of the club's heyday inevitably feature the extraordinary Big in Japan, comprising the shaven-headed Jayne Casey, Scotsman Bill Drummond, Holly Johnson, Ian Broudie, Budgie (Peter Clarke) and Dave Balfe, who all became famous for doing other things beyond the cramped but exciting walls of Eric's. Will Sergeant of Echo & The Bunnymen vividly remembers sharing a Christmas bill with Iggy Pop in 1979. When Iggy was prevented from completing his trademark walk over a packed crowd of 600, he was forced to crawl across the heads of punters because the ceiling was so low. The club closed in March 1980 when

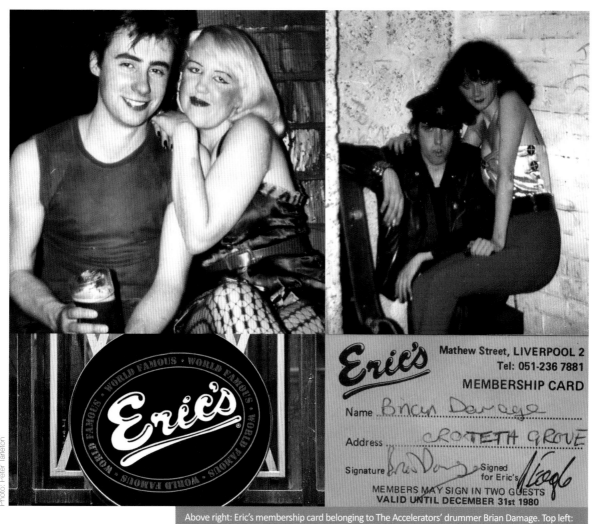

Photo: Peter Tarleton

Eric's
Mathew Street, LIVERPOOL 2
Tel: 051-236 7881
MEMBERSHIP CARD
Name Brian Damage
Address CROXTETH GROVE
Signature
Signed for Eric's
MEMBERS MAY SIGN IN TWO GUESTS
VALID UNTIL DECEMBER 31st 1980

Above right: Eric's membership card belonging to The Accelerators' drummer Brian Damage. Top left: photographer Melanie Smith back in the day with Glen Matlock when The Rich Kids played Eric's. Top right: Eric's regular Vanessa Pimblett shares a truly rock 'n' roll moment with The Clash's Mick Jones

the subject of a drugs raid by police, but the building has continued as a music venue under other names into the 21st-century, re-opening (briefly) as Erics in 2011. Eric's enduring appeal has been the subject of both a musical' (2008) and a book, All the Best Clubs Are Downstairs, Everybody Knows That... (2009).

LOCATION 436: the building still stands but the club does not at 9 Mathew Street, postcode L2 6RE

"**People talk about The Cavern or the Marquee or CBGB's... ERIC'S was one of those places for a very strong generation of musicians**"

ANDY MCCLUSKEY
Whose OMD first came into being at Eric's

Merseyside

Liverpool 3
The Beatles Story visitor attraction

Located within Liverpool's Albert Dock, The Beatles Story will transport you into the life, times, culture and music of the Fab Four. Open seven days a week, it is now on two sites – the second a little way north on the waterfront at Pier Head.

LOCATION 437: Britannia Vaults, Albert Dock, postcode L3 4AD, and Pier Head, postcode L3 1DG

Liverpool 8
Central reservation inspiration

One of the most memorable and controversial No.1 singles in pop history began as a rhyme made up by local lad Holly Johnson as he hurried along Princes Avenue, Toxteth, to a Frankie Goes to Hollywood rehearsal. On arrival at the rehearsal, Johnson immediately laid down a vocal on to a one-note bassline from bass guitarist Mark O'Toole and drummer Peter Gill and 'Relax' was on its two-year journey to the top of the UK chart in 1984.

LOCATION 438: two miles south-east of the city centre on Princes Avenue, Toxteth, postcode L8 2UP

"One day in the winter of 1982, I was late for rehearsals, walking very quickly along the central reservation, and I made up this LITTLE RHYME in my head, which was 'Relax, don't do it'"

HOLLY JOHNSON

Liverpool 7
Percy Phillips' recording studios

An unassuming red-bricked house at 38 Kensington was the family home and business address for record producer Percy Phillips. Harmonising and playing into one microphone in Phillips' tiny studio, The Quarry Men recorded two songs straight to vinyl, but not before each group member had stumped-up the three shillings and sixpence demanded by Phillips in advance. This 1958 session featured John Lennon, Paul McCartney, George Harrison, John Lowe and Colin Hanton, recording Buddy Holly's 'That'll Be the Day' and a McCartney/ Harrison composition, 'In Spite of All the Danger'. This remarkable location displays a glass image to commemorate these Kensington recordings above the front door where five excited young musicians passed through on that day in 1958. Other local clients included Billy Fury, The Swinging Blue Jeans, Ken Dodd and Brian Epstein.

LOCATION 439: a mile east of the city centre on the A57, 38 Kensington, postcode L7 8. Status: private residence

Liverpool 3
The Mersey surfer cover

The Royal Liver Building, with the rather fanciful addition of Mersey surfer Ian Broudie, features as the backdrop to the cover of The Lightning Seeds' 1997 album Like You Do... Best of The Lightning Seeds.

LOCATION 440: Pier Head, postcode L3 1HT

Liverpool 8
A Sentimental Journey to the Empress pub

Between the Liverpool districts of Toxteth and Dingle stands the Empress pub - a two-minute walk from Ringo Starr's former homes in Madryn Street and Admiral Grove. The distinctive tall, thin pub is immortalised on the cover of Ringo's first solo album Sentimental Journey, a fact tastefully engraved into the glass below the stone arch in the centre of the building.

LOCATION 441: 93 High Park Street, Toxteth, L8 3UF

The Starkey family's local with Ringo's home on the right

Liverpool 8
Ringo's childhood home

When Ringo Starr was a young boy, his family split up. As a result, he and his mother moved a short distance from his birthplace to a smaller property in Admiral Grove when he was five. Richard Starkey suffered poor health, accompanied by frequent hospital visits, and was mostly schooled at home. As a teenager he was visited here by a friend, who would, like himself, go on to find fame with a name change from Priscilla White to Cilla Black. Ringo celebrated his 21st birthday and prepared for his wedding at Admiral Grove, the house that remained his Liverpool base until The Beatles became chart-toppers for the first time in 1963.

LOCATION 442: 10 Admiral Grove, postcode L8 8BH. Status: private residence

Merseyside

Liverpool 8
Ringo's birthplace

Richard Starkey (aka Ringo Starr) was born at 9 Madryn Street on July 7, 1940. At 10 shillings a week, the rent on the small terraced property was just too expensive and the family were forced to move the short distance to a more modest, affordable house in Admiral Grove.

LOCATION 443: 9 Madryn Street, Toxteth, postcode L8 3TT. Status: private residence, and the subject of a good deal of heated debate about its future as one of 16 houses saved in a mass demolition of the area's run-down Victorian properties

Liverpool 12
Casbah queues in the suburbs

The extraordinary basement Casbah club in a Victorian house in the West Derby area of Liverpool carries a very strong Beatles imprint. The house and club, owned by the family of Pete Best, the early Beatles drummer, was not only a music venue for all the various early Quarry Men and Silver Beatles line-ups, it also contains (even today) artistic interior decoration painted by John Lennon and Paul McCartney. John painted the Aztec pattern on the ceiling and carved his name on the wall while Paul painted a room with rainbows. A giant spider decorated another wall, while the remaining band members set about painting stars across ceilings and the tiny bar. On August 29, 1959, the Casbah opened its doors for the first time as a coffee bar. Performances by all the latest Liverpool groups brought long queues down the road, attracted by the novelty of rock 'n' roll music, sandwiches, coffee and Coca-Cola laid on by Mona Best, Pete's mother. As Paul McCartney remembers, "The Casbah was the place where all that started. We helped paint it and stuff. We looked upon it as our personal club."

LOCATION 444: the Casbah Coffee Club is still a venue for live music and open seven days a week for tours. Reached by taking the A5089 West Derby Road east out of the city centre at 8 Haymans Green, postcode L12 7JG

A giant spider, or was it a beetle, created by a Beatle on the wall of the Casbah club

Liverpool 15
John Lennon's first home

An unusual auction at The Cavern Club in 2013 saw John Lennon's first home on Newcastle Road sell for £480,000, despite a market value of less than half that figure.

An American Beatles fan was the successful bidder and new owner of the largely unchanged terraced home where John's mother Julia Lennon brought up her son from 1940 until he lived with his Aunt Mimi a couple of miles away in Menlove Avenue five years later. "I lived in 9 Newcastle Road. I was born on the 9th of October. It's just a number that follows me around," said John Lennon, who later penned and released a single '#9 Dream' in 1975.

LOCATION 445: 9 Newcastle Road, Wavertree, postcode L15 9HP. Status: private

Lennon lived at No.9, was born on the 9th day of October, and this single peaked at No.9 on the US Billboard singles chart

John Lennon
#9Dream · What You Got

Liverpool 15
A tour of Penny Lane

The extended Penny Lane area of Liverpool was the childhood haunt of John Lennon and Paul McCartney and title and subject of The Beatles' 1967 single. This area of Liverpool is best experienced sound-tracked by the song on your MP3 player as you visit each of the places name-checked by the song, a guided tour with lyrics of mostly McCartney's memories. The shelter in the middle of the roundabout where the pretty nurse sells her poppies is directly linked to the roundabout at the top of Penny Lane, where the building in the middle was a bus shelter, waiting room and public convenience. On the corners at the roundabout are where both the barber and the banker were described in 'Penny Lane'. The fireman referred to in the lyrics of the song no doubt worked in the fire station where Allerton Road meets Mather Avenue. Even though this was half a mile from Penny Lane itself, it was on the bus route Paul McCartney would take to school every day when heading towards Penny Lane roundabout from his home in Forthlin Road. Bordered on one side of Penny Lane is St Barnabas Church, where the young McCartney was a member of the choir. Paul was best man at his brother Mike's wedding here in 1982, a ceremony that attracted sizeable crowds to get a glimpse of the returning Beatle.

LOCATION 446: Tony Slavin's barber shop is at 11 Smithdown Place, off Penny Lane, and on the same block is the original bank (now a doctor's surgery). Begin your tour from here and head south for the full effect. Postcode: L15 9EH

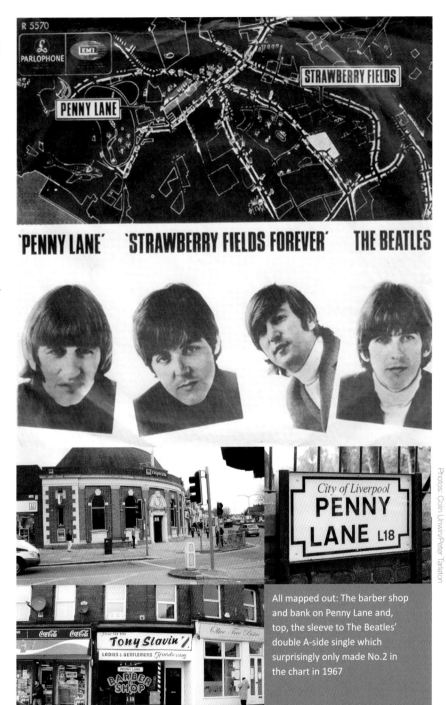

Photos: Colin Unwin/Peter Tarleton

All mapped out: The barber shop and bank on Penny Lane and, top, the sleeve to The Beatles' double A-side single which surprisingly only made No.2 in the chart in 1967

Merseyside

Liverpool 18
Forthlin Road: Paul McCartney's childhood home

Photo: Peter Tarleton

No.20 Forthlin Road: Paul McCartney's bedroom was immediately above the front door

The McCartney family home in Forthlin Road was where Paul and his brother Michael were raised by their father after their mother tragically died in 1956, the year after they moved in. Now maintained in all its quaint 1950s glory by the National Trust, the small terraced house is a visitor attraction open to the public. 'Let It Be', for Paul's mother Mary, 'When I'm Sixty-Four', about his father Jim, 'Love Me Do' and 'I Saw Her Standing There' were just some of more than one-hundred songs written by the teenage Lennon and McCartney in the tiny front room. The two would sometimes bunk off school and enter the empty house during the day. As Paul had no key he would make for the back of the house, climb up the drainpipe and enter through the open toilet window, before running downstairs to let John carry in their guitars. Paul's bedroom was situated above the front door. From this window, years later, he would witness the growing number of fans arriving to try to catch a glimpse of a Beatle. They would camp out all night and take mementos - even a wing mirror from Paul's car - and by 1964 the McCartney family were forced to move to a spot 25 miles away from Forthlin Road, which has continued to be a pilgrimage point for fans from all over the world.

LOCATION 447: 20 Forthlin Road, Allerton, postcode L18 9TN. Status: open for pre-booked public tours

Liverpool 15
George Harrison's childhood home

George Harrison grew up in a small terraced house, the youngest of three brothers and one sister. When George was a boy, the rent was 10 shillings per week, and before his father Harold landed a job as a bus conductor the family were forced to rely on welfare payments. Harold Harrison also spent a period in the Navy and brought some interesting records home. One vivid memory George recalled from his childhood at Arnold Grove was listening to 'One Meat Ball' by American Josh White.

LOCATION 448: 12 Arnold Grove, postcode L15 8HP. Status: private residence

George Harrison's 12 Arnold Grove birthplace is the orangey brick house in the middle of this terrace

Photo: Colin Unwin

Liverpool 25
Mendips: John Lennon's childhood home

Mendips, the house belonging to John Lennon's Aunt Mimi and Uncle George, was where he came to stay after his parents separated when John was just five years old. The suburban semi on Menlove Avenue was his home from 1945 until 1963. With all the fixtures and fittings that decorated the place in Lennon's time there, the house is now a beautifully restored shrine owned by the National Trust and open to the public. Underlining the Oasis obsession with their hero John Lennon, the Britpop band's single 'Live Forever' pictured Mendips on its front cover and many similarly enthusiastic Beatles fans, including Bob Dylan, have enjoyed the house tour, experiencing an insight into the lifestyle of the young Lennon. John's small bedroom was where, along with Paul McCartney, he sat and wrote future Beatles songs including 'Please, Please Me'. His bedroom was above the house's front porch, an area the boys would use to play their guitars, directed to go there by Mimi, who was not fond of the noise the two generated inside Mendips. Menlove Avenue was also the spot where Mimi's sister and John's mother Julia was killed when knocked down by a car when hurrying to catch a bus at the Menlove Avenue bus stop on July 15, 1958. In 2012, the Government's Tourism & Heritage Minister John Penrose announced that Mendips, along with Paul McCartney's childhood home on Forthlin Road, had become Grade II-listed buildings, ensuring their preservation for generations to come.

LOCATION 449: 251 Menlove Avenue, postcode L25 7SA. Status: open for pre-booked public tours

Photo: Peter Tarleton

John Lennon's home, where he lived as a schoolboy, art student and Beatle until 1963

" **[In 2009], a guided group arrived by bus and I saw that BOB DYLAN WAS AMONG THEM...** when we reached John's bedroom, Bob Dylan spotted the volume of Just William, which was one of John's favourite books. Dylan was fascinated by the book, and I remember thinking, 'I'm standing in John Lennon's bedroom with Bob Dylan.' It was a totally surreal moment **"**

COLIN HALL
Mendips' custodian

Merseyside

Liverpool 24
"Above us only sky" at John Lennon Airport

Liverpool's largest Beatles monument is Liverpool John Lennon Airport. The gateway to tourists arriving in the city, the airport name is aptly branded with the additional slogan "above us only sky", a line from Lennon's solo No.1 hit, 'Imagine'. The airport adopted Lennon's name in 2002 at a ceremony attended by Yoko Ono, when she unveiled the statue of her late husband by local sculptor Tom Murphy. The seven-foot-tall bronze overlooks the check-in hall on the first floor. The walls of the airport buildings are decorated with Beatles images and display cases of the group's clothing. Outside the terminal building is a giant Yellow Submarine. This 25-tonne model stands on the traffic island at the airport entrance. The 16-metre-long sculpture, representing the underwater craft featured in the song and movie Yellow Submarine, was built originally in 1984 for Liverpool's International Garden Festival by a group of 80 apprentices from the world-famous Cammell Laird shipyard.

LOCATION 450: seven miles south-east of the city, in Speke, postcode L24 1

Liverpool 21
The Beatles' Litherland murals

On the side end of a nice little house and adjoining wall on Croxteth Avenue, leading into the large roundabout that connects Princess Way and Church Road is the Beatles' mural. It is the work of Belfast Loyalist Mark Ervine and Republican Danny Devenny who joined forces to create the striking mural, commissioned by Riverside Housing Group to mark its 80th birthday, in 2008. This collaboration by artists from both sides of Northern Ireland's political divide celebrates Litherland's

important part in the Beatles' story in a spot which is one of the many gateways into the city of Liverpool.

LOCATION 451: the mural is on a wall and one side of a nice little end of terrace house at 5 Croxteth Avenue, Litherland. It faces the large roundabout connecting Princess Way and Church Road. Postcode L21 6NA

Photo: Peter Tarleton

Merseyside

Liverpool 25
St Peter's Church: Where it all began for The Beatles

Church Road, Woolton, boasts three important locations for fans of The Beatles wishing to make a pilgrimage to Liverpool in search of the group's earliest moments. Here you will also find the spot where The Beatles' saddest song first took flight in the imagination of Paul McCartney. The Beatles' story effectively began in the field outside St Peter's Parish Church in Woolton village on July 6, 1957. The occasion was a fete to mark the crowning of the local Rose Queen, which involved decorated floats, stalls, a police dog display and live music by local skiffle group The Quarry Men. This was the day when 15-year-old Paul McCartney first watched John Lennon and his group in action before being introduced to him later that night across the road in St Peter's Church Hall. Also in the audience to witness The Quarry Men's outdoor performance was a seething Aunt Mimi. Lennon's Aunt was not best pleased to witness her darling John performing as a Teddy Boy, with his hair in a quiff, bootlace tie and tight-fitting jeans. The Lennon-McCartney introduction was made by Ivan Vaughan, a member of John's Lennon's Quarry Men who played the youth club dances at the church hall. That night Paul, noticing that John (taught by his mother Julia) played banjo chords on his guitar, wasted no time in showcasing his own skills with the guitar, playing impressive versions of Eddie Cochran's 'Twenty Flight Rock' and Little Richard's 'Long Tall Sally', which prompted John and the others to ask him to join The Quarry Men. Within a month or two, he was playing in the band (taking over from banjo player Rod Davis, who was leaving anyway) and taking the stage at St Peter's Church Hall. The building, though modernized, stands as it did in 1957 and the outside wall carries a commemorative plaque to mark the day that John first met Paul. The hall's wooden stage where it all began was rescued by Liverpool City Council and is now an exhibit at the new Museum of Liverpool. Retracing your steps back to the church from the hall takes you to the churchyard and a couple of significant graves in Beatles folklore. The Eleanor Rigby gravestone marks the spot where the former scullery maid, who died aged 44 in 1939, could hardly have imagined leaving such a powerful legacy. Although Paul McCartney was reportedly influenced in choosing a name for his song of the same name when acting with Eleanor Bron in the movie Help!, the graveyard was a place both he and Lennon frequented when sunbathing in their teenage years. McCartney was also guided in the creation of the hit's title and lyrics by a Bristol name plate, but in all probability the gravestone was the starting point for what became the band's 10th chart-topping single. As the lyrics describe, the real Eleanor's final years may possibly have been lonely, but earlier she had lived a relatively normal life and was married at one time to a railway foreman. She was born in the street behind Menlove Avenue, where John Lennon grew up, and reports suggest John would sit in front of Eleanor Rigby's headstone fascinated by the word ''ASLEEP'', which is inscribed in the lower half of the impressive stone work. Weirdly, just two rows away from Eleanor Rigby's headstone lies the body of a John McKenzie, possibly a subconscious connection to the song's ''Father McKenzie'' character who also featured in McCartney's lyrics.

LOCATIONS 452, 453, 454 and 455:
St Peter's Church (and the field in which The Quarry Men performed) is in Church Road, Woolton, postcode L25 6DA. Both the Eleanor Rigby and 'Father McKenzie' gravestones are in the churchyard (pictured on the page opposite) at the same address. To find the hall and plaque, leave St Peter's Church return to Church Road, turning right, and soon after, left into the church hall behind the Simon Peter Centre, postcode L25 5JF. Currently, the famous stage is on exhibition at the Museum of Liverpool at Pier Head, Liverpool Waterfont, postcode L3 1DG

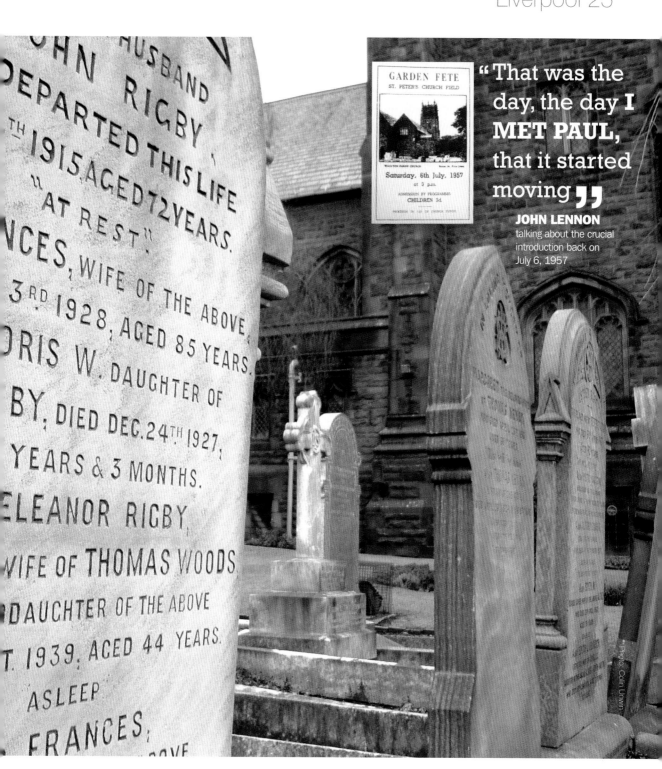

GARDEN FETE
ST. PETER'S CHURCH FIELD

WOOLTON PARISH CHURCH

Saturday, 6th July, 1957
at 3 p.m.

ADMISSION BY PROGRAMME
CHILDREN 3d

PROCEEDS IN AID OF CHURCH FUNDS

" That was the day, the day **I MET PAUL,** that it started moving "

JOHN LENNON
talking about the crucial
introduction back on
July 6, 1957

JOHN RIGBY HUSBAND
DEPARTED THIS LIFE
1915 AGED 72 YEARS.
" AT REST "

NCES, WIFE OF THE ABOVE,
3 RD 1928, AGED 85 YEARS.

ORIS W. DAUGHTER OF
BY; DIED DEC. 24TH 1927,
YEARS & 3 MONTHS.

ELEANOR RIGBY,
WIFE OF THOMAS WOODS,
DAUGHTER OF THE ABOVE
T. 1939, AGED 44 YEARS.

ASLEEP

FRANCES,

Photo: Colin Unwin

"John... lived next door to Strawberry Field, which was a Salvation Army place for kids. And he used to bunk over to this little **MAGIC** garden that he used to sort of play in 🙶

PAUL McCARTNEY
from The Beatles Anthology

Liverpool 25
Lennon's escape into Strawberry Field

All that remains structurally from the childhood days when John Lennon would play in the grounds of the children's orphanage are the still iconic red Strawberry Field gates and wall signs and an overgrown area of bushes and brambles. But there is a real sense of atmosphere about the place even now. The Salvation Army property was demolished and rebuilt but now lies vacant in the large rambling fields that once backed on to John's home at Mendips. He would squeeze through the hedge at the bottom of Aunt Mimi's garden and play in the area around the Victorian orphanage at Strawberry Field. This was a magical place for the young Lennon, where his imagination later conjured up The Beatles' earliest psychedelic song, 'Strawberry Fields Forever'.

Like everyone else who is haunted by the song's lyrics, Lennon's widow Yoko and son Sean Ono Lennon paid a visit to the children at the Strawberry Field orphanage and grounds in 1984.

LOCATION 456: Beaconsfield Road, Woolton, postcode L25

Inset: The long-gone Strawberry Field orphanage as it was back in the days of John Lennon's childhood

Main picture: The much-visited gates and autographed sign at the entrance to Strawberry Field

Photos: Salvation Army / Peter Tarleton

Merseyside

THE BEATLES
Ringo Starr made his official debut here on 18th August 1962

Photo: Peter Tarleton

Port Sunlight
Hulme Hall Beatles debut for Ringo

There's good evidence to suggest that Hulme Hall in Port Sunlight is the birthplace of The Beatles. What is certainly a fact is that on August 18, 1962, for the first time, The Beatles were officially John, Paul, George and (Pete Best replacement) Ringo. After diligently rehearsing for two hours, the new line-up kicked off their Hulme Hall gig (the local horticultural society's dance) at 10pm. On a later visit to Hulme Hall on October 27, that same year, The Beatles gave their earliest radio interview, broadcast on local hospital radio station Radio Clatterbridge.

LOCATION 457: Port Sunlight is on the western back of the River Mersey. Hulme Hall is at 23 Bolton Road, Port Sunlight, postcode CH62 5DH

The mop-top hairstyle was yet to evolve, but what became the famous line-up of John, Paul, George and Ringo played their first official gig in front of 500 at Hulme Hall, just before their first hit single release

THE BEATLES

LOVE ME DO

Born on MERSEYSIDE

Jacqui Abbott, vocals, The Beautiful South (b. 10 Nov 1973, St Helens)

Marc Almond (b. 9 Jul 1957, Southport)

Ian Astbury, vocals, The Cult (b. 14 May 1962, Heswall)

Rick Astley (b. 6 Feb 1966, Newton-le-Willows)

Cilla Black (b. 27 May 1943, Liverpool)

Roy Boulter, drums, The Farm (b. 2 Jul 1964, Liverpool)

Ian Broudie, The Lightning Seeds (b. 4 Aug 1958, Liverpool)

Tim Brown, bass, The Boo Radleys (b. 26 Feb 1969, Wallasey)

Pete Burns, Dead or Alive (b. 5 Aug 1959, Port Sunlight)

Mel C (Melanie Chisholm), Spice Girls (b. 12 Jan 1974, Whiston)

Les Chadwick, bass, Gerry & The Pacemakers (b. 11 May 1943, Liverpool)

Paul Draper, vocals/guitar, Mansun (b. 26 Sep 1970, Liverpool)

Aynsley Dunbar, drummer (b. 10 Jan 1946, Liverpool)

Brian Epstein, manager (b. 19 Sep 1934, Liverpool, d. 27 Aug 1967)

Tom Evans, singer-songwriter, Badfinger (b. 5 Jun 1947, Liverpool, d. 19 Nov 1983)

Billy Fury (b. 17 Apr 1940, Liverpool, d. 28 Jan 1983)

Peter 'Ped' Gill, drums, Frankie Goes to Hollywood (b. 8 Mar 1964, Liverpool)

Franny Griffiths, keyboards, Space (b. 1 Jul 1970, Liverpool)

Steve Grimes, guitar, The Farm (b. 4 Jun 1957, Liverpool)

George Harrison (b. 25 Feb 1943, Liverpool, d. 29 Nov 2001)

Paul Heaton, vocals, The Housemartins/The Beautiful South (b. 9 May 1962, Bromborough)

Michael Holliday, singer (b. 26 Nov 1924, Liverpool, d. 29 Oct 1963)

Peter Hooton, vocals, The Farm (b. 28 Sep 1962, Liverpool)

Carl Hunter, bass, The Farm (b. 22 Apr 1965, Bootle)

Tony Jackson, vocals/bass, The Searchers (b. 16 Jul 1938, Liverpool, d. 18 Aug 2003)

Holly Johnson, vocals, Frankie Goes to Hollywood (b. 9 Feb 1960, Liverpool)

Simon Jones, bass, The Verve (b. 29 May 1972, Wigan)

Billy J. Kramer (b. 19 Aug 1943, Bootle)

Ben Leach, keyboards, The Farm (b. 2 May 1969, Liverpool)

John Lennon (b. 9 Oct 1940, Liverpool, d. 8 Dec 1980)

Dave McCabe, vocals, The Zutons (b. 1980, Liverpool)

Nick McCabe, guitar, The Verve (b. 14 Jul 1971, St Helens)

Paul McCartney (b. 18 Jun 1942, Liverpool)

Jim McCarty, drums, The Yardbirds (b. 25 Jul 1943, Liverpool)

Andy McCluskey, vocals/guitar, Orchestral Manoeuvres in the Dark (b. 24 Jun 1959, Heswall)

Ian McCulloch, vocals, Echo & The Bunnymen (b. 5 May 1959, Liverpool)

Ian McNabb, vocals, The Icicle Works (b. 3 Nov 1960, Liverpool)

John McNally, guitar, The Searchers (b. 30 Aug 1941, Liverpool)

Stuart Maconie, broadcaster (b. 13 Aug 1961, Whiston)

Les Maguire, piano, Gerry & The Pacemakers (b. 27 Dec 1941, Wallasey)

Freddie Marsden, drums, Gerry & The Pacemakers (b. 23 Nov 1940, Liverpool)

Gerry Marsden, vocals, Gerry & The Pacemakers (b. 24 Sep 1942, Liverpool)

Lee Mavers, vocals, The La's (b. 2 Aug 1962, Liverpool)

Damon Minchella, bass, Ocean Colour Scene (b. 1 Jun 1969, Liverpool)

Joey Molland, guitar, Badfinger (b. 21 Jun 1947, Liverpool)

Brian 'Nasher' Nash, guitar, Frankie Goes to Hollywood (b. 20 May 1963, Liverpool)

Nigel Olsson, drums, Elton John Band (b. 10 Feb 1949, Wallasey)

Keith O'Neill, drums, Cast (b. 18 Feb 1969, Liverpool)

Mark O'Toole, bass, Frankie Goes to Hollywood (b. 6 Jan 1964, Liverpool)

David 'Yorkie' Palmer, bass, Space (b. 7 Apr 1965, Liverpool)

Sean Payne, drums, The Zutons (b. 1978, Liverpool)

John Peel, broadcaster (b. 30 Aug 1939, Heswall, d. 25 Oct 2004)

Mike Pender, vocals, The Searchers (b. 3 Mar 1942, Liverpool)

John Power, vocals, Cast/The La's (b. 14 Sep 1967, Liverpool)

Russell Pritchard, guitar, The Zutons (b. 22 May 1979, Liverpool)

Heidi Range, Sugababes (b. 23 May 1983, Liverpool)

Paul Rutherford, vocals, Frankie Goes to Hollywood (b. 8 Dec 1959, Liverpool)

Will Sergeant, guitar, Echo & The Bunnymen (b. 12 Apr 1958, Liverpool)

Chris Sharrock, drums, The Icicle Works (b. 30 May 1964, Bebington)

James Skelly, guitar/vocals, The Coral (b. 1980, Birkenhead)

Sice (Sice Rowbottom), vocals, The Boo Radleys (b. 18 Jun 1969, Wallasey)

Ringo Starr (b. 7 Jul 1940, Liverpool)

Liam 'Skin' Tyson, guitar, Cast (b. 7 Sep 1969, Liverpool)

Peter Wilkinson, bass, Cast (b. 9 May 1969, Liverpool)

Rock Atlas

Norfolk

*N*orfolk has Beatles and Nirvana for starters and is lyrically bracketed in the same line and league as Ibiza by David Bowie. Norfolk, or the "Norfolk Broads" as Bowie sang on 'Life on Mars', might be some kind of geographical rock extremity but never off the map when it comes to fondly remembered locations. Motörhead's giant mock-up Luftwaffe bomber stage set lies abandoned somewhere in Diss, The Stranglers like to be beside the seaside at Hunstanton, blue plaques abound in Norwich and the remote rock 'n' roll village of West Runton all contradict the notion that The Singing Postman is the county's most iconic contribution to the music map of Britain. Unique as he was, the guitar-toting postie was actually born in Lancashire. The most famous current rock 'n' roll resident has to be Seasick Steve. If America's most celebrated blues hobo rents out a country cottage here and stays for more than a year, you know Norfolk has got something special.

Born in NORFOLK

Cathy Dennis, singer-songwriter (b. 25 Mar 1970, Norwich)

Ed Graham, drums, The Darkness (b. 20 Feb 1977, Great Yarmouth)

Myleene Klass (b. 6 Apr 1978, Gorleston)

Beth Orton (b. 14 Dec 1970, East Dereham)

Tony Sheridan, (b. 21 May 1940, Norwich)

Roger Taylor, drums, Queen (b. 26 Jul 1949, Dersingham)

Hunstanton
Funk photo call for the men in black

The Stranglers named their 2004 album Norfolk Coast and were logically snapped by New York rock photographer Harrison Funk for the front cover, standing on Hunstanton beach.

LOCATION 458: the beach is west of the B1161 at the end of Hunstanton's Promenade, postcode PE36 5BF

"I took my treasure to the Norfolk Coast", as the lyrics to the title track say

Norwich
Pablo Fanque marks his place in Sgt Pepper

A blue plaque honours an extraordinary Norwich citizen name-checked by The Beatles in their Sgt Pepper's Lonely Hearts Club Band track 'Being for the Benefit of Mr Kite'. Born in Norwich in 1796, Pablo Fanque was Britain's first black circus proprietor and the man responsible for hiring the Hendersons, an act also included in the song inspired by a 19th-century circus poster purchased in an antique shop by John Lennon. Fanque also enjoys a mention on 'Ritz', a 1974 Cockney Rebel track from their Top 10 album The Psychomodo.

LOCATION 459: the plaque is on the wall of the John Lewis building, All Saints Green, Norwich, postcode NR1 3LX

Norwich
Orford Cellar: 'The Cavern for East Anglia'

On March 6, 2010, a plaque was unveiled in Norwich to mark the spot where the city's underground venue, The Orford Cellar, once hosted gigs by the likes of Jimi Hendrix, Rod Stewart, Eric Clapton, David Bowie and Elton John. The unveiling was carried out by the lead singer of favourite local performers at the club, Lucas and The Emperors, who, together with the illustrious list above, were name-checked on this Norwich Heritage & Economic Regeneration Trust (HEART for short) roll of honour. Lucas recalled playing the hot, sweaty club "every other week" and one local fan who had

campaigned for the plaque, Fred Agombar, described the place as "The Cavern for East Anglia". The Hendrix visit is perhaps remembered with most affection. According to one Cellar regular, January 25, 1967 saw a queue snaking back as far as The Bell Hotel at nearby Orford Hill. They had all turned up to see the new wild man of rock for the princely sum of seven shillings and sixpence.

LOCATION 460: the blue wall plaque is at 11 Orford Hill in Norwich city centre, postcode NR1 3QD

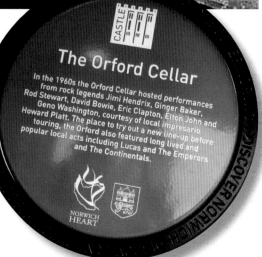

Top: The Orford Cellar in its heyday attracted long queues of rock fans anxious to see acts such as The Jimi Hendrix Experience, who made a barnstorming appearance there in January 1967

Norfolk

Norwich
Nirvana at the Arts Centre

They would become reluctant Nineties superstars, but US grunge rockers Nirvana made an early impact in Norwich in 1989. Booked by the founder of the city's Wilde Club, Barry Newman, the band wowed a capacity 200-plus crowd at the Norwich Arts Centre a few months after the first release of their album Bleach. Norwich's rock fans had, in the main, turned out for Seattle band Tad that night, with the lesser-known Nirvana (and Brain Drain 69) providing support. The Wilde Club can also point to early appearances by Oasis, Coldplay, Snow Patrol and Muse. In 1991, the converted church was the setting for a dramatic gesture by Manic Street Preacher Richey Edwards when challenged by journalist Steve Lamacq about his music. The guitarist, grabbing a razor blade, cut the reply "4 Real" into his bare arm, an act that later required a hospital visit and 17 stitches.

LOCATION 461: Norwich Arts Centre is in the city centre at Reeves Yard, St Benedict's Street, St Swithins Church. Postcode: NR2 4PG

Norwich
Perfect timing for The Beatles' only Norwich gig

Seventeen-hundred lucky teenagers were present the day The Beatles made their only appearance in Norwich. On May 17, 1963, the Grosvenor Rooms were the setting for a concert timed perfectly by local promoters Ray Aldous and Peter Holmes. Securing a booking with a band who had yet to begin their run of chart-topping recordings, the two 33-year-olds were able to negotiate a pricey but affordable £250 fee with Beatles manager Brian Epstein. By the time The Beatles arrived in Norwich, they were No.1 in both the singles and albums charts and played two 20-minute sets to a delirious audience inside the former ballroom. Obviously on a tight schedule and still tighter budget,

John, Paul, George and Ringo manhandled all their own equipment on arrival, carried out a soundcheck and then watched a movie at the nearby ABC cinema before taking to the stage. Afterwards, there was no overnight stay in a hotel for them. Aldous and Holmes recall the four chatting with fans over a hurriedly consumed fish and chip supper at Valori's in Rose Lane before heading south to begin a third nationwide tour in Slough.

LOCATION 463: a plaque is all there is to mark this gig, where the Grosvenor Rooms once stood in Prince of Wales Road in the city centre. Postcode: NR1 1NS

Just back from a short holiday in the Canary Islands, The Beatles play Norwich, their one and only gig in the city. No doubt with a warm glow inside, local promoter Ray Aldous looks on, standing to the left of Ringo's drum kit

Sheringham
Childhood home of The Singing Postman

Norfolk had its very own singing sensation in the mid-to-late Sixties. 'Hev Yew Gotta Loight Boy?' was the signature song by Greater Manchester-born Allan Smethurst. The Singing Postman, as he was called, shifted more records in his adopted county of Norfolk in the mid-Sixties than The Beatles and The Stones but his music failed to translate nationally into chart success aside from two Top 20 EPs. He was exposed to the thick Norfolk accent – his trademark vocal sound - from birth as his mother was from the Norfolk village of Stiffkey. His childhood, from age two, was then spent on the Norfolk coast at Sheringham.

LOCATION 462: the Smethurst family home was at 48 Cliff Road, Sheringham, postcode NR26 8BJ. Status: private residence

He's escaped into Suffolk! ... pictured in Coddenham

West Runton
Motörhead's bomber and Elvis at the far pavilion

Demolished in 1986, West Runton Pavilion was one of British rock's farthest flung outposts. A difficult enough journey for music fans from Norwich, the Pavilion nevertheless boasted a towering list of acts. As the blue plaque on West Runton's Village Inn describes, the Pavilion "hosted concerts by legendary pop, rock and punk artists from Chuck Berry, T.Rex and Black Sabbath [incorrectly as it turns out!] to the Sex Pistols and The Clash". This revered venue and the nearby Royal Links Pavilion at Cromer even have their own lovingly created book and website, What Flo Said, authored by Julie Fielder. Rarely visited by music paper scribes, West Runton village did however draw occasional visits from the NME's Ian Penman to report from "Norfolk's only hot hop", notably when Elvis Costello & The Attractions appeared in 1980.

Some bands generously resisted the temptation to scale down their live show to fit the Pavilion's intimate surroundings. Motörhead famously included West Runton on their touring schedule in 1980. They even brought a version of the vast "bomber" stage set, pictured on their No.1 album No Sleep 'til Hammersmith, to the Norfolk seaside venue. The 40-ft framework representing a Luftwaffe bomber is, according to Motörhead's Lemmy in John Harris' excellent book Hail! Hail! Rock 'n' Roll, now "holding up a shed" [or is that "holed-up in a shed"?] in nearby Diss. Locals regale their friends with tales of visiting rock stars mingling with fans in The Village Inn. Some even managed a game of pool with Lemmy and John Otway, who once staged a rather hazardous gig in the corner by the dartboard.

LOCATION 464: West Runton lies just north of the A149 on the north Norfolk coast. The plaque at The Village Inn (a short walk from the ex-Pavilion) is in Water Lane, postcode NR27 9QP.

Inside and outside the 1,400-capacity West Runton Pavilion

Photo: Syd Shelton

Rock Atlas
Northamptonshire

*T*he county that gave birth to Radiohead's Thom Yorke was also where top music broadcasters 'Whispering' Bob Harris and Jo Whiley both uttered their first words. Here, deep in the Northamptonshire countryside, Britain's honey-voiced folk songstress Sandy Denny chose to live with her fellow Fairport Convention band member and husband Trevor Lucas. A reminder of Corby's industrial heritage is poignantly documented by Big Country's 'Steeltown', and Kettering can possibly claim to have some of the most excitable fans in pop history. In the autumn of 1972, fans of the Bay City Rollers caused what some reported as a riot, eclipsing anything the local Granada had seen from earlier visits by pop's bad boys The Rolling Stones and Gene Vincent. And pre-dating that was some equally scandalous behaviour at Northampton's ABC cinema back in the Sixties, which hosted an infamous performance by P.J. Proby. The American singer famously split his trousers, causing nationally reported outrage necessitating action by the local constabulary. The policeman involved in dealing with the Proby incident that night and arresting the tight-trousered publicity seeker? None other than 'Whispering' Bob Harris's dad!

Corby
Big Country's 'Steeltown'

The town's population was boosted by the migration south of thousands of Glaswegians in the post-war Fifties. Corby was an iron-and steel-making hotbed before decline in production and large-scale unemployment in the Eighties. The band Big Country eloquently documented the promise of a new town and new life 'built on sand' by their fellow Scots on 'Steeltown', a track featured on the No.1 album of the same name in 1984.

LOCATION 465: an Asda supermarket now stands on the appropriately named Phoenix Parkway, the site where the steelworks' blast furnaces once stood. Postcode: NN17 5DT

Eighties devastation for Corby: documented on Big Country's chart-topping album

Byfield
Sandy Denny at The Twistle

This is the village where Sandy Denny, husband and fellow Fairport Convention band member Trevor Lucas, their daughter Georgia and Watson the Airedale Terrier lived in the mid-Seventies. Their Byfield home was affectionately known as The Twistle by Sandy's friends. The couple's orange and lime green VW Beetle and Rover cars were familiar sights around the local highways and byways and across the county boundary in the nearby Oxfordshire village of Cropredy, where the band's Dave Swarbrick and Dave Pegg had bought local properties. The large cottage in Byfield was where Sandy Denny lived and worked in the adjacent converted barn for the last four years of her troubled and frequently hedonistic life. Byfield Village Hall was the setting for her final public appearance in April 1978, shortly before her death later that same month.

LOCATION 466: Byfield is midway between Daventry and Banbury on the A361. The Village Hall location is The Green, postcode NN11 6UT

Below: The first lady of British folk-rock: Sandy Denny at her home in Byfield

Bottom: The picture-postcard cottage once shared by Sandy, Trevor, Georgia and Watson

Photo: Brian Cooke (courtesy of Island Records)

Photos x 2: Andrew Batt

Northamptonshire

Kettering
Rollermania at the Granada

On October 25, 1974, the Bay City Rollers visited Kettering's art deco Granada cinema. "Fan behaviour unlike anything seen since the height of Beatlemania" was how Q magazine later listed this notorious appearance by a group who were, at the time, rocketing up the chart with their fifth consecutive Top 10 single, 'All of Me Loves All of You'. The fans who didn't faint that day (and there were many who did) mobbed the band, trapping them in the Granada manager's office before a rescue operation by Kettering's police force. Thirteen-year-old Kettering schoolgirl Sara Simms remembers being a BCR fanatic in 1974. "We used to go to the Granada quite a lot for what the Evening Telegraph called the Junior Reader Club. It's not really changed that much inside, even though it is now a bingo hall. I can remember arriving and it being packed with girls, and a few boys all with BCR tops, scarves, or the whole kit on. I had a scarf on which I embroidered their names and you had to wear that round your wrist not round your neck, a rosette with Eric's face on it (my favourite) and one of their tops. The screaming was deafening, and I remember the security guards trying to stop people standing up during the concert, but they gave up in the end and we all stood on the seats, and at the end of the concert everyone rushed down to the front." In the two decades before the Granada's Rollermania experience, the venue also played host to the likes of Gene Vincent and The Rolling Stones and featured as a destination on Dusty Springfield's first solo tour of Britain.

LOCATION 467: the building in Kettering's High Street still stands, but its purpose, like so many others, has changed. The Granada is now a bingo hall. Postcode: NN16 8ST

Born in
NORTHAMPTONSHIRE

Daniel Ash, guitar, Bauhaus (b. 31 Jul 1957, Northampton)
Richard Coles, keyboards, The Communards (b. 23 Jun 1962, Northampton)
Bob Harris, broadcaster (b. 11 Apr 1946, Northampton)
David J. Haskins, Bauhaus (b. 24 Apr 1957, Northampton)
Kevin Haskins, drums, Bauhaus (b. 19 Jul 1960, Northampton)
Jim King, saxophone, Family (b. 5 May 1942, Kettering)
Peter Murphy, vocals, Bauhaus (b. 11 Jul 1957, Northampton)
Jo Whiley, broadcaster (b. 4 Jul 1965, Northampton)
Thom Yorke, vocals, Radiohead (b. 7 Oct 1968, Wellingborough)

Definitely not a library: Northampton's home to indie rock

Photo: Peter Tarleton

Northampton
The Roadmender returns

The reason Northampton's premier live music venue looks more like a public library than a nightclub is because the structure was once school buildings. Heavy-hitters The Stone Roses, Oasis, Radiohead and Metallica have all played the Roadmender, and after closure in 2005 these days it's back open again attracting artists such as Fish, Saxon and Adam Ant.

LOCATION 468: in the centre of the town, 1 Lady's Lane, postcode NN1 3AH

Northampton
'Uncle Len' books The Beatles

The town's ABC cinema saw two visits by The Beatles in 1963, on March 27 (on a tour they were originally billed as supporting Americans Chris Montez and Tommy Roe before Beatlemania reversed the pecking order) and later that same year on November 6, by which time they were undisputed headliners and chart-toppers with their first LP Please Please Me. The ABC was run by 'Uncle Len' Webster, as he was known, who cornered the market in Sixties beat groups as the town had no other music venues with any decent capacity at that time. The Rolling Stones, The Kinks and Marianne Faithfull all played the place.

LOCATION 469: at the busy Abington Square. The still magnificent art deco auditorium is currently the Northampton Jesus Centre, postcode NN1 4AE

Northumberland

Holy Island
The Brethren become Lindisfarne

In 635 AD, Saint Aidan journeyed from Scotland and founded a monastery on Northumberland's Holy Island, which became an evangelical base for the Christian faith. When Newcastle folk-rock group The Brethren chose Lindisfarne as their new name, they became more famous than the island itself when their Fog on the Tyne album topped the UK chart in 1972. "We chose the name Lindisfarne after the small tidal island off Newcastle – it's completely cut off at high tide; consequently the pubs stay open all day without fear of police action," said Lindisfarne's Ray Jackson, interviewed by Record Mirror in 1972.

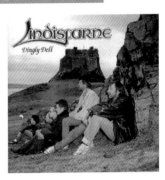

LOCATION 470: five miles east of the A1 at Beal. Take the Lindisfarne Causeway to the island. Postcode: TD15 2SH. The island, its priory and craggy hilltop castle are only accessible when the tide permits.

With the lowest density population of any English county, rural Northumberland is unsurprisingly a tad thin on the ground when it comes to rock locations or venues. Nevertheless, the inspirational landscape has created a region of great folk tradition, steeped in the unique music of the small pipes and other local instruments played by expert exponent Kathryn Tickell, who, on her many side projects, has recorded and performed with north-east rock star Sting. Although born a few miles down the road in Newcastle, Sting taught the secondary school children of Cramlington in Northumberland before a career in The Police beckoned. Out at sea, the island tourist attraction that is Lindisfarne inspired the name of one of Britain's much-loved folk-rock bands and Hexham was the birthplace of Libertines and Babyshambles rock idol Pete Doherty.

Born in NORTHUMBERLAND

Dave Cliff, jazz guitar (b. 25 Jun 1944, Hexham)
Pete Doherty (b. 12 Mar 1979, Hexham)
Robson Green, actor/singer, Robson & Jerome (b. 18 Dec 1964, Hexham)
Kathryn Tickell (b. 8 Jun 1967, Wark on Tyne)

Pete Doherty was born in Northumberland to parents employed by the British Army

Rock Atlas
Nottinghamshire

*N*ottingham University was the unannounced opening gig on Paul McCartney's first Wings tour back in 1972. Still in the Seventies… no music-related paragraph including the word 'Nottingham' can fail to feature Paper Lace. The band, who still includes one Carlo Santanna in their ranks and who topped both the UK and US pop charts, even managed to join forces with Nottingham Forest football club and storm the chart with the men from the City Ground. Nottingham's other club, Notts County, had their own musical claim to fame in 1969 when hosting Britain's first football stadium pop festival. One indoor venue that has worked hard to put the county on the map of rock 'n' roll worthiness is the star magnet that is Nottingham's Rock City, and Retford's Porterhouse also gets more than a passing mention, although now only, alas, in a historically gone-but-not-forgotten type of way.

Nottingham
Pop and blues at Meadow Lane

Presented by Stirling Enterprises, Nottingham can claim to have staged the first outdoor rock gig in a football stadium. Notts County's Meadow Lane ground was the setting for the 11-hour Pop & Blues Festival on May 10, 1969. Headline attractions were Fleetwood Mac, The Tremeloes and Marmalade, with up-and-coming Pink Floyd sandwiched further down the bill between The Move and Keef Hartley. Despite being headliners, Fleetwood Mac played an early set to enable themselves to fulfill a second booking later that day in Bangor, north Wales. Having reportedly printed 40,000 tickets, the organiser's enterprising but perhaps too eclectic bill attracted just 2,000 paying customers. Despite the low attendance, local promoters weren't daunted and in July the same year The Nice, Yes, King Crimson and Status Quo played what was billed as the '12-Hour Happiness' at Nottingham Racecourse, followed a

Retford
New beginnings at the Porterhouse

The Porterhouse was where Ultravox played one of their earliest gigs with Midge Ure, U2 got some vital Nottinghamshire feedback in 1980 and New Order began their live transformation from the dark end of Joy Division in 1981. Run by the now legendary Londoner Sammy

year later by the Nottingham Festival of Blues and Progressive Music at Victoria Embankment, starring Family, Taste and Mungo Jerry. "Woodstock comes to Nottingham", as the advertising put it at the time.

LOCATIONS 471, 472 and 473: the three festival venues were Notts County football club, Meadow Lane, postcode NG2 3HJ. Nottingham Racecourse, postcode: NG2 4BE. Victoria Embankment, postcode: NG2 2GF

Jackson, Motörhead and The Clash were among big names persuaded to stop by when heading north on their tour schedules. Jackson also booked AC/DC for only their second appearance on British soil back in May 1976.

LOCATION 474: no longer a music venue, the site is at 20 Carolgate, in the centre of Retford, postcode DN22 6BU

Photo: WEBWings Nottingham University Exchange

On the road with the McCartney family and band

Nottingham
Wings' secret debut

With no definite idea where they were heading, Paul McCartney's new band Wings journeyed north looking for places to play in the early spring of 1972. Incredibly, the superstar ex-Beatle had originally fancied playing Ashby de la Zouch as he liked the sound of the town's name, but their extraordinary journey in a van up the M1 eventually took them to the grand entrance of Nottingham University on February 8. When an enquiry was made at the Students' Union asking whether Wings could play, the then social secretary, a disbelieving Elaine

Woodhams, went outside little expecting to see Paul McCartney and family and band sitting patiently in their transit van. Arrangements were hurriedly made, some very basic advertising flyers pinned up and a 40-pence-per-ticket price agreed upon before 800 astonished fans watched the historic gig in the University's Portland Ballroom the next day. As Elaine Woodhams explained, ''The word went round like wildfire, just from the blackboard notice up in the bar.'' McCartney's take on the whole idea? ''We decided we'd just go on the road with no plans; no hotels booked, no gigs booked, a complete blank canvas. So we set off with the band, the family, the dogs,

the babies – up the motorway. We headed north and saw a sign that said Ashby de la Zouch so we got off the motorway there and asked where the nearest uni was.'' His first stage appearance since The Beatles continued with the eleven-gig tour in 15 days, eventually winding up at Oxford University on February 23. These days Nottingham University commemorates the still much talked-about Wings gig with a plaque in The Portland Dining Room.

LOCATION 475: a mile or two west of the city centre, the Portland Ballroom (now Portland Dining Room) is at University Park, postcode NG7 2RJ

Born in NOTTINGHAMSHIRE

Rob B (Robert Birch), vocals, Stereo MCs (b. 11 Jun 1961, Ruddington)

David Boulter, keyboards, Tindersticks (b. 27 Feb 1965, Nottingham)

Jake Bugg, singer-songwriter (b. 28 Feb 1984, Clifton, Nottingham)

Mark Colwill, bass, Tindersticks (b. 12 May 1960, Nottingham)

Elton Dean, saxophonist (b. 28 Oct 1945, Nottingham, d. 11 Feb 2006)

Bruce Dickinson, vocals, Iron Maiden (b. 7 Aug 1958, Worksop)

Corinne Drewery, vocals, Swing Out Sister (b. 21 Sep 1959, Nottingham)

Andy Fletcher, keyboards, Depeche Mode (b. 8 Jul 1961, Nottingham)

Nick Hallam, DJ/producer, Stereo MCs (b. 11 Jun 1960, Nottingham)

Dickon Hinchliffe, Tindersticks (b. 9 Jul 1967, Nottingham)

Simon Katz, guitar, Jamiroquai (b. 16 May 1971, Nottingham)

Alvin Lee, vocals/guitar, Ten Years After (b. 19 Dec 1944, Nottingham, d. 6 Mar 2013)

Al Macaulay, drums, Tindersticks (b. 2 Aug 1965, Nottingham)

Dave Manders, vocals/guitar, Paper Lace (b. 4 Aug 1947, Nottingham)

Ian Paice, drums, Deep Purple (b. 29 Jun 1948, Nottingham)

John Parr (b. 18 Nov 1954, Worksop)

Graham Russell, guitar/vocals, Air Supply (b. 11 Jun 1950, Nottingham)

Stuart Staples, vocals/guitar, Tindersticks (b. 14 Nov 1965, Nottingham)

Chris Urbanowicz, guitar, Editors (b. 22 Jun 1981, Aslockton)

Philip Wright, drums, Paper Lace (b. 9 Apr 1946, Nottingham)

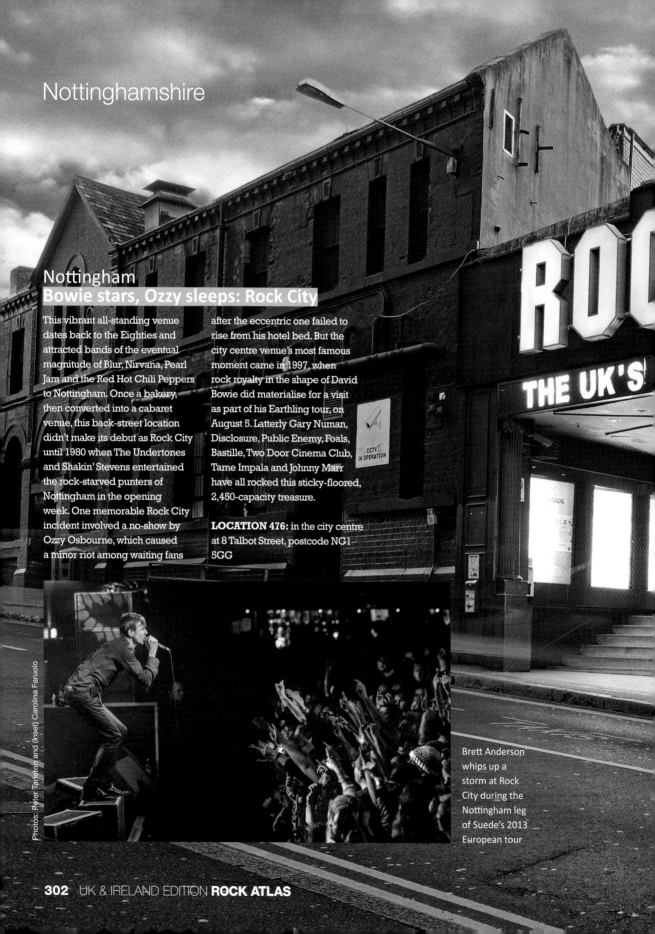

Nottinghamshire

Nottingham
Bowie stars, Ozzy sleeps: Rock City

This vibrant all-standing venue dates back to the Eighties and attracted bands of the eventual magnitude of Blur, Nirvana, Pearl Jam and the Red Hot Chili Peppers to Nottingham. Once a bakery, then converted into a cabaret venue, this back-street location didn't make its debut as Rock City until 1980 when The Undertones and Shakin' Stevens entertained the rock-starved punters of Nottingham in the opening week. One memorable Rock City incident involved a no-show by Ozzy Osbourne, which caused a minor riot among waiting fans after the eccentric one failed to rise from his hotel bed. But the city centre venue's most famous moment came in 1997, when rock royalty in the shape of David Bowie did materialise for a visit as part of his Earthling tour, on August 5. Latterly Gary Numan, Disclosure, Public Enemy, Foals, Bastille, Two Door Cinema Club, Tame Impala and Johnny Marr have all rocked this sticky-floored, 2,450-capacity treasure.

LOCATION 476: in the city centre at 8 Talbot Street, postcode NG1 5GG

Brett Anderson whips up a storm at Rock City during the Nottingham leg of Suede's 2013 European tour

Photos: Peter Tarleton and (inset) Carolina Faruolo

ʀK CITY

EST LIVE VENUE & CLUB

alt-tickets
box office
0871 3100 000
www.alt-tickets.co.uk
Open 9am-8pm, Mon to Sat
Book online 24/7
Tickets for concerts across Nottingham & the UK

Oxfordshire

*T*he epicentre of the vibe created by folk-rock pioneers and mainstays Fairport Convention is the village of Cropredy, where their annual festival has been going forever. The same rural summer sunshine their festival appears to guarantee has drawn Traffic, XTC, Paul Weller and Mike Oldfield to seek out Oxfordshire rural retreats for the creation of some of these artists' finest work. In keeping with its history as a place where cerebral activity has thrived, the city of Oxford has produced a calibre of band famed for their thoughtful, intricate lyrics. Foals, Stornoway, Supergrass and Radiohead top the list of a wave of music, much of which has been nurtured in the small area of the city called Jericho. The county's greatest claim to rock immortality and worldwide musical acclaim came when schoolboys Thom Yorke, Colin Greenwood, Ed O'Brien, Phil Selway and Jonny Greenwood formed a group at Abingdon School that would later become a music obsession for some and a terrific earner worldwide for the British music industry. East of Oxfordshire is the palatial estate where the county's most famous rock resident, George Harrison, lived, gardened, filmed and recorded for the greater part of his life before his death in 2001.

Chipping Norton
Elton John: The Pied Piper of Chipping Norton

An NME report in 1975 by Steve Turner nominated the launch party for Elton John's new label Rocket Records as one of the most notable media events of the decade. In keeping with the train-themed label logo, Elton laid on a football special with disco and ferried the press and guests from London's Paddington to Oxfordshire. Alighting at the Oxfordshire station of Kingham, the media scrum then followed Elton - acting, as Turner put it, "as a 20th-century Pied Piper" - through the streets, complete with marching band, to the local hall for much merrymaking before the return trip to Paddington. At this time the residents of Chipping Norton were hardly unfamiliar with the sight of rock and pop legends visiting the town. Edwin Starr, Status Quo, Duran Duran, Gerry Rafferty, Jeff Beck, Fairground Attraction and Alison Moyet are just some of the musicians that recorded or rehearsed at Chipping Norton Recording Studios from 1972 to 1999.

LOCATION 477: Chipping Norton is about 20 miles north-east of Oxford on the A44. The grade II-listed building that once housed the recording studios is at 28 New Street, postcode OX7 5LJ

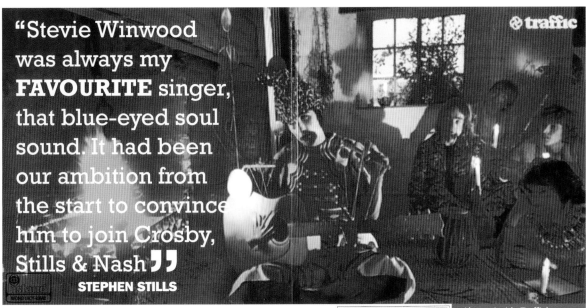

"Stevie Winwood was always my **FAVOURITE** singer, that blue-eyed soul sound. It had been our ambition from the start to convince him to join Crosby, Stills & Nash "
STEPHEN STILLS

Aston Tirrold
Traffic go back to the country

Nestled in the Oxfordshire countryside is the secluded white cottage surrounded by farmland where the group Traffic escaped to gain some rural inspiration and rehearse new material in 1967. The idyllic spot, complete with beehives, was tucked away down a dirt track, with stunning views from the makeshift cement platform rehearsal stage where the group would play on warm summer evenings. The stone-floored cottage had no running water and no electricity at the start of their three-year rented residence, but the band members set about creating their own unique lifestyle, with many visitors dropping by despite the geographical isolation of the place. Eric Clapton, Pete Townshend, John Bonham, Ginger Baker and Joe Cocker were all house guests. Leon Russell even premiered a new song he'd composed called

'Superstar' on the cottage piano, and Stephen Stills "trudged across the moors", as he put it, in a vain attempt to get Traffic's Steve Winwood to join Crosby, Stills & Nash. By 1969, rock fans everywhere had become aware of Traffic's music haven, following the release of the Mr. Fantasy and Traffic albums and numerous press reports about the band's "back to the country" commune. Rolling Stone magazine reported the experience in depth, with Winwood pictured outside the cottage on the front cover.

LOCATION 478: south of Aston Tirrold, where Spring Lane meets the A417, there's a lane on the opposite side of the A417 which in turn branches off right into a dirt track leading to Sheepcot Farm. Postcode: OX11 9DS. Status: private residence

Above: inside Traffic's cottage and left, on the cover of Rolling Stone

" I think the sound of the room is very interesting, like every room has its own **CHARACTER**, and the room in the cottage where we do rough takes of the songs has its own special quality "
STEVE WINWOOD
talking to Rolling Stone in 1968

Oxfordshire

Cropredy
Fairport's convention in the sun

Music festivals featuring Fairport Convention in the village of Cropredy can be dated back to 1976. The band's bass-playing founder member Dave Pegg and his family settled in the village and Fairport's Cropredy convention started life as a private back garden event with a few hundred guests. What began as the end of the band (they played what they believed to be their final outdoor gig at Cropredy in 1979) was actually a rebirth with a burgeoning fanbase seeded and grown through decades of tours and recordings. Their festival has now expanded to stretch over three days and attracts up to 20,000 at the annual August get-together. Joining Fairport Convention on the bill in recent years have been folk favourites Seth Lakeman, John Martyn and Ralph McTell, plus Steve Winwood, Supergrass and, broadening the scope of the event, even Alice Cooper.

LOCATION 479: the current festival site is east of the village of Cropredy, immediately over the Cropredy Bridge which spans the River Cherwell and Oxford Canal, postcode OX17 1PQ. Check out the extremely helpful Cropredy section of the website www.fairportconvention.com

Cropredy's imaginative 2013 bill included Alice Cooper, complete with the usual pyrotechnics, python and guillotine

Attendances of 20,000 come to Cropredy each summer to pay homage to Fairport Convention and an assortment of acts in addition to the usual folk favourites

Photos: www.fairportconvention.com

Oxfordshire

Henley-on-Thames
Dusty Springfield's memorial stone

Henley is the town where Dusty Springfield lived out the final years of her life and the parish church of St Mary the Virgin is a much-visited spot for her loyal fans. Here a funeral congregation, including Lulu, Elvis Costello and the Pet Shop Boys, came to pay their last respects to the iconic singer after her death in 1999. There is a memorial stone in the churchyard where some of her ashes are buried, the remainder having been scattered by her brother Tom Springfield in Ireland. Go to the Rock Atlas Lislarkin (Republic of Ireland) entry and the Greater London W8 section for additional information on these Dusty memorials.

LOCATION 480: St Mary the Virgin churchyard is on the A4130 (Hart Street) in the centre of Henley-on-Thames. Postcode: RG9 2AU

Oxford
Supergrass on 'Shotover Hill'

The Supergrass 1999 album includes a track about local beauty spot, 'Shotover Hill'. The band's Gaz Coombes describes the whereabouts of this 557-ft-high location: "It's actually a hill in Wheatley and we used to go up there and the travellers used to be there and we used to get a bit of smoking done and see all these mad travellers with their dogs. It's just a little story about that, remembering walking up the hill and coming back down three hours later after a few smokes and it's raining. It was a really beautiful place as well, and it's a very visual song. It talks about how you can see the glow of the caravans and they're smoking stuff and you can smell it all. It's looking back to our youth. We all remember it really well, so it was good to get together and write about it."

LOCATION 481: east of Oxford, Old Road, postcode OX3 8TB

Oxford
'Creep' video at The Zodiac

Formerly called the Co-op Dining Hall, The Venue and then The Zodiac, this 1,000-plus-capacity music theatre was where Radiohead's 'Creep' video was shot on the old main stage. The band's management company were responsible for funding the venue's re-opening in 1995. Oxford's premier music spot now continues to do business, re-named as the O2 Academy.

LOCATION 482: the O2 Academy, 190 Cowley Road, postcode OX4 1UE

Henley-on-Thames
George Harrison's Friar Park estate

The so-called quiet Beatle's estate at Friar Park is strongly associated with his hugely successful debut solo album All Things Must Pass. One track in particular, 'Ballad of Sir Frankie Crisp (Let It Roll)', acts as a guided tour of Friar Park's 120-room, Neo-Gothic mansion's caves, maze, woods and "Ye long walks of Coole and Shades", as George Harrison puts it. Frank Crisp was an earlier owner of Friar Park who designed the gardens and began a collection of whimsical statues and gnomes, a trend embraced by Harrison (a keen gardener), who included some of his garden gnomes on the All Things Must Pass album cover shot at Friar Park. Harrison purchased the estate in 1970 and lived there until his death in 2001. His debut album wasn't the only chart-topper recorded at the estate's studio. Shakespear's Sister's No.1 single 'Stay' and their album, Hormonally Yours, was recorded there.

LOCATION 483: heading west from the centre of Henley-on-Thames, follow Market Place into Gravel Hill. The private Friar Park estate begins on the right after the right-hand turn to Hop Gardens. Postcode: RG9 2EH

Below: an old postcard of Friar Park and right, George Harrison in his beloved garden with the Victorian neo-Gothic mansion in the background

Photo: Terry O'Neill/Getty Images

Oxfordshire

Oxford
Radiohead's South Park homecoming

With their album Amnesiac top of the chart a month earlier, Radiohead made a triumphant homecoming appearance at Oxford's South Park in July 2001. Torrential rain failed to dampen the spirits of 42,000 adoring fans, who also witnessed performances by fellow local lads Supergrass plus Beck, Sigur Rós and Humphrey Lyttelton. Radiohead's Phil Selway reflects:

"It's what you dream of really. Having a show like that in what was my local park at the time was quite something. Looking out into the audience and seeing the pandemonium is an image that will stay with me."

LOCATION 484: south of the A420 Headington Road at Cheney Lane, postcode OX3 7QJ

Fans arriving early for the eventually wet but triumphant Radiohead homecoming in Oxford's South Park

Born in OXFORDSHIRE

Adam Clayton, bass, U2 (b. 13 Mar 1960, Chinnor)
Gareth 'Gaz' Coombes, vocals, Supergrass (b. 8 Mar 1976, Oxford)
Rob Coombes, keyboards, Supergrass (b. 27 Apr 1972, Oxford)
Thea Gilmore (b. 25 Nov 1979, Oxford)
Gary Glitter (Paul Gadd) (b. 8 May 1944, Banbury)
Colin Greenwood, bass, Radiohead (b. 26 Jun 1969, Oxford)
Jonny Greenwood, guitar/keyboards, Radiohead (b. 5 Nov 1971, Oxford)
Tom Hingley, vocals, Inspiral Carpets (b. 9 Jul 1965, Oxford)
Ed O'Brien, guitar, Radiohead (b. 15 Apr 1968, Oxford)
Mick Quinn, bass/vocals, Supergrass (b. 17 Dec 1969, Oxford)
Tim Rice-Oxley, guitar, Keane (b. 2 Jun 1976, Oxford)
'Legs' Larry Smith, drums, Bonzo Dog Doo-Dah Band (b. 18 Jan 1944, Oxford)
Vivian Stanshall, vocals Bonzo Dog Doo-Dah Band (b. 21 Mar 1943, Oxford, d. 5 Mar 1995)
Nik Turner, saxophone/vocals, Hawkwind (b. 26 Aug 1940, Oxford)

Shipton-on-Cherwell
Weller at The Manor

Now the private property of the Marquess of Headfort, The Manor at Shipton-on-Cherwell was once a rural residential recording studio owned by Richard Branson, ostensibly to service his Virgin Records stable of artists. The place gave the right amount of freedom and inspiration that enabled Mike Oldfield to create his 17-million-copy-shifting album Tubular Bells. It also famously fitted the bill perfectly when a mellowing Paul Weller, seeking a new base to record some folkier material in 1993, hit upon The Manor for his new album Wild Wood. Weller remembers:"The Manor was just really magical. In fact, everyone who came down sensed it." His next album, Stanley Road, was another

product of the the Manor's rural vibe, this time with a guest appearance by Steve Winwood, who had himself returned to some traditional British roots music during Traffic's immersion in the Oxfordshire countryside three decades earlier. Apparently, Traffic's Jim Capaldi had tipped off Winwood about Weller's Wild Wood and he was approached to play at The Manor on Stanley Road's 'Woodcutter's Son' and 'Pink on White Walls'. The Strawbs, Gong and XTC made tracks there more than once before Radiohead and Cast became The Manor's last bookings in 1995.

LOCATION 485: two miles north of Kidlington, postcode OX5 1JL

Oxford
Supergrass and Radiohead take off in Jericho

Jericho is a historic suburb of Oxford, just a short walk north-east of the city centre, and is a place where A&R people would flock to see new bands. In 1986, The Jericho Tavern witnessed the very first gig by local boys On A Friday, who would soon become Radiohead, and a performance by Supergrass in 1994 was so good it instantly bagged them a recording contract. Built in 1818, The Jericho continues to promote great live music in this quiet corner of Oxford. It was local record shop the Manic

Hedgehog that gave On A Friday the name for their final demo tape. It included tracks that would resurface on the band's Pablo Honey debut album, released under their new band name Radiohead.

LOCATION 486: a short walk north-east of the city centre, The Jericho Tavern is at 56 Walton Street, postcode OX2 6AZ

> " It's such a **WEIRD** place and it's very important to my writing "
> **THOM YORKE**
> describes Oxford in an early interview

The Jericho Tavern now has a PRS For Music plaque to mark the spot where Supergrass bagged their first recording contract

Mapledurham
The first Black Sabbath album cover

The ghostly cloaked figure on the front cover of Black Sabbath's debut album is standing in a winter landscape in front of Mapledurham Mill, on the River Thames. The building, which dates back to the 15th century, was photographed from the lawns of Mapledurham House.

LOCATION 487: a short distance west of the A4074, north-west of Reading. Postcode: RG4 7TR. Status: public paid admission

Mapledurham Mill and a cloaked friend are all you need to recreate this famous Black Sabbath photo shoot

Rock Atlas

Rutland

Despite a population of just 35,000, Britain's smallest county delivers an excellent smattering of Rock Atlas entries from music heavyweights The Who, The Glitter Band, Geno Washington and Kasabian. The Seventies gave Rutland its most famous rock'n'roll connection when Rutland Weekend Television and the best ever Beatles parody, The Rutles (both fictitious creations of Neil Innes and Eric Idle), hit our TV screens.

Nasty, Stig, Dirk and Barry – The Rutles were a by-product of Rutland Weekend Television

Exton
Marmalade down on the farm

The resourceful farm folk of Home Farm spotted a non-agricultural use for their two large, linked Dutch barns back in the Seventies. Hired out for barn dances, they went a stage further and cheekily coaxed a number of impressive chart acts to play down on the farm. Marmalade, who boasted eight Top 10 singles, and The Glitter Band, with six of their own, were "regularly on Top of the Pops and playing in front of hundreds of people on our farm," remembers farm manager's son Jamie Healey, who was 11 years old at the time.

LOCATION 488: Home Farm, Exton, north of the A606 between Oakham and Stamford, postcode LE15 8AZ

Normanton
Kasabian's 'mash-up' farm

Leicestershire's multi-award-winning band Kasabian seemingly escape to Rutland at any given opportunity. Aside from having a liking for the county's pubs (Oakham's Railway pub is said to be a particular favourite), Normanton, near Rutland Water, has come to be the band's creative bolt-hole. Described by vocalist Tom Meighan as "our quiet, private place", the farm at Normanton was the location for a party

> " A big, psychedelic MASH-UP on a farm "

SERGIO PIZZORNO
Kasabian's guitarist describes the band's debut hit album, created at Normanton

the band were invited to attend before they hit big in 2004. They found the setting so much to their liking, they moved in and recorded debut album Kasabian there.

LOCATION 489: on the south-east shore of Rutland Water and south of the A606 between Oakham and Stamford. Postcode: LE15 8RP

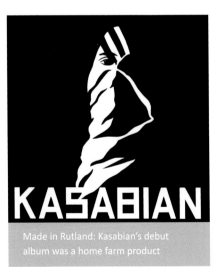

Made in Rutland: Kasabian's debut album was a home farm product

Stretton
Geno Washington and the Ram Jam Inn

When Geno Washington left his native Indiana to travel from the UK as a member of the US Air Force, he managed to gain a reputation as a part-time soul singer. When discharged as an airman, Washington fronted Geno Washington and The Ram Jam Band, who promptly established themselves as mainstays of the live circuit and chart stars during 1966 and '67. The band were named after the Ram Jam Inn, situated on the A1 at Stretton, a handy stopping point for bands dragging themselves north and south up Britain's busiest road before the completion of the M1 motorway. Amazingly, Geno and his merry men never actually set foot in the place. Interviewed by Brian Southall in 2011, Geno Washington explains: "In those days it was a pub-cum-restaurant with a petrol station next to it. We never stopped there but were looking for a name for the band and we went through about 2,000 names and none of them sounded right. We were coming down the A1 and just happened to see this place called Ram Jam and we started laughing about the name. We just thought it was a silly fucked-up name, but by the time

we got back to London we were still laughing at the name Ram Jam so we thought 'Hey, if we are still laughing about some shit from two hours ago that must be a good name.' So we named ourselves The Ram Jam Band featuring Geno Washington."

LOCATION 490: Great North Road, Stretton, postcode LE15 7QX

Geno and his band never did step inside the Ram Jam Inn

Exton Park & Cottesmore
The Who relax in Rutland

The Who were once regular visitors to Rutland during the period their tour manager Bob Pridden lived at Fort Henry in Exton Park. The band availed themselves of the local hospitality and were frequently spotted in the mid-Seventies rehearsing (Exton Village Hall),

recording (Bob Pridden's Fort Henry studio) and drinking (The Sun Inn at Cottesmore). When staying with Pridden at Fort Henry, local pub, The Sun Inn was a particular favourite of Keith Moon. In 1975, teenage local music fan Vernon Stokes was star-struck on seeing Moon walk into the gents toilets at The Sun Inn. He remembered accidentally peeing down his own trouser leg, which led Moon to

comment in an understanding kind of way, "Hey, that's rock 'n' roll!", leaving the boy from Oakham with a memory he's never forgotten.

LOCATIONS 491 and 492: Bob Pridden's Fort Henry is the mock-gothic folly on the Exton Park estate, postcode LE15 8AN. The Sun Inn pub is at 25 Main Street, Cottesmore, postcode LE15 7DH

Rock Atlas

Shropshire

The county of birth for proper rock legend Ian Hunter of Mott the Hoople. Shropshire's county town Shrewsbury was where DJ John Peel spent his somewhat reluctant school days and, additionally, was where the locals witnessed three appearances by The Beatles in less than five months. The second of these visits coincided with a particularly significant day in the life of Lennon and McCartney's song-writing partnership.

Shrewsbury
Lennon & McCartney pen their first No.1

The Beatles made three visits to Shrewsbury, all in less than five months. December 14, 1962 saw them arrive for their first performance, at the town's Music Hall. Their third and final appearance was on April 26, 1963 at the same venue. However, the second Shrewsbury concert was to be the most significant - for them at least. Arriving in the back of their bus on the Helen Shapiro tour on February 28th 1963, as the coach transporting the group completed its journey from York to Shrewsbury's Granada cinema, John Lennon and Paul McCartney completed their latest composition, 'From Me to You'. A pivotal release in Beatles history, the song would register as the group's first number one hit and top the singles chart in the same week of their final visit to the town. Both of the town's Beatles venues are now Grade II-listed buildings.

LOCATION 493: now Shrewsbury's Museum & Art Gallery, Music Hall is at The Square, postcode SY1 1LH. The building that was once the Granada cinema is now a bingo hall, 6 Castle Gates, postcode SY1 2AG

Shrewsbury
Ian Hunter's childhood home

Before gravitating to London and before Mott The Hoople, Shrewsbury was where young Ian Hunter Patterson grew up. After the Mott The Hoople years, Ian Hunter, as he'd become by then, later released a steady stream of solo albums including the 1996 offering The Artful Dodger, which featured the autobiographical '23A, Swan Hill'. His teenage address, the song paints a less than romantic picture of a place where it was always raining that he wanted a way out of.

LOCATION 494: 23a Swan Hill, town centre, postcode SY1 1NQ. Status: private residence

Born in
SHROPSHIRE

Michael Chetwood, keyboards, T'Pau (b. 26 Aug 1954, Telford)
Dick Heckstall-Smith, saxophonist (b. 16 Sep 1934, Ludlow, d. 17 Dec 2004)
Ian Hunter, vocals/guitar, Mott the Hoople (b. 3 Jun 1939, Oswestry)
Paul Jackson, bass, T'Pau (b. 8 Aug 1961, Telford)
Stephen Jones, Babybird (b. 16 Sep 1962, Telford)
Ronnie Rogers, guitar, T'Pau (b. 13 Mar 1959, Shrewsbury)

Somerset

*T*his is where it would appear more musical merrymaking goes on outdoors than anywhere else. Early pioneering rock festivals began at Glastonbury, Shepton Mallet and Bath. Somerset was the place to be as the '60s gave way to the '70s. The first UK act to top the US chart, Acker Bilk, was born, bred and lived in the village of Pensford, some familiar pictures of The Beatles were snapped on Somerset's golden sands and the Fab Four made a fish and chip shop in Taunton famous during a detour on their Magical Mystery Tour. The spiritual Somerset landscape comes complete with trip-hop, Wurzels, Peter Gabriel's solo inspiration, a Tudor 'pile' that gave Radiohead the shivers, Kylie singing down the village pub and Anthony Newley's televisual hijacking of the quaintly named village of Gurney Slade.

Photo: Peter Tarleton

The large marble memorial to Eddie Cochran, in the grounds of St Martin's Hospital

Bath
Eddie Cochran's memorial

In 1960, Eddie Cochran died from the injuries suffered in a car crash in Chippenham at St Martin's Hospital in Bath. Prominently displaying the words 'Three Steps to Heaven', a large marble memorial to the American rock 'n' roll star is situated in the hospital's meditation garden. There's also a smaller memorial a few steps away in the form of a sundial presented by "his many fans from Bristol". Cochran's body was returned to California, where he is buried at Forest Lawn Cemetery, Cypress.

LOCATION 495: situated on Clara Cross Lane off the B3110, postcode BA2 5RP

Somerset

Bath
Nashers has it covered

The wonderfully named Nashers independent record shop, with American Dream Comics upstairs for good measure, is the enticing emporium featured on the cover of Van Morrison's 2002 album Down the Road.

LOCATION 496: 72 Walcot Street, Bath, postcode BA1 5BD

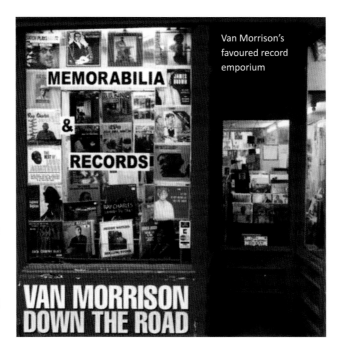

Van Morrison's favoured record emporium

Bath
Led Zeppelin rock the Recreation Ground

Perhaps the attendance wasn't large by today's standards - MC John Peel even offered the crowd a lift back to London in his camper van - but the Bath Festival of Blues was an important rock milestone back on a balmy summer's day in 1969. Set in the Recreation Ground and surrounded by the splendour of Bath's Georgian architecture, this spot was notable for Led Zeppelin's earliest festival appearance. Local opinion was fearful of such a large youth invasion. However, the powers that be were so impressed with the behaviour of the 12,000 fans that they offered, those that wished to, an impromptu sleepover.

LOCATION 497: bordered by Great Pulteney Street and Pulteney Road. Status: now home to Bath Rugby Club. Postcode: BA2 4DS

Frome
Vinyl Heaven

Music lovers in this small market town are spoilt with not one but two record shops. Raves from the Grave's owner had so much stock he opened a second shop next door selling only vinyl and accurately named it Vinyl Heaven. And that's not all. Raves from the Grave also has a shop in Weymouth Street, Warminster, in the neighbouring county of Wiltshire. Here you'll find six rooms of vinyl and enough space to regularly host live music events.

LOCATION 498: 18a and 20 Cheap Street, Frome, postcode BA11 1BN

" **Our music range covers all tastes, from MANTOVANI to MOTÖRHEAD** "

ANDREW BIRCH
Shop manager

Glastonbury
The Waterboys' spiritual awakening

Turned on by the mythical literature he read in the early Eighties, Waterboys singer-songwriter Mike Scott was a frequent visitor to Glastonbury the place, not just the festival. This "awakening", as he puts it, filtered through to the lyrics of a spiritual journey on the band's 1993 hit single 'Glastonbury Song'. A much more 'mud and music' Glastonbury song was recorded by Warwickshire duo Nizlopi a decade later.

LOCATION 499: Glastonbury Tor sits atop its green hill east of the town of Glastonbury, just north of the A361. Postcode for nearby Wellhouse Lane is BA6 8BL. Status: owned by the National Trust and open to the public

Gurney Slade
The weird world of Anthony Newley

The theme to 1960 weird comedy The Strange World of Gurney Slade by Max Harris provided TV immortality for the village of Gurney Slade. The show's central character was Anthony Newley and the metronomic tune's TV exposure led to a No.11 chart hit.

LOCATION 500: north of Shepton Mallet on the A37, postcode BA3 4TQ

"**Everyone** was sworn to **SECRECY**, even the staff didn't know about it "

LAUREN GODDARD
Ring O' Bells landlady talking to the BBC about the Kylie appearance

Photo: Sun Newspaper Group

Photo: Sun Newspaper Group

Compton Martin
Kylie and Coldplay down the pub

A seven-month-long secret kept by pub landlord and landlady Reuben and Lauren Goddard ended on August 19, 2010 when Kylie Minogue performed at the Ring O Bells pub in this tiny north Somerset village. Locals assumed the pub's blackboard advertising "For One Night Only! – Kylie Minogue" was either a hoax or a tribute performer night but were shocked when they realised their pub had been selected for a Parlophone company outing to witness the label's artists Kylie, Tinie Tempah, Eliza Doolittle and Morning Parade in action. If that wasn't enough, the pub also had Coldplay perform there on December 17, 2013.

LOCATION 501: on the A368 Bath to Weston-super-Mare road, postcode BS40 6JE

Yes, it really is Kylie Minogue performing among the beams, horse brasses and a few lucky pub regulars at the Ring O Bells, a pub gig matched by Coldplay (above) three years later

Somerset

Pilton
The Glastonbury experience

These days, Glastonbury is a true British institution in the same league as the Henley Regatta, the Chelsea Flower Show and Wimbledon fortnight. Alright, Glastonbury hasn't yet got a Royal enclosure, but our best-loved rock festival's creator Michael Eavis has probably pondered over whether it should have. It's been an incredible journey for the man who started it all from his Worthy Farm back in 1970. Excited by the possibilities thrown up by the nearby 1970 Bath Festival of Blues, Eavis set about creating an outdoor festival of his own in a money-making bid to rid himself of a £5,000 overdraft. The early festivals did not go down well with all of his neighbours. Some Somerset locals took exception to the invasion of hippies, whose cause was not helped by a lunatic fringe who would wander the nearby villages under

" There are **LITTLE SERVICES** here nearly every weekend, ashes sprinkled on the land... This is where they want to be throughout eternity. Nice, isn't it? 〞

MICHAEL EAVIS
Rock's famous farmer

the influence of LSD, naked but for top hats and Wellington boots. Established as the elder statesman of rock festivals, Glastonbury now produces £100 million annually in tourism and trade for the south-west of England. Typical of the festival's varied bill, 2014 had two more incredible performances to add to the Glastonbury memory banks from headliners Metallica and Dolly Parton. The 900-acre farm, with its 30 permanent festival staff, attracts 137,000 music fans and support staff numbering an additional 40,000. Despite the very greenest of profiles, festival fans amazingly still regularly leave behind 1,650 tonnes of waste to be cleaned up afterwards.

LOCATION 502: the Glastonbury festival site is actually at Pilton not Glastonbury, postcode BA4 4BY

Somerset

Beckington
Morrissey's 'Murder at The Wool Hall'

In 1987, The Smiths recorded their final studio album Strangeways, Here We Come at Beckington's Wool Hall. A single taken from the album, 'I Started Something I Couldn't Finish', carried an etching in the vinyl by Morrissey that name-checked The Wool Hall and a pseudonym the singer used before he became a Smith in a fake movie title. 'MURDER AT THE WOOL HALL (X) STARRING SHERIDAN WHITESIDE' was etched into the 7-inch and 12-inch singles on release at the same time Morrissey had returned to The Wool Hall to create his first solo offering, Viva Hate. Other notable working visitors to the studios down the years include Joni Mitchell, Paul Weller and Stereophonics. Van Morrison recorded so frequently there that he bought the place in 1994.

LOCATION 503: The Wool Hall is up Church Street from the centre of Beckington village, postcode BA3 6TA

Producer Stephen Street and Morrissey at The Wool Hall at the time the latter's debut solo album Viva Hate was being created in late 1987

Solsbury Hill
Peter Gabriel's inspirational turning point

The ancient hill fort was a favourite place for jogger and walker Peter Gabriel and immortalised in his 1977 hit single 'Solsbury Hill'. An obvious spiritual source of strength to Gabriel, the hill offers excellent views of Bath and the surrounding countryside from its summit. 'Solsbury Hill' is a symbol of Gabriel's career turning-point from Genesis band member to solo musician.

LOCATION 504: east of the A46 near the village of Batheaston, postcode BA1 7RA

Shepton Mallet
Britain's very own Woodstock

With an artists' taxi service provided by Hells Angels, dodgy weather conditions that halted proceedings and traffic chaos, the Bath Festival of Blues & Progressive Music in 1970 was the closest thing to Woodstock that Britain could muster. Promoter Freddie Bannister's ambitious project drew a 150,000 attendance, prompting the first use of viewing screens for the benefit of fans some way from the action. Bannister also cleverly tapped into the huge surge in popularity of American groups. The Byrds, Frank Zappa, Johnny Winter, Steppenwolf and Jefferson Airplane, plus Woodstock 'veterans' Santana, Canned Heat and Country Joe, joined forces with top homegrown rock favourites Pink Floyd and Led Zeppelin for what many now consider to be the finest British festival bill of all time.

"I'm going to **WARM UP** my hands on the amplifier, they're totally numb 🔊
FRANK ZAPPA
at Shepton Mallet

LOCATION 505: Royal Bath & West Showground, south of Shepton Mallet, postcode BA4 6QN

Weston-super-Mare
Beatles and Oasis photo shoots

The Beatles are visually linked with this traditional seaside resort courtesy of photographer Dezo Hoffmann's 1963 shots of John, Paul, George and Ringo pictured in Victorian stripy swimsuits and straw boaters. Hoffmann also captured the group donkey-riding on the beach at Brean Down, go-karting and suited and booted at the Royal Pier Hotel during a week of concerts at Weston-super-Mare's Odeon cinema. Beatles fans Oasis used Weston-super-Mare's Grand Pier (devastated by fire in 2008 but reopened two years later) as the backdrop to the group photo on their 1995 single 'Roll With It'.

LOCATIONS 506, 507 and 508: Royal Pier Hotel, postcode BS23 2EJ; Brean Down beach; postcode TA8 2RS, Grand Pier, postcode BS23 1

The Beatles, snapped by local Weston-super-Mare photographer G D Smith. Inset: Oasis visit the famous Beatles photo shoot location for one of their own

Somerset

St Catherine
The house that gave Thom Yorke the shivers

More than half of Radiohead's first chart-topping album OK Computer was recorded in the isolated splendour of St Catherine's Court, which has also attracted the likes of New Order and The Cure. Thom Yorke reportedly found the 16th-century haunted house rented out to Radiohead by owner and actress Jane Seymour distinctly unsettling.

LOCATION 509: east of the A46, north of Bath. Grade I-listed St Catherine's Court is a private home rented out for weddings, events and recordings in the hamlet of St Catherine. Postcode: BA1 8HA

Yatton
Stackridge headquarters

Yatton is the epicentre of folk-rock band Stackridge's world. Their crowd-pleaser, 'Purple Spaceships over Yatton', also features as the title of the 2006 Best Of album for a group whose appreciation enjoyed something of a reawakening in the Noughties, four decades on from their omnipresence on the early '70s festival scene.

LOCATION 510: three miles east of the M5 on the B3133, north of Congresbury, postcode BS49 4DH

Taunton
The Beatles stop for fish and chips

In a scene cut from the original Magical Mystery Tour movie, The Beatles, and the rest of the coach's passengers, stopped in Taunton to grab some fast food at Smedley's fish and chip shop. The 'lost' film clip did the rounds during the re-release of the 1967 movie on DVD, which now makes this establishment (now named The Phoenix) possibly the most rock 'n' roll chippy in Britain.

LOCATION 512: formerly Smedley's, now The Phoenix Chinese Takeaway & Fish Bar, 108 Roman Road, postcode TA1 2BJ

The Beatles ordering their favourite haddock and chips, on September 15, 1967 in Taunton

Portishead
Trip-hop town

The small town on the banks of the River Severn is now most famous as the name of the Mercury Prize-winning band who cornered the market in the darker side of '90s trip-hop. Although based in nearby Bristol, Portishead were named by band member Geoff Barrow, who grew up in the town and was referred to as "that bloke from Portishead" so frequently that the phrase stuck when creating the band name.

LOCATION 511: at the end of the A369, west of Bristol, postcode BS20 7BY

Welcome to our world: band members Beth Gibbons and Geoff Barrow

Born in SOMERSET

Geoff Barrow, Portishead (b. 9 Dec 1971, **Walton in Gordano**)

Acker Bilk, clarinet (b. 28 Jan 1929, **Pensford**, d. 2 Nov 2014)

Ritchie Blackmore (b. 14 Apr 1945, **Weston-super-Mare**)

Adge Cutler, The Wurzels (b. 19 Nov 1931, **Portishead**, d. 5 May 1974)

Debbie Googe, bass, My Bloody Valentine (b. 24 Oct 1962, **Yeovil**)

PJ Harvey (b. 9 Oct 1969, **Yeovil**)

John Parish, musician PJ Harvey (b. 11 Apr 1959, **Yeovil**)

Peter Salisbury, drums, The Verve (b. 24 Sep 1971, **Bath**)

Curt Smith, vocals/bass, Tears for Fears (b. 24 Jun 1961, **Bath**)

Staffordshire

S lash grew up in Blurton, Stoke-on-Trent, and recommends his grandmother's mince pies, his old chum Lemmy was born just down the road, and a third rock 'n' roll hellraiser, Ozzy Osbourne, bought a country retreat and tried manfully to settle down in the village of Ranton. Add to that a Hollywood festival coming to Little Madeley and the mighty Northern Soul meccas The Golden Torch and the Heavy Steam Machine and you have a county brim-full of legendary music locations. And, lest we forget, the name most likely to encourage local bigwigs to erect a plaque in his honour would be the Port Vale FC-loving Robbie Williams, who was born in Stoke and grew up in the cheery atmosphere of Burslem's Red Lion pub, one of many points of interest on a tourist trail created to celebrate the singer's 40th birthday in 2013.

Made in Stoke: On his return to Stoke, Slash recorded a live performance at Victoria Hall, and on another visit was inducted into the 6 Towns Music Hall of Fame. Here he accepts the 6 Towns award made by The Gold Disc.com, flanked by his uncle (left) and 6 Towns Radio presenter Terry Bossons

Stoke-on-Trent
Slash comes home

When American guitarist and rock legend Slash set out on his first solo tour, there was one venue that was an obvious choice for recording a live album. The result was Made in Stoke 24/7/11, captured for posterity at the city's Victoria Hall, less than five miles from his former childhood home at Blurton. Interviewed by GQ magazine, Slash recalled with some relish, "My grandmother made great mince pies and my dad would take me for long walks in the countryside. I loved it."

LOCATION 513: Victoria Hall is in the city centre, in Bagnall Street, postcode ST1 3AD

Staffordshire

Little Madeley
The Grateful Dead come to Hollywood

On May 23, 1970, American rock band The Grateful Dead played their first gig outside the US at the grandly named Hollywood Rock Festival. On a stage adorned by a 20-foot-high red and gold-coloured phallic symbol, the festival line-up also featured a second West Coast band, The Flying Burrito Brothers, a career-defining performance by Mungo Jerry, strong sets from Traffic and Family and a special guest appearance from blind guitarist José Feliciano, who arrived in style on the festival site, chauffeur-driven in a Jaguar. Unsurprisingly, the local pubs in the area did fantastic business with almost 30,000 fans descending on the place. The Crewe Arms at Madeley Heath was particularly popular and was drunk completely dry within a few hours of opening.

LOCATION 514: east of the village of Madeley, a short distance west of the M6 off the A525. Postcode: CW3 9JT

Photos: The Tone

Above: Bussed up to Staffordshire overnight, the Grateful Dead's long set began at 4.30am with their first number 'Casey Jones'

Stoke-on-Trent
Northern Soul at The Golden Torch

This prominent building was purchased as the Regal cinema by new owner Chris Burton in 1965 and was christened as a music venue by Billy J Kramer and The Dakotas. The Golden Torch's popularity as a soul venue was first sparked by an enthusiastically received appearance by Inez & Charlie Foxx in 1967. Subsequent highlights, in Burton's opinion, included performances by Major Lance, Oscar Toney, Jr, Junior Walker and The Stylistics. The Drifters and Edwin Starr also made it to Tunstall, where a record attendance was set in 1973 when 1,300 soul fans crammed in. A second Northern Soul hotbed could be found in the Potteries in Hanley, where the Heavy Steam Machine did good business without ever quite upstaging The Golden Torch.

LOCATION 515: sadly only the former site of The Golden Torch remains. The building is at Hose Street, Tunstall, postcode ST6 5AL

Ranton
Ozzy's 'Atrocity Cottage'

The delightfully named Bullrush Cottage was where Ozzy Osbourne lived with his equally delightfully named first wife Thelma Mayfair until the early 1980s. Here he would unwind from the rigours of rock stardom by firing off his shotgun and racing his motorbike and cars across the local fields and lanes. Not adverse to a bit of home improvement while at Bullrush Cottage, Ozzy organised the building of a home studio and turned his hand to creating the waterfall that feeds the front garden pond. Ozzy was a loyal supporter of local pub the Hand & Cleaver, where he spent almost as much time as he did back at 'Atrocity Cottage', as Ozzy and friends nicknamed his country home.

LOCATION 516: both the cottage and pub are a few miles west of Stafford in Butt Lane, Ranton, postcode ST18 9JZ. Status: Bullrush Cottage is a private residence

Stoke-on-Trent
The Robbie Williams tourist trail

Vacating their conventional three-bedroom semi in Burslem in 1976, the two-year-old Robert Williams and family moved to their new home farther along the same road. The Red Lion pub became the family home for a teenage Robbie Williams until mum and dad, landlady Jan and landlord Pete, separated. Burslem is one of Stoke-on-Trent's six towns in the Potteries, which also includes Tunstall, where Robbie subsequently lived with his mother and sister Sally in Greenbank Road. The singer's family connections to his local football club are strong. "I've been a Port Vale fan all my life. When I was younger I was in the Railway Paddock and I used to dream about sitting in the chairman's box," Robbie said recently. His father was licensee at the football ground's Vale Park social club and Robbie is reported to have invested £240,000 in the club he has supported since he was a child, living within sight of the stadium's floodlights at the Red Lion on Moorland Road. The singer's 40th birthday in 2013 was the que for Stoke-on-Trent to honour its famous son with a plaque and celebrate with a Robbie Williams tourist trail taking in Tunstall's Newfield Street, where his grandparents used to live, Victoria Park Road, where he spent the first two years of his life, Victoria Park, where he honed his football skills, his Mill Hill Primary School in Sunnyside Avenue, St Margaret Ward

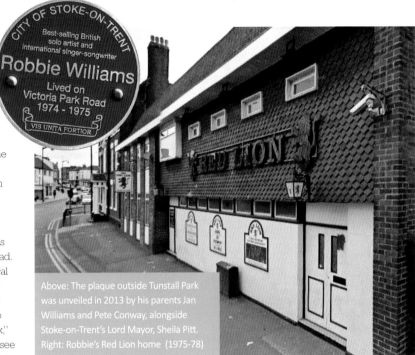

Above: The plaque outside Tunstall Park was unveiled in 2013 by his parents Jan Williams and Pete Conway, alongside Stoke-on-Trent's Lord Mayor, Sheila Pitt. Right: Robbie's Red Lion home (1975-78)

Catholic College (now Academy), Little Chell Lane, which he attended from 1985 to 1990, Greenbank Road, where he lived when he joined Take That, and Scotia Road, name-checked in 'The '80s a song on the Rudebox album. Then it's off to Burslem for the second leg of the tour, which incorporates Queens Theatre, Wedgwood Place, where Robbie made his stage debut as the Artful Dodger in Oliver!, Vale Park, home of Port Vale, the angel at Old Town Hall, rumoured to be the inspiration for his most popular song 'Angels' and the Red Lion on Moorland Road. In addition to all

this geographical adulation, roads in a new Middleport estate are set to be named after some of his hit songs, including Angels Way, Candy Lane and Supreme Street.

LOCATIONS 517 and 518: the Red Lion, 3 Moorland Road, near to the crossroads with the main A50 in Burslem, postcode ST6 1DJ. The recently unveiled plaque to the left of the gates to Tunstall Park (a football kick away from his childhood home), near the corner of the park where Queen's Avenue meets Victoria Park Road, postcode ST6 6DX

Born in STAFFORDSHIRE

Mick Dyche, guitar, Sniff 'n' The Tears (b. 1951, Burton-upon-Trent)
Graeme Edge, drums, The Moody Blues (b. 30 Mar 1941, Rocester)
Richie Edwards, bass, The Darkness (b. 25 Sep 1974, Lichfield)
Mel Galley, guitar, Whitesnake (b. 8 Mar 1948, Cannock, d. 1 Jul 2008)
Fran Healy, vocals/guitar, Travis

(b. 23 Jul 1973, Stafford)
Glenn Hughes, bass/vocals, Deep Purple/Black Sabbath/Trapeze/Black Country Communion (b. 21 Aug 1951, Cannock)
Joe Jackson (b. 11 Aug 1954, Burton-upon-Trent)
Lemmy (Ian Kilmister), vocals, Motörhead (b. 24 Dec 1945, Stoke)

Robert Lloyd, vocals, The Nightingales (b. 5 Jun 1959, Cannock)
Andy Moor, DJ (b. 16 Jan 1980, Stoke)
Jackie Trent (b. 6 Sep 1940, Newcastle-under-Lyme)
Jonathan Wilkes (b. 1 Aug 1978, Stoke-on-Trent)
Robbie Williams (b. 13 Feb 1974, Stoke-on-Trent)

Suffolk

*T*he relative lack of large towns in Suffolk meant that Ipswich managed to monopolise booking just about every act worthy of a place in the A-Z of rock legends back in the day. In fact, such was the standing of the town's famous Gaumont that it even has its own rock-related biography written about it. The county can also brag about attracting the likes of John Peel to its bosom for 33 happy years of residency and giving birth to that 21st-century hit-making machine The Darkness, and it has the closest piece of mainland to another Peel-related location, pirate station BIG L. Felixstowe pier was start point for Britain's largest chain of independent record stores, Andy's Records, whose HQ became based in Bury St Edmunds, and five miles out of Southwold lies the setting for Suffolk's very own miniature impression of Woodstock, Latitude Festival, which stages its three days of music, poetry and comedy every July.

Great Finborough
John Peel country

West of Stowmarket lies the village of Great Finborough, where John Peel lived, worked and received numerous guests from the world of music. The thatched cottage where he often broadcast BBC programmes from his home studio also contained the much-loved DJ's world-famous record collection. Peel Acres is just a short stroll from St Andrew's Church, where John is buried. His York stone gravestone bears an epitaph few would be surprised at: '"Teenage dreams so hard to beat", a line from Peel's all-time favourite record, 'Teenage Kicks' by The Undertones, and is also adorned by a representation of the badge of his beloved Liverpool FC

LOCATION 519: Peel Acres is a private residence. St Andrew's churchyard can be located just north of the centre of the village by heading up Church Road. Postcode: IP14 3AD

Photo: Peter Tarleton

Born in SUFFOLK

Dina Carroll (b. 21 Aug 1968, Newmarket)
Alan Davey, bass, Hawkwind (b. 11 Sep 1963, Ipswich)
Brian Eno (b. 15 May 1948, Woodbridge)
Kate Jackson, The Long Blondes (b. 16 Sep 1979, Bury St Edmunds)
Charlie Simpson, Busted (b. 7 Jun 1985, Woodbridge)
Tim Westwood, DJ, presenter (b. 3 Oct 1957, Lowestoft)

Felixstowe
Radio London's final broadcast

On August 14, 1967, off-shore pirate station Radio London played its final record. "Big L time is three o'clock - Radio London is closing down" came the announcement that millions of pop fans had dreaded as 'A Day in the Life' by The Beatles brought to an end three years of broadcasts from converted mine-sweeper the Galaxy. When the British government introduced legislation outlawing the off-shore broadcasts, it led to all nine DJs and three engineers leaving the ship for good. Among the Big L contingent picked up and dropped off at Felixstowe quayside was DJ John Peel. From Felixstowe, the party made their way to Ipswich to catch a train to London's Liverpool Street station, where 1,000 angry demonstrating fans had assembled.

LOCATION 521: The Dock, postcode IP11 3SY

Gillingham
The Darkness formed at auntie's pub

The Swan pub and motel was the spot where Justin and Dan Hawkins formed retro-glam rockers The Darkness. The brothers had already been in a band, Empire, which hadn't exactly set the world alight, but on Millennium Eve they dramatically began the new century with a new resolution and confidence that would lead to No.1 album Permission to Land in 2003. Surrounded by family and friends at their aunt's pub that night, the two Hawkins brothers recall someone selecting Queen's 'Bohemian Rhapsody' on The Swan's jukebox. "I jumped up and started doing this interpretive mime," recalled Justin, which prompted Dan to see his brother in a new light and as a potential frontman in their new project. "We formed The Darkness there and then," Justin later admitted to Mojo magazine.

LOCATION 520: just outside Beccles on the Suffolk and Norfolk county border on Loddon Road. Postcode: NR34 0LD

Back to his roots: Ed Sheeran poses with one of the lucky secret gig ticket-holders outside the Steamboat Tavern, a pub he played "a bunch of times" before becoming a global superstar

Ipswich
Ed Sheeran at the Steamboat Tavern

Award-winning singer-songwriter Ed Sheeran returned to a venue at the root of his success when he played a secret gig at the Steamboat Tavern in Ipswich on May 5, 2014. With the pub doors opening at 10am to allow the 100 lucky ticket-holders inside, Sheeran took to the stage at 10.45 for a 45 minute acoustic gig. The two-time BRIT Awards-winner grew up in the Suffolk market town of Framlingham, where he purchased a farm in 2012. Unsurprisingly, once the tickets for the tiny gig had been put on sale via Sheeran's Facebook page all were snapped up in 10 minutes. The Steamboat gig was one of three in the same day with a second appearance in London and a third, finally, in Dublin that night. Aside from this unique appearance by an international superstar, the Steamboat prides itself on its live music schedule which showcases purveyors of punk, folk-rock, blues and jazz on various days throughout the week.

LOCATION 522: the Steamboat Tavern is a short distance south of Ipswich city centre on the banks of the River Orwell at 78-80 New Cut West, postcode IP2 8HW

"I haven't played this venue in almost FIVE YEARS - it's nice to come back to where it first started"
ED SHEERAN

Suffolk

Ipswich
Rock greats at the Gaumont

Maybe due to its relative isolation as a large town in a vast rural area, Ipswich appears to have cornered the market in attracting just about every rock legend down the years. More recently re-named the Regent after years as the Gaumont, this grand venue has witnessed seminal gigs by a list that reads like a roll call of pop's heavyweights. Little Richard, Chuck Berry, Buddy Holly, Lonnie Donegan, the Rolling Stones, Dusty Springfield, The Kinks, The Beatles, The Byrds, Black Sabbath, KISS, The Cure and Britpop pioneers Suede all trod the Gaumont's boards. There was even a Nineties Motown 'Dancing in the Streets' package tour which, unlike countless recent tribute shows, actually featured originals Martha Reeves, Edwin Starr and Freda Payne. You do get the feeling that if Elvis had ever come to England, this remarkable venue would have been his first port of call. The rather beautiful theatre even has its own biography, titled From Buddy to The Beatles: When the Regent Rocked, authored by BBC Suffolk's Stephen Foster with photographer Dave Kindred. An 18-year-old Dave volunteered to cover The Beatles' 1964 Ipswich press call and admits he made an expensive mistake. "The Beatles were only with us for a few minutes, they were polite but bored. My colleague had purchased two copies of A

Photo: Stephen Davies

The Byrds meet the kids: "The Gaumont manager organised competitions at the Saturday morning children's cinema the week before a "pop" show. The competition winners would meet the top band backstage before the show. This threw up a strange mix of young children and a bunch of rock stars who were taking something stronger than Smarties." Photographer Dave Kindred

Photo: Dave Kindred

Hard Day's Night earlier in the day and took the opportunity to get them both autographed. He gave one away to a girlfriend. In around 2005, my colleague sold his remaining album at Christie's, which sold for over £20,000. A couple of years later a "Bring Your Rock Memorabilia" day was held at a venue in Ipswich and they paid around £12,000 for an autographed copy of A Hard Day's Night from an Ipswich lady. I presume that was the second copy."

LOCATION 523: the town centre, 3 St Helen's Street, postcode IP4 1HE

Ipswich

In at the deep end: Led Zeppelin's swimming pool gig

Although the town's Baths Hall had been used for dances and a number of concerts before, Led Zeppelin's appearance in 1971 was certainly the most spectacular use of this old swimming pool. Not without some degree of trepidation did both the packed crowd and the band themselves enter a rock venue designed for aquatic water sports. The promoters, Nanda and Ron Lesley, had the usual conversion plan in place for the arrival of a band at the height of their powers, just about to release what would become their third chart-topping album – Four Symbols (Led Zeppelin IV). First they organised the emptying of the pool's water before constructing a framework to lay the wooden boards that would cover the huge pool and support the capacity crowd. Some fans recall Zeppelin's Robert Plant joking with the crowd about their safety as the makeshift floor began to bounce as the night's entertainment reached its raucous conclusion. But the gig passed off with no serious incidents and the promoters even recall sitting down with Jimmy Page and Robert Plant for a chat and a cup of tea after the couple's biggest Ipswich concert. There were other memorable nights at this swimming pool venue. Included among the highlights? Kenny Ball's shows (he loved the bouncing floor, apparently). The Spencer Davis Group, a real favourite with the Ipswich fans, Zoot Money, whose wild behaviour extended to climbing up the curtains, according to Nanda, and the one and only noise complaint when Status Quo played the Baths Hall.

LOCATION 524: St Matthew's Baths Hall, in St Matthew's Street, closed in 1984 and became offices and currently houses a gym, fronted by a new Tesco Express store. Postcode IP1 3EW

PETER GRANT in association with NANDA and RON LESLEY
★ PROUDLY PRESENT AT BLUESVILLE ★
BATHS HALL - IPSWICH
TUESDAY, NOV. 16
FOR ONE APPEARANCE ONLY
★ ★ ★ ★ ★ ★ ★ ★ ★
INTERNATIONALLY FAMOUS
LED ZEPPELIN
★ ★ ★ ★ ★ ★ ★ ★ ★
TICKETS £1 EACH ON SALE DAILY
AT BATHS HALL BOX OFFICE, IPSWICH (TEL. IPSWICH 53882)
AND ON NIGHT PERFORMANCE 8 – 11 P.M.

"I don't know whether the 12-foot end's this one or that one. GOD HELP US! I'm sure you must have had a town hall!"
ROBERT PLANT
bantering with the Ipswich fans

Suffolk

Damon Albarn battled a torrential rain storm at Latitude in 2014 but kept smiling with a terrific performance, according to press reports

Photo: Latitude / Marc Sethi

A sci-fi water boatman brings a familiar touch of weirdness to the Latitude Festival

Southwold
Latitude: 'More than just a music festival'

As their slogan suggests, Latitude is a festival where artists, comedians, poets, dancers and writers engage and entertain alongside a music bill that has seen Henham Park's picturesque setting secure Snow Patrol, Arcade Fire, Franz Ferdinand, the Pet Shop Boys, Florence + The Machine and Damon Albarn since the festival began in 2006. Old festival-going romantics might be forgiven for thinking they have been transported back to 1969 and Max Yasgur's farm in New York state: Latitude's woodland and lake form a backdrop creating a miniature Woodstock deep in the Suffolk countryside, five miles from Southwold.

LOCATION 525: Henham Park is flanked by the A12 on its eastern perimeter and the A145 to the west. Postcode: NR34 8AN

Surrey

A handy distance for wealthy rock star commuters into London, Keith Moon, John Lennon, Ringo Starr, Eric Clapton and Stephen Stills have all lived the rock royalty lifestyle in some of Surrey's most attractive properties. The affluent county can also boast what's generally accepted as the largest audience to watch Bob Dylan when his Bobness played Blackbushe Aerodrome. Birth county of such luminaries as Roger Waters, Paul Weller, Petula Clark and Peter Gabriel, it even has a Bow Wow Wow beauty spot, Christmas Cottage, where Genesis got their act together, and a cracking family-orientated annual festival, GuilFest. And let's hear it for the town of Woking, which seems to have given birth to more pop people than any place that size has any right to.

Camberley
Dylan's aerodrome picnic at Blackbushe

A crowd of 175,000 rock fans turned up at this Surrey airfield in 1978 to see Bob Dylan top the bill in what promoter Harvey Goldsmith advertised as 'The Picnic at Blackbushe Aerodrome'. Present-day pilgrims might find it tough to work out exactly where the stage would have been where the great man (bedecked in top hat) performed on that July weekend. The exact position where Dylan, supported by local boy made god Eric Clapton, Joan Armatrading, Graham Parker and The Rumour and Lake, performed is a short stroll due north of the aerodrome control tower. On the day of the concert, a sea of humanity stretched from the fence near the A30 to a stage with no giant screens. Even a privileged ligger like Ringo Starr complained he couldn't see anything from his VIP vantage point. Still, at least Dylan gave good audio value for money for £6-a-head ticket-holders crammed together on the runway: watching from what seemed like miles away, Dylan disciples witnessed a three-hour-long performance. Most fans who were at Blackbushe that day seem to recall the fantastic atmosphere and friendly, trouble-free vibe. Unfortunately most also remember the huge problems in leaving the aerodrome afterwards. Total chaos ensued with the site gridlocked for hours, which prompted many fans to sleep in their cars until morning.

LOCATION 526: on the A30, three miles west of Camberley, postcode GU17 9LQ

> **"He rang my agent. Not his manager, Dylan HIMSELF personally. That was great. The idea of it 🙲"**

JOAN ARMATRADING
recalls her invitation
to play Blackbushe

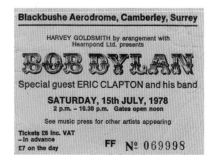

Chertsey
Keith Moon and Vince Clarke's grand designs

Possessor of the largest kit in rock, The Who's larger-than-life drummer Keith Moon lived at 'Tara', a home built of pyramids and named by the original owner after the southern mansion in Gone with the Wind. The eccentric structure, with eight-foot-high metal gates adorned with musical notes, was party central during Moon's ownership between 1971 and 1975, when he sold the place to Kevin Godley. The 10cc man then sold in turn to Erasure's Vince Clarke, who demolished the place but, to his credit, created an equally eccentric rock star fantasy home featuring a futuristic snail shell-like house and recording studio. Still standing as it did in the '70s at the bottom of the winding drive to the house is a building that was a familiar and much-loved part of Keith Moon's life in the Seventies, his handily placed local hostelry, the Golden Grove pub.

LOCATION 527: St Ann's Hill Road, Chertsey, postcode KT16 9EN. Status: no longer rock-star-owner occupied and a private residence

Above: The rather wonderful home created by Vince Clarke and (inset top) the rather odd home of Keith Moon that once stood on the same plot of land in Chertsey

Surrey

"There were **GHOSTS** and I had wonderful bursts of creativity there "
STEPHEN STILLS

Elstead
Sellers, Starr and Stills at Brookfield

A beautiful estate made remarkable by the property-buying chain that saw Peter Sellers sell to Ringo Starr, who sold to Stephen Stills. The 15th-century oak-beamed house, complete with Japanese deer pond, waterfowl and stables, was owned by Sellers when he married Britt Ekland. The actor added a cinema above the garage and, at vast expense, imported a beautiful front door all the way from Italy. Rumour has it that Ringo later 'adapted' the door by cutting a cat flap in it for the family's Siamese cats. During Ringo's time, the

place was the location for a meeting convened in January 1969 to attempt to get The Beatles back together to finish the Let It Be album. George Harrison was the defector summoned to Brookfield and the attempt to 'get back' was successful, with the four switching recording from the "cold and not very nice atmosphere" at Twickenham, as George put it, to their studio at Savile Row. When Stephen Stills first rented, then bought the house from Ringo, his period in Surrey coincided with a rich vein of form in 1970, sparked by the atmosphere around the estate. "Brookfield House was a magical place," he later admitted. Escaping the infighting surrounding

supergroup Crosby, Stills, Nash & Young back in the States, Stills set about writing and recording his first solo album, commuting from Brookfield up to London's Island Studios, where both Eric Clapton and Jimi Hendrix contributed to the LP. A second burst of activity two years later saw Stills fly in his new band Manassas for rehearsals before they hit the road to tour. Manassas band member Chris Hillman recalled how much the three months of foggy, cold British weather affected a bunch of musicians more used to the sun of California. He also remembers being visited by Bernie Leadon of The Eagles, who played him cuts from the band's debut album, which they were

Photo: Henry Diltz

recording in London with producer Glyn Johns at the time. Through all the rock 'n' roll changes at Brookfield, one thing was constant: the presence of the estate's gardener John. A calming influence over all he met, Stills even wrote a song about him. 'Johnny's Garden' appeared on the first Manassas album, but it wasn't the only legacy left by the pipe-smoking herbalist that had a profound effect on all Brookfield's tenants: Peter Sellers based his performance of Chance the Gardener on John in the 1979 movie Being There.

LOCATION 528: Fulbrook Lane, Elstead, postcode GU8 6LG. Status: private residence

Above: Peter Sellers returns to Brookfield to visit Stephen Stills and the subject of Stills' song 'Johnny's Garden', John the gardener. Right: According to Graham Nash, 'Love the One You're With' from Stills' solo album was conceived at a party at Brookfield when Stills, former occupant Ringo Starr and Billy Preston (who came up with the phrase) were present

STEPHEN STILLS

Surrey

Ewhurst
'Layla' and other assorted love songs at Eric Clapton's Hurtwood

"When I drove down there, I felt I was entering Hobbit land." That's Eric Clapton describing the final mile of the spectacular road to his Hurtwood Edge home. Clapton first spotted Hurtwood Edge when searching for properties in Country Life magazine. Impressed by how well positioned the place was, set into the side of a hill with balcony and terrace overlooking great views towards the south coast, he took the advice of his manager Robert Stigwood and bought it for £30,000. His first proper home and close to his childhood home in Ripley, Clapton moved into this 1910 Italian-styled villa in 1969 and it was here he wrote 'Layla' for Pattie Boyd, who later became his wife at Hurtwood. The house became love nest, band rehearsal HQ for Delaney & Bonnie and Friends and Derek and The Dominos and home to the reclusive guitarist during his darkest days when addicted to drugs. Memphis-born Domino, Bobby Whitlock, recalled writing songs with Clapton by the fireside at Hurtwood, and then heading up to the Windmill pub for beer and sausages, although 'Layla', Clapton's signature song and the standout track on Derek and The Dominos' album Layla and Other Assorted Love Songs, was one song Clapton worked on alone in his bedroom. When Eric finally did marry Pattie, in 1979, a party to celebrate the occasion at Hurtwood saw Mick Jagger, George Harrison, Paul McCartney, Denny Laine, Ginger Baker and Lonnie Donegan join Eric on stage for a jam in the garden. Among the many earlier magical moments witnessed by this beautiful place, one in particular stands out. Friend and neighbour George Harrison wrote 'Here Comes the Sun' at Hurtwood one beautiful spring morning when the two friends were down the bottom of the garden at the top of a large paddock. There's more: The house provided the necessary seclusion when supergroup Blind Faith needed to put in the days of rehearsal ahead of their legendary Hyde Park debut in 1969. And one of Clapton's best-known songs was quickly written at Hurtwood one evening in 1976 when he was impatiently waiting for Pattie Boyd to get ready and choose the right outfit for a night out. That song he referred too as nothing more than a "ditty" was 'Wonderful Tonight' - not quite the romantic love song we all thought!

LOCATIONS 529 and 530: between Ewhurst and Shere, the private grade II-listed residence Hurtwood Edge, postcode GU6 7NW, and the Windmill pub at Pitch Hill, which adjoins the estate's gardens at postcode GU6 7NN on Ride Way

Both written about girlfriend Pattie Boyd, two of Eric Clapton's best-known songs, 'Layla' and 'Wonderful Tonight', were written at Hurtwood

Guildford
Fun for all the family at GuilFest

Guilfest was started in 1992 by local businessman and festival fan Tony Scott. This annual mid-July festival doesn't make any cutting-edge or cult claims. It's possibly Britain's most family-orientated music festival, attracting tens of thousands of fans to line-ups featuring pop and rock's more enduring bands. In 2014, the wide-ranging bill included Fun Lovin' Criminals, The Boomtown Rats, Kool & The Gang, Human League and Norman Jay. Among the many bonus attractions for music fans is the 150-foot beer tent that serves up the festival's very own brew, GuilFest bitter. Despite attracting 45,000 fans, who grooved to music on 13 stages, the 2014 festival was blighted by bad weather and the firm behind it were reported to have gone bust in September that year.

LOCATION 531: a short walk north of the centre of Guildford at Stoke Park, London Road (A3100), postcode GU1 1SW

Guildford
National anthem calms Beatles fans

When The Beatles made their only concert appearance in Guildford on June 21, 1963, their fans' screaming had reached new levels of high volume. So piercing was the noise at the end of their last number that the Odeon's management decided to drown out the din by playing an extremely loud recording of the national anthem over the PA system in an attempt to calm everyone down. The art deco Odeon was a sumptuous cinema often used for concerts in the Sixties with red upholstered, wide, shallow seats and a rich red carpet up to the foyer into the auditorium. Very few of the seats were actually sat in that night for the two performances The Beatles made, supported by a bill including Lance Fortune, Rockin' Henri and The Vikings with Michael London. Lynne Ball, a local schoolgirl from the nearby Bellfields estate, has familiar memories of the concert. "My then boyfriend (now husband)

Chris bought us 7/6d tickets for my 15th birthday present. We were up in the balcony and the one thing I really remember is that everyone was screaming so much that you could barely hear them singing. Afterwards we waited outside to try and catch sight of them leaving. Paul and John waved out of the window at the side of the building to great excitement, and then they rapidly left by car with just a quick glimpse. Unfortunately we missed the last bus and had to walk home and I got into huge trouble!"

LOCATION 532: the Odeon was demolished in 2002 but once stood at the corner of Epsom Road and Jenner Road, postcode GU1 3JQ. Almost opposite the old Odeon site in London Road, a new concert hall and entertainment centre – G Live – has now replaced the Civic Hall and caters for Guildford's music fans

Reigate
Bow Wow Wow 'Go Wild in the Country'

In a 1981 reconstruction of Manet's famous painting Le Déjeuner sur l'herbe, Bow Wow Bow posed for the cover of their See Jungle! See Jungle! Go Join Your Gang, Yeah. City All Over! Go Ape Crazy album (and the following year's 'Last of the Mohicans' EP) at a location discovered by photographer Andy Earl. The Surrey beauty spot, overlooked by the North Downs, is a 200-acre woodland area but not the most private place for a photo shoot involving a degree of nudity. Although the cover failed to get used in the UK and US, it presents a much seen image due to the controversial nudity of singer Annabella Lwin, who was only 15 at the time. Earl recalls Malcolm McLaren's concept: "He came up with the idea of copying Déjeuner on Saturday and we shot it on Monday. I drove round Surrey looking for locations in my old Land Rover and found this spot at Priory Park, near Reigate."

LOCATION 533: south of Reigate town centre. Accessed via Park Lane at the park's western side, postcode RH2 7RL

Andy Earl's Priory Park photo shoot was conceived by Malcolm McLaren, who wanted to reproduce 'the Luncheon on the Grass' scene depicted in Édouard Manet's masterpiece from the mid-19th century

Surrey

Ripley
Eric Clapton's childhood home

Britain's most famous exponent of the electric guitar was born and raised in the comparative comfort of the Surrey stockbroker belt. This historic village had a great pull on Eric Clapton's affections in a non-musical sense. Aside from being born here and raised by his grandparents, Ripley was a significant place in the formation of the game of cricket, which Clapton enthusiastically plays and watches. In fact, the 250-year-old local cricket club is situated on the village green, reputed to be England's largest.

LOCATION 534: 1 The Green (postcode GU23 6AJ) is in the centre of the village, off the B2215. Status: private residence

Photo: David Roberts

The young Eric Clapton's Ripley home

PAUL WELLER 22 DREAMS

Ripley
Black Barn Recording Studio has the "vibe"

"More vibe than you can shake a stick at" and "bucketloads of vibe" is how this rural recording studio advertises itself. Anyone needing to witness how that vibe translates visually can see clearly what has attracted the likes of Joss Stone, Bo Diddley, The Who and Gary Numan to the Surrey countryside. The album cover for 22 Dreams, by local boy Paul Weller, is the perfect calling card. The 2008 release's sleeve depicts the idyllic setting where he spent a year recording the 21 tracks.

LOCATION 535: the private studios are near Dunsborough Park, just north of Ripley High Street, beyond The Half Moon Inn, postcode GU23 6AL

The control room at Black Barn and Paul Weller's 2008 album cover depicting the idyllic setting in which the music was recorded

Weybridge
Lennon's Kenwood and Ringo's Sunny Heights

The house where John Lennon lived at the height of Beatlemania between 1964 and 1968, Kenwood was so much associated with this period in '60s music culture that the house sign is reported to have been sold at auction in 2003 for a staggering $20,400. The 1.5-acre property dates back to 1913, when it was appropriately built by Love & Sons. Some of Lennon's home-movie footage shot at Kenwood later turned up on the Imagine: John Lennon movie and the cover of The Beatles' sixth chart-topping album, Rubber Soul, was photographed in the garden. Inside the house an old circus poster Lennon had bought in Sevenoaks, Kent, decorated the living room wall. On one particular Kenwood get-together, he and Paul McCartney turned the characters named in the poster into the Sgt Pepper track 'Being for the Benefit of Mr Kite'. The St George's Hill estate on which Kenwood stands also provided homes to newly minted '60s pop stars Tom Jones and Cliff Richard. A year after John Lennon's move to the estate, the newly married Ringo Starr followed suit, buying nearby Sunny Heights on South Road. When Lennon and first wife Cynthia divorced, Kenwood was sold to chart-topping hits songwriter Bill Martin, who penned 'Puppet on a String', 'Congratulations' and 'Back Home'. In 2012, Kenwood was offered for sale by estate agents Knight Frank for a guide price of £15 million. The property, little changed from Lennon's day, includes the split-level garden terraces, six bedrooms, six reception rooms and six bathrooms but with the added luxury of a comparatively new indoor swimming pool and sauna.

LOCATION 536: from Weybridge station take the B374 south, turning left into South Road and straight on to Cavendish Road, which curves to the left, before turning into Wood Lane and Kenwood, postcode KT13 0JU. Sadly, for both residents and visitors, a spate of burglaries led to the construction of security gates at the entrance to the entire St George's Hill estate, preventing anything but distant viewing of these Beatles bases

Top: A recent picture of John Lennon's former home. Above: The Beatles captured in suede in the garden at Kenwood by photographer Robert Freeman

Surrey

Woking
The Jam's 'Town Called Malice'

The Jam's single 'a Town Called Malice' is reported to have been based on Woking, a town much changed since the young Paul Weller kicked a ball about in his local streets. The title of his best-known solo album, Stanley Road, is the Woking back street where he grew up. His former two-up, two-down Victorian family home is a distant memory as the road has been redeveloped as a one-way street with offices and flats. Joining Stanley Road is Walton Road, where the teenage Weller played some of his first gigs at the then Working Men's Club, now the Woking Liberal Club. Half a mile away, on the other side of the railway line, there's an extraordinary sculpture which honours The Jam's Woking connections. A trio of huge oak columns, weighing 7.7 tonnes and almost 20-foot high, represent the three band members, Weller, Bruce Foxton and Rick Buckler, and form the centrepiece to a new multi-storey building development. A small plaque at the foot of the sculpture informs the visitor that the artwork is titled "The Space Between" and its creator is East Sussex artist Richard Heys. At the sculpture's unveiling by the band's drummer Buckler in 2012, Heys revealed that his inspiration for the piece came from local children's interpretation of The Jam's music during workshops at St John the Baptist School, Bishop David Brown School and Woking High School.

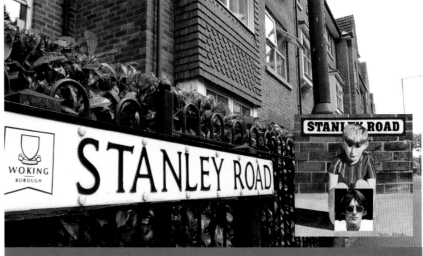

Above: Stanley Road today. Below: The Jam's oak sculpture was the work of artist Richard Heys, who consulted band members, local residents and schoolchildren on the artwork's concept

Photo: David Roberts

LOCATIONS 537, 538 and 539: Woking Liberal Club, 23 Walton Road, postcode GU21 5DL, is just a short walk away from the one-time Weller family home in Stanley Road, postcode GU21 5DJ. The Jam sculpture is near the centre of Woking in a piazza in the middle of a three-sided new building development on Guildford Road, postcode GU22 7PX

> "I'm **PROUD** that The Jam has inspired this great piece of artwork for Woking **"**
> **PAUL WELLER**

Photo: Martin Downham

Wotton
Genesis 'Trespass' at Christmas Cottage

Christmas Cottage was where Genesis first began to work productively as a unit. The property was owned by the parents of Richard MacPhail, who became the band's tour manager, and in the winter of 1969/70 the remote location created the required togetherness to develop and hone writing and rehearsing skills, culminating in the release of Trespass, which according to guitarist Mike Rutherford was the only Genesis album where all band members were involved in writing every track. The spacious Surrey cottage, on Sheephouse Lane in the village of Wotton, is slightly remodelled these days and more accessible than in Genesis's time. Back then they'd manhandle instruments and equipment - including a Hammond organ, a home-built Leslie cabinet, Hohner electric piano and a mellotron borrowed from King Crimson - by hand from vehicles up the hill to the cottage. They even cut a gap in the property's wooden fence to shorten the journey. When Tony Stratton-Smith took over management of the band and signed them to the Charisma label for the princely sum of ten pounds a week, Genesis never looked back. They released Trespass, left Christmas Cottage for London and added new drummer Phil Collins.

LOCATION 540: Christmas Cottage is in the village of Wotton between Dorking and Abinger Hammer, Sheephouse Lane, postcode RH5 6QL. Status: private residence

Having left Decca, Genesis created their first album for Charisma while at Christmas Cottage in the Surrey countryside

Born in SURREY

Mick Avory, drums, The Kinks (b. 15 Feb 1944, East Molesey)
Rick Buckler, drums, The Jam (b. 6 Dec 1955, Woking)
Eric Clapton (b. 30 Mar 1945, Ripley)
Petula Clark (b. 15 Nov 1932, Epsom)
Gus Dudgeon, producer (b. 30 Sep 1942, Woking, d. 21 Jul 2002)
Bruce Foxton, bass/vocals, The Jam (b. 1 Sep 1955, Woking)
Peter Gabriel (b. 13 Feb 1950, Chobham)
Simon Gallup, bass, The Cure (b. 1 Jun 1960, Duxhurst)
Dana Gillespie, folk/pop singer (b. 30 Mar 1949, Woking)
Dave Greenslade, keyboardist (b. 18 Jan 1943, Woking)
Dan Hawkins, guitar, The Darkness (b. 12 Dec 1976, Chertsey)
Justin Hawkins, vocals/guitar, The Darkness (b. 17 Mar 1975, Chertsey)

Glyn Johns, producer (b. 15 Feb 1942, Epsom)
Steve Lillywhite, producer (b. 1955, Egham)
Nick Lowe (b. 24 Mar 1949, Walton-on-Thames)
Rick Parfitt, vocals/guitar, Status Quo (b. 12 Oct 1948, Woking)
Jimmy Pursey, vocals, Sham 69 (b. 9 Feb 1955, Hersham)
Andrew Ridgeley, guitar/vocals, Wham! (b. 26 Jan 1963, Windlesham)
Mike Rutherford, guitar, Genesis (b. 2 Oct 1950, Guildford)
Lol Tolhurst, drums/keyboards, The Cure (b. 3 Feb 1959, Horley)
Roger Waters, bass/vocals, Pink Floyd (b. 6 Sep 1943, Great Bookham)
Paul Weller (b. 25 May 1958, Woking)
Pete Wiggs, keyboards, Saint Etienne (b. 15 May 1966, Reigate)

Sussex: East

*B*righton proves to be a prominent centre of music culture through its once infamous (now just famous) connection to the mods and rockers pitched battles of the sixties, later popularly documented in The Who's Quadrophenia album and movie. A city stuffed full of lively music venues, it has two of the more extraordinary places to take in the live music experience. The architectural splendour of the Dome was where ABBA enjoyed their career-defining Eurovision Song Contest win and Brighton's pebble beach has rattled to a series of huge gigs witnessing the DJ decks dexterity of local resident Norman Cook. The city even has a large enough pool of talent to boast its very own pavement-starred Walk of Fame. Farther afield, the county's shoreline hosted David Bowie's 'Ashes to Ashes' video shoot, and Bexhill's seafront sets the scene for Keane's Strangeland album cover and East Sussex's grandest homes and gardens provided newsworthy residences for Paul McCartney, Brian Jones, Jimmy Page and farmer Roger Daltrey, who likes nothing better than walking the Sussex Weald. The county also throws up the quirkiest of locations. Seek out the secluded church and its pump organ featured on a British Sea Power track written about the East Sussex coastline and its dramatic Seven Sisters.

Brighton
The Walk of Fame

Based on the popular American concept of awarding pavement stars to celebrities, songwriter and producer David Courtney brought the idea to Brighton's Marina in 2002. A trail of plaques honour current and former residents Norman Cook, Annie Nightingale, Zoe Ball, Gaz Coombes, Steve Ellis, Levellers, Kevin Rowland, Leo Sayer, Dusty Springfield, Brighton Eurovision winners ABBA and Brighton's mod figureheads The Who.

LOCATION 541: Brighton Marina, 18 Waterfront, postcode BN25 5WA

One of many artists drawn to live in Brighton, the Dexy's Midnight Runners lead vocalist lived at Flat 5, No.12 Sussex Square, Kemptown, in the mid-'90s

Photo: Peter Tarleton

Bexhill-on-Sea
Keane-on-Sea

Bexhill-on-Sea features heavily in Keane's music and artwork for their album Strangeland and the band's single 'Sovereign Light Café', both released in 2012. Even the video for the single was shot here. Rob Chenery (Creative Director of design consultancy Tourist) explained, "We wanted the Strangeland sleeve to come across as quite familiar yet abstract at the same time. One of the band's favourite images was a view of some apartments taken from the shoreline, which was shot at first light when only one or two lights were visible in the apartments." The image used for the single cover pays homage to the seafront café on Bexhill Parade where the band would meet as teenagers.

LOCATIONS 542, 543 and 544: the café (postcode TN39 3DX), Strangeland buildings (postcode TN3DX) and De La Warr Pavilion (postcode TN40 1DP) are all on Bexhill seafront

Inset pictures: Bexhill-on-Sea on the cover of Keane's chart-topping album and spin-off single. Main picture: the band at the town's seafront arts and entertainment centre, De La Warr Pavilion

Brighton
John Peel at The Prince Albert

A memorial to the much-loved DJ John Peel in the form of a vast mural dominates the side wall of the Prince Albert pub in Frederick Place. Never one to big himself up, Peel might well have shied away from such a giant-sized tribute and would no doubt have disapproved of the subject of the Banksy artwork that shares the wall with him. An additional painting depicts his beloved Liverpool's arch-rivals Manchester United, represented by an image of George Best.

LOCATION 545: The Prince Albert is on the corner of Trafalgar Street and Frederick Place, postcode BN1 4ED

Photo: Janet Bateman

A giant-sized tribute to John Peel at The Prince Albert

MUSIC FROM THE SOUNDTRACK OF THE WHO FILM

QUADROPHENIA

Brighton
Quadrophenia mod spots

The spiritual home of Mod culture, Brighton is still a place you can shop for all the right gear while soaking up the atmosphere of the Sixties scene so grittily portrayed in The Who's 1973 rock opera and 1979 movie Quadrophenia. The Lanes and North Laine are shoppers' paradises and the seaside city appears to positively encourage scooter runs and Mod weekenders these days: a far cry from almost half a century ago when teenagers on Lambrettas and Vespas would gather by word of mouth all points south of Crawley and Croydon on the A23 to weekend in Brighton. Fashion, dancing and scooters were the mods' main obsessions but their violent clashes with gangs of rockers (or greasers) were what made front-page news. The Brighton Sea Life centre, formerly the seafront aquarium, was the setting for

one of the bloodiest battles in 1964, restaged as a scene in Quadrophenia. The movie's famous sex scene when mod Jimmy (played by Phil Daniels) and girlfriend Steph (Leslie Ash) get it together in a narrow alley is still down Little East Street (off East Street) and the hotel where bellboy Ace (Sting) worked is the magnificent Grand, which dominates the seafront.

LOCATIONS 546, 547 and 548: all the above can be explored within a short distance of Brighton's seafront. The Sea Life Brighton is on Marine Parade, postcode BN2 1TB, the Little East Street alley is at postcode BN1 1HT, the Grand Hotel (now The Grand Brighton) is 97-99 King's Road, postcode BN1 2FW

Contestants for the 1974 Eurovision Song Contest, including Sweden's ABBA and the UK's Olivia Newton-John, pose for a pre-contest press picture outside Brighton's Royal Pavilion

Photo: RTE Stills Library

Brighton
'Waterloo' at the Dome

The Dome is where ABBA's 'Waterloo' claimed victory in the 1974 Eurovision Song Contest. In the same year Leonard Cohen played the place, and two years earlier Pink Floyd gave a debut performance here of Dark Side of the Moon. The Dome is in Brighton's cultural quarter close to the Royal Pavilion. The Dome's concert hall is still used for all forms of arts and entertainment and there are guided tours of this iconic building that include a rare glimpse of the unusual tunnel that links the concert hall to the Royal Pavilion.

LOCATION 549: Brighton Dome is on Church Street, postcode BN1 1UE

Photo: Peter Tarleton

Sussex: East

Brighton
Fatboy Slim's Big Beach parties

Local resident and DJ Norman Cook provided Brighton with its best-attended musical event when a larger than anticipated 250,000 attended his Fatboy Slim concert on the beach in the summer of 2002. Subsequent events, branded the Big Beach Boutique, have attracted more modest but manageable crowds to the seafront. The former member of The Housemartins took a new alias in 2008 when calling his act BPA – Brighton Port Authority. In 2013, Cook opened his very own Big Beach Cafe at Hove Lagoon.

LOCATION 550: Brighton beach, postcode BN2 1TB

Burwash Common
Farmer Daltrey's country manor

Always a keen angler, The Who's lead singer Roger Daltrey achieved a lifelong ambition when he got to manage his very own trout fishery on the 400-acre farm he calls home. Daltrey originally purchased the 20-room, 400-year-old Holmshurst Manor property in 1972 for the excellent views it afforded some of East Sussex's most beautiful countryside. But, having taken on the place, he thrived in the day-to-day running of the estate, instantly catching the farming bug. Accepted by the locals after decades living and working in the area, he has now become something of an authority on the fishery business and cattle management.

LOCATIONS 552 and 553: Lakedown Trout Fishery is just north of the A265 at Swife Lane, postcode TN21 8UX. Holmshurst Manor is at postcode TN19 7JP

"I love walking on the Sussex Weald" said Roger Daltrey in a Times interview in 2008

Lullington
British Sea Power's church song

The smallest church in Sussex (some say smallest in England) is featured in the 2003 British Sea Power song about this part of East Sussex. The 20-seat flint building, which dates from the 13th century, sits atop a wooded hill above the Cuckmere Valley. Band member Hamilton added the melancholy organ part to 'The Smallest Church in Sussex' by sneaking inside the tiny Church of the Good Shepherd to play the pump organ.

LOCATION 551: Lullington is a tiny hamlet, a short stroll east of the village of Alfriston. Postcode: BN26 5QY

British Sea Power at the Church of the Good Shepherd

Hartfield
Brian Jones' 'House at Pooh Corner'

News reports still circulate more than 40 years after the death of Rolling Stone Brian Jones about the mysterious circumstances surrounding his passing at his Cotchford Farm estate. In 1969, the guitarist and founder member of the band was discovered dead, aged 27, in the swimming pool of the house once owned by author A.A. Milne. The 16th-century building is the House at Pooh Corner that Milne wrote about in his Winnie the Pooh stories. The innocent world of children's literature is at odds with Jones' rock 'n' roll lifestyle, which, at varying levels, included loud music annoying the neighbours and sending his Vespa scooter through the front window of local Hartfield pub The Haywaggon Inn. Recent wear and tear on the infamous

swimming pool at Cotchford Farm prompted a dubious sale of underwater rock memorabilia when recent owners elected to sell the pool's tiles to Jones fans priced at £100 each. A second tenuous music connection to Cotchford Farm comes courtesy of Kenny Loggins' whimsical song 'House at Pooh Corner', also recorded by the Nitty Gritty Dirt Band.

LOCATION 554: south on the B2026 out of the village of Hartfield, turning right on to Cotchford Lane, postcode TN7 4DN. Status: private residence

Cotchford Farm: little changed since Brian Jones owned the place

Hastings
Sex Pistols and Stones on the pier

Burnt to a cinder in 2010 and requiring multi-million-pound investment to return it to its former glory, Hastings pier was a thriving business when Britain's top pop and rock groups played the pier ballroom. Gene Vincent, Jimi Hendrix, Pink Floyd, The Hollies, The Who, Tom Jones and Genesis all performed there in the '60s and '70s, with The Rolling Stones making four appearances at an entertainment centre that offered the usual pier activities. The Stones were booked for the Saturday of the infamous 1964 Bank Holiday weekend when mods and rockers ran riot at the seaside resort the Monday following. Just as controversial, by reputation at least, an early Sex Pistols appearance at the pier made such an impression on one young music fan that she set about forming a band (X-Ray Spex) and changing her name to Poly Styrene. The July 1976 gig saw the Pistols bizarrely supporting Budgie, and two years later X-Ray Spex were a star attraction at the pier themselves.

LOCATION 555: Hastings pier (tentatively scheduled for a full reopening in 2015) is situated close by White Rock (A259). Postcode: TN34 1EU

Hastings
John Martyn: 'Over The Hill'

'Over the Hill' is a single and track from John Martyn's 1973 album Solid Air. The song was written by Martyn when, as passenger on a train returning to Hastings, he caught sight of his home behind the town's East Hill. The cliffside house afforded great views. Two decades after he made his home in the seaside town, Martyn played an impromptu gig on the beach – an idea hatched during a lunchtime drink or two at The Lord Nelson. He'd just returned from a US tour, the weather was favourable and there was electricity on tap for his guitar courtesy of one of the boat huts. He played all afternoon before carrying a wellington boot around the crowd to collect money for local charities.

LOCATION 556: 10 Coburg Place, postcode TN34 3HY

Peasmarsh
McCartney's country estate

From modest investment in a few farm buildings in the 1970s, Paul McCartney's impressive East Sussex estate now extends to a vast 933 acres with traditional farm livestock plus the country's largest population of wild boar. Waterfall was the property he purchased back in 1973 and the McCartney II track 'Waterfalls' was said to have been inspired by his new home. So secluded was the house that after a while McCartney had a 70-ft tower constructed to enable the family to see above the densely wooded surrounding area. It was here in the tower that McCartney got the tragic news that his friend and former Beatle John Lennon had died, in 1980. By this time the McCartney family had outgrown their original home and later moved into the state's renovated Blossom Farm, which boasted its own elevated position and striking rural views. Away from the estate, an old converted windmill owned by McCartney near the village of Icklesham served as a recording studio. Protected by a dry moat, Hog Hill Mill was where the then surviving Beatles reunited to set about recording 'Free as a Bird' in 1994. Despite the redevelopment of certain old buildings and the newly created annexes and cabins it is undoubtedly the secluded beauty of this part of East Sussex that has retained Paul McCartney as a resident for almost 40 years.

LOCATION 557: north-west of the A259 and the coastal town of Rye, on Starvecrow Lane. Postcode: TN31 6UU. Status: private residence

> " He kept his original Hofner guitar from his Beatles days in a **SECRET PANEL** underneath the floor. There was a small circular hook that he pulled... and a bit of the floor came up, seamlessly **"**

AN INVITED GUEST
talking to the London Evening Standard about the windmill studio

Pett Level
David Bowie on the beach

David Bowie on the beachWith added solarisation effects, the beach and cliffs at Pett Level were the backdrop for David Bowie's 1980 'Ashes To Ashes' video. In May that year the secluded shoreline was invaded by Bowie in a Pierrot clown outfit, a bulldozer and a number of weirdly attired extras courtesy of London's Blitz Club, who under Steve Strange's artistic guidance, were assembled outside London's Hilton hotel in the early morning of the shoot before being transported by coach to the East Sussex coast.

LOCATION 558: the shoreline between Rye and Hastings, a few miles off the A259. Postcode: TN35 4EH

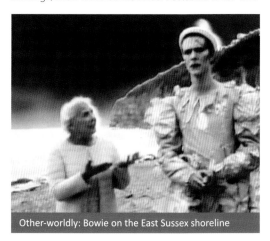
Other-worldly: Bowie on the East Sussex shoreline

Born in SUSSEX: EAST

Tony Banks, keyboards, Genesis (b. 27 Mar 1950, **East Hoathly**)
Tom Chaplin, vocals/guitar, Keane (b. 8 Mar 1979, **Battle**)
Dave Clarke, DJ/producer (b. 19 Sep 1968, **Brighton**)
Shirley Collins, folk singer (b. 5 Jul 1935, **Hastings**)
Simon Fuller, manager/TV producer (b. 17 May 1960, **Hastings**)
Dave Greenfield, keyboards, The Stranglers (b. 29 Mar 1949, **Brighton**)
Dan Hipgrave, guitar, Toploader (b. 5 Aug 1975, **Brighton**)

Annie Holland, bass, Elastica (b. 26 Aug 1965, **Brighton**)
Peter 'Spider' Stacy, whistle/harmonica/vocals, The Pogues (b. 14 Dec 1958, **Eastbourne**)
Suggs (Graham McPherson), vocals, Madness (b. 13 Jan 1961, **Hastings**)
David Van Day, vocals, Dollar/Guys 'n' Dolls (b. 28 Nov 1956, **Brighton**)
Johnny Wakelin, singer-songwriter (b. 1939, **Brighton**)
Samantha Womack (née Janus), UK entry, 1991 Eurovision Song Contest (b. 2 Nov 1972, **Brighton**)

Sussex: West

The South Downs sweep down to the sea to a spot rock pirate Keith Richards calls both home and 'God's Little Acre'. The West Sussex countryside was an inspiration to Cat Stevens and also provided the right environment for the young Paul Weller to nail a life-changing spot of song-writing and Paul McCartney to shoot a 1979 Christmas video down the pub. The county's Bluebell Railway presented Elton John with a location that gave a passable impression of an American railroad station for the cover of his second hit album, and West Sussex gave birth to Britain's most brilliantly monikered punk poet Attila the Stockbroker, born in the genteel town of Southwick.

Ashurst
A 'Wonderful Christmastime' at The Fountain Inn

The Fountain Inn was the location for the video shot to promote Paul McCartney's 1979 single 'Wonderful Christmastime'. A packed pub saw McCartney hamming it up festive style at the piano in the Fountain's dining room, and outside the then whitewashed frontage displayed a large sign advertising the now defunct Portsmouth-based Brickwoods Brewery. Despite making quite an impact, it is doubtful whether McCartney visited the pub more than once, unlike Ashurst resident Sir Laurence Olivier, who from 1973 until his death in 1989 was something of a regular customer.

LOCATION 559: The Fountain Inn is just off the B2135 in the village of Ashurst, four miles north of Steyning. Postcode: BN44 3AP

Bernie Taupin (left) and Elton John (right) make a Horsted Keynes connection

Horsted Keynes
Elton's Tumbleweed Connection

Situated on the delightful Bluebell Railway, Horsted Keynes station is the spot where Elton John's cover photo for Tumbleweed Connection was shot. The station buildings and platforms have changed little since Elton, lyricist Bernie Taupin and photographer David Larkham made the trip in 1970 to capture images for the gatefold LP. The station is a throwback to Britain's pre-war steam era but could pass for a railroad halt in the American West and was a good fit for Elton's country-themed album.

LOCATION 560: public station, east of the B2028, less than two miles outside the village of Horsted Keynes, postcode RH17 7BB

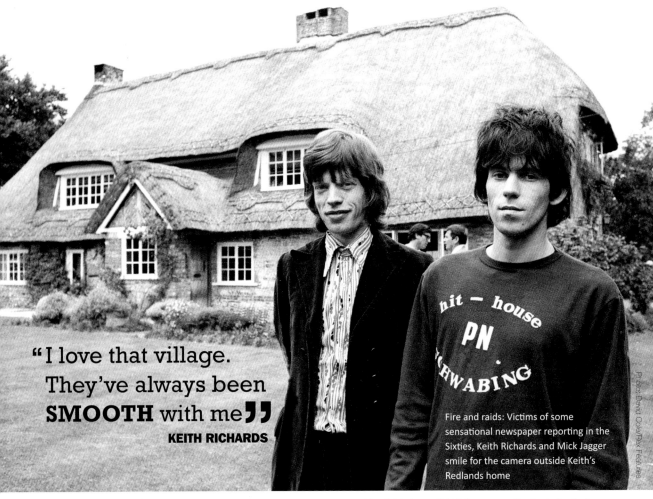

"I love that village. They've always been **SMOOTH** with me"
KEITH RICHARDS

Fire and raids: Victims of some sensational newspaper reporting in the Sixties, Keith Richards and Mick Jagger smile for the camera outside Keith's Redlands home

Photo: David Cole/Rex Features

West Wittering
Redlands: Keith Richards' 'God's Little Acre'

Keith Richards' home base in Britain since 1966 is Redlands, the Elizabethan farmhouse in the West Sussex coastal countryside discovered by a house-hunting Richards when he and his Bentley took a wrong turning, winding up at Redlands, which was miraculously for sale. From spotting the place to buying it took from midday to evening that same day, a whirlwind of activity that involved a return trip to London to grab the necessary £20,000 cash for a transfer of the deeds in front of the picturesque house's fireplace that night. Redlands was the setting for the most publicised drugs bust in rock history involving Keith, Mick Jagger and friends. On that winter's evening on February 12, 1967,

one friend, Marianne Faithfull, was to suffer the indignity forever associated with that Mars bar story, a rock myth according to the gallant Richards. More productively, the house was where Rolling Stones classic 'Jumpin' Jack Flash' was born, a song inspired by Redlands gardener Jack Dyer's early morning activities. In an interview with the Independent in 2000, he referred to his thatched and moated property and the nearby village as 'God's Little Acre'. The genuine article when it comes to proper rock star status, Richards is a popular figure in these parts. He generously forked out £30,000 to help renovate the community's West Wittering Memorial Hall in the village centre, at the junction of Rookwood Road and Elms Lane.

LOCATION 561: north out of West Wittering on the B2179, left into Redlands Lane, postcode PO20 8QE. Status: private residence

Midhurst
Cat Stevens' change of direction

When Cat Stevens suffered an almost fatal bout of tuberculosis in 1968, he was hospitalised for a lengthy period at Midhurst's King Edward VII Hospital. However uncomfortable his slow period of recuperation, Stevens would look back on the period and admit to a significant side-effect. It gave the singer-songwriter, who had already charted with 'Matthew and Son' and 'I'm Gonna Get Me a Gun', a period to reflect on his intensive life as a young pop star and begin a new direction in his career. The three months spent in bed and outside in the hospital's beautiful grounds were followed by a further nine months spent recovering at home. The enforced absence from the music business produced a move away from commercial pop songs to a reflective, acoustic phase. During this period of recovery, he wrote more than 30 new songs. These new folk-based offerings didn't go down well with his then producer Mike Hurst, which in turn led to a departure from Deram Records. Island Records were more appreciative, signing the new Cat Stevens and releasing Mona Bone Jakon, which began a sequence of Island album releases that peaked with Catch Bull at Four, a US chart-topper.

LOCATION 562: King's Drive, postcode GU29 0BJ, due west of the A286 north of Midhurst. Status: the hospital and grounds are in the process of being redeveloped as a residential site

"**I got into meditation, deep in the Sussex countryside, and that began my EARNEST SEARCH for the road, and ultimately, to find out what's at the end of it**"
CAT STEVENS

Born in
SUSSEX: WEST

Brett Anderson, vocals, Suede (b. 29 Sep 1967, Haywards Heath)

Attila the Stockbroker (John Baine) poet/musician (b. 21 Oct 1957, Southwick)

Jeremy Cunningham, bass, Levellers (b. 2 Jun 1965, Cuckfield)

Robin Goodridge, drums, Bush (b. 10 Sep 1966, Crawley)

Antony Hegarty, vocals, Antony and The Johnsons (b. 1971, Chichester)

Tom Odell, singer-songwriter (b. 24 Nov 1990, Chichester)

Luke Pritchard, vocals, The Kooks (b. 2 Mar 1985, Worthing)

Leo Sayer (b. 21 May 1948, Shoreham-by-Sea)

Bob Stanley, keyboards, Saint Etienne (b. 25 Dec 1964, Horsham)

Nick Van Eede, vocals, Cutting Crew/producer (b. 14 Jun 1958, Cuckfield)

Bruce Welch, guitar, The Shadows (b. 2 Nov 1941, Bognor Regis)

Selsey Bill
Paul Weller's seaside holiday scribblings

"Save up their money for a holiday, to Selsey Bill or Bracklesham Bay", as The Jam's 'Saturday's Kids' goes. Paul Weller wrote 'The Eton Rifles' while holidaying in his parents' caravan at the seaside headland of Selsey Bill. Both songs surfaced on Setting Sons, the band's 1979 album. The southern-most spot on the West Sussex coast also gets an honourable mention in 'Driving in My Car', where, Madness admit they've "even been to Selsey Bill".

LOCATION 563: Selsey Bill seafront, postcode PO20 9DB

"**I was in a CARAVAN down at Selsey. I went away for a week with me girlfriend. And I knew then it was going to be something special**"
PAUL WELLER
on writing 'The Eton Rifles'

Tyne & Wear

*T*he first beat boom sensation to come out of the north-east, The Animals were so inextricably in thrall to the music of America's southern states that in the mind of vocalist Eric Burdon the River Tyne became the Mississippi. They covered Timmy Shaw's R&B hit 'Gonna Send You Back to Georgia', tailoring it to namecheck a local suburb of Newcastle on 'Gonna Send You Back to Walker'. Bizarrely, the Walker version, only a B-side in the UK, was an A-side hit single in the US. Not surprisingly, the band's bass player Chas Chandler's association with Jimi Hendrix sees him dominate Tyne & Wear's Rock Atlas entries based on the legendary guitarist's six extraordinary appearances in the area. Then there's the discovery of Sting in Gosforth, The Police man's debut at the canny new community music centre Sage Gateshead, and the South Shields shenanigans of Angelic Upstarts. The region also gave stage debuts to Tommy Steele and Nirvana and created the necessary romantic grittiness to inspire modern-day folk songs about the Tyne, Corstorphine Town, Jarrow and Spanish City from Lindisfarne, The Nice, Splinter, Alan Price and Dire Straits respectively. And finally to Sunderland: Underexposed in the first edition of Rock Atlas, readers have been quick to flag up a wonderful list of legendary music venues including the Bay, Locarno, El Cubana, Wetheralls and the Rink.

Gosforth
Sting 'discovered' at The Gosforth Hotel

It was while working as a Virgin Records PR man that Andy Worrall 'discovered' Sting in the upstairs performance room in this small blue-tiled traditional pub in Gosforth. Locally famous as the place where the first copies of the comic Viz were sold, The Gosforth Hotel hosted folk and jazz nights, and on the night in question in 1976 Sting was playing with jazz-pop band Last Exit. Impressed by the bass player from nearby Wallsend, Worrall approached Sting and the band's manager, Sting's first wife Frances Tomelty, to find out where he might bring his head of A&R to see them again. Although that gig did not result in a recording contract - not commercial enough according to Virgin - Sting did subsequently get offered a deal and signed his publishing over to Virgin. Not long after this The Police were formed and in 1978 their first hit, 'Can't Stand Losing You', entered the singles chart.

Worrall's association with Sting didn't end there: "A few years later I was again involved with Sting when, in a dispute between him and Virgin regarding his publishing, I was called to London to attend a court hearing to recount the beginnings of this story. The case was settled out of court. So The Gosforth Hotel is a landmark in Sting's career."

LOCATION 564: The Gosforth Hotel is still going strong, at the junction of High Street and Salters Road, postcode NE3 1DH

“ I'm from Wallsend, which is the **POSH** part of Tyneside ”

STING
Proud to be making his debut at the Sage in 2009 jokes about his roots

Photo: Mark Savage

Gateshead
The Sage: The north-east's community music centre

Granted, the Sage may not have much rock heritage to speak of, but the sci-fi-like structure built on post-industrial wasteland next to the River Tyne is worthy of a mention for its stunning architectural contribution alone. The-designed live music and music education centre was opened in 2004 and fittingly celebrated its fifth birthday with a concert featuring two of the north-east's most accomplished recording artists, rock star Sting and traditional musician Kathryn Tickell. Performers at Sage Gateshead tend to be at the more cerebral end of the rock music spectrum with

Elbow, Morrissey, Robert Plant, Goldfrapp, Herbie Hancock, Crosby, Stills & Nash and the Pet Shop Boys all playing the 1,640-seat venue since its opening by the Queen. Aside from the concert hall, this remarkable building's library of music, access to rehearsals, listening posts and the internet is open to the public daily, free of charge.

LOCATION 565: on the regenerated south bank of the River Tyne at St Mary's Square, Gateshead Quays, postcode NE8 2JR

Tyne & Wear

Heaton
Chas Chandler and Jimi Hendrix at Second Avenue

Animals founder member Chas Chandler grew up in Heaton, and despite moving to London when success beckoned as a pop star and then a manager, he returned frequently to the solid-looking terraced house on Second Avenue. His most famous client as a manager was Jimi Hendrix, and when the wild man of rock played in the north-east in 1967 Chandler, saving money on hotel bills, took Hendrix home to stay at his parents' flat at No.35, where a plaque marks the spot. Without a home telephone, Chandler would walk to the local public call box to make contact with London. It was here he discovered his client was on his way to massive popularity when he got the news that 'Hey Joe' had rocketed up to No.6 in the singles chart. In addition to enjoying Mrs Chandler's hospitality, unsubstantiated reports suggest that Hendrix also took to the streets to complete a spot of busking on nearby Chillingham Road.

LOCATION 566: the plaque at 35 Second Avenue, Heaton, is two miles north-east of Newcastle city centre. Postcode: NE6 5XT

Newcastle
Lindisfarne's 'Fog on the Tyne'

The song 'Fog on the Tyne', included on the album of the same name that featured a 19th-century illustrated view of the river and city on the cover, became a Geordie theme tune in the mid-Seventies. It gave local band Lindisfarne (named after the nearby Northumberland island) national fame when the album shot to No.1, becoming the top-seller in 1972 by any UK act. The song was 'revisited' when Lindisfarne and England's Geordie footballing hero Paul Gascoigne teamed up to release a new version in World Cup year, 1990. Promoted this time by a video set in Geordieland, the single made No.2 in the chart but thankfully didn't herald a new career in pop for the irrepressible Gazza.

LOCATIONS 567 and 568: the Gazza and Lindisfarne 'Fog on the Tyne (Revisited)' video was shot on the banks of the River Tyne around the Tyne Bridge, postcode NE1 3. The special plaque honouring Lindisfarne band member and songwriter Alan Hull, who died in 1995, is outside City Hall, Northumberland Road, postcode NE1 8SF

Lindisfarne co-founder Ray Jackson at the unveiling of a plaque honouring band member and songwriter Alan Hull in 2012. The plaque is located outside City Hall, where Lindisfarne played more than 130 concerts

Photo: The Journal

Newcastle
'Wild' Animals A'GoGo

The A'GoGo must have been quite a place. Mourning its passing even became nationally famous thanks to an eloquent conversation about the club by Bob Ferris and Terry Collier in north-east TV sitcom Whatever Happened to the Likely Lads. Local R&B chart stars The Animals got their big break (and their name due to their "wild" stage antics) at the Club A'GoGo when they began a residency at the city centre Percy Street venue in 1963. By this time the club had already established itself in north-east folklore, hosting performances by a number of emerging acts from London including The Rolling Stones. Local youngsters Bryan Ferry, AC/DC's Brian Johnson, Lindisfarne's Rod Clements, Jimmy Nail and Sting were frequent fans of the venue and the many blues-rock bands that played the A'GoGo. Geordie teenagers then began playing the place themselves with The Warriors (featuring Jon Anderson) and The VIPs (who became Spooky Tooth) making quite an impact alongside a young Bryan Ferry fronting his band The Gas Board. On March 10, 1967, The Jimi Hendrix Experience made their first Newcastle appearance, playing two sets at the club's linked venues the Young Set and then the Jazz Lounge. Hendrix repeated his ceiling-puncturing act from a recent South Shields performance, this time spectacularly leaving his guitar hanging from the roof at the climax of the gig. The variety of exciting acts at the A'GoGo was staggering. Captain Beefheart, John Mayall, The Spencer Davis Group (once memorably joined on stage by Alan Price), Wilson Pickett and Nina Simone satisfied audiences that evolved from R&B to mod.

LOCATION 569: the club buildings were demolished in 1983 and replaced by the Eldon Garden shopping centre, postcode NE1 7RA

> My favourite memory of the A'GoGo was the night my mate and me were right in front of the stage watching Steampacket when this guy came between us and put a hand on each of our shoulders, he then put one foot on the stage, which was about four feet high, and said "Give us a push up lads." It was a slightly inebriated Long John Baldry, but we managed to get him on stage with a helping hand from Rod Stewart. And he still sounded great.
> Geordie teenager Ian Dalgliesh

> The standout [gig] for me was when The Animals played Newcastle City Hall and introduced 'House of the Rising Sun' for the first time. They were on the undercard to Chuck Berry that night and after a couple of verses Eric Burdon said 'Ladies and gents – Mr. Alan Price,' and slowly the band left the stage while Alan went into a six-or-seven minute organ solo which almost took the roof off. I was very disappointed when the single they released didn't have it on. Anyway, I went back to the A'GoGo that night and managed to get a quick word with [Animals guitarist] Hilton Valentine. I ended up having a 4am breakfast with Chuck Berry, who earlier taught me how to spoil good whisky by putting Coca-Cola in it. Then came a conversation about the blues over steak and eggs, and he paid for it all, despite his reputation for being tight with his money.
> Peter O'Donnell, roadie and self-confessed groupie for local Geordie band The Jetstreams

> I lay in my bed that night with my ears ringing and my world view significantly altered.
> Sting's memory of the Hendrix gig at the A'GoGo in March 1967

> I was in my mid-teens and used to go to the Club A'GoGo, which had a very low ceiling. Hendrix - I hadn't seen anything like it - leapt with the guitar and it went through a ceiling tile. But get this, he let it go and continued playing while it hung from the ceiling.
> Jimmy Nail

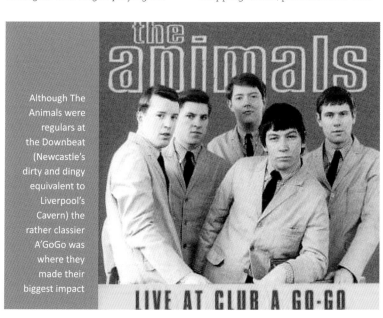

Although The Animals were regulars at the Downbeat (Newcastle's dirty and dingy equivalent to Liverpool's Cavern) the rather classier A'GoGo was where they made their biggest impact

Tyne & Wear

South Shields
Hendrix in the Cellar

With its low ceiling and revolving stage, the New Cellar Club was one of the north-east's most passionately supported music venues. When this enterprising club moved from Beach Road to Thomas Street, Cream were booked for the grand opening. But it was the appearance of The Jimi Hendrix Experience two months later on February 1, 1967 that local rock fans still rave about to this day. According to the Experience's bass guitarist Noel Redding, they were just about to launch into opening number 'Foxy Lady' when Hendrix's 200-watt amp blew-up. But despite the resulting frantic unplugging and plugging in, the trio went down a storm. In the confined space, Hendrix managed to shove his guitar through the ceiling and then narrowly avoid crashing into the Cellar wall when the revolving stage was activated to remove the band from view at the end of a sensational gig witnessed by under 100 fans.

LOCATION 570: now a dental clinic, the New Cellar Club (later renamed the Chelsea Cat and The Wave) was at 8 Thomas Street, postcode NE33 1PU

The Jimi Hendrix Experience play the New Cellar Club for £71 and five shillings

Photo: Fletschers Fotos

❝ Hendrix mingled with the people before he went on. I remember him being quiet, but when the band came on stage he was mind-blowing. His guitar was scraping the ceiling, playing with his teeth. Unbelievable. After that we followed him till he died. ❞
16-year-old East Boldon schoolboy Mick Jackson

❝ Sounds which had never been heard on this Earth before, it was all very amazing, a new breed of music had been born. I remember departing the club quite literally gob-smacked. ❞
21-year-old engineer Graham Cook

❝ My one main outstanding memory was of [Hendrix], on his own, kicking off an absolutely killer version of Muddy Waters' 'Catfish Blues', a slow, sensual, lascivious, wicked blues with guitar licks the like of which the world had never heard up to that point (or so it seemed to us). ❞
19-year-old Dave Bainbridge, guitarist with local support band that night, The Bond

Newcastle
Five nice bridges on a Nice album

A dramatic river's-eye view of the Tyne Bridge decorates the cover of Five Bridges, The Nice's most successful album, released in 1970. Peaking at No.2 in the UK chart and recorded with a full orchestra, this creation in five movements is synchronized to what were, at the time, the city's five bridges and was commissioned for the Newcastle Arts Festival.

LOCATION 571: the five bridges spanning the Tyne at the time of the release of Five Bridges were the Tyne Bridge, Swing Bridge, High Level Bridge, King Edward VII Bridge and Scotswood Bridge. The Tyne Bridge postcode is NE1 3

South Shields
Splinter's Costafine Town

'Costafine Town' provided South Shields duo Splinter with their only hit single. The place they sang about is actually spelt 'Corstorphine Town' and is little more than a short stretch of road near the banks of the River Tyne. The track, which features guitar work and production by George Harrison, evokes days gone by when this area was commercially busy and the local pub, the Commercial Hotel, was thriving.

LOCATION 572: south of the centre of South Shields, postcode NE33 1SQ

South Shields
A pig's head flies at Bolingbroke Hall

They don't play gigs like this one at Bolingbroke Hall anymore. The 21st-century health and safety police would have had a field day at venues booking Angelic Upstarts. On a snowy Friday night in March 1978, the Northumbrian agitators made another of their increasingly headline-grabbing performances. Creating an indelible impression on the punk memory banks, the South Shields audience witnessed a performance of the provocative Upstarts favourite 'Police Oppression'. During the song they were accompanied on stage by their manager Keith Bell, who held a pig's head aloft, which eventually got booted into the steaming hot crowd.

LOCATION 573: in the centre of South Shields, in Bolingbroke Street, postcode NE33 2SS

Newcastle
Riverside UK debut for Nirvana

Riverside was the first venue on Nirvana's first tour of the UK. The October 23, 1989 gig was typical of the far-sighted Riverside, who also managed to book early appearances by Pearl Jam, Red Hot Chili Peppers and Nine Inch Nails. The place seems to have anecdotes to burn, with Buster Bloodvessel once causing a complete power outage when shooting lager over the audience and soaking the electrics at a Bad Manners gig.

LOCATION 574: The Close, Quayside, postcode NE1 3RQ

Tyne & Wear

Sunderland
Tommy Steele debuts at The Empire

The Empire Theatre was the location for Tommy Steele's debut on November 5, 1956 as part of a variety bill that gave the Sunderland public their first taste of the rock 'n' roll phenomenon. So new was this exciting craze that the electric guitars and amplifiers used that night attracted the attention of the local fire brigade, who threatened to prevent Steele performing. The go-ahead was only given with the proviso that a fireman sit on stage armed with a blanket and fire bucket to prevent the band bursting into flames. Steele's famously thrilling debut was thankfully fire free, attracting six curtain calls. The Empire witnessed a second sensational rock 'n' roll debut a year later when Marty Wilde made his bow. By the time The Beatles played the Empire in 1963 variety was pretty much dead, but happily this striking century-old building is still open for business.

LOCATION 575: 4-5 High Street West, on the corner of Garden Place in the city centre. Postcode: SR1 3EX

Sunderland
World's best bands at The Bay Hotel

In 1969, having bought his way out of the Royal Navy's Fleet Air Arm, Geoff Docherty was working as a doorman at Whitburn's Bay Hotel when he hit upon the idea of booking some live music. With a budget of £50 a band, he promptly trebled that spend on the Bay's first gig, persuading established Midlands outfit Family on January 6 that year to head north. His confident approach worked and it was standing room only for a whole bunch of household name appearances at this seafront ballroom. Newcomers Free were next up, but it wasn't long before Tyrannosaurus Rex, Country Joe & The Fish, Jethro Tull, The Nice, Led Zeppelin, The Who and Pink Floyd were playing the place. Docherty had turned into a master at music promotion – he even travelled to London to seek out the underground Floyd to secure their services. "I walked out of the office in Mayfair [London] and my head was spinning thinking 'Crikey! We've got Pink Floyd coming to Sunderland!'" Doherty recalls. Somehow, he produced a conveyor belt of great bands for Sunderland's rock-starved music fans. The Bay's 800 capacity was cramping his style by the summer of '69 and he branched out, promoting King Crimson and The Who at the 3,000 capacity Locarno Ballroom. Following the lead of the great US promoter at the time, Bill Graham, Docherty's next marketing masterstroke was to avoid booking rock bands into a staid old dance hall called the Locarno by changing its name to the Fillmore North. The place where it all started, the Bay, was demolished more than a decade ago and at least one local music fan says it should have become a world heritage site! In its place stand a bunch of non-descript apartments that occupy the space where some of the world's best bands came to Wearside.

LOCATIONS 576 and 577: the Bay Hotel (demolished in 2003) stood on the seafront at the corner of Whitburn Bents Road and South Bents Avenue, postcode SR6 8AE. The Locarno (aka the Fillmore North) has also been demolished and is now the site of a Tesco superstore on the Newcastle Road, postcode SR6 0DA

Sunderland
The Beatles go it alone at The Rink

The Rink, or Top Rank Suite, was a mecca for dancing back in the early Sixties, but it was put to a new and much more exciting use as Sunderland's mums and dads gave way to their kids on Tuesday nights when beat groups came to town. On May 14, 1963, The Beatles made their second and final appearance in Sunderland, having already performed on a variety bill supporting Helen Shapiro at the Empire earlier that year. Unusually, this time they were the only act on the bill, returning to Sunderland as chart-toppers. Their 'From Me to You' single was in the middle of a six-week stay at No.1, and despite a lack of any support on the night, The Beatles were by now well able to look after themselves. But the Rink's audience wasn't all screaming in adoration and John, Paul, George and Ringo needed all their experience to handle an unruly element near the stage. According to 18-year-old Seaham Harbour apprentice mechanic Mick Bute, a foul-mouthed section of the crowd shouted abuse at John Lennon. "McCartney had to get hold of Lennon to put his guitar strap back on his shoulder as he was just about to jump into the crowd and have a go." Aside from this historic night, Bute echoes a recommendation by many other music fans when nominating one of Sunderland's best ever gigs. "My own favourite would have to be the two shows I saw at the Rink by The Small Faces. I can still hear the awesome power of the band and Marriott's incredible voice."

LOCATION 578: another building in rock history that has been demolished. The site where the Rink once stood is on Park Lane near the bus station. Postcode SR1 3NX

Whitley Bay
Spanish City inspiration for Dire Straits

The dome atop the Empress Theatre and ballroom still stands as a reminder of the hugely popular Spanish City fairground featured in Dire Straits' 1981 hit single 'Tunnel of Love'. The fairground provided the young Mark Knopfler with his first exposure to loud rock 'n' roll music. The song, which also name-checks the nearby town of Cullercoats, is not the only locally connected composition by songwriter Knopfler, who grew up in nearby Blyth. His 'Going Home' theme from the Local Hero soundtrack is played at the start of every Newcastle United home match at their St James' Park football ground.

LOCATION 579: Whitley Bay is about 10 miles north-east of Newcastle city centre, postcode NE26. The impressive domed ballroom at Spanish City still stands near the junction of Marine Avenue and the Promenade, postcode NE26 1LX

"It was just a little fun fair on the coast, but to us it was INFUSED with all kinds of things "

MARK KNOPFLER

Born in TYNE &WEAR

Michael Algar, AKA 'Olga', vocals/guitar, The Toy Dolls (b. 21 Sep 1962, South Shields)

Ruth-Ann Boyle, vocals, Olive (b. 26 Apr 1970, Sunderland)

Eric Burdon (b. 11 May 1941, Walker)

Chas Chandler (b. 18 Dec 1938, Heaton, d. 17 Jul 1996)

Cheryl Fernandez-Versini (née Tweedy), Girls Aloud (b. 30 Jun 1983, Newcastle upon Tyne)

Rod Clements, bass, Lindisfarne (b. 17 Nov 1947, North Shields)

Simon Cowe, guitar, Lindisfarne (b. 1 Apr 1948, Jesmond Dene)

Bryan Ferry (b. 26 Sep 1945, Washington)

Geordie (Kevin Walker), guitar, Killing Joke (b. 18 Dec 1958, Newcastle upon Tyne)

Janick Gers, guitar, Iron Maiden (b. 27 Jan 1957, Hartlepool)

Ginger (David Walls), vocals, The Wildhearts (b. 17 Dec 1964, South Shields)

Trevor Horn, producer (b. 15 Jul 1949, Houghton-le-Spring)

Alan Hull, Lindisfarne (b. 20 Feb 1945, Newcastle upon Tyne. d. 17 Nov 1995)

Lee Jackson, bass/vocals, The Nice (b. 8 Jan 1943, Newcastle upon Tyne)

Ray Jackson, Lindisfarne (b. 12 Dec 1948, Wallsend)

Brian Johnson, vocals, AC/DC (b. 5 Oct 1947, Dunston)

Ray Laidlaw, drums, Lindisfarne (b. 28 May 1948, North Shields)

Lauren Laverne, presenter (b. 28 Apr 1978, Sunderland)

Danny McCormack, bass, The Wildhearts (b. 28 Feb 1972, South Shields)

Hank Marvin, guitar, The Shadows (b. 28 Oct 1941, Newcastle upon Tyne)

Ross Millard, guitar/vocals, The Futureheads (b. 22 Jul 1982, Sunderland)

Jimmy Nail (b. 16 Mar 1954, Benton)

Paul Smith, vocals, Maximo Park (b. 13 Mar 1979, Billingham)

John Steel, drums, The Animals (b. 4 Feb 1941, Gateshead)

Dave Stewart, musician /producer (b. 9 Sep 1952, Sunderland)

Sting (b. 2 Oct 1951, Wallsend)

Andy Taylor, Duran Duran (b. 16 Feb 1961, Cullercoats)

Neil Tennant, Pet Shop Boys (b. 19 Jul 1954, Gosforth)

Becky Unthank, The Unthanks (b. 1 Sep 1985, Ryton, Gateshead)

Rachel Unthank, The Unthanks (b. 1 Sep 1977, Ryton, Gateshead)

Hilton Valentine, guitar, The Animals (b. 21 May 1943, North Shields)

Chris Wilkie, guitar, Dubstar (b. 25 Jan 1973, Gateshead)

"Those walks on my way home from Vieux Carré jazz club – the River Tyne in my mind became the Mississippi and I was convinced I was already there. I was already in New Orleans before I'd ever left my home town."
Eric Burdon

Warwickshire

*T*his is the county that gave birth to the mighty musical Broughton brothers Edgar and Steve. The West Midlands Ocean Colour Scene boys get out and about in local public parks and gardens and the village of Tanworth-in-Arden is an idyllic mecca for Nick Drake fans. And two-fifths of Britpop trail-blazers Suede were from the Warwickshire village of Tiddington.

Shot in Leamington Spa: The album title was a play on words in homage to the Muscle Shoals recording studio in America's southern state of Alabama

Leamington Spa
Moseley Shoals snapped at the Jephson memorial

Ocean Colour Scene's first hit album Moseley Shoals was 100% home-grown. Moseley Shoals was the Ladywood, Birmingham, studio where the band (three of whom were born in and around the Moseley district) recorded the 1996 release and made their base. The locally sourced album also featured a cover with the band snapped in front of the Jephson memorial in nearby Leamington Spa's Jephson Gardens. Dr Henry Jephson was a Warwickshire doctor and philanthropist who died in 1878.

LOCATION 580: Moseley Shoals studio is in the Ladywood district of Birmingham and set for demolition. Jephson Gardens is a public park near the centre of Leamington Spa, accessed from The Parade. Postcode: CV32

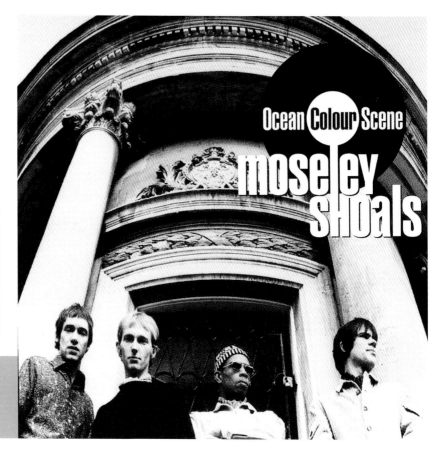

Sheltered by an old oak tree: Nick Drake's ashes are interred in the churchyard at St Mary Magdalene

Photo: Peter Tarleton

Tanworth-in-Arden
Nick Drake's churchyard shrine

Largely overlooked by record-buyers when alive, Nick Drake is now pigeon-holed and revered as the shy genius of English songwriting. The three albums released in his lifetime have left a small but much-written-about canon of work. Suicide was the verdict of the coroner when Drake's short life ended in November 1974. Although born in Burma, Tanworth-in-Arden is the village where he spent his childhood at the family estate Far Leys. A short walk from the large Queen Anne house takes you to the village churchyard. Here, sheltered by an ancient oak tree, a gravestone marks the spot where Nick's ashes were interred under the oak's branches in this idyllic spot, much visited by a steady stream of "very sweet young people" as his sister, actress Gabrielle Drake, describes them. In accordance with the notice on the tree, "Fans are requested to pay their respects by leaving only small tokens or flowers." The area is often covered by all manner of tiny ephemera. Most moving of all are the words on the reverse of Nick Drake's headstone, from his song 'From the Morning': "Now we arise. And we are everywhere."

LOCATION 581: churchyard of St Mary Magdalene, Tanworth Green, East Side, postcode B94 5AL. Far Leys is situated in Bates Lane, a short distance west out of Tanworth-in-Arden. Status: private residence

Lapworth
Ocean Colour Scene amid the topiary

The cover of the 1999 album One from the Modern shows the Ocean Colour Scene boys relaxing at the delightful public gardens at Packwood House, amid the topiary.

LOCATION 582: the Yew Garden, Packwood House, Lapworth, near Solihull, postcode B94 6AT

Born in WARWICKSHIRE

Edgar Broughton, guitar/vocals, Edgar Broughton Band (b. 27 Oct 1947, Warwick)

Steve Broughton, drums, Edgar Broughton Band (b. 20 May 1950, Warwick)

Neil Codling, keyboards, Suede (b. 5 Dec 1973, Tiddington)

Nicholas 'Razzle' Dingley, drums, Hanoi Rocks (b. 2 Dec 1960, Royal Leamington Spa, d. 9 Dec 1984)

Simon Gilbert, drums, Suede (b. 23 May 1965, Tiddington)

Arthur Grant, bass guitar, Edgar Broughton Band (b. 14 May 1950, Leamington Spa)

June Tabor, folk singer (b. 31 Dec 1947, Warwick)

Simon Taylor-Davis, Klaxons (b. 18 Jun 1982, Warwick)

Justin Welch, drums, Elastica (b. 4 Dec 1972, Nuneaton)

West Midlands

*T*rying to avoid the sweeping generalisation that shy, sensitive folk singers are pretty thin on the ground and heavy, strident rock predominates in Britain's second city is difficult. No shrinking violets, these world famous made-in-Birmingham types: The Moody Blues, The Move, ELO, Judas Priest, Black Sabbath, Slade, UB40, Duran Duran, Traffic, The Spencer Davis Group, Fine Young Cannibals and Steel Pulse have all contributed hugely to British music's timeline. Birmingham pays a Hollywood Boulevard-style tribute to some of these rock legends with its Walk of Stars, as does nearby Coventry, honouring its own with a Walk of Fame and trail around the haunts associated with the city's distinctive 2-Tone movement. The 2-Tone city even has its own museum dedicated to the genre, with, amongst its enlightening exhibits, its very own recreation of a rude boy's bedroom. And Coventry, responsible for Chuck Berry's 'My Ding-a-Ling'? Who'd have thought it? Finally, let's hear it for Wolverhampton, which still holds a Northern Soul torch and boasts one of the country's grandest and most chaotic venues judging by newsworthy visits from Morrissey, Slipknot and Slade.

Birmingham 1
Ozzy, Noddy and Tony: Stars on Broad Street

Birmingham's pavement tributes to local rock legends Ozzy Osbourne, Noddy Holder and Tony Iommi run the length of Broad Street. Recent additions to the Walk of Stars have been Bev Bevan, Beverley Knight and Joan Armatrading, in what is an on-going process honouring local stars with stars. Reports suggest that the next top musician to be honoured in this way will be Jeff Lynne.

LOCATION 583: Broad Street in Birmingham city centre. Noddy Holder's star is near the junction with Berkley Street, Ozzy Osbourne's is at Canal Bridge, and the Tony Iommi star is outside Symphony Hall, postcode B1 2HF. For a complete guide to all the Walk of Stars locations download the Broad Street app or visit their website

" I'm so thrilled to have this STAR. It means more to me than the one I have in Hollywood "
OZZY OSBOURNE

Ozzy's star was presented to him by the city's mayor in front of a crowd of more than 1,500 fans

Photo: Broad Street Business Improvement District

The Best of
UB40

Volume One

Birmingham 5
UB40 down The Eagle & Tun

Handily placed for a drink by the band, whose record label DEP International was close by in Digbeth, the Eagle & Tun pub has served more than one key role in UB40's history. Providing cover photos for the band's Best Of albums and the location for the filming of video 'Red Red Wine', the Victorian red brick building became the main meeting place for fans with the walls decked with UB40 photos. This popular community pub's future is uncertain, although there are positive plans to integrate the place into a public plaza linking the high-speed rail lines and Midland Metro.

LOCATION 584: 12 Banbury Street, postcode B5 5RH

Coventry
Stars on the Walk of Fame

The Specials, The Selecter, Hazel O'Connor, Pete Waterman, Vince Hill and Stereo Nation's Tarseme Singh (Taz) are Coventry's musical sons and daughters honoured with a pavement star on the city's Walk of Fame.

LOCATION 585: the stars are arranged diagonally across Priory Place in Coventry city centre. Postcode CV1 5SQ

Coventry
The birthplace of 2-Tone

A house on Albany Road was home to Specials founder Jerry Dammers and the general base and office for the 2-Tone record label. Here the band members would meet to perform DIY production-line tasks, rubber-stamping the titles on the record sleeves of the first 2-Tone record releases. The building, which carries a plaque marking the birthplace of 2-Tone above the front bedroom window, is one of a number of locations included in a 2-Tone trail featuring 11 distinctive black and white plaques dotted around the city. For more information on the trail, which includes additional Rock Atlas entries at the University and Tiffany's, visit the www.2tonecentral.co.uk website.

LOCATION 586: the 2-Tone office was west of the city centre at 51 Albany Road, postcode CV5 6

"Our office was a complete TIP! Everything was run from the little bedroom at Jerry's house in Albany Road **"**

LYNVAL GOLDING

Photo: John Coles

The Specials' Lynval Golding and Coventry ambassador and plaque sponsor Pete Chambers outside the former 2-Tone bedroom office in Albany Road

Photos: John Coles

Coventry
The Coventry Music Museum

It's fitting that a place as unique and different as Coventry should have a museum devoted to the outstanding contribution to popular music this small city has made. The fact that it is an independent museum means that so much of what's good about the place has been achieved through donations and, crucially, the hard work of a dedicated band of volunteers. The museum is the lifelong vision of Coventry music historian and journalist Pete Chambers and his wife Julie. The whole idea got off the ground with a 2-Tone-specific exhibition of memorabilia at the Coventry University students' union where, appropriately enough, Specials band members Jerry Dammers and Horace Panter first got acquainted and Selecter band member Pauline Black was a student. As 2-Tone is Coventry's primary music export to the wider world, it's not surprising that this vibrant genre bags one half of the museum's

exhibition areas. But Coventry's music history is broader and wider and older. AD60 and the Roman occupation is where the pre-pop journey begins and visitors can tune in to 'The Coventry Sound' via a reproduction record shop listening booth, learn about local singing sensation Frank Ifield, see memorabilia relating to Dave Swarbrick's folk-rock career, be reminded just how successful a pop svengali Pete Waterman has been and immerse themselves in the sounds and instruments associated with a second Coventry-related genre, bhangra.

LOCATION 591: less than two miles east of the city centre, The 2-Tone Village is at The Courtyard, 74-80 Walsgrave Road, postcode CV2 4ED. The museum, Wall of Fame, café and 2-Tone shop are open Thursday-Sunday each week. For further details on the museum, an 11-plaque 2-Tone trail, accompanying book and app, visit the Coventry Music Museum website: www.covmm.co.uk

West Midlands

Coventry

Chuck Berry and Pink Floyd: A night to remember at the Locarno

Chuck Berry's biggest, although certainly not his best, hit single was recorded during a live performance at Coventry's Locarno on Smithford Way. Recorded at the Lancaster Arts Festival on February 3, 1972, 'My Ding-a-Ling' became a novelty chart-topper later that same year, only prevented from bagging the Christmas No.1 spot by the equally dubious 'Long Haired Lover from Liverpool' by Little Jimmy Osmond. Chuck's concerts could be patchy or even downright disastrous on occasion, but reports suggest that this performance in Coventry (in part recorded and later bizarrely released as The London Chuck Berry London Sessions) was one of his very best. So good was his appearance that night, supported by Billy Preston and up-and-coming skinhead outfit Slade, that an entirely separate concert later that night was delayed while Chuck enjoyed his evening with a capacity crowd he had eating out of his hand. Festival organisers had sold 2,000 tickets for a second concert featuring Pink Floyd, which eventually got underway at 2.30am the next morning after the ballroom had been cleared of Chuck's fans to allow in the damp and freezing Floyd fans forced to queue outside. Accounts suggest that Floyd's performance was equally momentous, performing a new album of material then called Eclipse, which a year later was retitled and released as The Dark Side of the Moon. At the end of the decade, the Locarno had a name change to Tiffany's, where, just like Chuck, another 'live' No.1 hit was recorded by The Specials. Some of the five tracks contributed to 'The Special A.K.A. Live!' EP, the band's first chart-topper, which hit the top spot in February 1980.

LOCATION 592: the Locarno ballroom at Smithford Way survived a namechange to Tiffany's and is now the city's Central Library, postcode CV1 1FY

Photo: David Trinder

" Chuck opened with 'Roll Over Beethoven' but only got as far as "I'm gonna write" before the enthusiastic audience took over singing the song "
Dave Barker, whose wife (then girlfriend) got to speak to the great man after the gig

" He spent about quarter-of-an-hour setting up the singing with the girls doing 'my' and the boys 'ding-a-ling'. The set was fantastic, overran by about an hour and Chuck clearly was having a ball "
26-year-old systems analyst Alex Hicks, who also thought unknowns Slade were "brilliant"

" 'Can you PLEASE leave the building! We've got 2,000 people outside waiting for the Pink Floyd concert.' You can imagine the derision with which that comment was greeted! On the side stage Chuck is saying 'I can handle 'em. I can handle 'em.' But they wouldn't let him back on, and finally we realised that no amount of 'We want Chuck.' was going to bring him back "
16-year-old student Rob Porter who, with no night buses, was forced to walk all the way home to Walsgrave

" I remember waiting outside with hundreds of other increasingly irate Floyd fans while the stragglers from Chuck's show (mostly ageing Teds if my memory is correct) were cleared from the building "
Local Pink Floyd fan Mick Osler

" Leaving the Locarno you either caught the lift or walked six flights of stairs with glass windows all the way down. From there you could see the crowd for Pink Floyd, three or four deep as far as the Market Tavern Pub "
21-year-old Tile Hill tyre fitter Danny Elliott

" We had done a local pub gig that night and had arrived at the Locano at about 11pm to see Pink Floyd, only to be told that the doors would not open until midnight as Chuck Berry was over-running "
22-year-old gas fitter and roadie for Coventry band Asgard Bob Mansfield

" A truly magical place to see live acts. I went many times in the 70's and 80's and saw such bands as Strawbs, Mott the Hoople, Specials, Jam, Clash (twice), Stranglers, Squeeze, and most memorably on 9, December 1971, Led Zeppelin. It was tragic when they closed the place down and converted it into a library. I can honestly say that whenever I visit now to borrow a book, my mind travels back to those heady days and glorious nights of old! "
Ian Hallam mourns the passing of The Locarno

Above: The glass entrance for Pink Floyd fans and exit for Chuck Berry fans on the extraordinary night in 1972. Main picture: Chuck Berry performing at the Locarno in 1972. Organisers wanted him off the stage to start a late-running Pink Floyd concert that same night, but Chuck was having none of it

West Midlands

UB40 outside the pub where they made their debut in 1979 and returned in 2011 for the unveiling of a PRS for Music plaque to mark the occasion

Birmingham 14
Hare & Hounds debut for UB40

On February 9, 1979, UB40 played their first gig at the Hare & Hounds pub in the Birmingham suburb of Kings Heath, a fact recognized by the unveiling of a plaque on October 4, 2011. Still a vibrant music venue today, it lists Roy Ayers, Basement Jaxx, Ed Sheeran, Ellie Goulding and First Aid Kit as performers down the years.

LOCATION 587: five miles south of Birmingham city centre at 106 High Street, Kings Heath. The plaque is on the York Road side of the building. Postcode B14 7JZ

Birmingham 4
Duran Duran's pub formation

The Hole in the Wall (now The Confession Box) was the pub where Duran Duran were formed. One lunchtime back in 1978, John Taylor and Nick Rhodes met over a few drinks to plot the future of the band named after a character in the 1968 movie Barbarella. The duo then created their 'manifesto', as Nick Rhodes described it, at the Rum Runner nightclub, adding Simon Le Bon and making their chart debut in 1981.

LOCATION 588: Dale End, postcode B4 7LN

Birmingham 21
Steel Pulse's Handsworth revolution

A hotbed of reggae music, Handsworth was where Steel Pulse main man David Hinds grew up and formed the band while still at Handsworth Wood School. A milestone British reggae album release in 1978, Handsworth Revolution and its title track were a rallying cry to the black community in this vibrant inner-city area. Steel Pulse's Selwyn Brown put it like this: "We feel comfortable there because there's a sort of community spirit which we can't really find anywhere else."

LOCATION 589: north-west of the city centre, postcode B21

Opened in 1938, the grand Grade II-listed Wolverhampton Civic Hall and Morrissey's solo debut from 1988

Wolverhampton
Free Morrissey debut at Wolves Civic Hall

Although Morrissey stressed it was never his intention to cause chaos, mayhem ensued when he made his solo concert debut in Wolverhampton in a highly unusual free concert at Wolverhampton Civic Hall. Doubling as a farewell to The Smiths (ex-Smiths Mike Joyce and Andy Rourke formed the majority of his backing band that night), this December 22, 1988 gig invited free entry to anyone wearing a Smiths or Morrissey T-shirt. This meant that the ticketless gig became an extraordinarily emotional event, with just as many fans outside as inside the hall. Other chaotic concerts at the 3,000-capacity Civic include just about every appearance by local outfit Slade. In 2000, the place hit the headlines when Slipknot's Sid Wilson clambered on to the 20-ft-high balcony and stage-dived into the crowd, breaking a woman fan's leg in the process.

LOCATION 590: still a thriving music and entertainment venue at 12 North Street, postcode WV11RD

" It was Wolverhampton, it wasn't London and it wasn't Manchester, which I thought was an important GESTURE. It was free, which, for someone of my status, is unheard of 🗩🗩

MORRISSEY

Wolverhampton
Northern Soul at The Catacombs

One of the least northerly of the legendary Northern Soul clubs, The Catacombs sounds like a subterranean system of tunnels but was actually a bare brick-walled first-floor club. Utilising the former lead-smelting works furnace alcoves as the perfect atmospheric, dark and sweaty environment, the venue enjoyed a comparatively long existence from 1967 until its closure in 1974. Despite its fame as the epicentre of the Black Country's passionate soul community, The Catacombs also hosted the best underground rock groups such as Man and Caravan, and even David Bowie made an appearance back in 1969. As is frequently the case with iconic, much-loved music venues, it's hard to see how such a slab of a building can have meant so much to so many Northern Soul fans. Deserving of a plaque, it duly got one when the Wolverhampton Civic Society, who had previously limited its plaque budget to local dignitaries, created its 96th blue cast-iron memorial for the wall at the original Catacombs site in Temple Street.

LOCATION 593: the site of the original club and its plaque is in the centre of Wolverhampton on Temple Street, postcode WV2 4AQ

Born in WEST MIDLANDS

Kelli Ali (aka Kelli Dayton), vocals, Sneaker Pimps (b. 30 Jun 1974, Birmingham)

Astro (Terence Wilson), trumpet/vocals, UB40 (b. 24 Jun 1957, Birmingham)

Martin Barre, guitar, Jethro Tull (b. 17 Nov 1946, Birmingham)

Ritch Battersby, drums, The Wildhearts (b. 29 Jun 1968, Birmingham)

Blaze Bayley, vocals, Iron Maiden (b. 29 May 1963, Birmingham)

Bev Bevan, drums, The Move/Electric Light Orchestra (b. 24 Nov 1944, Birmingham)

John Bradbury, drums, The Specials (b. 16 Feb 1953, Coventry)

Jim Brown, drums, UB40 (b. 20 Nov 1957, Birmingham)

Trevor Burton, guitar, The Move (b. 9 Mar 1949, Birmingham)

Terry 'Geezer' Butler, bass, Black Sabbath (b. 17 Jul 1949, Birmingham)

Ali Campbell, vocals, UB40 (b. 15 Feb 1959, Birmingham)

Robin Campbell, guitar, UB40 (b. 25 Dec 1954, Birmingham)

Rob Cieka, drums, The Boo Radleys (b. 4 Aug 1968, Birmingham)

Paul Clifford, bass, The Wonder Stuff (b. 23 Apr 1968, Birmingham)

Andy Cox, guitar, Fine Young Cannibals (b. 25 Jan 1956, Birmingham)

Graham Crabb, drums, Pop Will Eat Itself (b. 10 Oct 1964, Sutton Coldfield)

Steve Cradock, guitar/keyboards, Ocean Colour Scene (b. 22 Aug 1969, Birmingham)

Fyfe Dangerfield, vocals, Guillemots (b. 7 Jul 1980, Moseley)

'K.K.' Downing, guitar, Judas Priest (b. 27 Oct 1951, West Bromwich)

Earl Falconer, bass, UB40 (b. 23 Jan 1957, Birmingham)

Simon Fowler, vocals, Ocean Colour Scene (b. 25 Apr 1965, Meriden, Solihull)

Steve Gibbons, vocals/guitar, The Uglys (b. 13 Jul 1941, Birmingham)

Roland Gift, vocals, Fine Young Cannibals (b. 28 May 1961, Birmingham)

Goldie (b. 19 Sep 1965, Walsall)

Kelly Groucutt, bass/vocals, Electric Light Orchestra (b. 8 Sep 1945, Coseley, d. 19 Feb 2009)

Rob Halford, vocals, Judas Priest (b. 25 Aug 1951, Sutton Coldfield)

Terry Hall, vocals, The Specials (b. 19 Mar 1959, Coventry)

Oscar Harrison, drums/keyboards, Ocean Colour Scene (b. 15 Apr 1965, Birmingham)

Norman Hassan, percussion, UB40 (b. 26 Jan 1958, Birmingham)

Ian Hill, bass, Judas Priest (b. 20 Jan 1951, West Bromwich)

Vince Hill (b. 16 Apr 1937, Coventry)

David Hinds, vocals/guitar, Steel Pulse (b. 15 Jun 1956, Birmingham)

Noddy Holder, vocals/guitar, Slade (b. 15 Jun 1946, Walsall)

Miles Hunt, vocals, The Wonder Stuff (b. 29 Jul 1966, Birmingham)

Frank Ifield (b. 30 Nov 1937, Coventry)

Tony Iommi, guitar, Black Sabbath (b. 19 Feb 1948, Birmingham)

Beverley Knight (b. 22 Mar 1973, Wolverhampton)

Jim Lea, bass/keyboards, Slade (b. 14 Jun 1949, Wolverhampton)

John Lodge, vocals/bass, The Moody Blues (b. 20 Jul 1945, Birmingham)

Jeff Lynne, The Move/Electric Light Orchestra/Traveling Wilburys (b. 30 Dec 1947, Birmingham)

Phil Lynott, vocals/bass, Thin Lizzy (b. 20 Aug 1949, West Bromwich, d. 4 Jan 1986)

Clinton Mansell, vocals, Pop Will Eat Itself (b. 7 Jan 1963, Coventry)

Tony Martin, vocals, Black Sabbath (b. 19 Apr 1957, Birmingham)

Nick Mason, drums, Pink Floyd (b. 27 Jan 1944, Birmingham)

Brian Matthew, radio presenter (b. 17 Sep 1928, Coventry)

Adam Mole, guitar, Pop Will Eat Itself (b. 8 Apr 1962, Stourbridge)

Hazel O'Connor (b. 16 May 1955, Coventry)

Ozzy Osbourne (b. 3 Dec 1948, Birmingham)

Carl Palmer, drums, Crazy World of Arthur Brown/Emerson, Lake & Palmer (b. 20 Mar 1950, Birmingham)

Dave Pegg, bass, Fairport Convention (b. 2 Nov 1947, Birmingham)

Brian Pendleton, guitar, The Pretty Things (b. 13 Apr 1944, Wolverhampton, d. 16 May 2001)

Jason Pierce, vocals/guitar, Spiritualized (b. 19 Nov 1965, Rugby)

Mike Pinder, keyboards/vocals, The Moody Blues (b. 27 Dec 1941, Birmingham)

Robert Plant (b. 20 Aug 1948, West Bromwich)

Don Powell, drums, Slade (b. 10 Sep 1946, Bilston)

Mathew Priest, drums, Dodgy (b. 27 Apr 1970, Birmingham)

Roddy Radiation (Roderick Byers), guitar,

The Specials (b. 5 May 1955, Coventry)

Nick Rhodes, keyboards, Duran Duran (b. 8 Jun 1962, Moseley)

John Rostill, bass, The Shadows (b. 16 Jun 1942, Birmingham, d. 26 Nov 1973)

Kevin Rowland, vocals/guitar, Dexy's Midnight Runners (b. 17 Aug 1953, Wolverhampton)

Mike Skinner, The Streets (b. 27 Nov 1978, Birmingham)

Richard Tandy, keyboards, Electric Light Orchestra (b. 26 Mar 1948, Birmingham)

Roger Taylor, drums, Duran Duran (b. 26 Apr 1960, Birmingham)

Glenn Tipton, guitar, Judas Priest (b. 25 Oct 1947, Blackheath)

Richard 'Fuzz' Townshend, drums, Pop Will Eat Itself (b. 31 Jul 1964, Birmingham)

Brian Travers, saxophone, UB40 (b. 7 Feb 1959, Birmingham)

Stephen Vaughan, bass, PJ Harvey (b. 22 Jun 1962, Wolverhampton)

Mickey Virtue, keyboards, UB40 (b. 19 Jan 1957, Birmingham)

Johnnie Walker, radio presenter (b. 30 Mar 1945, Solihull)

Pete Waterman, producer (b. 15 Jan 1947, Coventry)

Peter Overend Watts, bass, Mott the Hoople (b. 13 May 1947, Birmingham)

Carl Wayne, vocals, The Move (b. 18 Aug 1943, Birmingham, d. 31 Aug 2004)

Toyah Willcox (b. 18 May 1958, Birmingham)

Mervyn 'Muff' Winwood, The Spencer Davis Group (b. 15 Jun 1943, Birmingham)

Steve Winwood, (b. 12 May 1948, Birmingham)

Chris Wood, flute/saxophone, Traffic (b. 24 Jun 1944, Birmingham, d. 12 Jul 1983)

Roy Wood, The Move, Wizzard (b. 8 Nov 1946, Birmingham)

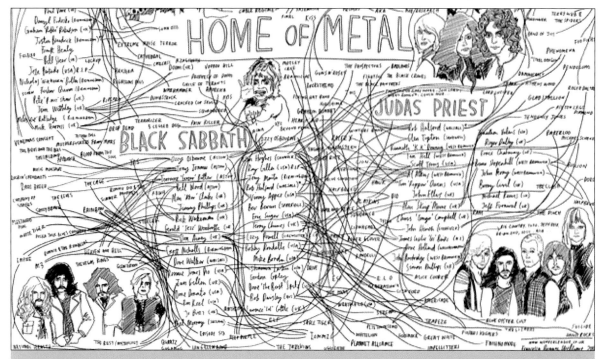

This family tree, illustrated by Bunny Bissoux, was part of the West Midlands' Home of Metal project. More than 200,000 people attended events across the Black Country, including an exhibition at Birmingham Museums and Art Gallery in 2011

Wiltshire

Wiltshire should be prefaced with the adjective wild! Long before the wild lions and tigers were introduced to Longleat's parkland, The Rolling Stones, Heinz and The Wild Boys and Billy J Kramer and The Dakotas all played al fresco dates at the stately home. Wilder still, scenes of mayhem ensued during a riotous Kinks gig at Salisbury's City Hall in 1965. And, so incendiary was the band's Neeld Hall, Chippenham, appearance that same year that the 900-strong audience chased all four Kinks off the stage to grab a piece of them, fuelled on nothing stronger than Coca-Cola, according to one eyewitness. Less chaotically there follow Wiltshire stories surrounding The Beatles filming Help!, ghostly goings-on for The Feeling, Peter Gabriel on Solsbury Hill, Eddie Cochran's tragic death, Buddy Holly in Woolworths, XTC's motoring nightmare, a Sting album cover and the arrival of Radiohead. The county has been blessed with a rich heritage of medium and small-sized venues. Devizes Corn Exchange was the place to encounter the best of British prog and glam rock in the '70s, while Swindon's Oasis was said to have been where Liam Gallagher got the idea for his band's name and the town's tiny Affair club once played host to The Clash when their original venue, the nearby Central Hall, caught fire!

Amesbury
The Beatles' hideaway hotel

While filming scenes on Salisbury Plain for their second movie Help!, The Beatles stayed at The Antrobus Arms Hotel, checking in on May 2 and out on May 6, 1965. Each day the four most famous pop stars on Earth were ferried to and fro in a black Austin Princess, which was ransacked overnight in the hotel garage by fans searching for cigarette ends and any other 'souvenirs' the band may have left behind.

LOCATION 594: Church Street, Amesbury, postcode SP4 7EU

Knighton Down
The Beatles stay mainly on the Plain

Knighton Down is the wild and windswept spot on Salisbury Plain where The Beatles filmed sequences for their second movie Help! The script demanded a remote location where the band could record their latest tunes while protecting Ringo from a bunch of baddies pursuing him, intent on removing his sacred ring. Used by the British Army to practise manoeuvres, Salisbury Plain provided not only some dismally cold spring weather but, owing to the generosity of the Royal Artillery, tanks for the storyline and real protection from over-enthusiastic fans on the days of filming.

LOCATION 595: near Larkhill army base. From the A303, head north on the A345, turning left to Larkhill. Knighton Down is a short ramble north-west

Box
Peter Gabriel's Real World

Real World is the world music label and studio complex created by Peter Gabriel. The residential recording studio has played host to a varied client list including Robbie Williams, the late Amy Winehouse, Tom Jones, Paolo Nutini, A-ha, Deep Purple, Laura Marling and Elbow. The place is also HQ for WOMAD and the world music recording label Real World Records.

LOCATION 596: midway between Chippenham and Bath on the A4, Real World is at Box Mill, Mill Lane, Box, postcode SN13 8PL. Status: private property

Swindon
XTC's Magic Roundabout

Swindon-born XTC band member Colin Moulding wrote 'English Roundabout', a track on the band's most successful album English Settlement. The song is about Swindon's famously large and convoluted motorists' nightmare, the so-called Magic Roundabout. Cue this four-minute insistent, choppy track to press and play as you travel through the roundabout for maximum effect.

LOCATION 597: best found by heading for the nearby Swindon Town football ground, postcode SN1 2ED

Wiltshire

Trowbridge
Radiohead debut at the Psychic Pig

Mark Johnston and George Hodgson's Psychic Pig club has enjoyed some great nights in three different venues around Trowbridge since its first event in 1984. Hardly the best attended but certainly the most famous gig came when, for a fee of £50, a group advertised as On a Friday turned up, only to announce that they would be christening a new band name. Thus in 1991, Radiohead were born at the Psychic Pig, impressing the organisers as much for their domestic neatness as the music played that night. Before leaving, Thom Yorke and co tidied the club and even washed up the dishes!

LOCATIONS 598, 599 and 600: the Psychic Pig venues in Trowbridge: Civic Hall, St Stephen's Place, postcode BA14 8AH; Trax nightclub, 46-47 Church Street, postcode BA14 The Hub, 2 Wicker Hill, postcode BA14 8JS

> " They were the **POLITEST** bunch of young men I have ever met **"**
>
> **GEORGE HODGSON**
> Radiohead booker

Salisbury
Buddy at Woolies

What is now Salisbury's Odeon cinema was formerly the Gaumont where Buddy Holly and The Crickets performed three shows on March 22, 1958. The Tudor revival, grade II-listed building is situated close by what was the Old George Hotel on the High Street, where Holly's entourage stayed. The singer, who visited Woolworths to buy a new pen to write a letter home to his folks, dropped into the store's new American soda bar, and described the hotel as "a real old, quaint place". The hotel's frontage can still be admired as the entrance to the town's shopping centre.

LOCATION XXX: Odeon, 15 New Canal, postcode SP1 2AA

Born in WILTSHIRE

James Blunt (b. 22 Feb 1974, **Tidworth**)
Rick Davies, vocals/ keyboards, Supertramp (b. 22 Jul 1944, **Swindon**)
Dave Dee (b. 17 Dec, 1943, **Salisbury**, d. 9 Jan 2009)
Dave Gregory, guitar, XTC (b. 21 Sep 1952, **Swindon**)
Justin Hayward, vocals, The Moody Blues (b. 14 Oct 1946, **Swindon**)
Mark Lamarr, presenter (b. 7 Jan 1967, **Swindon**)
Colin Moulding, bass, XTC (b. 17 Aug 1955, **Swindon**)
Colin Newman, vocals/ guitar, Wire (b. 16 Sep 1954, **Salisbury**)
Billie Piper, vocalist/ actress (b. 22 Sep 1982, **Swindon**)

Chippenham
Eddie Cochran's roadside memorial

A plaque beside the old Bristol to London main A40 road marks the place where influential rock 'n' roller Eddie Cochran was fatally injured in a car accident on April 16, 1960. The star had completed the final date of his British tour at the Bristol Hippodrome and the taxi driving him was heading east to London Heathrow Airport for his flight home to the USA. His fellow passengers, performer Gene Vincent, Cochran's fiancée Sharon Sheeley, deputy tour manager Patrick Tomkins and the driver, George Martin, all survived the crash. The plaque features an illustration of Cochran's Gretsch guitar which was in the taxi on the fateful night and later impounded at the local police station, where young police cadet David Harman (himself a pop star by 1965, named Dave Dee) was entrusted with taking care of the instrument. The guitar must have been sprinkled with stardust: just days before the accident the Gretsch had been carried to Cochran's waiting car in London by helpful 13-year-old fan Mark Feld, who later became Marc Bolan.

LOCATION 601: on the A4 in Chippenham, heading east after passing under the railway viaduct in the town, on the grass verge to the left of the road before heading up Rowden Hill, outside 36b Rowden Hill, postcode SN15 2AR

Daily Mirror

MON APR. 18 1968

2½d · · · No. 17,522

'ROCK' STAR DIES IN CRASH

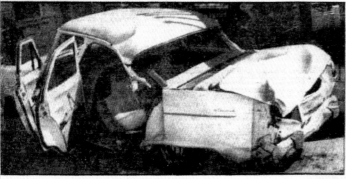

● PICTURED ABOVE: Singer Eddie Cochran.
LEFT: The wreckage of the car after the crash which killed him.

A MERICAN rock 'n' roll singing star Eddie Cochran died yesterday after a car taking him to London Airport crashed.

The crash happened late on Saturday night at Chippenham, Wilts.

Cochran, 21, was travelling to the airport by hire-car from Bristol, where he topped the bill last week in a stage variety show.

With him were three other passengers.

One was American singer Gene Vincent, 25, who starred with Cochran in the show.

Song Girl

Another was American girl songwriter Sharon Sheeley, 20. The third was theatrical agent Patrick Tompkins, 29, of Camberwell, London.

As the car went through Chippenham it suddenly spun in the road and crashed backwards into a concrete lamp-post.

Cochran was flung into the road

● GENE VINCENT

Flung out as car is wrecked

People living near, or heard the crash. They ran out in their nightclothes to help him and the others in the crash.

Cochran had severe head injuries.

Vincent was badly bruised and had slight head injuries. Miss Sheeley had a fractured pelvis.

By NED GRANT

and back injuries. Tompkins was bruised and shocked.

The car-driver—George Martin, of Blaenthorpe-road, Handville, Bristol—was unhurt.

The four injured passengers were taken to hospital at Bath.

And three, just after four o'clock yesterday afternoon, Cochran died.

Tompkins said in hospital last night "The crash happened so suddenly that I don't think any of us knew much about it."

Cochran, whose records have included "Summertime Blues" and C'mon Everybody, had been in Britain since January doing stage and TV work.

He was due to fly back to America yesterday, to do some filming.

Vincent—his first big hit was "Be-Bop-a-Lula"—was flying with Cochran to take a holiday.

So was British "rock" singer Vince Eager, 19.

He did not know of the crash until he called to collect his plane ticket at London Airport yesterday.

Then Eager was given a message from Bath about the crash.

He cancelled his flight and drove to Bath. There he saw the three injured people.

With Body

Last night a spokesman for Eager's manager—agent Larry Parnes—said the British singer would fly to America with Cochran's body after the inquest.

And Cochran's last record, called "Three Steps to Heaven," will be issued on schedule in Britain within a few days.

The toll: 30 dead 628 injured so far

AT least thirty people have been killed and 628 injured on the roads since the Easter Holiday started on Good Friday.

First reports of YESTERDAY'S ACCIDENTS showed that nine people were killed and 12 injured.

Provisional figures for GOOD FRI. DAY and SATURDAY announced by the Automobile Association were: Twenty-one dead and 616 injured.

Last year's figures for the same two days were: Fifteen dead and 456 injured.

Last night the Automobile Association made this urgent Bank Holiday appeal:

"An all-out effort will be required by everyone if the toll on the roads is not to be greater than last Easter

"Bank Holiday motoring conditions call for every bit of concentration on the part of drivers, cyclists and pedestrians.

"A second's carelessness could mean another lost life.

"The Margin of error allowed by congested roads and heavy traffic is so small that no one can afford the slightest mistake."

● See 'Bumper "Parade" to the Sea—Back Page.

Wiltshire

The Stones on the steps: Longleat 1964

Photo: Tony Keeley/Lebrecht Music & Arts

Longleat
Lord Bath's stately home goes pop

Always full of innovative ideas, Lord Bath (the 7th Marquess of Bath) came up with an ingenious plan in the early Sixties to raise some much-needed cash to help run the vast estate at Longleat. The novel introduction of lions to roam his parkland would wait until 1966. Two years earlier, he came up with a potentially more dangerous idea: outdoor pop concerts. A 1961 appearance by local clarinet chart-topper Acker Bilk proved successful enough before Billy J. Kramer and The Dakotas topped the first Longleat pop bill in May

1964, attracting 12,153 fans and causing traffic chaos stretching six miles from the historical house. Ill-equipped for his first pop invasion, the Marquess promised "stronger barriers and barbed wire" for any future event, and a month later a rain-swept concert by The Bachelors (arriving at Longleat with film actress Diana Dors) passed off more quietly. Confident that he was getting the hang of organising by now, the Marquess pulled off his biggest coup in August 1964 when 16,000 turned out to see The Rolling Stones performing "in person and on the steps" of his stately home, as the adverts proclaimed. More than 200 mostly female fans were treated for fainting by a team of nurses, incidents

never repeated as future Longleat concerts became rather sedate affairs. One more gig that year by Heinz and The Wild Boys (filling in for last-minute cancellations The Hollies) and 1965 appearances by Freddie and The Dreamers, The Seekers and Adam Faith failed to recapture the drama of the summer of '64. But the gamble of organising large-scale outdoor pop concerts had been prototyped at Longleat, and soon this exciting, new idea would take root in neighbouring Somerset, before mushrooming nationwide.

LOCATION 602: off the A36 between Bath and Salisbury (A362 Warminster to Frome road). Postcode: BA12 7NW

Stonehenge
A rock mecca for Stones, Byrds and Spinal Tap

A place of lunar and solar worship since 3100 BC, Stonehenge was a mecca for freaks and hippies in the Sixties, drawn to the most breathtakingly spiritual location in Britain. In 1968, Rolling Stones Mick Jagger and Keith Richards acted as perfect hosts for a tourist visit by American group The Byrds. Gram Parsons was clearly in awe of Mick and Keith and the trip to the famous stones precipitated Parsons exiting The Byrds when the remaining band members left for a controversial tour of South Africa. Leaving a South Kensington club in the early hours, the party headed west out of London in Richards' Bentley, walked the last stretch to the ancient standing stones and later breakfasted on kippers in a nearby Salisbury pub. By 1972, Stonehenge began to stage annual free pop festivals. Space-rockers Hawkwind made frequent appearances and attendance figures reached a peak in 1984 when 30,000 descended on the historic site. A year later, clashes between police and new-age travellers made the news headlines in the so-called 'Battle of the Beanfield'. This battlefield, a short distance from the stones, prevented the festival and summer solstice celebrations from taking place again following government intervention. There is no record of the band Spinal Tap having actually visited the ancient site, but their track 'Stonehenge' and its appearance in the movie This Is Spinal Tap included the hilarious, shambolic Stonehenge stage set, which prompted an angry Nigel Tufnel to describe the none-too-epic creation as "a Stonehenge monument on the stage that was in danger of being crushed by a dwarf".

LOCATION 603: north of the A303, close by its junction with the A344, postcode SP4 7DE

> " The famous Stonehenge trip we went on at three in the morning... desperately trying to **WIN FAVOUR** with our old friends Mick and Keith **"**
>
> **CHRIS HILLMAN**
> The Byrds

Salisbury
Dave Dee, Dozy, Beaky, Mick & Tich remembered

The Wiltshire group who topped the chart in 1968 with 'The Legend of Xanadu' are remembered with a Salisbury Civic Society blue plaque outside City Hall. The plaque was unveiled on the 40th anniversary of their most successful single release. The venue, which has hosted The Beatles, The Rolling Stones, Cream, David Bowie, Led Zeppelin and Pink Floyd, is still a great place to catch the best of British live music.

LOCATION 604: City Hall, Malthouse Lane, postcode SP2 7TU

Old Wardour Castle
Sting's all-Wiltshire affair

This 14th-century castle was the album cover location shoot for Sting's Ten Summoner's Tales. Inside the distinctive white ruin, Sting is pictured together with his Icelandic horse Hrímnir. The Police man's fifth solo album was an all-Wiltshire affair, recorded at his Elizabethan manor, Lake House, at Wilsford cum Lake. The 1993 release included one of Sting's best-loved songs, 'Fields of Gold'.

LOCATION 605: open to the public, Wardour Castle lies two miles south-west of Tisbury, postcode SP3 6RR. Lake House is a private, heavily protected house

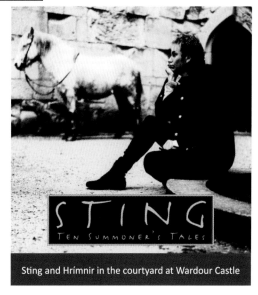

Sting and Hrímnir in the courtyard at Wardour Castle

Worcestershire

Cornering the market in locations linked to what most would agree to be among the top half dozen rock gods, Worcestershire has noteworthy Beatles, Elvis and Dylan connections and is the home county of Led Zeppelin's Robert Plant and John Bonham. The good Captain Beefheart once enjoyed high tea in Kidderminster and – astonishingly weird fact warning - Eric Clapton played a unique pub gig in front of four England cricket captains at the Crown pub in Martley.

Photo: David Roberts

Barnt Green

Elvis on the roof at Graceland

No tourist trip to Worcestershire is complete without a visit to Graceland. A mile or so east of Barnt Green and you are on the Old Birmingham Road heading south towards the M42. Look out for Graceland Garage and the life-size, guitar-playing Elvis Presley perched on the edge of the building's roof.

LOCATION 606: Graceland is at 283 Old Birmingham Road, postcode B60 1HQ

Born in WORCESTERSHIRE

Michael Ball (b. 27 Jun 1962, Bromsgrove)
John Bonham, drums, Led Zeppelin (b. 31 May 1948, Redditch, d. 25 Sep 1980)
Jim Capaldi, drums, Traffic (b. 2 Aug 1944, Evesham, d. 28 Jan 2005)
Nigel Clark, vocals/bass, Dodgy (b. 18 Sep 1966, Redditch)
Karl Hyde, vocals/guitar, Underworld

(b. 10 May 1957, Worcester)
Luke Johnson, drums, Lostprophets (b. 11 Mar 1981, Redditch)
Dave Mason, vocals/guitar, Traffic (b. 10 May 1946, Worcester)
Ray Thomas, flute/vocals, The Moody Blues (b. 29 Dec 1941, Stourport-on-Severn)
Clifford T. Ward (b. 10 Feb 1944, Stourport-on-Severn, d. 18 Dec 2001)

Photo: Peter Tarleton

The pub where cricket fan Eric Clapton played in front of an audience that included four England captains

Martley
Clapton at The Crown

Guitar god Eric Clapton played a bizarre gig as a result of losing a bet to his friend Ian Botham back in 1987. The result of the winning bet meant that the cricket legend was able to get Clapton to play for free at a gig of his choosing. Botham chose the wedding of the son of the landlord and landlady at his favourite pub, The Crown at Martley. Occurring on the eve of Worcestershire's County Championship match against Essex, it meant that both teams turned up at The Crown to witness Clapton's appearance. Supported by Chicken Shack guitarist Stan Webb, Clapton had the distinction of being cheered on by pub regulars, the wedding party and four former or future England cricket captains: Hussain, Gooch, Fletcher and a highly satisfied Botham.

LOCATION 607: deep in the Worcestershire countryside, approximately 10 miles north-west of Worcester on Berrow Green Road, postcode WR6 6PA

Kidderminster
Captain Beefheart and Marc Bolan at Frank's

A plaque put in place by the town's Civic Society marks the spot where Frank Freeman's Dancing Club hosted gigs by rock legends Captain Beefheart, Tyrannosaurus Rex and Fleetwood Mac between 1968 and 1971. Together with his wife Wynn and DJ John Peel, who was a staunch supporter of this unlikely named venue on his radio shows, the club gained a strong reputation across the Midlands and beyond. May 19, 1968 was the day Captain Beefheart and his Magic Band journeyed north to play this Kidderminster hotspot.

Entertained to tea, cucumber sandwiches and cakes by Frank and Wynn Freeman, and actually driven to the gig all the way from London by Peel, the good Captain enjoyed his short stay in Kidderminster. He took in the town's shoe shop and the next door Flamingo café where he relaxed over a few games played on the pinball machine. As John Peel later remarked in an interview with The Sun newspaper: "Frank's is the most amazing place. It's remarkable to find a club like this in the middle of nowhere."

LOCATION 608: look out for the extraordinary medieval-style door surrounded by blue-tiled bricks in Lower Mill Street, postcode DY11 6UU

Worcestershire

Tenbury Wells
The Beatles at The Bridge

With a population that wouldn't fill half the Royal Albert Hall, the small market town of Tenbury Wells was nevertheless the Joe Brown and The Bruvvers, Johnny Kidd and The Pirates and Screaming Lord Sutch location for a milestone gig for The Beatles. The visit coincided with the release of the Fab Four's first chart-topping single and they were booked for a £100 fee at the Bridge hotel's Riverside Dancing Club well before they were nationally famous. However, the club committee's foresight, or luck, saw The Beatles take to the stage on April 15, 1963 at the same time as single 'From Me to You' and album Please Please Me were on their short climbs to No.1. The ballroom had already witnessed well-received visits, but nothing could have prepared the organisers for the frenzied reception The Beatles enjoyed, stoked up by a fresh-in-the-memory TV appearance on ATV show Thank Your Lucky Stars. When John, Paul, George and Ringo took a pre-gig stroll down Teme Street, they experienced the growing hysteria that would soon become Beatlemania. They sneaked into local pub The Crow for a smoke and a drink, only to be turfed out by a landlord who took exception to their long hair. A mini pub crawl developed and next stop was The Royal Oak, before completing their tour of Tenbury at The Bridge, where at least one local was bought a pint of Wrekin bitter by George Harrison. Three days after the Bridge gig The Beatles were performing at London's Royal Albert Hall and confirmed as the best new music attraction in the country.

LOCATION 609: Tenbury Wells is 20 miles north-west of Worcester. The Bridge hotel is at 87 Teme Street, postcode WR15 8AE

Photo: Shropshire Star

Easter Monday 1963: The Beatles take a stroll in Tenbury Wells

" Looking back it was great that [The Beatles] did HONOUR our booking, as by the time they came to Tenbury they were worth thousands "

PAT LAMBERT
Dancing Club committee member

Photo: Peter Tarleton

Led Zeppelin fans who make a pilgrimage to Rushock bring drumsticks for the band's larger-than-life drummer

Rushock
John Bonham's drumstick shrine

One of rock's greatest characters and drummers, John 'Bonzo' Bonham, is remembered by a headstone in the village churchyard, close to the Bonham family home at Old Hyde Farm. Bonham, who died in 1980, lived for eight years at the farm at Cutnall Green he bought from the proceeds of his extraordinary career with Led Zeppelin. Old Hyde Farm appears in scenes from the band's mid-Seventies movie The Song Remains the Same. The prominent headstone at Rushock church is a regular place of pilgrimage for Bonham's legions of fans, who, appropriately, bring drumsticks to add to the growing collection decorating the spot.

LOCATION 610: east of the A442, south of Kidderminster, at St Michael's Parish Church, Rushock, Church Hill, postcode WR9 0NR

Bob Dylan, Robbie Robertson, Steve Winwood and Procol Harum were just some of the rock 'n' roll visitors to Witley Court. Right: Blonde on Blonde, the 1966 album Dylan released in the same month he played the Birmingham Odeon and visited Witley Court

Witley Court
Dylan goes ghost-hunting

Gutted by a fire in 1937, Witley Court was the setting for an extraordinary visit by Bob Dylan three decades later. The vast ruined, but still magnificent mansion was the subject of a ghost-hunting expedition by Dylan and his on-tour guitarist Robbie Robertson. Their guides for the night were Traffic band members Dave Mason and Jim Capaldi and local musician Kevyn Gammond. Dylan's vague recollections following this 1966 excursion suggest that Steve Winwood and his brother Muff were also present when he met his new friends one night at Birmingham club Elbow Room. They all drove the 25 miles from Birmingham to Witley Court in the early hours of the morning, but Dylan's presence was not enough to encourage any spooky activity, apparently. In 1967, Procol Harum's pre-video-days film to accompany their smash hit 'A Whiter Shade of Pale' was shot at Witley Court.

LOCATION 611: 10 miles north of Worcester on the A443, postcode WR6 6JT. Status: open to the public

> "We went to see a HAUNTED house, where a man and his dog burned up in the 13th century. Boy, that place was spooky "

BOB DYLAN recalls the trip to Witley Court in an interview with Rolling Stone

Yorkshire: East Riding

*T*he ceremonial county that includes the former Humberside city of Kingston upon Hull has pirates, Housemartins, The Beautiful South and the folk family Waterson to commend it. The nucleus of Bowie's Spiders from Mars (Mick Ronson and Trevor Bolder) was hatched in Hull and vocalist Lene Lovich and Fine Young Cannibals frontman Roland Gift grew up here, but sadly most of the venues that saw The Rolling Stones, Buddy Holly and many other ground-breaking rock acts visit the East Riding are long gone, including Hull's two Beatles locations, which saw the Fab Four arrive in 1962 and 1963 to play the Majestic Ballroom, returning again in '63 and '64 to play the ABC cinema.

Bridlington Bay
Pirate DJs brave the ocean waves

The choppy sea off the Yorkshire coast was home to the DJs of Radio 270 for 18 exciting months before government legislation outlawed their broadcasts in 1967. Dutch vessel Oceaan V11 had more than its fair share of choppy seas, and even the ship's final-day farewell party was a let-down when a North Sea storm prevented a number of staff members getting aboard for the sad goodbye. DJ Paul Burnett, who clearly never quite acclimatised to life on the ocean waves, once reportedly chucked up his breakfast live on air during the reading of a Radio 270 commercial for bacon! Aside from the physical discomfort experienced, those aboard also suffered a bomb threat, which fortunately turned out to be a hoax. The Oceaan V11, a former fishing vessel, was by far the smallest of all the pirate ships, and on a number of occasions was forced to leave her anchorage and seek shelter. Once the pirates were banned she was advertised for sale complete with record collection!

LOCATION 612: three miles east of Bridlington, postcode YO15 2PB

Born in YORKSHIRE: EAST RIDING

Trevor Bolder, bass, Uriah Heep/The Spiders from Mars (b. 9 Jun 1950, Hull, d. 21 May 2013)
Stan Cullimore, guitar, The Housemartins (b. 6 May 1962, **Hull**)
Dave Hemingway, The Beautiful South/The Housemartins (b. 20 Sep 1960, **Hull**)
Graham Jones, guitar, Haircut 100 (b. 8 Jul 1961, **Bridlington**)
Mick Ronson, guitar (b. 26 May 1946, Hull, d. 29 Apr 1993)
Dave Rotheray, guitar, The Beautiful South (b. 9 Feb 1963, **Hull**)
Lal Waterson, folk singer (b. 15 Feb 1943, Hull, d. 4 Sep 1998)
Mike Waterson, folk singer (b. 16 Jan 1941, Hull, d. 22 Jun 2011)
Norma Waterson, folk singer (b. 15 Aug 1939, **Hull**)

Hull
Mick Ronson's memorial stage

In the absence so far of a more fitting memorial to Hull's great rock star Mick Ronson, there is the Mick Ronson Stage, a slab of concrete with his name attached in Queen's Gardens, the park where he once worked as a gardener for the local council.

LOCATION 613: the Mick Ronson Stage is in the centre of the city at Queen's Gardens, 1 Paragon Street, postcode HU1 3DR

From gardener to rock star: Hull's Mick Ronson was born in the city's Beverley Road

Hull
The New Adelphi Club

Pulp, Oasis, Green Day, Franz Ferdinand and Radiohead have all played this remarkable 200-capacity venue in a three-bedroomed house in a terraced street. The New Adelphi Club celebrated its 30th birthday in 2014. A working men's club and laundry before 1984, it still prides itself in being able to host a diversity of live music in a safe environment.

LOCATION 614: still going strong at 89 De Grey Street, Hull, HU5 2RU

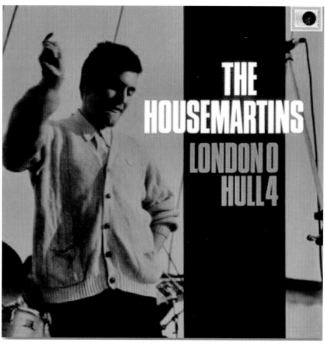

Hull
'The Rising of Grafton Street'

London 0 Hull 4 was the title of The Housemartins' 1986 album, a title prompted by the band's propensity to rate their live gigs in terms of football scorelines. A key figure in The Housemartins' growing success story, Merseyside-born singer-songwriter Paul Heaton moved to Hull in 1983 and made the city his base for the next 20 years. The spiritual home for first The Housemartins, then Heaton's commercially massive The Beautiful South, was No.87 Grafton Street. 'The Rising of Grafton Street' was the cheerfully upbeat instrumental track on The Beautiful South's 1990 album Choke.

LOCATION 615: The Grafton Hotel on Grafton Street is about three miles north of the city centre, west of the A1079. Postcode: HU5 2NP

"My favourite winter pub would be The Grafton... It's just great on a rainy day to hear dominoes and the old **CHARACTERS** who are really entertaining "
PAUL HEATON

Yorkshire: North

*R*ock legends Arthur Brown, David Coverdale, Chris Rea and Paul Rodgers all hail from England's largest rural county. It's the setting for busloads of fans descending on a remote Hendrix gig, The Rolling Stones' first show outside Greater London, Paul Simon's Scarborough Fair folk education, Welsh rock band Man's gloomy song story and album cover shoots for The Cure and Richard Hawley. All that plus a gem of a record shop and the hang-out of those Stainsby Girls.

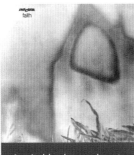

A suitably gloomy day at Bolton Priory

Bolton Abbey
Porl Thompson's ghostly Cure cover

A barely recognisable fog-shrouded image of Bolton Priory provides the cover of The Cure's 1981 album Faith. Musician and painter Porl Thompson (who had been an original member of The Cure in the late Seventies) was the cover designer for Faith. He subsequently re-joined the band in 1983 but left again in 2012, auctioning off his Cure memorabilia, guitars, clothes and photos to concentrate on his art, now as Pearl Thompson.

LOCATION 616: seven miles east of Skipton, north of the A59, postcode BD23 6EX

Kirklevington
Hendrix at the Kirklevington Country Club

A former petrol station and garage workshop was the setting for a remote haven for music fans near the small village of Kirklevington. Converted into a dance hall, Kirklevington Country Club did have one advantage: the main A19 ran right past it, providing easy access for teenagers who poured out of Middlesbrough at weekends to enjoy gigs by some of the UK's biggest names in the Sixties, Seventies and Eighties. Biggest of all perhaps was the appearance of Jimi Hendrix in January 1967. The legendary guitarist journeyed north to play The Kirk the day before a three-day booking at London's Mayfair and a memorable appearance on BBC TV's Top of the Pops.

" **The night Hendrix came I can remember loads of DOUBLE-DECKER BUSES coming from Stockton and Middlesbrough packed with people** "

TOM REAY
son of the club's owner

LOCATION 617: now residential housing, the site of the Kirklevington Country Club was on the old A19. Postcode: TS15

Photo: Middlesbrough Evening Gazette

OUTLOOK CLUB

FRIDAY, from MANCHESTER
IAN CRAWFORD and THE
BOOMERANGS
Members 5/6. Guests 7/6.
Members only after 9 p.m.
SATURDAY
RHYTHM AND BLUES
NORTH v. SOUTH
Fabulous Two-group Session
TOP TWENTY STARS
From MANCHESTER—
THE HOLLIES ("Just Like Me")
From LONDON—THE ROLLING
STONES ("Come On")
Doors open 7.30. Members only after
8.15 p.m. Members 7/6. Guests 10/-
Positively no admittance after
10.30 p.m.
52-60. CORPORATION ROAD
(Opp. Odeon). MIDDLESBROUGH.
Tel. 2261.

Not a tour by the Stones but a one-off flying visit supporting The Hollies about six weeks before they first hit the UK chart with debut single 'Come On'

COME ON
I WANT TO BE LOVED

the rolling STONES

Middlesbrough
The Rolling Stones head north to the Outlook

The Outlook was Middlesbrough's answer to London's Marquee Club, seemingly showcasing every national act seconds before they became megastars. On July 13, 1963, local legend John McCoy booked a double bill featuring "Top Twenty Stars from Manchester The Hollies" and "From London – The Rolling Stones". It was the first time the Stones had ventured outside their native Greater London concert circuit, with McCoy, the man later credited with hiring out the

nearby Kirklevington Country Club, securing the band for a £65 fee, which also included subbing their then leader, Brian Jones, for three packets of the band's favourite Player's cigarettes. Stevie Wonder and The Who were other inspired acquisitions for the basement venue below teenage fashion shop Young Outlook, which McCoy dubbed The Alcove to give it a separate identity. In addition to the club on Corporation Road, the Corporation Hotel was where

the Stones stayed overnight on their first exploration north, and also the location of the much-loved Hamilton's record shop.

LOCATION 618: in the town centre, the Outlook (52-60 Corporation Road) no longer exists as a club and the Corporation Hotel, where the Stones and many other Outlook-booked groups once stayed, is now Middlesbrough's tallest skyscraper. Postcode: TS1

Middlesbrough
Chris Rea "fell in love with a Stainsby girl"

His biggest hit up to 1985, Chris Rea's 'Stainsby Girls' was the vocalist/guitarist's tribute to his wife Joan. Stainsby girls, according to the song's lyrics, weren't the type who loved horses or stayed at home, but loved The Rolling Stones, which obviously met with the approval of Rea, born and bred in Middlesbrough. The Stainsby referred to in the song was Stainsby Secondary Modern School, now renamed Acklam Grange School.

LOCATION 619: the renamed school, which educated all those Stainsby girls, including Chris Rea's future wife Joan, is two miles south-west of the centre of Middlesbrough at Lodore Grove, Acklam, postcode, TS5 8PB

Yorkshire: North

Scarborough
Made in Sheffield, shot in Scarborough

The Stephen Joseph Theatre (Britain's first theatre in the round) appears on the cover of Richard Hawley's 2005 Coles Corner album. The real lovers' meeting place was actually in Sheffield, but Scarborough's town centre theatre was an ideal 21st-century substitute for the photo shoot.

LOCATION 620: in the centre of Scarborough at the junction of Westborough and Northway, postcode YO11 1JW

The actual (almost identical) Coles Corner lacked this substitute location's facility to light up the album cover wording

Born in YORKSHIRE: NORTH

Paul Banks, guitar, Shed Seven (b. 6 Jul 1973, **York**)

John Barry, film score composer (b. 3 Nov 1933, **York**, d. 30 Jan 2011)

Arthur Brown (b. 24 Jun 1942, **Whitby**)

Chris Corner, Sneaker Pimps/IAMX (b. **Middlesbrough**)

David Coverdale, vocals, Whitesnake (b. 22 Sep 1951, **Saltburn-by-the-Sea**)

Stuart Fletcher, bass, The Seahorses (b. 16 Jan 1976, **York**)

Vin Garbutt, folk singer (b. 20 Nov 1947, **Middlesbrough**)

Alistair Griffin, singer-songwriter (b. 1 Nov 1977, **Middlesbrough**)

Chris Helme, vocals, The Seahorses (b. 22 Jul 1971, **York**)

Richard March, bass, Pop Will Eat Itself (b. 4 Mar 1965, **York**)

Micky Moody, guitar, Juicy Lucy/ Whitesnake (b. 30 Aug 1950, **Middlesbrough**)

Chris Norman, vocals, Smokie (b. 25 Oct 1950, **Redcar**)

Charles O'Connor, Horslips (b. 7 Sep 1948, **Middlesbrough**)

Chris Rea (b. 4 Mar 1951, **Middlesbrough**)

Paul Rodgers, vocals/guitar, Bad Company/Free/Queen (b. 17 Dec 1949, **Middlesbrough**)

Pete Trewavas, bass, Marillion (b. 15 Jan 1959, **Middlesbrough**)

Charlie Whitney, guitar, Family (b. 24 Jun 1944, **Skipton**)

Pete York, drums, The Spencer Davis Group (b. 15 Aug 1942, **Redcar**)

Scotch Corner
Man's turtle tripping café

'Scotch Corner' is a nine-minute-plus track on Welsh band Man's most successful album Rhinos, Winos + Lunatics. According to the 1974 album's liner notes, the song was inspired by the band's encounter at the Scotch Corner transport café with a man who looked like a turtle who was on his way to the Lake District to commit suicide. Deke Leonard, Man guitarist and songwriter, explains: "It was a psychedelic experience. We were on our way back from Scotland and all tripping. We called in at the café on Scotch Corner. It was all a bit shabby. We noticed a guy who looked like a turtle. So it was inspired by being there but nothing actually happened."

LOCATION 621: an important refuelling point on the A1, Scotch Corner is approximately seven miles south of Darlington. Postcode: DL10 6NP

Photo: David Wala

Stockton-on-Tees
Vinyl flourishes at Sound It Out

Teesside's last remaining vinyl record shop survives and is the revered subject of a movie documentary made by local film-maker Jeanie Finlay. Sound It Out's vast range of "ABBA to Zappa" sleeves can be thumbed in the wonderfully ramshackle shop surroundings in the back streets of Stockton.

LOCATION 622: Stockton town centre, 15a Yarm Street, postcode TS18 3DR

Midlands band Superfood do an in-store performance at Sound It Out on Record Store Day 2014

Scarborough
Martin Carthy's folk lesson to Paul Simon

Once a medieval fair for tradespeople and now a more modest entertainment-based celebration, Scarborough Fair was the inspiration for a folk song made internationally famous by Simon and Garfunkel. Paul Simon first learned the old ballad on his folk exploration of Britain in the Sixties, when introduced to the song by London folk club regular Martin Carthy.

It was Carthy's 20th-century arrangement of the traditional ballad the American duo used when recording the track, which appeared first on their 1966 album Parsley, Sage, Rosemary and Thyme, then the Graduate film soundtrack LP in 1968. Covers and variations of the song run into the hundreds, including Bob Dylan's take on Carthy's arrangement of the traditional 'Scarborough Fair', which he recorded as 'Girl from the North Country' in 1963.

LOCATION 623: on the North Sea coast, Scarborough is Yorkshire's largest holiday resort. The present-day Scarborough Fair celebrations take place in the town in the month of September. Postcode: YO11 1JW

ROCK ATLAS UK & IRELAND EDITION **387**

Yorkshire: South

*T*here's a very real pride in the city of Sheffield that consumes the more thoughtful, local, musical wordsmiths Richard Hawley and Jarvis Cocker. The latter's poetry is literally writ large on the wall of a student hall while Hawley is a walking Sheffield information centre, name-checking the place in album titles and lyrics and once appropriately recording live in the city's Hawleys Tyres & Exhausts centre on Bridge Road. There's even a Hawley Street close by in a city centre crammed full of great clubs (The Leadmill, The Boardwalk) and great pubs, (The Grapes and The Pack Horse) that have witnessed the birth of The Clash through to the Arctic Monkeys. Northern Soul, electronica and Britpop all owe Sheffield a debt of gratitude for boosting their profiles and even the memories left by demolished music meccas The Limit and the King Mojo linger on powerfully thanks to online forums. If you like your legends of the rock variety, Sheffield does too. The first two acts to be accorded the honour of a star on the city's Walk of Fame were Joe Cocker and Def Leppard.

Doncaster
Never mind the Sex Pistols, here's the Tax Exiles

The Sex Pistols' first Doncaster appearance in 1976 was an event met with a good deal of indifference. On August 24, 1977, the Pistols' return to the Outlook club was only possible when the band changed their name to The Tax Exiles to avoid the ban that was widespread in British venues at the time. Despised nationwide by local authorities, but with three Top 40 singles under their belt, the band were still almost three months away from their Never Mind the Bollocks, Here's the Sex Pistols album release, which would enter the chart at No.1 on November 12. But as life-changing experiences go there was one particular gig at the Outlook during 1977's 'Summer of Hate' that Sheffield music fans still rave about today. A 75 pence ticket bought them a night to remember when The Ramones laid waste to the Outlook, supported by Talking Heads.

LOCATION 624: depressingly demolished, the Outlook was on Trafford Way, postcode DN1

Sheffield 2
Soul central at Samantha's

While Wigan had its Casino and Stoke had The Torch, Sheffield's Northern Soul hotspot was a long upstairs room above the city's Silver Blades ice skating rink. Catering for a wide cross-section of dance fans, Samantha's reigned supreme from 1973 to 1977, with resident DJ John Vincent manning the decks and turntables.

LOCATION 625: Samantha's (now the building operating as Stars Party Suites) is on the main A61 south out of Sheffield city centre on Queens Road, postcode S2 4DF

High Green
Champagne chart rundown at The Pack Horse

This is the pub where the Arctic Monkeys, and as many of their fans who could squeeze in with them, first heard the news they had made their chart debut at No.1. On Sunday October 23, 2005, requesting the landlord to switch on the chart rundown on the pub radio, the band settled down to toast their success at whichever point 'I Bet You Look Good on the Dancefloor' entered the Top 40. The noisy gathering were not disappointed.

LOCATION 626: the northernmost part of suburban Sheffield. The Pack Horse is at 23 Pack Horse Lane, High Green, postcode S35 3HY

"I think The Sugababes had a big tune out the same week and we just thought, 'There's no way this is gonna happen. It's great if we even got **TOP 10**.' And then they played the Sugababes tune at No.2 and everyone cheered. People were jumping on pool tables, and it were all champagne and nonsense 🔊🔊

ALEX TURNER
talking to Mojo magazine

Above: the single release that set everything in motion for the Arctic Monkeys

Below: The Pack Horse, where the band celebrated being No.1 for the first time. Their affinity for the place stretches beyond music. Guitarist Jamie Cook plays right back for the pub's football team, who played a Sunday League cup final in 2010 at Bramall Lane, home of Sheffield United

Photo: Peter Tarleton

Yorkshire: South

Sheffield 1
Grapes pub debut for the Arctics

Friday the 13th was the date of the Arctic Monkeys' first gig back in June 2003. The band had been playing together for 18 months prior to this subsequently historic booking but had no master plan mapped out to climb the slippery pole of rock stardom. But, confidence boosted by this and a second Grapes gig quickly led to the first Arctic Monkeys demo recordings. By October 2005 they were the nation's favourites, when 'I Bet You Look Good on the Dancefloor' hit the top of the singles chart.

" That was our first [gig], in this pub called The Grapes. About 30 people there, in this very TINY ROOM. There's bigger bathrooms than that room "

ALEX TURNER
Monkey frontman talking to Mojo

LOCATION 627: the 60-capacity upstairs venue is at the Grapes pub, 80 Trippet Lane, in the city centre, postcode S1 4EL

Early Monkeys starting point with a photo shoot for a radar piece in NME that gave the band its first national coverage: Friday the 13th didn't prove unlucky for the Arctic Monkeys

Photo: Dean Chalkey/NME

Photo: Peter Tarleton

Where it all began for Def Leppard and Steve Clark's headstone – a point of pilgrimage for Def Leppard fans

Photos: Peter Tarleton

Sheffield 2 and 6
Def Leppard connections

Def Leppard rehearsed for the first time in a redundant spoon factory for a £5 weekly rental, near Sheffield United's football ground at Bramall Lane. The location holds special memories for the band's bass player Rick Savage, who came close to making a career in football playing for United, despite supporting Sheffield Wednesday, the club located at Hillsborough, which in turn was the birthplace of their now deceased guitarist Steve Clark, buried in the nearby Wisewood Cemetery.

LOCATIONS 628 and 629: Stag Works (the former spoon factory turned rehearsal facility) is at 84 John Street, postcode S2 4QU. Steve Clark's black granite gravestone is plot 1697, section D, just inside the entrance of Wisewood Cemetery, Loxley Road, postcode S6 4TD

Sheffield 1
Joe Cocker and Def Leppard are Town Hall giants

Nominated by the city's residents and honoured with a pavement plaque are two world-famous music legends. Former gas fitter Joe Cocker, who was born in Sheffield and grew up at 38 Tasker Road, Crookes, has one and Sheffield's hard-rocking exports Def Leppard have the other. Both can be visited at the Sheffield Legends Walk of Fame, outside the Town Hall.

LOCATION 630: Pinstone Street, city centre, postcode S1 2HH

Photo: Peter Tarleton

Yorkshire: South

Sheffield 1, 3 and 8
Richard Hawley's guide to Sheffield

Postal districts 1, 3 and 8 don't cover the half of it, as can be seen from this section's introduction. Born in Sheffield, raised in the city suburbs of Pitsmoor and Kelham Island, musician and producer Richard Hawley takes every opportunity to reference local place names in the titles of his record releases. First came Lowedges (2003), then Coles Corner (2005), Lady's Bridge (2007) and Truelove's Gutter (2009). Even his 2001 album, Late Night Final, a title that echoed the cry of Sheffield newspaper vendors, carried a cover image of Hawley devouring the local paper in Castle Market's Sharon's Café. Continuing this local theme, Hawley chose Hawley's Tyres & Exhausts centre for the launch of his Lady's Bridge album.

LOCATIONS 631, 632, 633, 634, 635 and 636: Lowedges is a residential area around six miles south-west of the city centre, postcode S8 7. Cole's Corner was named after the sight of the old Cole Brothers department store in the city centre, where Fargate meets Church Street, postcode S1 2HE. The city's Lady's Bridge spans the River Don, postcode S3 8LB. Truelove's Gutter was named after the 18th-century publican Thomas Truelove, whose drains, according to historians, ran into the gutter of Castle Street, postcode S3 8LT. Sharon's Café was at 133 Castle Market in the city centre, postcode S1 2AF, before closing in 2013. Hawley's Tyres & Exhausts is at 53 Bridge Street, postcode S3 8NS

No stranger to performing in unusual places, Richard Hawley showcased his Lady's Bridge album in this appropriately named Sheffield 'Hawleys' venue

Richard Hawley Late Night Final

Above: Richard Hawley in Sharon's Café

66 Sheffield's couples, lovers, friends, mums and dads or whatever, would meet [there]. I've always found it quite a romantic notion - how many kids in Sheffield are knocking about as a result of a meeting at Coles Corner? **99**
Richard Hawley

66 It's a really ancient fording point. It was originally built out of wood in 1140 by a Norman prince, and it was rebuilt after the great Sheffield floods of the 1840s. The title is a metaphor too; it's about leaving the past behind **99**
Richard Hawley describes Lady's Bridge for Uncut magazine

66 I'm into local history and I was looking through manuscripts from the 1700s when I saw that street name - Truelove's Gutter - opposite where you once had a pub, the Black Swan. The Sex Pistols played there and it's now called The Boardwalk. So while I wasn't looking for the album title, it just appeared **99**
Richard Hawley, interviewed by Mojo magazine

Photo: Peter Tarleton

"A **HEADY COCKTAIL** of sweat, leather, sound and fury, beer and vodka and limes **"**

MARTIN FRY
of ABC describes The Leadmill

Photo: Jamie Boynton

Sheffield 1
"Sweat and leather" at The Leadmill

Gaining a reputation, according to NME, as a cross between a thrifty working men's club and Manchester's Haçienda, The Leadmill has enjoyed a starry three decades since first opening for business in 1980. Despite failing to book Madonna when offered the emerging superstar in 1983, the venue has established itself on the back of thousands of appearances by cool bands and staunch supporters. When Mel C made her solo debut at the club, she was cheered on by an appreciative crowd that included the remaining Spice Girls and David Beckham. Gil Scott-Heron, the Bay City Rollers, Rose Royce, the Sugarhill Gang with Grandmaster Melle Mel and just about every indie-guitar band under the sun have all graced the former flour mill.

LOCATION 637: a short stroll south of the city centre at 6 Leadmill Road, postcode S1 4SE

Far left: The rather grand outside and, above, Graham Coxon performing inside The Leadmill

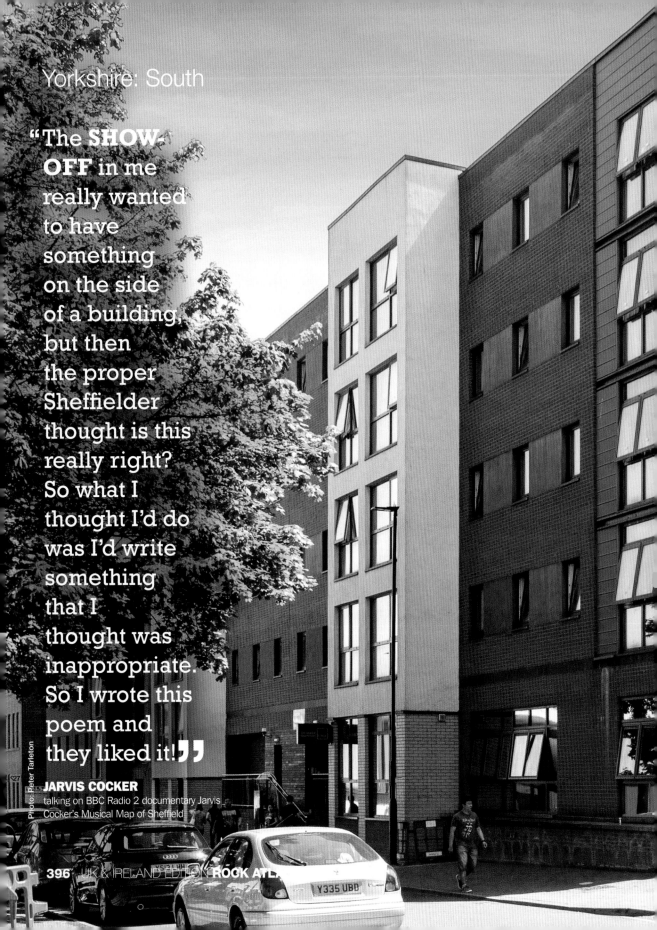

"The **SHOW-OFF** in me really wanted to have something on the side of a building, but then the proper Sheffielder thought is this really right? So what I thought I'd do was I'd write something that I thought was inappropriate. So I wrote this poem and they liked it!"

JARVIS COCKER
talking on BBC Radio 2 documentary Jarvis Cocker's Musical Map of Sheffield

Photo: Peter Tarleton

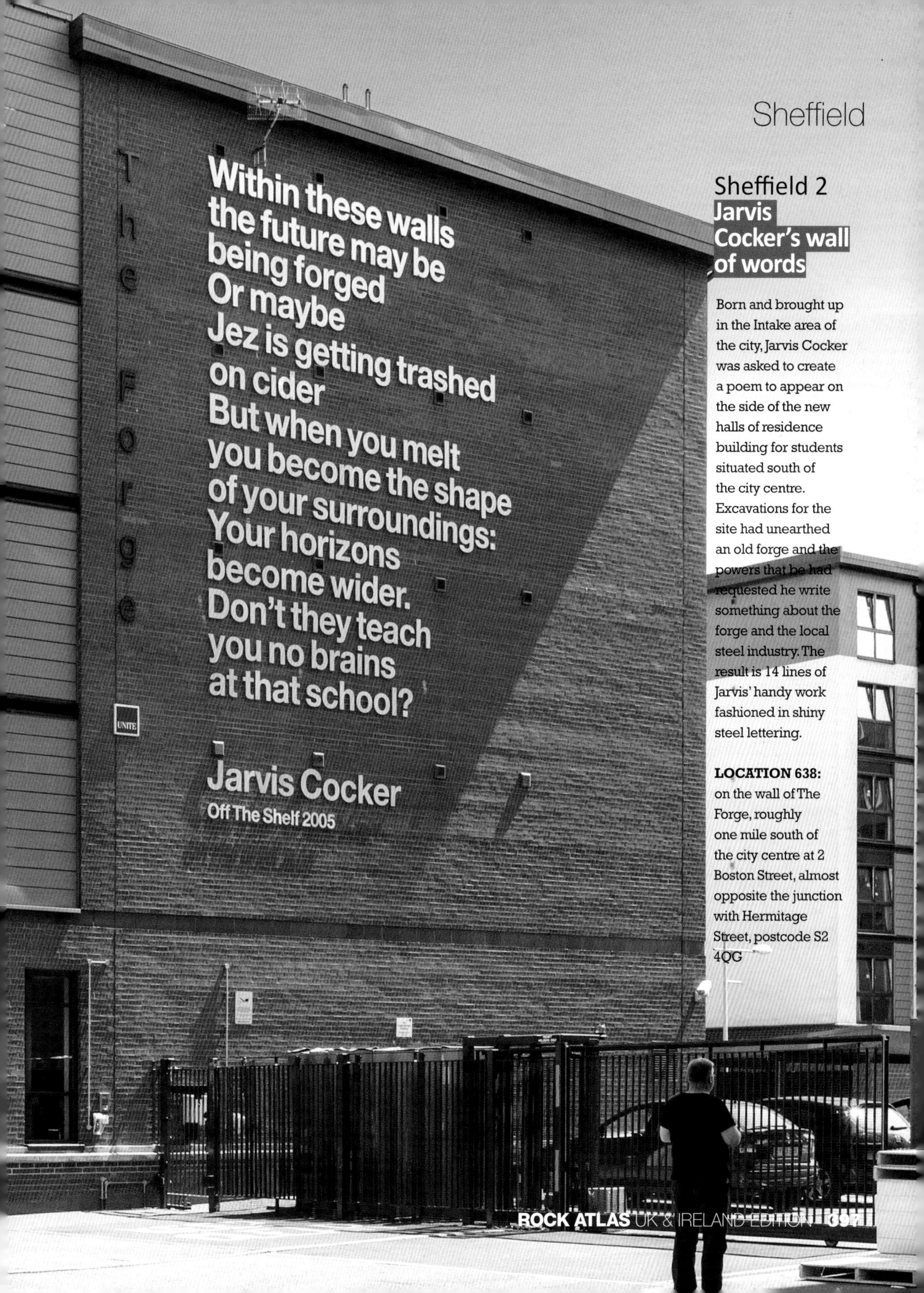

The Forge

**Within these walls
the future may be
being forged
Or maybe
Jez is getting trashed
on cider
But when you melt
you become the shape
of your surroundings:
Your horizons
become wider.
Don't they teach
you no brains
at that school?**

Jarvis Cocker
Off The Shelf 2005

UNITE

Sheffield 2
Jarvis Cocker's wall of words

Born and brought up in the Intake area of the city, Jarvis Cocker was asked to create a poem to appear on the side of the new halls of residence building for students situated south of the city centre. Excavations for the site had unearthed an old forge and the powers that be had requested he write something about the forge and the local steel industry. The result is 14 lines of Jarvis' handy work fashioned in shiny steel lettering.

LOCATION 638: on the wall of The Forge, roughly one mile south of the city centre at 2 Boston Street, almost opposite the junction with Hermitage Street, postcode S2 4QG

Yorkshire: South

Sheffield 1
Dark, sticky and glorious: The Limit

Sheffield had a certain number of nightclub licences, and for one to open another had to close. It's thought that was the inspiration for the appropriately named The Limit. From 1978, this small basement club played an essential part in the development of early Eighties synth pop and also hosted gigs from eventual legends Simple Minds, U2, local-turned-national favourites Cabaret Voltaire, Pulp and the Human League. Genre-specific nights, such as reggae on Wednesdays, saw The Limit create a healthily broad booking policy with Aswad, Steel Pulse and UB40 plus ska acts The Specials and The Beat. On big nights the capacity of 330 was dangerously trebled and the variety of music played and watched live meant that the club experienced its fair share of tribal violence from mods, goths, skinheads and punks all mingling together. Despite this, and the unbelievably beer-sticky carpet flooring, The Limit, along with its handily placed next door pie and chip shop, was for many Sheffield music fans the perfect location for a night out. Neil Anderson's book Take It to The Limit gives the full, sometimes gory, but always glorious story of the club's 13-year existence.

LOCATION 639: the building where The Limit stood is no more, replaced by the current apartment block at 70 West Street, near the junction with Carver Street in the city centre, postcode S1 4DZ

Sheffield 3
Soul and Hendrix at Stringfellow's Mojo

Soul music's Sixties popularity coincided with the opening of a new club catering for the very American style of music in a quiet road north of the city centre. The Mojo Club (or King Mojo) was situated in a Victorian bow-window-fronted house run by local youngster Peter Stringfellow, who later became the internationally famous celebrity nightclub owner. Stringfellow and his two brothers would advertise a records-only night once a week and hype up the playlist in the local paper. When hosting live acts, the place boasted Edwin Starr's first UK appearance and attracted the cream of US soul and R&B to this innovative new venture, which made its debut in 1964. Soon attracting a dedicated and enthusiastic mod clientele, the Mojo hosted The Who, The Kinks and The Small Faces at the out-of-town address in Pitsmoor Road. Much like Liverpool's Casbah Coffee Club, this residential road venue was decorated inside with pop art wall murals and posters, and when the psychedelic era arrived Stringfellow switched the musical emphasis, renaming the place The Beautiful King Mojo. Shortly after booking Jimi Hendrix, who was the subject of a botched drugs raid by the local constabulary, the club closed in February 1967 when some neighbours campaigned against the noise and nuisance caused by a hugely exciting venture in a rather inappropriate suburban location.

LOCATION 640: Pitsmoor Road is two miles north of the city centre, but the Pitsmoor Road junction with Roe Lane, where The King Mojo Club house once stood, is now a white-painted housing block, postcode S3 9AU

> "It was one bus into town, from town to the Wicker, another bus up Pitsmoor Road, maybe even another bus! You had to **REALLY WANT** to go to the Mojo Club!"
>
> **PETER STRINGFELLOW**

Photo: Peter Tarleton

Sheffield 3
The Clash debut at the Black Swan

Tucked away in a corner of the city centre, thus far safe from the developers' wrecking ball, is a music venue that has attracted Genesis, AC/DC, and, for their one and only Sheffield gig, the Sex Pistols. The Pistols' appearance coincided with the Black Swan's biggest claim to fame as the venue for The Clash's debut on July 4, 1976, with the Pistols as their support act. Now The Boardwalk, this lively venue's name went through earlier identities as the aforementioned Black Swan and the Mucky Duck for a period. During its half-century existence, the place has rolled with the times, successfully staying in business as it staged gigs by everyone from local-boy-made-rock-superstar Joe Cocker to dynamic glam-rockers The Sweet and, more recently, the likes of David Gray and Seasick Steve. At the time of writing the venue is closed and in limbo, awaiting the next chapter in its illustrious history.

LOCATION 641: at the corner of Bank Street and Snig Hill near the city centre. Postcode: S3 8NA

The Boardwalk still carries a visual reminder of its heyday in the Seventies, when it was regularly packed to the rafters as the Black Swan

Sheffield 11
Wham Bar debut for the Human League

Based at Hallam University's Psalter Lane campus, the Wham Bar (also known as Bar 2) was where local synth-pop legends the Human League performed live for the first time on June 12, 1978.

LOCATION 642: Psalter Lane campus was the smallest of three Hallam University campus locations at Brincliffe, a couple of miles south-west of Sheffield city centre.

Postcode: S11 9BG. Status: the site is currently under what appears to be lengthy redevelopment so a plaque commemorating the Human League's debut may be missing

Yorkshire: South

Photo: Peter Tarleton

Sheffield 10
Vinyl heaven at Record Collector

Sheffield band Little Man Tate bigged-up their local record shop by featuring it on the cover of their 2007 debut album About What You Know. The photo shoot captured the quartet rummaging in the vinyl half of Record Collector.

LOCATION 643: Record Collector can be visited on the A57, a couple of miles west of the city centre at 233 Fulwood Road, postcode S10 3BA

The largest independent record shop in Sheffield, Record Collector was established in 1978 by Barry Everard, who still runs the place today

Born YORKSHIRE: SOUTH

Rick Allen, drums, Def Leppard (b. 1 Nov 1963, Sheffield)

Nick Banks, drums, Pulp (b. 28 Jul 1965, Rotherham)

Paul Carrack (b. 22 Apr 1951, Sheffield)

Joanne Catherall, vocals, Human League (b. 18 Sep 1962, Sheffield)

Steve Clark, guitar Def Leppard (b. 23 Apr 1960, Sheffield, d. 8 Jan 1991)

Jarvis Cocker (b. 19 Sep 1963, Sheffield)

Joe Cocker (b. 20 May 1944, Sheffield)

Jamie Cook, guitar, Arctic Monkeys (b. 8 Jul 1985, High Green, Sheffield)

Joe Elliott, vocals, Def Leppard (b. 1 Aug 1959, Sheffield)

Glenn Gregory, vocals, Heaven 17 (b. 16 May 1958, Sheffield)

Richard Hawley (b. 17 Jan 1967, Sheffield)

Matt Helders, drums, Arctic Monkeys/Mongrel (b. 7 May 1986, Sheffield)

Jon McClure, Reverend and The Makers (b. 22 Dec 1981, Sheffield)

Steve Mackey, bass, Pulp (b. 10 Nov 1966, Sheffield)

Adrian McNally, The Unthanks (b. 28 May 1975, Chapeltown, Sheffield)

Ian Craig Marsh, keyboards, Heaven 17 (b. 11 Nov 1956, Sheffield)

Nick O'Malley, bass guitar, Arctic Monkeys (b. 5 Jul 1985, Sheffield)

Steve Rothery, guitar, Marillion (b. 25 Nov 1959, Brampton)

Kate Rusby (b. 4 Dec 1973, Penistone)

Rick Savage, bass, Def Leppard (b. 2 Dec 1960, Sheffield)

Russell Senior, guitar, Pulp (b. 18 May 1961, Sheffield)

Jon Stewart, guitar, Sleeper (b. 12 Sep 1966, Sheffield)

Peter Stringfellow (b. 17 Oct 1940, Sheffield)

Susanne Sulley, vocals, Human League (b. 22 Mar 1963, Sheffield)

Alex Turner, vocals/guitar, Arctic Monkeys (b. 6 Jan 1986, High Green, Sheffield)

Martyn Ware, Heaven 17 (b. 19 May 1956, Sheffield)

Mark White, guitar/keyboards, ABC (b. 1 Apr 1961, Sheffield)

Mick Whitnall, Babyshambles (b. 7 Nov 1968, Doncaster)

Chris Wolstenholme, bass, Muse (b. 2 Dec 1978, Sheffield)

Yorkshire: West

*W*est Yorkshire seems to have a strong attraction for American blues legends. Big Bill Broonzy and Champion Jack Dupree are remembered with fondness by the good folk of Glasshoughton and Ovenden, while BB King visited Dupree in Halifax, Sonny Terry and Brownie McGhee performed in the same town and Louis Armstrong played Batley. Then there's the story of Kurt Cobain and the Duchess of York's sofa, a beer named in honour of a visit to Ilkley by Jimi Hendrix, a fruit-fancying Michael Jackson in Halifax, the rain-lashed Krumlin Festival and the setting for the recording of one of rock's greatest live albums in Leeds, a city that also boasts a song-writing visit by Graham Nash and a special Mark Knopfler gig. Halifax was the location for Dusty Springfield's first solo debut, and it was local boy Don Lang who sang the theme tune to '50s BBC TV's ground-breaking show for teens, Six-Five Special. The Cribs have been honoured by a Hollywood-style star in Wakefield, Wintersett is something of a spiritual home for The Unthanks, and the county currently hosts one of Britain's best-attended festivals, which has seen Radiohead, Kings of Leon and just about every other act that you might describe as the world's biggest band play Bramham Park in recent years.

Glasshoughton
Big Bill Broonzy at the Cosy Cinema

In a small West Yorkshire town on the outskirts of Castleford, local music fans had an unexpected injection of the blues one Saturday night in June 1956 when the American legend Big Bill Broonzy played a one-off show at the Cosy Cinema, Glasshoughton. This unusual personal appearance occurred when the cinema owner called in a favour from a showbiz impresario friend. Broonzy, the Arkansas-raised grandson of a cotton-picking slave, had recently played a Leeds jazz club and was dispatched by the impresario from Leeds to the outskirts of Castleford, at Glasshoughton, to repay the favour.

LOCATION 644: following its closure, the Cosy Cinema became part of the Castletex textile factory before disappearing completely to make way for flats at Lagentium Plaza, Leeds Road, Glasshoughton. Postcode: WF10 4PP

Yorkshire: West

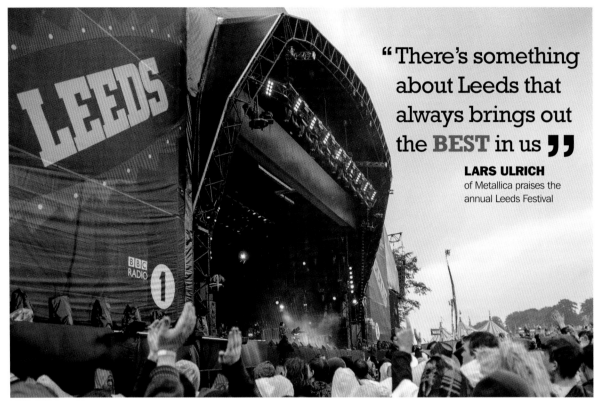

"There's something about Leeds that always brings out the **BEST** in us"

LARS ULRICH
of Metallica praises the annual Leeds Festival

Bramham Park
Home of the Leeds festival

Held on the same weekend in August as the annual Reading festival and sharing the same bill, the Leeds festival has been held at Bramham Park since 2003. It consistently attracts the best-known headline acts in the world and gets some heavyweight endorsement from rock's biggest names including Nicky Wire, who says: "If the Manic Street Preachers have a spiritual festival home then it is the Leeds festival. They have the most knowledgeable fans of rock music and an instinctive appreciation of intelligent music and entertainment."

LOCATION 645: the festival site is approximately five miles south of Wetherby at Bramham Park, accessed by leaving junction 45 of the A1M. Postcode: LS23 6N

Halifax
Dusty's debut on Broad Street

Already nationally famous as one-third of hit trio The Springfields and a panellist on BBC TV's Juke Box Jury, Dusty Springfield made her solo debut at the Odeon cinema on November 8, 1963. A "special guest star" addition to a bill featuring Freddie and The Dreamers, Brian Poole & The Tremeloes and The Searchers, the nervous Dusty performed what would become her first solo chart hit, 'I Only Want to be with You'. "I have never been so scared in all my life" said Dusty on making her world debut as a solo performer in Halifax.

LOCATION 646: the striking art deco cinema still stands (now a bingo hall) on the corner of Broad Street and Orange Street in the centre of Halifax, postcode HX1 1YA

A rare picture of Dusty in Halifax

Photo: www.smalltownsaturdaynight.co.uk

Halifax
Michael Jackson comes to town

When The Jacksons played the Civic Theatre, on February 19, 1979, Michael Jackson was already a solo superstar with five UK Top 10 singles and two US No.1s behind him. By all accounts his ego was very much under control on his visit to Halifax, only shyly requesting a bowl of fruit for the dressing room. Not so the rest of his brothers, two of whom had fallen out on the journey to the venue. The disharmony led to them allegedly refusing to perform until theatre manager Robbie Robinson read the riot act and the shame-faced Jacksons took to the stage and were, according to assistant manager Les Milner, "superb". Despite the management's problems that day, The Jacksons paved the way for more appearances by Motown and soul acts at the Civic with Martha Reeves, Freda Payne, The Supremes and Smokey Robinson all heading for this West Yorkshire pop hotspot.

LOCATION 647: in the town centre, the Civic Theatre, now renamed The Victoria Theatre, still stands at 2 Fountain Street, postcode HX1 1BP

Ilkley
Hendrix gig halted at the Troutbeck

The spa town of Ilkley was the unlikely final stopping point on a 1967 UK tour by The Jimi Hendrix Experience. On March 12, they played to a packed audience at the Troutbeck hotel, but the trio had barely got into their psychedelic stride when the local police force made a decision to halt the show. In an early act of health and safety enforcement, the trio and a 400-strong crowd were forced to file out into the cold evening air. Although subsequent Daily Express "riot" headlines were wide of the mark, some of the more disgruntled fans who

Photo: www.smalltownsaturdaynight.co.uk

The Jacksons' security guards insisted on "no pictures" during their Halifax visit: this shot of Michael backstage was the unique exception

had squeezed in to see their heroes did damage to some hotel furnishings. In 2008, the nearby Crescent Inn named a beer "Jimi's", created by brewer Moorhouse's, to commemorate the guitarist's stay at the hotel while in town to play the Troutbeck. "My recollection of Jimi was that he was quiet, polite, friendly and funny - and he enjoyed a nice cup of tea" said Danny Pollock, who booked Jimi Hendrix for the Troutbeck hotel.

LOCATIONS 648 and 649: a nursing home now occupies the buildings where the Troutbeck hotel once booked The Jimi Hendrix Experience at Crossbeck Road, postcode LS29 9JP. The Crescent Inn, where they once served Jimi's, is in Ilkley town centre on Brook Street, postcode LS29 8DG

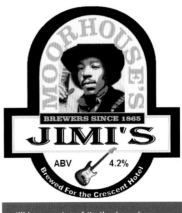

I'll have a pint of Jimi's please!

Yorkshire: West

Leeds
Kurt Cobain and the Duchess of York's sofa

Sandwiched between two John Peel sessions for the BBC, Nirvana played a gig on October 25th 1989 at the Duchess of York pub in Leeds city centre. The Seattle band's visit to Leeds gained legendary status when singer Kurt Cobain crashed out in the upstairs dressing room after the gig and slept the night on a piece of furniture that has since enjoyed an extended life as the most famous rock 'n' roll sofa in the world. The extended life was prolonged by Cobain's use of the rather tatty settee that had already attracted the autographs of many musicians relaxing on it in the pre and post-performance gigging hours at the pub. Originally purchased at auction for £6 by promoter John Keenan, the sofa's increasing fame and value as a national treasure was acknowledged by Sheffield's National Centre for Popular Music, who snapped it up for its collection. The Duchess, much loved for its patronage of emerging bands from all over the UK, closed for music business on March 26, 2000. Fittingly, Chumbawamba, billed with their famous lyric line "I Get Knocked Down" on tickets, were the last act to play The Duchess before renovations saw the building transformed into a fashion store.

LOCATION 650: despite The Duchess of York's demise, it's still possible to cast your eyes upwards to the first floor of what is now the Leeds branch of Hugo Boss and imagine Kurt Cobain curled up on that sofa at 71 Vicar Lane. Postcode: LS1 6QA

Holmfield
Beatles, Small Faces and R.E.M. at Holdsworth House

At the height of Beatlemania, and amid enormous security, the four Beatles and manager Brian Epstein celebrated John Lennon's 24th birthday here in the opulent surroundings of Holdsworth House Hotel. On the evening of October 9, 1964, the 17th-century Jacobean manor house, then known as the Cavalier Country Club, was the first overnight stop on The Beatles' first bill-topping tour. Earlier that day, they had opened the nationwide shows at the Bradford Gaumont, before heading out of the city to this country retreat, aided by a road block and accompanied by a police escort. Despite suffering a bout of toothache, Lennon, by all accounts, enjoyed his celebration meal before retiring to bed. He and Ringo Starr slept in a bedroom which is now one of the hotel's offices, while Paul McCartney and George Harrison were given the Ayrton Room, which these days is used for conferences. A popular haunt for rock stars and celebrities, the hotel's reputation and Beatles connection spread as far as Athens, Georgia, with R.E.M. booking in as guests during the American band's Yorkshire visit to play two £1.6 million-grossing gigs at Huddersfield's McAlpine Stadium in July 1995. On learning that the landlord of the local pub, The Ivy House, was a big R.E.M. fan, Michael Stipe and the rest of the band paid him a surprise visit. Later that same week hotel staff were astonished when a "so glad you are feeling better" fax came through from US President Bill Clinton and wife Hillary for bass player Mike Mills, who had recently undergone abdominal surgery. And the stories of rock royalty at Holdsworth House don't stop there. In the Sixties, John Lee Hooker and Cliff Richard both enjoyed stays and current owner Gail Moss (then a teenager) recalls The Small Faces checking-in and giving her a lift to school the next morning on their way to Halifax to do a spot of shopping.

LOCATION 651: Holdsworth House Hotel & Restaurant, near Holmfield, is three miles north of Halifax and seven miles west of Bradford, east of the A467. Postcode: HX2 9TG

" Although I wasn't a huge music fan I knew the band were just about the biggest in the world at the time, so imagine my son Nicholas' reaction when I rang him at boarding school to tell him the news that **E.R.M.** [sic] are coming to stay! "
GAIL MOSS

The Beatles arrive at Holdsworth House. The bill for two rooms, bed and breakfast and a slap-up birthday dinner for John Lennon was £42

Photo: www.smalltownsaturdaynight.co.uk

Photo: John Wharton

Krumlin
The mother of all rain-lashed festivals

It must have seemed like a great idea at the time. Pick August, traditionally the hottest month, find a peaceful piece of Yorkshire and find an equally hot line-up of established and up-and-coming acts. However, this storm-ravaged three-day festival in a moorland valley suffered power failures, a ramshackle running order, and medical treatment was required for hundreds of fans suffering from exposure. The Yorkshire Folk, Blues & Jazz Festival, to give it its proper name, did set out to provide a varied bill of acts as the name suggests, although how

many of the 30 or so artists showed up or finished performances is debatable. Well-received gutsy sets by Elton John and Georgie Fame helped save the first day following a hugely frustrating five-hour wait by fans for the festival to begin. Day two started promisingly enough with The Groundhogs, Alexis Korner and Graham Bond mentioned in dispatches for some classic British blues before the weather turned particularly nasty as Zoot Money and Alan Price brought proceedings to an inclement close on Saturday. The driving rain turned the site into

a freezing mudbath overnight, and when many of the big names advertised failed to appear or bailed out at the eleventh hour, the final Sunday line-up of acts was literally washed away. "Ginger Baker in fact turned up on the Sunday to play free of charge, not even asking for his expenses, but by that time the festival had been abandoned" said Walter Lloyd, Chairman of Civil Aid, who looked after the welfare of the 15,000 fans.

LOCATION 652: Krumlin, near Barkisland, six miles south-west of Halifax, postcode HX4 0AT

The somewhat exposed Krumlin Festival site before the heavens opened

Inset: Before the storm: The Groundhogs on stage at the Yorkshire Folk, Blues & Jazz Festival

Photo: University of Leeds

At the unveiling of the plaque by Roger Daltrey and Pete Townshend, Daltrey gave special thanks to the University unions that had given bands places to play back in the early Seventies when venues were thin on the ground

Leeds
The Who record the greatest ever live album

A blue plaque on the wall of the University of Leeds refectory marks the spot where The Who recorded what the commemorative disc says was "the most celebrated live album of its generation". And they're not exaggerating; Live at Leeds topped Q magazine's list of greatest live albums and even The New York Times weighed in with a "best ever" accolade. Despite the fact that The Who had to plug in to the refectory's kitchen electricity power point, the performance on February 14, 1970 at the 2,000-capacity art deco dining hall also charted in Q's list of loudest gigs. Reports suggest the band were even louder when they returned to Leeds to reprise their performance in 2006, although this time the kitchen plug sockets were not required. The University has another rock-related claim to fame. In February 2005, Sir Peter Blake opened a unique gallery dedicated to his music artwork at the University of Leeds' School of Music.

LOCATION 653: the plaque, unveiled by Pete Townshend and Roger Daltrey when they returned to perform Live at Leeds Again, is left of the entrance doors to the refectory building, Cromer Road, postcode LS1 1UH

"I have never taken drugs but I think I now know what a '**HIGH**' must be like. Colleagues suggest that I will have calmed down by Christmas and I ask... 'which Christmas?'"

JOHN STANDERLINE
Leeds University entertainments team member and student electrician on witnessing The Who's 1970 gig

Yorkshire: West

Ovenden
A blues legend settles in Yorkshire

The New Orleans-born bluesman Champion Jack Dupree settled in Britain permanently in 1959 and lived in this village on the outskirts of Halifax after meeting and marrying Yorkshire lass Shirley Harrison. Eleven years after his death in 1992, a wall plaque was unveiled in memory of the pianist who attracted a good few celebrity music pilgrims to make the trip to Ovenden. Local author Trevor Simpson recalls the first time he saw Champion Jack in George Street, Halifax:

"He was getting out of his American station wagon with lace curtains in the back and his name, 'Champion Jack Dupree – Blues Pianist – of New Orleans - LA - USA', emblazoned on each of two side doors in big gold leaf letters. He never locked the car before he strolled across the road into the Griffin pub and he left most people in the street open-mouthed and staring at the car in disbelief at what they had just seen. It was highly unusual to see a black guy at the time."

LOCATION 658: Champion Jack Dupree's home was at 173 Ovenden Way, two miles north of Halifax on the A629. The wall plaque is at the Dean Clough complex in the reception area, near the cafe for the Viaduct Theatre, postcode HX3 5AX

The son of a French black man and Cherokee Indian mother, the internationally acclaimed Champion Jack Dupree entertains members of the Halifax Women's Institute

" Eric Clapton came to visit us in Ovenden. John Lee Hooker and BB King also visited... and dad would do **GUMBO**, red beans with rice and black eyed peas with fish, which everyone loved "

GEORGIANA
Champion Jack Dupree's daughter, quoted from Trevor Simpson's Small Town Saturday Night books

Photo: www.smalltownsaturdaynight.co.uk

Yorkshire: West

Leeds
Mark Knopfler downsizes at The Town & Country Club

In the early Nineties, Dire Straits embarked on a record-shattering world tour witnessed by more than seven million fans in 25 countries. Less than a year later, on July 3, 1993, Dire Straits' frontman Mark Knopfler was back on the road, but this time to a one-off Dire Straits Information Service fans only gig with old friends and fellow Notting Hillbillies band members Brendan Croker and Steve Phillips. In aid of the Kirkstall Valley Association, Leeds, former Leeds University student Knopfler topped the Town & Country Club bill, which also included comedian Fine Time Fontayne and The Silver Donkey Band.

LOCATION 654: The Town & Country Club is now the O2 Academy, 55 Cookridge Street, postcode LS2 3AW

A rare photo of Mark Knopfler and Brendan Croker at The Town & Country Club, snapped by fan Alison Parsons, and Alison's standing-only ticket for the charity gig in 1993

Leeds
Graham Nash's "artistic bonanza"

In 1968, with his days in The Hollies numbered, Graham Nash would pass the time in hotel rooms while on tour writing the kind of songs The Hollies would mostly reject. During a Hollies residency in Leeds, Nash retreated to his Oulton Grove Motel room and wrote what would turn out to be three future Crosby, Stills & Nash songs in one night. 'Right Between the Eyes', 'Lady of the Island' and 'Teach Your Children' might have been an "artistic bonanza", as Nash described it in his autobiography Wild Tales, but the rest of The Hollies didn't want to know and pressed on with their vision of a 'new' way forward by working on an album of Bob Dylan covers.

LOCATION 655: now a Toby Carvery restaurant, Aberford Road, Oulton, postcode LS26 8EJ

Wintersett
Early inspiration for The Unthanks

The reservoir at Wintersett was the inspiration for the band name Rachel Unthank & The Winterset. The folk group's songwriter, producer and band member (and Rachel Unthank's husband) Adrian McNally grew up a couple of miles south of the West Yorkshire reservoir in the mining village of South Hiendley. In 2009, the band name was shortened to The Unthanks but Wintersett - note the place name's spelling with three 't's - still draws McNally and fellow Unthanks band member Chris Price back to the area where they both enjoyed a childhood, living three doors apart on the same street in South Hiendley. "There's a tiny real ale pub [near Wintersett] that Chris and I drink in whenever we're home to see our parents called the Anglers Retreat," says multi-instrumentalist McNally.

LOCATION 656: six miles south-east of Wakefield, the Anglers Retreat public house is a short walk from the reservoir at Ferry Top Lane, Wintersett, postcode WF4 2EB

Born in YORKSHIRE: WEST

Craig Adams, bass, The Mission (b. 4 Apr 1962, **Otley**)

Tasmin Archer, (b. 3 Aug 1963, **Bradford**)

Mel B (Melanie Brown) Spice Girls (b. 29 May 1975, **Leeds**)

Tom Bailey, vocals/keyboards, Thompson Twins (b. 18 Jan 1954, Halifax)

Corinne Bailey Rae (b. 26 Feb 1979, **Leeds**)

Nick "Peanut" Baines, keyboards, Kaiser Chiefs (b. 21 Mar 1978, Leeds)

Sarah Blackwood, vocals, Dubstar (b. 6 May 1971, **Halifax**)

Tim Booth, vocals, James (b. 4 Feb 1960, **Bradford**)

Billy Currie, Ultravox (b. 1 Apr 1950, **Huddersfield**)

Kiki Dee (b. 6 Mar 1947, **Bradford**)

Keith Emerson, keyboards, The Nice/Emerson, Lake and Palmer (b. 2 Nov 1944, **Todmorden**)

David Gedge, vocals, The Wedding Present (b. 23 Apr 1960, Leeds)

Robert Hardy, bass, Franz Ferdinand (b. 16 Aug 1980, **Dewsbury**)

John Helliwell, saxophone, Supertramp (b. 15 Feb 1945, Todmorden)

Nick Hodgson, drums, Kaiser Chiefs (b. 20 Oct 1977, **Leeds**)

Gary Jarman, bass/vocals, The Cribs (b. 20 Oct 1980, **Wakefield**)

Ross Jarman, drums, The Cribs (b. 22 Sep 1984, **Wakefield**)

Ryan Jarman, guitar/vocals, The Cribs (b. 20 Oct 1980, Wakefield)

Don Lang, vocals, Don Lang & His Frantic Five (b. 19 Jan 1925, Halifax, d. 3 Aug 1992)

Derek Leckenby, guitar, Herman's Hermits (b. 14 May 1943, Leeds, d. 4 Jun 1994)

Chris Moyles, radio DJ (b. 22 Feb 1974, **Leeds**)

Danny McNamara, vocals, Embrace (b. 31 Dec 1970, **Bailiff Bridge, Brighouse**)

Richard McNamara, guitar, Embrace (b. 23 Oct, 1972 **Bailiff Bridge, Brighouse**)

Bill Nelson, guitar/vocals, solo and Be-Bop Deluxe (b. 18 Dec 1948, **Wakefield**)

Robert Palmer (b. 19 Jan 1949, **Batley**, d. 26 Sep 2003)

Rhianna (Rhianna Kenny) (b. 7 Jan 1983,**Leeds**)

Simon Rix, bass, Kaiser Chiefs (b. 18 Oct 1977, **Leeds**)

Ed Sheeran (b. 17 Feb 1991, **Halifax**)

Shutty (David Shuttleworth) drums, Terrorvision, (b. 20 Mar 1967, Keighley)

Dave Stead, drums, The Beautiful South (b. 15 Oct 1966, Huddersfield)

Kimberley Walsh, Girls Aloud (b. 20 Nov 1981, **Bradford**)

Andrew "Whitey" White, guitar, Kaiser Chiefs (b. 28 Aug 1974, **Leeds**)

Ricky Wilson, vocals, Kaiser Chiefs (b. 17 Jan 1978, **Keighley**)

The star-struck Jarman brothers, who became The Cribs in 2001

Wakefield
Home town plaque for The Cribs

In 2011, The Cribs and their fans got the news that the local council were to honour the Wakefield band with a commemorative plaque in their home town. The band voiced their Wakefield pride most obviously on the 2005 track 'The Wrong Way to Be' and were immortalised with a Hollywood-style pavement plaque in the city centre for their contribution to the local music scene.

LOCATION 657: the star plaque is at the Bull Ring, just outside the Wakefield Visitor Centre in the heart of the town, postcode WF1 1HB

Scotland

*D*ripping in atmosphere, was how Madonna described the remote beauty of Scotland at the time of her Highland wedding to Guy Ritchie. The remoter corners of the Highlands have certainly drawn admiring visits from the most legendary rock stars. Lennon, McCartney, Page and Dylan have all holidayed, recuperated and rejuvenated themselves or bought into the Highland lifestyle. Johnny Cash had a soft spot for his 'ancestral home' in Fife, Joe Strummer has a forest on the Isle of Skye, and a small part of Prestwick has almost become hallowed ground as the only spot in Britain to have witnessed an appearance by Elvis Presley. But it's a matter of fact that indicates the country's passion for music. Outside of central London, statistics prove that the good folk of Inverness are Britain's most avid music fans. When it comes to shopping for albums, the Entertainment Retailers Association proved that the inhabitants of the Highland city bought, on average, three times the number of albums purchased by the apparently less fanatical music fans of places such as Wigan and Wolverhampton down south. There's no reduction in fanaticism where the actual music created by the country's musicians is concerned, either. Few groups have added "mania" to their moniker in the way Edinburgh's Bay City Rollers matched The Beatles after a year-long residency at the city's Top Storey Club set them on their way and gave the rest of the world Rollermania. Dundee can rightly claim to have hosted one of Queen's most memorable appearances remembered vividly today by dozens of fans who witnessed the live unveiling of 'Bohemian Rhapsody'. And give it up for Glasgow, where rock extrovert Alex Harvey, Postcard Records and Belle & Sebastian all contributed to their own hugely inspirational little worlds. From the tenement blocks of the Gorbals to the rugged quiet of Kintyre, Scotland oozes an eccentric mix of music stories, exemplified by Alex Harvey's recorded investigation to undercover the truth about the Loch Ness monster.

Aberdeen
The Beatles at the Beach

The Beatles' 1963 four-day tour of Scotland wound up here at the art deco seafront Beach Ballroom on January 6. Snow and freezing temperatures characterised the mini tour, which ended just after the band's first hit 'Love Me Do' hit its chart peak of No.17. More than one report suggests they got a mixed reaction, with even some booing during their performance. In 1967, The Who arrived at the Ballroom, but the venue would soon be too parochial for the rock age with the likes of Pete Townshend, Roger Daltrey, Keith Moon and John Entwistle taking on the world at Monterey, Woodstock and the Isle of Wight.

LOCATION 686: still standing and still doing business, although, alas, rarely as a rock 'n' roll venue these days, Beach Promenade, postcode AB24 5NR

A fee of just £45 secured The Beatles for their one and only appearance in Aberdeen at the Beach Ballroom

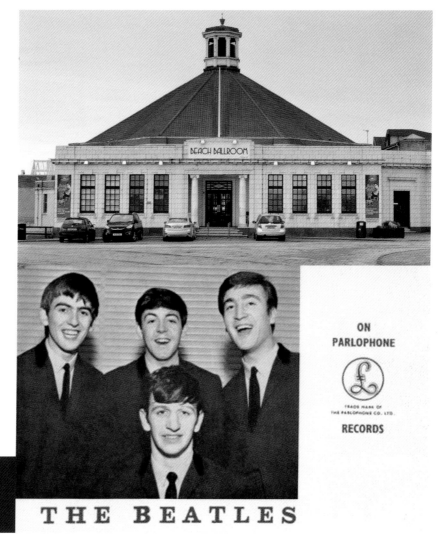

Aberdeen
Whole lotta soul at the Music Hall

Northern Soul didn't get much more northern than Aberdeen, and the passion for it in the Granite City has endured for five decades. Formerly the Assembly Rooms, Aberdeen's Music Hall was a favourite venue for devoted soul fans, who would travel extreme distances to dance to the right records. The place also attracted rock's finest. When Led Zeppelin visited in 1973, the council neglected to lay on the wherewithal for the required light show. Despite the lack of visual entertainment, the boisterous audience got good value for their £1 tickets. Zeppelin put on a gutsy performance one would expect from a band at the height of their powers. The rock gods may no longer visit Scotland's third largest city, but the Music Hall still attracts rock, pop and blues acts with Richard Thompson, John Mayall, Mike and The Mechanics and Kate Rusby all scheduled to appear at the time of writing.

LOCATION 687: Aberdeen Music Hall is still going strong on Union Street, in Aberdeen city centre, postcode AB10 1QS

Scotland

Balado
T in the Park

Growing rapidly since its debut at Strathclyde Country Park in 1994, T in the Park these days turns this Kinross-shire spot into Scotland's fifth biggest town when the annual festival arrives at Balado Park. Aside from attracting rock's biggest names, the festival has seen some exciting live collaborations down the years. In 2002, Noel Gallagher joined with Paul Weller, and 2005 saw Brandon Flowers guest with New Order. The airfield site attracts 85,000 music fans per day over the weekend each summer and is famous for its stunning sunsets over the Ochil Hills. In 2010, Madness even paused mid set and invited the crowd to turn round and admire the view. Appropriately enough for Scotland's biggest festival, Kilmarnock's Biffy Clyro and Paisley's Paolo Nutini were among the headliners in 2014.

LOCATION 688: Balado Park is accessed off the A91 near Kinross, postcode KY13

T in the Park opens its gates and becomes Scotland's fifth largest town every July

Cairnholy
Cope's Interpreter

Although partly inspired by Berkshire's Newbury bypass protests in the mid-Nineties, the setting for the dramatic cover of Julian Cope's 1996 album Interpreter is the group of standing stones known as Cairnholy I in south-west Scotland. As can be seen from the Callanish entry, Cope, a keen archaeologist, has also released albums with standing stone cover images from the Isle of Lewis.

LOCATION 689: near the village of Creetown (postcode DG8 7JH), Dumfries and Galloway, signposted from the A75 down a single-track road

Campbeltown
Paul McCartney's Kintyre hideaways

Purchased in 1966, High Park Farm was a hugely important location in Paul McCartney's life and music. It was here, while still a Beatle, he wrote 'The Long and Winding Road', said by some to have been inspired by the long and winding B842 in Kintyre that led to his farm. When post-Beatles depression set in he would escape to Scotland, but despite the farm's isolation the media were hungry to find out what McCartney was up to. He didn't take kindly to invasions of privacy from the media, and one over-zealous photographer from Life magazine who made it all the way to the farm had a bucket thrown at him by the exasperated McCartney. By the fag end of 1970 and the beginning of 1971, McCartney made the secluded, dilapidated, two-bedroom farmhouse his family home. A corrugated iron-roofed farmhouse extension was used to rehearse and record McCartney's new songwriting projects that would show up on albums Ram (credited to Paul and Linda McCartney) and Wild Life (his first album credited to Wings). A hand-drawn sign, "Rude Studio", over the door was the only indication that this was where McCartney, refreshed by his detachment from city life, was restoring his confidence and enthusiasm for song-writing after the dark, demoralising end

days of The Beatles. After leaving his new home to tour with Wings, McCartney returned to High Park in 1973 and set about writing Band on the Run. This time rehearsals were undertaken in the barn over the hill at Lower Ranachan, a second farm purchased by Paul and Linda, who would ride horseback the short distance to work each morning. In 1977, the area's best known claim to fame arrived in the shape of McCartney's biggest hit record, 'Mull of Kintyre'. A lasting memorial to Linda, who died from cancer in 1998, can be found in the form of a statue in Campbeltown, marking the happy times the McCartney family spent on this isolated but beautiful peninsula.

LOCATIONS 690, 691 and 692: the Linda McCartney statue is in the Memorial Garden in the library and museum grounds at Campbeltown, best found by taking the back gate from Shore Street, postcode PA28 6. The farms at High Park and Lower Ranachan are four miles out of Campbeltown, just north of the A83, postcode PA28 6NY. The Carskiey estate, photographed on the cover of the 'Mull of Kintyre' single, is east of Campbeltown, postcode PA28 6RU

WINGS

MULL OF KINTYRE

Right: the Campbeltown statue of Linda McCartney by sculptor Jane Robbins, and the cover of Paul McCartney's best-selling single, featuring Davaar Island viewed from the Carskiey estate, Mull of Kintyre

Callanish
Ultravox and Cope cover shots

The ancient Callanish Stones are pictured on covers for Ultravox's 1984 Top 10 album Lament and Julian Cope's 1995 Top 20 offering Jehovahkill. Both show illustrations of what archaeologists specifically name Callanish I to identify the group of stones among others in the local area. Callanish I and Callanish III were also locations for the

wintry filming of an Ultravox video featuring the band freezing to death while miming to 1984 hit single 'One Small Day'.

LOCATION 693: the village of Callanish (Calanais in Gaelic) and the stones are on the Isle of Lewis in the Western Isles, postcode HS2 9DY

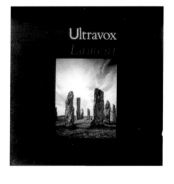

Scotland

Dunbar
Scotland's own radio pirates

Scotland's very own pirate radio station was anchored off the south-east coast. Debuting during the final seconds of New Year's Eve in 1965, the 61-year-old former Irish lightship, The Comet, was home to Radio Scotland 242 until government legislation signalled the end just 20 months later. Owing to a weak broadcasting signal, The Comet moved north from the Dunbar coast to first the west coast waters off Troon, then Ballywalter off County Down, before returning once more to Dunbar. Despite a two-million fan petition to the government, 242 ceased broadcasting in the summer of 1967. DJ's who worked on the station later finding national fame included Stuart Henry.

LOCATION 694: less than four miles off the coast from the East Lothian town of Dunbar, postcode EH42 1

On board the Comet

UNCLE'S man from Glasgow

A vital part of communicating with its listeners: 242 magazine featuring cover pics of The Comet, Lulu and Scottish actor and singer David McCallum

Dingwall
19 fans at The Beatles' remotest gig

Arguably the Fab Four's most remote gig occurred at Dingwall Town Hall as part of their Scottish mini-tour on January 4, 1963. According to Ken McNab's excellent The Beatles in Scotland, only 19 people turned out for their appearance. So sparsely attended was the gig that The Beatles packed up their gear early and journeyed five miles west with most of the audience (two Beatles by van, two on the bus) to a late-night dance at Strathpeffer Pavilion. Here at the Strath, local band The Chessmen were supporting Irish show band The Mel-Tones, attracting about 1,000 more punters than The Beatles had managed in Dingwall. Despite the poor attendance, John, Paul, George and Ringo appeared to enjoy their stay in the small town, bed-and-breakfasting in The National Hotel and partaking in a pre-gig beer or two at the Commercial Bar.

LOCATION 695: Dingwall is at the head of the Cromarty Firth. The Town Hall, Commercial Hotel and National Hotel are all in the High Street, postcode IV15 9RU

Durness
John Lennon's return to Sango Bay

The most north-westerly village on the British mainland is where the young John Lennon was packed off to enjoy summer holidays with his relatives in a croft overlooking Sango Bay. In 1969, he returned with his own children, Julian and Kyoko, and wife Yoko, full of nostalgia for this quiet corner of Scotland. Amazingly, the trip north from Surrey was undertaken with Lennon at the wheel of a hired Mini, stopping enroute at bed and breakfast accommodation in an attempt to normalise his family life. But, by the time they had made it to Edinburgh, the burnt out Mini's gearbox meant that a replacement car was called for. A far worse motoring disaster followed on arrival in Durness, before the vacation had hardly begun. While touring the Sutherland villages of Tongue and Loch Eriboll, the holiday came to an abrupt end when Lennon crashed the family's Austin Maxi on a narrow stretch of road near the Kyle of Tongue. The accident led to a five-day stay in the nearby Lawson Memorial Hospital for both John and Yoko. The couple made the most of the peace and quiet afforded them as a result of their injuries, which required numerous stitches due to the impact of the crash. While the rest of the world tuned in to hear the duo's new hit 'Give Peace a Chance', John and Yoko escaped the media excitement surrounding the Plastic Ono Band's debut and gratefully accepted their enforced relaxation. On July 6, John, Yoko and Kyoko were airlifted by helicopter to Inverness Airport before flying back to London in a private jet. Unhurt by the crash, Julian was collected earlier by his mother Cynthia. Surprisingly, the wrecked Austin Maxi was eventually shipped back south to the Lennon family home, Tittenhurst Park, where the car lay in the grounds as a souvenir sculpture of their Highland holiday and a reminder of John's appalling driving. More recently, a ceremony to mark the unveiling of three standing stones as a memorial to Lennon's visits to Durness was attended by his cousin Stan Parkes, who once shared those childhood holidays in Durness.

LOCATIONS 696 and 697: the croft where Lennon spent his childhood summers is marked by a blue plaque at 56 Sangomore, found by following the A838 east out of the centre of Durness. When the road turns south away from the sea, look for the white croft on the hill underneath the transmitter tower. Postcode: IV27 4PZ. The John Lennon memorial stones are to be found in the community garden in the village, overlooking the beach where Lennon played as a boy. Postcode: IV27 4PZ. The Lawson Memorial Hospital lies on Station Road, just north of the A9 in Golspie, postcode KW10 6SS

The Lennon family enjoy their Durness holiday, with Julian and Kyoko sporting tartan outfits purchased from Scotch House in Princes Street during the family's Edinburgh stopover

Dornoch
Madonna's secret service at Skibo Castle

When deciding on a wedding venue, Madonna has been quoted as saying: "Well first of all, Scotland is dripping in atmosphere. It is so beautiful." Under the cloak of secrecy, Jon Bon Jovi, Bryan Adams, Celine Dion and Sting all travelled to Sutherland for the rock wedding of the decade when Madonna married Guy Ritchie at Skibo Castle. The magnificent luxury hotel and estate was the setting for the wedding on December 22, 2000 and nearby Dornoch Cathedral saw the couple's son Rocco's christening a day earlier.

LOCATION 698: 40 miles north of Inverness on the A9, Skibo Castle is accessible to Carnegie Club members and wedding and hotel guests only. Postcode: IV25 3. Dornoch Cathedral is about seven miles east of the castle in the High Street

Scotland

Dundee
A Night at the Opera with Queen

Caird Hall's architectural magnificence has rock heritage to match. This imposing Grade A-listed building, with its Doric columned frontage, has seen the likes of Frank Sinatra (poorly attended and poorly received, apparently), The Beatles, Led Zeppelin, Elton John, David Bowie and U2 take the stage. One of Caird Hall's best nights must have been in 1974 when Deep Purple literally brought the house down. So loud were they that fragments of the ceiling fell off. But even that momentous night can said to have been topped a year later. Queen's appearance on December 13, 1975 was perfectly timed when their Night at the Opera Tour came to Dundee. Two weeks previously the band had topped the UK singles chart for the first time with 'Bohemian Rhapsody', a run that would continue that winter for nine weeks in total. The emerging superstars celebrated by tossing red roses into the crowd during the encore, but were soon brought back down to earth with a bump when their tour bus broke down and the AA were called to repair it.

LOCATION 699: Dundee's City Square, postcode, DD1 3BB

Grade A-listed and still packing in the crowds: the magnificent Caird Hall

One of the best gigs Scotland has ever witnessed is remembered in detail by the fans who were there…

❝ This gig was my first. The hall was absolutely jumping. 'Bohemian Rhapsody' was the opening number and the atmosphere was built up by the soundtrack playing to an empty stage through to the end of the operatic section. Then the band burst into action on the heavy guitar section with Freddie coming on in time for the vocals ❞
Kevin Malone, a 15-year-old St Saviours High School student back in 1975

❝ Three of us obtained tickets for the Queen gig – two from the sports department and another from the electrical department. That gentleman was Ricky Ross of Deacon Blue fame! When Queen played the operatic bit of 'Bohemian Rhapsody' the stage curtains were drawn to hide the band and that part was played on tape, and when the rock part started the curtains were drawn open. I don't think the technology was around at the time to allow them to play that bit live ❞
Colin Scott, 18-year-old shop assistant at Dundee's McGill Brothers department store

❝ I was at the Queen concert as was my wife, who I didn't know at the time! It was clear they were going to be superstars, it was a fantastic night and I've attended hundreds of concerts and this ranks in the top three ❞
Alex Gill, a 14-year-old schoolboy

❝ To say the crowd went wild is an understatement. Before the interval Freddie came on in a black satin cat suit. After the interval he wore a white satin cat suit. For the encore Freddie came out wearing a regal ermine cloak along with a crown on his head. He started throwing single roses into the crowd. I nearly got one for my girlfriend but unfortunately in the melee it was snatched out of my hand: gone forever! Post gig, the band stayed overnight in the very expensive and posh at the time Angus Hotel in Dundee. Any fans trying to break the cordon of his entourage when Freddie retired to the residents cocktail lounge were bluntly turned away when seeking autographs by his minder unless they had a concert programme or official Queen merchandise for Freddie to sign.❞
Peter Lyons, aged 22, who worked for a local architectural ironmongers

❝ I remember as Queen came on to the stage there was a big surge, the stage was surrounded and we were now about the fifth row of standing bodies but still a great view. Also magnesium-like flares went off on the front of stage at the same time. It was a brilliant concert. I remember not hearing properly for about two days after it ❞
Eighteen-year-old accountancy student Scott Leslie

CAIRD HALL - DUNDEE
SAT., Dec. 13, 1975, 7.30 p.m.
QUEEN
CENTRE AREA
£2.00
D   9
Tickets not exchanged or taken back.
This portion to be retained.

"The hall was absolutely **JUMPING** "

KEVIN MALONE
15-year-old schoolboy

" Freddie Mercury had the audience (myself included) in the palm of his hand and for the next couple of hours they blew everyone in the hall away. I do remember Freddie Mercury throwing roses into the crowd and the Steinway grand piano on the stage looked like a bar - laden with champagne glasses "
Seventeen-year-old Jonathan Hood who drove to the gig from Kirriemuir

" Freddie sat at the piano dressed in white satin shirt with the buttons mostly undone so you saw his hairy chest and matching white trousers with his long dark hair and black eye liner and on one of his hands he wore black polish on his nails with his couple of silver bangles on one of his wrists. We were all quite captivated by Queen on stage. My memories of that night are magical and I have always been proud to say that I was there that night "
Twenty-two-year-old office worker (and flu victim on the night of the gig) Carole Anderson

" A benefit of this era was the basic speaker systems and how guitarists made best use of them. A wall of sound is all I can remember - similar to Rory Gallagher. This was a band at their peak and they knew it. The audience knew it as well, and lapped it up. You come away from the gig, with ears ringing from the noise and delight at being allowed to see them perform. Deep Purple and Black Sabbath aside, I have never seen a band dominate a stage and audience as well and more importantly, appear to enjoy the experience themselves "
Fifteen-year-old schoolboy Frank Sturrock

" The crush at the front of stage made it a hard night's work for us, as we constantly had to pull people out who were in distress, some of them actually fainted but had no place to fall and just got bounced around with the crowd. Near the end of the show, I went out into the street for fresh air. I then saw a young girl sitting crying her eyes out. Turned out she was a diehard Queen fan and could not get a ticket. She was a tiny wee thing, about 12 or 13. I took her in and got her right down at the front of the stage and stood facing her, leaning back against the stage. Freddie Mercury was strutting around tossing roses into the crowd. I was then attracted to a scream, and as I turned I was head-butted in the face by a fan who then used me as a ladder and ran up and over my head on to the stage. Managing to grab HER ankles (yes, it was that wee tiny girl I brought in) I pulled her off stage but she was struggling like mad and then ripped my T-shirt off my back. I eventually subdued her with the help of a first-aider and we carried her out to the first-aid station. I spoke to her later on, when she had calmed down and asked her if she was OK and she replied that this was the best night of her entire life! "
Nineteen-year-old from Kirskton Kevin Logie, who along with his four brothers provided back-up for the road crew and stage security on the night

Scotland

Elgin
Chart stars head north to the Two Red Shoes Ballroom

The Beatles played their most northerly UK gig on January 3, 1963 when they took the stage at the Two Red Shoes Ballroom in the Grampian region of Scotland. The scheduled gig a day earlier, 15 miles south-east of Elgin in Keith, had been cancelled due to heavy snow and the Two Red Shoes Ballroom's Thursday night Elgin Folk Music Club hosted the Fab Four, although John Lennon almost missed the performance having dashed back south for a day. By October the place had another non-folk injection of excitement when Alex Harvey and His Soul Band came to town, and then the venue became a regular northern outpost on tours by chart stars The Four Pennies, The Honeycombs, The Moody Blues, The Nashville Teens and The Animals. Despite being great for dancing, the ballroom's 'L'-shaped floor layout was inconvenient for pop fans wanting a clear view of their idols on the frequent occasions the place was packed out. By July 1967, psychedelia came to Elgin with the venue grooving to the sounds and light show of The Pink Floyd, who performed their then current No.6 chart smash hit 'See Emily Play'.

LOCATION 700: the ballroom still stands and, until recently, was continuing in the entertainment business as the Red Shoes Theatre, 4-8 South College Street, postcode IV30 1EP

The rumours turned out to be true: Dave Grohl and Kurt Cobain play The Southern

Inset photo: Kai Mörk

Edinburgh
Nirvana in secret at The Southern

A charity gig featuring "very, very special American guests" (note the two "verys") was fly-posted as happening at this Edinburgh bar on December 1, 1991. The Southern was packed to bursting amid rumours that grunge gods Nirvana, who were touring Glasgow and Edinburgh, were in town and about to take the stage of this tiny bar and music venue. At the time the band were riding high in the albums chart courtesy of Nevermind, with single 'Smells Like Teen Spirit' released just days earlier. No-one was too surprised when a spokesman stood up amid The Southern's expectant punters to explain that a rumour was all it was and Nirvana would not be performing. But when the announcement had eventually succeeded in reducing the crowd to 20 an hour later, the remaining fans' disappointment turned to amazement as Nirvana's Kurt Cobain, Dave Grohl and Krist Novoselic wandered in. Cobain and Grohl performed a short but extraordinary acoustic set while Novoselic propped up the bar with a pint and watched alongside the rest of the gobsmacked audience.

LOCATION 701: a mile south of the city centre on the A7 at 22-26 South Clerk Street, Newington, postcode EH8 9PR

Johnny Cash at Falkland Palace

Edinburgh
Marillion's 'Heart of Lothian'

Marillion's song 'Heart of Lothian' refers to Edinburgh's Royal Mile in the lyrics and the stone mosaic Heart of Midlothian embedded in the pavement on this famous street running through the city. Local superstition dictates that to spit on the heart mosaic brings good luck. 'Heart of Lothian' appears on Marillion's 1985 concept album Misplaced Childhood.

LOCATION 704: the cobblestone heart is on the Royal Mile, outside the west door of St Giles' Cathedral. Postcode: EH1 1RE

Findhorn
Mike Scott's sanctuary

The Waterboys' 2003 album Universal Hall is named after the venue where the band have performed some of their most memorable gigs and where this album was recorded in the studio under the hall itself. The studio and the Findhorn Foundation spiritual sanctuary have seen The Waterboys' Mike Scott return regularly to this extraordinary coastal community. Scott has been a member of the local wedding band, ceilidh and jazz band and performed regular solo spots at this unique eco village, which he now calls home.

LOCATION 705: Universal Hall is near Findhorn, County Moray, postcode IV36 3TZ

Falkland
Johnny Cash's ancestral home

Falkland Palace was the location used for filming a Johnny Cash US TV Christmas special in 1981, but it was a place the legendary singing star was familiar with from a previous visit when he had good reason to explore the palace as a tourist. His considerable interest in the area was personal. Cash had met Major Michael Crichton-Stuart (hereditary keeper of Falkland Palace, the country retreat of the Stewart kings) on a 'plane journey and discovered that several places in the area around the village bore the name 'Cash'. Having researched his family tree, Cash had traced his family back to the 12th century, a connection that led him to believe that he was a direct descendant of the sister of King Malcolm VI. There's a commemorative bench inscribed "In recognition of the deep attachment the Cash family in America have for the Howe of Fife, where the name 'Cash' originated", and goes on to record the fact that Johnny and Rosanne Cash gave concerts in the town.

LOCATIONS 702 and 703: the palace is in the centre of Falkland, postcode KY15 7BY. The bench is on Brunton Green, Brunton Street, postcode KY15 7BQ

Scotland

"The house was built on the site of a kirk... that had burned down with all of its congregation inside... It's not an unfriendly place... It just seems to have **THIS THING...** 99

JIMMY PAGE
talking to Melody Maker in 1974

Front and rear views of Boleskine House, Jimmy Page's former home, overlooking Loch Ness

Foyers
Jimmy Page's Loch Ness retreat

On the eastern shore of Loch Ness lies the property once inhabited by Jimmy Page. The Led Zeppelin guitarist purchased and lived in a few noteworthy homes, but the secluded Boleskine House was acquired due to its connection with former owner Aleister Crowley. The notorious occultist and magician, who had lived in the house from 1899 to 1913, was a source of fascination for Page, who believed the man billed by the early 20th-century press as "the wickedest man in the world" was a misunderstood genius. Having bought the house in the early '70s, Page locked into the mysterious atmosphere of the estate when filming a night-time full Moon fantasy sequence in 1973 for the Led Zeppelin movie The Song Remains the Same. Satanist Charles Pace was commissioned by Page to recreate the Crowley décor by painting a series of murals in the house, but what had been little more than an infrequent retreat was vacated entirely by the rock star in 1991.

LOCATION 706: midway between the villages of Foyers and Inverfarigaig, Inverness, above the B852 loch-side road, Boleskine House (with cemetery on the opposite side of the road) is a private residence. Postcode: IV2 6XT

Glasgow
Oasis wow Alan McGee at King Tut's

"Quite possibly the finest small venue in the world" says the NME. This lively basement copied the name King Tut's Wah Wah Hut from a New York club when it opened in Glasgow city centre in 1990. Despite its limited space for only 300 punters, King Tut's' importance has continually exceeded its capacity, attracting exciting, emerging bands on the cusp of greatness. Scottish acts Travis, Texas, Biffy Clyro and Franz Ferdinand have all played significant gigs in their development as major music attractions at King Tut's. But it was the Oasis performance on May 31, 1993 that

helped give the place its legendary status and provided a crucial turning point for the unknown, unsigned Manchester band. In the audience that day, checking out Scottish band 18 Wheeler, was record label boss Alan McGee, who was so excited by the five-song set by Oasis that he decided to sign them up for his Creation Records set-up by the end of song three.

LOCATION 707: city centre, 272a St Vincent Street, postcode G2 5RL

Glasgow
Belle & Sebastian's Boho tea house

The cover photograph for Belle & Sebastian's 2003 album Dear Catastrophe Waitress was shot at the extraordinary Tchai-Ovna in Glasgow's West End. Inspired by the tea houses of the Czech Republic, Tchai-Ovna offers 80 varieties of tea, vegetarian food, hookah pipes and live music. Aside from Belle & Sebastian's obvious love of the place, fellow Glasgow indie bands Franz Ferdinand and Camera Obscura have also enjoyed a cuppa there.

LOCATION 708: a short walk from the university, Tchai-Ovna is at 42 Otago Lane, postcode G11 9PB

Refreshment all round at the Tchai-Ovna tea house

> " It's a real **HUB** for right-thinking poets, and wrong-playing jazzers "
>
> **STUART MURDOCH**
> Belle & Sebastian

Glasgow
Alex Harvey's "house of music"

The south side of Glasgow's River Clyde was once the impoverished Gorbals birthplace of one of Scotland's greatest rock legends. Famed for his extrovert blending of American blues and British musical hall and his trademark black-and-white-hooped T-shirts, Alex Harvey was born on Govan Road in 1935. Later the family moved the short distance to Durham

Street, where his younger brother Leslie formed The Kinning Park Ramblers with girlfriend Maggie Bell. Someone once chalked "This is the house of music" on the wall, and for good reason as Alex would eventually form The Sensational Alex Harvey Band and Maggie and Leslie would find fame of their own when creating blues-rock band Stone the Crows. In the mid-Seventies, around the same time Alex Harvey's fame was peaking with his first appearance on TV's Top of the Pops at the age of 40, the rough neighbourhood

of his childhood was disappearing. Redeveloped or demolished, his wartime homes made way for new, improved living conditions and the building of Glasgow's M8 motorway.

LOCATION 709: Alex Harvey's birthplace at 49 Govan Road is no longer standing and Durham Street is barely recognisable from the days of his youth. The old Harvey childhood locations are sandwiched between the River Clyde and the M8 south of the centre of Glasgow. Postcode: G51 1JL

Photo: Michael Mackinnon

Glasgow
Barrowlands' ceiling of stars

Barrowland Ballroom is a family affair. After fire gutted the first ballroom, built by the indomitable millionairess Maggie McIver, her family re-opened the new structure in 1960, and Maggie's grandson, Victor Cairns, still runs the business. With its iconic neon-signed frontage and 1,950-standing-capacity floor space, the Barrowland Ballroom is a Glasgow institution favoured by touring bands from Arcade Fire to The Zutons. In 1997, one performing superstar took away a fragment of Barrowland history. When David Bowie played the ballroom, the venue's manager, Tom Joyes, remembered him stopping during a pre-gig soundcheck when a porcelain star fell off the ballroom ceiling, narrowly missing his head. Without complaining, Bowie bent down, picked up the star and slid it into his pocket.

LOCATION 710: in the city centre at 244 Gallowgate, postcode G4 0TT

> " This is the most beautiful **CEILING**... I dream about this ceiling **"**
>
> **NICK CAVE**
> waxes lyrical about the starry Barrowlands ceiling

Above: Nick Cave & The Bad Seeds and Barrowlands' ceiling of his dreams

Opposite page: Same as it ever was: the famous ballroom has remained largely unchanged since the Sixties

Scotland

Glasgow
"The Sound of Young Scotland" at Postcard Records

"I remember the wardrobe, the singles were there. That was where Alan [Horne] kept the stock. He used the bedroom as an office and the phone was in the hall. People would phone to arrange to collect the singles and the artwork and all of that." That's how Edwyn Collins, former Orange Juice member, recalled Postcard Records when interviewed in the Glasgow Herald in 2009. Founded in 1979 by 19-year-old student Alan Horne, Postcard Records was a tiny, short-lived inspiration underpinned by the line "The Sound of Young Scotland", the motto printed on every record label. Like most great labels, its personality was determined by the person that ran it. The analogy describing Horne as Glasgow's Andy Warhol running the city's equivalent of Factory Records was about right. A larger-than-life character, he operated from a wardrobe in a small tenement apartment on West Princes Street. Up the stairs to the second floor trudged The Go-Betweens, Aztec Camera, Josef K and Orange Juice, the four bands that helped make a sea change in the rest of the UK's perception of Scottish pop music. After two short years, Postcard Records closed for business. Horne, who was headhunted by London Records, had been unable to capitalise on the musical change he had helped to develop. A&R scouts were beating a path north in large numbers, signing virtually any Scot clutching a guitar, and Postcard was brushed aside. The iconic label's disappearance was not forgotten by a stream of new bands years later, who revelled in the memory of what had been a golden period in the timeline of Scottish pop.

LOCATION 711: the flat was on the second floor at 185 West Princes Street, West End, Glasgow, postcode G4 9BZ

The first Postcard Records single release: 'Falling and Laughing' by Orange Juice in 1981, the label's drumming cat logo and its second-floor home on West Princes Street

Glasgow
Simple Minds at the Mars Bar

During most of 1978, Simple Minds were the resident Sunday night band at the Mars Bar. The tiny L-shaped club was the launchpad for the Glasgow band's burgeoning career as stadium rockers. While most live gigging at the time was of the high-energy post-punk or new wave variety, Simple Minds were all melodic melodrama, featuring Jim Kerr pushing a few Glasgow club boundaries by taking to the tiny stage in white jacket and make-up. It was at the Mars Bar that they

would perfect the 10 songs that would form their 1979 debut album Life in a Day. Their focused vision of what they wanted to achieve on a larger scale was evident by employing their own lighting and sound engineer, even at this early stage. The club, a popular meeting place for mod revivalists, was also forced into calling itself Countdown: the manufacturers of the famous chocolate bar were not happy, apparently.

LOCATION 712: the club burnt down but was once the centre of the universe for young Glasgow music fans at Howard Street, just off St Enoch Square, postcode G1 4

Invermoriston
Alex Harvey's monster investigations

Even the most sceptical scientist can't say with any certainty that the Loch Ness monster doesn't exist, and when Scottish music legend Alex Harvey has something to say on the subject, one is inclined to listen. So enthralled in the mystery was he that he recorded an album investigating the monster legend, which included his interviews with the loch-side villagers of Invermoriston. Buy the album and draw your own conclusions!

LOCATION 713: Invermoriston lies seven miles north of Fort Augustus on the northern side of Loch Ness, where the A82 meets the A887. Postcode: IV63 7YA

Alex Harvey's 1977 side project

Leith
Birthplace of The Proclaimers

Sunshine on Leith is the album and album track released by local duo The Proclaimers in 1988. The identical twin brothers Charlie and Craig Reid are the most Scottish-sounding of rock stars and enthusiastic supporters of their local Edinburgh football club Hibernian, where 'Sunshine on Leith' is blasted out on match days as something of a local anthem. Sunshine on Leith the musical, infused with the brothers' socialist ideology but not featuring the twins themselves, played to packed houses across Scotland in the Noughties.

LOCATION 714: Leith is the waterside port area of Edinburgh, postcode EH6

> **"**Now I'm nae telling you whether I've seen it or not but there's a **WATER BAILIFF** up there who's consulted about the movement of fish by experts all around the world and he's seen it 18 or 20 times **"**
>
> **ALEX HARVEY**
> interviewed by Sounds in 1977

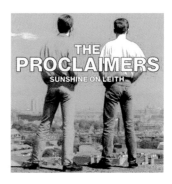

Scotland

Kirriemuir
Bon Scott's home town memorial

Kirriemuir is the small town where AC/DC frontman Bon Scott was born and spent the first six years of his life before emigrating to Australia. In May 2006, a Caithness stone memorial to the singer, who died in 1980, was unveiled in the town, watched by 500 of Scott's fans. The work of acclaimed local sculptor Bruce Walker, the stone pavement plaque lies in the town's Cumberland Close. Nearby is Bon Scott Place, a residential road in memory of the man who sported a "Scotland Forever" tattoo on his arm. Enhancing his Scottish folk hero credentials, he played the bagpipes on 1975's T.N.T. album track 'It's a Long Way to the Top (If You Wanna Rock 'n' Roll)' and was once voted rock's greatest frontman in Classic Rock magazine.

LOCATIONS 715 and 716: Kirriemuir is in eastern Scotland, about 20 miles north of Dundee. The memorial stone is at Cumberland Close, postcode DD8 4EF, and Bon Scott Place is at postcode DD8 4LD

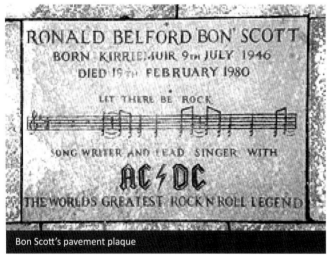
Bon Scott's pavement plaque

Keith
The Silver Beetles plaque

Fifty years after the event, a local heritage group commemorated an appearance by John Lennon, Paul McCartney and George Harrison as members of Johnny Gentle's backing group at this small town in the north-east of Scotland. The plaque is at the entrance to the modest little St Thomas' Hall, where the gig took place.

LOCATION 718: the plaque is near the junction of Chapel Street and Land Street, postcode AB55 5AL

Loch Lomond
On the bonnie banks with Runrig

The most sung-about of all Scotland's beauty spots, 'Loch Lomond' became the closing song at gigs by Celtic rock ambassadors Runrig. It gave them their biggest hit when their 2007 version raised funds for BBC TV's Children in Need, making No.9 in the singles chart. Revised and retitled down the years, this traditional folk song has been covered by Bill Haley & His Comets, AC/DC and Marillion, among others. The bonnie banks of Loch Lomond were also the setting for what ranks as the band's favourite concert, when close to 50,000 turned out to see them in the grounds of Balloch Castle in 1991.

LOCATION 717: Balloch Castle, on the banks of Loch Lomond in West Dunbartonshire, was the setting for Runrig's big Loch Lomond bash. Status: public country park, postcode G83

Stenness
Van Morrison's Philosopher's Stone

A trawl through the Van Morrison archives, his 1998 Top 20 album The Philosopher's Stone depicts the standing stones of Stenness on the cover. The 19-foot-tall megaliths are off the north-east tip of Scotland on Orkney's Mainland.

LOCATION 719: Stenness village, Orkney, postcode KW17

Lochearnhead
Simple Minds' Bonnie Wee Studios

In 1986, Simple Minds' success led them to invest in Dalkenneth House, a property on the banks of Loch Earn in Perthshire. Their retreat became the perfect bolt-hole for the band and work began on a purpose-built recording studio. The refreshing isolation created the ideal environment for writing and recording tracks for albums Street Fighting Years (1989), Real Life (1991) and Good News from the Next World (1995). The Bonnie Wee Studios got their name following a question posed by Jon Bon Jovi to Simple Minds' Jim Kerr about where the drums were recorded on tracks he'd heard: "In the bonnie wee studios" was Kerr's instant description, and from then on the name of the striking hexagonal building, designed and built by Gaia Architects, stuck. Architect Howard Liddell's final flourish on completion of the timber structure was to erect a "Simple Winds" weather vane.

LOCATION 720: Dalkenneth House is on the north side of Loch Earn. Status: now a private residence. Postcode: FK19 8PZ

> " Loch Earn is not far east of Loch Lomond, but it feels worlds away... My son James used to ask me if there was a monster in it, like Loch Ness, and I'd say yes – these lochs were **SO DEEP** that they all link together. I think I half believed it myself "
>
> **JIM KERR**

Nethy Bridge
Bob Dylan's highland home

In 2007, Bob Dylan added property owner to his existing Scottish connection of honorary degree at the University of St Andrews. The music icon spent a week in the spring of 2006 enjoying the five-star, bed-and-breakfast country comforts of Aultmore House in the Cairngorms. So delighted was he with the experience that he purchased the woodland estate and house, along with his brother, for £2.2 million. The 10-bedroom house's interior had previously been the location for BBC TV drama Monarch of the Glen. Since purchasing the place, sightings of Bob Dylan have been harder to come by than a glimpse of the elusive local ospreys and capercaillie.

Bob Dylan's Aultmore House, the perfect spot for hiking, biking, fishing and water sports

LOCATION 721: about 30 miles south-east of Inverness, Nethy Bridge is two miles east of the A95. Follow the B970 north out of Nethy Bridge. Postcode: PH25 3ED

Scotland

Paisley
Stealers Wheel's Ferguslie Park and Gerry Rafferty Drive

The title of Stealers Wheel's 1974 album Ferguslie Park came from a deprived area of Paisley where musical duo Gerry Rafferty and Joe Egan were born and raised. The housing estate has, with considerable investment, improved its reputation down the years. Don't try reading too much into the decision-making behind the album title; according to Egan it was "just a name we thought sounded good".

LOCATIONS 722 and 723: Ferguslie Park is north-west of Paisley. Postcode: PA3 1DW. Gerry Rafferty Drive is part of a housing development south of Glasgow Airport. Postcode: PA3 2PG

A council official displays the Paisley-born albums Ferguslie Park and Gerry Rafferty's City to City

Orbost
Joe Strummer's forest

An idea hatched backstage at the 1996 Glastonbury Festival led to Joe Strummer having a forest planted here in a remote corner of the Isle of Skye. The project was driven by a new company started a year later called Future Forests, founded by Strummer's friends Sue Welland and Dan Morrell. Concerned by the detrimental effect the music industry could be having on global warming through heavy tour transportation and the excessive CO_2 created in pressing and distributing his CDs, Strummer decided that he would become the world's first 'carbon neutral artist'. The result was a plantation of trees named Rebel's Wood. Morrell's belief was that planting trees to re-absorb harmful carbon dioxide was the way forward. If you are a Clash fan that likes hiking, check out just how Strummer's saplings have fared.

LOCATION 724: Isle of Skye, Orbost estate, near Dunvegan, postcode IV55 8ZB

The sign erected in memory of Joe Strummer

Photo: Joanna Dobson

Elvis' short, enforced stay in Scotland was a closely guarded secret, but these teenagers mobbed the air base once rumours started circulating locally

Prestwick
Elvis Presley's only visit to Britain

The 'secret' visit may only have lasted 80 minutes, but when the aircraft carrying Elvis Presley touched down at Prestwick Airport it was, as it turned out, a deeply significant moment. March 3, 1960 was the day music's greatest star made his first visit to Britain, which duly became the singer's only stay on British soil. The brief encounter was not a planned meet-and-greet-the fans visit, more born out of practicality, made possible due to Elvis' period in the military. Back in 1960, aged 25, he was a serving sergeant in the US Army, travelling from Germany to be demobbed back home and return to civilian life and his career in music and films. The flying visit to this small Scottish airport was simply for aircraft refuelling on the long journey home, but Elvis did nevertheless enjoy a brief experience of Scottish hospitality. After a few polite words with reporters, he sped away in a chauffeured limo to the NCO's mess and youth club on the US air base. This gave those teenagers lucky enough to be present that day the opportunity to thrust an autograph book or scrap of paper over the airport's chicken-wire fence. Some of the screaming fans even got to hold hands, and one or two of the more excitable girls even claimed they had managed to kiss their idol. Proud of the associated limelight that Elvis Presley brought to Prestwick, the airport has marked his visit with a plaque on the terminal building floor and the creation of an Elvis tribute bar in the departure lounge.

LOCATION 725: despite being 32 miles from Glasgow city centre on Scotland's west coast, the airport is now known as Glasgow Prestwick Airport at Graceland (nice touch) Arcade. Postcode: KA9 2PL

"The father of the American family I babysat for just said that there was a VIP coming in that evening. When he told me it was Elvis I could hardly believe it"

ANNE MURPHY
a 16-year-old Elvis fan

Scotland

Born in SCOTLAND

James Allan, vocals/guitar, Glasvegas (b. 21 Sep 1979, **Dalmarnock, Glasgow**)

Ian Anderson, vocals, Jethro Tull (b. 10 Aug 1947, **Dunfermline**)

Colin Angus, vocals/guitar, The Shamen (b. 24 Aug 1961, **Aberdeen**)

Roger Ball, saxophone, Average White Band (b. 4 Jun 1944, **Broughty Ferry, Dundee**)

Maggie Bell, solo/Stone the Crows (b. 12 Jan 1945, **Maryhill, Glasgow**)

Robert Bell, keyboards, The Blue Nile (b. 22 Aug 1952, **Glasgow**)

Guy Berryman, bass, Coldplay (b. 12 Apr 1978, **Kirkcaldy**)

Norman Blake, vocals/guitar, Teenage Fanclub (b. 20 Oct 1965, **Glasgow**)

Edith Bowman, DJ/presenter (b. 15 Jan 1974, **Anstruther, Fife**)

Stuart Braithwaite, guitar, Mogwai (b. 10 May 1976, **Dalserf, South Lanarkshire**)

Steve Bronski, keyboards, Bronski Beat (b. 7 Feb 1960, **Glasgow**)

Jack Bruce, bass/vocals, Cream (b. 14 May 1943, **Bishopbriggs, East Dunbartonshire**, d. 25 Oct 2014)

Paul Buchanan, vocals, The Blue Nile (b. 16 Apr 1956, **Edinburgh**)

Martin Bulloch, drums, Mogwai (b. 14 Aug 1974, **Bellshill, Glasgow**)

Charlie Burchill, guitar, Simple Minds (b. 27 Nov 1959, **Glasgow**)

David Byrne, vocals/guitar, Talking Heads (b. 14 May 1952, **Dumbarton**)

Isobel Campbell, cello/keyboards, Belle & Sebastian/solo (b. 27 Apr 1976, **Glasgow**)

Martin Carr, guitar, The Boo Radleys (b. 29 Nov 1968, **Thurso**)

Zal Cleminson, guitar, The Sensational Alex Harvey Band (b. 4 May 1949, **Glasgow**)

Richard Colburn, drums, Belle & Sebastian (b. 25 Jul 1970, **Perth**)

Edwyn Collins (b. 23 Aug 1959, **Edinburgh**)

Brian Connolly, vocals, The Sweet (b. 5 Oct 1945, **Hamilton**, d. 9 Feb 1997)

Mick Cooke, brass, Belle & Sebastian (b. 15 Dec 1973, **Dundee**)

Tommy Cunningham, drums, Wet Wet Wet (b. 22 Jun 1964, **Drumchapel, Glasgow**)

Justin Currie, vocals/bass, Del Amitri (b. 11 Dec 1964, **Glasgow**)

Stuart David, bass, Belle & Sebastian (b. 26 Dec 1969, **Dumbarton**)

Barbara Dickson (b. 27 Sep 1947, **Dunfermline**)

Lonnie Donegan (b. 29 Apr 1931, **Glasgow**, d. 3 Nov 2002)

Donovan (b. 10 May 1946, **Glasgow**)

Eddy Duffy, bass, Simple Minds (b. 30 Dec 1969, **Glasgow**)

Malcolm 'Molly' Duncan, saxophone, Average White Band (b. 24 Aug 1945, **Montrose**)

Andy Dunlop, guitar, Travis (b. 16 Mar 1972, **Lenzie, East Dunbartonshire**)

Sheena Easton (b. 27 Apr 1959, **Bellshill, Glasgow**)

Joe Egan, Stealers Wheel (b. 18 Oct 1946, **Paisley**)

Eric Faulkner, guitar, Bay City Rollers (b. 21 Oct 1953, **Edinburgh**)

Fish (Derek Dick), vocals, Marillion (b. 25 Apr 1958, **Dalkeith, Midlothian**)

Roddy Frame (b. 29 Jan 1964, **East Kilbride**)

Elizabeth Fraser, vocals, Cocteau Twins (b. 29 Aug 1963, **Grangemouth**)

Barry Fratelli (Barry Wallace), guitar, The Fratellis (b. 23 Apr 1979, **Glasgow**)

Jon Fratelli (John Lawler), vocals, The Fratellis (b. 4 Mar 1979, **Cumbernauld**)

Mince Fratelli (Gordon McRory), drums, The Fratellis (b. 16 May 1983, **Glasgow**)

Benny Gallagher, Gallagher & Lyle (b. 10 Jun 1945, **Largs, Ayrshire**)

Chris Geddes, keyboards, Belle & Sebastian (b. 15 Oct 1975, **Dalry, Ayrshire**)

Bobby Gillespie, vocals, Primal Scream/drums, The Jesus and Mary Chain (b. 22 Jun 1962, **Glasgow**)

Alan Gorrie, bass/vocals, Average White Band (b. 19 Jul 1946, **Perth**)

Clare Grogan, vocals, Altered Images (b. 17 Mar 1962, **Glasgow**)

Robin Guthrie, multi-instrumentalist, Cocteau Twins (b. 4 Jan 1962, **Grangemouth**)

Calvin Harris (b. 17 Jan 1984, **Dumfries**)

Alex Harvey (b. 5 Feb 1935, **Glasgow**, d. 4 Feb 1982)

Les Harvey, guitar, Stone the Crows (b. 13 Sep 1944, **Glasgow**, d. 3 May 1972)

Iain Harvie, guitar, Del Amitri (b. 19 May 1962, **Glasgow**)

Colin Hay, vocals, Men at Work (b. 29 Jun 1953, **Kilwinning, Ayrshire**)

Mike Heron, vocals, The Incredible String Band (b. 27 Dec 1942, **Edinburgh**)

Richard Hynd, drums, Texas (b. 17 Jun 1965, **Aberdeen**)

Stevie Jackson, guitar, Belle & Sebastian (b. 16 Jan 1969, **Glasgow**)

Bert Jansch, guitar, Pentangle (b. 3 Nov 1943, **Glasgow**, d. 5 Oct 2011)

Richard Jobson, vocals, The Skids/TV presenter (b. 6 Oct 1960, **Dunfermline**)

Ben Johnston, drums/vocals, Biffy Clyro (b. 25 Apr 1980, **Kilmarnock**)

James Johnston, bass/vocals, Biffy Clyro (b. 25 Apr 1980, **Kilmarnock**)

Malcolm Jones, guitar/pipes, Runrig (b. 12 Jul 1959, **Inverness**)

Graeme Kelling, guitar, Deacon Blue (b. 4 Apr 1957, **Paisley**, d. 10 Jun 2004)

Jim Kerr (b. 9 Jul 1959, **Glasgow**)

David Knopfler, guitar, Dire Straits (b. 27 Dec 1952, **Glasgow**)

Mark Knopfler, guitar, Dire Straits (b. 12 Aug 1949, **Glasgow**)

Annie Lennox (b. 25 Dec 1954, **Aberdeen**)

Alan Longmuir, bass, Bay City Rollers

(b. 20 Jun 1948, **Edinburgh**)

Derek Longmuir, drums, Bay City Rollers (b. 19 Mar 1951, **Edinburgh**)

Gerard Love, bass/vocals, Teenage Fanclub (b. 31 Aug 1967, **Motherwell**)

Lulu (Marie Lawrie) (b. 3 Nov 1948, **Lennoxtown, East Dunbartonshire**)

Graham Lyle, Gallagher & Lyle (b. 11 Mar 1944, **Bellshill, Glasgow**)

Calum Macdonald, vocals/drums, Runrig (b. 12 Nov 1953, **Lochmaddy, North Uist**)

Rory Macdonald, vocals, Runrig (b. 27 Jul 1949, **Dornoch, Western Isles**)

Billy Mackenzie, vocals, Associates (b. 27 Mar 1957, **Dundee**, d. 22 Jan 1997)

Dan McCafferty, vocals, Nazareth (b. 14 Oct 1946, **Dunfermline**)

Jimmy McCulloch, guitar, Wings (b. 4 Jun 1953, **Dumbarton**, d. 27 Sep 1979)

Chas McDevitt (b. 4 Dec 1934, **Eaglesham, Glasgow**)

Johnny McElhone, guitar, Altered Images/bass, Texas (b. 21 Apr 1963, **Bearsden, East Dunbartonshire**)

Ally McErlaine, guitar, Texas (b. 31 Oct 1968, **Glasgow**)

Alan McGee, record label boss/manager (b. 29 Sep 1960, **East Kilbride**)

John McGeoch, guitar/saxophone, Magazine (b. 25 Aug 1955, **Greenock, Renfrewshire**, d. 4 Mar 2004)

Raymond McGinley, guitar/vocals, Teenage Fanclub (b. 3 Jan 1964, **Glasgow**)

Lorraine McIntosh, vocals, Deacon Blue (b. 13 May 1964, **Glasgow**)

Robbie McIntosh, drums, Average White Band (b. 6 May 1950, **Dundee**, d. 23 Sep 1974)

Onnie McIntyre, guitar, Average White Band (b. 25 Sep 1945, **Lennoxtown, East Dunbartonshire**)

Les McKeown, vocals, Bay City Rollers (b. 12 Nov 1955, **Edinburgh**)

Shirley Manson, vocals, Garbage

(b. 26 Aug 1966, **Edinburgh**)

Paul Joseph Moore, keyboards, The Blue Nile (b. 19 Mar 1957, **Glasgow**)

Donnie Munro, vocals/guitar, Runrig (b. 2 Aug 1953, **Uig, Isle of Skye**)

Stuart Murdoch, vocals, Belle & Sebastian (b. 25 Aug 1968, **Ayr**)

Simon Neil, vocals/guitar, Biffy Clyro (b. 31 Aug 1979, **Irvine, North Ayrshire**)

Paolo Nutini (b. 9 Jan 1987, **Paisley**)

Brendan O'Hare, drums, Teenage Fanclub (b. 16 Jan 1970, **Cambuslang, Glasgow**)

Dougie Payne, bass, Travis (b. 14 Nov 1972, **Glasgow**)

Marti Pellow, vocals, Wet Wet Wet (b. 23 Mar 1965, **Clydebank**)

Frankie Poullain, bass, The Darkness (b. 15 Apr 1967, **Edinburgh**)

James "Optimus" Prime, keyboards, Deacon Blue (b. 3 Nov 1960, **Kilmarnock**)

Neil Primrose, drums, Travis (b. 20 Feb 1972, **Cumbernauld**)

Finley Quaye (b. 25 Mar 1974, **Edinburgh**)

Gerry Rafferty (b. 16 Apr 1947, **Paisley**, d. 4 Jan 2011)

Eddi Reader, vocals, Fairground Attraction (b. 29 Aug 1959, **Glasgow**)

Charlie Reid, The Proclaimers (b. 5 Mar 1962, **Leith**)

Craig Reid, The Proclaimers (b. 5 Mar 1962, **Leith**)

Jim Reid, vocals, The Jesus and Mary Chain (b. 29 Dec 1961, **Glasgow**)

William Reid, guitar/vocals, The Jesus and Mary Chain (b. 28 Oct 1958, **Glasgow**)

Brian Robertson, guitar, Thin Lizzy (b. 12 Sep 1956, **Clarkston, Glasgow**)

Ricky Ross, vocals, Deacon Blue (b. 22 Dec 1957, **Dundee**)

Bon Scott, vocals, AC/DC (b. 9 Jul 1946, **Kirriemuir**, d. 19 Feb 1980)

Mike Scott, The Waterboys (b. 14 Dec 1958, **Edinburgh**)

Tom Simpson, keyboards, Snow Patrol (b. 7 Jan 1972, **Angus**)

Jimmy Somerville, vocals, Bronski Beat/The Communards (b. 22 Jun 1961, **Glasgow**)

Sharleen Spiteri, vocals, Texas (b. 7 Nov 1967, **Bellshill, Glasgow**)

Al Stewart (b. 5 Sep 1945, **Glasgow**)

Hamish Stuart, vocals/guitar, Average White Band (b. 8 Oct 1949, **Glasgow**)

Stuart Sutcliffe, bass, The Beatles (b. 23 Jun 1940, **Edinburgh**, d. 10 Apr 1962)

Gavin Sutherland, bass/vocals, The Sutherland Brothers (& Quiver) (b. 6 Oct 1951, **Peterhead**)

Iain Sutherland, guitar/vocals, Sutherland Brothers and Quiver (b. 17 Nov 1948, **Ellon, Aberdeenshire**)

Dougie Thomson, bass, Supertramp (b. 24 Mar 1951, **Glasgow**)

Paul Thomson, drums, Franz Ferdinand (b. 15 Sep 1976, **Glasgow**)

Len Tuckey, guitar, Suzi Quatro Band/The Nashville Teens (b. 15 Dec 1947, **Aberdeen**)

KT Tunstall (b. 23 Jun 1975, **St Andrews, Fife**)

Midge Ure (b. 10 Oct 1953, **Cambuslang, Glasgow**)

Ewen Vernal, bass, Deacon Blue (b. 27 Feb 1964, **Glasgow**)

Nancy Whiskey (b. 4 Mar 1935, **Bridgeton, Glasgow**, d. 1 Feb 2003)

Robin Williamson, vocals, The Incredible String Band (b. 24 Nov 1943, **Edinburgh**)

Paul Wilson, bass, Snow Patrol (b. 20 Oct 1978, **Kinlochleven, Scottish Highlands**)

Pete Wishart, keyboards, Runrig (b. 9 Mar 1962, **Dunfermline**)

Stuart 'Woody' Wood, guitar, Bay City Rollers (b. 25 Feb 1957, **Edinburgh**)

Angus Young, guitar, AC/DC (b. 31 Mar 1955, **Glasgow**)

Malcolm Young, guitar, AC/DC (b. 6 Jan 1953, **Glasgow**)

Wales

*T*he Welsh have "voices sweeter than angels." This confirmation of what we all knew already comes from Led Zeppelin's Robert Plant, an Englishman who drew inspiration for the writing of some of rock's greatest tracks at a remote cottage in north Wales. The more urban parts of Wales also have their moments. The New York Times even once described Newport as 'The Seattle of the UK'. There's immense pride in the principality at producing a steady stream of cutting-edge to comic Welsh rock from John Cale to Goldie Lookin Chain. A fact flow of stories tell of the survival of the world's oldest record shop, Jerry Hall dressing up as a mermaid for Bryan Ferry, Kurt Cobain failing to cough up £3 to enter a Newport nightspot, Page and Plant's cottage industry, Joe Strummer's Vultures, a Byrds Welsh mining song, the world's first residential recording studios in the village of Rockfield, a lovely trip to Bangor by The Beatles, the Fab Four's final British concert and Tom Jones' green, green, grass of home.

Abergavenny
John Lennon's Juke Box Jury helicopter dash

The market town immortalised in the song 'Abergavenny', written and recorded by Marty Wilde in 1968, also hosted a newsworthy performance by The Beatles a few years earlier on June 22, 1963. Not until 10.30pm did the Fab Four take to the Town Hall Ballroom stage as John Lennon arrived late after filming a TV appearance on the BBC show Juke Box Jury earlier in the day. Lennon was flown in by helicopter from London and touched down at the best available makeshift heliport Abergavenny could offer, the nearby Pen-y-pound football ground. The group's hour-long performance in front of 600 fans was followed by an untroubled overnight stay at the Angel hotel.

LOCATIONS 659 and 660: Abergavenny is on the Welsh/English border off the A40. The Town Hall (postcode NP7 5HD) and the Angel hotel (postcode NP7 5EN) are both in Cross Street

Aberdare & Cwmaman
Birthplace of the Stereophonics

On the day of former Stereophonics band member Stuart Cable's funeral in 2010, thousands of fans brought Aberdare to a standstill as family and friends packed into the drummer's local St Elvan's Church. A short stroll from the church takes you past the town's 600-seater Coliseum, where the band played an early breakthrough gig as Tragic Love Company. Throwing off the shackles of their existence under this less than memorable moniker, a name change and steady rise to success as the Stereophonics quickly followed. Just over two miles south of Aberdare lies the coal-mining village of Cwmaman, where the original Stereophonics line-up met and went to school together: drummer Stuart Cable had lived in the same Cwmaman street as singer Kelly Jones. The nearby Workmen's & Social Club was the spot where the band made their earliest performance, and it was here they returned on December 14, 2007 to play a one-off acoustic homecoming gig for a BBC Radio 1 Live Lounge show presented by Jo Whiley.

LOCATION 661: Cwmaman Workmen's & Social Club is on Glanaman Road, postcode CF44 6LA

The band's 2003 No.1 album cover shows Kelly Jones' brother and dad enjoying some quality time at Cwmaman pub The Ivy Bush, where Kelly would later perform with an early incarnation of the Stereophonics

Blackwood
Manic Street Preachers' return for a 'home town ecstasy'

"It will be the smallest gig that we have played in a long time... severe nerves, but hopefully a night of home town ecstasy." That's how Manic Street Preachers guitarist Nicky Wire looked forward to an extraordinary homecoming gig at Blackwood's Miners' Institute on January 28, 2011. Twenty-five years since the Manic Street Preachers last played the town's Blackwood Little Theatre, the band returned to a building where they recalled playing countless games of snooker as teenagers. The tiny Miners' Institute hosted an emotional appearance for both the Manics and 180 lucky fans, broadcast live on BBC Radio 2. A mile or so east of Blackwood, Oakdale Comprehensive School was where James Dean Bradfield, Richey Edwards, Nicky Wire and Sean Moore first forged friendships that would lead to the formation of the internationally famous band. Vocalist and guitarist Bradfield still returns to his home town regularly: "My opticians is still in Blackwood, I still go to Lui's Plaice now and again, and I'm up to see my dad all the time."

LOCATION 662: this former coalminers' meeting place has been transformed into a local community function centre. Blackwood is 12 miles north of Newport and the M4 motorway. The Miners' Institute is in Blackwood High Street, postcode NP12 1BB

Photo: henrygrossman.com

Bangor
Flower power in north Wales: The Beatles break cover

Little had been seen of The Beatles since they quit concert performances in 1966. So, by 1967's 'Summer of Love', when they made headlines with a trip to north Wales, all that pent-up Beatlemania was released once more on the largely bewildered seaside resort of Bangor. The purpose of the visit on August 25, was to take in the lectures of Maharishi Mahesh Yogi, leader of the Spiritual Regeneration Movement, who was holding a conference at Normal College Bangor. University Student landlady Edna Pritchard takes up the story: '"The Maharishi was sitting in the darkened

"Cyn [Cynthia] and I were thinking of going to Libya, until this came up. **LIBYA OR BANGOR?** Well, there was no choice, was there? 🥇🥇

JOHN LENNON

Left: Jane Asher, Paul McCartney, John Lennon, Cynthia Harrison, Maharishi Mahesh Yogi, Pattie Boyd, George Harrison, Ringo Starr and Maureen Starkey

Right: student landlady Edna Pritchard (centre) attending the 40th anniversary reunion of The Beatles' two-day trip to Bangor, with John Lennon seemingly looking down on her approvingly

Cardiff
The end of the road for The Beatles and The Kinks

The Beatles' appearance at Cardiff's Capitol cinema on December 12, 1965 was the last on British soil in front of a paying audience. The Cardiff concerts – there were two 30-minute sets on the day – were the final date of a tour on which they were supported by The Moody Blues and fellow Liverpool acts The Koobas and Beryl Marsden. Although 25,000 fans applied for tickets, only 5,000 were lucky enough to witness what would turn out to be a last chance to see The Beatles perform a regular concert in the UK. Two previous visits to the Capitol cinema had already occurred when The Beatles toured with Roy Orbison and Gerry and The Pacemakers in May 1963 and again in November 1964, when Sounds Incorporated and Mary Wells were among the supporting bill. Similar hysterical receptions to those that greeted The Beatles at the Capitol were also experienced by early teen idols Bill Haley and His Comets in the Fifties and the Bay City Rollers in the Seventies. The venue also witnessed a famous on-stage bust-up that ended a bill-topping package tour by The Kinks in May 1965. So serious was the altercation between drummer Mick Avory and guitarist Dave Davies that Davies needed hospital treatment and the band failed to complete the remaining dates on the tour.

LOCATION 664: demolished in 1983, there's a new Odeon cinema at the Capitol shopping centre. Postcode: CF10 2HQ

hall and he could see the teenagers looking through the windows. 'Let them all come in' he said. He was holding a dahlia in his hand and he slowly plucked off the petals. He couldn't quite pronounce 'dahlia' as we would and said 'A darrlia is a darrlia is a darrlia' and other mumbo jumbo.'' Unimaginable today, but The Beatles' entourage, including Mick Jagger and Marianne Faithfull, all travelled by train on the 3.15pm out of London's Euston Station, bound for Bangor. If the crowds of fans and reporters were enthusiastic to once again see the Fab Four at Euston, they were in full hysterical mode by the time the train arrived in Bangor. Taxied without mishap to their spartan

dormitory accommodation at the vacant college, The Beatles even managed to slip out for a late-night meal at the Senior Chinese restaurant, but awoke the next morning to find the college gardens stripped of all the flowers by the growing hordes of flower-power fans. The 10-day-long visit was cut short on August 27 when Paul McCartney took the telephone call that broke the news that Brian Epstein had been found dead. The extraordinary trip to north Wales had been the first The Beatles had undertaken without their manager.

LOCATION 663: Hugh Owen Hall, Bangor University, Gwynedd, postcode LL57 2DG

Wales

Ewloe
Second coming delay by The Stone Roses

One of several locations booked for work on The Stone Roses' Second Coming album, this remote, converted 12-room north Wales brewery base saw no conclusion to recordings during the band's two stays in 1992. It's supposed to be the difficult second album syndrome that most bands suffer from, and The Stone Roses turned the whole business of creating one of the most eagerly awaited albums in rock history into a media-infatuated marathon event. The Rolling Stones' mobile recording unit was hired, John Leckie tried to produce, but it would be a further two years until Second Coming finally arrived in record shops. Others sampling The Old Brewery's Angelshare Studios' hospitality who were more productive during their stays include John Martyn, Mansun, Roy Harper and The Farm.

LOCATION 665: on the B5125, Angelshare Studios no longer operate from The Old Brewery, Ewloe, postcode CH5 3BZ

Arcade to arcade: Spillers then (in the old Queens Arcade) and now (in Morgan Arcade)

Cardiff
The world's oldest record shop

Founded in 1894 and still selling music, Spillers Records is the family business originally opened by Henry Spiller in Queens Arcade, Cardiff. The world's oldest independent record shop moved to 'new' premises in the late 1940s and Spillers' current location is still in the Welsh capital's city centre. Threatened with almost certain closure in 2006, the shop's loyal supporters - most notably local band the Manic Street Preachers-campaigned successfully for its continued presence.

LOCATION 666: the city centre at 31 Morgan Arcade, postcode CF10 1AF

> "**WE LIKE RECORDS**, tea, instores, and if you bring us biscuits from Wally's deli (in the arcade next to us) we'll like you a lot 🎵🎵

The Spillers website staff biography

Barafundle Bay
Gorky's Pembrokeshire

The splendidly named but unfortunately now defunct Gorky's Zygotic Mynci hailed from Pembrokeshire and titled their 1997 album Barafundle after the beautiful bay and beach pictured on a postcard in the centre of the cover. The band was formed by three students at Welsh-speaking Bro Myrddin Welsh Comprehensive School in Carmarthen. The album, pictured left, was recorded at Studio Ofn, Llanfaelog, Anglesey.

LOCATION 667: six miles south of Pembroke, closest postcode SA70

Holyhead
Roxy Music's siren of the sea

Roxy Music's Bryan Ferry began dating Jerry Hall when she was chosen to model for the cover of Roxy's fifth album. The Texan was photographed as the Siren for the album of that name, released in late 1975. No digital fakery for this shoot: Hall, the photographer, make-up artist and Ferry all travelled to this wild spot for what proved to be one of rock's most memorable images.

LOCATION 668: north-west Anglesey at South Stack, reached by the A55. The exact location can be found by taking the bridge to the lighthouse and descending left to the rocks below. Postcode: LL65 1YH

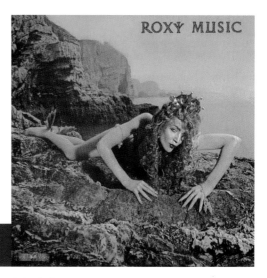

Rock reference: the RSPB centre at Ellin's Tower can be seen at the top of the cliffs

Newport
Joe's Vultures take off at Pentonville

Newport was the place where Turkish-born Joe Strummer first picked up a guitar and began performing. It was in this second-floor flat at Pentonville, Newport, that Strummer, known to all at the time as John "Woody" Mellor, lived in the early Seventies. Buying his first guitar for £12 and learning his first chords courtesy of fellow student Steve Richards, Strummer spent this period in Wales as a student and occasional performer at the students' union, along with frequent visits to absorb the West Indian music on offer at local open-mike club Silver Sands, in Pill. The Newport flat was the base where he formed his first band, The Vultures. Just over a month before his death in 2002, Strummer returned to Wales to play a gig with his band The Mescaleros at TJ's in Clarence Place. A plaque, unveiled by his widow Lucinda Tait, commemorates his time at the Pentonville flat where he took his first steps towards his life as a genuine rock legend in The Clash.

LOCATION 669: the flat and plaque are close to the city centre, west of the River Usk at 12 Pentonville, postcode NP20 5HB. Status: private residence

> **" When Joe was living in his flat in Newport he recorded the FIRST SONG that he ever wrote, 'Crummy Bum Blues' "**
>
> **RICHARD FRAME**
> fellow student and housemate tells a story in Pat Gilbert's recently published biography

Mold
The Beatles wander free in north Wales

Although by now gaining massively in popularity, The Beatles were still a few months away from registering their first No.1 single and album when they played Mold Assembly Rooms on January 24th 1963. Nevertheless, the sold-out 200-capacity venue was smaller than most they were playing at this point but did give enthusiastic fans an intimate view of the soon-to-be international superstars. The Fab Four were still relatively free to wander where they pleased and popped into the Y Pentan (then the Cross Keys pub) for a pre-gig drink. After the show, John Lennon, Paul McCartney and Ringo Starr visited Holywell's Beaufort Arms (back then the Talbot hotel) to unwind: McCartney even spent half an hour entertaining the locals with an impromptu stint on the pub piano. Leaving immediately after the gig, George Harrison missed the late night pub visit, choosing instead to visit his auntie, who lived six miles away in Hawarden, on the way home.

LOCATIONS 670, 671 and 672: Mold Assembly Rooms in the High Street (postcode CH7 1AS) is now a bank. Y Pentan Bar & Restaurant is at 3 New Street, Mold, postcode CH7 1NY. The Beaufort Arms, now a residential building, is at 26 Well Street, Holywell, postcode CH8 7PL

Wales

Machynlleth
Page and Plant at Bron-Yr-Aur

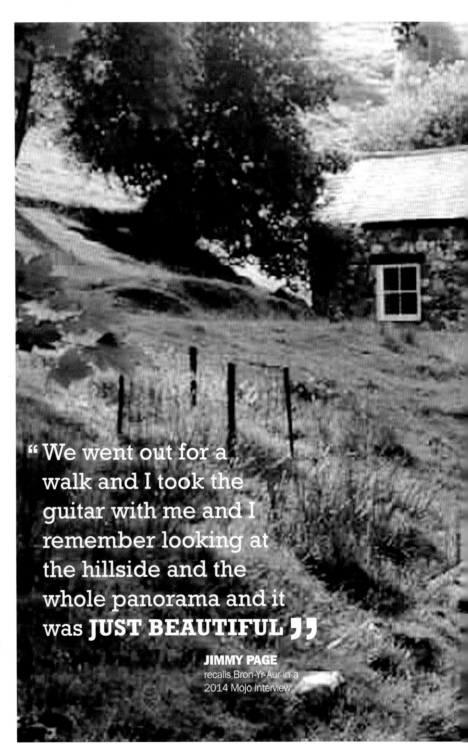

The rewards from the relentless workload undertaken by Led Zeppelin for the band's first hectic three years of success were not only financial. By 1970 they had enough power to determine their own way forward away from the hurly-burly of the music business. Stepping off the treadmill of writing while touring, a period of time dedicated solely to creating new material began at this remote cottage up a bumpy mountain lane. Relaxing into their natural surroundings, Jimmy Page and Robert Plant wrote a number of songs that would end up on Led Zeppelin III (including the incorrectly spelt 'Bron-Y-Aur Stomp'), their fourth album and Physical Graffiti. Immortalised as an instrumental album track on Physical Graffiti, Bron-Yr-Aur was a cottage that Plant had remembered from childhood family holidays in north Wales. Page, accompanied by girlfriend Charlotte Martin, and Plant by wife Maureen, their baby daughter Carmen and Strider the family dog, shared their rustic environment with Led Zeppelin roadies Clive Coulson and Sandy MacGregor. With no running water or electricity, the luxury of a weekly bath was only achievable by visits to the local Glyndwr Hotel in Doll Street, Machynlleth.

LOCATION 673: leave the market town of Machynlleth heading north, turning left on to the A493 and then almost immediately right up a lane that climbs towards Bron-Yr-Aur. Status: private residence. Postcode: SY20 8QA

" We went out for a walk and I took the guitar with me and I remember looking at the hillside and the whole panorama and it was **JUST BEAUTIFUL** 🙶

JIMMY PAGE
recalls Bron-Yr-Aur in a 2014 Mojo interview

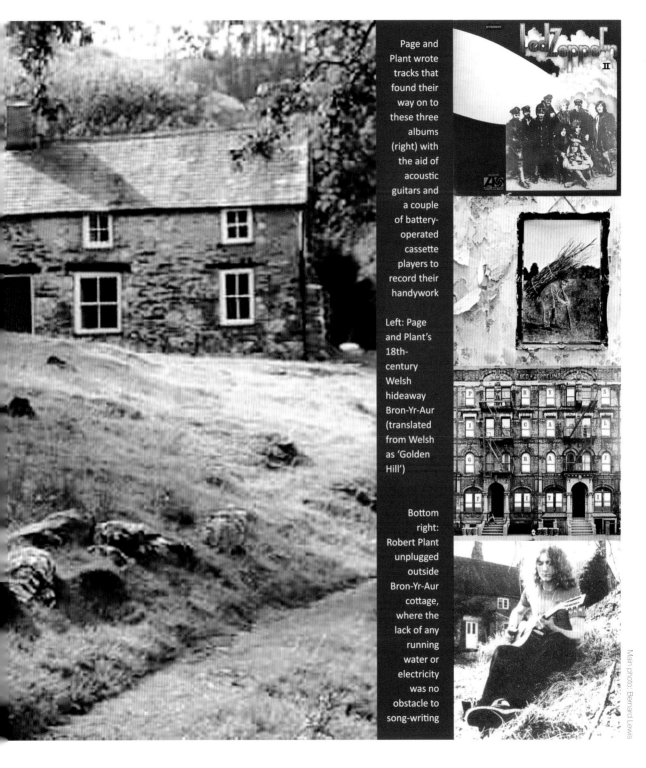

Page and Plant wrote tracks that found their way on to these three albums (right) with the aid of acoustic guitars and a couple of battery-operated cassette players to record their handywork

Left: Page and Plant's 18th-century Welsh hideaway Bron-Yr-Aur (translated from Welsh as 'Golden Hill')

Bottom right: Robert Plant unplugged outside Bron-Yr-Aur cottage, where the lack of any running water or electricity was no obstacle to song-writing

Main photo: Bernard Lewis

Wales

Newport
The Stone Roses coat of arms

The bridge in Newport from where Houdini once famously jumped in 1913 was a point of artistic inspiration for Stone Roses guitarist John Squire. The band's long-awaited Second Coming album saw them spend a good deal of time in the nearby Rockfield recording studios, and when complete in 1994 Squire searched around for graphic imagery for the cover of the album's first single release, 'Love Spreads'. The sleeve carries a photo of one of the bridge's Newport coats of arms: the civic badge of Newport City Council, formerly the coat of arms of the former county borough. The red chevron and cherub heraldry became so associated with the band at one point that Roses fans were reported removing the badges from the bridge.

The Newport civic badge and coat of arms

LOCATION 674: Newport (or Town) Bridge is in the city centre, Clarence Place, on the B4591, postcode NP19 0AE

Porthmadog
On the beach: the Manics go north

Virtually an all-Welsh creation, Manic Street Preachers' 1998 No.1 album This Is My Truth Tell Me Yours was recorded at Monnow Valley and Rockfield Studios in Monmouth and the cover artwork was shot at Black Rock Sands. This north Wales beach created a breathtakingly dramatic location for the photo shoot, but it's a surprise perhaps that the south Wales trio and photographer didn't take the shorter journey to the equally photogenic Gower Peninsula.

LOCATION 675: head for Morfa Bychan, two miles south-west of Porthmadog at Black Rock Sands beach. Postcode: LL49 9YB

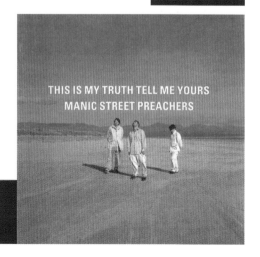

Quotation courtesy of Labour politician Aneurin Bevan, beach courtesy of Black Rock Sands

" Courtney Love's band Hole were sound-checking just before the doors opened when this blond, straggly haired geezer came up... I said to him, 'If you're coming in, it'll be £3.' He said to me, 'No man, I'm here to see Courtney; you see my accent?' I told him again it was three quid when Simon Phillips came rushing over going, 'No, no, it's all right John, **IT'S KURT COBAIN!**"

JOHN SICOLO
owner and founder of TJ's, interviewed by BBC Wales

At TJs to see Courtney: Kurt Cobain snapped at the legendary Newport gig by Hole, in 1991

Newport
Kurt Cobain gatecrashes a Hole gig

TJ's was the inspirational Newport venue owned and run by the mercurial John Sicolo. Although hosting a conveyor belt of up-and-coming bands such as Oasis, Green Day, The Offspring and Primal Scream, TJ's' stella moment involves a significant rock romance. It is said to be the place where Kurt Cobain proposed to Courtney Love when the couple visited the Newport nightspot in 1991. Courtney's band Hole were playing a gig organised by promoter Simon Phillips. Catatonia's 'Mulder and Scully' hit single video was shot at the venue in 1998 and one-time Newport resident Joe Strummer made one of his last stage appearances at TJ's before his death in 2002.

LOCATION 676: in the city centre east of the River Usk at 14-18 Clarence Place, postcode NP19 0AE. TJ's closed after the death of John Sicolo, who passed away in 2010

Wales

Pontypridd & Treforest
Tom Jones' 'Green, Green Grass of Home'

The Treforest Working Men's Club was where 17-year-old Tom Jones made his singing debut, but it wasn't until a gig at the Pontypridd YMCA six years later that he began to think he might make a career out of singing. Here in 1963, billed as Tommy Scott, with a backing band called The Senators, he filled in for the actual Tommy Scott who had failed to appear for the night in question. After a few drinks as Dutch courage, paper mill worker Jones stepped in as "Tommy" at the request of The Senators to fulfil the booking and did a good enough job to stay as lead singer. In 2008, a demo tape of Jones recorded in the YMCA toilets (no doubt for the best possible acoustics) was auctioned at Christie's in London. The recording, which later sold for £2,500, was catalogued by the auction house as "a rare ¼-inch reel-to-reel master-tape recording of Tom Jones, 1962, on one reel of Emitape, featuring four un-released tracks, tracks comprise: 1 'Don't Pretend', 2 'Time Alone' 3 'What About Me', 4 'That's What Love Can Do'". Local working men's clubs in the mining villages were where 'Jones the Voice' gained a reputation for soulful singing, and at a 1964 performance at Cwmtillery's Top Hat he was 'discovered' by songwriter and Jones' future manager Gordon Mills. The Kingsland Terrace house in Treforest where Jones was born Thomas Jones Woodward still stands, as does his subsequent childhood home in Laura Street in the small village of Treforest, south-east of Pontypridd. When superstardom came calling, Jones moved to California and, recalling his teenage years phoning a stream of girlfriends, including his future wife, managed to purchase and ship the old red telephone box that stood at the end of Laura Street to his new L.A. home. To celebrate the singer's 65th birthday in 2005, a concert was held at nearby Ponty Park (Ynysangharad Park), at which he wowed a 20,000-strong crowd.

LOCATIONS 677, 678 and 679: Pontypridd (where the town centre now honours Tom Jones by displaying the 'Green, Green Grass of Home' lyrics in the pavement) is due west off the A470. The YMCA is at Taff Street, postcode CF37 4TS. The house where Tom Jones was born is a mile south-east of Pontypridd in the village of Treforest at 57 Kingsland Terrace, postcode CF37 1RX. Less than a mile away is his childhood home at 44 Laura Street, postcode CF37 1NW. Status: private residences

"I spent the first 24 years of my life in Wales and **I LOVED IT** and have never really left. So I would want to be buried in Glyntaff cemetery in Pontypridd – all of my forefathers are there "

TOM JONES
talking to the Western Mail

Photo: Terry O'Neill/Getty

Tom Jones returns to the land of his forefathers, the green, green grass of home, and his birthplace at 57 Kingsland Terrace, Treforest

Wales

Photo: Don Hunstein/Sony BMG Music Entertainment

Roger McGuinn was turned on to 'The Bells of Rhymney' when working on a Judy Collins album in 1963. In 1965, he turned the song into a jingle-jangle Byrds classic on their Mr Tambourine Man album

Rhymney
A striking Welsh miners story borrowed by The Byrds

This Caerphilly village is the location name-checked in one of the stand-out tracks on The Byrds' Mr Tambourine Man album, released in 1965. The song which describes the General Strike in the spring of 1926 and its crippling effect on the local mining industry has been frequently covered by American folk artists and also north Wales band The Alarm, who included the song as a B-side to their 1984 hit single 'The Chant Has Just Begun'. The song's lyrics date back to a poem written by Rhymney-born former miner Idris Davies and the lines, first published in 1938, eventually attracted the attention of American protest singer Pete Seeger, who set the words to music. In addition to Rhymney's bells, those in Newport and Caerphilly, the brown bells of Merthyr, black bells of Rhondda, grim bells of Blaina, loud bells of Neath, moist bells of Swansea,

green bells of Cardiff and silver bells of Wye are all referred to in the song. In 2007, Welsh folk musician Huw Williams visited Pete Seeger in New York to research the origins of the song for a BBC documentary. The American folk legend had never seen Davies' original publication Gwalia Deserta, which included the poem, but had stumbled across a Dylan Thomas book which included 'The Bells of Rhymney' in a chapter on Welsh poetry. Once Seeger had added his music, the song struck a chord with the American folk community. Before his time in The Byrds, Roger McGuinn had been turned on to the song while contributing arrangements and guitar parts to Judy Collins' 1963 album Judy Collins 3. This disc's tracks 'The Bells of Rhymney' and 'Turn! Turn! Turn!' were adapted by McGuinn into the jingle-jangle style he was developing,

and sparkled as key contributions to The Byrds' ground-breaking folk-rock album Mr Tambourine Man which appeared two years later. And that's not all. McGuinn describes how some musical cross-pollination began with 'The Bells of Rhymney' and resulted in a Beatles track on their Rubber Soul album, released six months later in December 1965: "George [Harrison] had listened to The Byrds' version of 'The Bells of Rhymney', the Pete Seeger song, and on it I had done the riff with the Rickenbacker going de-de-de, de-de-de, so he took that and made the tune 'If I Needed Someone' out of it."

LOCATION 680: St David's Church, where the bells of Rhymney still chime, is situated in Rhymney village High Street, which is on the B4257 east of Merthyr Tydfil. Postcode: NP22 5NG

Swansea
Pete Ham remembered

Badfinger band member Pete Ham is remembered by a blue plaque in his home city. The Swansea-born songwriter, who co-wrote Harry Nilsson's transatlantic chart-topping hit 'Without You' (also a UK No.1 for Mariah Carey), penned many other hits including Badfinger's 'No Matter What' and 'Day After Day'. Tragically, Ham committed suicide in 1975. The plaque was unveiled by his daughter Petera, who never had the opportunity to know her father. The plaque's position in Ivey Place is significant. Before Badfinger, Pete's band were The Iveys, who, rumour has it, practised in the vicinity back in 1961.

Apple Records outfit Badfinger, with Pete Ham (right), who had a run of three UK Top 10 singles in two years from 1970

LOCATION 681: Swansea railway station, Ivey Place, postcode SA1 1NX

Rhyl
The Beatles make their Welsh debut

In the summer of 1962, July 14, was the date of The Beatles' first paid gig on Welsh soil, at the seaside resort of Rhyl. The town's Regent Dansette Ballroom was the venue for this historic appearance, a fact commemorated by an unusual artistic mosaic at Rhyl railway station, created by the town's Youth Forum. Still performing at this time with Pete Best on drums, the band's Welsh debut was a few months short of their first chart entry and they took time out to tout for extra concert appearances. There is a report of them crossing the Foryd Bridge to the old Clwyd Hotel (now The Harbour) to unsuccessfully scrounge a cabaret appearance. Work was more plentiful a year later when John, Paul, George and now Ringo returned as UK chart-toppers for two more Rhyl gigs on consecutive nights. This time they played to an adoring, screaming audience at the now-demolished Ritz Ballroom, with overnight luxury accommodation provided by Rhyl's Westminster Hotel bridal suite.

LOCATION 682: the Regent Dansette Ballroom, now shops, is at 38 High Street, and the Westminster Hotel still dominates the seafront at 11-12 East Parade, postcode LL18 3AH

Wales

Rockfield
The world's first residential recording studio

Rockfield claims to be the world's first residential recording studio. Since opening in 1965, artists as diverse as Del Shannon, Iggy Pop, Echo and The Bunnymen, The Undertones, Teenage Fanclub, Coldplay, KT Tunstall and Paolo Nutini have recorded there. And, you don't have to be in a band to stay at Rockfield. The complex offers bed-and-breakfast and self-catering accommodation for visiting this attractive corner of the Welsh countryside. Seasoned rock fans will associate Dave Edmunds most with the place; his 'I Hear You Knocking' spent six consecutive weeks at the top of the singles chart in 1970 and helped put both the studio and the associated Rockfield label on the music map. Perhaps the studio's grandest moment came in 1975 when, while working on new album A Night at the Opera, Queen recorded 'Bohemian Rhapsody' there. Even Rockfield's outdoor acoustics pop up on one album. Not the only rock band to find inspiration in poet Samuel Taylor Coleridge's 19th-century-published work Kubla Khan, Canadian trio Rush recorded their epic, 11-minute 'Xanadu' for 1977 album A Farewell to Kings in an early-morning marijuana haze in the Rockfield courtyard to capture the dawn chorus of birdsong.

"**We were watching Marx Brothers movies at Rockfield and we got a sense that they could go anywhere they WANTED, they were so in control of their medium. And we felt the same sort of spirit: we had discovered our power as a group**"

BRIAN MAY
of Queen, talking to The Daily Telegraph

LOCATION 683: less than two miles north-west of Monmouth on the B4233. Go left just before the village of Rockfield at Amberley Court, off Rockfield Road. Postcode: NP25 5ST

Prestatyn
Jam for the Fab Four at the Royal Lido

They wouldn't feature on any list of all-time greatest band riders, but The Beatles were only just enjoying their first entry on the UK singles chart when they ordered Prestatyn's Royal Lido to bring them a pre-gig plateful of jam sandwiches. An informative circular record disc-styled plaque remembering John, Paul, George and Ringo's November 24, 1962 gig marks the spot where the Royal Lido (now renamed The Nova Centre) stood. Less than a year later, on August 31, 1963, The Rolling Stones played their first concert outside England at the Royal Lido Ballroom.

LOCATION 684: The Nova Centre, Central Beach, postcode LL19 7EY

Born in WALES

Verden Allen, keyboards, Mott the Hoople (b. 26 May 1944, **Crynant**)
Shirley Bassey (b. 8 Jan 1937, **Tiger Bay, Cardiff**)
Andy Bell, guitar, Beady Eye/Oasis/Ride (b. 11 Aug 1970, **Cardiff**)
Tony Bourge, guitar/vocals, Budgie (b. 24 Nov 1948, **Tiger Bay, Cardiff**)
James Dean Bradfield, vocals/guitar, Manic Street Preachers (b. 21 Feb 1969, **Pontypool**)
Huw Bunford, guitar, Super Furry Animals (b. 15 Sep 1967, **Cardiff**)
Stuart Cable, drums, Stereophonics (b. 19 May 1970, **Aberdare,** d. 7 Jun 2010)
John Cale (b. 9 Mar 1942, **Garnant**)
Phil Campbell, guitar, Motörhead (b. 7 May 1961, **Pontypridd**)
Euros Childs, vocals, Gorky's Zygotic Mynci (b.16 Apr 1975, **Freshwater East**)
Cian Ciaran, keyboards, Super Furry Animals (b. 16 Jun 1976, **Bangor**)
Julian Cope, vocals, The Teardrop Explodes/solo (b. 21 Oct 1957, **Deri**)
Spencer Davis, guitar, The Spencer Davis Group (b. 17 Jul 1939, **Swansea**)
Duffy (b. 23 Jun 1984, **Nefyn**)
Dave Edmunds (b. 15 Apr 1944, **Cardiff**)
Richey Edwards, vocals/guitar, Manic Street Preachers (b. 22 Dec 1967, **Blackwood**, presumed dead 2008)
Sian Evans, vocals, Kosheen (b. 9 Oct 1973, **Caerphilly**)
Andy Fairweather Low (b. 2 Aug 1948, **Ystrad Mynach**)
James Frost, guitar, The Automatic (b. 22 Aug 1986, **Cowbridge**)
Green Gartside, vocals, Scritti Politti (b. 22 Jun 1955, **Cardiff**)
Mike Gibbins, drums, Badfinger (b. 12 Mar 1949, **Swansea**, d. 4 Oct 2005)
Roger Glover, bass, Deep Purple (b. 30 Nov 1945, **Brecon**)
Iwan Griffiths, drums, The Automatic (b. 4 Dec 1985, **Cowbridge**)

Ron Griffiths, bass, Badfinger (b. 2 Oct 1946, **Swansea**)

Pete Ham, guitar, Badfinger (b. 27 Apr 1947, **Swansea**, d. 24 Apr 1975)

Robin Hawkins, vocals/bass, The Automatic (b. 14 Dec 1986, **Cardiff**)

Mary Hopkin (b. 3 May 1950, **Pontardawe**)

Dafydd Ieuan, drums, Super Furry Animals (b. 1 Mar 1969, **Bangor**)

Owen If (Ian Rossiter), drums, Stereo MCs (b. 20 Mar 1959, **Newport**)

Katherine Jenkins (b. 29 Jun 1980, **Neath**)

Kelly Jones, vocals/guitar, Stereophonics (b. 3 Jun 1974, **Cwmaman**)

Paul Jones, bass, Catatonia (b. 5 Feb 1960, **Colwyn Bay**)

Richard Jones, bass, Stereophonics (b. 23 May 1974, **Cwmaman**)

Tom Jones (b. 7 Jun 1940, **Treforest**)

Jon Lee, drums, Feeder (b. 28 Mar 1968, **Newport**, d. 7 Jan 2002)

Deke Leonard, guitar, Man (b. 18 Dec 1944, **Llanelli**)

Eddie MacDonald, bass, The Alarm (b. 1 Nov 1959, **St Asaph**)

Cerys Matthews, vocals, Catatonia (b. 11 Apr 1969, **Cardiff**)

Donna Matthews, guitar/vocals, Elastica (b. 2 Dec 1971, **Newport**)

Sean Moore, drums, Manic Street Preachers (b. 30 Jul 1968, **Pontypool**)

Grant Nicholas, vocals/guitar, Feeder (b. 12 Nov 1967, **Newport**)

Mike Peters, vocals/guitar, The Alarm (b. 25 Feb 1959, **Prestatyn**)

Ray Phillips, drums, Budgie (b. 1 Mar 1949, **Ely, Cardiff**)

Guto Pryce, bass, Super Furry Animals (b. 4 Sep 1972, **Cardiff**)

Nigel Pulsford, guitar, Bush (b. 11 Apr 1963, **Newport**)

Gruff Rhys, vocals, Super Furry Animals (b. 18 Jul 1970, **Haverfordwest**)

Aled Richards, drums, Catatonia (b. 5 Jul 1969, **Carmarthen**)

Mark Roberts, guitar, Catatonia (b. 3 Nov 1969, **Llanrwst**)

Sasha, DJ/producer (b. 4 Sep 1969, **Bangor**)

Andy Scott, guitar, The Sweet (b. 30 Jun 1949, **Wrexham**)

Burke Shelley, vocals/bass, Budgie (b. 10 Apr 1947, **Tiger Bay, Cardiff**)

Rick Smith, keyboards, Underworld (b. 25 May 1959, **Ammanford**)

Shakin' Stevens (b. 4 Mar 1948, **Ely, Cardiff**)

Steve Strange, Visage (b. 28 Apr 1959, **Newbridge**)

Matt Tuck, vocals/guitar, Bullet for My Valentine (b. 20 Jan 1980, **Bridgend**)

Bonnie Tyler (b. 8 Jun 1951, **Skewen**)

Ricky Valance (b. 10 Apr 1939, **Ynysddu**)

Ian Watkins, vocals, Lostprophets (b. 30 Jul 1977, **Merthyr Tydfil**)

Nicky Wire, bass, Manic Street Preachers (b. 20 Jan 1969, **Tredegar**)

Paula Yates, presenter (b. 24 Apr 1959, **Colwyn Bay**, d. 17 Sep 2000)

Twice top of the albums chart as a member of Catatonia, Cerys Matthews was born in Cardiff, grew up in Swansea and attended schools in Llanelli and Fishguard

Wales

White Grit
Ronnie Lane settles down on the farm

So nomadic was Faces rock star Ronnie Lane that it comes as a real compliment to the rolling hills of east Wales to have him settle down on a border farm here. Rock stars made a habit of escaping to the country during the Seventies, and the former Small Faces and Faces man did it in considerable style. Famed for his wonderfully conceived but ultimately financially draining The Passing Show, where he and Slim Chance toured the country circus style with big top, Lane's nomadic tendencies did at least lead to an idyllic home life based in the countryside. After a recent trip to Ireland, he and wife Kate yearned for the country life, found the perfect 100-acre property in Wales and paid for the deeds with a plastic bag full of cash. Next he set about creating a mobile studio, where he recorded Anymore for Anymore, his debut album as Ronnie Lane's Slim Chance. The American Airstream trailer bought at a staggering £250,000 for this purpose later turned up on the cover of his 1976 album One for the Road. Ronnie became a sheep farmer by day, recording music by night in his mobile unit, or even in the open air. Pete Townshend and Eric Clapton (plus Steve Marriott for an abortive Small Faces reunion) would visit. "Eric took to Fishpool [Farm] like a duck to water," remembers Ronnie's wife Kate. "He liked driving a 4x4 over a sheer drop, it was marvellous boys stuff." Ronnie and friends would often frequent the local hostelries and perform the odd gig at The Miners Arms in Priest Weston and the Drum and Monkey in Bromlow (now Abel's Harp). These appearances helped repay the locals for their acceptance of the London east end rock star in this tight-knit rural community, on the Welsh border with England's Shropshire.

LOCATION 685: just inside the Welsh border, close by the village of White Grit, Fishpool Farm is north of Hyssington, north of the A488, postcode SY5 0JN. Status: private residence

Sheep farmer and recording artist Ronnie Lane at Fishpool Farm in 1974

Photo: Allan Ballard/Scopefeatures.com

Northern Ireland

Whether it be 'The Troubles', local hero George Best or simply the atmosphere of the place, Belfast has a lengthy back catalogue of songs featuring the city in the title. Simple Minds' 'Belfast Child', Don Fardon's football favourite 'Belfast Boy' and Boney M's 'Belfast' are three of the most enduring hits. And Orbital duo Paul and Phil Hartnoll were inspired to name their instrumental hit 'Belfast' after playing the demo at 4am on a car stereo driving home from a gig in the city. No-one does a better job at eulogising the province generally than Van Morrison, whose deep-seated attachment to places discovered in his youth reveal themselves in beautiful lyrics narrated on Van tracks like 'Cyprus Avenue' and 'Coney Island'. There's a classic Led Zep cover shoot on the rugged coast, the tale of Pearly Spencer, The Beatles' best attended UK gig and the scandalous lack of a plaque to commemorate the Derry location that enabled The Undertones to shake the world.

Belfast
Stones and Led Zep: drama at Ulster Hall

Built in 1859, Ulster Hall's foundations were tested to the limit when The Rolling Stones made their first visit to Northern Ireland on July 31, 1964. The 1,200-capacity venue was wildly oversubscribed as 3,000 fans packed the hall, causing suffocating panic and forcing the termination of the Stones' performance after just 12 minutes. No surprise, then, that when Mick, Keith, Brian, Bill and Charlie returned in January and September a year later Ulster Hall was out of bounds for a group whose shows were igniting mass states of hysteria among fans throughout Britain. Their 1965 appearances were made at the ABC theatre, and although hysteria was contained some fans queued for two days and nights to be sure of bagging tickets to see their idols. Rioting of a much more serious kind coincided with an equally memorable visit by Led Zeppelin on March 5, 1971. Rock fans who braved a particularly bad night of sectarian unrest on the surrounding streets witnessed Jimmy Page's live introduction of the famous double-necked Gibson guitar and the debut performance of 'Stairway to Heaven', almost nine months ahead of its release on their fourth album. As you enter the hall look out for a plaque, inside the main doors, in memory of Belfast's Fifties chart star Ruby Murray.

> " The Stones made The Beatles look like the OLD TIME music hall "
>
> **BELFAST TELEGRAPH, 1964**

LOCATION 726: in Belfast city centre at 1-7 Bedford Street, postcode BT2 7

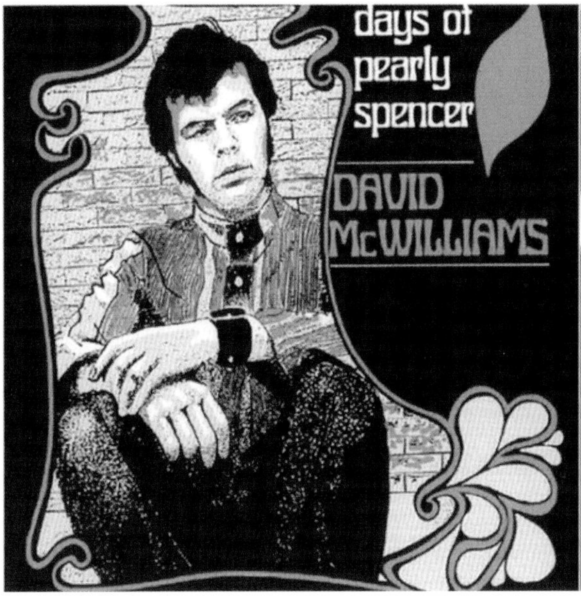

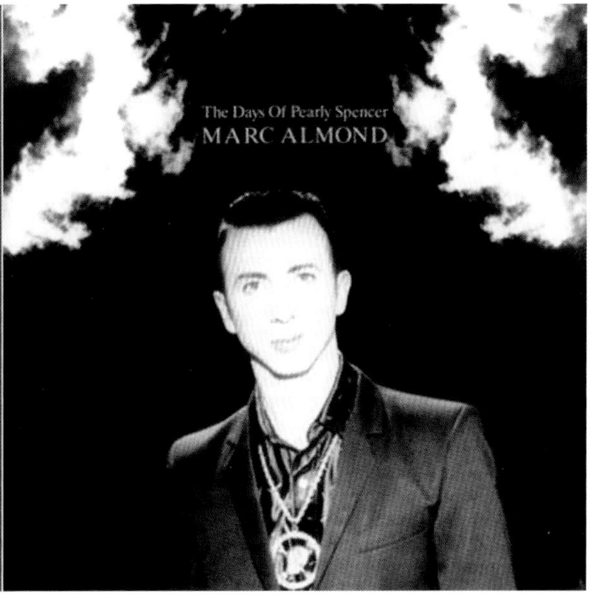

Ballymena
The homeless Pearly Spencer

Although familiar and much loved by anyone who possessed a pair of ears in the Sixties, 'The Days of Pearly Spencer' was inexplicably never a UK hit for David McWilliams when released as a single in 1967, despite topping the French hit parade at the time. Sensitive to the plight of society's disadvantaged, McWilliams wrote the song about one particular homeless man he encountered in his home town of Ballymena, where he grew up on the Rectory estate. The poignant tale of an impoverished life in County Antrim was covered in some style in 1992 by Yorkshireman Marc Almond, and this time McWilliams' song shot to No.4 in the UK singles chart.

LOCATION 727: the Rectory estate is less than a mile north of the centre of Ballymena, postcode BT43

Belfast
Snow Patrol's Duke of York debut

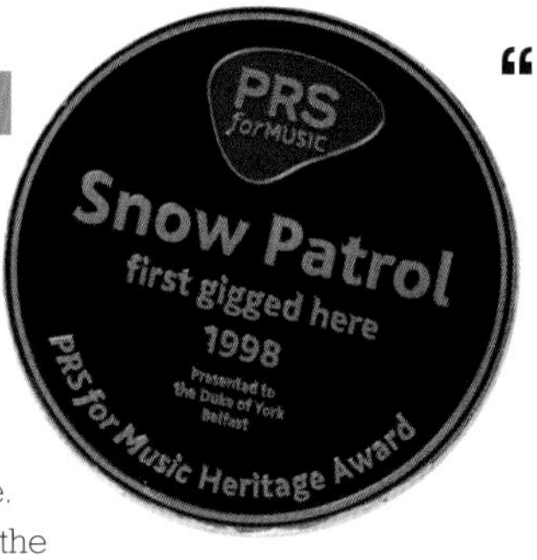

Situated down a cobbled alleyway, the Duke of York bar is where Snow Patrol played their first gig in 1998. To celebrate the fact, there's a PRS plaque on the outside wall of this attractive venue. When band members returned to the spot for the plaque unveiling in 2010 they found the place little changed and recalled doing two nights, one acoustic and one as a full band, in front of a tiny gathering.

LOCATION 728: in the historic Half Bap area of Belfast, the Duke of York is at 7-11 Commercial Court, postcode BT1 2NB

> "We never sold out the Duke of York, and to be honest, getting 30 people back then was a **GOOD NIGHT**. To be playing for up to 40,000 people now is incredible for us"

GARY LIGHTBODY
Snow Patrol vocalist

Northern Ireland

Belfast
Them are big news at The Maritime

The Ulster History Circle's blue plaque is a constant reminder to everyone that the city's Maritime Hotel was the focal point responsible for nurturing not just local bands but an entire music genre. Back in 1964, it begat Belfast's own Celtic take on rhythm and blues and the distinctive sound of local boys Them, featuring the young Van Morrison. The opening of the Maritime as a music venue coincided with the new band's unveiling in a now legendary Belfast newspaper ad campaign: 'Who Are? What Are? THEM', immediately followed by a debut appearance at Maritime's new Club Rado. Formerly a police station and a seaman's hostel, the city centre building's new role as Belfast's equivalent to Liverpool's Cavern saw a stream of increasingly confident young bands converge on the 200-capacity club, which soon began to pack twice that number in when queues stretched around the block. Bands with no previous place to play, or those enthusiastically assembled overnight in the beat boom, included The Aztecs, The Mad Lads, The Fugitives, The Few, Five by Five, The Method, The Deltones, The Lovin' Kind and The Alleykatz.

> "Them **LIVED** and died on the stage at the Maritime Hotel **"**
> **VAN MORRISON**

LOCATION 729: the inspirational Maritime Hotel once stood in College Square North. Its position is marked by a shiny blue plaque on an uninspiring brick wall opposite the junction with Hamill Street and Killen Street. Postcode: BT1 6

Belfast
The Belfast Music Exhibition

A hub of the city's music activity, the Oh Yeah music centre, named after the 1996 Ash hit single 'Oh Yeah', is housed in a three-storey warehouse that includes the Belfast Music Exhibition. Highlights of this visitor attraction include Ash frontman Tim Wheeler's Flying V guitar and the Fender guitar on which Snow Patrol's Gary Lightbody wrote 'Run' and 'Chasing Cars'. Music fans visiting the city requiring a visual potted history of Northern Ireland's pop music scene should head here first to discover all there is to know about artists as diverse as Clodagh Rodgers and Stiff Little Fingers.

LOCATION 730: located in a former bonded whiskey warehouse in the heart of Belfast at the Oh Yeah music centre, 15-21 Gordon Street, postcode BT1 2LG

Tim Wheeler with his Golden Gibson Flying V, which is now a popular exhibit at the Oh Yeah music centre

Photo: Carrie Davenport

"We lived in a pretty FUNKY neighbourhood "

VAN MORRISON
talking to Rolling Stone in 1970

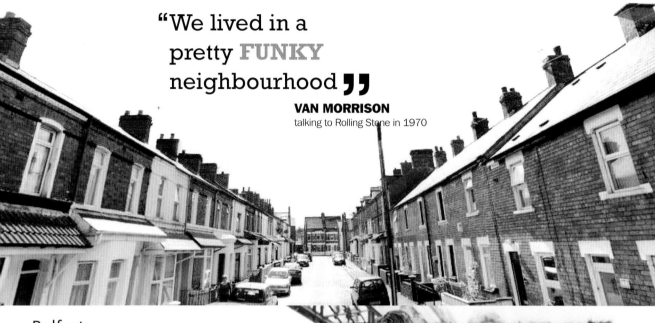

Belfast
The streets and avenues of Van Morrison's childhood

A small brass plaque to the right of the door of No.125 Hyndford Street discreetly indicates that this was the home of the young Van Morrison from 1945 until he was 16. Years before the plaque, fans of Them, Morrison's hugely popular Belfast R&B export to the world in the Sixties, would chalk the walls of the small terraced home with their own mark of appreciation: "Them's House". Fond of evoking places and activities from his youth in song, there's no better example than Morrison's narration on the track 'On Hyndford Street', from his 1991 No.5 album Hymns to the Silence. His childhood home is pictured on the back of the album cover and the track takes the listener on a journey to nearby Abetta Parade, Cyprus Avenue (the title of another Van track), Fusco's ice-cream parlour (on Woodstock Road), Orangefield (his secondary school), St Donard's church (on Bloomfield Road) and a little further afield to Beechie River, Cherryvalley, North Road bridge, the Castlereagh Hills, Cregagh Glen and Holywood (a bus journey for the young Morrison north-east of the city on the coast). One of Van's most popular tracks, 'Cyprus Avenue' appears on his 1968 album

Astral Weeks. This tree-lined avenue is a short stroll from his modest Hyndford Street home but a world away in property prices and was a mystical, romantic place for Van the budding songwriter to escape to.

LOCATIONS 731, 732, 733, 734, 735, 736 737 and 738: 125 Hyndford Street (postcode BT5 5) is one mile south-east of the city centre. Most of the other locations name-checked by Van Morrison in song are within walking distance of his childhood home, including Cyprus Avenue, postcode BT5 5NT. Fusco's is still serving ice-cream at 369 Woodstock Road, postcode BT6 8PU

Van the (young) man: Them would congregate at Van's Hyndford Street home, on the right beyond the telegraph pole

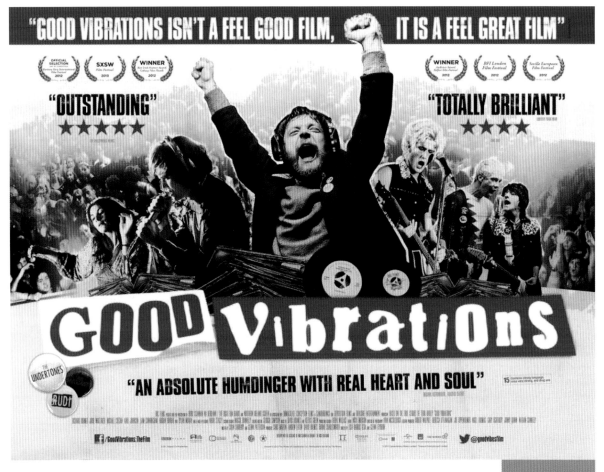

Belfast
'Teenage Kicks' at Wizard Sound Studios

The Undertones recorded their career-defining hit 'Teenage Kicks' at Wizard Sound Studios, a short walk from Belfast city centre. On June 16, 1978, they recorded a four-track EP's worth of material for the £108 it cost to hire the tiny studio. Belfast record label Good Vibrations in Great Victoria Street was where the band, along with other young outfits The Moondogs and The Outcasts, were signed. Where these bands once popped in and out of the Good Vibrations office, Belfast folk now book holidays and rent cars at the newly erected Norwood House, where the label and record shop once did its business. If accessing the city by using the M3 motorway, look out for the mural featuring The Undertones' '"Teenage kicks all through the night" lyric line, which spans the wall beneath the flyover at Bridge End, to the east of the city.

LOCATIONS 739, 740 and 741: Wizard Sound Studios were at Exchange Place, off lower Donegall Street, postcode BT1 2. South of the city centre was where the Good Vibrations label operated from a record shop (now demolished) at 102 Great Victoria Street, postcode BT2 7BE. The M3 'Teenage Kicks' flyover mural is under a mile east of the city at Bridge End, postcode BT5 4

Released in 2013, Good Vibrations the movie tells the story behind Belfast's punk-rock scene and the role played by the scene's pivotal character Terri Hooley, who founded the famous shop and created the label

Belfast
The Ruby Murray mural

Moltke Street and Benburb Street were where the young Ruby Murray grew up. Britain's top chart star in 1955, Ruby's achievement of five hit singles in one week's Top 20 that year is a record unsurpassed by any female singer to this day. The shy girl who made her TV debut aged just 12 is immortalised off the Donegall Road by an informative biographical mural in nearby Maldon Street.

LOCATION 742: Ruby Murray's original homes in Moltke Street and 49 Benburb Street are no longer standing. The mural is opposite the Methodist church in Maldon Street. All three locations join the Donegall Road in an area a mile or so south-west of the city centre. Postcode: BT12 6

Ruby Murray (March 29, 1935 - December 17, 1996) was a popular singer born in Moltke Street and brought up in the Village. Her characteristic hoarse voice was a result of an operation on her throat in early childhood. She toured as a child singer, and first appeared on television at the age of 12. Her first single was 'Heartbeat', which reached the UK top 5 in 1954.

The next, 'Softly, Softly', reached number 1 in 1955, a year in which Murray achieved the rare feat of having five singles in the top twenty at the same time. Ruby still holds the record for the most hit records in the Top Twenty at the same time; beating Madonna and the Beatles.

Belfast
Simple Minds' 'Belfast Child'

"Enniskillen was, I think, the catalyst to the song." So said Jim Kerr, describing the 1989 Simple Minds single 'Belfast Child', which was based on the traditional Irish folk tune 'She Moves Through the Fair'. With lyrics by the band's Glasgow-born singer, the chart-topper was a poignant updating of the ballad, prompted by the recent escalation of violence during 'The Troubles' in the province at the time. Where most late-Eighties pop promo videos were selling records using exotic Caribbean locations as backdrops, the 'Belfast Child' video was soberly filmed in and around the city's derelict and disappearing landscape. Shot in black and white, Simple Minds perform the song against the backdrop of the once thriving Harland and Wolff shipyard and on top of a Belfast rubbish dump, interspersed with glimpses of depressingly decaying streets and the Stormont parliament buildings.

LOCATION 743: the increasingly redundant shipyard area is a short distance north-east of the city centre, postcode BT3 9DU

Coney Island
Van the day tripper

A biographical spoken-word poem set to a sweeping orchestral accompaniment, 'Coney Island' first featured on Van Morrison's 1989 album Avalon Sunset. Not an island at all but a small group of seaside bungalows and a beach on the County Down coast, Coney Island is one location on the frequently made journeys out of his home city of Belfast name-checked by Van as day trip destinations of his youth. Downpatrick, St John's Point, Strangford Lough, Shrigley, Killyleagh, Lecale and Ardglass all get a mention as his narration recalls favourite pastimes: birdwatching, reading the Sunday papers and snacking on mussels and potted herring.

LOCATION 744: Van Morrison's Coney Island is 30 miles south-east of Belfast. To emulate Van's car trips to the seaside, head for Downpatrick and then follow the A2 coastal road round to Coney Island. Postcode: BT30 7UQ

Photo: Ritchie McLardy

Photo: Pete Nash

Belfast
Beatles are record-breakers at The King's Hall

While the Ritz cinema at Fisherwick Place was the first to host a concert by them in 1963 (demolished and now Jurys Inn hotel), The King's Hall is Northern Ireland's only venue still standing that played host to The Beatles. Reassuringly, the cavernous King's Hall looks much the same from the outside as it did back on November 2nd 1964 when the Fab Four made the second of only two visits to Northern Ireland. The King's Hall provided enough space for The Beatles to attract their largest British concert audience when 17,500 fans, no doubt excited by the summer release of the A Hard Day's Night movie and LP, crammed into the venue for two capacity attendances of 8,750, witnessing an early and late evening show. Belfast Beatles fan Ed McCann attended the late evening show and recalls one now famous incident: "A local paper had run an article that the boys liked jelly babies and Lennon

and McCartney were playfully ducking to and fro trying to avoid the downpour of jelly babies thrown by their adoring fans." During their visit all four Beatles tucked into The King's Hall's catering, scoffing a selection of north Irish bread and a pot of tea served by waitress Susy Crymble, who was treated to their impromptu rendition of the Everly Brothers hit 'Wake Up Little Susie'. Also working for the catering company that day was May Majury, who, despite getting John, Paul, George, Ringo and manager Brian Epstein's autographs, was dismayed that they didn't pay their half crown (12 pence) bill. May eventually got over her indignation at the incident when, years later, the signatures realised an astronomical value unthinkable at the time.

LOCATION 745: about three miles south-west of the city centre on Lisburn Road, postcode BT9 6GW

The cavernous King's Hall, where 17,500 Beatles fans attended the two shows on November 2, 1964. Top right and left: Programme cover for The Beatles' record-breaking King's Hall date in 1964 and 14-year-old Ritchie McLardy's ticket to The Beatles' second show

Londonderry
Early Undertones at Bull Park and the Casbah

The Undertones' five members came together to form a band in Derry in 1975, and three years later they had broadened their horizons and caught the punk epidemic, marking their recording debut with 'Teenage Kicks' in Belfast's Wizard Sound Studios. Closer to home, two important locations of activity for the band were Derry's now demolished Casbah, little more than a portacabin on a bomb site, and Bull Park, where the five friends once played football as kids. The park was the setting for a group photo taken for the cover of their first LP and where they played an outdoor gig in 1978. Surprisingly, there is still no plaque on the walls of the Foyleside shopping centre, where the mighty Casbah once helped five lads from Derry to shake the world.

LOCATIONS 746 and 747: the north wall of Bull Park is the spot where the band were photographed for their debut album sleeve. The park is on the B524 Lone Moor Road near the city centre, postcode BT48 9. The Casbah was at the top of Orchard Street, where it turns left at Bridge Street at the junction

The Undertones at Bull Park line up for the cover of their debut album

" For us getting up on stage at the Casbah on a Friday night, SLIGHTLY BOMBED on three pints of beer, it was pure, utter escapism. Our audience, i.e. our mates, didn't really need us on a Friday night to get up and lecture them about what was politically and socially going on... For them it was the same thing, three pints of Guinness and hallelujah here comes Saturday morning "

FEARGAL SHARKEY

Northern Ireland

Portballintrae
Houses of the Holy at the Giant's Causeway

The Giant's Causeway is an extraordinary rock formation and World Heritage site situated on the northern coastline of Northern Ireland, a place that captured the imagination of graphic artists Hipgnosis when creating a new album cover for Led Zeppelin in 1973. In the days before effortless photo montaging on screen in a comfy design studio, creative types (and their models) actually braved all weathers to snap the best images for covers, like the superb sci-fi landscape for the band's Houses of the Holy album. Here's how Hipgnosis designer Storm Thorgerson remembered the photo shoot: "The photo for the cover of Led Zeppelin's Houses of the Holy was taken at the Giant's Causeway in Northern Ireland. At 4am every morning for a week, three adults and two children were sprayed silver and gold from head to toe and driven to the location to await a glorious sunrise that never happened."

LOCATION 748: less than four miles by road north-east of Portballintrae in County Antrim, on the B147 at 44a Causeway Road, postcode BT57 8SU

Top: Inspired by Arthur C. Clarke's book Childhood's End, Hipgnosis designer Aubrey 'Po' Powell hand-tinted the black and white photo and used cutouts of the children to make a collage for the finished result. Above: 21-st century US rock band Imagine Dragons were also inspired by the Giant's Causeway when settling on an image for their 2012 hit debut album Night Visions

Born in NORTHERN IRELAND

Derek Bell, multi-instrumentalist, The Chieftains (b. 21 Oct 1935, Belfast, d. 17 Oct 2002)

Eric Bell, guitar, Thin Lizzy (b. 3 Sep 1947, Belfast)

Michael Bradley, bass, The Undertones (b. 13 Aug 1959, Londonderry)

Jake Burns, vocals/guitar, Stiff Little Fingers (b. 21 Feb 1958, Belfast)

Andy Cairns, vocals/guitar, Therapy? (b. 22 Sep 1965, Ballyclare, Co. Antrim)

Vivian Campbell, guitar, Def Leppard (b. 25 Aug 1962, Belfast)

Henry Cluney, guitar, Stiff Little Fingers (b. 4 Aug 1957, Belfast)

Nathan Connolly, guitar, Snow Patrol (b. 20 Jan 1981, Belfast)

Phil Coulter, songwriter (b. 19 Feb 1942, Londonderry)

Nadine Coyle, Girls Aloud (b. 15 Jun 1985, Londonderry)

Peter Cunnah, vocals, D:Ream (b. 30 Aug 1966, Londonderry)

Billy Doherty, drums, The Undertones (b. 10 Jul 1958, Enniskillen)

Candida Doyle, keyboards, Pulp (b. 25 Aug 1963, Belfast)

Fyfe Ewing, drums, Therapy? (b. 1 Nov 1970, Larne, Co. Antrim)

Mark Hamilton, bass, Ash (b. 21 Mar 1977, Lisburn)

Neil Hannon, The Divine Comedy (b. 7 Nov 1970, Londonderry)

David Holmes, DJ/producer (b. 14 Feb 1969, Belfast)

Bobby Kildea, bass, Belle & Sebastian (b. 14 Mar 1972, Belfast)

Gary Lightbody, vocals/guitar, Snow Patrol (b.15 Jun 1976, Bangor, Co. Down)

Mark McClelland, bass guitar, Snow Patrol (b. 30 Mar 1976, Belfast)

Henry McCullough, guitar, Spooky Tooth/Wings (b. 21 Jul 1943, Portstewart)

Michael McKeegan, bass, Therapy? (b. 23 Mar 1971, Larne, Co. Antrim)

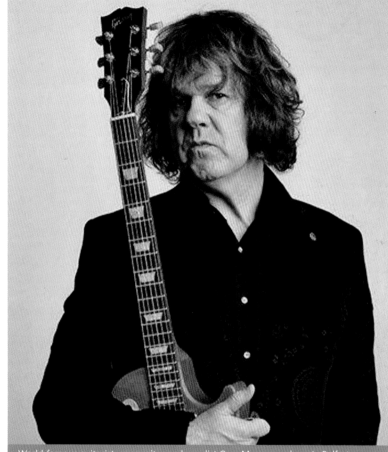

World-famous guitarist, songwriter and vocalist Gary Moore was born in Belfast and grew up on Castleview Road, to the extreme east of the city

Ali McMordie, bass, Stiff Little Fingers (b. 31 Mar 1959, Belfast)

Rick McMurray, drums, Ash (b. 11 Jul 1975, Downpatrick)

David McWilliams, singer-songwriter (b. 4 Jul 1945, Belfast, d. 8 Jan 2002)

Gary Moore, guitar (b. 4 Apr 1952, Belfast, d. 6 Feb 2011)

Van Morrison (b. 31 Aug 1945, Belfast)

Ruby Murray (b. 29 Mar 1935, Belfast, d. 17 Dec 1996)

Damian O'Neill, guitar, The Undertones (b. 15 Jan 1961, Londonderry)

John O'Neill, guitar, The Undertones (b. 26 Aug 1957, Londonderry)

Jonny Quinn, drums, Snow Patrol (b. 26 Feb 1972, Bangor, Co. Down)

Clodagh Rodgers (b. 5 Mar 1947, Ballymena, Co. Antrim)

Feargal Sharkey (b. 13 Aug 1958, Londonderry)

Tim Wheeler, vocals/guitar, Ash (b. 4 Jan 1977, Downpatrick)

Eric Wrixon, Them/Thin Lizzy/The People (b. 29 Jun 1947, Belfast)

Republic of Ireland

*I*f Dublin is the logical homing-in point for music fans who congregate in the tourist-friendly Temple Bar, there are plenty of music venues punching above their weight farther afield, particularly in Clonakilty, Limerick and a proper rock pilgrimage point at Slane Castle. When County Clare's Lisdoonvarna Festival (so good Christy Moore wrote a song about it) halted, Slane Castle began to dominate the festival scene; thus began U2's castle connections, supporting Thin Lizzy at Slane in 1981 and famously using Moydrum and Carrigogunnell for cover album shots. A late developer, Ireland's rock heritage had its legacy based in the folk and highly successful showband culture, but the country would appear to be streets ahead of the UK when it comes to honouring its own. Phil Lynott, Joe Dolan and Rory Gallagher are all remembered by their statues. 'Foreigners' Noel Redding and Ronnie Wood came to live, The Rolling Stones came to tea and The Beatles paid a flying visit, with John Lennon returning to buy an island off the west coast. Then there's Horslips' haunted house, Sebadoh's Harmacy, "Van the Man's" Veedon Fleece cover, The Waterboys' inspirational base on Galway Bay, a Script video, US West Coast obsessives The Thrills and a plethora of U2 locations in keeping with the adoration afforded to one of the world's biggest rock acts.

Ardfield
Noel Redding: County Cork's adopted son

When Noel Redding moved to Ardfield in 1973 he didn't lead the rock reclusive lifestyle - he embraced everything the local community had to offer. The former Jimi Hendrix Experience bass guitarist purchased Dunowen House, a farmhouse built in 1771 located a short stroll from the sea, and helped support a thriving music scene in the area. The villagers' fondness for the rock star born in Folkestone, Kent, was illustrated by the Ardfield plaque they erected in his memory after his death in 2003. Redding's funeral service was held at the Catholic church in Clonakilty and his ashes were scattered in the gardens at his Dunowen home.

LOCATION 749: Ardfield, County Cork, is a hamlet on the Atlantic coast, five miles south of Clonakilty. The Noel Redding memorial plaque is on a wall outside O'Mahoney's pub

Athlone
Unforgettable Fire at Moydrum Castle

Built in the 17th century, the ruined Moydrum Castle provided the spectacular landscape featured on the cover of U2's 1984 album The Unforgettable Fire. The cover shoot for what would become the band's second No.1 album includes Bono, The Edge, Larry Mullen, Jr and Adam Clayton in the foreground of the ivy-covered structure, photographed by Anton Corbijn. A second ruin, Carrigogunnell Castle, is pictured on the vinyl album back cover and in the CD booklet.

LOCATION 750: Athlone is in County Westmeath in the centre of Ireland. On the Athlone bypass (N6), head east and turn left after the next junction after the town centre turn-off. Then turn right, following a sign to Mount Temple. After more than two miles, turn right at the junction just before two red-brick properties. Continue up the hill to the next corner. The castle is on the right. Carrigogunnell Castle is a mile north of Clarina, off the N69 west of Limerick

A symbol of British power, Moydrum Castle was the target for an Irish Republican Army attack when set on fire in 1921

Ballincollig
Rory Gallagher's sunburst headstone

St Oliver's Cemetery at Ballincollig is where guitarist Rory Gallagher was buried following his death in 1995, aged just 47. The unusual sunburst-style headstone is shaped to mimic the 1972 award he received for International Guitarist of the Year. Before the funeral at this peaceful place outside the city where he lived, crowds numbering 15,000 lined the streets of Cork for the funeral procession to pay their last respects to a true Irish rock legend.

LOCATION 751: Ballincollig is west of Cork city. The cemetery is signposted on Model Farm Road. As you enter, go past the little house on the left and turn right

The distinctive Rory Gallagher headstone at St Oliver's Cemetery

Boherlahan
Horslips' haunted house of bales

Set in a "rural hinterland" according to the local property agents, Longfield House was the base for the recordings of Celtic rockers Horslips' debut album Happy to Meet… Sorry to Part in autumn 1972. Hiring The Rolling Stones' mobile unit, the band booked the 18th-century County Tipperary house, recording in the drawing room, cellar and library. Perfecting the old house's acoustics proved a problem. Improvising, they used the neighbouring farm's hay bales and loaned the stage curtains from Trinity College Players Theatre in Dublin as sound baffles. All remote old houses rented for get-away-from-it-all rock music recordings are reportedly haunted and Longfield House was no exception, although the band were probably more materially irritated by the vast numbers of insects that plagued the place once they had escaped from the imported, infested hay bales.

LOCATION 752: in the centre of the lush Golden Vale near the village of Boherlahan, five miles north of Cashel, off the R660 in County Tipperary

Blackrock
East Ireland to West Coast for The Thrills

Thrills band members Conor Deasy and Daniel Ryan were born next door to each other in the east coast town of Blackrock. The nucleus of the band and friends famously decamped to California in their late teens, seeking out the roots of their obsession with US West Coast musical heroes. The resulting formation of The Thrills and release of their debut album So Much for the City in 2003 led to one in six homes in Ireland owning a copy.

LOCATION 753: Blackrock, County Dublin, is six miles south of the centre of Dublin, found by taking the N11 then N31 out of the city

Republic of Ireland

Ballyshannon
Rory Gallagher's birthplace statue

Although blues-rock guitar hero Rory Gallagher's childhood (from the age of three) was spent in Derry and then Cork, where he formed Taste, Ballyshannon was his birthplace. Although he never had the chance to return and perform in the town once he became internationally famous, Ballyshannon's favourite son is immortalised in a life-size statue in the town centre. What is said to be the oldest town in Ireland has hosted the Rory Gallagher Festival annually for many years, attracting thousands of music fans to this west Ireland spot. In another memorial to the great man, the building where his mother both sang and acted for the Abbey Players was renamed the Rory Gallagher Theatre in his honour.

LOCATION 754: Ballyshannon is close to Ireland's west coast in County Donegal. The statue is positioned in the town centre where Main Street and Market Street fork

The intense stage pose of Rory Gallagher captured brilliantly by sculptor David Annand

Cashel
Album title snapped by Sebadoh

American band Sebadoh visually adopted this town in County Tipperary when the cover of their 1996 album Harmacy pictured a pharmacy in Cashel's Main Street. While on tour in Ireland,,the band's multi-instrumentalist Jason Loewenstein snapped a number of photos on the road. Bandmate Lou Barlow, talking to reporter Michael Stutz, recalled: "We did a little tour of Ireland and Jason took this picture of this totally run-down pharmacy from the van window and the pharmacy was just run down to the point where the 'P' had actually fallen off – really big letters, too, and when we were looking for pictures for the album he had a lot of pictures that he had taken and we chose three of his photographs for the album. And when we saw the pharmacy picture we're like, 'That's it, that's the ******* title right there!'"

LOCATION 755: O'Dwyer's Pharmacy, 34 Main Street. Cashel is off the M8 Dublin to Cork motorway

Bray
Dr Strangely Strange's 'Garden of Eden'

A tranquil spot where the local angling club is based is the setting for the cover of Dr Strangely Strange's Kip of the Serenes album. Produced by Joe Boyd, the psychedelic folk group's 1969 debut release came in a sleeve picturing the band assembled in the trickling waters of the River Dargle, a spot well known for producing some of Ireland's biggest sea trout. Recalling his obviously happy childhood on the banks of the Dargle, Dr Strangely Strange band member Tim Goulding eloquently recalls: "Us three kids spent our days in this Garden of Eden on the banks of a Guinness-brown torrent in winter and a stately trickle in the summer."

LOCATION 756: the River Dargle and Dargle Valley are near Bray, County Wicklow

Clane
Ronnie Wood's home from home at Sandymount

A good pint of Guinness and a decent snooker table were always essentials in the Ronnie Wood lifestyle. Two good reasons why the former Faces guitarist made Sandymount House his rural home when the money rolled in from The Rolling Stones' lucrative Steel Wheels Tour in 1989/90. He converted the property's outbuildings into an art studio, a film and tape archive and his own pub (Yer Father's Yacht) and set about breeding racehorses. Outside a statue of Elvis Presley greets house guests, which have included Slash, David Bowie, Bob Dylan, Jerry Lee Lewis and the remaining Stones, who all convened here for early work on 1994 album Voodoo Lounge. Wood's sanctuary in the lush County Kildare countryside is bordered by the Grand Canal and was a real home from home for the musician and talented painter, who as a child grew up on the banks of the Grand Union Canal, at Yiewsley, in north-west London.

LOCATION 757: two miles north of the M8 and two miles south of Clane, Sandymount House is at the 16th lock and bridge on the Grand Canal, County Kildare

Cork
U2 at The Montenotte hotel

It would be more than a year before U2 would enjoy their first UK chart entry, but in February 1980 the quartet were already registering their second Irish chart-topper. On the 4th of this month they played Cork City's Country Club Hotel (now The Montenotte hotel) and were snapped in front of the Cork City skyline by NME freelance photographer David Corio on the building's roof. Corio's pictures of the fresh-faced future rock legends are now displayed in the hotel's lobby, but the most memorable shot was used to great effect years later on the book cover U2 by U2 and greatest hits album and DVD U218 Singles, published and released in 2006.

LOCATION 758: Middle Glanmire Road, north-east of the city centre

David Corio had never heard of U2 when dispatched for his first overseas photo shoot for NME in 1980

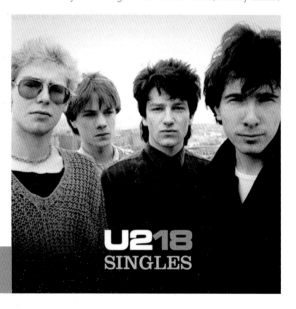

Republic of Ireland

Castlemartyr
The Rolling Stones stop for tea

The quiet village of Castlemartyr played host to the world's most
controversial pop stars when The Rolling Stones broke their journey en
route to Cork on January 8, 1965. The Austin Princess ferrying them to two
evening performances at Cork's Savoy theatre stopped outside what is
now the village greengrocer to enable the five Stones to avail themselves
of some Castlemartyr refreshment. While the two older band members,
Charlie Watts and Bill Wyman, headed for tea at Mrs Farrell's eating house,
Mick Jagger, Keith Richard and Brian Jones made for a winter warmer or
two at Barry's Bar. The village is little changed since their visit, a fact proved
by a brief scene in Charlie Is My Darling, the Stones' cult movie of their
riotously received three-day Irish tour. The picture (right) shows the Stones
and manager Andrew Loog Oldham being filmed in a scene from the movie
as their train speeds through Ireland.

LOCATION 759: one of two villages in County Cork with this name, the
Castlemartyr the Stones visited is about 25 miles east of Cork on the N25.
The bridge end of Main Street is where they stopped. Barry's Bar is now
Pat Shortt's, owned by the Irish celebrity of that name, but Mrs Farrell's
establishment is long gone

" Our sort of **SUCCESS** is a first-class ticket to a lot of things. On the other hand, there's not much physical **FREEDOM** 🔊🔊

BRIAN JONES
Ireland, 1965

Marc Sharratt/Rex Features

Republic of Ireland

Photo: Diarmud O'Sullivan

Clonakilty
English rock and folk legends at De Barra

A very musical town and nicknamed 'Bohemia by the sea' by The Irish Times, Clonakilty has a number of hostelries doubling as rock and folk venues. The atmospheric De Barra has the highest profile due to English singer-songwriter Roy Harper's 2004 DVD Beyond The Door being recorded there and, until his death in 2003, legendary Jimi Hendrix Experience bass guitarist Noel Redding's regular Friday night performances. Both musicians moved to this south coast region to set up home and The Noel Redding Band's 1975 debut album was affectionately titled Clonakilty Cowboys. Among the music memorabilia on display is Noel's signature Fender bass, photos, letters, gold discs, a number of traditional Irish folk instruments and Roy Harper's Mojo magazine Hero award. There is a plaque commemorating Redding's life outside the front door of De Barra and every May since he died the place hosts the Noel Redding Experience festival, celebrating all things Noel. Shanley's, Mick Finns, O'Donovan's Hotel, Scannells Bar and The Back Door are just some of the venues which also contribute to the town's commendable musical heritage, which includes the International Guitar Festival.

LOCATION 760: Clonakilty is on the N71 in west Cork. De Barra is on the R588 in the town centre at 55 Pearse Street

ROY HARPER
BEYOND THE DOOR

Top: The Elephant Family charity makes an impact on this De Barra regular and (above) the DVD Roy Harper recorded at this Clonakilty venue

Cork
Kurt Cobain's Irish roots

In August 1991, Nirvana played Sir Henry's bar, a support slot for Sonic Youth that went down well with the Cork audience that night but which also led to a spiritual revelation for frontman Kurt Cobain. Recalling the day vividly, here is how he explained the experience to rock music writer Jon Savage two years later. "[The Cobains] came from County Cork, which is a weird coincidence, because when [Nirvana] toured Ireland, we played in Cork and the entire day I walked around in a daze. I'd never felt more spiritual in my life. It was the weirdest feeling, and I have one friend who was with me who could testify to this. I was almost in tears the whole day. Since that tour, which was about two years ago, I've had like a sense that I was from Ireland."

LOCATION 761: Sir Henry's once stood on South Main Street, before closure in 2003 and demolition

Dorinish Island
Lennon's "island off Ireland"

After spotting a newspaper "for sale" headline advertising "an island off Ireland", John Lennon purchased Dorinish Island in Clew Bay, off the west coast in 1967 for £1,700. On instructions from Lennon, The Beatles' "Mr Fixit", Alistair Taylor, travelled to Ireland and outbid a crowd of more than 30 locals to secure the place for Lennon. The then uninhabited island was visited by Lennon, who shipped a psychedelically painted caravan to the 19-acre plot of land for him, wife Cynthia and son Julian to sleep in. A year later, he visited again with new partner Yoko Ono and the couple looked forward to building a cottage and spending holidays in their off-shore Irish bolt-hole. But time ran out on a planning permission option and, after Lennon's death, Yoko sold Dorinish in 1984 to a local farmer who now grazes his sheep on it. When in the area to visit the island, John and Yoko stayed at the Mulranny Park Hotel, with views of the Atlantic Ocean over Clew Bay. This grand 81-bedroom Victorian hotel has appropriately themed the room the couple once used (now offered as the John Lennon Suite) in tribute to the Beatle who so loved this quiet Irish outpost.

"The most PEACEFUL place on Earth"
JOHN LENNON
describes Dorinish Island

LOCATION 762: a 20-minute boat ride from the mainland at Westport, Dorinish is one of 365 islands in Clew Bay, off the west coast of County Mayo. The Mulranny Park Hotel is at 1 Mulranny Road, off the N59, County Mayo

The realistic battered replica guitar in its elevated wall position in Temple Bar

Dublin 2
The Rory Gallagher Strat sculpture

A detailed and realistic replica of bluesman Rory Gallagher's iconic, battered 1961 Fender Stratocaster guitar is fixed to the wall that bears his name in one of Dublin's busiest spots. The actual-size bronze cast sculpture at Rory Gallagher Corner was unveiled as a tribute to the guitarist in 2007, a ceremony attended by Dublin Mayor Catherine Byrne and a rock god in the form of U2 guitarist The Edge. Rory's guitar was said to be the first Fender Stratocaster purchased in Ireland. As a measure of his enduring popularity, Rory's DVD, Live at Montreux, was top of the Irish chart at the time of the Strat's unveiling. "His legacy will live on in hundreds of bands in this country," as The Edge put it at the unveiling of the Stratocaster in Temple Bar.

LOCATION 763: the Strat sculpture is at Rory Gallagher Corner on East Essex Street, just beside Meeting House Square, Temple Bar, Dublin 2

Republic of Ireland

Photos: Chrysalis/John Prew and David Roberts

Cork
The Rory Gallagher tour

The town where Rory Gallagher grew up has a number of
significant locations connected to the Irish guitar hero. Currently,
there's even a petition rename Cork's airport after him. A
Gallagher tour of the city would best start chronologically at
Crowleys Music Centre, the shop where the budding guitarist
purchased his first Fender Stratocaster in 1963 and where a wall
plaque informs visitors that Rory once lived on the same street.
Then head for the Long Valley bar, where his band Taste were
said to have formed, and Leader's, the shop where Gallagher
bought his trademark check shirts. A Rory Gallagher sculpture
by his childhood friend Geraldine Creedon was unveiled in 1997
in what is now Rory Gallagher Place (formerly Paul Street Plaza)
and a café named Taste, complete with replica Stratocaster,
is a good place to pause before continuing your tour at Cork

City Library's Rory Gallagher Music Room, which displays
memorabilia from the man's short career and opened in the
same year as the café, in 2004. He also once played at the still
elegant building that housed the Savoy theatre and may well
have been one of the fans who squeezed into the venue for the
legendary Rolling Stones shows on January 8, 1965.

LOCATIONS 764, 765, 766, 767, 768, 769 and 770: all within
walking distance and with the northernmost first. Crowleys Music
Centre is north over the river at 29 MacCurtain Street. Then head
back west to Leader's at 76-77 North Main Street. Next stop is
back east to Rory Gallagher Place and then south to the Savoy
theatre at 108 St Patrick's Street. Then head south to the Long
Valley bar at 10 Winthrop Street and continue south across the
southern section of the River Lee to the Taste café at 4 Union
Quay. End your tour by heading west again over the river to Cork
City Library on Grand Parade

Opposite, top left: The man himself - a 1976 record company press shot of Rory Gallagher

Opposite, top right: The Savoy theatre is still operating as a live music venue. Where once The Rolling Stones famously trod this stage, now the likes of the Wu-Tang Clan and Mumford & Sons attract the famously enthusiastic Cork music fans

Above: Rory Gallagher Place: the setting for a tribute sculpture to the guitarist by Geraldine Creedon

Right: Leader's, where Rory Gallagher once purchased his trademark check shirts

Republic of Ireland

Dublin 1
The Beatles escape to the Gresham Hotel

The venue for The Beatles' only performances in the Republic of Ireland, the now demolished Adelphi cinema, may be long gone but Dublin's Gresham Hotel, where the Fab Four stayed, continues to thrive. Their visit coincided with the release of No.1 EP, featuring the tracks 'I Saw Her Standing There', 'Misery', 'Anna (Go to Him)' and 'Chains'. Arriving at Dublin Airport shortly after midday on November 7, 1963, John, Paul, George and Ringo were driven away to the Gresham before heading to the Adelphi for a press conference ahead of two sold-out concerts at 6.30 and 9pm at the 2,304-capacity cinema. Their relatively sedate journey to the hotel from the airport was in stark contrast to the manner in which they found themselves transported back to the Gresham after the concert curtain came down at 11pm. All four Beatles exited the Adelphi via the back entrance in Prussia Street, where a waiting Evening Herald newspaper van whisked them back to their hotel in the wake of scenes approaching riot status. The mayhem had begun earlier when fans attending the first evening performance clashed with those pushing their way enthusiastically in for the second show of the night. In the chaos that followed, windows were smashed, at least one car in the streets outside was set ablaze and others were overturned.

LOCATIONS 771 and 772: the Adelphi cinema (now demolished and replaced with a car park for Arnotts department store) was at 98-101 Middle Abbey Street. The Gresham Hotel is still standing at 23 Upper O'Connell, Dublin 1

" I have real **TANGIBLE** sight and sound and smell memories of things like The Beatles: very heavy velvet draped curtains, a leather pointed boot sticking out under the curtain and the place going ballistic "

BOB GELDOF
recalls his experience as a
12-year-old at the Adelphi

Republic of Ireland

Dublin 1
Ireland's largest indoor rock venue

Ireland's largest venue is the 14,500 capacity 3Arena. Before the site's 2007 refurbishment and renaming it was as The Point that it had built a reputation in the Nineties as the country's foremost music venue, hosting the Eurovision Song Contest three times and the MTV Europe Awards. The former dockside train depot has attracted worldwide talent of the calibre of Bob Dylan, David Bowie, Bruce Springsteen, Oasis, R.E.M., Nirvana, U2, Coldplay, Def Leppard, Beyoncé and Kings of Leon, with local boys Westlife hitting the headlines with 12 sold-out shows in 2007.

LOCATION 773: north side of the River Liffey at the end of North Wall Quay, Dublin 1

Dublin 2
Rock treasures at the Hard Rock Café

Fittingly dominated by U2 memorabilia, Dublin's Hard Rock Café includes an original U2 Zoo TV Tour Trabant car suspended from the restaurant ceiling. A shirt worn by Elvis in the '50s, a Madonna jacket, a rather beautiful rug from Jimi Hendrix's London apartment and Paul McCartney's Beatles boots are just some of the treasures on display.

LOCATION 774: 12 Fleet Street, in the heart of the Temple Bar area, Dublin 2

Dublin 2
The Phil Lynott statue

Thin Lizzy, variously advertised as The Tin Lizzie and Thin Lizzie and promoted as a new supergroup featuring former members of Them, The Dreams, Skid Row, Orphanage, Sugarshack and The Trixons, played their first gigs in and around Dublin in 1970. Early venues St Anthony's, Liberty and St Aidan's Halls, Glasnevin Tennis Club and the Town & Country and Countdown clubs helped propel the band to the world stage after the release of their breakthrough hit 'Whiskey in the Jar'. The English-born Lizzy frontman, bass guitarist and solo star Phil Lynott died aged just 36 in 1986 but is rock royalty to Dublin's music fans, where his statue stands close to two of his favourite haunts, the Zodiac Club and the Bailey pub in Upper Duke Street. Unveiled in 2005 by his mother Philomena, the statue was created by Paul Daly and cast in bronze by Leo Higgins. Famously vandalised and removed in May 2014, it was happily restored to its original position by August that same year. Lynott, who grew up on Leighlin Road, Crumlin, used his beloved Dublin as the backdrop to the video for his solo single 'Old Town' in 1982.

LOCATION 775: the statue stands just north of St Stephen's Green, outside Bruxelles bar on Harry Street, Dublin 2

West Bromwich-born, Irish to the core and immortalised in bronze: Phil Lynott

Photo: Stephen Wallis Photography www.stephenwallis.ie

Philip P Lynott 1949-1986

Dublin 2
The Dubliners start at O'Donoghue's

The Dubliners band were formed at O'Donoghue's bar on Merrion Row and have returned to this shrine to Irish music regularly. Also associated closely with O'Donoghue's are those other Irish folk favourites The Fureys, who hailed from Ballyfermot to the west of the city.

ÉIRE 48c

THE DUBLINERS

2006

LOCATION 776: 15 Merrion Row is near the north-east corner of St Stephen's Green

An appropriate way for the Rock Atlas tourist to write home with The Dubliners stamp adorning your postcard

Dublin 2
The Script 'Breakeven' at Whelan's

Since 1989, when Whelan's morphed into a music venue, Bloc Party, Nick Cave, Arctic Monkeys, The Magic Numbers and Jeff Buckley have all played the place where a pub has stood since 1771. Dubliners The Script shot the video for their 2008 single 'Breakeven' at Whelan's and out and about in Dublin. Script band members Danny O'Donoghue and Mark Sheehan met in the Liberties area of Dublin and songs like their first single, the anthemic 'We Cry', were inspired by the people and streets of their home city.

LOCATION 777: 25 Wexford Street, Dublin 2

Dublin 2
U2's 'Beautiful Day' on the roof

The Clarence Hotel was famously purchased by U2's Bono and The Edge in 1992. The pair are regular visitors and famously used the hotel's rooftop as the stage when the band previewed new tracks 'Elevation' and 'Beautiful Day' for broadcast on BBC TV's Top of the Pops in 2000. By the time the quartet arrived to perform on September 27 at 3pm, the wind and rain that had failed to deter thousands of fans lining the surrounding streets and bridges was replaced, appropriately, by a beautiful day's sunshine.

LOCATION 778: in the west end of the city's cultural quarter Temple Bar, south side of the River Liffey on Wellington Quay, Dublin 2

Dublin 2
Horslips' Celtic rock on Crow Street

An art gallery in Crow Street was the beginning of the story for Ireland's innovative folk-rockers Horslips. In the early Seventies they rehearsed and played their first gigs at Galerie Langlois, a gallery owned by Brendan Langlois-Kennedy, an artist friend of the band. The building is now part of the music, food, fashion and arts community of shops at Crow Street Bazaar.

LOCATION 779: at 7 Crow Street, Temple Bar, Dublin 2

Dublin 2
Irish Top 12 honoured on the Wall of Fame

The Wall of Fame was launched in 2005 when music broadcaster Dave Fanning flicked a switch to light up the images of 12 Irish music legends on a unique tribute in Dublin's Temple Bar. The wall is made up of a permanent exhibition of illuminated photographs illustrating 12 of Ireland's greatest musicians. Not a definitive list, say the organisers, those currently selected for their commercial success and pioneering and influential contributions are Christy Moore, Paul Brady, Luke Kelly, Phil Lynott, Rory Gallagher, Dolores O'Riordan, Bob Geldof, Shane MacGowan, Sinéad O'Connor, The Undertones, Van Morrison and U2.

LOCATION 780: in the popular Temple Bar area at the junction of Curved Street and Temple Lane South, Dublin 2

Dublin 2
Bono's Fitzwilliam Street video apology

The U2 video for 1998 hit 'Sweetest Thing' was filmed entirely in Fitzwilliam Place and north-east on Upper Fitzwilliam Street and Lower Fitzwilliam Street. Bono's personal apology in song to his wife Ali, whose birthday he had forgotten, is delivered with a good deal of humour in one take in the Kevin Godley-directed carriage ride.

LOCATION 781: between St Stephens Green, and Lower Fitzwilliam Street, Dublin 2

Dublin 2 & 4
U2 recording studios and message walls

Two districts of Dublin with a history of inspirational work where some of rock's greatest ever recording moments were committed to tape. Hanover Quay Studios has been the most used of U2's recording bases this century. Situated by the still waters of the Grand Canal Dock since 1994, the band's creative hub may face relocation soon as redevelopment of the old South Docks has been gathering pace over recent years. A wall of graffiti messages from visiting fans wanting to leave their mark is situated between the studio and the neighbouring concrete works. Years earlier, Windmill Lane Recording Studios was where the first three U2 albums were recorded in their entirety. They were the first rock band to record at the Irish traditional music set-up subsequently used by Kate Bush and the Spice Girls and purchased by Van Morrison in 2006. Although U2 no longer frequent these studios, now mostly used for TV and multimedia work, the original graffiti walls with thousands of messages still remain. In 1989,

Windmill Lane Recording Studios moved from Windmill Lane to Ringsend Road, where the band continued recording and mixing their albums. Also used by U2 for recordings and tour rehearsals is The Factory on Barrow Street. In 1994, Windmill Lane Recording Studios was the battleground for one of Mick Jagger and Keith Richards' most notorious rows during tense recordings for The Rolling Stones' Voodoo Lounge album. Appropriately, their festering animosity was brought to a head during the development of 'I Go Wild', a song that would end up as one of the album's single releases.

LOCATIONS 782, 783, 784 and 785: all within a short distance of each other, the original site for the Windmill studios is south of the River Liffey at 4 Windmill Lane, Dublin 2, and later a few streets east at 20 Ringsend Road, Dublin 4. The Factory is in the next road at 35a Barrow Street, Dublin 4, and Hanover Quay Studios is over the canal at Hanover Quay, Dublin 4

Still a tourist trap for music fans today, the original site of Windmill Lane studios

Dublin 5
Larry Mullen, Jr's childhood home

U2 drummer Larry Mullen, Jr's home was at 60 Rosemount Avenue, Artane. This was the venue for a band meeting after the 14-year-old Mullen advertised for musicians on the Mount Temple Comprehensive School notice board in 1976. This led to the formation of U2 and rehearsals in compliant teacher Mr McKenzie's class.

LOCATION 786: 60 Rosemount Avenue, Artane, is a private residence about five miles north-east of the city centre, between the R107 and R105

Dublin 10
Claddagh Road beginnings for The Fureys

World-famous Irish band of brothers The Fureys came from a family of travelling people who settled in Claddagh Road, which provided the folk group with the title of their 1994 album, the last recorded with Finbar Furey. "My father played the fiddle and the pipes; my mother played melodeon and five-string banjo. She was a wonderful singer as well... I can remember when we moved into our new house in Ballyfermot. My father singing in the empty rooms. We lived and breathed music," recalled Finbar.

LOCATION 787: Claddagh Road is about six miles west of Dublin city centre at Ballyfermot, Dublin 10

Dublin 11
Bono's childhood home

This is the house where young Paul Hewson changed into U2 frontman Bono (he had the box room bedroom). After Mum and Dad Hewson sold the place in 1986, the new owners were enjoying their first Christmas in the house when a concerned Bono is said to have turned up and enquired how they were coping with U2 fans making a pilgrimage to the place. In the U2 video for the 2005 chart-topping single 'Sometimes You Can't Make It on Your Own', a hooded Bono is filmed walking down Cedarwood Road vocalising an emotional tribute to his late father. Across the road is the house where the Rowen family lived. Bono's childhood friend Derek Rowen and his kid brother Peter also made their own unique mark on rock history. Peter was the blonde youngster pictured on U2 album covers Boy (1981) and War (1983) and Derek (aka Guggi), along with Bono and Gavin Friday, formed Irish punk band Virgin Prunes in 1977.

LOCATION 788: a private residence, 10 Cedarwood Road is four miles north of the centre of Dublin, found by taking the N2 out of the city, then right at the R103, then left on to Grove Park Road. Turn right and then left into Cedarwood Road

Above: Bono still returns to Cedarwood Road to check on the occupants of No.10 and film the odd music video

Below: Bono's young Cedarwood Road neighbour, Peter Rowen, was paid in Mars bars for this modelling assignment

Republic of Ireland

Howth
Phil Lynott and U2 in County Fingal

The peaceful seaside peninsula north-east of Dublin is where Phil Lynott once lived and is now buried at the local cemetery, St Fintan's, which is much visited by fans. A short stroll up the coast brings you to the home, White Horses, he bought for his mother Philomena, who acts as curator of a good deal of memorabilia and the enthusiastic and hard-working secretary of the Phil Lynott fan club. A Dublin tourism plaque is positioned above the front door of the house describing "Philip Parris Lynott" as "singer, songwriter, musician and poet". Back towards the north of the peninsula is Glen Corr, the home that the Thin Lizzy frontman purchased with the proceeds from the band's great commercial success in the '70s and '80s. U2 also appreciated the isolation of this beautiful spot. They rented what The Edge described as a 'tiny little house' at Howth to rehearse ahead of recording the band's 1983 LP, War and played a few early gigs at Howth's Community Centre and Howth Presbyterian Church hall back in the late '70s.

LOCATIONS 789 and 790: the east coast peninsula near Howth at County Fingal. For Glen Corr, head left at the R105 and R106 crossroads on to Howth Road, then left on to Claremont Road to the entrance to Glen Cross, which is a private residence. St Fintan's Cemetery is on the right on Carrickbrack Road. Phil Lynott is buried at Row 1, Plot 13. White Horses faces the beach on Strand Road, opposite the Sutton Dinghy Club

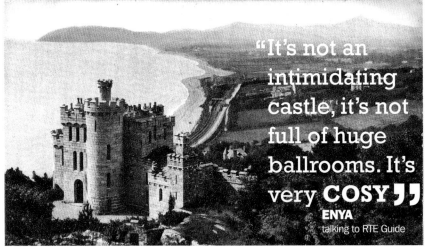

"It's not an intimidating castle, it's not full of huge ballrooms. It's very COSY"
ENYA
talking to RTE Guide

Killiney
Bono and Enya in 'Bel Eire'

Around 10 miles south-east of Dublin is Ireland's own Laurel Canyon-like scattering of rock and pop star properties nicknamed Bel Eire. Bono's elevated estate hugs the coast, while fellow U2 bandmate The Edge has a property at nearby Killiney Hill Road. Other musicians in love with the area include current property owners Van Morrison and Lisa Stansfield and former residents Jim Kerr and Chris de Burgh. Most spectacular of the Bel Eire rock pads is Ayesha Castle, renamed Manderley by its owner Enya due to the singer's love of the Daphne du Maurier book Rebecca, in which the house played a central role. These rock star pads are very private places and you will not gain access unless you are a family member or (in Bono's case) a world leader!

LOCATIONS 791 and 792: in County Dublin, where Bono's private estate is 10 miles south of the city of Dublin on the R119 coastal Vico Road, at the junction with Strathmore Road. The property is best viewed from the beach as Bono's privacy is protected by large gates. Enya's similarly private Ayesha Castle is on nearby Victoria Road

Howth
Van's Veedon Fleece backdrop

The grassy landscape depicted on the cover of Van Morrison's 1974 LP Veedon Fleece is in the grounds of Sutton House Hotel. The mansion is now a private residence and was the place overlooking Dublin Bay where Morrison holidayed when he first arrived back in Ireland after a gruelling 1973 tour. His three-week vacation, with fiance Carol Guida in October, led to a wave of song-writing that culminated in the release of Veedon Fleece a year later.

LOCATION 793: eight miles north-east of Dublin city centre, Sutton House, Shielmartin Road, Howth, north shore of Dublin Bay, County Fingal

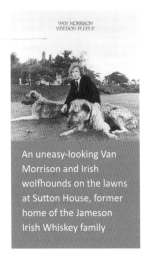

An uneasy-looking Van Morrison and Irish wolfhounds on the lawns at Sutton House, former home of the Jameson Irish Whiskey family

Limerick
Dolan's: a music mecca every night of the week

Anyone wanting to sample second hand the atmosphere at Dolan's could do worse than check out the 2007 DVD recorded at the venue by accordion maestro Sharon Shannon and her Big Band. Dolan's comprises three venues, two outdoor areas, a traditional Irish pub and a restaurant and boasts live music in the bar seven nights a week. In addition to showcasing all that is good about traditional Irish music, this mecca for music has hosted top-quality acts from farther afield including The Magic Numbers, Biffy Clyro, Kasabian, Alabama 3, Snow Patrol, Franz Ferdinand, Duffy and Imelda May.

LOCATION 794: 3/4 Dock Road, on the south side of the River Shannon, west of the city centre

Dolan's traditional Irish pub and the 300-capacity music venue which attracts bands of the calibre of Kasabian to Limerick

Republic of Ireland

Spiddal
The Waterboys' HQ

Spiddal House, in the village of Spiddal, forms the backdrop to the group photo on the cover of The Waterboys' 1988 album Fisherman's Blues. Spiddal House was discovered by the band's Mike Scott and rented as a perfect location for completing work on what would turn out to be the Celtic rockers' best-selling album. The cover photo was taken towards the end of recording in May that year and features the band members and recording personnel involved during an idyllic couple of months spent by the band in this seaside spot overlooking Galway Bay. Jam sessions, including at least one fair-weather appearance on the house's flat roof, games of football and regular appearances at local watering hole Hughes and the Quays bar (where new-found friends The Saw Doctors were playing every Tuesday) provided the happy atmosphere that enabled the band to complete Fisherman's Blues. Eager to draw on the magical surroundings again, The Waterboys returned to record all of the follow-up Room to Roam, which name-checks the location on the album's track 'Spring Comes to Spiddal'.

LOCATION 795: Moycullen Road on the coast of Galway Bay

Slane
Slane Castle: Ireland's premier outdoor music venue

Home to the 8th Marquess Conyngham, Lord Henry Mount Charles, and, for a short while, U2 when recording their album The Unforgettable Fire in 1984, Slane Castle is Ireland's premier outdoor concert venue, attracting the world's biggest rock bands. Few venues can match a history of concert headliners that have included Neil Young (1993), The Rolling Stones (1982 and 2007), U2 (1983 and 2001), Bob Dylan (1984), Bruce Springsteen (1985), Queen (1986), David Bowie (1987), Guns N' Roses (1992), R.E.M. (1995), The Verve (1998), Robbie Williams (1999), Bryan Adams (2000), Stereophonics (2002), Red Hot Chili Peppers (2003), Madonna (2004), Oasis (2009), Kings of Leon (2011) and Bon Jovi and Eminem (2013). It all began with headliners Thin Lizzy in 1981.

LOCATION 796: about 30 miles north of Dublin where the N2 meets the N51, Slane Castle is just over half a mile from the village of Slane in County Meath. From Slane, head up the hill towards Navan. The castle is on the left

"Their musical journey is special. They have openly admitted that Thin Lizzy was one of their primary influences and they opened the first Slane in 1981. Thirty years later that had a **POIGNANCY TO ME** "

LORD HENRY MOUNT CHARLES
announces Kings of Leon as 2011 Slane Castle headliners

Photo: Slane Castle Ltd

Republic of Ireland

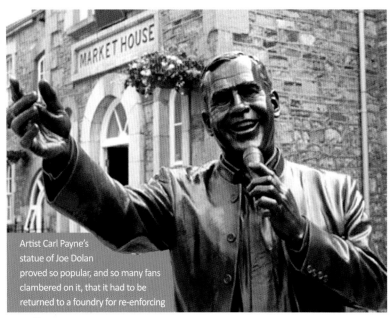

Artist Carl Payne's statue of Joe Dolan proved so popular, and so many fans clambered on it, that it had to be returned to a foundry for re-enforcing

Mullingar
Joe Dolan Bridge and statue

One of Ireland's most successful pop stars, Joe Dolan, was born and based in Mullingar, where the cover of his debut album was photographed. The Answer to Everything (1964) cover depicts Joe and The Drifters Showband in the grounds of Belvedere House, a Georgian mansion and 160-acre estate on the shores of Lough Ennell. After his death, Dolan was buried at Walshestown Cemetery near Mullingar and honoured with a statue in the centre of the town, which drew 6,000 fans at its unveiling in 2008. Local fondness for the entertainer didn't stop there: the final link in the Mullingar ringroad was named after him when the 540-metre Joe Dolan Bridge was opened in 2010.

LOCATIONS 797, 798 and 799: the statue is on the square at the corner of Pearse Street and Mount Street, in front of Canton Casey's pub and the tourist information office in Mullingar. Belvedere House, gardens and park are open to the public, best accessed by taking Lynn Road south out of Mullingar for approximately six miles. Joe Dolan Bridge links Clonmore Business Park to the Lynn roundabout on Tullamore Road and spans the flood plains of the River Brosna and Lacy's Canal

Lislarkin
Dusty Springfield's clifftop memorial

The dramatic Atlantic coastal Cliffs of Moher is the spot where Tom Springfield scattered his sister Dusty's ashes in 2007, more than seven years after her death. This very dramatic location is said to have been a favourite of the iconic pop star, whose family roots were in Tralee, County Kerry, where her mother grew up.

LOCATION 800: take the R478 about 30 miles south-west of Galway, on the west coast, and head for Lislarkin in County Clare

Born in the
REPUBLIC OF IRELAND

Leo Barnes, saxophone, Hothouse Flowers (b. 5 Oct 1965, Dublin)
Mary Black (b. 22 May 1955, Dublin)
Bono, Paul Hewson, (b. 10 May 1960, Dublin)
Tim Booth, vocals/guitar, Dr Strangely Strange (b. 6 Sep 1943, Co. Kildare)
Ciarán Bourke, The Dubliners (b. 18 Feb 1935, Dublin, d. 10 May 1988)
Brendan Bowyer, vocals, The Royal Showband (b. 12 Oct 1938, Waterford)
Paul Brady (b. 19 May 1947, Strabane, Co. Tyrone)
Ciarán Brennan, guitar/vocals Clannad (b. 4 Mar 1954, Gweedore)
Máire Brennan, vocals, Clannad (b. 4 Aug 1952, Gweedore)
Pete Briquette, bass, The Boomtown Rats (b. 2 Jul 1954, Dublin)
Nicky Byrne, Westlife (b. 9 Oct 1978, Dublin)
Eamonn Campbell, The Dubliners (b. 29 Nov 1946, Drogheda)
Seán Cannon, The Dubliners (b. 29 Nov 1940, Galway)
Eamon Carr, Horslips (b. 12 Nov 1948, Kells, Co. Meath)
Davy Carton, vocals, The Saw Doctors (b. 10 Apr 1959, Tuam, Co. Galway)
Philip Chevron, guitar, The Pogues (b. 17 Jun 1957, Dublin, d. 8 oct 2013)
Con Cluskey, The Bachelors (b. 18 Nov 1941, Dublin)
Dec Cluskey, The Bachelors (b. 23 Dec 1942, Dublin)
Sonny Condell, Tír Na Nóg/Scullion (b. 1 Jul 1949, Newtownmountkennedy)
Kevin Conneff, The Chieftains (b. 8 Jan 1945, Donore, Co. Meath)
Andrea Corr, vocals/tin whistle, The Corrs (b. 17 May 1974, Dundalk)
Caroline Corr, drums/vocals, The Corrs (b. 17 Mar 1973, Dundalk)
Jim Corr, keyboards, The Corrs (b. 31 Jul

1964, Dundalk)

Sharon Corr, vocals/violin, The Corrs (b. 24 Mar 1970, Dundalk)

Gerry Cott, guitar, The Boomtown Rats (b. 15 Oct 1954, Dublin)

Cathal Coughlan, vocals, MicrodisneyThe Fatima Mansions (b. Cork)

Mary Coughlan (b. 5 May 1956, Co. Galway)

Simon Crowe, drums, The Boomtown Rats (b. 14 Apr 1955, Dublin)

Conor Deasy, vocals, The Thrills (b. 31 Dec 1969, Dublin)

Barry Devlin, Horslips (b. 27 Nov 1946, Newry, Co. Down)

Joe Dolan (b. 16 Oct 1939, Mullingar, d. 26 Dec 2007)

Val Doonican (b. 3 Feb 1927, Waterford)

Brian Downey, drums, Thin Lizzy (b. 27 Jan 1951, Dublin)

Ronnie Drew, The Dubliners (b. 16 Sep 1934, Dún Laoghaire, d. 16 Aug 2008)

Keith Duffy, Boyzone (b. 1 Oct 1974, Dublin)

Noel Duggan, guitar/vocals, Clannad (b. 23 Jan 1949, Gweedore)

Pádraig Duggan, mandolin/vocals, Clannad (b. 23 Jan 1949, Gweedore)

Kian Egan, Westlife (b. 29 Apr 1980, Sligo)

Enya (Enya Brennan) (b. 17 May 1961, Gweedore, Co. Donegal)

Siobhán Fahey, Shakespears Sister/Bananarama (b. 10 Sep 1958, Dunshaughlin, Co. Meath)

Johnny Fean, Horslips (b. 17 Nov 1951, Dublin)

Mark Feehily, Westlife (b. 28 May 1980, Sligo)

Jerry Fehily, drums, Hothouse Flowers (b. 28 Aug 1963, Bishopstown, Cork)

Shane Filan, Westlife (b. 5 Jul 1979, Sligo)

Johnnie Fingers, (John Moylett) keyboards, The Boomtown Rats, 10 Sep 1956, Dublin)

Gavin Friday (b. 8 Oct 1959, Dublin)

Eddie Furey, The Fureys (b. 23 Dec 1944, Dublin)

Finbar Furey, The Fureys (b. 28 Sep 1946, Dublin)

George Furey, The Fureys (b. 11 Jun 1951, Dublin)

Paul Furey, The Fureys (b. 6 May 1948, Dublin, d.17 Jun 2002)

Rory Gallagher (b. 2 Mar 1948, Ballyshannon, d. 14 Jun 1995)

Stephen Gately Boyzone (b. 17 Mar 1976, Dublin, d. 10 Oct 2009)

Bob Geldof, vocals, The Boomtown Rats (b. 5 Oct 1951, Dublin)

Liam Genockey, drums, Steeleye Span (b. 12 Aug 1948, Dublin)

Tim Goulding, Dr Strangely Strange (b. 15 May 1945, Dublin)

Mikey Graham Boyzone (b. 15 Aug 1972, Dublin)

Michael Hogan, bass, The Cranberries (b. 29 Apr 1973, Moyross)

Noel Hogan, guitar, The Cranberries (b. 25 Dec 1971, Moyross)

Graham Hopkins, drums, Therapy? (b. 20 Dec 1975, Dublin)

Richard James, aka Aphex Twin (b. 18 Aug 1971, Limerick)

Seán Keane, The Chieftains (b. 12 Jul 1946, Dublin)

Ronan Keating, Boyzone (b. 3 Mar 1977, Dublin)

Luke Kelly, The Dubliners (b. 17 Nov 1940, Dublin, d. 30 Jan 1984)

Mark Kelly, keyboards, Marillion (b. 9 Apr 1961, Dublin)

Fergal Lawler, drums, The Cranberries (b. 4 Mar 1971, Limerick)

Jim Lockhart, Horslips (b. 3 Feb 1948, Dublin)

Bob Lynch, The Dubliners (b. 18 May 1935, Dublin, d. 2 Oct 1982)

Shane Lynch, Boyzone (b. 3 Jul 1976, Dublin)

Drew McConnell, bass, Babyshambles (b. 10 Nov 1978, Dublin)

Brian McFadden, Westlife (b. 12 Apr 1980, Dublin)

Barney McKenna, banjo, The Dubliners (b. 16 Dec 1939, Dublin, d. 5 Apr 2012)

Imelda May (b. 10 Jul 1974, Dublin)

Paddy Moloney, The Chieftains (b. 1 Aug 1938, Dublin)

Matt Molloy, The Bothy Band/The Chieftans/Planxty (b. 12 Jan 1947, Ballaghaderreen, Co. Roscommon)

Christy Moore (b. 7 May 1945, Dublin)

Leo Moran, guitar, The Saw Doctors (b. 9 Nov 1964, Tuam, Co. Galway)

Larry Mullen, Jr, drums, U2 (b. 31 Oct 1961, Artane, Dublin)

Tony Murray, guitar, The Troggs (b. 26 Apr 1943, Dublin)

Fiachna Ó Braonáin, guitar, Hothouse Flowers (b. 27 Nov 1965, Dublin)

Colm Ó Cíosóig, drums/keyboards, My Bloody Valentine (b. 31 Oct 1964, Dublin)

Sinéad O'Connor (b. 8 Dec 1966, Glenageary, Co. Dublin)

Daniel O'Donnell (b. 12 Dec 1961, Kincasslagh, Co. Donegal)

Danny O'Donoghue, vocals, The Script (b. 3 Oct 1980, Dublin)

Leo O'Kelly, Tír Na Nóg (b. 27 Nov 1949, Dublin)

Liam Ó Maonlaí, vocals/keyboards, Hothouse Flowers (b. 7 Nov 1964, Monkstown)

Dolores O'Riordan, vocals, The Cranberries (b. 6 Sep 1971, Limerick)

Gilbert O'Sullivan (b. 1 Dec 1946, Waterford)

Peter O'Toole, bass, Hothouse Flowers (b. 1 Apr 1965, Dublin)

Paddy Reilly, The Dubliners (b. 18 Oct 1939, Rathcoole, South Dublin Co.)

Damien Rice (b. 7 Dec 1973, Celbridge, Co. Kildare)

Garry Roberts, guitar, The Boomtown Rats (b. 16 Jun 1954, Dublin)

Sharon Shannon (b. 12 Nov 1968, Ruan, Co. Clare)

John Sheahan, The Dubliners (b. 19 May 1939, Dublin)

Mark Sheehan, vocals/bass, The Script (b. 29 Oct 1981, Dublin)

John Stokes, The Bachelors (b. 13 Aug 1940, Dublin)

Louis Walsh, manager/talent show judge (b. 5 Aug 1952, Kiltimagh, Co. Mayo)

Terry Woods, mandolin/guitar, The Pogues (b. 4 Dec 1947, Dublin)

Rock Atlas

Rock Atlas

Rock Atlas